Youth Justice Law a

Kate Aubrey-Johnson is a children's rights barrister and mediator. She is a tenant at Garden Court Chambers. She practised for ten years as a criminal and prison law barrister specialising in representing children. As a mediator, she specialises in special educational needs mediation. Kate is author of *Making Mediation Work For You* (LAG, 2012). She joined Just for Kids Law in 2014 and established the Youth Justice Legal Centre. She regularly writes, lectures and delivers training on youth justice law and chairs the Ministry of Justice working group on quality of youth justice advocacy. Before becoming a barrister, Kate worked as a youth worker and founded an educational and environmental charity working in Uganda.

Shauneen Lambe is a barrister in England and Wales and an attorney in the USA. She is a partner in Impact – Law for Social Justice, a consultancy that supports those considering using the law for social change. Shauneen is the co-founder and former CEO of Just for Kids Law (2005–2018). Her work included supervising Just for Kids Law's strategic litigation team which successfully changed the law to benefit many children and young people and starting up the Youth Justice Legal Centre as a centre of excellence in youth justice law. Prior to working in the UK, Shauneen worked at the Louisiana Crisis Assistance Center representing those facing the death penalty.

Jennifer Twite was called to the Bar in 2006. She specialised in defending children and vulnerable adults in criminal proceedings for almost a decade before becoming Head of Strategic Litigation at Just for Kids Law in 2015. In that role she has helped change the way the law treats children, notably in the context of the joint enterprise doctrine and the disclosure of criminal records. Jennifer is co-author of the bi-annual youth justice update *Legal Action*. She regularly trains professionals in youth justice law.

Available as an eBook at www.lag.org.uk/bookshop/ebooks

LAG eBook

The purpose of Legal Action Group is to promote equal access to justice for all members of society who are socially, economically or otherwise disadvantaged. To this end, it seeks to improve law and practice, the administration of justice and legal services.

Youth Justice Law and Practice

Kate Aubrey-Johnson
Shauneen Lambe and Jennifer Twite

Legal researchers: Laura Cooper and Katya Moran

LAG the access to justice charity
Legal Action Group
2019

This edition published in Great Britain 2019
by LAG Education and Service Trust Limited
National Pro Bono Centre, 48 Chancery Lane, London WC2A 1JF
www.lag.org.uk

British Library Cataloguing in Publication Data
a CIP catalogue record for this book is available from the British Library.

FSC www.fsc.org MIX Paper from responsible sources FSC® C020438

This book has been produced using Forest Stewardship Council (FSC) certified paper. The wood used to produce FSC certified products with a 'Mixed Sources' label comes from FSC certified well-managed forests, controlled sources and/or recycled material.

print ISBN 978 1 908407 32 0
eBook ISBN 978 1 912273 17 1
Bundle (print + ebook) ISBN 978 1 912273 36 2

Typeset by Refinecatch Limited, Bungay, Suffolk
Printed in Great Britain by Hobbs the Printers, Totton, Hampshire

For
Jonah, Erin, Amala,
Frankie,
Aisling, Cian, Caitlín

and to all the children we haved worked with over the years who helped us develop our thinking and kept us committed.

Foreword

Professor David Ormerod QC (Hon), Law Commissioner for England and Wales

This book deals with a subject of fundamental importance. Children who come into contact with the criminal justice system are some of the most vulnerable in our society. Whenever a child appears before the criminal courts the implications are profound – not only for that child's immediate future but for the likelihood of future contact with the criminal justice system throughout his or her life. It really matters that we get it right for children. Getting it wrong can have far reaching consequences for the child and society.

It is vital therefore that all those working with children in the system have a clear understanding of the law and its impact on children. Securing that understanding is not always easy. First, there are many who might assume knowledge on the basis that the youth court system has evolved from the more familiar adult one; but that ignores the numerous significant differences that exist, and that children should be treated entirely differently to adults. Secondly, the law is technical and derives from a wide range of sources, including guidelines, protocols and circulars which are not always widely known, even among legal practitioners. This guide will be an invaluable resource to assist lawyers, judges and all professionals working in the youth justice system access the legally accurate information they require to ensure children's rights are protected. It is a very worthy successor to the hugely popular *Defending Young People*.

Two outstanding features of this book that will make it instantly popular with practitioners are worth highlighting. First, the authors are to be congratulated on rendering such a vast amount of material so accessible to a wide readership. There are useful overviews at the start of each chapter, the text is written in a clear style and is not overly cluttered with unnecessary citations. Secondly, the authors bring their vast expertise and experience to bear by providing intensely practical checklists on numerous topics including: meeting the young client for the first time (para 8.91), talking to adolescents (para 3.6); how to approach an age determination (para 2.52); and available sentences (paras 17.9–17.31).

As one would expect, the book has many other impressive qualities. It offers authoritative and comprehensive coverage of the law, evidence procedure and sentencing (with 200 pages alone on sentencing as it affects children). It goes far beyond that with focused discussions of context (e.g. the background to 'looked after children' and the significance of race); the broader issues under the UN and European Conventions; and, what the practitioner needs to know about other disciplines (eg how to instruct mental health experts and intermediaries). There is also a wealth of useful references to helpful materials including numerous guides on subjects such as out of court disposals, modern slavery and police detention as well as appendices of some of the core source materials in full. The text is up-to-date, including references to 2019 case law, and deals with important topical matters arising in the courts, with a particularly good example being the explanation of the Modern Slavery Act 2015 and its impact in county lines cases.

As a Law Commissioner I have been concerned for some time about key issues that affect how the criminal justice system treats children, in particular in our work on Unfitness to Plead and the Sentencing Code and Criminal Records. I welcome this book which has, at its core, such a powerful message about ensuring access to justice for children. More than anything, this handbook demonstrates that children should always be represented by lawyers who have a good understanding of the youth justice law and the specific needs of the children they represent. I hope it will ensure that the all those working in the criminal courts are knowledgeable, sensitive and responsive to the needs of children.

David Ormerod QC (Hon)
Law Commissioner for England and Wales
Professor of Criminal Justice, University College London

Preface

Society evolves and the landscape of traditional thought shifts. It wasn't until the 1930s that paediatrics became a universally accepted specialist area of medicine. Nowadays it is impossible to imagine a medical system that doesn't provide specialist care for children through practitioners trained for the purpose. We have spent the best part of the last 15 years advocating for specialist representation for children in the criminal justice system – after almost all other areas of law recognise and require such specialisation. We have done so because we believe it is essential. We hope, by the fact that you are reading this book, that you believe this too.

We have written this book because we believe that every child, including those in the criminal justice system, deserves the best possible legal representation. This is achieved when children are represented by lawyers who are specially trained and knowledgeable about the particular needs of their clients.

We want this book to be a guide and assist anyone working with a child in criminal proceedings. We hope it will be used by solicitors and barristers, judges and magistrates, youth offending teams and social workers, police officers and other professionals, parents, guardians but most of all, we have written this book for the benefit of children. To ensure children are not treated in the same way as adults in the criminal justice system and that they are diverted from the criminal justice system wherever possible.

In 2006 Shauneen Lambe and Aika Stephenson founded Just for Kids Law because they had seen at first hand that the youth justice system was not addressing the underlying causes of offending. The holistic model of representation that they developed addressed children's education, learning difficulties, mental health conditions, living arrangements, future employability and immigration. Alongside this they set out to train criminal lawyers in becoming child specialist criminal lawyers.

Since then, much more is understood about the prevalence of children with speech, language and communication difficulties in the justice system. And although the numbers of children in the criminal justice system have been steadily declining, it is often the most troubled children, with complex needs, who are being brought before the courts. Alongside this we now know that looked after children and children from black, Asian and minority ethnic backgrounds are disproportionately overrepresented.

In 2014, we set up the Youth Justice Legal Centre to provide accessible, legally accurate information about youth justice law, to deliver training, offer advice and provide guidance. We hope that the Youth Justice Legal Centre continues to provide this service and support to professionals working on the frontline with some of our society's most vulnerable children.

We would like to express our gratitude to the authors of *Defending Young People* – Mark Ashford, Alex Chard and Naomi Redhouse. In our early days practising in the youth court, we all carried around our well-thumbed, dog-eared copies of their book. It was like a bible to many, shining a spotlight on the importance of understanding the very different approach needed when representing children in criminal proceedings. We hope this book can build on the work they have done to establish youth justice as a specialism. We have written this book with the aim of it being an accessible handbook – we hope it will help to support the next generation of specialist youth justice lawyers.

Writing a legal handbook on criminal law relating to children has been no easy feat. There are many people who made this book possible, first and foremost are our friends and families. Who provided childcare, sacrificed weekends away and holidays, and became somewhat cynical when they were told the book was 'nearly finished'. We're grateful to you all. Most of all to Lewis, David and Greg. Thank you.

Quite simply, this book would not have been possible without our publisher Esther Pilger. She has encouraged and nurtured this book into existence. It is a huge achievement!

We would like to offer our particular thanks to our proof readers, Aika Stephenson, Greg Ó Ceallaigh, Professor Kathryn Hollingsworth, Claire Sands, Kate O'Raghallaigh, Dr Sinéad Marriott, Chris Bath, Greg Stewart, Kaushik Ramdhary, Anya Lewis, Brenda Campbell QC, Jo Cecil, David Emmanuel QC, Frances Searle, Julia Krish, Dr Laura Janes, Chris Stacey and Adam Straw. Our thanks to Tim Bateman and Neal Hazel for their fantastic research to create the

'Beyond youth custody – youth justice timeline', which provides an invaluable overview of the historical developments in youth justice.

Thank you to the volunteers and legal researchers who made writing the book possible and for their painstaking help checking the references. An enormous thank you to Laura Cooper, Katya Moran, Alex Temple, Ruth McGregor-Hamann, Karolina Rychlicka, Sally Gunn, Alex Cheah, Bartosz Kruk, Julia Jenson and Emma Checkley.

A particular thank you to our colleagues at Just for Kids Law for keeping us calm, relevant and topical.

Kate Aubrey-Johnson
Shauneen Lambe
Jennifer Twite

March 2019

Contents

Table of cases

R v Podola (Guenther Fritz Erwin) [1960] 1 QB 325, [1959] 3 WLR 718, [1959] 3 All ER 418, [1959] 10 WLUK 78, (1959) 43 Cr App R 220, (1959) 103 SJ 856, CA — 4.88, 4.92, 12.30

R v Powell (Michael John) [2006] EWCA Crim 3, [2006] 1 WLUK 158, [2006] 1 Cr App R 31, [2006] Crim LR 781, (2006) *Times*, January 17 — 5.44, 6.62

R v Pritchard (1836) 7 C & P 303, [1836] EngR 540, (1836) 173 ER 135 — 4.84, 4.85, 4.86, 4.92, 12.30

R v Rashid (Yahya) [2017] EWCA Crim 2, [2017] 1 WLR 2449, [2017] 1 WLUK 259, [2017] 1 Cr App R 25, [2017] Crim LR 418 — 4.42, 12.46

R v Rehman (Zakir) [2005] EWCA Crim 2056, [2005] 7 WLUK 523, [2006] 1 Cr App R (S) 77, [2005] Crim LR 878, (2005) *Times*, September 27 — 21.36

R v Robertson (Eric John) [1968] 1 WLR 1767, [1968] 3 All ER 557, [1968] 7 WLUK 127, (1968) 52 Cr App R 690, (1968) 133 JP 5, (1968) 112 SJ 799, CA — 4.88

R v Robinson (Kenneth Mark) [1993] 1 WLR 168, [1993] 2 All ER 1, [1992] 11 WLUK 400, (1993) 96 Cr App R 418, (1993) 14 Cr App R (S) 448, (1993) 157 JP 125, [1993] Crim LR 143, (1993) 157 JPN 93 — 17.31

R v Robson (Kevin) [2006] EWCA Crim 1414, [2007] 1 All ER 506, [2006] 6 WLUK 579, [2007] 1 Cr App R (S) 54, (2006) 170 JP 637, [2006] Crim LR 935, (2007) 171 JPN 123 — 2.15, 17.31

R v Russell (Ian) [1990] 12 WLUK 5, [1993] RTR 249, CA — 24.166

R v S [2000] 1 Cr App R (S) 18 — 21.78

R v Secretary of State for the Home Department ex p A (a juvenile) [2000] UKHL 4, [2000] 2 AC 276, [2000] 2 WLR 293, [2000] 1 All ER 651, [2000] 1 WLUK 675, [2000] 2 Cr App R (S) 263, (2000) 164 JP 141, [2000] Prison LR 13, [2000] Crim LR 321, [2000] COD 209, (2000) 97(6) LSG 33, (2000) 144 SJLB 82, (2000) *Times*, January 28 — 21.98

R v Sheffield Crown Court ex p Clarkson [1986] 11 WLUK 229, (1986) 8 Cr App R (S) 454 — 18.54

R v Simsek (Onur) [2015] EWCA Crim 1268, [2015] 6 WLUK 142, (2016) 180 JP 192 — 24.8, 24.30

R v Slocombe (Nicholas) [2005] EWCA Crim 2997, [2006] 1 WLR 328, [2006] 1 All ER 670, [2005] 11 WLUK 625, [2006] 1 Cr App R 33, (2005) *Times*, December 6 — 25.79, 25.80

R v Smith (Steven) and others [2011] EWCA Crim 1772, [2012] 1 WLR 1316, [2012] 1 All ER 451, [2011] 7 WLUK 542, [2012] 1 Cr App R (S) 82, [2011] Crim LR 967 — 24.184

R v South Hackney Juvenile Court ex p B (a minor) [1983] 3 WLUK 201, (1983) 77 Cr App R 294 — 8.132

R v South Tameside Magistrates Court ex p Rowland [1983] 3 All ER 689, [1983] 5 WLUK 26, (1984) 148 JP 202, QBD — 8.159

R v Steed (Gareth) [1990] 5 WLUK 72, (1990–91) 12 Cr App R (S) 230, [1990] Crim LR 816, CA — 2.19, 2.20, 2.45, 2.52

Table of statutes

Table of statutory instruments

Table of European and international legislation

Table of abbreviations

ABE	Achieving Best Evidence
ACPO	Association of Chief Police Officers
ACRO	ACRO Criminal Records Office
ADCS	Association of Directors for Children's Services
ADHD	attention deficit hyperactivity disorder
AGI	anti-gang injunction
AMHP	approved mental health professional
APP	Accredited Professional Practice
ASBI	anti-social behaviour injunction
ASBO	anti-social behaviour order
ASD	autism spectrum disorders
ASBCPA 2014	Anti-social Behaviour, Crime and Policing Act 2014
BA 1976	Bail Act 1976
BAME	black, Asian and minority ethnic
BMA	British Medical Association
BTP	British Transport Police
C&YP	children and young people
CA 2004	Children Act 2004
CAMHS	Child and Adolescent Mental Health Service
CBO	criminal behaviour order
CCA 1968	Criminal Appeal Act 1968
CCE	child criminal exploitation
CCRC	Criminal Cases Review Commission
CDA 1998	Crime and Disorder Act 1998
CICA	Criminal Injuries Compensation Authority
CJA 2003	Criminal Justice Act 2003
CJIA 2008	Criminal Justice and Immigration Act 2008
CJPOA 1984	Criminal Justice and Public Order Act 1984
CJS	criminal justice system
CO	confiscation order
COE	Council of Europe
CPD	Criminal Practice Direction
CP(I)A 1964	Criminal Procedure (Insanity) Act 1964
CPS	Crown Prosecution Service
CQC	Care Quality Commission
CR	community resolution

CRC	Committee on the Rights of the Child
CRC	criminal record certificate
CrimPD	Criminal Practice Directions
CrimPR	Criminal Procedure Rules 2015
CSAE	child sexual abuse and exploitation
CYPA 1933	Children and Young Persons Act 1933
CYPA 1963	Children and Young Persons Act 1963
CYPA 1969	Children and Young Persons Act 1969
DPP	Director of Public Prosecutions
DSCC	Defence Solicitor Call Centre
DTO	detention and training order
ECHR	European Convention of Human Rights
ECRC	enhanced criminal record certificate
ECtHR	European Court of Human Rights
EHCP	education, health and care plan
EU	European Union
FASD	foetal alcohol syndrome disorders
FCA	Financial Conduct Authority
fMRI	functional magnetic resonance imaging
GSS	Gudjonsson suggestibility scale
HOCR	Home Office Counting Rules
HRA 1998	Human Rights Act 1998
HSE	Health and Safety Executive
IF	intensive fostering
IPCC	Independent Police Complaints Commission
IPP	Imprisonment for Public Protection
IPSO	Independent Press Standards Organisation
ISS	intensive supervision and surveillance
ISSP	intensive supervision and surveillance programme
LAA	Legal Aid Agency
LASPO 2012	Legal Aid, Sentencing and Punishment of Offenders Act 2012
MCA 1980	Magistrates' Court Act 1980
MHA 1983	Mental Health Act 1983
MOJ	Ministry of Justice
MRI	magnetic resonant imaging
MSA 2015	Modern Slavery Act 2015
MST	multi-systemic therapy
NFA	no further action
NOMS	National Offender Management Service
NPCC	National Police Chiefs' Council
NPM	National Preventive Mechanism
NRM	National Referral Mechanism
NSPCC	National Society for the Prevention of Cruelty to Children
ODD	oppositional defiant disorder
OFSTED	Office for Standards in Education, Children's Services and Skills
OOCD	out of court disposal
OPCAT	Optional Protocol to the Convention against Torture and other Cruel, Inhuman or Degrading Treatment or Punishment

OTP	Operation Turning Point
PA 1997	Police Act 1997
PACE	Police and Criminal Evidence Act 1984
PCA 1953	Prevention of Crime Act 1953
PCA 2009	Policing and Crime Act 2009
PCC(S)A 2000	Powers of Criminal Courts (Sentencing) Act 2000
PNC	Police National Computer
PND	Police National Database
PO	parenting order
PTPH	Plea and Trial Preparation Hearing
PTSD	post-traumatic stress disorder
PSR	pre-sentencing report
RI	Registered Intermediary
RLAA	remanded to local authority accommodation
RO	referral order
ROA 1974	Rehabilitation of Offenders Act 1974
ROTL	Release on Temporary Licence
RUI	release under investigation
SAR	subject access request
SCA 1981	Senior Courts Act 1981
SCH	secure children's home
SCPO	serious crime prevention order
SEN	special educational needs
SHPO	sexual harm prevention order
SOA 2003	Sexual Offences Act 2003
STC	secure training centre
SGVA 2006	Safeguarding Vulnerable Groups Act 2006
UASC	unaccompanied asylum-seeking child
UKVI	UK Visas and Immigration
UN	United Nations
UNCRC	United Nations Convention on the Rights of the Child
VCS	Victim Contact Scheme
VOO	violent offender order
VPS	Victim Personal Statement
WHO	World Health Organization
WISC	Wechsler Intelligence Scale for Children
YCS	Youth Custody Service
YDA	youth detention accommodation
YJB	Youth Justice Board
YJCEA 1999	Youth Justice and Criminal Evidence Act 1999
YJLC	Youth Justice Legal Centre
YOI	young offender institution
YOT	youth offending team
YRI	youth restorative intervention
YRO	youth rehabilitation order

PART 1

Children in the criminal justice system

CHAPTER 1

Overview of the youth justice system in England and Wales

continued

Key points

- This book describes 'children' as under 18-year-olds, in line with the United Nations Convention on the Rights of the Child (UNCRC) which the UK has ratified.
- The youth justice system in England and Wales evolved out of the adult criminal justice system.
- The age of criminal responsibility is 10 years old, England and Wales has a particularly low age of criminal responsibility in comparison with most other European countries.
- Children have special status. The rights protected by the UNCRC can be brought into litigation in various ways.
- The number of children in the youth justice system and in custody has been falling in the last decade.
- However, the children in the youth justice system can be acutely vulnerable and a high proportion have complex needs, and there is an over-representation of looked-after children and children from black, Asian and minority ethnic backgrounds.
- There are different statutory bodies responsible for children in the youth justice system; and there are different statutory frameworks, duties and protections for children than there are for adults.

Introduction

1.1 In England and Wales children aged between 10 and 17 years (see paras 1.4–1.5 on definition of children), who are accused of infringing the criminal law, are dealt with by the youth justice system. This is defined in law as 'the system of criminal justice in so far as it relates to children and young persons.'[1]

1.2 The youth justice system in England and Wales evolved out of an existing criminal justice system which was designed for adults. This can still be reflected in the way in which children who come into contact with the justice system are treated today. Although in some respects our youth justice system has developed distinct processes, in many ways it mirrors the adult criminal justice system, for example:

- the way in which allegations are investigated by the police;

1 Crime and Disorder Act (CDA) 1998 s42(1).

- the court processes involved in deciding whether a child committed a criminal act; and
- some of the places where we detain children who are deprived of their liberty

are similar for both children and adults.

1.3 There are, however, distinct rules which provide specific rights and protections for children in the criminal justice system, and these will be explored below.

A child in law – the definition of children in England and Wales

1.4 The United Nations Convention on the Rights of the Child (UNCRC) provides the following definition, 'a child means every human being below the age of eighteen years unless under the law applicable to the child, majority is attained earlier.'[2] The age of majority is attained at 18 in England and Wales.[3]

Terminology in this book

1.5 For the purposes of this book the term 'child' or 'children' is used to describe those aged 17 years and younger. Some legislation makes a distinction between a 'child' and a 'young person' (see para 1.7 on children and young persons) but this book describes children as under 18-year-olds in line with the UNCRC.

1.6 Many teenagers may not be happy to hear themselves described as a 'child', but in a criminal justice context this reflects the special status and international protections to which they are entitled (see, for example, paras 1.38–1.39 on UNCRC).

Children and young persons

1.7 In England and Wales, some legislation makes a distinction between a 'child', someone aged under 14, and a 'young person' as someone who has attained the age of 14 and is under the age of 18 years.[4]

2 United Nations Convention on the Rights of the Child (UNCRC) Article 1.

3 Family Law Reform Act 1969 s1. Reduction of Age of Majority from 21 to 18.

4 See Children and Young Persons Act (CYPA) 1933 s107(1) and Children and Young Persons Act 1969 s70(1). Also see Judicial College, 'The Youth Court Bench Book' (August 2017) p1.

However, more recent legislation has reflected the UNCRC definition and describes a 'child' as a person under the age of 18.[5]

Juvenile

1.8 When a child is accused of a crime and is dealt with at the police station, the legislation refers to an 'arrested juvenile'. The Police and Criminal Evidence Act 1984 (PACE) defines an 'arrested juvenile' as anyone who 'appears under the age of 18'.[6] The Magistrates' Court Act 1980 s29(1)(a) also refers to 'juvenile' to describe a person under the age of 18. While 'juvenile justice' remains a commonly recognised term internationally, in England and Wales 'youth justice' is more commonly used.

Young adults

1.9 There is an emerging view that young adults, aged 18 to 25, should be considered as a distinct group from older adults.[7] Young adults can share the same vulnerabilities and developing as children. Young adults can be at greater risk of adverse outcomes from contact with the criminal justice system and it can increase the risk of re-offending. (See paras 17.41–17.50 on turning 18 and sentencing young adults.)

A brief history of the youth justice system in England and Wales[8]

Beginnings

1.10 Prior to 1838, children in contact with the penal system were treated in the same way as adults.

1.11 The first penal institution set up exclusively for juveniles, Parkhurst Prison, opened on the Isle of Wight in 1838.

5 For example, Children Act 1989 s105(1), Legal Aid, Sentencing and Punishment of Offenders Act 2012 s91(6), Police and Criminal Evidence Act 1984 (PACE) s37(15) (as amended by Criminal Justice and Courts Act 2015 s42).

6 PACE s37(15).

7 Justice Committee, *Young adults in the criminal justice system* (HC 2017–19, 419); Howard League for Penal Reform and Transition to Adulthood (T2A) Alliance, 'Judging maturity' (2017) at: https://howardleague.org/wp-content/uploads/2017/07/Judging-maturity.pdf.

8 The overview of the historical developments in youth justice are from: T Bateman and H Neal, 'Beyond youth custody – youth justice timeline', at: www.beyondyouthcustody.net/policy/youth-justice-timeline/.

1.12 The first legislation to distinguish children and adults for criminal purposes was the Juvenile Offenders Act 1847. This distinguished children by allowing those under 14 years to be charged with lesser offences than their adult counterparts and therefore allowing them to be tried in the magistrates' court rather than the Crown Court.

1.13 Over the next 50 years, there was continued development in keeping children who were detained for criminal purposes separate from adults, either on remand or once sentenced.

Early to late twentieth century

1.14 The Children Act 1908 established for the first time a separate 'juvenile court' which dealt with children who were brought before the courts for both crime and welfare issues. The special provisions for 'juvenile offenders' within this Act applied to those under 16 years of age. The Children and Young Persons Act (CYPA) 1933 required courts to have regard to children's 'welfare'. The welfare principle is still in force today and remains one of the guiding principles of the current youth justice system, nearly 85 years later (see para 1.68–1.71 for more on the welfare principle).

1.15 The CYPA 1933 raised the age of criminal responsibility to eight years and abolished the death penalty for those under the age of 18 years. In 1961, a report commissioned by the government, *The Ingleby report,* recommended raising the age of criminal responsibility from eight to 12 years. In response to that report, in 1963 the age of criminal responsibility was raised from eight to ten years.[9] The Children and Young Persons Act 1969 intended to raise the age of criminal responsibility from ten to 14 years; however, this part of the Act has never been implemented and so the age of criminal responsibility in England and Wales has remained at ten years despite criticism from campaigners and international bodies (see paras 1.55–1.63 on the age of criminal responsibility in England and Wales).

Modern day

1.16 The Children Act 1989 saw the creation of what was to become the modern-day youth court. The juvenile court was separated into two different courts to deal with children depending on whether they faced criminal proceedings or welfare matters: the legislation created a 'family proceedings court' (subsequently absorbed into the single

9 CYPA 1933 s50 as amended by CYPA 1963 s16(1).

Family Court); leaving the 'juvenile courts' to deal purely with criminal matters; in 1991, the juvenile court was renamed the youth court.[10]

1.17 The Crime and Disorder Act (CDA) 1998 introduced a 'principal aim' for the youth justice system – which is the prevention of offending (see para 1.67 on the principal aim).[11] This principal aim was part of the government response to public outcry about the behaviour of children and young people in the aftermath of the murder of the toddler Jamie Bulger by two ten-year-old boys in 1993.[12]

1.18 The CDA 1998 also created the Youth Justice Board (YJB), which became the non-departmental public body responsible for national implementation of good practice and monitoring of the newly formed youth offending teams (YOTs) (see para 1.75 on the YJB).

1.19 Much of the sentencing regime that is in place today was devised and implemented in the last few years of the twentieth century and the beginning of the twenty-first century under the New Labour government. This included the creation of:

- referral orders (ROs) (a community order which diverts 'young offenders' from courts to panels of lay people who have responsibility for designing and overseeing these disposals) (see chapter 19 for referral orders);
- anti-social behaviour orders (ASBOs) (subsequently replaced by criminal behaviour orders; and anti-social behaviour injunctions) (see chapter 24 for ancillary orders);
- intensive supervision and surveillance programmes (ISSPs) (a rigorous community alternative to custody) (see chapter 20); and
- detention and training orders (DTOs) (custodial sentences which are restricted to blocks of a minimum of four months and a maximum of 24 months (see paras 21.71–21.116 on detention and training orders).

1.20 In 2008, the Criminal Justice and Immigration Act 2008 replaced the variety of community orders that existed at the time, bar referral orders, with one community sentence called the youth rehabilitation order (YRO) – intensive supervision and surveillance became an optional component of a YRO (see chapter 20 for YROs).[13]

10 Criminal Justice Act 1991 s70(1).

11 CDA 1998 s37(1).

12 Fortin, J, *Children's rights and the developing law*, 2009, Cambridge University Press, p680.

13 Bateman T, Hazel N, 'Beyond youth custody – youth justice timeline: www.beyondyouthcustody.net/policy/youth-justice-timeline/.

International law relevant to the youth justice system in England and Wales

United Nations Convention on the Rights of the Child

Introduction

1.21 The domestic law affecting children in the justice system must always be considered alongside extensive provisions in international human rights law. One of the most important treaties for all children, including those in the youth justice system, is the UNCRC. The UN General Assembly adopted the convention on 20 November 1989 and it came into force in the UK in 1992. The UNCRC sets out, in 54 Articles, a range of rights specific to children. The treaty has been ratified by 195 countries, making it the most widely ratified international human rights treaty in history; the only UN member state that has not ratified the convention is the USA. The rights set down in the UNCRC apply to all children, no matter what their legal status or individual circumstances.

UNCRC in domestic law

1.22 Although the UK government has ratified the UNCRC and it came into force in 1992, it has not been incorporated into domestic law. This means that the rights contained in the UNCRC are not directly enforceable in English. However, it can be used by judges to interpret ambiguous legislation, develop common law principles and to interpret and apply the European Convention on Human Rights (see paras 1.27–1.36 on the weight of UNCRC in domestic law).

1.23 UK government publicly states that its policies and practices must comply with the UNCRC:

> The United Nations Convention on the Rights of the Child (UNCRC) is an international human rights treaty that grants all children and young people (aged 17 and under) a comprehensive set of rights. The UK signed the convention on 19 April 1990, ratified it on 16 December 1991 and it came into force on 15 January 1992. All of our policies and practices must comply with the UNCRC and we report to the United Nations every 5 years to show this.[14]

14 Department of Education, Government Equalities Office, Office for Disability Issues, *Policy paper 2010 to 2015 government policy: equality, Appendix 6,* 2015: www.gov.uk/government/policies/creating-a-fairer-and-more-equal-society/supporting-pages/the-united-nations-convention-on-the-rights-of-the-child-uncrc.

However, it is not always the case that all legislation or policies comply with the UNCRC.

1.24 The Crown Prosecution Service legal guidance on young offenders states:

> Crown Prosecutors will have regard to their obligations arising from the European Convention of Human Rights, the United Nations 1989 Convention on the Rights of the Child and the United Nations 1985 Standard Minimum Rules for the Administration of Juvenile Justice (the Beijing Rules).[15]

1.25 The Sentencing Council's *Sentencing children and young people: definitive guideline* states:

> Domestic and international law dictate that a custodial sentence should always be a measure of last resort.[16]

This reflects the obligations under the UNCRC Article 37(b). The defence lawyer can raise these principles around the UNCRC to the Crown Prosecution Service (CPS) or by the courts (see also para 1.27 below).

1.26 A broader analysis of the UK government's commitment to the UNCRC can be found in 'UNCRC how legislation underpins implementation in England'.[17] Where it is stated that international treaties are not automatically incorporated into UK law and that the UK will not ratify a treaty 'unless the government is satisfied that domestic law and practice means that it can comply'.[18]

Weight of UNCRC in domestic litigation

1.27 In the domestic courts, the UNCRC has successfully been used to support legal challenges to how children are treated in the criminal justice system and in children's rights challenges more broadly. In 2003, in the case of *R v G*,[19] Lord Steyn observed that the fact that the UK had ratified the UNCRC which 'imposes both procedural and substantive obligations on state parties to protect the special provision of children in the criminal justice system.' The UNCRC makes it

15 www.cps.gov.uk/legal-guidance/youth-offenders.

16 Sentencing Council, *Sentencing children and young people: definitive guideline*, 2017, para 1.3.

17 Department for Children, Schools and Families, 'The United Nations Convention on the Rights of the Child: How legislation underpins implementation in England', 2010, available at www.gov.uk.

18 Para 1.2.

19 *R v G* [2003] UKHL 50.

impossible to ignore 'the special position of children in the criminal justice system' and that ignoring it 'is not acceptable in the modern civil society'.[20]

1.28 The fact that the UNCRC has been ratified but not incorporated into domestic law means that it is not possible to take direct legal action against a policy or law where there is a perceived breach of the UNCRC, but it is still possible to argue that the protections set out in the UNCRC are observed, and taken into consideration, before the courts. For example, where a European Convention of Human Rights (ECHR) Article is engaged, the European Court of Human Rights (ECtHR) has said the ECHR must be interpreted in conjunction with the UNCRC, where it is relevant.[21] Therefore, in domestic litigation the UNCRC can be referred to inform the interpretation of an ECHR right:

> [The] United Nations Convention on the Rights of the Child 1989 ('UNCRC'), . . . is not only binding in international law; it is reflected in the interpretation and application by the European Court of Human Rights of the rights guaranteed by the European Convention: see, for example, *V v United Kingdom* [1999] 30 EHRR 121 [sic]; to that extent at least, therefore, it must be taken into account in the interpretation and application of those rights in our national law.[22]

1.29 In *Neulinger v Switzerland* the ECtHR observed:[23]

> The Convention cannot be interpreted in a vacuum but must be interpreted in harmony with the general principles of international law. Account should be taken . . . of 'any relevant rules of international law applicable in the relations between the parties' and in particular the rules concerning the international protection of human rights.

1.30 What is:

> . . . not in dispute is that the Convention rights protected in our domestic law by the Human Rights Act can also be interpreted in light of international treaties such as the UNCRC.[24]

1.31 Sometimes the domestic courts can be resistant to relying on UNCRC when there is no direct ECHR right engaged. See, for example, *T v Secretary of State for Justice*:[25]

20 At para 53.
21 *V v UK* (2000) 30 EHRR 121.
22 *R (R) v Durham Constabulary* [2005] UKHL 21, para 26.
23 *Neulinger v Switzerland* (2010) 28 BHRC 706, para 131.
24 *R (SG) v Secretary of State for Work and Pensions* [2015] UKSC 16, para 83.
25 *T v Secretary of State for Justice* [2013] EWHC 1119 (Admin), para 32.

> We are not persuaded that the UNCRC can be employed to assist the interpretation of section 31 of the 1933 Act, let alone the Beijing Rules, which are not binding in International law when these instruments post-date it by some six decades. No Strasbourg right is in contention. Nor has the legislation translated the relevant parts of the UNCRC or the Beijing rules into domestic law. . . . Section 31 must be interpreted without the assistance of the international instruments he has identified.

1.32 Lady Hale (President of the Supreme Court) has said that 'even if an international treaty has not been incorporated into domestic law our domestic legislation has to be construed so far as possible so as to comply with the international obligations we have undertaken'.[26] In *ZH (Tanzania) v Secretary of State for the Home Department,* the Supreme Court stated that Article 3 (best interests of the child principle) 'is a binding obligation in international law, and the spirit, if not the precise language, has also been translated into our national law.[27]

1.33 In the case of *HH, PH, F-K,*[28] the Supreme Court recognised that Article 3 are correctly applied when the components of Article 12 (right to be heard) are fully respected. This was a case that did not involve the children in the legal proceedings directly, rather it concerned the proposed extradition of their parents.

1.34 Article 8 (Right to a private and family life) is frequently relied upon for children's rights arguments. In *HC v Secretary of State for the Home Department*[29] it was established that:

> . . . once it is accepted that Article 8 is engaged, the Secretary of State cannot resist the application of the principles contained in the UNCRC. It should be recalled that the Home Department, over 11 years ago, accepted that: 'Where children in custody are concerned the provisions of the Convention (UNCRC) are available to inform the content of ECHR Article 8' (*R (SR) v Nottingham Magistrates' Court* [2001] EWHC Admin 802 para 65).[30]

26 *Smith v Secretary of State for Work and Pensions and another* [2006] UKHL 35, para 78.

27 *ZH (Tanzania) v Secretary of State for the Home Department* [2011] UKSC 4, para 23.

28 *HH, PH, F-K* [2012] UKSC 25, para 82 –85.

29 *R (HC) v Secretary of State for the Home Department* [2013] EWHC 982 (Admin).

30 *R (HC) v Secretary of State for the Home Department* [[2013] EWHC 982 (Admin) para 80.

1.35 Article 14 of the ECHR (Protection from discrimination) has also been found to trigger interpretation in line with the UNCRC. In the case of *Mathieson*[31] the Supreme Court found the child's best interests had not been considered when stopping disability payments to parents whose child was in hospital.

Examination by the UN Committee on the Rights of the Child

1.36 The UK (as with every state that has ratified the UNCRC) is required to report to the Committee on the Rights of the Child on the measures they have adopted to implement the UNCRC every five years. The state party's own report is followed by a report from the Committee, known as 'concluding observations' which set out areas of concern and make recommendations.

1.37 The latest report from the Committee about the UK was delivered in July 2016 and in it the Committee raised an extensive list of concerns. In relation to youth justice, it recommended that the government address a number of issues including that the UK:

1) raise the minimum age of criminal responsibility 'in accordance with acceptable international standards';
2) ensure that children in conflict with the law are always dealt with in the juvenile justice system and that diversion measures do not appear on children's criminal records;
3) abolish imposition of mandatory life imprisonment for offences that are committed by those under the age of 18;
4) establish the statutory principle that detention should be used as a last resort for the shortest possible period of time and that detention is not used to discriminate against certain groups of children
5) ensure that child detainees are separated from adults in all detention settings;
6) immediately remove all children from solitary confinement, prohibit the use of solitary confinement in all circumstances;
7) improve access to education and health services for children in the custodial estate.[32]

31 *Mathieson v Secretary of State for Work and Pensions* [2015] UKSC 47.

32 Concluding Observations on the Fifth Periodic report of the United Kingdom of Great Britain and Northern Ireland CRC/C/GBR/CO/5.

Articles of the UNCRC most relevant to children in the criminal justice system

1.38 The particular Articles of the UNCRC that apply most often in criminal justice context are as follows.

- Article 3.1: This is known as the 'best interests' principle, this applies where children are both directly and indirectly involved in administrative and judicial proceedings.[33] (See paras 1.72–1.74 'best interests' principle test.)

  In all actions concerning children, whether undertaken by public or private social welfare institutions, courts of law, administrative authorities or legislative bodies, the best interests of the child shall be a primary consideration.
- Article 12:

  1. States Parties shall assure to the child who is capable of forming his or her own views the right to express those views freely in all matters affecting the child, the views of the child being given due weight in accordance with the age and maturity of the child.

  2. For this purpose, the child shall in particular be provided the opportunity to be heard in any judicial and administrative proceedings affecting the child, either directly, or through a representative or an appropriate body, in a manner consistent with the procedural rules of national law.
- Article 37:

  States Parties shall ensure that:

  (a) No child shall be subjected to torture or other cruel, inhuman or degrading treatment or punishment. Neither capital punishment nor life imprisonment without possibility of release shall be imposed for offences committed by persons below eighteen years of age;

  (b) No child shall be deprived of his or her liberty unlawfully or arbitrarily. The arrest, detention or imprisonment of a child shall be in conformity with the law and shall be used only as a measure of last resort and for the shortest appropriate period of time;

  (c) Every child deprived of liberty shall be treated with humanity and respect for the inherent dignity of the human person, and in a manner which takes into account the needs of persons of his or her age.

  In particular, every child deprived of liberty shall be separated from adults unless it is considered in the child's best interest not to do so and shall have the right to maintain contact with his or her family through correspondence and visits, save in exceptional circumstances;

33 General Comment 14 – Best Interest of the Child Article III 13(a) page 5: https://www2.ohchr.org/english/bodies/crc/docs/gc/crc_c_gc_14_eng.pdf.

(d) Every child deprived of his or her liberty shall have the right to prompt access to legal and other appropriate assistance, as well as the right to challenge the legality of the deprivation of his or her liberty before a court or other competent, independent and impartial authority, and to a prompt decision on any such action.'

- Article 40:

1. Parties recognize the right of every child alleged as, accused of, or recognized as having infringed the penal law to be treated in a manner consistent with the promotion of the child's sense of dignity and worth, which reinforces the child's respect for the human rights and fundamental freedoms of others and which takes into account the child's age and the desirability of promoting the child's reintegration and the child's assuming a constructive role in society.

2. To this end, and having regard to the relevant provisions of international instruments, States Parties shall, in particular, ensure that:

(a) No child shall be alleged as, be accused of, or recognized as having infringed the penal law by reason of acts or omissions that were not prohibited by national or international law at the time they were committed;

(b) Every child alleged as or accused of having infringed the penal law has at least the following guarantees:

(i) To be presumed innocent until proven guilty according to law;

(ii) To be informed promptly and directly of the charges against him or her, and, if appropriate, through his or her parents or legal guardians, and to have legal or other appropriate assistance in the preparation and presentation of his or her defence;

(iii) To have the matter determined without delay by a competent, independent and impartial authority or judicial body in a fair hearing according to law, in the presence of legal or other appropriate assistance and, unless it is considered not to be in the best interest of the child, in particular, taking into account his or her age or situation, his or her parents or legal guardians;

(iv) Not to be compelled to give testimony or to confess guilt; to examine or have examined adverse witnesses and to obtain the participation and examination of witnesses on his or her behalf under conditions of equality;

(v) If considered to have infringed the penal law, to have this decision and any measures imposed in consequence thereof reviewed by a higher competent, independent and impartial authority or judicial body according to law;

(vi) To have the free assistance of an interpreter if the child cannot understand or speak the language used;

(vii) To have his or her privacy fully respected at all stages of the proceedings.

3. States Parties shall seek to promote the establishment of laws, procedures, authorities and institutions specifically applicable to

children alleged as, accused of, or recognized as having infringed the penal law, and, in particular:

(a) The establishment of a minimum age below which children shall be presumed not to have the capacity to infringe the penal law;

(b) Whenever appropriate and desirable, measures for dealing with such children without resorting to judicial proceedings, providing that human rights and legal safeguards are fully respected.

4. A variety of dispositions, such as care, guidance and supervision orders; counselling; probation; foster care; education and vocational training programmes and other alternatives to institutional care shall be available to ensure that children are dealt with in a manner appropriate to their well-being and proportionate both to their circumstances and the offence.

1.39 Other possible Articles of the UNCRC that might be relevant in the context of children in the criminal justice system are:

- Article 16 – right to a private life;
- Article 19 – protection from violence, abuse and neglect;
- Article 20 – right to special protection if parents are not caring for children (provision of care); and
- Article 28 – right to education.

UNCRC General Comments and other supporting rules

1.40 As well as the UNCRC, the UN has created other rules and comments that can be used as guidance in interpreting the UN Convention on the Rights of the Child. These rules, as Lady Hale has observed: 'although not binding on member states, must be taken into account in the interpretation and application of those rights in our national law'.[34] Furthermore, in *Mathieson* the Supreme Court supported the idea that the 'general comments' provided by the UNCRC analysis are 'authoritative guidance'.[35]

1.41 These supporting rules and relevant general comments include:

1) UN Standard Minimum Rules for the Administration of Juvenile Justice System ('Beijing Rules') (1985);[36]

34 *R (R) v Durham Constabulary* [2005] UKHL 21, para 26.

35 *Mathieson v Secretary of State for Work and Pensions* [2015] UKSC 47, para 39 referring to *R (SG) v Secretary of State for Work and Pensions* [2015] UKSC 16, [2015] 1 WLR 1449 at paras 105–106, Lord Carnwath described the committee's analysis as 'authoritative guidance'.

36 United Nations Standard Minimum Rules for the Administration of Juvenile Justice System (Beijing Rules), 1985: http://www.un.org/documents/ga/res/40/a40r033.htm

2) UN Guidelines for the Prevention of Juvenile Delinquency ('Riyadh Guidelines') (1990);[37]
3) UN Rules for the Protection of Juveniles Deprived of their Liberty ('Havana Rules') (1990);[38]
4) UN Committee on the Rights of the Child – General Comment No 6: Treatment of unaccompanied and separated children outside their country of origin (2005);[39]
5) UN Committee on the Rights of the Child – General Comment No 8: The right of the child to protection from corporal punishment and other cruel or degrading forms of punishment (2006);[40]
6) UN Committee on the Rights of the Child – General Comment No 10: Children's rights in juvenile justice (2007);[41]
7) UN Committee on the Rights of the Child – General Comment No 13: The right of the child to freedom from all forms of violence (2011); [42]
8) UN Committee on the Rights of the Child General – General Comment No 14: On the right of the child to have his or her best interests taken as a primary consideration – Art 3(1) (2013);[43]

37 United Nations Guidelines for the Prevention of Juvenile Delinquency (The Riyadh Guidelines), 1990: http://www.un.org/documents/ga/res/45/a45r112.htm.

38 The United Nations Rules for the Protection of Juveniles Deprived of their Liberty (Havana Rules), 1990: https://www.unodc.org/pdf/criminal_justice/United_Nations_Rules_for_the_Protection_of_Juveniles_Deprived_of_their_Liberty.pdf.

39 UN Committee on the Rights of the Child – General Comment No 6, Treatment of unaccompanied and separated children outside their country of origin, 2005: https://www2.ohchr.org/english/bodies/crc/docs/GC6.pdf.

40 UN Committee on the Rights of the Child – General Comment No 8, The right of the child to protection from corporal punishment and other cruel or degrading forms of punishment, 2006: https://www2.ohchr.org/english/bodies/crc/docs/CRC.C.GC.13_en.pdf.

41 UN Committee on the Rights of the Child – General Comment No. 10, Children's rights in juvenile justice, 2007: www2.ohchr.org/english/bodies/crc/docs/CRC.C.GC.10.pdf.

42 UN Committee on the Rights of the Child – General comment No 13, The right of the child to freedom from all forms of violence, 2011: https://www2.ohchr.org/english/bodies/crc/docs/CRC.C.GC.13_en.pdf.

43 UN Committee on the Rights of the Child General comment No 14 on the right of the child to have his or her best interests taken as a primary consideration – Article 3(1), 2013: www2.ohchr.org/English/bodies/crc/docs/GC/CRC_C_GC_14_ENG.pdf.

9) UN Committee on the Rights of the Child – General Comment No 15: On the right of the child to the enjoyment of the highest attainable standard of health (2013).[44]
10) UN Guidelines on Justice in Matters involving Child Victims and Witnesses of Crime (2009).[45]

European Convention on Human Rights and Human Rights Act 1998

Background

1.42 The UK was one of the first member states to ratify the Convention in 1951.

1.43 The ECHR does not specifically mention children, but the rights set down within it are applicable to everyone, whatever their age. The idea that children are human beings, who are entitled to rights, is an important one. The rights contained in the UNCRC are additional to these general human rights, and they flow from the fact that 'childhood is entitled to special care and assistance'.[46] See, for example, *Zherdev v Ukraine*,[47] in which the ECtHR found that a child was subjected to 'degrading' treatment contrary to Article 3 by being kept handcuffed and wearing just his underwear for at least two and a half hours and, subsequently, by being placed in a cell with adult detainees for three days.[48]

1.44 The rights contained in the ECHR were incorporated into domestic law by the Human Rights Act (HRA) 1998, which came into force on 2 October 2000. The implementation of the HRA 1998 has enabled children and adults to enforce rights identified in the ECHR in the English courts.

1.45 The ECtHR recognises the child-specific international conventions when making decisions that relate to children and young people – for example, *Neulinger v Switzerland*[49] (see para 1.29 on enforcing UNCRC rights and the weight of the UNCRC in domestic law).

44 UN Committee on the Rights of the Child – General comment No 15 on the right of the child to the enjoyment of the highest attainable standard of health, 2013: https://undocs.org/CRC/C/GC/15.

45 The United Nations Guidelines on Justice in Matters involving Child Victims and Witnesses of Crime, 2009: www.unicef.org/eca/UNDOC-UNICEF_Model_Law_on_Children.pdf.

46 UNCRC, preamble.

47 [2018] ECHR 87.

48 *Zherdev v Ukraine* (2017): http://hudoc.echr.coe.int/eng?i=001-173088.

49 *Neulinger v Switzerland* (2010) 28 BHRC 706, paras 131 and 135.

Relevant Articles of the ECHR

1.46 The particular ECHR rights that are often engaged in youth justice are:

- Article 2 – right to life;
- Article 3 – freedom from degrading or inhuman treatment;
- Article 4 – servitude;
- Article 5 – liberty;
- Article 6 – right to a fair trial (including the right to effectively participate);
- Article 7 – retroactivity;
- Article 8 – right to respect for private and family life;
- Article 14 – discrimination.

1.47 The ECtHR is clear that children's rights cannot be diluted in the name of rehabilitation or reform. Indeed, children must be given greater rights and protections than adults in the criminal justice system:

> [Children] facing criminal charges and trial are as fully entitled as adults to benefit from all the Convention requirements for a fair trial. Great care must always be taken to ensure that this entitlement is not diluted by considerations of rehabilitation or of reform. These are considerations which should be in addition to all the procedural protections available. Fair trial and proper proof of guilt are absolute conditions precedent.[50]

1.48 The right to a fair trial includes the right to effectively participate.[51] The ECtHR has stated in *Martin v Estonia* that the right of a child to effectively participate means that due regard must be given to their vulnerabilities at all stages of contact with the criminal justice system and not just at trial:[52]

> The right of an accused minor to effective participation in his criminal trial requires that the authorities deal with him with due regard to his vulnerability and capacities from the first stages of his involvement in a criminal investigation and, in particular, during any questioning by the police. The authorities must take steps to reduce as far as possible his feelings of intimidation and inhibition.

(See para 4.15–4.30 on capacity, effective participation and fitness to plead).

50 *Nortier v Netherlands* (1994) 17 EHRR 273, concurring opinion of Judge Walsh, para 2.

51 *V v UK* (2000) 30 EHRR 121, para 84; and *SC v UK* (2005) 40 EHRR 10 para 33.

52 *Martin v Estonia* (2013) ECHR 493, para 92.

1.49 The ECtHR also recognised that these vulnerabilities do not expire exactly on the turning of 18:

> Although in the present case the applicant reached the age of eighteen three weeks before his arrest, the Court considers that the reasons for which the special treatment of minors is required – such as the person's level of maturity and intellectual and emotional capacities – do not cease immediately once the legal age is reached. Therefore, the considerations based on those factors could maintain some of their relevance, although their importance decreased as time passed.[53]

Guidelines of the Committee of Ministers of the Council of Europe on child-friendly justice

1.50 The Council of Europe (COE) has created various standards and guidelines in the field of 'child-friendly justice'. These standards aim at improving the justice system and adapting it to the specific needs of children, a process which, the COE says, entails creating a justice system which guarantees respect for and the effective implementation of all children's rights.[54] The most extensive set of standards on child-friendly justice are contained in the *Guidelines of the Committee of Ministers of the Council of Europe on child-friendly justice* adopted by the Committee of the Ministers of the Council of Europe in 2010.[55]

1.51 Although these guidelines not binding in domestic law, they set out best practice based on international and European standards. They provide important guidance on how the government and professionals can ensure children's effective access to justice and appropriate treatment in criminal justice processes.

1.52 The COE is different from the EU and it is anticipated the UK will still be a member of this Council if it is no longer a member of the EU post-Brexit.

Charter of Fundamental Rights of the European Union

1.53 The Charter of Fundamental Rights of the European Union brings together in a single document the fundamental rights protected in the EU. It became legally binding on the EU with the entry into force of the Treaty of Lisbon in December 2009. Under the Charter, member

53 *Martin v Estonia* (2013) ECHR 493, para 92.

54 Council of Europe, *Child-friendly justice*, 2017: www.coe.int/en/web/children/child-friendly-justice.

55 Council of Europe, Guidelines of the Committee of Ministers of the Council of Europe on child-friendly justice, 2010: https://rm.coe.int/680462cf3.

states of the EU must act and legislate consistently with the Charter, and the EU's courts will strike down legislation adopted by the EU's institutions that contravene it. The Charter applies to the institutions of the EU and its member states when implementing EU law.

1.54 It is not clear what status the Charter will have post-Brexit.

The age of criminal responsibility in England and Wales

1.55 The age of criminal responsibility in England and Wales is ten years old.[56]

1.56 For more than 800 years, the presumption of 'doli incapax' provided an important safeguard for children under the age of 14.[57] Under this doctrine, there was a conclusive presumption that under-ten-year-olds were– incapable of knowing that what they had done, therefore incapable of committing an offence. There was also the *rebuttable* presumption for those aged over ten were doli incapax. For children aged ten to 13, this presumption could be rebutted by proving that a child who had committed an act prohibited by the criminal law knew that he or she was doing something that was wrong. The prosecution had to prove that the child appreciated that his or her action was 'seriously wrong' at the time of the offence, rather than just being 'merely naughty'. The rebuttable presumption and defence of doli incapax was abolished for children aged ten and over by the CDA 1998 s34.[58] For more information on doli incapax see paras 4.5–4.7.

1.57 England, Wales and Northern Ireland have a particularly low age of criminal responsibility in comparison to many other European countries. In Scotland the minimum age of criminal responsibility is eight, but this is set to rise to 12 years.[59] In Europe, the average age of criminal responsibility is 14,[60] and the only other country in Europe that holds children criminally liable from such a young age is Switzerland.[61]

56 CYPA 1933 s50. Raised from 8 in 1963. Also see para 1.15 on the history of youth justice system.

57 Fortin J, *Children's rights and the developing law*, 2009, Cambridge University Press, p688.

58 Also see *R v T* [2009] UKHL 20.

59 Age of Criminal Responsibility Bill 2018 is currently in the legislative process before the Scottish parliament.

60 Howard League for Penal Reform, 'Punishing children', 2008, p6.

61 Child Rights International Network, *Minimum ages of criminal responsibility in Europe*: https://www.crin.org/en/home/ages/europe.

1.58 UNCRC Article 40(30(a) states that state parties shall 'establish a minimum age below which children shall be presumed not to have the capacity to infringe the penal law'. The UN Committee of the Rights of the Child has repeatedly criticised the UK for keeping the age of criminal responsibility unjustifiably low, most recently in 2016 (see para 1.37 on the UK's examination by the UN Committee on the Rights of the Child).[62] Support that the UNCRC sees the age of criminal responsibility as above ten is set out in detail in the CRC's General Comment No 10[63] which states that it is not 'internationally acceptable' to set an age of criminal responsibility below 12.

1.59 The 'Beijing Rules' on Juvenile Justice Rule 4[64] offer guidance for countries on setting the age of criminal responsibility – they state that this age shall not be set too low 'bearing in mind the facts of emotional, mental and intellectual maturity'.[65] The commentary to Rule 4 goes into more detail as to what is meant by 'too low'; it is noted that:

> In general, there is a close relationship between the notion of responsibility for delinquent or criminal behaviour and other social rights and responsibilities (such as marital status, civil majority, etc).[66]

1.60 In the case of *T and V v UK*,[67] the ECtHR was asked to consider whether the age of criminal responsibility in England and Wales was so low at ten years as to constitute 'inhumane or degrading treatment or punishment' and, as such, to be in breach of Article 3 of the ECHR. When the Court in Strasbourg decided the case in 1999, it found that:

> . . . there is not yet a commonly accepted minimum age for attribution of criminal responsibility in Europe. Whilst most of the Contracting States have adopted an age-limit which is higher that in force in England and Wales, other States, such as Cyprus, Ireland, Liechtenstein and Switzerland attribute criminal responsibility from a younger age.[68]

62 Concluding Observations on the Fifth Periodic report of the United Kingdom of Great Britain and Northern Ireland CRC/C/GBR/CO/5.

63 UNCRC, General Comment No 10: children's rights in juvenile justice 2007, para 32: www2.ohchr.org/english/bodies/crc/docs/CRC.C.GC.10.pdf.

64 United Nations Standard Minimum Rules for the Administration of Juvenile Justice System (Beijing Rules), 1985: http://www.un.org/documents/ga/res/40/a40r033.

65 'Beijing Rules' on Juvenile Justice Rule 4, Commentary.

66 'Beijing Rules' on Juvenile Justice Rule 4, Commentary.

67 *V v UK* (2000) 30 EHRR 121.

68 *T and V v UK* (2000) 30 EHRR 121, para 73.

1.61 This being the case, the low age in England and Wales was not so disproportionatley different as to be a breach of Article 3. The court stated:

> . . . it is legitimate when deciding whether a certain measure is acceptable under one of its provisions to take account of the standards prevailing amongst the member States of the Council of Europe.[69]

The court noted that the ECHR was a living instrument, meaning that this judgment was not fixed in stone and the positon might alter if the 'common standard' within member states changed.[70]

1.62 Since the judgment in this case, Cyprus, Ireland and Liechenstein have raised the age of criminal responsibility, meaning that only the UK and Switzerland have retained their very low ages of criminal responsibility. Successive governments have stated that they have no intention of raising the age of criminal responsibility. Most recently, in response to a private member's bill in the House of Lords, the government stated:[71]

> This Government take the view that children aged 10 and above are able to differentiate between bad behaviour and serious wrongdoing and can therefore be held accountable for their actions.

1.63 Despite conceding that '[we] are aware that most European countries have a higher minimum age of criminal responsibility, and that the United Nations considers 12 to be the minimum acceptable age', governments continues to justify the low age of criminal responsibility in England and Wales, because '[we] believe that each country must make a judgment based on its own circumstances and procedures'.[72]

Relevant ages and the criminal law

1.64 In England and Wales the age of majority, the age at which a person legally becomes an adult is 18 years, having been reduced from 21 years by the Family Law Reform Act 1969.[73]

69 *T and V v UK* (2000) 30 EHRR 121, para 72.

70 *T and V v UK* (2000) 30 EHRR 121, para 74.

71 Lady Vere for the Government in the House of Lords 08/09/17: https://hansard.parliament.uk/lords/2017-09-08/debates/D3E4D198-43BB-4B60-9FF0-CFF5B0EA1CB6/AgeOfCriminalResponsibilityBill(HL) at column 2209.

72 Lady Vere for the Government in the House of Lords 08/09/17: https://hansard.parliament.uk/lords/2017-09-08/debates/D3E4D198-43BB-4B60-9FF0-CFF5B0EA1CB6/AgeOfCriminalResponsibilityBill(HL) at column 2211.

73 Family Law Reform Act 1969 s1.

1.65 It is important to note that the age of majority can be different from:

- age for consenting to medical treatment;
- age of sexual consent;
- marriageable age;
- school leaving age;
- age for consuming alcohol;
- age of being able to drive;
- voting age; and
- age of purchasing cigarettes.

1.66 Having different permissible ages can lead to legal anomalies. For example, in England and Wales the age of sexual consent is 16 yet the age of criminal responsibility is ten years old. This means that children under the age of 16 who engage in consensual sexual activity (or even photograph themselves naked) can fall foul of the criminal law, not because the act is criminal *per se* but because it is a crime to be involved in sexual activity with a child below the legal age of consent. This apparent anomaly in the law can cause children to be criminalised and stigmatised for acts that would not be crimes if they were adults. As such, offences in law that were designed to *protect* children can also be used to punish them.

Principles of the youth justice system in England and Wales

Preventing offending

1.67 There are a number of principles, in legislation and government policy, which make the youth justice system distinct from the adult criminal justice system. One of the most important of these is the principle established by CDA 1998 s37, which states:

> . . . it shall be the principal aim of the youth justice system to prevent offending by children and young persons.

There is no equivalent principle in relation to adults and so this sets those in the youth justice system very much apart from the adult criminal justice system.

The welfare principle

1.68 Another key principle that distinguishing children in the criminal justice system from adults is the 'welfare principle' which was enshrined in law by CYPA 1933 s44:

> Every court in dealing with a child or young person who is brought before it, either as an offender or otherwise, *shall have regard to the welfare of the child or young person* and shall in a proper case take steps for removing him from undesirable surroundings, and for securing that proper provision is made for his education and training [emphasis added].

1.69 The 'welfare principle' applies to every court. The 'welfare principle' applies to all children who come before the courts as witnesses and victims as well as defendants.

1.70 The 'welfare principle' extends to certain authorities who 'must ensure their functions are discharged having regard to the need to safeguard and promote the welfare of children'.[74] The specific statutory bodies, in relation to the youth justice system, include:

- the local authority or district council;[75]
- the police;[76]
- the youth offending team;[77] and
- the governor or director of a secure training centre or youth offending institution.[78]

1.71 There is no definition of 'welfare' within CYPA 1933 but it must be the court's 'paramount consideration' when dealing with issues about a child's 'upbringing'.[79] In the context of family proceedings having regard to a child's welfare includes the court taking into account:

- the wishes and feelings of the child concerned;
- the child's physical, emotional and educational needs;
- the likely effect on the child if circumstances changed as a result of the court's decision;
- the child's age, sex, backgrounds and any other characteristics which will be relevant to the court's decision;
- any harm the child has suffered or maybe at risk of suffering;

74 Children Act (CA) 2004 s11(1).
75 CA 2004 s11(1)(a)–(b).
76 CA 2004 s11(1)(h)–(i).
77 CA 2004 s11(1)(k).
78 CA 2004 s11(1)(l).
79 CA 1989 s1(1).

- capability of the child's parents (or any other person the courts find relevant) at meeting the child's needs;
- the powers available to the court in the given proceedings.[80]

The 'best interests' principle

1.72 One of the most important aspects of the UNCRC that applies in a criminal context is the 'best interests' principle. Article 3.1 states:

> In all actions concerning children, whether undertaken by public or private social welfare institutions, courts of law, administrative authorities or legislative bodies, the best interests of the child shall be the primary consideration.

1.73 This best interests principle was considered by the ECtHR, which stated:

> . . . there is currently a broad consensus – including in international law – in support of the idea that in all decisions concerning children, their best interests must be paramount.[81]

1.74 In *Mathieson* the Supreme Court approved the UN Committee on the Rights of the Child's articulation of the 'best interests' principle in General Comment 14,[82] which is described as a threefold concept:

> The first aspect of the concept is the child's substantive right to have his best interests assessed as a primary consideration whenever a decision is made concerning him.
>
> The second is an interpretative principle that, where a legal provision is open to more than one interpretation, that which more effectively serves his best interests should be adopted.
>
> The third is a 'rule of procedure', described as follows:
>
>> 'Whenever a decision is to be made that will affect a specific child, an identified group of children or children in general, the decision-making process must include an evaluation of the possible impact (positive or negative) of the decision on the child or children concerned . . . Furthermore, the justification of a decision must show that the right has been explicitly taken into account . . .'[83]

80 CA 1989 s1(3).

81 *Neulinger v Switzerland* (2012) 54 EHRR 31 para 135.

82 www2.ohchr.org/English/bodies/crc/docs/GC/CRC_C_GC_14_ENG.pdf.

83 *Mathieson v Secretary of State for Work and Pensions* [2015] UKSC 47 para 39.

Statutory bodies

The Youth Justice Board

1.75 The Youth Justice Board for England and Wales (YJB) is a non-departmental public body established by the CDA 1998. Its primary function is to monitor the operation of the youth justice system and the provision of youth justice services.[84] While the YJB is responsible for overseeing the performance of youth justice services including multi-agency youth offending teams (YOTs), the YJB does not deliver or manage these services. The YJB also has a legal duty to advise the Secretary of State on matters relating to the youth justice system including to:

- report on how the youth justice system is operating and how the principal aim of the system might most effectively be achieved including steps to prevent offending;
- publish information about the youth justice system;
- identify, commission research and share examples of good practice;
- make grants to local authorities and others for the purposes of the operation of the youth justice system; and
- enter into agreements for the provision of 'youth detention accommodation'.[85]

Youth Offending Teams

1.76 Every local authority has the duty to ensure that youth justice services are available in their area.[86] To fulfil this duty, local authorities are required to establish multi-disciplinary youth offending teams (YOTs), in some areas these are now called the Youth Offending Service (YOS). Every local police force and health authority can make payments towards the costs incurred by the YOTs.

1.77 The CDA 1998 dictates that a YOT shall include at least one of the following:

- someone from probation services;
- someone with experience of social work;
- a police officer;

84 The YJB's functions are set out in CDA 1998 s41.

85 CDA 1998 ss41(5) and see Youth Justice Board for England and Wales: Strategic Plan 2018–2021 p6.

86 CDA 1998 s38(1).

- a person nominated by the health authority; and
- a person with experience of education work.[87]

YOTs can also include other people that the local authority think are appropriate.

1.78 It is the duty of the YOT to co-ordinate the provision of youth justice services in their area.[88] YOTs have responsibility for any child in the local area who is in contact with the criminal justice system. The Legal Aid, Sentencing and Punishment of Offenders Act (LASPO) 2012 gave courts the power to decide, if there is a dispute, which local authority should be responsible for a child or young person. If the child is remanded, the court must designate the responsible local authority.[89] Once the court has designated a local authority, that local authority *must* receive the child.[90]

1.79 The work performed by YOTs includes:

- providing appropriate adults at the police station;
- supervising rehabilitation programmes;
- giving and supervising cautions and conditional cautions;
- recommending bail packages;
- placement of remanded children in local authority accommodation;
- recommendations for pre-sentence reports;
- implementation of referral orders;
- supervising youth rehabilitation orders;
- supervising detention and training orders; and
- supervising any licence requirements.[91]

Mechanisms of accountability

Children's Commissioner

1.80 The office of the Children's Commissioner was created by section 1 of the Children Act 2004. The post was established to promote awareness of the views and interests of all children in England. The role was strengthened in 2014 to 'promoting and protecting children's rights' including promoting awareness of children's views and interests.[92] The Children's Commissioner is tasked to have 'particular regard' to

87 CDA 1998 s39(5).
88 CDA 1998 s39(7).
89 LASPO 2012 s92(2).
90 LASPO 2012 s92(2) and (4).
91 CDA 1998 s38(4).
92 CA 2004 s2(1).

children who are living away from home, are in social care, or others whose rights are likely to be infringed[93] – children in care, in the youth justice system and in the custodial estate would fall within this remit.

1.81 In order to carry out its functions, the Children's Commissioner advises other bodies on how to act compatibly with the rights of children; advises government; and considers new policy and legislation which may affect children. The Commissioner investigates complaints procedures and advocacy services for children. The Commissioner also has responsibility for monitoring the implementation of the UNCRC in England.[94] In this regard, the Commissioner is empowered to carry out inspections of the secure estate, including interviews with staff and detained children.[95] However, in the discharge of these functions the Commissioner may not conduct investigations into the cases of individual children in the discharge of the primary function.[96]

1.82 Following a programme of visits throughout the secure estate, in the 2017–18 the Commissioner highlighted a lack of specialist mental health and education provision in the secure estate.[97]

Prisons Inspectorate

1.83 HM Inspectorate of Prisons monitors the treatment of people deprived of liberty in England and Wales.[98] This is not limited to prisons, and includes police and court custody suites, immigration detention, customs custody and military detention. All parts of the secure estate, where children are held, are included – such as young offender institutions and secure training centres. Secure juvenile accommodation, inside and outside of the prison estate are inspected by the Prisons Inspectorate on behalf of the YJB. Inspections of Secure Training Centres are carried out jointly with OFSTED (Office for Standards in Education, Children's Services and Skills), which also has responsibilities in this area.[99]

1.84 As a general rule, inspections are unannounced, and all youth offender institutions holding children are inspected annually (rather

93 CA 2004 s2(4).

94 CA 2004 s2(3)(i).

95 CA 2004 s2E.

96 CA 2004 s2(5).

97 Office of the Children's Commissioner, 'Year in Review 2017/18' (July 2018): www.childrenscommissioner.gov.uk/wp-content/uploads/2018/07/CCO-Year-in-Review-2017-18.pdf.

98 Prison Act 1952 s5A.

99 HM Inspectorate of Prisons, 'Terms of Reference': www.justiceinspectorates.gov.uk/hmiprisons/about-hmi-prisons/terms-of-reference/.

than every five years for adult facilities). Immigration Removal Centres detaining children must be inspected at least every two years.[100]

1.85 Since 2008, the Prisons Inspectorate has produced a yearly, thematic report on the experience of 12 to 18-year-olds in custody. The latest report for children in custody 2016/17 finds that the situation is 'bleak'.[101] The annual report for the same period found that 'there was not a single establishment that we inspected in England and Wales in which it was safe to hold children and young people'.[102] The speed of decline in standards and safety was described as 'staggering', because as recently as 2013/14 'nine out of 12 institutions were graded as reasonably good or good for safety'.[103]

National Preventive Mechanism

1.86 The UK is required to set up a 'National Preventive Mechanism' (NPM) as a signatory of the Optional Protocol to the Convention against Torture and other Cruel, Inhuman or Degrading Treatment or Punishment (OPCAT). This international human rights treaty was ratified in 2003. The role of the NPM is to visit places of detention and monitor the treatment and conditions of detainees.[104] In the UK, the NPM consists of 21 statutory bodies, including both the Children's Commissioner and the Prisons Inspectorate. Other bodies which follow the detention of children in England and Wales within the framework of the NPM are the Care Quality Commission (CQC) and OFSTED.[105]

1.87 The NPM produces an annual report on monitoring places of detention, which draws at least in part on work produced by its member bodies. The 2016/17 report contains a separate section

100 HM Inspectorate of Prisons, 'Inspections Framework' (May 2017): www.justiceinspectorates.gov.uk/hmiprisons/wp-content/uploads/sites/4/2014/02/1.-INSPECTION-FRAMEWORK-May-2017-1.pdf, p11.

101 HM Inspectorate of Prisons 'Children in Custody 2016–17' (2017): www.justiceinspectorates.gov.uk/hmiprisons/wp-content/uploads/sites/4/2017/11/6.3903_HMIP_Children-in-Custody-2016-17_FINAL_WEB_221117.pdf, p6.

102 HM Inspectorate of Prisons, 'Annual Report 2016–17' (2017): www.justiceinspectorates.gov.uk/hmiprisons/wp-content/uploads/sites/4/2017/07/HMIP-AR_2016-17_CONTENT_201017_WEB.pdf, p9.

103 HM Inspectorate of Prisons, 'Annual Report 2016–17' (2017): www.justiceinspectorates.gov.uk/hmiprisons/wp-content/uploads/sites/4/2017/07/HMIP-AR_2016-17_CONTENT_201017_WEB.pdf, p9.

104 National Preventive Mechanism: https://www.nationalpreventivemechanism.org.uk/about/background/.

105 National Preventive Mechanism members: https://www.nationalpreventivemechanism.org.uk/members/.

about the situation of children in detention. For this period the report notes the continued fall of children in custody throughout the UK. However, it raises concern about the increasing over-representation of children from black, Asian and minority ethnic backgrounds, rising from 29.7 per cent in 2011 to 41.5 per cent in 2016. Members of the NPM were also alarmed by evidence that increasingly vulnerable children were being placed in detention, with incidents of self-harm doubling over the same period.[106]

Probation Inspectorate

1.88 The Probation Inspectorate is the 'source of fair comment for ministers and the public on the effectiveness of the work of probation and youth offending services'.[107] It dates back to 1936 and similarly to the bodies described above, discharges its duties by way of inspection. Inspections by the Probation Inspectorate are announced in advance and carried out in liaison with the service being inspected. A selection of youth offending services are inspected every year on the basis of risk. It is not feasible to inspect all services on an annual basis, so the calendar of inspections is determined with regard to 'volume, performance information and the date since last inspection'.[108]

The secure estate

Introduction

1.89 The 'secure estate' is the generic name given to places that children can be detained when their liberty is taken from them by the court – this can be either when they are remanded awaiting the outcome of a criminal case or sentenced to a custodial sentence.[109] Children can also be detained at the police station or remanded by

106 National Preventive Mechanism, '8th Annual Report 2016/17': https://s3-eu-west-2.amazonaws.com/npm-prod-storage-19n0nag2nk8xk/uploads/2018/02/6.4122_NPM_AR2016-17_v4_web.pdfpp15–16.

107 HM Inspectorate of Probation, 'About HMI Probation' (2014): www.justiceinspectorates.gov.uk/hmiprobation/about-hmi-probation/.

108 HM Inspectorate of Probation, 'When and how we inspect' (2018): www.justiceinspectorates.gov.uk/hmiprobation/about-our-work/when-and-how-we-inspect/.

109 www.gov.uk/government/collections/secure-estate-for-young-people-contact-details.

local authorities if refused bail (see paras 6.192–6.202 on children and the police).[110]

1.90 The UK has one of the highest rates of incarcerating children in Europe. This number has decreased by 71 per cent in recent years, from a peak of over 3,000 in 2007 to just under 1,000 in 2016.[111] There has been a steady reduction in the number of children in custody since 2003 – however provisional data for 2017–18 predicts a slight increase in the numbers of children entering custody.[112]

1.91 When a child or young person under 18 is remanded or sentenced to custody, the Ministry of Justice Placement Service decides where he or she should be detained (see paras 11.112–11.119). This will be at:

- a secure children's home (SCH);
- a secure training centre (STC); or
- a young offender institution (YOI) (if the child is a boy and 15 years or older[113]).

Secure children's homes

1.92 SCHs are run by local authorities, voluntary organisations or privately owned organisations.[114] Just under half of the children living in SCHs have been placed by there by the local authority on welfare grounds; the remaining half are on remand or sentenced children placed by the Youth Custody Service (YCS) (see paras 11.113–11.117 on the YCS) with a few children on a secure placement remanded to local authority accommodation (see paras 11.91–11.111 on secure remands to local authority accommodation).[115] According to the Secure Children's Home Network:

110 LASPO 2012 ss91–104.

111 Youth Justice Board, Bromley Briefings Summer 2016 – statistics, p6; and HM Prison and Probation Services, 'Monthly Youth Custody Report – July 2018': www.gov.uk/government/statistics/youth-custody-data.

112 Youth Justice Board, 'Annual Report and Accounts 2017/18' (2018): https://assets.publishing.service.gov.uk/government/uploads/system/uploads/attachment_data/file/726302/YJB_Annual_Report_and_Accounts_2017–18.pdf, p12.

113 https://assets.publishing.service.gov.uk/government/uploads/system/uploads/attachment_data/file/647093/Placement_Guidance_Sept_2017_YCS.pdf para 31.

114 Through Children Act 1989 Schs 5 and 6 as amended by Criminal Justice and Public Order Act 1994 s19.

115 Children accommodated in secure children's homes: 31 March 2018, Department for Education and National Statistics: https://assets.publishing.service.gov.uk/government/uploads/system/uploads/attachment_data/file/714071/SCH_2018_Text.pdf.

> There are 15 individually managed Secure Children's Homes throughout England and Wales encompassing a range of services within a secure environment that support the individual needs of the children in its care. They provide placements for boys and girls aged between 10 and 17 and include full residential care, educational facilities and healthcare provision. A very high level of intensive help is offered to each young person, with low children to staff ratios. The secure children's homes work closely with multi-agency partners to deliver individualised care plans.[116]

1.93 In the context of criminal placements, SCHs tend to be used for girls and younger boys, typically those under 13, and who are deemed the most vulnerable.[117] Guidance from the YCS suggests that young age, low levels of maturity, inability to function in large groups, and requirements for high levels of support are considerations which may make children particularly suited to placement in a SCH.[118] Children can be detained in a SCH because they are remanded to youth detention accommodation (YDA) or receive a custodial sentence; they may also be placed in a SCH on a care order.

Secure training centres

1.94 STCs were historically privately run custodial settings, run on government contracts. There are three STCs: Medway, Oakhill and Rainsbrook. Following a BBC Panorama exposé in January 2016 revealing abuse of children at Medway, the centre was taken over by the National Offender Management Service (NOMS).[119]

116 Secure Children's Homes, 'Welcome to the Secure Children's Homes website' (2018): www.securechildrenshomes.org.uk/.

117 Ministry of Justice, 2017: https://www.gov.uk/guidance/secure-childrens-homes-contact-details.

118 Youth Custody Service, 'The Youth Custody Service Placement Team – Overview of operational procedures' (2017): https://assets.publishing.service.gov.uk/government/uploads/system/uploads/attachment_data/file/647093/Placement_Guidance_Sept_2017_YCS.pdf, para 20.

119 National Preventive Mechanism, '7th Annual Report 2015/16' (2017): https://s3-eu-west-2.amazonaws.com/npm-prod-storage-19n0nag2nk8xk/uploads/2017/01/NPM-annual-report-corrected.pdf, p14.

1.95 Typically STCs are used for young boys, or older boys who have been found to be vulnerable.[120] STCs are governed by Secure Training Centre Rules.[121]

Young offender institutions

1.96 These are facilities where the YJB has contracted with the prison service to provide custodial placements for boys from the age of 15 to 21. There are five YOIs in England and Wales – Cookham Wood, Feltham, Parc, Werrington and Wetherby.[122]

1.97 YOIs who detain children operate within many of the same rules and policies as prisons for adults. While sentenced children will be subject to the YOI Rules. YOIs are governed by Young Offender Institution Rules[123] with the aim of the YOI to:

> . . . help offenders to prepare for their return to the outside community.
> (2) The aim mentioned in paragraph (1) shall be achieved, in particular, by–
> (a) providing a programme of activities, including education, training and work designed to assist offenders to acquire or develop personal responsibility, self-discipline, physical fitness, interests and skills and to obtain suitable employment after release;
> (b) fostering links between the offender and the outside community; and
> (c) co-operating with the services responsible for the offender's supervision after release.'[124]

Numbers of children in the criminal justice system

1.98 One of the recent stories of the youth justice system in England and Wales is the steady reduction of children entering the criminal justice system. In 2007, there were over 110,800 first time entrants (children who received their first youth caution or court conviction); in 2017

120 Youth Custody Service, 'The Youth Custody Service Placement Team – Overview of operational procedures' (2017): https://assets.publishing.service.gov.uk/government/uploads/system/uploads/attachment_data/file/647093/Placement_Guidance_Sept_2017_YCS.pdf, para 20.

121 Secure Training Centre Rules 1998 SI No 472.

122 https://www.gov.uk/guidance/young-offender-institution-contact-details.

123 Young Offender Institution Rules 2000 SI No 3371.

124 Young Offender Institution Rules 2000 SI No 3371 r3.

this had fallen to around 16,500.[125] This represents a decrease of 79 per cent over the last ten years.

1.99 In the year ending March 2017, there were around 74,800 arrests of children aged ten to 17 for notifiable offences[126] the numbers of children re-offending has also steadily fallen over those years.

1.100 The average youth custody population in 2016/17 was around 870, however 45 per cent were children from black, Asian and minority ethnic (BAME) backgrounds as compared to 18 per cent of the general population.[127] 'Looked after' children are also over-represented in custody.[128]

Children in the criminal courts

Introduction

1.101 Any child charged with a criminal offence and taken to court will have his or her case heard in the youth court – unless the child is jointly charged with an adult, there is no youth court sitting or the offence is so serious the case will be sent to the Crown Court.

Detention during court proceedings

1.102 There is a presumption that people awaiting the outcome of a criminal case will be granted bail. Children who are refused bail at court are remanded to local authority accommodation (RLAA) (see paras 11.83–11.94 for RLAA) unless they meet one of two sets of conditions for youth detention accommodation (see paras 11.95–11.119).

1.103 There is a cost implication for detaining children in the secure estate. SCHs are the most expensive of the placements and average £204,000 a year per child. STCs are the next most expensive averaging £163,000 per year per child. The least expensive of the

125 https://assets.publishing.service.gov.uk/government/uploads/system/uploads/attachment_data/file/726302/YJB_Annual_Report_and_Accounts_2017–18.pdf page 13.

126 Youth Justice Statistics 2016/17 England and Wales, Ministry of Justice, p9.

127 Youth Justice Statistics 2016/17 England and Wales, Ministry of Justice, p34.

128 The National Protocol on Reducing Criminalisation of LAC and Care Leavers https://assets.publishing.service.gov.uk/government/uploads/system/uploads/attachment_data/file/758873/The_National_Protocol_on_Reducing_Unnecessary_Criminalisation_of_LAC_and_Care_Leavers__002_.pdf page 5.

provision in the secure estate are the YOIs, averaging £75,000 per year per child.[129]

Youth court

Overview

1.104 There is a clear principle that cases involving child defendants should be tried and sentenced in the youth court wherever possible (see chapter 8 for more detail about youth court procedure).[130] A youth court is a specially constituted magistrates' courts where criminal cases concerning children aged between ten and 17 are heard by one district judge or three lay magistrates.[131]

1.105 The youth court is generally believed to be the best place for children to be tried because it is the court best suited to meet their needs, it is less formal than the adult court and it affords greater privacy – there is no jury and the public are excluded.[132] There are, however, some concerns about cases being tried in the youth court – that despite the benefits of the youth justice system it is vital that children benefit from the same due process protections as adults and that these must not be diluted in the name of rehabilitation or reform.

Fewer youth courts sitting

1.106 Youth courts are constituted in a local area 'as often as may be necessary for the purpose of exercising any jurisdiction conferred on them by or under this or any other Act'.[133] As there a fewer children are being brought before the courts (see para 1.105 on the numbers of children in the criminal justice system), the number of youth court sittings has been diminishing. This means that children are more frequently appearing before the adult magistrates' court for bail and remand decisions as there is not always a youth court sitting when a child is brought in custody from a police station (see para 9.6 on children in adult magistrates' court for first appearance).

129 Written question 23107, 19 January 2016.

130 *Sentencing children and young people: definitive guideline*, para 2.1.

131 CYPA 1933 s45(1).

132 *Sentencing children and young people: definitive guideline*, para 2.1.

133 CYPA 1933 s47(1).

1.107 The court closure programme[134] means that children often have to travel long distances to attend court, raising issues where children have to cross gang boundaries or lack the means to cover travel costs to attend court.

Children in adult courts

Adult magistrates' court

1.108 Children charged jointly with adults who appear in the adult magistrates' court (see paras 9.7–9.9) on children jointly charged with adults). The adult magistrates' court has the power to remit a child for trial in the youth court, even if charged with an adult.[135]

1.109 A child may appear in the adult magistrates' court where their age is in dispute. In cases involving victims of trafficking and modern slavery the court should presume the victim is a child if their age is not certain but they may be under 18 years.[136] Good practice would suggest courts should remit the case to the youth court until the issue of age is determined[137] (see paras 2.24–2.51 on age disputes).

Crown Court

1.110 It has long been recognised that the Crown Court should be reserved for the most serious cases involving children by international obligations, case law and government policy.[138] There are limited circumstances when children are sent to the Crown Court for trial:

- when charged with a homicide;
- when subject to a minimum statutory sentence (eg firearms);[139]
- when charged with a 'grave crime' and a youth court has determined that if convicted, a sentence beyond its powers should be available;[140]

134 https://www.gov.uk/government/news/government-announces-changes-to-court-estate.

135 Magistrates' Court Act 1980 s29(2).

136 Modern Slavery Act 2015 s51.

137 CYPA 1933 ss46(1)(c) and 99(1).

138 *Sentencing children and young people: definitive guideline*, para 12.2.

139 Powers of Criminal Courts (Sentencing) Act 2000 s91(1B), (1C).

140 Powers of Criminal Courts (Sentencing) Act 2000 s91.

- when charged with an adult defendant who has been sent to the Crown Court and it has been determined that the case should be kept together;[141]
- those deemed to be dangerous offenders can be sent to Crown Court for trial or sentence;[142]
- in certain cases involving serious or complex fraud or certain cases where children are witnesses if the Director of Public Prosecutions (DPP) gives notice that the case is to be tried in the Crown Court.

(See paras 8.129–8.158 on allocation and mode of trial.)

1.111 Children can now be sent from the youth court to the Crown Court for sentence[143] (see paras 17.11–17.13 on committal for sentence).

1.112 A trial in the Crown Court incurs all of the formality that exists for adults on trial for serious criminal offences and can be 'intimidating and inhibiting'[144] for children and young people.

1.113 The UK has been criticised a number of times by the ECtHR about trying very young children in the adult criminal courts (see paras 4.14 – 4.19 effective participation in criminal proceedings).

Sentencing of children

1.114 The Sentencing Council's *Sentencing children and young people: definitive guideline*[145] provides definitive guidelines to courts when sentencing children:

- the court must have regard to the principal aim of the youth justice system – to prevent offending by children and young people and the welfare of the child or young person;[146]
- sentencers must be aware of obligations under a range of international conventions when sentencing under 18s;[147]
- the importance of avoiding the 'criminalisation' of children and young people;[148]

141 *Sentencing children and young people: definitive guideline*, para 2.11; and Magistrates' Court Act 1980 s24.

142 *Sentencing children and young people: definitive guideline*, paras 2.3–2.7.

143 Criminal Justice and Courts Act 2015 s53.

144 *Panovits v Cyprus* [2008] ECHR 1688; and *T and V v UK* (2000) 30 EHRR 121, para 85.

145 *Sentencing children and young people: definitive guideline.*

146 *Sentencing children and young people: definitive guideline*, paras 1.1–1.2.

147 *Sentencing children and young people: definitive guideline*, para 1.3.

148 *Sentencing children and young people: definitive guideline*, paras 1.3 and 1.4.

- offending by children is often a phase that passes rapidly;[149]
- the chronological, emotional and developmental age of the child is significant and the sentence will be different depending on whether the child or young person is at the lower end of the age bracket, in the middle or towards the top end.[150]

1.115 The new guidelines reflect a very conscious change in terminology from 'youth' and 'young offender' in the 2009 guidelines to 'children and young people' in the 2017 guidelines. The guidelines require sentencers to consider more deeply the background, circumstances and vulnerability of children in the youth justice system, with increased attention drawn to the importance of considering developmental age as well as chronological age (see chapter 16 overview of youth sentencing).

Criminal records

1.116 Although we know that offending by children is often a phase which passes rapidly,[151] a child or young adult's opportunity to reintegrate and assume a constructive role in society[152] in England and Wales is often hindered by his or her criminal record (see chapter 25 on criminal records). Although there are shorter rehabilitation periods for offences to become spent or filtered, childhood offending can remain on a child's record until his or her 100th birthday. The proportionality of this and whether it breaches a child's ECHR Article 8 right to private and family life.[153] The Supreme Court has recently ruled that in some respects the current regime is disproportionate and therefore in compatible with Article 8.[154]

149 *Sentencing children and young people: definitive guideline*, para 1.7.
150 *Sentencing children and young people: definitive guideline*, paras 1.5, 1.12, 4.9 and 4.10.
151 *Sentencing children and young people: definitive guideline*, para 1.7.
152 UNCRC Article 40(1).
153 www.supremecourt.uk/cases/uksc-2017-0170.html.
154 *R (P, G and W) v Secretary of State for the Home Department* [2019] UKSC 3.

CHAPTER 2

Age and age disputed defendants

continued

Key points

- The age of criminal responsibility in England and Wales is 10 years old.
- The courts will consider both the chronological age of the defendant, as well as their emotional and cognitive maturity.
- The significant age thresholds for sentencing are 12, 15 and 18 years old
- If a defendant turns 18 during proceedings, the youth court retains the power to continue proceedings, including sentencing him or her as a child.
- When the court finds the defendant to be a different age to what they originally thought, the court may keep or transfer the case.
- The court has the power to deem a defendant's age, and should take into account relevant evidence including any age assessment, background information or other evidence and physical appearance. (Physical appearance is very rarely sufficient to determine age by itself).
- When the defendant's age is disputed, the local authority may conduct an age assessment. Where age is unclear the court should usually adjourn proceedings to obtain evidence or an age assessment, rather than deeming the defendant's age on insufficient evidence.
- Where the age of the defendant has not yet been established, the court should usually treat the defendant as a child if he or she claims to be a child, unless and until it has been otherwise established. Where the defendant is suspected of being a victim of trafficking the courts must assume that the defendant is under 18 until an assessment is conducted.
- A court's determination of age is not binding on other courts and may be reassessed.
- In all such proceedings the court must consider the defendant's welfare (unless and until the defendant has been deemed an adult).

Introduction

2.1 The age of the defendant is relevant throughout the criminal process. This is particularly so when the defendant is a child or claims to be a child. Any defence lawyer should consider the age of the client at the date of the offence; at charge; at first appearance; and at conviction and sentence. It is not only important to consider whether the defendant is a child or an adult, but the defendant's specific age at the relevant times, as there are different provisions for children of different ages.

2.2 The court has the power to decide or 'deem' the age of the defendant where there is any question or dispute over the defendant's age (see paras 2.31–2.34). It is important, where there is any doubt as to the defendant's true age, that proper consideration is given to the age determination.

2.3 This chapter deals with the relevance of age at different parts in the proceedings, as well as the appropriate procedures when age is disputed.

Relevance of age

Age of criminal responsibility

2.4 The age of criminal responsibility is 10 in England and Wales. Children and Young Persons Act (CYPA) 1933 s50 provides that 'It shall be conclusively presumed that no child under the age of ten years can be guilty of an offence'[1] (also see paras 1.55–1.63 on the age of criminal responsibility in England and Wales). This does not prevent the police creating crime records about offences that children are suspected of committing when they are below the age of ten (see paras 25.12–25.17 on police national databases).

Emotional and psychological age

2.5 Children's chronological age may not reflect their cognitive functioning. When considering sentencing a child, the child's emotional and developmental age and maturity is at least as important as the child's chronological age (see paras 16.21–16.23 on sentencing, age and maturity).

2.6 Similarly, when considering other aspects of the court process, such as whether the child can effectively participate, the child's developmental age is likely to be the most important consideration. (See chapter 4 on effective participation and fitness to plead.)

1 Children and Young Persons Act (CYPA) 1933 s50.

Relevance of age – which court?

2.7 The youth court's powers are restricted to hearing cases for those who are under the age of 18,[2] although the court can continue to hear cases, provided that the defendant was under 18 when proceedings began (see paras 2.10–2.14 below). The adult magistrates' court has no jurisdiction to hear cases where the defendant is under 18, other than in specific circumstances[3] (see para 9.1 on children in the adult magistrates' court). The Crown Court has jurisdiction to hear cases for any child provided the child has been allocated to the court (see paras 8.97–8.160 on allocation).

Turning a significant age threshold

Overview

2.8 The significant age thresholds in criminal cases involving child defendants are 12, 15 and 18. This is because there are different sentencing powers for people aged ten to 11, those aged 12–14, and those aged 15–17 (see paras 17.31–17.60 on relevance of age and available sentences). The exact age of the defendant is also relevant for:

- bail applications (see chapter 11);
- allocation of the case for trial (see paras 8.97–8.158 on allocation);
- any modifications necessary to ensure that the child can effectively participate.

2.9 Often the court will consider both chronological age, as well as the emotional and psychological maturity of the defendant (see paras 13.54–13.71 on trials, age as a relevant characteristic).

Turning 18 during proceedings

2.10 Where a defendant is a child at the start of the proceedings, but turns 18 before the conclusion of the proceedings, the youth court has the discretion to continue to deal with the case[4] or to send the case to be heard in the adult magistrates' court[5] either on bail or in custody.[6] If

2 CYPA 1933 s 45.
3 CYPA 1933 s46(1).
4 CYPA 1963 s29.
5 Powers of Criminal Courts (Sentencing) Act (PCC(S)A) 2000 s9(1).
6 Magistrates' Courts Act 1980 s128.

the defendant turns 18 after a finding of guilt the youth court may remit to the adult magistrates' court for sentence,[7] or may proceed to sentence in the youth court,[8] and in such circumstances the defendant can be sentenced as a child or as an adult[9] (see paras 17.29–17.51 on relevance of age and turning 18).

2.11 Theoretically, if sent to the adult magistrates' court, the allocation rules would allow either-way offences to be allocated to the Crown Court. However, in such circumstances that may be a reason against exercising the court's powers to remit. In *R (Denny) v Acton Youth Court*[10] the court's remittal of an 18-year-old to the adult magistrates' court following a conviction in the youth court for robbery was found to be unlawful as the matter was indictable only for an adult, and therefore the adult magistrates' court did not have jurisdiction to hear it.[11]

2.12 The relevant date for determining the start of proceedings is the date the charge is put to the defendant,[12] and mode of trial is decided,[13] which is usually the first appearance. The date of arrest is not relevant to determining the start of proceedings.[14] Once the defendant has turned 18, any additional charges cannot be heard in the youth court even if they relate to charges being heard there already.[15]

2.13 Therefore, if the defendant is still a child at the time of the first appearance, the defendant will have the first appearance in the youth court and can remain in that court until the case is concluded, even if that means having a trial in the youth court when the defendant is 18 years old.

2.14 The date that the child first surrendered to bail is not relevant, rather the hearing at which the plea and venue are considered. In *R v Ford*[16] the defendant first appeared before the youth court aged 17 but that appearance was adjourned to the day after his 18th birthday, when he pleaded guilty to an offence contrary to Offences Against the Person Act 1861 s18 and the youth court committed his matter

7 PCC(S)A 2000 s9(1).
8 CYPA 1963 s29.
9 *A v DPP* [2002] EWHC 403 (Admin).
10 In *R (Denny) v Acton Youth Court* [2004] 2 All ER 901.
11 In *R (Denny) v Acton Youth Court* [2004] 2 All ER 901, Maurice Kay LJ at para 9.
12 *R v Vale of Glamorgan Juvenile Justices ex p Beattie* (1986) 82 Cr App R 1.
13 *R v Islington North Juvenile Court ex p Daley* [1983] 1 AC 347, per Lord Diplock, and *R v Ford (Lewis)* [2018] EWCA Crim 1751.
14 *R v Uxbridge Youth Court ex p H* (1998) 162 JP 327.
15 *R v Chelsea Justices ex p DPP* [1963] 3 All ER 657.
16 [2018] EWCA Crim 1751.

for sentence. They had no jurisdiction to do so, as the matter was indictable only in respect of an adult, and on the date that he came before the court for plea and allocation he was 18.[17]

Sentencing

2.15 The age of the defendant on the date of conviction determines the court's sentencing powers.[18] Therefore if the defendant was under 18 on the date of pleading guilty or being found guilty the court is limited to imposing a referral order; a youth rehabilitation order; or detention and training order (and other disposals available to children). Where the defendant turned 18 between the start of proceedings and pleading or being found guilty the youth court retains a discretion to sentence the defendant as a child (see paras 17.42–17.43),[19] but otherwise he/she will be sentenced as an adult. However, the defendant's age at the date of the offence must be considered when deciding what the appropriate sentence should be (see paras 16.21–16.23 on sentencing, age and maturity).

Mistake as to age

Retaining jurisdiction

2.16 CYPA 1933, s99(1) provides that:

> an order or judgment of the court shall not be invalidated by any subsequent proof that the age of that person has not been correctly stated to the court, and the age presumed or declared by the court to be the age of the person so brought before it shall, for the purposes of this Act, be deemed to be the true age of that person . . .

2.17 If, during proceedings, it transpires that the defendant is, in fact, not the age the court initially believed him or her to be, the court can either transfer the case to the appropriate court (from the adult magistrates' to the youth court, or vice versa), or retain the case.

17 The judgment relied on *R v Islington Juvenile Court ex p Daley* (1992) 75 Cr App R 280.

18 *R v Dennis Obasi* [2014] EWCA 581; *R v Ghafoor (Imran Hussain)* [2002] EWCA Crim 1857; *R v Danga (Harbeer Singh)* [1992] QB 1996; *R v Robson* [2007] 1 Cr App (S) 54; *R v CB* [2013] EWCA Crim 2494.

19 CYPA 1963 s29.

2.18 Where a youth court is hearing a case where it believed the defendant was a child, but it transpires is an adult, the youth court can continue to hear the case, if they think it 'fit to do so'.[20] Where the adult magistrates' court is hearing a case, having believed that the defendant was an adult, but it later transpires, that the defendant is a child, the court can continue to hear the case, if they think it 'fit to do so'.[21] In the authors' view it would usually be appropriate to transfer the case back to the relevant court when it is clear that the defendant is a different age to what was previously believed, especially as the youth court is a specialist court and because of the duties the court owes to the child's welfare.[22]

Sentencing

2.19 In the case of *R v Steed (Gareth)*[23] the Court of Appeal held that a sentence passed on the defendant could not be appealed even though it transpired that the sentencing court was mistaken as to the age of the defendant, and had passed a sentence that was unlawful given the defendant's true age. Whilst this seems to be in keeping with CYPA 1933 s99(1) which states that an order of the court is not invalidated where it transpires there was a mistake as to age, it is difficult to reconcile with the court's welfare duties to children[24] to allow a child to be sentenced as an adult. It can no longer be considered the correct approach.

2.20 A more recent case suggested that the court would allow an appeal, based on the fact that the sentencing court made a mistake as to the defendant's age. In *R v H*[25] the appeal was allowed and a shorter sentence of a detention and training order was imposed, after the Court of Appeal found that the offender was 15 years old, not an adult as previously believed. However, the case of *Steed* does remain good authority for the proposition that, where a dispute arises as to a defendant's age, the case should be adjourned so that enquiries can be made.

20 CYPA 1933 s48(1).
21 CYPA 1933 s46(1)(c)
22 CYPA 1933 s44.
23 *R v Steed (Gareth)* (1990–91) 12 Cr App R (S) 230, [1990] Crim LR 816.
24 CYPA 1933 s44.
25 [2013] EWCA Crim 344.

Court not bound by previous decisions

2.21 Once a court has made a decision as to the defendant's age, that decision, while not usually to be reopened at each hearing, does not bind future courts. In *R (N) v Staines Magistrates' Court*,[26] Mr Justice Cranston suggested that a court was not bound by a previous decision as to age:

> That remedy is provided by section 99 of the Children and Young Persons Act 1933. At any point a court can make an assessment as to the age of a person appearing before it. That being the case, it seems to me that the best course is for the Crown Court to make an assessment, as a matter of urgency, of this claimant's age . . .[27]

2.22 Therefore, while proceedings are ongoing, the court could make a fresh decision. This may be appropriate if further evidence comes to light, or if the previous court made a decision that was clearly erroneous.

2.23 In *R (M) v Hammersmith*[28] the youth court erroneously decided that M was an adult and sent him to the Crown Court for trial. One of the consequences upon M of being determined to be an adult was that he was remanded into custody in an adult prison. The Crown Court, while having the power to make their own decision as to M's age, did not have the power to remit the matter back to the youth court even if they found M to be a child, following *R (W) v Leeds Crown Court*.[29] Therefore, there was no effective remedy for M other than to judicially review the magistrates' finding that he was a child. He did so, and the High Court quashed the determination of age and the decision to send him to the Crown Court for trial, and remitted the matter back to the youth court.

Age disputed defendants

Unaccompanied minors (foreign nationals)

2.24 Most commonly, age disputes arise in cases of children travelling to the UK (often unaccompanied) without documentation, or documentation that is difficult to validate. Those children who arrive

26 *R (N) v Staines Magistrates' Court* [2009] EWHC 3081 (Admin).

27 *R (N) v Staines Magistrates' Court* [2009] EWHC 3081 (Admin), at para 20.

28 *R (M) v Hammersmith Magistrates' Court* [2017] EWHC 1359 (Admin).

29 *R (W) v Leeds Crown Court* [2011] EWHC 2326 (Admin).

alone are often referred to as 'unaccompanied minors' or 'UASCs' (unaccompanied asylum-seeking children). In most of these cases, and certainly where the child is unaccompanied, the local authority in which the child is located owes a duty to the child as a 'child in need', and will have to provide accommodation and other support.[30] If the local authority does not accept the age the person claims to be, then it is incumbent upon that local authority to do an age assessment (see para 2.39 below on the Association of Directors for Children's Services (ADCS) guidance).

2.25 The Crown Prosecution Service's (CPS) legal guidance on 'youth offenders'[31] includes the following guidance:

> Where the defendant appears to have entered the UK without satisfactory evidence of identity and age, additional evidence should be available from UKBA or the local authority.

2.26 The relevant local authority – which is frequently represented through the YOT for the first appearance at the youth court – should be contacted immediately when a putative child who has no family in the UK comes before the courts. Local authorities have duties to "children in need"[32] in their area, and unless and until they have assessed the individual to be an adult, in accordance with a lawful process compliant with the ADCS guidance, they also have a duty to arrange to provide the child with an address, capable of supporting a bail application with a support package under Children Act (CA) 1989 ss20 and 22.

Modern slavery and child trafficking

2.27 In any case involving an unaccompanied minor or foreign national, the defence lawyer should consider whether there is any reason to believe that the person has been trafficked or is the victim of modern slavery. This may give rise to possible defences, relevant mitigation, or a challenge as to whether it is in the interests of justice to prosecute him or her (see paras 13.14–13.53 on trafficked children). It may

30 CA 1989 s20.

31 CPS Guidance 'young offenders'.

32 A 'child in need' is defined by CA 1989 s17(10): 'he is unlikely to achieve or maintain, or to have the opportunity of achieving or maintaining, a reasonable standard of health or development without the provision for him of services by a local authority under [CA 1989], or his health or development is likely to be significantly impaired, or further impaired, without the provision for him of such services; or he is disabled'.

also be important because the child may still be under the control of the traffickers at the time the matter comes to court.

2.28 Offences such as theft (eg pick pocketing), cultivation of cannabis, offences related to prostitution and immigration offences are offences known to be committed by trafficking victims.

Presumption of age

2.29 Where the court has reasonable grounds to believe that a person may be a victim of human trafficking, and the person may be a child, until an assessment of the person's age is carried out the court must assume that the person is a child.[33]

2.30 The Council of Europe Convention of Action against Trafficking in Human Beings,[34] Article 10(3), which was cited in *L and others*,[35] states:

> When the age of the victim is uncertain and there are reasons to believe that the victim is a child, he or she shall presume to be a child and shall be accorded special protection measures pending verification of his/her age.

Determining age

Introduction

2.31 When a person whose age is disputed appears before the court, the court has a power to determine the person's age. CYPA 1933 s99(1) allows any court to deem the age of a person before it:

> [T]he court shall make due inquiry as to the age of that person, and for that purpose shall take such evidence as may be forthcoming at the hearing of the case, but an order or judgment of the court shall not be invalidated by any subsequent proof that the age of that person has not been correctly stated to the court, and the age presumed or declared by the court to be the age of the person so brought before it shall, for the purposes of this Act, be deemed to be the true age of that person . . .[36]

33 Modern Slavery Act 2015 s51.

34 Adopted by the Committee of Ministers of the Council of Europe on 3 May 2005.

35 *R v L, HVN, THN, T* [2013] EWCA Crim 99.

36 CYPA 1933 s99(1).

2.32 In *R v L, HVN, THN, T*[37] the Court of Appeal, commenting on CYPA 1933 s99(1), stated:

> This provision directs the court to 'make due inquiry' about the defendant's age, and 'take such evidence as may be forthcoming at the hearing of the case' for this purpose. Similar provisions require the court addressing the age question to consider 'any available evidence'.[38]

2.33 The court's other powers to determine age are:

- Magistrates' Court Act 1980 s150(4);
- Criminal Justice Act 1982 s1(6);
- Power of Criminal Courts (Sentencing) Act 2000 s164(1); and
- Criminal Justice Act 2003 s305(2).

These all provide the court with powers to determine the age of an individual before the court if relevant for exercising the court's powers under the relevant Act.

2.34 In each of the provisions, the court is given the power to determine age 'after considering any available evidence.' It is submitted that the comments above in the case of *R v L* are also relevant when the court is determining age under one of the other provisions in a different Act.

Procedure for determining age

2.35 Local authorities and the UK Visas and Immigration (UKVI)/immigration services have to grapple with the issues arising from age-disputed individuals regularly, and therefore there is a wealth of case-law in other jurisdictions that should be considered by criminal practitioners faced with this issue.

Age assessments

Overview

2.36 In the judgment of *R (A) v Croydon LBC*,[39] the Supreme Court held that, for the purposes of the Children Act 1989 at least, a child's age is an objective fact, that admits only one right answer.[40]

37 *R v L, HVN, THN, T* [2013] EWCA Crim 99.

38 *R v L, HVN, THN, T* [2013] EWCA Crim 99, para 21.

39 [2009] UKSC 8 [2009] 1 WLR 2557.

40*R (A) v Croydon LBC* [2009] UKSC 8, [2009] 1 WLR 2557, see Lady Hale at para 33 and Lord Hope at para 54.

Age should not be determined by appearance alone

2.37 It is well established that the physical appearance of a child is a poor indicator of age. For this reason, a visual assessment is not sufficient or appropriate.[41] In *R v L, HVN, THN, T,* the Lord Chief Justice stated:

> The facial features of the defendant may provide a clue or two, but experience has shown that this is very soft evidence indeed and liable to mislead. What we do know is that young people mature at different ages, and that their early life experiences can sometimes leave them with a misleading appearance. We also appreciate that young people from an ethnic group with which the court is unfamiliar may seem older, or indeed younger, than those from ethnic groups with which the court has greater experience. Therefore when an age issue arises, the court must be provided with all the relevant evidence which bears on it.[42]

Merton-compliant age assessments

2.38 The basic principles about how age could be fairly assessed were first set out in the case of *R (B) v Merton LBC.*[43] Since then there has been a wealth of jurisprudence, as helpfully summarised in *R (MVN) v Greenwich LBC.*[44] These principles include:

- Ensuring that the individual has appropriate support during the interview, and an appropriate interpreter.
- The assessment takes into account more than just a child's physical characteristics, and should not be carried out in a custodial setting.
- It is essential that the putative child has the opportunity to respond to matters considered adverse before a decision is reached.

2.39 These principles are now enshrined in guidance published by the ADCS.[45] The ADCS has also agreed and published a joint protocol with the Home Office on the process by which age disputes are to be determined where they arise in the immigration context.[46]

41 *R (M) v Hammersmith Magistrates' Court* [2017] EWHC 1359 (Admin).

42 *R v L, HVN, THN, T,* para 22.

43 [2003] EWHC 1689 (Admin).

44 [2015] EWHC 1942 (Admin).

45 ADCS Age Assessment guidance, October 2015: http://adcs.org.uk/assets/documentation/Age_Assessment_Guidance_2015_Final.pdf.

46 ADCS and Home Office Joint Working Guidance, April 2015: https://assets.publishing.service.gov.uk/government/uploads/system/uploads/attachment_data/file/432724/Age_Assessment_Joint_Working_Guidance__April_2015__Final_agreed_v2_EXT.pdf.

Association of Directors for Children's Services guidance and joint protocol

2.40 The ADCS guidance sets out that age assessments should not be conducted routinely, and that only where there is reason to believe that the individual is not the age that they purport to be should it be necessary to carry out a formal age assessment.

2.41 If the local authority does not accept the purported age of the individual, then they must nevertheless treat that individual as a child while conducting an age assessment. An age assessment carried out in line with the guidance and case-law is usually referred to as a 'Merton-compliant' age assessment (after the case of *R (B) v Merton LBC*, above).

2.42 Age assessments should not usually be carried out in a custodial setting; should not be based on appearance alone; and will usually involve taking background details from the individual. The assessment should be carried out by two social workers, trained for the task.

2.43 The local authority will have to take its own view about the age of the person, drawing on its experience and acquired expertise applying the ADCS guidance, and has the power to ask the child to obtain relevant documentation, seeking experts' verification of any documents where appropriate.

Weight of age assessments in the criminal court

2.44 In *N v Staines Magistrates Court*[47] Mr Justice Cranston explained that, where they have been appropriately carried out, age assessments are usually considered to have some weight by the courts, and while the criminal court is not bound to follow the result of a Merton-compliant age assessment, it should consider them carefully. This reflects the approach taken by immigration tribunals.

Adjournments for further enquiries

2.45 Where the age of the defendant is unclear it is usually appropriate to adjourn for further enquiries to be made.[48] Pressing ahead can cause procedural problems if it later transpires that the individual is a child. For example, in the case of M,[49] while the Crown Court may have

47 [2009] EWHC 3081 (Admin).

48 *R v Steed* [1990] 12 Cr App R (S) 230.

49 *R (M) v Hammersmith Magistrates' Court* [2017] EWHC 1359 (Admin).

been able to revisit the decision as to M's age, it did not have the power to remit the matter back to the youth court if it found that M was a child.[50] The Crown Court therefore faced the possibility of being required to pass a sentence upon M which did not reflect his true age. Thus, real injustice can be caused to an age-disputed person if the matter is not adjourned, and resolved, at an early stage.

2.46 In *R v O*[51] the Court of Appeal criticised the court, defence and prosecution for all failing to recognise that O was a child. All parties owe a duty to the child, and should ensure that the court makes proper enquiries.

Bail

2.47 Where matters are adjourned to facilitate further enquiries, bail will need to be considered. If the age-disputed defendant is to be presumed a child until a proper assessment can be made, the defendant must be treated as a child for the purposes of any such bail and remand decision, in order to ensure that his or her rights are protected.

2.48 Under the ADCS guidance, local authorities must treat an age-disputed individual as a child, unless and until they have made a decision that they are an adult.

2.49 This approach was endorsed by the High Court in *M*. The court quashed the decision of the magistrates' court to remand M as an adult. The High Court was prepared to treat M as a child, despite no final decision having been made as to his age. The High Court ordered that M was remanded to local authority accommodation pursuant to the bail regime for children under the Legal Aid, Sentencing and Punishment of Offenders Act 2012 (LASPO), pending his remittal to the magistrates' court for re-determination of his age.[52]

Benefit of the doubt

2.50 The CPS guidance suggests that children should have the benefit of the doubt if their age is not clear:

> Where it is not clear whether the young person is a child (ie under 18 years of age) then in line with the United Nations Convention of the Rights of a Child, the benefit of the doubt should be given and the

50 *R (W) v Leeds Crown Court* [2011] EWHC 2326 (Admin).

51 [2008] EWCA Crim 2835.

52 *R (M) v Hammersmith Magistrates' Court* [2017] EWHC 1359 (Admin).

young person should be treated as a child. This is reinforced in the Council of Europe Convention on Action against Trafficking in Human Beings.[53]

2.51 This is supported by the UN Committee on the Rights of the Child: General Comment No 10 (2007) children's rights in juvenile justice, which states:

> 39. . . . A child without a provable date of birth is extremely vulnerable to all kinds of abuse and injustice . . .
>
> If there is no proof of age, the child is entitled to a reliable medical or social investigation that may establish his/her age and, in the case of conflict or inconclusive evidence, the child shall have the right to the rule of the benefit of the doubt.[54]

Age assessment procedure checklist

2.52 It is suggested that the following approach should be taken when dealing with an age-disputed defendant, taking into account the case-law above:

1) Where a dispute arises about the defendant's age, it will usually be appropriate for the court to adjourn proceedings for enquiries to be made as to the age of the individual.[55] This may be for the prosecution or defence to obtain documents or other evidence; it may also allow the court to ascertain the local authority's view as to the individual's age (see paras 2.40–2.42 on ADCS guidance above).
2) While the matter is being adjourned for further enquiries to be made, the court should treat the individual as if he or she were a child, until the court has made a decision as to the age[56] (see paras 2.47–2.51 above).
3) All existing age assessments, evidence or views of the local authority should be put before the court. While the court is not bound by the local authority's view, it should be aware that Merton-compliant age assessments should be given substantial weight by the courts[57] (see para 2.44 above).

53 CPS Guidance on Youth Offenders.

54 CPS Guidance & The UN committee on the Rights of the Child: General Comment No 10 (2007) Children's Rights in juvenile justice, para 39.

55 *R v Steed, R v L, HVN* [2013] EWCA Crim 991.

56 *R (M) v Hammersmith Youth Court* [2017] EWHC 1359 (Admin).

57 *R (N) v Staines Magistrates' Court* [2009] EWHC 3081 (Admin).

4) The court should be aware that, as held in *R (AM) v Solihull LBC*,[58] the views of a teacher or family member who has spent significant amounts of time with the child may have more weight than observations in the 'artificial' environment of an interview room. That same rationale will be relevant in the context of a criminal courtroom.
5) It is not appropriate for the criminal court to order the local authority or youth offending team (YOT) to carry out an age assessment. YOTs may not have the expertise to carry out Merton-compliant age assessments. The local authority should follow the appropriate guidance (see paras 2.40–2.43 on ADCS guidance above) to determine whether to carry out an age assessment. Any evidence or age assessment gathered by the local authority can then be placed before the court (see paras 2.44 above).
6) Where there continues to be doubt over the age of the individual, the benefit of the doubt should be given to the individual, who should be presumed to be a child[59] (see paras 2.50–2.51 above).
7) The court can deem an individual to be an age at any point of proceedings.[60] Therefore a court is not bound by a previous court's decision and can reconsider the age determination should more information come to light (see paras 2.16–2.22 above on mistake as to age).

Welfare-related duties

2.53 When defendants whose age is disputed come before the criminal courts, the defendant may already be known to the local authority or UKVI/immigration services who may have already conducted an age assessment. If the defendant is not yet known to the authorities, it may be important to ensure that the authorities are aware of them as soon as possible for their own welfare.

2.54 Where the individual concerned may be a child and does not have a suitable address, the local authority should be alerted that there is a

58 [2012] UKUT 00118 (IAC).

59 CPS Guidance; and The UN committee on the Rights of the Child: General Comment No 10 (2007) Children's Rights in juvenile justice, para 39.

60 CYPA 1933 s99; and *N v Staines Magistrates' Court* [2009] EWHC 3081 (Admin).

child in need in their area. This should be done as soon as possible, ideally when the child is at the police station, so that there is sufficient time to find accommodation to allow for a bail application to be made. It might be expected that the youth offending team as part of the local authority should notify children's services.

2.55 The police, defence lawyer and the court all have duties to consider the welfare of the child and should check that the local authority has been notified and is complying with its duties. The local authority should be reminded of the need to provide support and accommodation under CA 1989 ss20 and 22.

CHAPTER 3

Relevance of background for children in the criminal justice system

continued

Key points

- Most children in the youth justice system are adolescents (as defined by the American Academy of Pediatrics).
- Many children in the youth justice system have communication, speech and language difficulties. Research published by the Children's Commissioner for England in 2012 showed that 60–90 per cent of children going through the criminal justice system have significant problems with speech and language or other communication difficulties.
- Many children in the youth justice system have learning difficulties or learning disabilities, mental health problems and mental illness
- Many children in the criminal justice system have experienced abuse or neglect
- BAME children are overrepresented in the criminal justice system
- Looked after children are overrepresented in the criminal justice system
- Evidence of all of these things will be relevant when it comes to: diverting children out of the criminal justice system, procedures and modifications for court processes, ensuring that children can effectively participate in the system and for mitigation in sentencing (if needed).

Introduction

3.1 The background of a child – the child's health, education, family living arrangements and other information about the child's background – is particularly important when representing children in the criminal justice system. It should be a priority of a lawyer representing a child to find out as much as he or she can about the background of the child.

3.2 Understanding a child's background is important for:

1) communication;
2) approach to police interviews;
3) exclusion of police interviews at trial;
4) making representations in relation to informal diversions or out of court disposals;
5) effective participation in the interview or court process;

6) fitness to plead;
7) taking instructions and gathering a full understanding of the child's circumstances;
8) resisting adverse inferences from a child's failure to give evidence;
9) any relevant defences;
10) mitigation;
11) additional support with things such as health, housing, social services, education, immigration.

3.3 Most children in the youth justice system are adolescents. According to the American Academy of Pediatrics, adolescence can be defined as the years from puberty to adulthood, and may be divided into three stages:

- *early* adolescence, generally ages 11 to 14;
- *middle* adolescence, ages 15 to 17; and
- *late* adolescence, ages 18 to 21.[1]

There is a developing scientific theory that adolescence may continue into the mid-20s.[2] Scientific developments, including magnetic resonance imaging (MRI) scans have been able to demonstrate that adolescent brains continue to develop and change structurally often into the early 20s (see paras 3.31–3.34 on greater understanding of the adolescent brain). Alongside hormonal changes, this knowledge may help explain why adolescents engage in riskier behaviour than adults (see para 3.35 on risk-taking behaviour).

3.4 Many children in the criminal justice system will have speech, language and communication needs,[3] and there are far higher levels of learning difficulties and mental illness among children in the youth justice system compared to the general population (see paras 3.40–3.44 on neurodevelopment disorders).[4] Children who come into

1 www.healthychildren.org/English/ages-stages/teen/Pages/Stages-of-Adolescence.aspx.

2 https://thinkneuroscience.wordpress.com/2014/01/22/adolescent-brain-development/.

3 Royal College of Speech and Language Therapy, at: www.rcslt.org/about/young_offenders_and_criminal_justice/intro.

4 One-third of children in custody have identified special educational needs (Gyateng et al, 2013: 39). Approximately 30 per cent of children who have 'persistent offending histories' in custody have IQs of less than 70, signifying a learning disability (Rayner et al, 2008, cited in Hughes et al, 2012: 26). Of a sample of 13- to 18-year-old offenders in custody and the community, 31 per cent were found to have mental health problems, compared to ten per cent of the wider population (Jacobson et al, 2010: 68).

contact with the youth justice system often come from complicated backgrounds:

> ... with poor parental employment records, low educational attainment, early experience of offending by other family members, experience of abuse and/or neglect, negative influences from peer associates and the misuse of drugs and/or alcohol.[5]

3.5 Research also shows disproportionately high numbers of children from black, Asian and minority ethnic (BAME) backgrounds, with 45 per cent of children in custody being from BAME backgrounds while making up only 18 per cent of the population[6] (see paras 3.96–3.99 on racial disparity). 'Looked after' children are five times more likely to be cautioned or convicted than children in the general population,[7] 38 per cent of children in young offender institutions (YOIs) and 52 per cent in secure training centres (STCs) are looked after children[8] (see paras 3.87–3.95 on looked after children). Many of the children in the youth justice system have had little or no engagement in education.[9]

Effective communication

3.6 Communicating effectively with children who come into contact with the criminal justice system is incredibly important. It is essential that a child being treated as a suspect by the police, and a child defendant at court, understands what is happening to him or her. The American Psychological Association offers professionals 'Tips for talking with adolescents' – copied in overleaf text box.[10]

5 Sentencing Council, *Sentencing children and young people: definitive guideline*, 2017, para 1.13: www.sentencingcouncil.org.uk/wp-content/uploads/Sentencing-Children-and-young-people-Definitive-Guide_FINAL_WEB.pdf.

6 Youth Justice Statistics 2016/17 England and Wales, Ministry of Justice, page 34.

7 'Review of the Youth Justice System in England and Wales' by Charlie Taylor (2016), para 76: https://yjlc.uk/wp-content/uploads/2016/12/Review-of-the-Youth-Justice-System.pdf.

8 'Review of the youth justice system in England and Wales' by Charlie Taylor (2016), para 4.

9 'Review of the youth justice system in England and Wales' by Charlie Taylor (2016) para 8; Youth Justice Board, 'Barriers to engagement in education, training and employment' (2006); HM Inspectorate of Prisons, 'Children in Custody 2014–2015' (2016).

10 www.apa.org/pi/families/resources/develop.pdf.

Tips for talking with adolescents

- **Engage adolescents with non-threatening questions.** Choosing only one or two questions at a given time, ask adolescents questions that help them to define their identities. For example, whom do you admire? What is it about that person that makes them admirable? What do you like to do in your free time? What do you consider to be your strengths? What are your hopes for the future? What have you done in your life that you feel proud of (even if just a little)?
- **Listen nonjudgmentally (and listen more than you speak).** This enables the adolescent to realize that you value his or her opinions, and thus to trust you more (Forgatch & Patterson, 1989).
- **Ask open-ended questions.** Ask questions that require more than a yes or no response; this helps the adolescent think through ideas and options (Hill & O'Brien, 1999).
- **Avoid 'why' questions.** 'Why?' questions tend to put people on the defensive (Plutchik, 2000). Try to rephrase your questions to get at what the adolescent was thinking rather than the reason for something the adolescent has said or done. For example, instead of asking, 'Why did you say that?' say instead: 'You seemed to be really trying to get across a point when you did that. Can you tell me more about what you meant?'
- **Match the adolescent's emotional state, unless it is hostile.** If the adolescent seems enthusiastic or sad, let your responses reflect his or her mood. Reflecting someone's mood helps the individual feel understood (Forgatch & Patterson, 1989).
- **Casually model rational decision-making strategies.** Discuss how you once arrived at a decision. Explain, for example, how you (or someone you know well) defined the problem, generated options, anticipated positive and negative consequences, made the decision, and evaluated the outcome. Keep in mind that the adolescent has a relatively short attention span, so be brief. Choose a topic that is relevant to adolescents (eg, deciding how to deal with an interpersonal conflict, identifying strategies for earning money for college) (Keating, 1990).
- **Discuss ethical and moral problems that are in the news.** Encourage the adolescent to think through the issues out loud. Without challenging his or her point of view, wonder aloud about how others might differ in their perspective on the issue and what might influence these differences (Santilli & Hudson, 1992).

Source: American Psychological Association offers professionals 'Tips for talking with adolescents'.

3.7 Defence lawyers should be aware that children might view them as working alongside the police or the court. Many child defendants say they distrust their lawyer, seeing them as part of the system, perceiving them to be one of the adults who are 'against them' (this might also include, depending on their circumstances, their parents, teachers, youth offending team (YOT) workers and social workers).

3.8 Children, and particularly adolescents, use different parts of their brain when making decisions than adults (see paras 3.30–3.35 on the adolescent brain) – a child's lawyer should be conscious of this when working with a child in the youth justice system. Decisions made at the police station and in court proceedings may have consequences for the rest of the child's life. The lawyer will also have to establish how to work most effectively with the child's appropriate adult (see paras 6.108–6.118) or supporting adult (see paras 8.29–8.41 on supporting adults, parents and guardians) when making decisions about their case

3.9 Children may be more likely to respond emotionally rather than rationally (see 3.30–3.35 on adolescent brain development), therefore establishing rapport and trust are particularly important. Children can become easily distracted or bored. Alternatively, they may mask a lack of understanding (see paras 3.66–3.70 on speech and language difficulty). Defence lawyers should proceed at a pace that works for the child, rather than for the adult. Remembering to take regular breaks and monitoring the child's concentration and when they need a break, even if it is only for a few minutes. The Sentencing Council acknowledges that a child's lack of maturity may mean they struggle to conduct themselves appropriately, this can be brought to a court's attention.

> The court should consider the reasons why, on some occasions, a child or young person may conduct themselves inappropriately in court (eg due to nervousness, a lack of understanding of the system, a belief that they will be discriminated against, peer pressure to behave in a certain way because of others present, a lack of maturity etc) and take this into account.[11]

11 Sentencing Council, *Sentencing children and young people: definitive guideline*, 2017, para 1.15.

Working with children

3.10 Work with children requires:

- *Building a rapport.* Find a common or shared interest, show interest in them and their life. Avoid appearing under time pressure, and spend some time chatting before talking about the case and asking formal questions.
- *Gain the trust of a child.* Defence lawyers should be conscious of how their behaviour and actions could be interpreted. For example, children often comment that seeing their lawyer talking to the prosecution confirms their view that their lawyer is working for the police or the court.[12] It is always best to tell the child who you are going to speak to whether it is the custody sergeant, officer in the case, prosecutor, YOT or the court staff and explain why you are doing it. Be aware that the appearance of friendship with a police officer, prosecutor or a judge could lead to isolating your client.
- *Empathy.* The one thing we all share is that we were all children once. By empathy we mean remembering what it was like to be a child. Remember the power and authority that adults had over us, remember how we felt about adults and people in authority. Empathising enables us to check in with a child about how they feel about the process.
- *Simplify language.* Without being patronising, try to recognise use of jargon and shortcuts in language (acronyms, sections of statute, legal terms) which may alienate a child (or the child's supporting adult). Avoid, leading questions and tag questions (two questions in one).
- *Ask your client to explain back to you what you have explained to them.* Avoid asking 'Do you understand?' and don't presume, because they say they understand, that they actually do. Children's understanding of language is not fully developed so they may not be aware that they haven't understood. The responsibility lies with the professional to explain what is going to happen and the decisions the child needs to make, rather than expecting a child to tell you they haven't understood.
- *Avoid being judgmental.*
- *Explicitly inform the child you are on their side.*

12 'Evidence at the Independent Parliamentarians Inquiry into Youth Justice'.

Importance of background

Background and effective participation

3.11 The background and circumstances of a child will be highly relevant to assessing whether a child is able to effectively participate in the court process and/or is fit to plead (see chapter 4 on effective participation, special measures and fitness to plead).

3.12 If a defence lawyer has concerns relating to a child's ability to effectively participate it might be safest not to allow the child to answer questions during the police interview or not to enter a plea to the court.

- Ask the court to grant you an adjournment as you believe that you need to instruct an expert (psychiatrist or psychologist) (see chapter 12).
- Get signed authority from your client for a release of their records (see text box below for template).
- Consider whether background requires you to investigate; fitness to plead, effective participation, modifications to the court process (see chapter 4).
- Consider whether the background of your client and the offence for which they are charged should mean making representations to the Crown Prosecution Service (CPS) that prosecution is not in the public interest (see chapter paras 7.132–7.137 for more information on written representations to the CPS).

Suggestibility and compliance

3.13 Research shows that adolescents are over-represented among those who falsely confessed in response to interrogation.[13] The Gudjonsson suggestibility scale (GSS) is a psychological test that measures suggestibility. It was created in 1983 by psychologist Gisli Gudjonsson. The GSS allows psychologists to identify individuals who may be susceptible to giving false accounts of events when questioned. The GSS might be useful to assist in a situation where a child is facing interrogation or to assist in excluding evidence that may be false or unreliable due to the child's suggestibility and compliance.

3.14 Suggestibility, in criminal proceedings, often relates to the likelihood of false confessions or providing inaccurate information when asked by those in authority even when the answers are not true.

13 Amicus Brief for the American Psychological Association.

3.15 Compliance is the likelihood of acting in a manner that someone else asks, even if it is contrary to what the person wants to do. For example, compliance would be relevant to whether a child acted under duress and how likely the specific child might be to comply with a request that came from another person. Suggestibility and compliance can be addressed by a psychologist report.

Child's background and sentencing

3.16 The Sentencing Council's *Sentencing children and young people: definitive guideline*[14] highlights the factors that may diminish the culpability of children. These factors may also be relevant to assessing culpability even at the police station, in relation to decisions about Out of Court Disposals or decisions to charge (prosecute), as well as sentencing.

3.17 See paras 3.40–3.102 for more detail on common background issues and chapter 16 for an overview of the relevant sections of the *Guidelines* that apply in relation to background and sentencing.

3.18 This places a responsibility on defence and prosecution lawyers, as well as courts, to address any of the factors that may lead to specific groups of children being unnecessarily criminalised or more severely sentenced.

Sources of background information

3.19 A defence lawyer should ensure they make a thorough investigation into the child's background.

3.20 There are many sources that are useful to a lawyer in beginning to build a picture of a child's background and circumstances. Children are not always the best narrators of their circumstances for various reasons, which could include:

- they are embarrassed;
- they don't consider them relevant; and
- they are not aware that they have a vulnerability.

3.21 Sources who can help build the picture include, but are not limited to:

- parents/family;

14 *Sentencing children and young people: definitive guideline*, 2017.

- for looked after children – their social worker, key worker or the local authority;
- YOTs;
- schools – check with the school as to whether there are any school exclusions, special educational needs;
- GP – will be aware of any medication prescribed, referrals to other services, childhood illnesses, current physical and mental conditions, family history;
- Child and Adolescent Mental Health Service (CAMHS);
- support workers.

Gaining the child's consent

3.22 In order to obtain information about a child from third parties such as the child's GP, school and social services, the child must provide his or her consent to the sharing of the information.

Sample records request

3.23 A sample catch-all authorisation/release can be as follows:

> I ________________date of birth __/__/__ give my authorisation for any and all records held about me to be released to my solicitors ____________________________. This includes but is not limited to medical, school and social service records.
> Signed:
> Date:
> Witnessed:
> Date:

Medical records

3.24 Records held by a child's GP should also contain other medical referrals and services (including tangential referrals such as speech and language support, physiotherapy or psychological support). They may also contain information that is relevant to the child's background, such as whether they have ever been on an 'at risk' register by their local authority – where they have been considered at risk of neglect or ever been looked after by the local authority. These records may be more complete than others if a child has moved from a different geographical area.

Educational records

3.25 Educational records should be available for all children, but will be most relevant for those who have a learning difficulty or disability which calls for special educational provision and are supported by external professionals such as a speech and language therapist or in-class assistance but their difficulty or disability is not considered so serious as to require an Educational and Health Care Plan (EHCP) (see para 3.26).[15]

Education and health care plan (formerly statement of special educational needs)

3.26 Children who have a learning difficulty or disability which calls for special educational provision to be made are described as having 'special educational needs' (SEN).[16] A child of compulsory school age has a learning difficulty if the child has a significantly greater difficulty in learning than the majority of others of the same age.[17] Special educational provision will need to be made for a child or young person with a disability which prevents or hinders him or her from making use of facilities of a kind generally provided for others of the same age in mainstream school or mainstream post-16 institutions.[18]

3.27 The current guidance to be applied can be found in *Special educational needs and disability code of practice 0–25 years*,[19] which replaces the *SEN code of practice*.

3.28 Defence lawyers will find the EHCP a useful source of information if representing a child in criminal proceedings with an EHCP.

Obtaining expert reports

3.29 An expert report may be required to help inform the court whether the child is fit to plead or able to effectively participate. Alternatively, the report may provide advice on any modifications that would be required for the child defendant to effectively participate including whether to seek the support of an intermediary for communications assistance. It

15 https://www.gov.uk/children-with-special-educational-needs.

16 Children and Families Act 2014 s20(1).

17 Children and Families Act 2014 s20(2)(a).

18 Children and Families Act 2014 s21(1).

19 https://assets.publishing.service.gov.uk/government/uploads/system/uploads/attachment_data/file/398815/SEND_Code_of_Practice_January_2015.pdf.

may also provide information relevant to mitigation. (See chapter 12 on instructing a mental health expert or an intermediary.)

Child and adolescent brain development

Greater understanding of the adolescent brain

3.30 'Until about 15 years ago it was assumed that the vast majority of brain development takes place in the first few years of life.'[20] The development of MRI and functional magnetic resonance imaging (fMRI), the moving image version of MRI, has enabled scientists to gain a greater understanding of the physiology of children's brain and the changes and evolving structure of the adolescent brain.

3.31 The evidence shows that children and young people's brains are continually changing and developing, and that this continues into their early 20s. The scientific support for these findings is based on a combination of neuro-science, endocrinology (study of hormones) and psychology:

> Science confirms that older adolescents behave differently to adults because their minds operate differently, their emotions are more volatile, and their brains are anatomically immature.[21]

3.32 Neuroscience reveals that changes in important neural circuits continue past 20 years of age. The prefrontal cortex (which is especially important in relation to judgment, decision-making and impulse control) is the slowest to mature:

> the prefrontal cortex loses grey matter during adolescence. It has been proposed that this decline in grey matter volume partly reflects an important neurodevelopmental process: the loss of connections between brain cells (synapses) during development. This process, which is known as synaptic pruning. [22]

3.33 By contrast, the amygdala (an area of the brain responsible for reward and emotional processing) develops during early adolescence.[23] The amygdala's dominance over the frontal lobe may cause adolescents to

20 https://thinkneuroscience.wordpress.com/2014/01/22/adolescent-brain-development/.

21 American Medical Association, Amicus Brief in the case of *Roper v Simmons* 543 US 551 (2005) the Supreme Court of the United States.

22 https://thinkneuroscience.wordpress.com/2014/01/22/adolescent-brain-development/.

23 Brainwaves –The Royal Society – Module 4 Neuroscience and the law (2011) – A neuroscientific perspective on brain development and criminal responsibility.

be more prone to react with gut instincts. In adult brains, the frontal lobe offers a check on the emotions and impulses originating from the amygdala. The imbalance may account for the 'risk taking behaviour characteristic of adolescence'.[24] Emotional maturity is likely not to happen until the maturation of the cognitive processes of the prefrontal cortex and the emotional processing in the amygdala.[25]

3.34 The physiological structure of the adolescent brain is similar to the physical manifestation of mental disability within an adult brain. Completing what is 'a strong base of emerging evidence highlighting consistent and universal differences in the judgment and consequential thinking processes between children and young people and adults'.[26]

Greater risk-taking behaviour

3.35 Adolescence represents a phase of increased impulsivity, sensation-seeking and risk-taking behaviour.[27] *Sentencing children and young people: definitive guideline* recognises this at para 1.5:

> Children and young people are not fully developed and they have not attained full maturity. As such, this can impact on their decision making and risk taking behaviour it is important to consider the extent to which the child or young person has been acting impulsively and whether their conduct has been affected by inexperience, emotional volatility or negative influences. They may not fully appreciate the effect their actions can have on other people and may not be capable of fully understanding the distress and pain they cause to the victims of their crimes. Children and young people are also likely to be susceptible to peer pressure and other external influences and changes taking place during adolescence can lead to experimentation, resulting in criminal behaviour. *When considering a child or young person's age their emotional and developmental age is of at least equal importance to their chronological age (if not greater)* [emphasis added].

24 The Royal Society, *Neuroscience and the law*, Brainwaves 4, December 2011, p13.

25 University of Birmingham Institute of Applied Social Studies School of Social Policy, 'Maturity, young adults and criminal justice: a literature review' (2011).

26 The Minimum Age of Criminal Responsibility – a Medico-Legal Perspective Enys Delmage (2013), at p108.

27 The Minimum Age of Criminal Responsibility – a Medico-Legal Perspective Enys Delmage (2013).

Developmental immaturity

3.36 The rapid growth in knowledge and understanding of adolescent brain development has led the Law Commission to call for a new defence of 'developmental immaturity', their reasoning was based upon '[c]linical advances in our understanding of the brains of children and adolescents reveal that the natural physical development of the brain continues throughout childhood and adolescence and may not be fully mature until the individual reaches their early 20s. Increasingly research findings confirm that juveniles aged under 16 demonstrate inadequate functional and decision making'.[28] (See paras 4.117–4.120 for more on the Law Commission's position with regards to fitness to plead.)

Information about mental disorders

3.37 There are two main diagnostic 'manuals' that are used by mental health practitioners and offer a common language and standard criteria for the classification of mental disorders. These can provide a legal practitioner with assistance in understanding mental disorders that might be affecting a child client.

DSM-5

3.38 DSM-5 stands for the *Diagnostic and statistical manual for mental disorders* (fifth edition, 2013). DSM-5 is an American diagnostic manual and is often considered 'as a universal authority for psychiatric diagnosis'.[29] DSM-5 may be referred to by practitioners who are familiar with the American mental health system.

ICD-10

3.39 ICD-10 stands for the *International statistical classification of diseases and related health problems*. This manual is a medical classification list established by the World Health Organization (WHO) and completed in 1992. It is more widely referred to by international medical practitioners.

28 *Unfitness to plead*, Law Commission (2016) – Chapter 7, Natural developmental immaturity, para 7.35.

29 https://www.ivcc.edu/uploadedFiles/_faculty/_mangold/DSM%205.pdf.

Neurodevelopment disorders

3.40 NHS England defines a neurodisability as:

> [A]n umbrella term for conditions associated with impairment involving the nervous system and includes conditions such as cerebral palsy, autism and epilepsy; it is not uncommon for such conditions to co-occur. Children with a neurodisability have a range of impairments but many have complex and continuing needs and as a result are frequent users of the health service at all levels, community, primary care inpatient and outpatient settings.[30]

3.41 There has been a significant amount of research into the over-representation of neuro-disabled children in the youth justice system. In 2012, the Office of the Children's Commissioner published *Nobody made the connection – the prevalence of Neurodisability on young people who offend.*[31] The specific neurological disorders considered in the report are: learning disabilities; specific learning difficulties; communication disorders; attention deficit hyperactivity disorder (ADHD); autistic spectrum disorders (ASD); acquired/traumatic brain injury (TBI); epilepsy; and foetal alcohol syndrome disorders (FASD).

3.42 The relevant findings of the study include:

- A learning disability[32] is defined by three criteria: an IQ score of less than 70; significant difficulties with everyday tasks; and onset prior to adulthood.
- Generalised learning disability is significantly more common in young people in custody, with research studies suggesting a prevalence of 23–32 per cent, compared to 2–4 per cent of the general population.
- Specific reading difficulties, such as dyslexia, appear significantly more common in young people who offend, with research studies suggesting a prevalence of between 43 and 57 per cent, compared to around ten per cent of the general population.
- Studies of speech and language skills in young offenders in the UK have demonstrated that many have impairment in both receptive and expressive language skills, with incidence rates reported to be as high as 60–90 per cent.

30 NHS England standard contract for paediatric neurodisabilities.

31 'Nobody made the connection: the prevalence of neurodisability in young people who offend', Office of the Children's Commissioner, October 2012.

32 New terminology now calls this an intellectual disability and can be diagnosed with an IQ around 70.

- Prevalence rates of ADHD in young offenders have varied across studies, dependent on the methodology of the study. However, rates of ADHD are significantly greater in both male and female young offenders in comparison with the general population, with one systematic review suggesting rates of 11.7 per cent for males and 18.5 per cent for females. This compares to around one to two per cent commonly identified in the general population of young people, rising to three to nine per cent when the broader DSM-IV criteria for ADHD is applied.
- Very few studies report the prevalence of ASD within a represent ative population in youth custody. Only one such study was identified, which suggested an incidence rate of 15 per cent. This compares with reported rates of between 0.6 and 1.2 per cent in the general population.
- Rates of TBI among the general population have been identified as being between five and 24 per cent, with self-report measures of TBI often finding higher prevalence rates. This compares with rates of 65 to 76 per cent among populations in youth custody.
- FASD is an umbrella term encompassing several different diagnostic categories related to permanent birth defects resulting from prenatal alcohol exposure due to maternal consumption of alcohol during pregnancy. Traits include: characteristic facial features; reduced height, weight, and/or head circumference; and damage to the central nervous system. A few international studies exploring the prevalence of FASD in young offenders suggest a higher rate in comparison to the general population, with rates of 10.9 to 11.7 per cent compared to 0.15 per cent.[33]

3.43 The report also raised a concern that a significant number of neurodisabilities had been undiagnosed prior to the child entering the secure estate or receiving a community sentence.[34] The Children's Commissioner at the time, Maggie Atkinson, commented in her foreword that:

> The failure to identify such disorders is a tragedy in many ways. It directly, certainly negatively affects the lives of the victims of these children's crimes, of the children themselves, their families, the

33 From the Executive Summary, 'Nobody made the connection: the prevalence of neurodisability in young people who offend', Office of the Children's Commissioner, October 2012.

34 Foreword by the Children's Commissioner, 'Nobody made the connection: the prevalence of neurodisability in young people who offend', Office of the Children's Commissioner, October 2012.

services seeking to change offenders' lives for the better, and wider society.[35]

If the police or courts are made aware of a child's neurodisability, it may enable a defence lawyer to explore the possibility of an alternative intervention that may avoid criminalising a child unnecessarily.

3.44 Failure to identify and treat these conditions at an early stage could be reasons that children are entering the youth justice system. Lawyers should be alert to any signs of neurodisability and seek an expert opinion if needed to support or diagnose a neurodisability (see chapter 12 on instructing an expert).

Common conditions that affect children in the youth justice system

Attention deficit hyperactivity disorder

Overview

3.45 Attention deficit hyperactivity disorder, commonly known as 'ADHD', is characterised by persistence in symptoms of inattention, hyperactivity and impulsivity. ADHD is common among both male and female young offenders, at 11.7 and 18.5 per cent, respectively.[36] A diagnosis of ADHD might be found within an EHCP, or through the GP's medical records. However, many adolescents with atypical ADHD may not have a diagnosis. Neurodevelopmental disorders are less likely to be diagnosed in girls who tend to mask their symptoms more effectively. It may be that contact with the youth justice system will be the first time that behaviour has reached the level of concern that referrals are made.

3.46 There is medication that can be prescribed for ADHD; that prescription will have to come from a psychiatrist or medical practitioner, it is somewhat controversial and may have negative side effects. Some children may choose not to take the medication.

Representing children with ADHD

3.47 Child defendants with ADHD can very easily lose focus, it is important to bear this in mind when taking instructions from a child with

35 Foreword, nobody made the connection: the prevalence of neurodisability in young people who offend, Office of the Children's Commissioner, October 2012.

36 Nobody made the connection: the prevalence of neurodisability in young people who offend, Office of the Children's Commissioner, October 2012.

ADHD. It is often important to remind those decision-makers in the criminal justice system, police officers and courts (whether judiciary or jury) that these characteristics stem from a medical condition that affects the child's behaviour.

3.48 Regular breaks will need to be considered but it might also be beneficial to provide the police or court with a greater understanding of the condition, this will usually be by adducing expert evidence, in the form of a written report or live evidence. Medical descriptions of conditions such as ADHD can be found in the DSM-5 or ICD-10 (see paras 3.38–3.39 for explanation on DSM-5 and ICD-10) which might be useful to have for the court.

3.49 Another manifestation of ADHD that can be commonly misconceived is a child's body language, which may manifest with constant fidgeting and an inability to remain still. Again it is important to remind the police or the court that this is a result of a medical condition rather than disrespect for the proceedings.

Adverse inferences and ADHD

3.50 See paras 13.78–13.80 on adverse inferences for failing to give evidence in court.

3.51 Where a child with ADHD is unable to give a full comment, give a police interview or give evidence in court, it may be possible to resist an adverse inference being drawn from the child's failure to give evidence.[37] It will be important to have an expert report to provide advice to the court. In *R v Billy Joe Friend*,[38] the Court of Appeal concluded that had the trial judge had expert evidence about the appellant's ADHD, the judge would not have ruled in favour of drawing any adverse inference, certainly in respect of the failure to give evidence. The Court of Appeal made this observation:

> [T]hat it was undesirable for him to give evidence because of his intellectual and cognitive deficits and his ADHD.

The court concluded that it was clear that had the judge known the true position, he would not have ruled in favour of drawing any adverse inference.[39] (See paras 13.72–13.80 on adverse inferences and chapter 12 on instructing an expert.)

37 CJPOA 1984 s 35.

38 [2004] EWCA Crim 2661.

39 *R v Dixon* [2013] EWCA Crim 465.

Intermediary for a child with ADHD

3.52 The case of *R v Sevenoaks Youth Court*[40] examined a youth court's failure to provide a child with ADHD as well as other behavioural difficulties, with an intermediary. The High Court ruled:[41]

> [W]hen trying a young child, and most particularly a child such as 'C' who is only 12 with learning and behavioural difficulties, notwithstanding the absence of any express statutory power, the Youth Court has a duty under its inherent powers and under the Criminal Procedure Rules to take such steps as are necessary to ensure that he has a fair trial, not just during the proceedings, but beforehand as he and his lawyers prepare for trial. He must be given such help as he needs . . . he will need particular help to decide if he is to give evidence, and if so he will need help to do so. It is in the highest degree unlikely that this level of help can be given by a lawyer, however kind and sympathetic she may be. He needs someone to befriend and to help him, both during the trial itself and in preparation for it. In short, he needs an intermediary. Furthermore, if an intermediary is to be effective, 'C' must know the intermediary and have confidence in him or her. Such trust will not be established if their first meeting is on the morning of the trial. Moreover, the court will have to adopt its procedures to ensure that the hearing is fair to 'C' by using simple language, by taking breaks, by taking any and all such steps as are necessary. Experienced justices sitting in Youth Courts are well able to ensure the fairness of the proceedings.

3.53 For more a fuller discussion on intermediaries for child defendants, see paras 12.36–12.55 on instructing an intermediary.

Conduct disorder or oppositional defiant disorder

3.54 According to the *Royal College of Psychiatrists:*

> Children with a conduct disorder may get involved in more violent physical fights, and may steal or lie, without any sign of remorse or guilt when they are found out. They refuse to follow rules and may start to break the law. They may start to stay out all night, and play truant from school during the day. Teenagers with conduct disorder may also take risks with their health and safety by taking illegal drugs or having unprotected sexual intercourse . . . Children who behave like this will often find it difficult to make friends and have difficulties understanding social situations.[42]

40 *R v Sevenoaks Youth Court* [2009] EWHC 3088 (Admin).

41 At para 17.

42 www.rcpsych.ac.uk/healthadvice/parentsandyoungpeople/parentscarers/behaviouralproblems.aspx.

3.55 Oppositional defiant disorder (ODD) is a less severe, but equally persistent, conduct disorder in younger children. It is a childhood disorder that is defined by a pattern of hostile, disobedient and defiant behaviours directed at adults or other authority figures. ODD is also characterised by children displaying angry and irritable moods, as well as argumentative and vindictive behaviours.

3.56 Treatment for these conditions takes the form of therapeutic support, which can be undertaken with the family, in the school or broader community setting The Royal College of Psychiatrists says.

> The treatment may include social skills groups, behavioural therapy and talking therapy. These therapies can help the child to appropriately express themselves in different situations and manage their anger more effectively.[43]

Autism spectrum disorders

Overview

3.57 The collective term autism spectrum disorders (ASD), will now include Asperger syndrome (a form of high-functioning autism which may not present with language difficulties) within the spectrum. ASD conditions represent a wide spectrum of impairment and characteristics which vary from person to person and from the non-verbal to highly articulate but will usually have persistent difficulties with social interactions and communication and markedly restricted and repetitive patterns of behaviours, activities and interests since early childhood.

3.58 Certain features of ASD may predispose children to offend, such as: social naivety, misinterpretation of social cues and poor empathy. ASD can manifest itself in very concrete and rigid thinking and obsessive and repetitive behaviour. In particular, children with ASD may have poor interactions with adults in positions of authority.

3.59 Autism is a lifelong condition; there is no medication for ASD or any 'cure' as such, however social skills training can help putting in tools to manage various situations.

Representing children with ASD

3.60 Practitioners communicating with a child with ASD should avoid using metaphors, as concrete thinking can lead to literal

43 www.rcpsych.ac.uk/healthadvice/parentsandyoungpeople/parentscarers/behaviouralproblems.aspx.

interpretation of phrases. For example, idioms such as 'get your skates on' and 'reading between the lines' are kinds of metaphors that could be misinterpreted by children with ASD. Lawyers must also ensure that questions during police interview or cross-examination are closely monitored and that there are no leading questions or tag questions.

3.61 It will often be the case that a child defendant with ASD should have an intermediary to be able to effectively participate in the trial process. The Advocate's Gateway offers guidance for the lawyers representing a child with ASD with its guidance *Planning to question someone with an autism spectrum disorder.*[44]

3.62 There is also guidance produced by the National Autistic Society, including a booklet, *Autism: the National Autistic Society guide for criminal justice professionals* to give a greater understanding of ASD to criminal justice professionals.[45]

Learning disability

Overview

3.63 A learning disability is defined by the Department of Health as a 'significant reduced ability to understand new or complex information, to learn new skills (impaired intelligence), with a reduced ability to cope independently (impaired social functioning), which started before adulthood'.[46]

3.64 The Wechsler Intelligence Scale for Children (WISC) is the most widely used form of IQ testing for those aged six to 16-years-and-11-months. The WISC-V takes 45–65 minutes to administer. It generates a Full Scale IQ (formerly known as an intelligence quotient or IQ score) that represents a child's general intellectual ability, verbal and non-verbal. It also provides five primary index scores: Verbal Comprehension Index; Visual Spatial Index; Fluid Reasoning Index; Working Memory Index; and Processing Speed Index. These indices represent a child's abilities in discrete cognitive domains:

- Verbal Comprehension – verbal expression, comprehension, language, abstract reasoning;

44 www.theadvocatesgateway.org; and www.theadvocatesgateway.org/images/toolkits/3-planning-to-question-someone-with-an-autism-spectrum-disorder-including-asperger-syndrome-2016.pdf.

45 www.autism.org.uk.

46 https://assets.publishing.service.gov.uk/government/uploads/system/uploads/attachment_data/file/250877/5086.pdf.

- Visual Spatial – visual spatial reasoning, integration and synthesis, attention to visual detail, visual-motor integration;
- Fluid Reasoning – understand underlying conceptual relationships, understand visual representations of concepts;
- Working Memory – concentration, attention, ability to hold on to and mentally manipulate information;
- Processing Speed – psychomotor control & speed, learning, short term memory.

Representing children with learning disabilities

3.65 Avoid leading questions as these are too complex – some children with a lower cognitive position may not have the IQ to foresee that questions could lead them to self-incriminate. They lack cognitive strategies to sidestep questions or to see where the questions could lead to.

Speech, language and communication difficulty

Overview

3.66 The Communication Trust estimates that 10 per cent of children have speech, language and communication needs. However, the evidence indicates that 60 per cent of children in the custodial estate will have speech and language difficulties. And research published by the Children's Commissioner for England in 2012 showed that 60–90 per cent of children going through the criminal justice system have significant problems with speech and language or other communication difficulties[47] Many of these go unidentified by schools and parents.[48]

3.67 As a child's age increases, good 'surface' language skills or clear speech might make everyday conversation manageable but could still mean that the child is masking underlying speech and language difficulties. Practitioners should be particularly alert to children who are familiar with legal and court jargon, as this can give the appearance of 'street smart' and 'savvy' but can simply come from exposure and can convincingly mask an underlying communication difficulty.

47 *Nobody made the connection: the prevalence of neurodisability in young people who offend* (London: Children's Commissioner for England 2012), p9.

48 'Doing justice to speech, language and communication needs', The Communication Trust, November 2014;

Representing children with communication difficulties

3.68 All children, but particularly those with communication difficulties, will need lawyers taking instructions or asking questions in examination-in-chief or cross-examination to:

- speak clearly;
- use simple language;
- avoid leading questions;
- ensure that there are regular breaks;
- avoid tag questions (two questions in one).

3.69 If a child defendant has a speech or language difficulty, the child might need support from an intermediary a majority of whom are speech and language therapists (see paras 12.36–12.52 on instructing an intermediary during the legal process). The law relating to the appointment of intermediaries is getting more complicated, however there is support for the claim that, where needed, support should be provided to help a child defendant understand the case against him or her, for; the giving of instructions, listening to the trial, to understand and challenge witnesses and for the giving of evidence. Even if an intermediary is not granted, additional support should be provided. See the recent amendment to the Criminal Practice Directions paragraphs 3F.12 and 3F.13 serve to highlight the merit in an application for a support worker or other companion who can provide assistance when it has not been necessary to appoint an intermediary, but a defendant may benefit from some additional support to understand the proceedings.[49]

3.70 Where a child has severe communication difficulties, an intermediary can consider using visual aids to support communication. See the Advocate's Gateway – *Using communication aids in the criminal justice system* (Toolkit 14).[50]

Mental illnesses

Depression

3.71 The DSM-5 diagnostic criteria for adult depression is:

49 www.judiciary.uk/wp.content/uploads/2018/08/crim-pd-2015-no-7-oct-2018.pdf.

50 The Advocates Gatewaytoolkits14 using-communication-aids-in-the-criminal-justice-system.

> Five (or more) of the following symptoms have been present during the same 2-week period and represent a change from previous functioning; at least one of the symptoms is either (1) depressed mood or (2) loss of interest or pleasure.
>
> 1. Depressed mood most of the day, nearly every day, as indicated by either subjective report (eg, feels sad, empty, hopeless) or observation made by others (eg, appears tearful). (Note: In children and adolescents, can be irritable mood.)
> 2. Markedly diminished interest or pleasure in all, or almost all, activities most of the day, nearly every day (as indicated by either subjective account or observation).
> 3. Significant weight loss when not dieting or weight gain (eg, a change of more than 5% of body weight in a month) or decrease or increase in appetite nearly every day. (Note: In children, consider failure to make expected weight gain.)
> 4. Insomnia or hypersomnia nearly every day.
> 5. Psychomotor agitation or retardation nearly every day (observable by others, not merely subjective feelings of restlessness or being slowed down).
> 6. Fatigue or loss of energy nearly every day.
> 7. Feelings of worthlessness or excessive or inappropriate guilt (which may be delusional) nearly every day (not merely self-reproach or guilt about being sick).
> 8. Diminished ability to think or concentrate, or indecisiveness, nearly every day (either by subjective account or as observed by others).
> 9. Recurrent thoughts of death (not just fear of dying), recurrent suicidal ideation without a specific plan, or a suicide attempt or a specific plan for committing suicide.[51]

3.72 In a report published by Young Minds and Prison Reform Trust in 2013, *Turning young lives around* the researchers state:

> Evidence from the UK and international studies shows that between a third and a half of children in custody have a diagnosable mental health disorder such as depression, which is particularly prevalent in girls.[52]

3.73 The predominance of depression and other mental health disorders in children in the criminal justice system means that practitioners need to be alert to the symptoms to ensure a child, who is a defendant, is given the appropriate support and that the court is aware of the potential consequences of the condition on any particular child.

51 Pearson Clinical DSM5 Diagnostic Criteria Major Depressive Disorder.

52 Turning Young Lives Around – Prison Reform Trust: www.prisonreformtrust.org.uk/Portals/0/Documents/turningyounglivesaroundFINAL.pdf.

Bipolar disorder

3.74 Young Minds, a leading charity championing the wellbeing and mental health of young people, defines bipolar disorder as follows:

> Bipolar disorder is a disorder in which your mood can switch between extremes of happiness and depression, with episodes lasting for days or even weeks on end. It affects 1 in 100 people and tends to begin later in adolescence with symptoms usually starting between the ages of 15 and 19 in young people.[53]

3.75 The symptoms of bipolar disorder 'can come and go' according to Young Minds, but the symptoms to look out for include:

- extreme mood swings;
- manic episodes such as talking a lot, racing thoughts, over confidence, increased activity;
- difficulty with concentration;
- low mood;
- decreased energy;
- disturbed sleep;
- reduced appetite;
- thoughts of self-harm;
- psychosis.[54]

Psychosis

3.76 Psychosis is a mental health problem that causes people to perceive or interpret things differently from those around them. This might involve hallucinations or delusions.

3.77 The two main symptoms of psychosis are:

- hallucinations – where a person hears, sees and, in some cases, feels, smells or tastes things that aren't there; a common hallucination is hearing voices;
- delusions – where a person has strong beliefs that aren't shared by others; a common delusion is someone believing there is a conspiracy to harm them.

3.78 The combination of hallucinations and delusional thinking can cause severe distress and a change in behaviour. When someone is

53 Young Minds – conditions – bipolar disorder.

54 Young Minds – conditions – bipolar disorder.

experiencing the symptoms of psychosis it is often referred to as having a psychotic episode.[55]

3.79 Psychosis may be a symptom of schizophrenia, but it can also be brought on by other conditions, such as bipolar (see paras 3.74–3.75) or from drug use or withdrawal from drugs or medications.

Post-traumatic stress disorder

3.80 Post-traumatic stress disorder (PTSD) is defined as delayed and/or protracted response to a stressful event or situation of an exceptionally threatening or catastrophic nature.[56] PTSD is often associated with flashbacks; these may or may not be a link to an alleged offence for a person in the criminal justice system. A core symptom of PTSD is hypervigilance, which means person is constantly primed for fight or flight as constantly anticipating danger. PTSD is also commonly associated with emotional numbness or dissociating and someone absenting themselves so they may therefore having little or no memory of the alleged incident. Symptoms of PTSD include detachment from people, disturbed sleep and reduced appetite.

3.81 If a practitioner believes that a child in the criminal justice system is suffering from PTSD, it is important to apply for an assessment by a mental health professional. PTSD can be referred to in mitigation and may be relevant to sentencing disposal.

Deprivation and neglect

3.82 Deprivation can have profound effects on a child's development: The British Medical Association (BMA) published a report in 2014 titled *Young lives behind bars: the health and human rights of children and young people detained in the criminal justice system*. In an overview of the report, Dr John Chisolm, Chair of the BMA Medical Ethics Committee, stated:

> Many of the children and young people who end up in the criminal justice system come from chaotic backgrounds, and are often victims of violence, abuse or neglect. They are unable to thrive socially, emotionally or physically, and are among the most vulnerable individuals in our society long before they reach detention.[57]

55 NHS UK – conditions – psychosis.

56 ICD-10.

57 British Medical Association – *Young Lives Behind Bars* (2014).

3.83 The report talks about development in science leading to a greater understanding of 'the neurobiology of deprivation'.[58] As mentioned previously, rapid developments in neuroscience have enabled researchers to look in considerable detail at the impacts of environment on child brain development. Given the extreme plasticity of the young brain, these environments can have lifelong implications. It seems likely that early exposure to abuse or deprivation, particularly if it is sustained, can lead to brain alterations that are linked to emotional and behavioural difficulties.[59]

Attachment difficulties

3.84 Attachment theory was developed by John Bowlby (1907–1990), a child psychiatrist and psychoanalyst who looked at mother–child attachment relationships providing psychoanalytical theory on the impact on a child of separation and loss.

3.85 Generally the term 'attachment disorder' refers to the absence or distortion of age appropriate social behaviors with adults. Attachment disorder is rare. There are two types: one is overly friendly and does not discriminate familiar adults with strangers; the other has no interest in attachment figures. Mistrustful and angry is an attachment difficulty.

3.86 A child with attachment difficulties is more likely to have social problems with peers and teachers and other adults in positions of trust. These children can be mistrustful and angry toward their parents and adults and are unable to regulate their emotions.[60]

Looked after children

3.87 Looked after children are over-represented in the criminal justice system – 38 per cent of children in YOIs and 52 per cent in STCs have been in care.[61]

3.88 The Sentencing Council has recognised the special status of looked after children in the criminal justice system.[62] it is not just

58 At p25.

59 At p25.

60 Elgar, Knight, Worrall, and Sherman, 2003.

61 Prison Reform Trust, *In care, out of trouble. an independent review chaired by Lord Laming* (London: Prison Reform Trust, 2016).

62 *Sentencing children and young people: definitive guideline.*

children who are in foster care or children's homes who may have had experience of the care system, children who live with extended family members may have been placed there through the family courts – it is the lawyer's duty to explore this part of a child's background either with an accompanying adult or the YOT.[63]

3.89 *Sentencing children and young people: definitive guideline states:*

> Evidence shows that looked after children and young people are over-represented in the criminal justice system.[64] When dealing with a child or young person who is looked after the court should also bear in mind the additional complex vulnerabilities that are likely to be present in their background. For example, looked after children and young people may have no or little contact with their family and/or friends, they may have special educational needs and/or emotional and behavioural problems, they may be heavily exposed to peers who have committed crime and they are likely to have accessed the care system as a result of abuse, neglect or parental absence due to bereavement, imprisonment or desertion. The court should also bear in mind that the level of parental- type support that a looked after child receives through the criminal justice process may vary, and may be limited. For example, while parents are required to attend court hearings, this is not the case for social workers responsible for looked after children and young people.[65]

3.90 The guideline highlights that looked after children are often brought to court for offences that are minor in nature and for behaviour, that if it happened in the family environment would be unlikely to end up in the criminal justice system.

> In some instances a looked after child or young person (including those placed in foster homes and independent accommodation, as well as in care homes) may be before the court for a low level offence that the police would not have been involved in, if it had occurred in an ordinary family setting.[66]

3.91 Sentencers are also told to consider the impact that custody will have on the leaving care rights of a child 'and whether this impact is proportionate to the seriousness of the offence'.[67]

3.92 Two recent reports sought to examine why looked after children are over-represented in the youth justice system. The first, by the Prison

63 *Sentencing children and young people: definitive guideline.*

64 Department for Education, 'Outcomes for children looked after by local authorities in England', as at 31 March 2014, Statistical First Release 49/2014.

65 *Sentencing children and young people: definitive guideline,* para 1.16.

66 *Sentencing children and young people: definitive guideline,* para 1.16.

67 *Sentencing children and young people: definitive guideline,* para 1.17.

Reform Trust, titled *Keeping children in care out of trouble*, was a review 'to examine the reasons for, and how best to tackle, the over representation of children in care, or with experience of care, in the criminal justice system in England and Wales'.[68] The second, by the Howard League for Penal Reform, looked at the over-criminalisation of children in care homes. This report found, among other things, that:

- 'Looked after' children living in children's homes are being criminalised at excessively high rates compared to all other groups of children, including those in other types of care.
- Staff in children's homes are too frequently calling out the police, often over minor incidents.
- Exposure to the criminal justice system affects the already damaged life chances of these highly vulnerable children.[69]

3.93 In response to these reports the government released a *National Protocol on Reducing Criminalisation of Looked After Children and Care Leavers.*[70] It is co-published by 3 government departments; Department for Education, Home Office and the Ministry of Justice. The Protocol clearly states that its aim is to reduce the contact that looked after children have with the criminal justice system, noting that

> Coming into contact with the criminal justice system tends to increase the likelihood of offending, and children and young people, especially the most vulnerable, such as looked after children, should be diverted from it wherever possible[71]

3.94 For the first time, the 'best interest principle' set out in UNCRC Article 3(1)[72] has been written into domestic legislation. Children and Social Work Act 2017 s1(1)(a) states:

> (1) A local authority in England must, in carrying out functions in relation to looked after children, relevant children and former relevant children and young people have regard to the need – (a) to *act in the best interests* . . . [emphasis added].

3.95 A lawyer involved with a child who is care-experienced or is still in care, or who should be in care needs to be aware of the circumstances

68 www.prisonreformtrust.org.uk/Portals/0/Documents/In%20care%20out%20of%20trouble%20summary.pdf.

69 Howard League for Penal Reform, Criminal Care – Children's Homes and Criminalising Children,

70 National protocol on reducing criminalisation of looked after children, November 2018.

71 Para 1.5.

72 See paras 1.72–1.74 on best interests.

around their situation and also of the policy and research in relation to these children to make representations, where appropriate to divert a child from the criminal justice system where they are being criminalised unnecessarily or where the circumstances would amount to substantial mitigation.

Racial disparity and children in the criminal justice system

3.96 *Sentencing children and young people: definitive guideline* requires an advocate and the court to consider racial disparity as a contributing factor to a child being in the youth justice system.

> There is evidence to suggest that black and minority ethnic children and young people are over-represented in the youth justice system.[73] The factors contributing to this are complex. One factor is that significant proportion of looked after children are from a black and minority ethnic background.[74] A further factor may be the experience of such children and young people in terms of discrimination and negative experiences of authority. When having regard to the welfare of the child or young person to be sentenced, *the particular factors which arise in the case of black and minority ethnic children and young people need to be taken into account*. [emphasis[75]

3.97 In 2017, David Lammy MP published an independent review into the treatment of, and outcomes for BAME individuals in the criminal justice system. The Lammy Review highlighted the current failings of the youth justice system and makes a number of important recommendations on how best to redress the disproportionate representation of BAME children in the criminal justice system. Despite making up just 14 per cent of the overall population, over 40 per cent of young people in custody are from BAME backgrounds. The BAME proportion of child prisoners has risen from 25 per cent to 41 per cent in the decade 2006–2016; in September 2018 over 50 per cent of the remand population of under 18-year-olds were from BAME backgrounds.[76]

73 Ministry of Justice *Black, Asian and Minority Ethnic disproportionality in the Criminal Justice System in England and Wales* (2016)

74 National Statistics, *Children looked after in England including adoption 2015 to 2016* (National table, figure B1).

75 *Sentencing children and young people: definitive guideline* Para 1.18f.

76 'Independent review into the treatment of, and outcomes for black, Asian and minority ethnic (BAME) individuals in the criminal justice system: final report' by David Lammy MP, 2017.

3.98 The Lammy Review highlights that arrest rates are higher across all ethnic groups when compared to their white peers,[77] and that young men from BAME are more likely to be tried in the Crown Court than their white equivalents.[78] At the Crown Court, BAME defendants were more likely than white defendants to receive prison sentences for drug offences, even when factors such as past convictions are taken into account.[79]

3.99 The Lammy Review also makes pioneering recommendations for judges, prosecutors and prisons. The Review recommends that all sentencing remarks in the Crown Court should also be published, making justice more transparent for victims, witnesses and offenders, and addressing the 'trust deficit' between BAME individuals and the justice system.[80]

Child victims of trafficking, criminal exploitation, modern slavery or sexual exploitation

3.100 Many children in the criminal justice system are not identified as potential victims of trafficking, criminal exploitation, modern slavery or sexual exploitation and are charged with criminal offences and treated like defendants when they should be treated as victims, this includes children who have been brought into what are called 'county lines' cases (see paras 13.14–13.53 for defences available to trafficked children).

3.101 A child who is coerced or forced to commit a crime by the trafficker, or may be compelled to commit a criminal offence as a direct consequence of having been trafficked, is entitled to rely on the Modern Slavery Act 2015 s45(4) defence (although some criminal offences including murder and manslaughter are excluded[81]). The practical step is to ask the police or the YOT or one of the referral agencies to make a referral to the National Referral Mechanism (see paras 13.48–13.51). If recognised as a victim of modern slavery, the

77 'Independent review into the treatment of, and outcomes for black, Asian and minority ethnic (BAME) individuals in the criminal justice system: final report' page 5.

78 Page 12.

79 Page 5.

80 Recommendation 13.

81 Modern Slavery Act 2015 Sch 4.

referral process will generate a 'conclusive grounds decision' and the CPS will review their decision to prosecute in the light of this.

3.102 The CPS guidance makes clear that child trafficking is first and foremost a child protection issue and that the use of a child in a criminal enterprise is a form of child abuse. The Code for Crown Prosecutors requires that they consider the best interests of children and young people when assessing whether it is in the public interest to prosecute:[82]

> Where there is a credible suspicion that the child or young person might have been trafficked and exploited through criminal activity, then that would generally provide a defence of duress. Clear evidence of trafficking should result in the young person not being prosecuted, and less clear evidence should at least prompt further enquiries. Prosecutors must work with law enforcement and organisations that support child victims of trafficking to ensure that all relevant information is available and that all appropriate assessments are undertaken.[83]

3.103 If the defendant is a child victim of trafficking/slavery, the extent to which the crime alleged against the child was consequent on and integral to the child being a victim of trafficking/slavery must be considered.[84] In some cases, the criminal offence is a manifestation of the exploitation[85] (see paras 13.14–13.54 for defence and fuller description of trafficking).

82 www.cps.gov.uk/publication/full-code-test.

83 CPS Legal Guidance on Human Trafficking, Smuggling and Slavery: www.cps.gov.uk/legal-guidance/human-trafficking-smuggling-and-slavery.

84 www.cps.gov.uk/legal-guidance/human-trafficking-smuggling-and-slavery.

85 See *L, HVN, THN and T* [2013] EWCA Crim 991, para 20.

CHAPTER 4

Effective participation, special measures and fitness to plead for child defendants

continued

Key points

- England and Wales has a particularly low age of criminal responsibility compared to the rest of Europe. In England and Wales, children can be held criminally responsible from the age of 10.
- The criminal justice system, legal processes and procedures can be complex. Defence lawyers must ensure their child clients are able to effectively participate in their trial, this is a key part of their right to a fair trial.
- Developmental immaturity combined with the prevalence neurodisabilities and mental illness means that child defendants are more likely to have difficulties with effectively participating in the legal processes than adults.
- The criminal justice system in England and Wales has not developed a child specific competency framework for children to understand their capacity.
- Lawyers and courts therefore have to rely on outdated and adult-focused procedures if a child is unable to understand the legal processes. This has continued by the Law Commission.
- There are modifications that are available to help a child to effectively participate in the legal processes.

Introduction

4.1 England and Wales has a very low age of criminal responsibility – the UK is an outlier in this regard in Europe.[1] There is a presumption in English law that all children from the age of 10 can be criminally responsible for their actions.[2] Given what we know about child and adolescent brain development[3] and the prevalence of children with neurodisabilities and mental illness in the youth justice system[4] this can lead to real difficulties in how to assess and ensure children are able to effectively participate in criminal proceedings.

1 See paras 1.55–1.62 on the age of criminal responsibility.

2 See paras 4.5–4.7 on abolition of doli incapax below.

3 See paras 3.30–3.34 on the importance of background and adolescent brain development.

4 See chapter 3 on relevance of background.

4.2 Unlike other areas of law in England and Wales,[5] or other countries[6] there is no formalised framework for assessing the capacity of children in criminal cases.[7] All children over the age of 10 are presumed to have the capacity to participate in criminal proceedings. In 2016 the Law Commission published a report *Unfitness to Plead*,[8] providing analysis and recommendations about the legal test and procedure to be followed when a defendant cannot effectively participate and lacks capacity to be tried.[9]

4.3 In a case involving any vulnerable defendant, including a child, consideration needs to be given to the defendant's individual needs, and in particular whether the defendant is fit to plead;[10] whether the defendant can effectively participate;[11] and what modifications or special measures may be necessary to ensure that the defendant is participating effectively.[12] These are considerations for any vulnerable defendant, including vulnerable adults. All children should be considered vulnerable by virtue of their age,[13] and many are doubly vulnerable as they may have extra needs due to underlying difficulties. The court should be reminded of its welfare duties towards children,[14] which may be another reason to consider modifications.

4.4 This chapter discusses vulnerable defendants in relation to capacity; effective participation; modifications and special measures; and fitness to plead. Chapter 12 deals with the practicalities of instructing mental health experts and intermediaries in cases where a child's capacity and ability to effectively participate are brought into question.

The abolition of doli incapax

4.5 The old rule of doli incapax required the prosecution to prove that any child between the ages of 10 and 13 knew that what he or she was

5 See Mental Capacity Act 2005 s3 for interpretation of capacity in civil legal proceedings.
6 For example, competency to face trial in the USA.
7 See paras 4.8–4.13 on capacity.
8 *Unfitness to Plead*, Law Commission (Law Com No 364) 12 January 2016.
9 See para 4.128 for the defence of developmental immaturity recommended by the Law Commission.
10 See paras 4.69–4.116 on fitness to plead.
11 See paras 4.14–4.30 effective participation below.
12 See paras 4.31–4.57 modifications and special measures
13 Criminal Practice Direction 3D.1: 'vulnerable includes those under 18 years of age'.
14 See para 4.55 on welfare and paras 1.68–1.71.

doing was seriously wrong.[15] The abolition of doli incapax as a rebuttable presumption in 1998[16] compounded the problem of how to deal with younger children (aged ten to 13) who lacked capacity.

4.6 In a paper in 2006, the Royal College of Psychiatrists[17] noted that it is extremely difficult to set a definitive age of criminal responsibility given that the processes of intellectual, emotional, social and physical development of children are highly complex, multi-faceted and uneven. The report argues that an enormously wide range of factors – both environmental (such as experiences of abuse and neglect) and biological (such as genetic and neuro-cognitive deficits), and the interaction between them – can impact different rates of development (see paras 3.30–3.34 on child and adolescent brain development).

4.7 The current procedures to deal with effective participation and fitness to plead have met with some criticism. The Law Commission in their 2016 report *Unfitness to plead* recommended a defence of developmental immaturity (see below at paras 4.117–4.120). However, the government have not implemented this suggestion to date, so at present legal practitioners must navigate their way through the complex system that is currently in force.

Capacity

Overview

4.8 Capacity or mental capacity has a legal definition in other areas of the law.

4.9 In civil proceedings, decisions about a person's capacity are governed by the Mental Capacity Act (MCA) 2005. Section 2(1) states that a person lacks capacity to make a decision if the person has an 'impairment of or disturbance in the function of their mind or brain' (either temporary or permanent), and as a result the person cannot do *one or more* of the following:

- understand the information relating to this particular decision;
- retain the information for long enough to make this decision;
- weigh up the information involved in making this decision;
- communicate his or her decision in any way.

15 See para 1.51 on the abolition of the rebuttable presumption of doli incapax.

16 Crime and Disorder Act 1998 s34: 'The rebuttable presumption of criminal law that a child aged 10 or over is incapable of committing an offence is hereby abolished'.

17 Royal College of Psychiatrists, OP56 2006.

4.10 In a civil context, this means a person may have capacity to make certain decisions and not others.

Grisso criteria

4.11 In parts of the USA, the juvenile justice system looks at decisional capacity to decide whether a child defendant is 'competent' to stand trial. There is an established 'competency' framework that has been developed by psychologist Thomas Grisso.[18]

Screening children for capacity and participation difficulties in criminal cases

4.12 Capacity is yet to become established as a measure of a child's ability to stand trial in England and Wales. The Law Commission's report *Unfitness to Plead* discusses the importance of identifying capacity issues among young defendants:

> Early identification of young defendants with participation difficulties is key to ensuring suitable and effective procedures in the youth court. We therefore recommend in principle that all defendants appearing for the first time in the youth court should be screened for participation difficulties.[19]

4.13 Although the Law Commission's recommendations have not been brought into law, the authors of this book believe that their guidance offer can best practice for legal practitioners and can be referred to wherever a defence lawyer is representing a child who is in court for the first time. The Royal College of Psychiatrists have recommended that assessments of child defendants take place as a matter of course.[20]

Origins of effective participation

European Court of Human Rights jurisprudence

4.14 The concept of 'effectively participating' in criminal proceedings began with the European Court of Human Rights (ECtHR) decision in *Stanford v UK*,[21] which held that in order for the accused to have a

18 See www.yjlc.uk/grisso-criteria.

19 *Unfitness to Plead*, Law Commission (Law Com No 364) 12 January 2016, para 1.104.

20 www.rcpsych.ac.uk/files/pdfversion/op56.pdf.

21 [1994] ECHR 6.

fair trial, 'Article 6 [of the European Convention on Human Rights (ECHR)] guarantees the right of an accused to participate effectively in a criminal trial'.[22]

4.15 'Effective participation' was referred to in relation to children in the criminal justice system in the case of *V v UK*.[23] The ECtHR found that the public trial of two boys aged 11 but with functional ages of eight- or nine-year-olds in the Crown Court, breached their Article 6 right to a fair trial. The court made the following observations:

> [T]hat the applicant's trial took place over three weeks in public in the Crown Court. Special measures were taken in view of the applicant's young age and to promote his understanding of the proceedings: for example, he had the trial procedure explained to him and was taken to see the courtroom in advance, and the hearing times were shortened so as not to tire the defendants excessively. Nonetheless, the formality and ritual of the Crown Court must at times have seemed incomprehensible and intimidating for a child of eleven, and there is evidence that certain of the modifications to the courtroom, in particular the raised dock which was designed to enable the defendants to see what was going on, had the effect of increasing the applicant's sense of discomfort during the trial, since he felt exposed to the scrutiny of the press and public . . . There is considerable psychiatric evidence relating to the applicant's ability to participate in the proceedings.[24]

4.16 The ECtHR found that:

> . . . it is essential that a child charged with an offence is dealt with in a manner which takes full account of his age, level of maturity and intellectual and emotional capacities, and that steps are taken to promote his ability to understand and participate in the proceedings.[25]

The court ruled that:

> . . . the applicant was unable to participate effectively in the criminal proceedings against him and was, in consequence, denied a fair hearing in breach of Article 6 para 1.[26]

The court noted that when a child is on trial, proceedings should be conducted in such a way as to reduce as far as possible the child defendant's feelings of intimidation and inhibition.[27]

22 *Stanford v UK* [1994] ECHR 6, para 26.
23 *V v UK* [2000] 30 EHRR 121.
24 *V v UK* [2000] 30 EHRR 121, paras 88–89.
25 *V v UK* [2000] 30 EHRR 121, para 86.
26 *V v UK* [2000] 30 EHRR 121, para 91.
27 *V v UK* [2000] 30 EHRR 121, para 85.

4.17 *SC v UK*[28] was a case that followed on from *V v UK*, SC was 11 years old, he was charged with attempted robbery and tried in the Crown Court. He had a significant degree of learning difficulties and his intellectual functioning was more consistent with a six- to eight-year-old, rather than an 11-year-old. He had been assessed by psychiatrists and found fit to plead. In SC's case, modifications were put in place to facilitate his ability to effectively participate in line with the Criminal Practice Directions (CrimPD), that was introduced after *V v UK* (see appendix C and paras 4.20–4.30). SC sat with his social worker throughout the trial; although he was tried in public, in the Crown Court, steps were taken to ensure that the procedure was as informal as possible, for example, the legal professionals did not wear wigs and gowns.

4.18 The ECtHR found that despite the modifications to the court process, there had been a breach of SC's ECHR Article 6(1) right to a fair trial because he had been unable to effectively participate in his trial. The ECtHR stated that:

> '[E]ffective participation' presupposes;
>
> 1. that the accused has a broad understanding of the nature of the trial process and of what is at stake, including the significance of any penalty which may be imposed . . .
> 2. the accused should be able to follow what is said by the prosecution witnesses and,
> 3. if represented, to explain to his own lawyers his version of events, to point out any statements with which he disagrees and make them aware of any facts which should be put forward in his defence.[29]

4.19 Further, the ECtHR found that:

> . . . when a decision is taken to deal with a child who risks not being able to participate effectively because of his youth and limited intellectual capacity, rather than some other form of disposal directed primarily at determining the child's best interests and those of the community, it is essential that he be tried in a specialist tribunal which is able to give full consideration to, and make proper allowance for, the handicaps under which he labours, and to adapt its procedures accordingly.[30]

28 *SC v UK* [2005] 40 EHRR 10.

29 *SC v UK* [2005] 40 EHRR, para 33.

30 *SC v UK* [2005] 40 EHRR, para 35.

Criminal practice direction for vulnerable defendants

Background

4.20 In 2000 the then Lord Chief Justice, Lord Bingham CJ, issued a practice direction in respect of the trial of young defendants in the Crown Court in order to respond to the ECtHR's finding in *V v UK* (see paras 4.15–4.16 above).

4.21 In 2013, the practice direction was modified to extend beyond young defendants to 'vulnerable people in court'. All children are vulnerable by virtue of their age, and therefore any reference to vulnerable defendants includes all children. The CrimPD Part 3D–G (reproduced in appendix C) includes a section on intermediaries, modifications[31] and on special measures.[32]

Duty to raise the practice direction on vulnerable defendants

4.22 The duty to raise the issues set out in CrimPD Part 3D–G lies with legal representatives and with the court itself. The Criminal Procedure Rules (CrimPR) 2015 state that 'the court has a responsibility to facilitate the participation of any person, including the defendant'.[33] Criminal Procedure Rules r3.11(c)(v) state that:

> . . . in order to manage a trial or an appeal, the court may require a party to identify what arrangments are desirable to facilitate the participation of any other person including the defendant.

4.23 In *R v H*,[34] the Court of Appeal said that there was a need for the court to observe the CrimPD whether or not the representatives for the defendant raise concerns about the trial process; and it was the duty of both counsel (including the prosecution) to assist the court to do so.[35] However, the Court of Appeal went on to state that failures to comply with the practice direction would not automatically render a conviction unsafe.

4.24 More recently, in the case of *R v Grant Murray*[36] the then Lord Chief Justice emphasised that it is

> . . . the judge's duty to 'take every reasonable step to encourage and facilitate the participation of vulnerable defendants' (CrimPR rr3.9(3)(a)

31 See paras 4.31–4.37.

32 See paras 4.43–4.56.

33 Criminal Procedure Rules 2015 SI No 1490 r3.9(3)(b).

34 [2006] 150 SJ 571.

35 *Archbold* 2017 4–162.

36 [2017] EWCA Crim 1228.

> and (b)) so that they may give their best evidence, comprehend the proceedings and engage fully with his or her defence. The pre-trial and trial process should, so far as necessary, be adapted to meet those ends.[37]

The Court of Appeal accepted that:

> ... further improvements can be made to the procedure so as to ensure a proper focus on the needs of a vulnerable defendant at the earliest possible stage in the proceedings.[38]

Pre-trial and preparation hearings

4.25 As mentioned above, the Court of Appeal accepted in 2017 that not all lawyers or judges are considering the practice direction for vulnerable defendants, even in serious criminal charges with very young defendants.

4.26 The practice direction applies not only to the trial of vulnerable defendants, but also to the pre-trial stages:

> The pre-trial and trial process should, so far as necessary, be adapted to meet those ends.[39]

4.27 The Court of Appeal aims to remedy any failure to consider modifications for child defendants by amending the PTPH form, stating:

> ... to ensure a proper focus on the needs of a vulnerable defendant at the earliest possible stage in the proceedings. The court therefore asked the Criminal Procedure Rules Committee to review the form used for the PTPH hearing; this form has proved an effective and vital means of identifying the issues that are likely to arise at the trial. The Committee had been asked to include within the form a check list of all the relevant matters that need to be considered when young persons are to be tried in the Crown Court. As the form will require the judge to give reasons for departing from the Practice Direction, focus on the needs of young defendants will be intense. The Committee has agreed to make revisions to the form.[40]

4.28 At the time of writing, no such changes have yet been made to the Plea and Trial Preparation Hearing (PTPH) form, but it should be considered good practice to raise these matters at any PTPH with a child or vulnerable defendant and ensure that the practice direction has been fully considered.

37 *R v Grant Murray and others* [2017] EWCA Crim 1228, para 109.
38 *R v Grant Murray and others* [2017] EWCA Crim 1228, para 227.
39 *R v Grant Murray and others* [2017] EWCA Crim 1228, para 109.
40 *R v Grant Murray and others* [2017] EWCA Crim 1228, para 227.

4.29 The Court of Appeal emphasised that it would generally be considered misconduct to take on a case where an advocate is not trained to represent a child defendant:

> It would be difficult to conceive of an advocate being competent to act in a case involving young witnesses or defendants unless the advocate had undertaken specific training.[41]

4.30 The Bar Standards Board (BSB), the regulatory authority for barristers in England and Wales, introduced in 2018 a requirement for barristers intending to represent children in the youth court to register their competence to do so.[42]

Modifications and special measures

Overview

4.31 The court should use the modifications in the practice directions, statutory special measures and any other adaptations that are appropriate in order to ensure a child can effectively participate.

4.32 In *R v Grant Murray* the Court of Appeal confirmed:

> . . . if confirmation is needed, that the principles in *R v Lubemba* [2014] EWCA Crim 2064 (in which the court highlighted best practice for vulnerable witnesses) apply to child defendants as witnesses in the same way as they apply to other vulnerable witnesses.[43]

4.33 The modifications in the criminal practice direction are not exhaustive, and there remains a common law power to ensure a vulnerable defendant can effectively participate. The modifications contained in the current version of the CrimPD Part 3D–G were summarised by the Lord Chief Justice as:

1) There should be the provision of an intermediary for the purposes of preparation for the trial and during the trial and a pre-trial visit arranged where appropriate.[44]

41 *R v Grant Murray and others* [2017] EWCA Crim 1228, para 226.

42 The rule change is contained within Rule S59 of the BSB Handbook and the specialist skills, knowledge and attributes necessary to work effectively with vulnerable children are set out in the BSB's *Youth Proceedings competences* and guidance.

43 [2017] EWCA Crim 1228, para 226.

44 CrimPD [2015] EWCA 1567 3F.3

2) Subject to the need for appropriate security arrangements, and if practicable, the trial should be held in a courtroom in which all the participants are on the same or almost the same level[45] and a vulnerable defendant, especially if young, should normally, if the defendant wishes, be free to sit with members of his or her family or others in a like relationship[46], and with some other suitable supporting adult such as a social worker, and in a place which permits easy, informal communication with the defendant's legal representatives.[47]
3) The wearing of robes and wigs should take account of the wishes of a vulnerable defendant.[48]
4) The conduct of the trial should be according to a timetable which takes full account of a vulnerable defendant's ability to concentrate with frequent and regular breaks, if necessary.[49]
5) The trial judge should ensure, so far as practicable, that the whole trial is conducted in clear language that the defendant can understand and that evidence in chief and cross-examination are conducted using questions that are short and clear.[50] The conclusions of the 'ground rules' hearing should be followed, and advocates should use and follow the advocates' 'toolkits'.[51]

4.34 The Court of Appeal found in the case of *R v Walls*[52] that when appropriately utilised, modifications and special measures should allow vulnerable defendants to effectively participate as opposed to going straight to a finding of unfit to plead:

> Plainly consideration should be given to the use of these powers or other ways in which the characteristics of a defendant evident from a psychological or psychiatric report can be accommodated with the trial process so that his limitations can be understood by the jury, before a court takes the very significant step of embarking on a trial of fitness to plead.[53]

45 CrimPD [2015] EWCA 1567–3G.7.
46 CrimPD [2015] EWCA 1567–3G.8.
47 CrimPD [2015] EWCA 1567–3G.8.
48 CrimPD [2015] EWCA 1567–3G.12.
49 CrimPD [2015] EWCA 1567–3G.10.
50 CrimPD [2015] EWCA 1567–3G.10.
51 *R v Grant Murray and others* [2017] EWCA Crim 1228, para 110.
52 [2011] EWCA Crim 443, para 37.
53 *R v Walls* [2011] EWCA Crim 443, para 37.

Intermediaries

4.35 The role of an intermediary is set out in Youth Justice and Criminal Evidence Act (YJCEA) 1999 s29(2) which states:

> The function of an intermediary is to communicate–
> (a) to the witness, questions put to the witness, and
> (b) to any person asking such questions, the answers given by the witness in reply to them,
>
> and to explain such questions or answers so far as necessary to enable them to be understood by the witness or person in question.

4.36 CrimPD 3F.1 states that:

> Intermediaries facilitate communication with witnesses and defendants who have communication needs.

4.37 An intermediary is often a speech and language therapist who has been trained to assist with communication with vulnerable people in criminal proceedings.

4.38 In *C v Sevenoaks Youth Court*[54] the magistrates felt they had no statutory power to order an intermediary to support a 12-year-old defendant with complex mental health problems throughout his trial in the youth court. His lawyers judicially reviewed the decision and the High Court found:

> In my judgment, when trying a young child, and most particularly a child such as 'C' who is only 12 with learning and behavioural difficulties, notwithstanding the absence of any express statutory power, the Youth Court has a duty under its inherent powers and under the Criminal Procedure Rules to take such steps as are necessary to ensure that he has a fair trial, not just during the proceedings, but beforehand as he and his lawyers prepare for trial. He must be given such help as he needs to understand the case against him; he must be helped to give his own side of the story as his proof of evidence is drawn up; it may be that he needs help to speak to his lawyers, let alone to the court; he will need help to follow the case as it proceeds; he would need help to decide whether to question the cadet whom he is alleged to have attacked; whether to accept his identification or to attack his credibility; he will need to decide what line to take with his co-defendant, 'P', depending on the evidence he gives; he will need particular help to decide if he is to give evidence, and if so he will need help to do so. It is in the highest degree unlikely that this level of help can be given by a lawyer, however kind and sympathetic she may be. He needs someone to befriend and to help him, both during the trial itself and in preparation for it. In short, he needs an intermediary.

54 [2009] EWHC 3088 (Admin).

> Furthermore, if an intermediary is to be effective, 'C' must know the intermediary and have confidence in him or her. Such trust will not be established if their first meeting is on the morning of the trial.[55]

4.39 In *AS v Great Yarmouth Youth Court*[56] a judicial review of a decision of the youth court to refuse a defendant an intermediary, the High Court stated:

> I have some difficulty in understanding how the justices were able to reach that view. I do not see how without the assistance of an intermediary, or at least some other person alert to the claimant's difficulties, the court would necessarily realise that the claimant was put in unusual difficulty by complex questions and might react in the manner that I have indicated by not answering the question because he was thinking about earlier questions. Such a reaction by a defendant could lead a court wrongly to conclude that he was dissembling or prevaricating because he had no answer to the proper questions that were being put. A registered intermediary could help him to overcome those difficulties, could ensure that the questions asked of him were simple and that he had adequate time to respond, and could alert the court to the difficulties which he faced in answering them.[57]

4.40 However, since these cases, more recent case-law and amendments to the Criminal Practice Directions, perhaps because of financial considerations, have restricted the provision of intermediaries for vulnerable defendants for the whole of their trials (see paras 12.36–12.55, on instructing intermediaries and their policies towards support for evidence only versus whole trials.)

4.41 In *R (OP) v The Secretary of State for Justice and others*, a 2014 case about the provision of a Registered Intermediary (RI) for a defendant throughout the course of the whole trial. The High Court found that:

> . . . there are likely to be two roles during a trial for which an intermediary is fitted. The first is founded in general support, reassurance and calm interpretation of unfolding events. The second requires skilled support and interpretation with the potential for intervention and on occasion suggestion to the Bench associated with the giving of the defendant's evidence. The first is a task readily achievable by an adult with experience of life and the cast of mind apt to facilitate comprehension by a worried individual on trial. In play are understandable emotions: uncertainty, perhaps a sense of territorial disadvantage,

55 [2009] EWHC 3088 (Admin), para 17.
56 [2011] EWHC 2059 (Admin).
57 [2014] EWHC 1944 (Admin).

> nervousness and agitation. The second requires developed skills of the type contemplated by inclusion in the WIS scheme.[58]

See also *R v Biddle*[59] where the judge refused an application for an intermediary for the whole trial and the Court of Appeal noted the solicitors must not have had concerns about the defendant's communication ability because they didn't send a representative to assist in court.

4.42 Furthermore, recent changes to the Criminal Practice Direction re-iterate that it will be rare that an intermediary will be appointed to a defendant throughout the trial:

> 3F.12 The court may direct the appointment of an intermediary to assist a defendant in reliance on its inherent powers (*C v Sevenoaks Youth Court* [2009] EWHC 3088 (Admin)). There is however no presumption that a defendant will be so assisted and, even where an intermediary would improve the trial process, appointment is not mandatory (*R v Cox* [2012] EWCA Crim 549). The court should adapt the trial process to address a defendant's communication needs (*R v Cox* [2012] EWCA Crim 549). It will rarely exercise its inherent powers to direct appointment of an intermediary but where a defendant is vulnerable or for some other reason experiences communication or hearing difficulties, such that he or she needs more help to follow the proceedings than his or her legal representatives readily can give having regard to their other functions on the defendant's behalf, then the court should consider sympathetically any application for the defendant to be accompanied throughout the trial by a support worker or other appropriate companion who can provide that assistance. This is consistent with CrimPR 3.9(3)(b) (see paragraph 3D.2 above); consistent with the observations in *R v Cox* (see paragraph 3D.4 above), *R (OP) v Ministry of Justice* [2014] EWHC 1944 (Admin) and *R v Rashid* [2017] EWCA Crim 2; and consistent with the arrangements contemplated at paragraph 3G.8 below.[60]

Other special measures

4.43 'Special Measures' were introduced by YJCEA 1999, primarily to assist victims and witnesses. While special measures are usually used for witnesses and victims, some may be appropriate to be considered for the defendant, especially where the defendant is herself or himself a witness. Under the doctrine of equality of arms, the court should consider whatever special measures are appropriate to ensure that the defendant can effectively participate in the

58 Paras 34–36.

59 [2019] EWCA Crim 86.

60 CrimPD 2015 Amendment No 7 [2018] EWCA 1760.

proceedings, and where the defendant is a child, also consider its statutory duty to consider the child's welfare.[61]

4.44 There is significant overlap between special measures and the modifications available in the CrimPD but special measures have a statutory footing in the YJCEA 1999. However, for child defendants, in addition to the statute and the criminal practice direction the court has inherent common law powers to ensure trials are conducted fairly, as explicitly set out in the case of *C v Sevenoaks* (see para 4.38 for common law powers).

4.45 The special measures that are available in the Act to witnesses are:

- the use of screens;[62]
- giving evidence in private[63] (achieved by clearing the public gallery);
- removal of wigs and gowns;[64]
- live link;[65]
- ABE recorded evidence in chief;[66]
- the use of intermediaries for witnesses;[67]
- other communication[68] aids such an interpreter or other aids or techniques.

4.46 Child witnesses are automatically eligible for any of these special measures, and that includes children giving evidence for the defence.[69] But the statute specifically excludes the defendant's eligibility for most of them. There is now a power to grant the defendant the ability to give evidence over live link[70] (see paras 4.50–4.53 on live link), and the power to grant the defendant an intermediary (see paras 4.35–4.42).

4.47 While it is difficult to imagine a situation where it might be appropriate to have an ABE recording of the defendant's evidence in chief, it is useful to be aware of the provisions available to witnesses in case a defence lawyer wants to argue for an ABE for a child defendant under common law powers (see further paras 5.16–5.20 on child witnesses for more information on special measures).

61 CYPA 1933 s44.
62 YJCEA 1999 s23.
63 YJCEA 1999 s25.
64 YJCEA 1999 s26.
65 YJCEA 1999 s24 and s33A.
66 YJCEA 1999 s27.
67 YJCEA 1999 s29.
68 YJCEA 1999 s30.
69 YJCEA 1999 s16.
70 YJCEA 1999 s33A.

Ground rules hearing (GRH)

4.48 Discussion of ground rules must take place in all trials where an intermediary is to be used.[71] This is to ensure that all the parties are aware of what needs to be done to facilitate communication in trials of vulnerable defendants and/or vulnerable witnesses. A GRH will usually takes place before the day of trial, this is preferable to give advocates time to adapt their questions to the witnesses' needs. It may be helpful for a trial practice note of boundaries to be created at the end of the discussion to ensure that the agreed ground rules are complied with.[72]

4.49 The Advocate's Gateway[73] provides detailed toolkits on assisting vulnerable defendants and witnesses in court. They have toolkits on ground rules hearings to assist advocates.[74] The CrimPD states that:

> These toolkits represent best practice. Advocates should consult and follow the relevant guidance whenever they prepare to question a young or vulnerable witness or defendant.[75]

Live link

4.50 It is possible for a child defendant to give their evidence via live link if it will assist with their effective participation, as the aim is to reduce as far as possible the child's feelings of intimidation and inhibition. (see para 4.16 for the ECtHR judgment on effective participation).[76] YJCEA 1999 s33A[77] provides:

> The court, may on the application of the accused (if a youth), give a live link direction–only if his ability to participate effectively in the proceedings as a witness giving oral evidence in court is *compromised by his level of intellectual ability or social functioning* and in the interests of justice and live link will allow him to participate more effectively [emphasis added].

71 CrimPD 3E.2.

72 CrimPD 3E.3.

73 www.theadvocatesgateway.org.

74 The Advocates Gateway Toolkit 1: Ground rules hearings and the fair treatment of vulnerable people in court.

75 CrimPD 3D.7.

76 *V v UK* [2000] 30 EHRR 121, para 85.

77 As inserted by Police and Justice Act 2006 s47, SI 2006 No 3364, which came into force on 15 January 2007.

4.51 The CrimPD reinforces this stating:

> A vulnerable defendant who wishes to give evidence by live link, in accordance with YJCEA 1999 s33A, may apply for a direction to that effect; the procedure in CrimPR 18.14–18.17 should be followed.[78]

4.52 CrimPR 18.14–18.17 is the Defendant's Evidence Direction.

4.53 It is not just the giving of evidence over live link that is an option available to a vulnerable defendant, in exceptional circumstances, to ensure effective participation, a court can order that a defendant can hear the whole of the trial via live link.[79]

First names

4.54 The Youth Court Protocol[80] states that children should be referred to by their first names in the youth court.[81] In the authors' view, children should also be called by first names in the Crown Court as the purpose is to reduce feelings of intimidation and inhibition and to facilitate effective participation.

Welfare considerations

4.55 While the court needs to ensure that all vulnerable defendants effectively participate in their trial, it owes extra duties to child defendants. Children and Young Persons Act 1933 s44 states that *every court* shall have regard to the welfare of the child appearing before it whether appearing as a defendant or otherwise. Therefore when considering the modifications that should be put in place for a child defendant the court must consider, not only the CrimPD, but also the court's statutory duty to consider the welfare of the child (see paras 1.68–1.71 on the welfare principle).

Effective participation

Overview

4.56 The ECtHR jurisprudence discussed at paras 4.14–4.19 above dealt with cases involving children facing a trial in the Crown Court. The

78 CrimPD 3G.11.

79 *R v Ukpabio* [2007] EWCA Crim 2108.

80 See para 8.19 on youth court procedure and Youth Court Protocol para 5.

81 Youth Court Bench Book, August 2017, para 11, p109.

court held in the case of *SC* that child defendants should be tried in a 'specialist tribunal' (see para 4.19).

4.57 However, there still may be cases where children will not be able to effectively participate even when they appear before the youth court. The Criminal Practice Direction for vulnerable defendants (CrimPD Part 3D–G) also applies in the youth court, and it should not be assumed that just because the court is a youth court that no further modifications will need to be made.

4.58 In the case of *R (P) v West London Youth Court*[82] the High Court ruled that neither youth nor limited intellectual capability would necessarily lead to a breach of Article 6 ECHR, the crucial question being whether the tribunal hearing the case was able to adapt its procedures so that the defendant could participate effectively in the proceedings. The court has a continuing jurisdiction to grant a stay if it becomes apparent during the course of proceedings that a defendant is incapable of effectively participating but the starting point should be to consider what modifications could enable a child to effectively participate.[83] See paras 4.65–4.68 below about staying proceedings.

4.59 Practical steps which may be taken to facilitate participation in a youth court were set out in *R (P) v West London Youth Court*. They include:

- keeping the defendant's level of cognitive functioning in mind;
- using concise and simple language;
- having regular breaks;
- taking additional time to explain court proceedings;
- being proactive in ensuring the defendant understands the ingredients of the charge;
- explaining and ensuring the defendant understands the ingredients of the charge;
- explaining the possible outcomes and sentences;
- ensuring that cross-examination is carefully controlled so that questions are short and clear and frustration is minimised.[84]

4.60 An intermediary, to facilitate communication, can and should be used for children with communication difficulties being tried in

82 [2005] EWHC 2583 (Admin).

83 *Archbold* 2020 4–86.

84 [2005] EWHC 2583 (Admin) para 26.

the youth court[85] (see fuller discussion at paras 4.35–4.42 on intermediaries).

4.61 In *C v Sevenoaks*[86] the High Court found that the youth court:

> . . . will have to adopt its procedures to ensure that the hearing is fair to 'C' by using simple language, by taking breaks, by taking any and all such steps as are necessary. Experienced justices sitting in Youth Courts are well able to ensure the fairness of the proceedings.

Staying proceedings due to inability to effectively participate

4.62 If a defendant is unable to effectively participate despite modifications, the proceedings would be a breach of ECHR Article 6[87] and therefore should be stayed as an abuse of process.

4.63 Courts are reluctant to stay proceedings as it does not provide an opportunity to identify whether or not a child defendant has done the acts alleged. In *CPS v P*[88] the High Court ruled 'that proceedings should be stayed as an abuse of process before fact-finding *only* if no useful purpose at all could be served by finding the facts' [emphasis added].[89] Given that this will rarely be the case, the High Court recommended that the youth court use the same procedures as used when a defendant is unfit to plead (see paras 4.67–4.69 below on switching procedures in the youth court).

4.64 This causes particular problems in the youth court, as the statutory procedures for fitness to plead do not apply in the youth court or the adult magistrates' court (see paras see paras 4.69–4.83 on procedure for fitness to plead in the youth court or adult magistrates' court).

4.65 The courts have therefore cobbled together a process to deal with vulnerable defendants who are unable to effectively participate in trials in the youth court, even with modifications. This is an unsatisfactory solution, combining legislation and case-law trying to fix this complex situation – and because it has not been addressed specifically by the legislature, it often leads to more problems than solutions (see paras 4.117–4.120). The Law Commission's report

85 *C v Sevenoaks Youth Court* [2009] EWHC 3088 (Admin).
86 [2009] EWHC 3088 (Admin).
87 *V v UK; SC v UK.*
88 [2007] EWHC 946 (Admin).
89 Para 56.

Unfitness to plead made the following observations on the ineffectiveness of the status quo:

> The most fundamental deficiency of the current summary system is that there is no statutory procedure to consider a defendant's unfitness to plead or capacity for effective participation. Although psychiatrists and psychologists not infrequently report that a defendant in the summary courts, particularly in the youth court, is 'unfit to plead', this concept has no formal application in the summary courts.[90]

The Law Commission goes on to recommend a statutory framework for proceedings in the adult magistrates' court and youth court,[91] this recommendation has not been followed up to date.

Standard of proof in determining effective participation

4.66 The standard of proof to be applied when determining whether the trial of a vulnerable defendant would be an abuse of process because he or she would be unable to effectively participate to the extent required by ECHR Article 6 is the balance of probabilities.[92]

Switching procedures in youth court

4.67 As discussed above in *CPS v P*,[93] the High court suggested that the youth court should consider effective participation first, then if it decides a child defendant cannot effectively participate, consider whether to switch to consideration of whether the child has done the acts alleged. In *CPS v P*, the High Court held that the district judge in the youth court was wrong to stay proceedings. The consideration of whether the defendant has done 'the acts alleged' is the same procedure as is used in the youth court to consider if a child is unfit to plead (see paras 4.69–4.81 on procedure for fitness to plead in the youth court or adult magistrates' court).

4.68 The court in *CPS v P* found that even if an order (hospital or guardianship) seems unlikely, there might be other advantages in continuing to complete the fact finding process. If the court found that the child did the acts alleged, it might be appropriate to alert the

90 *Unfitness to Plead*, Law Commission (Law Com No 364) 12 January 2016, para 7.13: https://s3-eu-west-2.amazonaws.com/lawcom-prod-storage 11jsxou24uy7q/uploads/2016/01/lc364_unfitness_vol-1.pdf.

91 Para 7.55.

92 See *TP v West London Youth Court* [2005] EWHC 2583 (Admin), para 14.

93 [2007] EWHC 946 (Admin).

local authority to the position with a view to the consideration of care proceedings. If the court found that the child had not done the acts alleged, the proceedings would be brought to an end by a finding of not guilty.[94]

Fitness to plead in the youth court (and adult magistrates' court)

Overview

4.69 The legislation that governs the fitness to plead procedure in the Crown Court, the Criminal Procedure (Insanity) Act (CP(I)A) 1964 ss4 and 4A, does not apply in the youth court or in the adult magistrates' court. However, in the case of *P v Barking Youth Court*[95] the High Court stated that an adult magistrates' court or youth court can follow a very similar procedure to that in the Crown Court by using Mental Health Act (MHA) 1983 s37(3) and Powers of Criminal Courts (Sentencing) Act (PCCSA) 2000 s11 (see paras 4.87–4.99 for more on the fitness to plead procedure in the Crown Court,).

4.70 The High Court said that the procedure achieves 'much the same effect'[96] as the fitness to plead process in the Crown Court:

> . . . a complete statutory framework for the determination by the Magistrates' Court . . . of all the issues that arise in cases of Defendants who are or may be mentally ill or suffering from severe mental impairment in the context of offences which are triable summarily only.[97]

4.71 The criteria for exercising powers vested in the MHA 1983 s37(3) are considerably less strict and more flexible than the statutory framework governing the issues of fitness to plead in the Crown Court:

> That is to say, to determine whether the Claimant did the acts alleged against him and then, in the light of such medical evidence as they have before them, to make such orders, if any, as they think fit under section 37(3) of the Mental Health Act.[98]

4.72 MHA 1983 s37(3) provides as follows:

94 *CPS v P* [2007] EWHC 946 (Admin).
95 [2002] EWHC 734 (Admin).
96 *R (Varma) v Redbridge Magistrates' Court* [2009] EWHC 836 (Admin), para 10.
97 *P v Barking Youth Court* [2002] EWHC 734 (Admin), para 10 cited in *R (Varma) v Redbridge Magistrates' Court* [2009] EWHC 836 (Admin), para 14.
98 *R (Varma) v Redbridge Magistrates' Court* [2009] EWHC 836 (Admin), para 24.

> Where a person is charged before a magistrates' court with any act or omission as an offence and the court would have power, on convicting him of that offence, to make an order under subsection (1) above in his case as being a person suffering from mental illness or severe mental impairment, then if the court is satisfied that the accused did the act of made the omission charged, the court may, if it thinks fit, make such an order without convicting him.

4.73 The 'order under subsection (1)' is either a hospital order or a guardianship order. They are both available to magistrates in any case where the offence carries imprisonment on summary conviction,[99] providing that the necessary medical evidence required by subsection (2) is present and providing (as required by subsection 2(b)) (see para 4.77) that the court is of opinion that such an order is the most suitable method of disposing of the case. Practitioners should note that a guardianship order is only available for defendants aged over 16 (see para 4.80).

4.74 Powers of Criminal Courts (Sentencing) Act 2000 s11 provides:

> If, on the trial by a magistrates' court of an offence punishable on summary conviction with imprisonment, the court–
>
> (a) is satisfied that the accused did the act or made the omission charged, but
>
> (b) is of the opinion that an inquiry ought to be made into his physical or mental condition before the method of dealing with him is determined,
>
> the court shall adjourn the case to enable a medical examination and report to be made, and shall remand him.

4.75 MHA 1983 s37(3) allows the court to pass the order on a defendant who is found to have done the act but who is suffering from a mental illness or severe mental impairment, without having been convicted.[100]

4.76 There is no requirement for a child to effectively participate in a fact-finding hearing as the process is not criminalising but part of the protective jurisdiction and, as such, ECHR Article 6 rights are not engaged.[101]

4.77 MHA 1983 s37(2) provides that the court must be:

> . . . satisfied, on the written or oral evidence of two registered medical practitioners, that the offender is suffering from mental disorder and that either –

99 MHA 1983 s37(1).

100 *R (Singh) v Stratford Magistrates' Court* [2007] EWHC 1582 (Admin), para 30.

101 *CPS v P* [2007] EWHC 946 (Admin), para 55 referring to *Re H* [2002] EWCA Crim 2988.

(i) the mental disorder from which the offender is suffering is of a nature or degree which makes it appropriate for him to be detained in a hospital for medical treatment and appropriate medical treatment is available for him; or
(ii) in the case of an offender who has attained the age of 16 years, the mental disorder is of a nature or degree which warrants his reception into guardianship under this Act;

4.78 Therefore, proceedings in the youth court will need two medical reports, however these can be from any registered medical practitioners, there is no requirement that one is MHA 1983 s12 approved, as there is in the crown court.

Disposals in the youth court (or adult magistrates' court)

Hospital order

4.79 MHA 1983 s37(1) sets out the requirements of a hospital order, which are the same as in the Crown Court (see paras 4.106 and 22.28–22.36 on hospital orders) while an adult magistrates' or youth court can only pass a hospital order, they cannot impose a hospital order with restrictions, which can only be passed by the Crown Court.

Guardianship order

4.80 A guardianship order places a defendant under the guardianship of a local social services authority or of such other person approved by a local social services authority as may be so specified.[102] Guardianship orders are only available for children aged 16 or over and require the written or oral evidence of two registered medical practitioners that the defendant is suffering from mental disorder.[103] (For a fuller discussion of guardianship orders see paras 22.17–22.26).

Other orders

4.81 An absolute discharge or a supervision order is not available in the youth court or the adult magistrates' court as a disposal under PCC(S)A 2000 s11/MHA 1983 s37.

4.82 If the youth court or adult magistrates' court thinks a hospital order with a restriction order should be considered, MHA 1983 s43

102 MHA 1983 s37(1).
103 MHA 1983 s37(2)(ii)(b).

allows the youth court or adult magistrates' court, when a child is over the age of 14, to send the case up to the Crown Court if all the section 37 criteria are met and it appears to the court, having regard to the nature of the offence, the antecedents of the offender and the risk of his committing further offences if set at large, that if a hospital order is made a restriction order should also be made (see paras 22.38–22.42).

Problems with the procedure

4.83 Problems with the procedure include the following:

- The current legislative framework that is to be applied in the courts of summary jurisdiction only applies to imprisonable offences.
- The disposals available are limited to a hospital order and a guardianship order. A hospital order would often not be applicable to someone with a learning difficulty or other kinds of conditions such as autism spectrum disorders (see para 22.28–22.36 for criteria for a hospital order).
- Guardianship orders, which are the only community disposal available under the statutory framework, only apply to those who are over the age of 16 (see para 4.80 above for the criteria for a guardianship order).
- The court is required to bear in mind the circumstances, including the nature of the offence and the character and antecedents of the defendant, and the other methods of dealing with him or her in considering whether this order is the 'most suitable method of dealing with the case'. The problem is that there is no clear legislative framework for the court to follow and even whether the process is a trial of the act(s) or a criminal trial is not clear.

Fitness to plead in the Crown Court

Background

4.84 The law relating to unfitness to plead addresses what should happen when a defendant who faces criminal prosecution is unable to engage with the process because of the defendant's mental or physical condition. The law aims to balance the rights of the vulnerable defendant with the interests of those affected by an alleged offence and the need to protect the public. The test for fitness was first introduced in *R v Pritchard* in 1836.[104] The test remains remarkably similar today.

Pritchard criteria

4.85 In the case of *Pritchard*, a 'deaf mute' was found not fit to plead. The criteria that were applied were whether a defendant has the ability to:

1) understand the charge(s);
2) decide whether to plead guilty or not guilty;
3) follow the course of proceedings;
4) instruct a lawyer;
5) challenge a juror.

Added to that, in the 21st century, which was not available in the 19th century as a right, was the ability to:

6) give evidence in the defendant's defence.[105]

If it is established that the defendant cannot do *any one* of the above six things that was beyond the defendant's capabilities, then the court should find a defendant unfit to plead.[106]

Giving evidence in own defence

4.86 The ability to give evidence on his own behalf was not available to a defendant in 1836 therefore it is not addressed in the *Pritchard* criteria. It is now a relevant criteria when considering fitness to plead see *R v Diamond*[107] Thomas LJ states:

> . . . in *M (John)* [2003] EWCA Crim 3452 where the defendant suffered from a serious impairment to his short term memory. The court approved the direction of the judge that the jury could find unfitness to plead if the defence could establish on a balance of probabilities any one of six things that was beyond the appellant's capabilities; '(1) understanding the charges; (2) deciding whether to plead guilty or not; (3) exercising his right to challenge jurors; (4) instructing solicitors and counsel; (5) following the course of the proceedings; (6) giving evidence in his own defence'.

104 (1836) 7 C&P 303.

105 *R v John M* [2003] EWCA Crim 3452.

106 *R v M (John)* [2003] EWCA Crim 3452, see para 20.

107 [2008] EWCA Crim 923.

Procedure

4.87 The procedure to determine fitness to plead in the Crown Court is a two-stage process that is set out in CP(I)A 1964 ss4 and 4A.[108] These only apply in the Crown Court. (For the procedure in the youth court or adult magistrates' court, see paras 4.69–4.83 above.)

Burden and standard of proof

4.88 It is usually a defence lawyer who raises the issue of fitness to plead. If this is the case, the onus is on the defence to prove that a defendant is not fit on the balance of probabilities.[109] However, there are occasions where the issue may be raised by the prosecution and the defence disputes that the defendant is unfit. In this situation, the burden is on the prosecution,[110] and the prosecution's standard of proof is beyond a reasonable doubt.[111]

Timing

4.89 The court should be alerted to the issue as soon as possible.[112] Credit for a guilty plea should not be lost if there needs to be adjournment for reports to assess fitness.[113] While not desirable, the issue can be raised at any point before the verdict, and all parties have a duty to consider the defendant's fitness.[114]

Stage 1: Determination

4.90 The decision as to whether or not a defendant is unfit to plead is one for a judge alone, without a jury.[115]

4.91 The court shall not make a determination that a defendant is unfit to plead except on the written or oral evidence of two or more registered medical practitioners, at least one of whom is approved under section 12.[116] The court will consider the *Pritchard* criteria

108 CP(I)A 1964 ss4, 4A (as amended by the Domestic Violence, Crime and Victims Act 2004).

109 *R v Podola* [1960] 1 QB 325, p350.

110 *R v Podola* [1960] 1 QB 325.

111 *R v Robertson* [1968] 1 WLR 1767, p1773C–E.

112 Criminal Procedure Rules rr1.1 and 1.2.

113 Sentencing Council, *Sentencing children and young people: definitive guideline*, 2017, para 5.16.

114 *Orr* [2016] EWCA Crim 889.

115 CP(I)A 1964 s4(5).

116 CP(I)A 1964 s4(6).

including the ability to give evidence and consider whether the defendant is fit to plead or not.

Expert evidence

4.92 In the case of *R v Walls*[117] the Court of Appeal stated:

> . . . we consider that, save in clear cases, a court must rigorously examine evidence of psychiatrists adduced before them and then subject that evidence to careful analysis against the *Pritchard* criteria as interpreted in *Podola*. Save in cases where the unfitness is clear, the fact that psychiatrists agree is not enough, as this case demonstrates; a court would be failing in its duty to both the public and a defendant if it did not rigorously examine the evidence and reach its own conclusion.

4.93 This follows the case of *P*,[118] which stated:

> Accordingly, it is my view that, in most cases, the medical evidence should be considered as part of the evidence in the case and not as the sole evidence on a freestanding application.

4.94 There is no requirement that both experts need to be instructed by the defence. It will usually be essential in order to get an adjournment for the requisite time in order to commission reports. However, the court is likely to issue case management directions. It is common for the defence to serve their first report on the prosecution and the court if it says that the defendant is not fit to plead, and then for the prosecution to instruct their own expert to assess the defendant. Where the prosecution's expert agrees, then the court will have the evidence of two medical practitioners, and there is no need for a further report. Where there is disagreement, or where the first report is written by a psychologist (see para 4.95 about psychologists and paras 12.15–12.21), then there will be a need for further reports.

Registered medical practitioners

4.95 A psychologist will usually not be a 'registered medical practitioner' as they are doctors by virtue of a PhD, not through medical qualification. However, a defence lawyer may still need a report prepared by a psychologist for testing for a learning disability or difficulty or other conditions (see chapter 12 instructing an expert paras 12.15–12.21).

4.96 A section 12 approved medical practitioner is 'a practitioner approved for the purposes of this section by the secretary of state as having special experience in the diagnosis or treatment of mental

117 [2011] EWCA Crim 443, para 38.

118 [2007] EWHC 946 (Admin), para 53.

disorder'.[119] They can also be a 'registered medical practitioner who is an approved clinician'[120] with special experience in the diagnosis or treatment of a mental disorder.

Stage 2: finding of fact

4.97 Once a determination of unfitness has been made by a judge, the trial shall not proceed or further proceed, but it shall be determined by a jury, on the evidence, whether they are satisfied the accused did the act or made the omission charged against him or her as the offence. If the jury are so satisfied, they shall make a finding that' the accused did the act or made the omission charged against him or her'.[121] If not so satisfied, they shall return a verdict of acquittal.[122]

The role of the lawyer

4.98 When a person has been found not fit to plead and the matter is to proceed by way of a trial of the issue rather than the usual criminal process, the lawyer in that process is no longer the lawyer acting on the instructions of the person accused but becomes appointed to put forward the case for the defence. 'The duty under s4A(2) is a duty personal to the court which must consider afresh the person who is to be appointed; it should not necessarily be the same person who has represented the defendant to date'[123] The responsibility of the lawyer appointed by the court is very different from a lawyer who is acting on behalf of a defendant and taking instructions from their client. It is probably better for the advocate to have experience and training of having worked with defendants with disabilities. (See *R v Norman*.[124])

Remands to hospital

4.99 The court can remand a defendant to hospital even before there has been a finding that the defendant is not fit to plead. MHA 1983 s35 allows the court to remand the defendant to hospital for a report to be prepared on his or her mental condition or the defendant can be hospitalised for treatment.

119 CP(I)A 1964 s12(2).
120 CP(I)A 1964 s12(3).
121 CP(I)A 1964 s4A(3).
122 CP(I)A 1964 s4A.
123 *R v Norman* [2008] EWCA Crim 1810, para 34.
124 [2008] EWCA Crim 1810.

Limitations after a finding of unfitness to plead

4.100 There can be tactical disadvantages for a defendant having a trial of the issue. These might include:

- The protections guaranteed under ECHR Article 6 (right to fair trial) are not applicable in a trial of the issue.
- Trials of the issue are only a trial of the acts (*actus reus*) rather than of a mental element (*mens rea*) which is a prerequisite for many offences.[125]
- In most cases which involve a trial of the issue, if the defendant is found unfit to plead he or she will not be able to give an account of events. In cases where an account is important to show the defendant was not involved in the acts alleged, an account by the defendant themselves might be helpful.[126]
- Some of the defences that are available for certain offences are not available to a defendant who has been found not fit to plead. For example the defendant cannot raise diminished responsibility, loss of control or lack of specific intent as a defence.[127] It also causes difficulty with the issue of secondary participation.[128]

4.101 Given the above difficulties with being found unfit to plead, there may be a tactical reason not to raise unfitness to plead at the outset.

The legislation states that:

> If, having regard to the nature of the supposed disability, the court are of opinion that it is expedient to do so and in the interests of the accused, they may postpone consideration of the question of fitness to be tried until any time up to the opening of the case for the defence.[129]

4.102 There is nothing procedurally, nor in statute, to prevent a joint trial of fit and unfit defendants in certain circumstances.[130] However, an application for severance can be made if it is thought a joint trial would be prejudicial, either by the lawyer for the defendant who has been found unfit or by the defence lawyers for the 'fit' defendants.

125 See *Archbold* 2018 4–237.

126 See *Archbold* 2018 4–237.

127 *R v Antoine* [2000] UKHL 20.

128 *Archbold* 2018 4–237a.

129 CP(I)A 1964 s4(2).

130 *R v B, W and others* [2008] EWCA Crim 1997.

Disposals after trial of the issue

4.103 A person who is found to have 'done the act' is not 'found guilty', therefore the usual 'sentencing options' are not available. The measures that are available to the court and the person found to have done the act are set out in the CP(I)A 1964.

4.104 There are three options available to the court for a defendant who has been found unfit to plead. These are:

- section 5(2)(a) – a hospital order (with or without a restriction order);
- section 5(2)(b) – a supervision order; or
- section 5(2)(c) – an order for absolute discharge.

Hospital order

4.105 If the offence is one in which the sentence is fixed by law and the court have power to make a hospital order, the court shall make a hospital order with a restriction order.[131]

4.106 A hospital order made under MHA 1983 s37 is available in the youth, adult magistrates court and Crown Court. MHA 1983 s37 enable the court to 'authorise his [the defendant's] admission to and detention in such hospital as may be specified in the order'. The conditions required for a hospital order are that the court must be satisfied, on the written or oral evidence of two registered medical practitioners, that the offender is suffering from a mental disorder (see paras 22.28–22.36).

Interim hospital order

4.107 In some instances, it will be possible for the child to be remanded to hospital before sentence or for an interim hospital order to be made.

A hospital order with a restriction order

4.108 Where it appears to the Crown Court, having regard to the nature of the offence, the antecedents and the risk of committing further offences, that it is necessary for the protection of the public from serious harm so to do, the court may order that the offender shall be subject to the special restrictions known as 'a restriction order'. (For a fuller discussion see paras 22.38–22.42).

131 CP(I)A 1964 s5(3).

4.109 A restriction order shall not be made in the case of any person unless at least one of the registered medical practitioners has given evidence orally before the court.

4.110 The meaning of the restriction is that the patient shall continue to be liable to be detained by virtue of the relevant hospital order unless the secretary of state orders that he is allowed to be discharged.[132] While a person is subject to a restriction order the responsible clinician shall at such intervals (not exceeding one year) examine and report to the secretary of state on that person; and every report shall contain such particulars as the secretary of state may require.

Supervision order

4.111 Under CP(I)A 1964 Sch 1A a supervision order means that the 'supervised person' must be under the supervision of a social worker or a probation officer (this presumably includes any youth offending team (YOT) officer though the Act does not specifically state the YOT as YOTs did not exist when the Act came into force. YOTs often have probation officers within them and social workers and so may be able to supervise a child on a supervision order. The supervision order is for a period specified, not to exceed two years. The supervision order may specify that the person undergo treatment by a medical practitioner with a view to the improvement of his or her mental condition.[133] (For a fuller discussion see paras 22.49–22.55).

4.112 The court should only make a supervision order, when, having regards to all the circumstances of the case, the order is the most suitable way of dealing with the person found to have done the act or omission charged if satisfied on the written or oral evidence of two or more registered medical practitioners (at least one of whom is duly registered) that the mental condition of the supervised persons may be susceptible to treatment but does not warrant a hospital order.

4.113 The court must also be satisfied that the supervising officer is willing to undertake the supervision and that arrangements have been made for any treatment that is specified.

4.114 A supervision order may include certain requirements relating to the residence of the supervised person.[134]

132 MHA 1983 ss35–36, 38.
133 CP(I)A 1964 Sch 1A Part 2(4).
134 CP(I)A 1964 Sch 1A.

Absolute discharge

4.115 An absolute discharge has the same meaning as an absolute discharge when someone has been convicted of an offence.

Ancillary orders and notification requirements

4.116 Ancillary orders can be given, even though a defendant is not found guilty (see chapter 24 on ancillary orders). Notification requirements (often referred to as the Sex Offender Register) will also apply – these apply automatically (see paras 25.76 25.81 on notification requirements).

Unfitness to Plead: Law Commission review

4.117 The Law Commission in 2016 undertook a lengthy review of the procedures surrounding fitness to plead and effective participation. They concluded that 'the current law in this area is outdated, inconsistently applied and can lead to unfairness.'[135] The Law Commission 'make recommendations for reform of the whole unfitness to plead framework. Our recommendations aim to modernise the law, making it fair, effective and accessible.'

4.118 In summary, the report recommends:[136]

- a new legal test to accurately identify those who are unable to participate effectively in their trial;
- an alternative hearing to scrutinise the allegations for such defendants;
- new disposals that are 'robust and effective' for such defendants, allowing more 'constructive support' and greater powers to monitor progress;
- a statutory scheme for the adult magistrates' and youth court in line with the Crown Court;
- a new defence for child defendants relating to developmental immaturity.[137]

4.119 At the time of writing, the Law Commision had received no further response from the government about unfitness to plead since 30

135 www.lawcom.gov.uk/project/unfitness-to-plead/.
136 www.lawcom.gov.uk/project/unfitness-to-plead/.
137 www.lawcom.gov.uk/project/unfitness-to-plead/.

June 2016, when the government provided an interim response, which stated:

> We are considering your report in detail, and will continue to work with your officials to provide a response to your recommendations in this area. We note the Commission's recommendations regarding the youth court, and we will consider these in the light of Charlie Taylor's report on the youth justice system. Our wider consideration of whether to accept the recommendation to extend unfitness to plead to all magistrates' courts will take this into account.[138]

4.120 The letter goes on to declare that 'it is unlikely that there will be space to include any recommendations we accept on unfitness to plead in our next legislative window'.

138 http://data.parliament.uk/DepositedPapers/Files/DEP2016-0605/Mike_Penning_Government_interim_response_on_Unfitness_to_Plead.pdf.

CHAPTER 5

Children as victims and witnesses

continued

Key points

- Being a witness in the criminal justice system is a daunting experience, for adults, let alone for children who often have to go through uncomfortable processes.
- Children Act 2004 s11 requires that the police and the National Crime Agency, among others, must make arrangements for ensuring that their functions are discharged, having regard to the need to safeguard and promote the welfare of children.
- Special protections are afforded to child victims and witnesses in the criminal justice system.
- All professionals should familiarise themselves with the special protections available to child witnesses and victims to ensure that their experience of the criminal justice system is as positive as is possible in the circumstances.

Introduction

5.1 The criminal justice system is a daunting place for anyone – it can be intimidating for adults, but for children and especially children with disabilities, who make up a significant percentage of those involved in the criminal justice system, there are additional factors that can make the process traumatic (see chapter 3 on the importance of background, paras 3.45–3.102 for more detailed breakdown of common disabilities and disadvantages). While most of this book focuses on children as defendants, it is less familiar for defence lawyers to think about the numbers of children who have contact with the criminal justice system as victims and witnesses. Child victims and witnesses far outweigh the number of child defendants. Victim Support, the charity for victims of crime, says:

> In England and Wales, more than one in ten children aged 10 to 15 are victims of crime, and there were around 373,000 incidents of violent crime against children and young people last year.[1]

5.2 This chapter will discuss child victims and witnesses at all stages of the youth justice system, including: fundamental rights of children; the Victims' Code; child victims and witnesses at the police station; court proceedings.

1 www.victimsupport.org.uk/more-us/why-choose-us/specialist-services/children-and-young-people.

Fundamental rights

5.3 The UN Convention on the Rights of the Child (UNCRC) applies to all children whether they are defendants, victims or witnesses (see chapter 1 for an overview of the youth justice system; and paras 1.38–1.39 for more on the Articles of the UNCRC). The obligation to act in the best interest of a child must be a *primary consideration* for any law court or administrative authority (UNCRC Article 3.1). Many children who come into contact with the criminal justice system as victims and witnesses may never actually go to court, however their best interests must be a primary consideration every step of the way – whether that is through any investigation, at the police station or informal enquiries.

5.4 There are also domestic obligations on authorities around children in contact with the criminal justice system. Children Act 2004 s11 requires that the police and the National Crime Agency (section 11(1)(h), (i), (ia)), among others, must make arrangements for ensuring that their functions are discharged, having regard to the need to safeguard and promote the welfare of children (section 11(2)(a)) (see paras 1.68–1.71 for more on the welfare principle).

5.5 The National College of Policing National Strategy for the Policing of Children and Young People – 'Child Centred Policing'[2] applies as much to child victims and witnesses as it does to child defendants (see para 6.3 for child-centred policing).

5.6 It is crucial that in all encounters with the police, those below the age of 18 should be treated as children first.

Definition of a victim

5.7 The definition of 'victim' by the Crown Prosecution Service (CPS) is as follows:

> A person who has suffered harm, including physical, mental or emotional harm or economic loss which was directly caused by criminal conduct.

5.8 This definition includes:

- close relatives of a person whose death was directly caused by criminal conduct;

2 NPCC Child Centred Policing (2016).

- parents or guardians where the main victim is a child or youth under 18;[3]
- family spokespersons of victims with a disability or who are so badly injured they cannot communicate.

The Victims' Code

Overview

5.9 The Ministry of Justice has produced the 'Code of practice for victims of crime'[4] ('Victims' Code') which sets out enhanced entitlements for particular victims because they are more likely to require enhanced support and services through the criminal justice process. All child victims of crime are automatically eligible for the enhanced services provided to vulnerable victims of crime.[5]

Therapy or counselling

5.10 The Victims' Code entitles child victims (and presumably witnesses) to therapy or counselling.[6] Therapy may be considered beneficial for a victim and a witness at any time after being interviewed and before the court proceedings. This can take place before court proceedings, either with or without the support of the investigative team[7]. If done without the support of the investigative team, the police and the CPS must be made aware that therapy has been proposed, is being undertaken, or has been undertaken[8] so that consideration can be given to whether or not the provision of such therapy is likely to impact on the criminal case.[9]

3 Parents or guardians might be entitled to support and help, in addition to a child victim, as long as they are not suspected of being involved in any offence and it is in the child's best interests.

4 Ministry of Justice, 'Code of practice for victims of crime', 2015.

5 Victims' Code, p69.

6 Victims' Code, para 1.7.

7 Victims' Code, para 6.1; 'Provision of therapy to child witnesses'.

8 Victims' Code, para 6.2; 'Provision of therapy to child witnesses'.

9 Provision of therapy for child witnesses prior to a criminal trial: practical guidance (Home Office, Crown Prosecution Service and Department of Health, 2011).

5.11 The 'Provision of therapy for child witnesses prior to a criminal trial: practical guidance'[10] emphasises that the best interests of the child are paramount when deciding whether, and in what form, therapeutic help can be given. However, records of therapeutic work should be kept, as they may be relevant to the trial. A victim or witness should be aware that there may be full discussions between all agencies involved in the therapy and court case, and that evidence of that therapy may be produced at court.

5.12 It is important that any therapist is aware of an ongoing investigation as he or she must be conscious not to appear to coach the child in matters that might be relevant to the evidence that will be presented at court. Training or coaching of witnesses in criminal proceedings is not permitted.[11]

Complaints

5.13 Any person may draw to the attention of the authorities their safeguarding and child protection obligations. If a complaint is against a particular body, such as the police, it should follow their particular complaints procedure. Complaints about a failure to investigate and allegation can be made to the direct police station involved in the investigation[12] or the Independent Police Complaints Commission (IPCC); or complaints can be made against the CPS for a decision not to bring charges or to terminate proceedings through the Victims' Right to Review scheme.[13]

Child victims and witnesses at the police station

Overview

5.14 When a crime is reported to the police, a child victim or witness is entitled to written confirmation that a crime has been reported, including:

- the basic details of the offence;
- a clear explanation of what happens next;

10 Provision of therapy for child witnesses prior to a criminal trial: practical guidance (Home Office, Crown Prosecution Service and Department of Health, 2011).

11 *R v Momodou and Limani* [2005] EWCA Crim 177, para 61.

12 Victims' Code, Chapter 3: Children and young people, para 2.2.

13 www.cps.gov.uk/victims_witnesses/victims_right_to_review/index.html.

- a leaflet with information for victims of crime to work out what support is needed;

unless there is a request to the police not to send over those details.[14]

5.15 If, after an allegation of a crime is made, the police decide not to investigate that allegation, they have a duty to inform a victim within five working days of that decision.[15] A child victim or witness is entitled to know:

- whether the police have no suspect in a case;
- whether the suspect has been interviewed;
- whether the suspect has been released;
- whether the suspect is on police bail; and
- the reasons why and that the case is to be passed on to the CPS.[16]

Witness statements (including video recorded statements)

5.16 If the police are pursuing an allegation of a crime, they will require a child victim or witness to be interviewed, either to give a written witness statement or a video recorded statement.

ABE interviews

5.17 A video recorded statement is sometimes called an ABE, which stands for Achieving Best Evidence. Guidance is provided on how to best interview victims and witnesses: *Achieving Best Evidence in criminal proceedings: Guidance on interviewing victims and witnesses, and guidance on using special measures* (March 2011).[17] The stated purpose of the 2011 version of the guidance is to assist those responsible for conducting video-recorded interviews with vulnerable, intimidated and significant witnesses, as well as those tasked with preparing and supporting witnesses during the criminal justice process.

Video recording cross-examination

5.18 In some pilot areas of the country[18] cross-examination is being pre-recorded as well as evidence in chief. The power to do this is contained

14 Victims' Code, Chapter 3: Children and young people.

15 Victims' Code, Chapter 3: Children and young people.

16 Victims' Code, Chapter 3: Children and young people, para 1.6.

17 Achieving best evidence in criminal proceedings.

18 Section 28 was piloted in Leeds, Liverpool and Kingston-upon-Thames Crown Courts from December 2013.

in Youth Justice and Criminal Evidence Act (YJCEA) 1999 s28. The judiciary have introduced guidance on proper use of section 28 cross-examination.[19]

5.19 The witness will be advised to tell the truth, but will not take the oath. The interviewer will use an example, depending on the age of the witness, as to what is a truth or a lie.

Consent

5.20 It is generally presumed that any witness consents to giving evidence. The guidance states that the parents or carers of a child witness will be informed of any interview before it takes place – this requirement is independent of consent.[20] In exceptional circumstances, however, it may be necessary to interview a victim[21] without the knowledge of the parent or carer. Such circumstances include:

a) the possibility that the child would be threatened or otherwise coerced into silence;
b) a strong likelihood that important evidence would be destroyed;
c) the child in question did not wish the parent to be involved at that stage and is competent to take that decision;
d) the allegation may be one against a family member – such as domestic violence, forced marriage, genital mutilation.[22]

5.21 The guidance is clear that no pressure should be brought to bear on reluctant witnesses to talk to police or to give evidence, the function of the investigator in these circumstances is simply one of providing enough information to allow the potential witness to make an informed choice.[23]

5.22 The police will need to obtain the consent from the witness and/or the witness's parent or carer if they make any enquiries of other professionals (eg teachers, doctors, specialists) about the witness's communication needs. The witness and/or his or her parent or carer should be informed that what these third parties say may be referred to in an intermediary's court report, which will subsequently be seen by the prosecution and disclosed to the defence.[24]

19 https://www.judiciary.uk/wp-content/uploads/2017/09/guidance-on-the-use-of-s28-youth-justice-and-criminal-evidence-act-28092017–1.pdf.

20 Achieving best evidence in criminal proceedings, para 2.40.

21 Guidance says victim, no mention of witnesses.

22 Achieving best evidence in criminal proceedings, para 2.40.

23 Achieving best evidence in criminal proceedings, para 2.141.

24 Achieving best evidence in criminal proceedings, box 2.1.

Medical examinations

5.23 Sometimes medical examinations of a victim or witness will be needed, depending on the nature of the case. These will be performed by forensic physicians who are independent of the police. Their speciality will vary depending on the particular circumstances. The victim or witness may express wishes about the gender of the forensic physician, and these should be respected wherever possible.[25]

5.24 Urgent medical treatment will be given before a medical examination, but the forensic physician can recommend treatment for any injuries and can prescribe medication to treat any conditions, including, if necessary, emergency contraception.[26]

5.25 One of the aims of the medical examination is to recover evidence to support the victim's assertion that the alleged offence has taken place. Both external and internal areas of the complainant's body can be swabbed for samples that can be submitted for forensic examination.

5.26 The Legal Guidance for Crown Prosecutors says it is good practice to take urine or blood samples for the purposes of a toxicology report to establish levels of any alcohol or drugs.[27]

If the allegation is historic, it may not be appropriate to conduct a medical examination – this should be decided by a forensic physician. Doctors performing the medical examination should not ask questions about the alleged offence but should record any spontaneous comments that are made. It is essential to preserve the notes and records of medical examinations, as they become a part of disclosure if the case goes to court.[28]

Identification procedures

5.27 If the identity of a suspect is in dispute, a victim or witness might be asked to try to identify the person by looking at them. The regulations governing identification processes are set out in Police and Criminal Evidence Act 1984 (PACE) Code D. A video identification

25 Crown Prosecution Service legal guidance rape and sexual offences, chapter 9 forensic scientific and medical evidence.

26 Crown Prosecution Service legal guidance rape and sexual offences, chapter 9 forensic scientific and medical evidence

27 Crown Prosecution Service legal guidance rape and sexual offences, chapter 9 forensic scientific and medical evidence

28 Achieving best evidence in criminal proceedings, para 2.41.

should take place if it is possible[29] – but where this is not possible, a victim or witness might be asked to identify the suspect from an identification parade.

5.28 A pre-trial support person who is not a witness should accompany the child, unless the child does not want the support.[30]

5.29 It is good practice to video record any identification procedure where there is a child victim or witness.[31] If a pre-recorded video statement is going to be used in court, then it is best to ask questions about the identification procedure in that interview. This reduces the need for a child to have to give additional evidence at court outside of the pre-recorded interview.[32]

Support for children at the police station

5.30 Protections are available for children who are victims or witnesses of crime at the investigative stage of the process, in addition to those that are available throughout the court process. The protections have been designed to make the process less intimidating and to encourage full and open evidence on how to best interview victims and witnesses. The police should explain to child victims and witnesses and their parent or carer, about special measures at the earliest possible stage in the process; the police should make clear that the granting of special measures in the court process is ultimately for the court to decide.[33] (See chapter 4 paras 4.43–4.47 for further discussion of statutory special measures.)

5.31 When planning the investigation and interview stage of a criminal case, investigators must consider any request made by the child about support they would like through the process. The local children's services authority may have information relating to the child or information may be provided by other professionals consulted such as schools or medical practitioners. Other information might best be provided by the child's parent(s) or carer(s). The interviewing team will need to balance the need to obtain as much of this information as

29 PACE Code D para 3.14.

30 Achieving best evidence in criminal proceedings, Appendix J Identification Parades J1.

31 Achieving best evidence in criminal proceedings, Appendix J Identification Parades J5.

32 Achieving best evidence, para 3.132.

33 Achieving best evidence in criminal proceedings, para 4.9.

possible with its desire to conduct the interview as soon as is practicable.[34]

5.32 The investigative team may decide that an assessment of the child should be done before an interview can take place. This can include an initial assessment of whether an intermediary is needed for the interview. (See paras 4.35–4.37 for more about the role of an intermediary.) The police, with help from the parent or carer or professionals can identify the appropriate skills the intermediary would need to have to assist the person who is being questioned.[35]

5.33 At the investigative stage only Registered Intermediaries should be used. A Registered Intermediary will conduct their own assessment of the child. The use of an unregistered person as an intermediary should only be considered once the options for using a Registered Intermediary have been exhausted.[36]

5.34 Before an intermediary can assist with communication, he or she needs to conduct an assessment meeting with the witness. The criminal case is not discussed during assessment meetings. Intermediaries should never be on their own with a victim or witness and the criminal case is not discussed. A third party must be present for this assessment, usually that third party is a police officer but it may also be helpful to have a support person present.[37]

5.35 Where there is a major concern about the mental health of a witness, or information that suggests a witness has a mental disorder, consent for an early psychiatric assessment might be sought to establish whether the witness is able to give a reliable account of events.[38]

Interview supporters

5.36 As well as an intermediary, or as an alternative to an intermediary, an 'interview supporter' can also be used. An interview supporter is a person who is known to the victim or witness. He or she can be present during the interview to provide emotional support to the witness. Whether an interview supporter will be used will depend on the views of the witness as to whether he or she wishes another

34 Achieving best evidence in criminal proceedings, paras 2.44–2.60.

35 Achieving best evidence in criminal proceedings, para 2.117.

36 Achieving best evidence in criminal proceedings, para 2.199.

37 Achieving best evidence in criminal proceedings, paras 2.198, 2.201.

38 Achieving best evidence in criminal proceedings, para 2.121.

person to be present.[39] A witness supporter cannot be a witness in the case.

Witness Care Unit and witness care officer

5.37 The local Witness Care Units are units across England and Wales, run jointly by the police and the CPS, which act as a single point of contact for all witnesses in the criminal justice system. The unit will allocate a witness care officer, whose job it job to keep a witness/victim/parent informed about how the case is progressing. The witness care officer is also the person who should let someone know if he or she has to attend court to give evidence. The witness care officer is also the person who will discuss with the witness any support needs. He or she can arrange a visit to the court before the day of the trial. When the witness attends court to give evidence, the witness care officer will meet the witness. The witness care officer will accompany the witness to the court room when it is time to give evidence.

5.38 The Witness Care Unit should let a child victim or witness (or their family or carer) know whether a suspect has been granted bail or remanded in custody. The police should also let the witness know, if a suspect is arrested for breaching any bail conditions.[40]

5.39 At court there is the provision of Witness Service that is available for witnesses who are required to attend court. Witness Service should be available at the Crown Court as well as at adult magistrates' and youth courts. Witness Service provides a free, independent, impartial and confidential service, adapted to individual needs.

5.40 A victim or witness can be introduced to the prosecutor before he or she gives his or her evidence. Defence witnesses should meet the defence lawyer.[41] The trial judge has a discretion to meet with a witness if he or she considers it appropriate.

Refreshing memory

5.41 A victim or witness is entitled to refresh his or her memory before giving evidence at court – either from a written statement, a transcript

39 Achieving best evidence in criminal proceedings, para 2.201.

40 Victims' Code, Chapter 3, para 2.7.

41 Achieving best evidence in criminal proceedings, para 4.65.

of the video interview that they gave or by viewing the video recorded interview. A supporter can also be present when the witness views the video to refresh his or her memory of his or her pre-recorded interview, as well as being present in the live-link room for the giving of evidence.

5.42 It should be explained to supporters that preparation work is not guaranteed to be confidential: if the witness talks about the evidence, the supporter should make a note and notify the police of its contents.[42]

Going to court – a step-by-step guide

5.43 The Ministry of Justice has a YouTube channel with animations for children. There is an animation about the Victim's Code for under 18s.[43]

There is a Young Witness Pack available which can be given to child victims and witnesses. There is also a DVD available for children and/or their parents or carers called 'Going to court: a step-by-step guide to being a witness'; it can also be viewed online.[44]

Delays in court proceedings

5.44 Delays in the proceedings may have an impact on a child's ability to remember an event and therefore his or her competency (see para 5.55–5.62 below on competency of witnesses). If the child is unable to remember the actual incident and is only remembering his or her video, then the entirety of the child's evidence may be excluded.[45] In the case of *R v Barker*,[46] the Court of Appeal emphasised the importance to the trial and investigative process of keeping any delay in a case involving a child victim to an irreducible minimum.

5.45 There is often a great deal of waiting in the court process and it would be prudent to explain this at the outset to any child victim or witness.

42 Achieving best evidence in criminal proceedings, para 4.24.

43 www.youtube.com/watch?v=t8gMFYl6Nm4.

44 www.youtube.com/watch?v=aUOc0Sa1WMM.

45 *R v Powell* [2006] 1 Cr App R 31; and *R v Malicki* [2009] EWCA Crim 365.

46 [2010] EWCA 4.

Discontinuing proceedings

5.46 A child victim or witness is entitled to a meeting with a representative from the CPS in certain specified cases, who can explain decisions that have been made – for example, if they decide not to prosecute a case, or to change the charges that have been made against a suspect, or if they decide to stop the case during the trial or after pre-trial hearings.[47]

Reporting restrictions for victims and witnesses

5.47 Children and Young Persons Act (CYPA) 1933 s49 imposes reporting restrictions on cases that are heard in the youth court. The general rule is that proceedings in the youth court are not open to the public (CYPA 1933 s47) – although press representatives are permitted to attend the youth court and report on proceedings, they are automatically restricted from reporting the identity or any details that would lead to the identity of any child or young person involved in the proceedings, whether as a defendant, witness or victim (CYPA 1933 s49). Section 49 also applies to appeals from the youth court, including an appeal by way of case stated and proceedings in the adult magistrates' court for breach, revocation or amendment of a Youth Rehabilitation Order and appeals.

5.48 As the reporting restriction under section 49 is automatic, the youth court does not need to make an order. It may, however, make an order allowing reporting restrictions to be lifted if it is appropriate to do so to avoid injustice to the child.[48] (See chapter 14 on anonymity for more information on reporting restrictions for child defendants.)

5.49 Reporting restrictions for child victims and witnesses involved in any other criminal proceedings, primarily trials in the Crown Court which are not appeals from the youth court, are governed by YJCEA 1999 s45. Section 45A, introduced in 2015, enables a court to grant lifelong anonymity to child witnesses and victims so that no matter that relates to them may be included in any publication if it likely to lead to them being identified by member of the public. This includes name, address, school, place of work, any still or moving picture. The test for making a reporting restriction for a child victim or witness is: the court must be satisfied that fear or distress on the part of the victim

47 Victims' Code, Chapter 3: Children and young people, para 2.3.

48 CYPA 1933 s49(5)(a).

or witness in connection with being identified by members of the public as being a part of the proceedings is likely to diminish the quality of the evidence or the level of co-operation (YJCEA 1999 s45A(5)).

5.50 When considering whether section 45A(5) should apply, the court must take into account:

- the welfare of the child victim or witness;
- the nature and circumstances of the alleged offence;
- the age of the victim or witness;
- the background, circumstances, religious beliefs, political opinions of the victim or witness (if relevant);
- any behaviour towards the victim or witness by the accused or their friends or family;
- any views of the child victim or witness, where that child is under 16 the views of their 'appropriate person'.[49]

5.51 The court may make an order in relation to YJCEA 1999 s45A, having regard to the welfare of the person, interests of justice and the public interest avoiding substantial and unreasonable restriction on the reporting of the proceedings.[50] The application for such an order can be made by the lawyers for either party in the case or by the court itself of its own initiative.

5.52 The legislation also gives the court the power to make what is called an 'excepting direction', which overturns any part of the reporting restrictions in section 45A. The court can make an excepting direction if it is satisfied that it is necessary in the interests of justice to do so, or that the reporting restriction imposes a substantial and unreasonable restriction on the reporting of the case and it is in the public interest to remove or relax the restriction. An excepting direction can be made at the time of proccedings, or later by the same court or an appellate court.[51]

5.53 Breaching a reporting restriction, in other words reproting what is prohibited, whether by a corporate media entity or an individual, is a criminal offence.[52]

5.54 Reporting restrictions have been expanded to cover all online content and social media in addition to traditional print and broadcast media.[53]

49 YJCEA 1999 s45A(6).

50 YJCEA 1999 s45A(8).

51 YJCEA 1999 s45A(14).

52 YJCEA 1999 s49.

53 YJCEA 1999 Sch 2 para 3 – definition of publication.

Competency of witnesses

Generally

5.55 The question of competency of witnesses, particularly very young children, has developed rapidly since the introduction of the Youth Justice and Criminal Evidence Act in 1999 – the test for competence is set out in section 53(3). It provides:

> A person is not competent to give evidence in criminal proceedings if it appears to the court that [he or she] is not able to (a) understand questions put to [him or her] as a witness, and (b) give answers to them which can be understood.

5.56 The leading case, which addresses the competency of children to be witnesses is *R v Barker*.[54] In that case, the Court of Appeal stated:

> We must analyse and address the essential point in the appeal, that is the principles which apply nowadays when young children give evidence in criminal trials. Many accreted suspicions and misunderstandings about children, and their capacity to understand the nature and purpose of an oath and to give truthful and accurate evidence at a trial have been swept away.[55]

5.57 In *Barker* the appeal was raised about 'the evidence of a child as young as 4½ years, describing events said to have occurred when she was not yet 3 years old' and whether the conviction could be regarded as safe.[56] The Court of Appeal found that the conviction was safe, *Barker* has made it clear that children have the right to be heard in the criminal courts, however the issue of competency is specific to the particular child witness in each particular case – there are no longer any presumptions or preconceptions: 'in the end it is a decision about the individual child and his or her competence to give evidence in the particular trial'.[57] In *Barker,* the Court of Appeal found that the child witness need not:

1) understand the special importance that the truth should be told in court;
2) understand every single question or give a readily understood answer to every question as many adult witnesses would fail such a competency test.

54 [2010] EWCA Crim 4.

55 *R v Barker* [2010] EWCA Crim 4, para 33.

56 *R v Barker* [2010] EWCA Crim 4, para 3.

57 *R v Barker* [2010] EWCA Crim 4, para 39.

5.58 Dealing with it broadly and fairly, provided the witness can understand the questions put to him or her and can also provide understandable answers, he or she is competent.[58]

5.59 If a witness's competence is called into question, a decision will normally be required about whether the witness can be called to give evidence, before the trial begins, and, if so, it is the responsibility of the party who is calling the witness to satisfy the court that the witness is competent on a balance of probabilities.[59] This questioning usually takes place before the trial, but can take place during the trial but before giving evidence. A child witness should have explained to him or her that a competency hearing is not the giving of evidence in the trial itself and that depending on the outcome of the hearing he or she may or may not be questioned about the alleged incident. Competency questions to the child witness must be asked by the court, in the absence of the jury, if there is one,[60] in the presence of the prosecution and the defence. Courts may ask for expert advice about the witness's competence, for example from a psychologist who has examined the witness, or from a lay person who has special knowledge of the witness's abilities.[61]

5.60 When the court assesses the witness's competence, it must take into account any 'special measures' it could grant (see paras 4.43–4.47 for what special measures can be put in place). Special measures have fundamentally changed the competency assessment that must be performed by the court and has enabled many witnesses, who historically would not have been able to give evidence at court due to vulnerability, disability or age, an opportunity to participate in criminal proceedings. In *R v F*[62] the Court of Appeal made it clear that the test for competency of a witness had greatly evolved, due to the additional support now available to vulnerable and child victims and witnesses.

5.61 *Barker* emphasises that competency is distinct from credibility, a competent witness might not necessarily be a credible one but that should not preclude them from giving evidence, provided the witness is competent, the weight to be attached to the evidence is a matter for the jury.[63]

58 *R v Barker* [2010] EWCA Crim 4.
59 YJCEA 1999 s54(2).
60 YJCEA 1999 s54(4).
61 YJCEA 1999 s54(5).
62 [2013] EWCA 424.
63 *R v Barker* [2010] EWCA Crim 4, para 41.

5.62 A competency decision can be re-opened at the end of the evidence given by the child witness. Re-analysis of competency is not contained in statute but is a consideration available to the judge. 'clearly established in a number of decisions of this court (*R v MacPherson*; *R v Powell*; *R v M*; *R v Malicki*'.[64] The re-analysis of competency post-evidence is there as back-up if, for example, the child witness has been unable to give intelligible answers to questions in cross-examination, or a meaningful cross-examination was impossible. This back-up is useful, as the initial competency decision is made before the court has heard the witness answers in cross-examination, and so made before being able to decide the witness's ability or inability to be cross-examined. If having heard the evidence it is apparent from answers given in cross-examination a witness is not competent, the entirety of that witness's evidence can be excluded to ensure a fair trial.[65]

Victims or witnesses who have been abused

5.63 It is now recognised by the courts that child victims and witnesses who have been subject to abuse are frequently damaged young people and:

> They can be difficult, emotional, contradictory, aggressive and on some occasions wholly uncommunicative. they are nearly always wholly unused to giving evidence in court.[66]

The position is that these inconsistencies should usually be matters for juries as fact finders rather than for judges to call a halt to the case:

> Whether in any trial their evidence is so vitiated that it is unsafe to leave the case to the jury will be a matter of careful judicial assessment. However, the courts now have a far greater understanding than hitherto as to the difficulties that exist for vulnerable witnesses and the need for care in assessing whether inconsistent or varying accounts given on different occasions necessarily mean that the underlying allegation is untruthful or unreliable. These are often matters for juries rather than judges to assess because it will be vital for the fact finder to assess the reasons for the changes or the contradictions in the witness's evidence and whether they fatally undermine the prosecution's case as regards the counts on the indictment.[67]

64 *R v Barker* [2010] EWCA Crim 4, para 43.

65 *R v Barker* [2010] EWCA Crim 4, para 43; also *R v Powell* [2006] EWCA Crim 3.

66 *R v Uddin* [2014] EWCA Crim 2269, para 54.

67 *R v Uddin* [2014] EWCA Crim 2269, para 54.

5.64 It is also recognised that advocates need to be specially trained in handling vulnerable and child witnesses in criminal proceedings:

> . . . do not underestimate the difficulties of questioning vulnerable witnesses. It requires not only training, flexibility and sensitivity, but also time and patience.[68]

In *F* above, the Court of Appeal draws attention to the publication 'Raising the Bar: the handling of vulnerable witnesses, victims and defendants in court' which has now been absorbed by The Advocates Gateway. The Advocates Gateway provides specific toolkits for lawyers preparing to question children and very young children (those under 7).[69] In 2016 new training came into place for barristers to learn how to question vulnerable victims and witnesses.

Cross-examination of child witnesses

5.65 Having a child witness in a case might mean that the defence lawyers are not able to put their client's case to very young witnesses, as they would have to in traditional cases with adult witnesses. In *R v Edwards*[70] one of the grounds of appeal was that the defence lawyer 'could not explore inconsistencies, credibility and reliability, or fundamental material for cross-examination'. With the playing of ABE video as evidence in chief with only a few bland and general questions from him,[71] the Court of Appeal found that the judge was entitled to conclude that the child understood the questions put to her without the defence lawyer putting his client's version of the case to the witness. The defendant was able to put his defence to the jury in many different ways, including giving evidence himself.

5.66 The Criminal Practice Direction 2015 makes it clear that in relation to young and/or vulnerable people there may be a radical departure from traditional cross-examination; and that when the witness is young, the court may dispense with normal practice and restrict the advocate from putting his or her case where there is a risk that the vulnerable witness will not understand, will become distressed or acquiesce to leading questions. Where limitations on questioning are necessary and appropriate, they must be clearly defined.[72]

68 *R v F* [2013] EWCA 424, para 26.

69 Toolkit 6. Planning to question a child or young person and toolkit 7. Additional factors concerning children under 7 (or functioning at a very young age).

70 [2011] EWCA Crim 3028.

71 *R v Edwards* [2011] EWCA Crim 3028.

72 CrimPD 3E.4.

5.67 However, in *R v B*[73] the Court of Appeal stated:

> . . . our system is adversarial and it is a matter for the parties to present the evidence in the way which they consider best serves their case . . . they should be permitted to conduct and present the case to the jury without unnecessary interference.

Oaths

5.68 An adult witness will swear an oath before the court to tell the truth or affirm before they give evidence. YJCEA 1999 s50 states that a witness shall not give sworn evidence, unless the witness:

- has attained the age of 14 years; and
- has sufficient appreciation for the solemnity of the occasion and of the particular responsibility to tell the truth which is involved in taking the oath.[74]

5.69 There is a presumption that witnesses of 14 and over are to be sworn, unless evidence is offered suggesting that they do not understand those two matters.[75] The question of whether a witness is eligible to swear an oath or to affirm may be raised by the parties or the court. The procedure used to determine this question is the same as the procedure outlined above (para 5.59 for determining competence) (ie in the absence of the jury, with the help of any necessary expert evidence, and through questions from the court in the presence of the parties).

Special measures for child witnesses in court

5.70 'Special measures' for witnesses in court were introduced into legislation in YJCEA 1999. These statutory special measures are available equally to prosecution and defence witnesses. (See paras 4.43–4.47 for more on the range and function of special measures.)

5.71 If a child is a witness for the prosecution, the CPS with the police will make the application for the special measures required before the trial takes place – that way the child witness should know what has been granted before he or she turns up at court to give his or her

73 [2010] EWCA 313.

74 YJCEA 1999 s50.

75 YJCEA 1999 s55.

evidence. If a child is a witness for the defence, the defence lawyer will apply for the special measures.

5.72 The definition of vulnerable witnesses is set out in YJCEA 1999 s16 (as amended by the Coroners and Justice Act 2009). Children are defined as vulnerable by reason of their age[76] and any of the statutory special measures protections apply to all children appearing as defence or prosecution witnesses in criminal proceedings to assist them to give their evidence in court.

5.73 The primary rule in the case of a child witness contained in YJCEA 1999 s21 is that the court must give a special measures direction which complies with the following requirements:

a) it must provide for any relevant video recording of the child witness evidence in chief to be admitted;
b) it must provide for any evidence given by the witness in the proceedings which is not given by means of a video recording (whether in chief or otherwise) to be given by means of a livelink.

5.74 For all child witnesses, there is a presumption that they will give their evidence in chief by video recorded interview, and any further evidence by livelink unless the court is satisfied that this will not improve the quality of the child's evidence. (See paras 5.18–5.19 above for pilots of recorded cross examination evidence).

5.75 However, a child witness may opt out of giving his or her evidence by either video recorded interview or by livelink or both, subject to the agreement of the court. If the child witness opts out, then there is a presumption that they will give his or her evidence in court from behind a screen.

5.76 Should the child witness not wish to use a screen, he or she may also be allowed to opt out of using it, again subject to the agreement of the court. In deciding whether or not to agree to the wish of the child witness, the court must be satisfied that the quality of the child's evidence will not be diminished. Where a video recorded interview is made before a child witness's 18th birthday, the witness is eligible for video recorded evidence in chief and livelink special measures directions after his or her 18th birthday.

Application process for special measures

5.77 Criminal Procedure Rule 18.9 applies where, under section 21 or 22 of YJCEA 1999, the primary rule requires the court to give a special

76 YJCEA 1999 s16(1).

measures direction for a child witness or a qualifying witness. This means that the usual application process for special measures is not required.

5.78 The primary rule always applies unless the witness does not want it to apply and the court is satisfied that to omit a measure would not diminish the quality of the evidence or that the court is satisfied that to direct one of the measures usually applicable would not be likely to maximise the quality of the witness' evidence.

5.79 It is the responsibility of the lawyer for the party who wants to introduce evidence using special measures to notify the court as soon as is practicable that the witness is eligible for assistance. The lawyer must also provide the court with any information that the court might need to assess the witness's views if they do not want the primary rule to apply and to serve any video recorded evidence on the court and the other party.

5.80 The content of an application for special measures must; explain how the witness is eligible for assistance, why special measures would be likely to improve the quality of the witness's evidence, propose the measure (or measures) that would be likely to maximise the quality of that evidence, report any views that the witness might have expressed about assistance and the measure proposed, in a case where livelink is proposed the application must identify someone to accompany the witness while the witness gives evidence and name that person if possible and explain why that person would be an appropriate companion for the witness, including the witness's views. In a case where video recorded evidence is proposed the application must include the date and duration of the recording, which part the applicant wants admitted as evidence. If the applicant wants a hearing this should be asked for in the application. The criminal practice directions set out a form that this application should take.

5.81 In a case where a child witness does not want the primary rule to apply the person making the application must provide the court with any information that might be needed to assess the witness's views.

Application to vary or discharge the special measures application

5.82 If any party wants the court to vary or discharge a special measures direction they must apply in writing as soon as reasonably practicable after becoming aware of the grounds for doing so. The application to vary or discharge must be served on the court and the other party. The application must explain what material circumstances have changed since the special measure direction was given, explain why the direction should be varied or discharged and ask for hearing if needed. The court can vary or discharge a special measures direction of its own initiative.

Ground rules hearing

5.83 Discussion of ground rules must take place in all trials where there is an intermediary – see further para 4.48. Discussion of ground rules is good practice, even if no intermediary is used in all cases involving young witnesses. Discussion before the day of trial is preferable to give advocates time to adapt their questions to the witnesses needs. It may be helpful for a trial practice note of boundaries to be created at the end of discussion to ensure that the agreed ground rules are complied with.

Types of special measures available

5.84 YJCEA 1999 s19(2) states that:

> Where the court determines that the witness is eligible for assistance by virtue of section 16 or 17, the court must then determine whether any of the special measures available in relation to the witness (or any combination of them) would, in its opinion, be likely to improve the quality of evidence given by the witness; and if so determine which of those measures (or combination of them) would, in its opinion, be likely to maximise so far as practicable the quality of such evidence; and give a direction under this section providing for the measure or measures so determined to apply to evidence given by the witness.

The court is also able to consider any other special measures that are not enshrined in statute, if the court considers that it is in the interests of justice to do so. See also para 4.38 on the court's inherent powers.

5.85 The special measures available to vulnerable and child witnesses set out in the Act, include:

- Screens, these can be put around the witness stand to make sure that the witness is shielded from seeing the defendant; The screen must not prevent the witness from being seen or heard by the justices, judge or jury, legal representatives.
- Livelink; a livelink is a closed circuit television link which enables the witness to give evidence during the trial from outside the courtroom through this televised link. The witness may be within the court building or in a suitable location outside the court. The

court should normally permit the defendant to be able to see the evidence given by livelink to 'ensure a fair trial,'[77] The court should make a direction with regards to the witness supporter who accompanies the child witness in the livelink room.

- Evidence given in private. This section excludes from the court members of the public and the press (except for one named person to represent the press) in cases involving sexual offences or intimidation by someone other than the accused.[78] The court is not able to exclude the defendants or the defence lawyers.
- Removal of wigs and gowns by judges and barristers (only relevant at the Crown Court);[79]
- Video-recorded interview before the trial may be admitted by the court as the witness's evidence-in-chief, the video recording or any part of it may be excluded if the court is of the opinion that it is in the interest of justice not to admit parts or any of it in the circumstances of the case.[80] Coroners and Justice Act 2009 s103 relaxes the restrictions on a witness giving additional evidence in chief after the witness video-recorded interview has been admitted. See para 5.17 for more detail on ABE interviews in court;
- Video recorded cross examination[81] this part of the Act has not yet been brought into force but is being piloted in certain areas of the country. It is anticipated that it will be brought into force nationally.
- An intermediary may be appointed by the court to assist a child witness to give her evidence at court. This role is similar to the intermediary who provides communication assistance in the investigation stage.[82]
- Aids to communication may be permitted to enable a witness to give his or her best evidence whether through a communicator, interpreter or through a communication aid or technique, provided that the communication can be independently verified and understood by the court.[83]

77 *R v Camberwell Youth Court ex p D (a minor)* [2005] UKHL 4 para 27.
78 YJCEA 1999 s17.
79 YJCEA 1999 s26.
80 YJCEA 1999 s27(2).
81 YJCEA 1999 s28.
82 YJCEA 1999 s29.
83 YJCEA 1999 s30.

Editing ABE interviews

5.86 ABE interviews may be edited if there are parts of the interview that are ruled inadmissible. The court must be of the opinion that, parts or all of, the video recording is not in the interests of justice in the particular case.[84] However the court must consider whether the prejudice to the accused is outweighed by the desirability of showing the whole video recorded interview. The lawyers may argue this issue before the trial to ensure that any editing can be completed before the trial begins. The child victim or witness must be informed of any editing to the video. This will avoid the witness being surprised, suspicious or confused when the recording does not match precisely his or her recollection of the interview.

5.87 Witnesses are entitled to see a copy of their statement before giving evidence and that includes a video-recorded interview, unless the video has been ruled inadmissible.

5.88 Where a pre-recorded interview is relied upon for evidence in chief the child witness must be available at court for cross-examination, unless they are in a pilot scheme where the recording of cross-examination is in place.

Supporter at court

5.89 The supporter who accompanies the child in giving evidence should not be the same person who has supported the witness when recording their statement.[85]

5.90 A witness supporter in the livelink room with a child victim or witness should be completely independent of the witness and her family and have no previous knowledge of or personal involvement in the case. The supporter should also be trained and understand their obligations. This supporter can be from witness service.

Intermediaries at court[86]

5.91 As stated previously, the statutory introduction of intermediaries for witnesses is contained in YJCEA 1999 s29. The function of the intermediary is to communicate:

84 YJCEA 1999 s27(2).

85 ABE para 4.19.

86 See CrimPD 3F.

> to the witness, any questions put to the witness; and to any persons asking such questions, the answers given by the witness in reply to them; and to explain such questions or answers so far.[87]

Intermediaries are different from supporters: the intermediary will assist a child victim or witness with communicating his or her evidence to the court, whereas a supporter's role is to provide emotional support to the witness.[88] The fact that an intermediary was not used in interview is therefore not in itself evidence that one is not needed at trial.

5.92 There are two different kinds of intermediaries as defined by the Witness Intermediary Scheme ('WIS'):[89] (i) a Registered Intermediary ('RI'): this is a professional communications specialist who has been recruited, selected and accredited by the Ministry of Justice, and whose details are recorded on the Intermediary Register, the WIS's national database; and (ii) a Non-Registered Intermediary: this is an individual who has <u>not</u> been recruited, selected or accredited by the Ministry of Justice as an RI. The WIS does not use or appoint non-registered intermediaries, ie those intermediaries not on the Intermediary Register.

5.93 The use of intermediaries has grown enormously since they were first introduced in 2002. In *R v James Michael Watts*,[90] an appeal was taken on the basis of the levels of communication that were available by the complainants, who were women suffering various degrees of paralysis and lack of communication through cerebral palsy and motor neurone's disease. The Court found that competency differed from lack of communication and held that those who are competent to give evidence should be assisted to do so. The Court stated that there are situations where a witness may be fully competent but lack sufficient communication skills to give evidence without the help of an intermediary.

5.94 An assessment by an intermediary should be particularly considered where there is a vulnerable witness. See Criminal Practice Direction 3F.26 – an assessment should be considered if a child or young person under 18 seems unlikely to be able to recognise a problematic question or, even if able to do so, may be reluctant to say so to a questioner in a position of authority. The decision should be

87 Registered Intermediary Procedural Guidance 2011.

88 See ABE Guidance para 4.67.

89 The WIS is operated on behalf of the Ministry of Justice (MoJ) by the National Crime Agency (NCA) through its Specialist Operations Centre.

90 [2010] EWCA Crim 1824.

made on an individual basis in the context of the circumstances of the particular case.

5.95 A Registered Intermediary must keep full records of his or her involvement throughout the process, including notes of assessments. These are disclosable by the prosecution to the defence.[91] In the case of prosecution witnesses, the RI must inform the officer-in-charge of the case of anything that they become aware of which might undermine the case for the prosecution against the accused or which might assist the case for the accused.

5.96 The RI writes a report for the court. It provides advice and makes recommendations with examples to those who will question the witness about how most effectively to do it. A ground rules hearing is required in all intermediary trials, this will usually take place pre-trial but it should take place with the trial judge. In any event it must take place before the witness gives evidence to discuss the ground rules for intermediary use and how the examination of the witness is to be dealt with.[92] This should cover issues such as how the intermediary will signal to the court that the witness has not understood a question or needs a break in proceedings, and how questions should be phrased in order to maximise the quality of the witness's evidence.

5.97 The RI, having taken the intermediary declaration just before the witness gives evidence, assists during the giving of evidence. They sit alongside the witness in the livelink room (or stand next to them if they are giving evidence in court) in order to monitor communication. They intervene during questioning when appropriate and as often as appropriate in accordance with the ground rules and the recommendations in their report.[93]

5.98 If at any stage the RI who assessed the witness and wrote a report for the court is unable to continue in the case or to assist at trial or to assist at re-trial then there is a hand-over procedure between the first RI and a substitute who is sourced through the WIS matching service. The new RI must assess the witness and write their own report (which can, where appropriate, consist of adding an addendum to the existing report). The reason is that the interventions during evidence at trial must be based on th RI's own conclusions about the witness and not someone else's.[94]

91 Registered Intermediary Procedural Guidance 2011.

92 CrimPD 3E.2.

93 www.theadvocatesgateway.org/intermediaries#how-it-works.

94 www.theadvocatesgateway.org/intermediaries#how-it-works.

5.99 There is a great deal of information about intermediaries and the development of the communication support for vulnerable witnesses in court for more detailed information see The Advocates' Gateway: www.theadvocatesgateway.org.

Victim Personal Statement

Overview

5.100 The Victims' Code offers the chance for a victim of crime to make a victim personal impact statement.[95] This is explained as letting someone 'explain in your own words how you feel the crime has affected you'. A Victim Personal Statement (VPS) can be video recorded in the same way that a witness statement is. The code goes on to state:

> If the defendant is found guilty, you are entitled to say you would like your VPS to be read aloud or played (where recorded) in court.[96]

5.101 A victim is entitled to read it aloud themselves, or have someone else read it out. The Code states:

> Before deciding whether you wish to have your VPS read aloud or played in court, you will be advised about the possible consequences, including that your VPS could be reported on in the media. You could also be asked questions about your VPS in court by the defence.[97]

Victim Personal Statement at parole hearings

5.102 Where an offender has been given a life sentence, a victim of crime is also entitled to prepare a VPS for any parole board consideration. The Code states:

> You will be asked whether you want to make a Victim Personal Statement for the Parole Board to consider when they make the decision on whether to release the offender or move them to an open prison.[98]

95 Victims' Code, Victim Personal Statement, paras 1.12–1.22.

96 Victims' Code, para 1.20.

97 Victims' Code, para 1.20.

98 Victims' Code, para 6.12.

Expenses

5.103 A victim or witness is entitled to his or her expenses to be paid by the CPS. The Code states:

> You are entitled to be paid any expenses the Crown Prosecution Service has decided are due to you if you have attended court to give evidence not later than 10 working days after the Crown Prosecution Service has received a correctly completed claim form.[99]

Victim Contact Scheme

5.104 There exists a Victim Contact Scheme (VCS) for victims of crime where the suspect is found guilty of a violent or sexual offence and is given a prison sentence of 12 months or more or is given a hospital order. The VCS says a victim is entitled to:

- ask for conditions to be put on the offender if they are released that the offender is not allowed to make contact with you in any way;
- be told when the offender is released from prison or hospital and any conditions put on them which relate to you;
- be told about any other important information which the National Probation Service think you should be told;
- be told you can choose at any time not to take part in the VCS.[100]

5.105 For child victims it will normally be a parent or guardian who is told about the VCS.[101]

Restorative justice

5.106 The Victims Code offers the opportunity for a victim to be involved in restorative justice, but emphasises that this is voluntary. The Code explains that 'Restorative Justice lets you talk about what happened with the offender'[102] and takes place with 'someone who has been specially trained in Restorative Justice' who 'will be at any meeting

99 Victims' Code, para 4.2.
100 Victims' Code, para 6.2.
101 Victims' Code, para 6.5.
102 Victims' Code, para 7.1.

with the offender'.[103] If the offender is under the age of 18, restorative justice will be organised by the Youth Offending Team (YOT).

Compensation for victims of crime

5.107 The Code explains that some victims might be entitled to compensation. The Criminal Injuries Compensation Authority (CICA) is an organisation that deals with applications made under the Criminal Injuries Compensation Scheme. 'This Scheme is paid for by the Government to make payments to blameless victims of violent crime.'[104] If a victim is a child at the time of the incident, 'it is best if a responsible adult applies' for compensation, any compensation claim 'must be within 2 years of the incident occurring'.[105]

103 Victims' Code, para 7.2.
104 Victims' Code, para 8.1.
105 Victims' Code, para 8.2.

PART 2

Children as suspects and defendants

CHAPTER 6

Children and the police

continued

Key points

- Although the numbers of children in contact with the criminal justice system are declining, police still arrest many thousands of children each year.
- Police have particular duties in relation to children, these are mostly contained in the PACE Codes of Practice.
- The development of child friendly policing, as set out in the National Police Chiefs' Council *National Strategy for the Policing of Children and Young People*, is welcomed but it needs to be put into practice in every contact between children and the police
- Stop and search continues to be utilised disproportionately against children and young adults and black, Asian and minority ethnic people (BAME).
- Where possible children should not be arrested. When invited for a voluntary interview they should be told of their right to free and independent legal advice.
- Children should not be detained in police custody or cells unless absolutely necessary.
- The introduction of the 28 day bail limit has resulted in children being released under investigation, often for months, before a decision is made about whether to charge, offer or an out of court disposal or take no further action.

Introduction

6.1 In the year ending March 2017, 74,784 children were arrested in England and Wales.[1] In 2014, the All Party Parliamentary Group for Children Report on Children and the Police found that:

> Police forces nationally continue to carry out several thousand child arrests a year . . . Evidence was presented to the inquiry which suggested that many children and young people who are arrested find the experience highly stressful and traumatic.[2]

1 Youth Justice Statistics 2016/17, England and Wales, Youth Justice Board and Ministry of Justice, 25 January 2018.

2 All Party Parliamentary Group for Children 2013–2014 Report *'Its all about trust': Building good relationships between children and the police*, para 1.2.

6.2 The police have particular duties in relation to children who come into contact with the criminal justice system – these are set out in greater detail throughout this chapter. Additionally, there is a welfare principle which underpins the youth justice system (see para 1.68–1.71 on the welfare principle). The Children Act 2004 s11 places a specific duty on the police to discharge their obligations having regard to the need to safeguard and promote the welfare of children.[3] In practice, this means that the police need to make decisions that safeguard and promote a child's welfare, and failure may form the basis of legal challenges. There may be civil challenges to the lawfulness of the child's treatment at the police station or the admissibility of evidence obtained in the course of the police investigation in criminal proceedings.

6.3 In 2016 the National Police Chiefs' Council (NPCC) published '*Child centred policing: National Strategy for the Policing of Children and Young People*'. It includes the following key principles:

- It is crucial that in all encounters with the police those below the age of 18 should be treated as children first. All officers must have regard to their safety, welfare and well-being as required under Children Act 2004 ss10 and 11 and the United Nations Convention on the Rights of the Child (UNCRC).
- The vulnerability of children and young people should be identified and responded to effectively in order to protect them from harm.
- In all situations where children and young people come to the attention of the police, a full understanding of their circumstances should be sought. It is unusual for a young person to be involved in serious offending without being a victim of circumstances or offending themselves.
- Engagement should be positive and opportunities should be sought to enhance our relationship with them.
- Children are entitled to be treated differently from adults and there are special protections when they are at the police station, one of the most important of these entitlements is the right to an appropriate adult.
- The voices of children and young people should be heard and their opinions respected.[4]

3 Children Act (CA) 2004 s11(2)(a).

4 'National strategy for the policing of children and young people', National Police Chiefs' Council, 2016.

PACE and the Codes of Practice

6.4 Most police powers are governed by the Police and Criminal Evidence Act 1984 (PACE) . There are additional common law police powers and other police powers contained in different statutes, but PACE contains the most commonly used powers. PACE is supported by a number of Codes of Practice, 'which regulate police powers and protect public rights'.

6.5 The Codes of Practice are regularly updated and must be readily available at all police stations for consultation by police officers, police staff, detained persons and members of the public (particularly an appropriate adult – see paras 6.108–6.131 for more on the role of the appropriate adult):

- Code A – Code of Practice for the exercise by police officers of statutory powers of stop and search;
- Code B – Code of practice for searches of premises by police officers and the seizure of property found by police officers on persons or premises;
- Code C – Code of practice for the detention, treatment and questioning of persons by police officers;
- Code D – Code of practice for the identification of persons by police officers;
- Code E – Code of practice on audio recording interviews with suspects;
- Code F – Code of practice on visual recording with sound of interviews with suspects;
- Code G – Code of practice for the statutory power of arrest by police officers;
- Code H– Code of practice in connection with the detention, treatment and questioning by police officers of persons under section 41 of and Schedule 8 to, the Terrorism Act 2000.

6.6 Breach of the Codes of Practice may result in disciplinary action against police officers or entitle a suspect to damages.

Stop and search powers

6.7 The police have powers to stop people without having to arrest them, including the power to stop and ask them to account for what they are doing and the power to stop and search people and vehicles (PACE Codes A and H). See further paras 6.13–6.15.

6.8 There is evidence that shows that stop and search powers are used disproportionately on males who are from black Asian and minority ethnic backgrounds (BAME). The independent review into the treatment of, and outcomes for BAME individuals in the criminal justice system (CJS) by David Lammy MP cites 'Grievances over policing tactics, particularly the disproportionate use of Stop and Search, drain trust in the CJS in BAME communities'.[5]

6.9 Data collated by the Metropolitan Police shows the disproportionate use of stop and search on young males and more specifically young black males,[6] who only make up a small percentage[7] of the general population.

6.10 Supervising officers are required to monitor the use of stop and search and 'must consider in particular where there is any evidence that they are being exercised on the basis of stereotyped images or inappropriate generalisations'.[8] Supervisors must also examine whether the records reveal any trends or patterns which give cause for concern by the compilation of comprehensive statistical records of stop and searches at force, area and local level, and if so take appropriate action to address any disproportionate use of powers.[9]

6.11 Children in contact with the criminal justice system often say that the use of stop and search is a power that they feel the police use inappropriately and disproportionately. It is important for professionals working with children in the criminal justice system to understand the impact that police stop and searches can have.

6.12 Research analysing ten years of police, crime and other data from London concluded that the effect of stop and search in reducing crime is marginal at best.[10]

5 'The Lammy Review: An independent review into the treatment of, and outcomes for Black, Asian and Minority Ethnic individuals in the Criminal Justice System', published 8 September 2017, p17.

6 At: www.met.police.uk/sd/stats-and-data/met/stop-and-search-dashboard.

7 According to 2011 census data, black people make up 3% of the general population in England and Wales. Office for National Statistics data for 2017 suggests 11.5% of the London population are black (this includes men and women of all ages), therefore young black males represent only a small percentage of the population in London.

8 PACE Code A, para 5.1.

9 PACE Code A, para 5.3.

10 Does stop and search deter crime? Evidence from ten years of London-wide data, Ben Bradford, Matteo Tiratelli and Paul Quinton, The British Journal of Criminology, Volume 58, Issue 5, 13 August 2018, pages 1212–1231.

Stop and account

6.13 The police can stop members of the public and ask them to account for themselves. This practice, known as 'stop and account', enables the police to stop a person at any time and ask what they are doing, why they are in an area and/or where they are going. There is no age restriction on who the police can ask to stop and account, even though the age of criminal responsibility is ten.

6.14 Stop and account is not a power based in statute. There is no requirement for an officer who has asked someone to stop and account to record the encounter or to give the person a receipt.[11] There is no requirement for the police to inform the person stopped that they are free to leave.[12] Police forces have a discretion whether to monitor that stop and account is being used disproportionately.[13]

6.15 During a stop and account encounter, the police have no authority to compel the person to answer questions and there is no corresponding legal requirement for the person to answer the police questions. There is no power to stop a person in order to find grounds for a search, however, not answering police questions during stop and account could create the reasonable grounds for suspicion necessary to conduct a stop and search of the suspect.

Stop and search under PACE s1

Overview

6.16 PACE s1 authorises the police to stop and search people in public. In this context, 'public' is defined as:

- any place to which at the time when he [a constable] proposes to exercise the power the public or any section of the public has access, on payment or otherwise, as of right or by virtue of express or implied permission; or
- in any other place to which people have ready access at the time when he proposes to exercise the power but which is not a dwelling.[14]

6.17 If a person being searched is in a garden or yard occupied with and used for the purposes of a dwelling, or on other land so occupied and

11 PACE Code A, para 4.12.

12 At: www.stop-watch.org/uploads/documents/Factsheet_-_Stop__Account.pdf.

13 PACE Code A, Notes for guidance, para 22A.

14 PACE s1(1)(a)–(b).

used, a constable may not lawfully search him unless the constable has reasonable grounds for believing:

- that he does not reside in the dwelling; and
- that he is not in the place in question with the express or implied permission of a person who resides in the dwelling.[15]

6.18 PACE contains no minimum age requirement for a person to be stopped and searched, this means that although children cannot be held criminally responsible until they are 10, they may be subjected to a police stop and search. The Metropolitan Police have issued guidance on how under 10 year olds should be treated if stopped and searched which states that children under 10 when found in possession of illegal items after a stop and search 'should be considered as an exploited victim rather than an offender.'[16]

6.19 In order to stop and search a person, the police officer must have 'reasonable grounds' to suspect that the person is either: carrying illegal drugs,[17] a weapon, stolen property or an item that is going to be used to commit certain offences.[18] Children under the age of 18 can also be stopped and searched if it is believed that they are carrying a firework[19] (there is a prohibition on any person under 18 possessing fireworks[20]).

6.20 Community Support Officers do not have powers of stop and search under PACE, but do have powers under other legislation including under the Terrorism Act 2000 (see Code A annex C for powers of community support officers).

6.21 There are also powers under the Terrorism Act 2000 s43 to stop and search a person the police 'reasonably suspect' of being a terrorist to find out if they have anything in their possession that may constitute evidence that they are a terrorist.

6.22 Terrorism Prevention and Investigation Measures Act 2011 Sch 5, para 3 grants powers to constables to search people who are subject to Terrorism Prevention and Investigation Measures (TPIM) notices in certain circumstances.[21]

15 PACE s1(1)(4).

16 www.met.police.uk/SysSiteAssets/media/downloads/central/advice/met/stop-and-search/position-statement-searching-children.PDF

17 Misuse of Drugs Act 1971 s23.

18 PACE s1(8) and (8A).

19 PACE s1(8B) and (8C).

20 Fireworks Regulations 2004 SI No 1836 reg 4.

21 See PACE Code A paras 2.18A–2.26 for additional detail.

Reasonable grounds for suspicion

6.23 Reasonable grounds for suspicion is explained in PACE Code A para 2.2 as a 'two part' legal test that the police must apply before they stop and search someone:

- Firstly, the officer must have formed a *genuine suspicion* in their own mind that they will find the object for which the search power being exercised allows them to search

and:

- Secondly, the suspicion that the object will be found must be *reasonable*. This means that there must be an *objective* basis for the suspicion – based on *facts, information and/or intelligence* which are relevant to the likelihood that the object in question will be found, so that a reasonable person would be entitled to reach the same conclusion that the object in question will be based on the same facts and information *and/or intelligence.*[22]

6.24 Reasonable suspicion can never be supported on the basis of personal factors.[23]

Search powers under Criminal Justice and Public Order Act 1994 s60

6.25 If an area is authorised by an officer ranked inspector or above as a designated area under Criminal Justice and Public Order Act (CJPOA) 1994 s60, any person or vehicle can be stopped and searched regardless of whether the police have *reasonable grounds for suspicion.*[24] An area can be designated a section 60 search area if the authorising officer reasonably believes that:

a) incidents involving serious violence may take place in any locality in the officer's police area, and that it is expedient to give an authorisation to prevent their occurrence; or
b) an incident involving serious violence has taken place in the officer's police area, a dangerous instrument or offensive weapon used in the incident is being carried in any locality in the officer's police area by a person and it is expedient to give an authorisation to find it; or
c) that persons are carrying dangerous instruments or offensive weapons in any locality in the officer's police area without good reason.

22 PACE Code A, para 2.2.
23 PACE Code A, para 2.2B.
24 CJPOA 1994 s60(4)(a)(b) and PACE Code A, paras 2.12–2.14.

6.26 The authorising officer may give an authorisation that the powers conferred by this section are to be exercisable at any place within that locality for a specified period not exceeding 24 hours.[25] If it appears to an officer of or above the rank of superintendent that it is expedient to do so, he may direct the period to continue for another 24 hours.[26]

6.27 In a section 60 designated area, if authorised by an officer of the rank of inspector or above,[27] a police officer also has the power to seize or demand the removal of any item of clothing the police officer believes is being worn by a person to conceal their identity.[28] The police must reasonably believe that someone is wearing an item wholly or mainly for the purpose of concealing identity.[29]

6.28 It is a criminal offence to fail to stop for a constable when required to do so in a section 60 designated area for a 'section 60 search'.[30] The maximum penalty for an adult is 1 month's imprisonment therefore this is not an offence for which a child can receive a custodial sentence.

Other search powers

Search at school premises

6.29 The police have the power to enter school premises and search the premises or any person on the premises for a blade, pointed article or offensive weapon.[31] The police officer must have a reasonable belief that an offence of having a blade or a point in a public place has been committed.[32]

Search of a vehicle

6.30 Police are entitled to search a vehicle under the same legislation and codes that they are entitled to search a person. This means that they must have reasonable grounds for suspicion under PACE s1(2) (see paras 6.23–6.24 on reasonable grounds for suspicion).

25 CJPOA 1994 s60(1)(b).
26 CJPOA 1994 s60(3).
27 PACE Code A, para 2.17.
28 CJPOA 1994 s60AA.
29 PACE Code A, para 2.15.
30 CJPOA 1994 s60(8).
31 Criminal Justice Act (CJA) 1988 s139B.
32 CJA 1988 s139B(1)(b).

Search of premises

6.31 The power to search people when they are in a building that is being searched is found in Code A paras 2.27–2.29.

Conduct of searches

Overview

6.32 As a last resort the police are entitled to use 'reasonable force' to carry out a search if it has been established that a person is unwilling to cooperate or is resisting the search.[33] The search must take place near where the person was first detained.[34] Before being searched the police officer must take reasonable steps to tell the person:

- that the person is being detained for the purposes of a search;
- the officer's name and police station (except in terrorist stop and search);
- a clear explanation as to the purpose of the search and the ground for suspicion;
- the legal power under which they are searching;[35]
- officers not in uniform must show their warrant cards;[36]
- that the person is entitled to a copy of the record of the search, which must be made at the time 'unless this is wholly impracticable'. If it isn't possible to get a copy of the record at the time of the search, a person is entitled to know how and where they can get a copy later.[37]

6.33 All stops and searches must be carried out with courtesy, consideration and respect for the person concerned.[38] Every reasonable effort must be made to minimise the embarrassment that a person being searched may experience.[39]

6.34 Where the exercise of the stop and search power requires reasonable suspicion, the thoroughness and extent of a search must depend on what is suspected of being carried, and by whom. If the suspicion relates to a particular article which is seen to be slipped into a person's

33 PACE s117 Code A, para 3.2.
34 PACE Code A, para.3.4.
35 PACE Code A, para 3.8.
36 PACE Code A, para 3.8.
37 PACE Code A, para 3.8(e).
38 PACE Code A, para 3.1
39 PACE Code A, para 3.1.

pocket, then, in the absence of other grounds for suspicion or an opportunity for the article to be moved elsewhere, the search must be confined to that pocket. In the case of a small article which can readily be concealed, such as a drug, which might be concealed anywhere on the person, a more extensive search may be necessary.[40]

Removal of clothing during searches

6.35 A police officer can ask a person to take off their outer coat, jacket or gloves at the scene of a stop and search.[41] There is no power to ask a person to remove more than their outer coat, jacket or gloves. If a police officer wants to request someone to take off more of their outer clothing or anything they're wearing for religious reasons, for example a veil or turban, they must take the person to a place out of public view, for example in a police van (see paras 6.92–6.109 on searches at the police station).[42] The exception to this is CJPOA 1994 s60AA which empowers a constable to require a person to remove any item worn to conceal identity (see para 6.27 above).

6.36 If the police wish to remove more than someone's coat, jacket, gloves, headgear or footwear, or any other item concealing identity, the police officer conducting the search must be the same sex as the person being searched[43] and may not occur in the presence of anyone of the opposite sex unless the person being searched specifically requests it. There is no duty for the police to ensure an appropriate adult is present unless it is a strip search.[44]

6.37 Refusing to comply with a stop and search may result in arrest for resisting or obstructing an officer in the execution of his or her duty.[45] Lawyers should consider whether the search was lawful in order to establish whether the officer was in fact executing their duty and therefore the elements of the offence made out.

6.38 The Youth Justice Legal Centre has produced a film on stop and search as a tool to explain to children and young people their rights and the powers the police are able to use when a stop and search takes place.[46]

40 PACE Code A, para 3.3.
41 PACE Code A, para 3.5.
42 PACE Code A, para 3.6 and PACE Code A notes for guidance 4.
43 PACE Code A, para 3.6.
44 see para 6.95 for definition of a strip search.
45 Police Act 1996 s89(2).
46 www.yjlc.uk/for-young-people.

Arrest

What is an arrest?

6.39 Arrest is governed by PACE Part 3. The term 'arrest' is not defined but a person is arrested if it is made clear to them, by what is said and done, that they are deprived of their liberty and are not free to go as they please. For an arrest to be lawful the police must comply with the duties set out in PACE Part 3.

Police powers of arrest

6.40 The police can arrest a child following the issue of a warrant by a court.[47] This is most likely to happen if the child has failed to attend a court hearing.

6.41 The police are given powers of summary arrest (arrest without a warrant) under PACE s24. A police officer may arrest a person without a warrant who is *about to commit* an offence or is *committing* an offence or who the police officer has reasonable grounds for suspecting *has committed* an offence.[48] Article 5 of the European Convention of Human Rights (ECHR) gives people the right to liberty and security, which means the police must exercise their powers of arrest in accordance with obligations under the Human Rights Act 1998.

6.42 The police may only use these powers of arrest if the police officer has reasonable grounds for believing it is necessary to arrest person, for any of the following reasons:

- to enable the name of the person in question to be ascertained (in the case where the constable does not know, and cannot readily ascertain, the person's name, or has reasonable grounds for doubting whether a name given by the person as his or her name is his or her real name);
- to enable the person's address to be ascertained;
- to prevent the person in question causing physical injury to himself or any other person; suffering physical injury; causing loss of or damage to property; committing an offence against public decency; or causing an unlawful obstruction of the highway;

47 Magistrates Courts Act 1980 s13.

48 PACE s24(1).

- to protect a child or other vulnerable person from the person in question;
- to allow the prompt and effective investigation of the offence; or of the conduct of the person in question; or
- to prevent any prosecution for the offence from being hindered by the disappearance of the person in question.[49]

6.43 The Code of Practice which governs the power of arrest is PACE Code G. It emphasises the importance of the right to liberty under the Human Rights Act 1998[50] and that an arrest must be both necessary and proportionate and that a police officer must consider whether the objectives can be met by other less intrusive means.[51]

6.44 The person who is being arrested must be informed, as soon as is practicable, after the arrest that he or she is under arrest.[52] This is required even when it is obvious that the person has been arrested.[53] Failure to inform the person that they are under arrest renders the arrest unlawful and any subsequent detention is arguably unlawful. Additionally the person arrested must be told the grounds for their arrest.[54]

Police caution upon arrest

6.45 A person who is arrested must be cautioned at the time of arrest or as soon as is practicable afterwards, unless it is impracticable to do so because of the person's condition or behaviour or because the person was cautioned immediately before being arrested.[55] The words of the caution that should be given are:

> You do not have to say anything. But it may harm your defence if you do not mention when questioned something which you later rely on in court. Anything you do say may be given in evidence.[56]

6.46 A person must be taken to a police station as soon as is practicable, after they have been arrested, if they are not there already.[57]

49 PACE s24(5).
50 PACE Code G, para 1.2.
51 PACE Code G, para 1.3.
52 PACE s28(1).
53 PACE s28(2).
54 PACE s28(3).
55 PACE Code C, section 10.
56 PACE Code C, para 10.5.
57 PACE s30(1A).

Arrest for further offences

6.47 Where someone is at the police station and it appears to the police that he or she should be arrested for another offence, the person must be arrested for that other offence.[58] The person must be cautioned again or reminded that he or she remains under caution.[59]

Breach of the peace

6.48 There is a common law power of arrest for breach of the peace. This arrest can be made by a police officer or member of the public. An arrest for breach of the peace can be made when a breach of the peace is committed or when the person believes that a breach of the peace is about to be committed in the immediate future. There is a breach of the peace whenever harm is actually done or is likely to be done to a person, to the person's property or a person is in fear of being harmed through an assault, an affray, a riot, unlawful assembly or other disturbance.[60]

Arrest of children

Generally

6.49 Police officers should avoid arresting children wherever possible to avoid their unnecessary detention – custody should only be used as a last resort.[61] Officers should pay particular regard to the timing of any necessary arrests of children and ensure that they are detained for no longer than needed and are only detained for the 'right reasons'.[62] Police officers can avoid arresting children by arranging for children to attend police stations for a voluntary interview (see paras 6.158–6.162 on voluntary police interviews). Arrests of children 'should be considered appropriately and used only where necessary.[63]

58 PACE s31.

59 PACE Code G, para 3.4.

60 *R v Howell* [1982] QB 416.

61 National Strategy for Police Custody, National Police Chiefs' Council, p7.

62 National Strategy for Police Custody, National Police Chiefs' Council, p11.

63 National Strategy for Police Custody, National Police Chiefs' Council p4.

No power to arrest under ten year olds

6.50 Since children under the age of 10 are under the age of criminal responsibility,[64] they cannot be deemed to have committed a criminal offence, therefore they can't be arrested for a criminal offence.

Child under ten detained at the police station

6.51 Although the police have no power to arrest children under the age of 10, the police do have the power to hold a child under 10 at the police station under Children Act 1989 s46. Where a constable has reasonable cause to believe that a child would otherwise be likely to suffer significant harm, the constable may remove the child to suitable accommodation and keep the child there.[65]

6.52 No child may be kept in police protection for more than 72 hours.[66]

Arrests at places of education

6.53 The guidance notes to PACE Code C (11D) state:

> Juveniles should not be arrested at their place of education unless this is unavoidable. When a juvenile is arrested at their place of education, the principal or their nominee must be informed.[67]

Arrest of children who have been remanded to local authority accommodation

6.54 The police have the power to arrest, without warrant, children who they have reasonable suspicion have failed to keep the conditions of a remand to local authority accommodation.[68]

Power of arrest for breach of anti-social behaviour injunction or anti-gang injunction

6.55 For police powers of arrest in relation breaches of anti-social behaviour injunctions (ASBIs) (see paras 24.53–24.98) and anti-gang injunctions (AGIs) (see paras 24.99–24.151).

64 CYPA 1933 s50.
65 CA 1989 s46(1)(a).
66 CA 1989 s46(6).
67 PACE Code C Notes for Guidance 11D.
68 Legal Aid, Sentencing and Punishment of Offenders Act (LASPO) 2012 s97(1).

Street bail

6.56 An arrested person may be released on 'street bail' without first going to the police station and informed that he or she must attend the police station at a date in the future.[69] There is no power to impose conditions on street bail.[70] If the police give 'street bail' to a child consideration should be given to their welfare and the police officer should make telephone contact with the parent or carer as soon as is practicable after street bail is granted.[71] The officer granting street bail must give the arrested person a written notice stating the offence and grounds for the arrest as well as the police station they must attend.[72]

Citizens' arrest

6.57 Powers of arrest for police community support officers and other civilians are limited to arresting someone who has committed, or for whom they have reasonable grounds for suspecting is about to commit, indictable offences. The person making the arrest must have reasonable grounds for believing the arrest is necessary to prevent the subject causing physical injury to themselves or someone else, damage property or making off before a constable can stop them and it must appear to the person making the arrest that it is not reasonably practicable for a constable to make it instead.[73]

Search and seizure on arrest

6.58 A constable may search an arrested person, in any case where the person has been arrested at a place other than a police station:

- if the constable has reasonable grounds for believing that the arrested person may present a danger to himself or herself, or others;
- to search the arrested person for anything which he might use to assist him to escape from lawful custody; or which might be evidence relating to an offence.[74]

6.59 A search for items to assist escape or for evidence must be reasonably required for the purpose of finding such an item.[75] The power

69 PACE s30A.
70 PACE s30A(4).
71 Home Office Circular 61/2003, para B(3)(1).
72 PACE s30B(1)–(3).
73 PACE s24A.
74 PACE s32(1)–(2).
75 PACE s32(3).

does not allow a constable to require the searched person to remove any of his clothing in public other than an outer coat, jacket or gloves, but they can search the person's mouth.[76] The presence of an appropriate adult during the search is not necessary.

6.60 On searching an arrested person, a constable may seize and retain anything he or she finds, if the constable has reasonable grounds for believing:

- that the person searched might use it to cause physical injury to himself or herself, or to any other person; or
- that the person might use it to assist him or her to escape from lawful custody; or
- that it is evidence of an offence or has been obtained in consequence of the commission of an offence.

The only exception to this is the items subject to legal privilege, which may not be seized.[77]

Search of premises following arrest

6.61 If the offence for which someone has been arrested is an indictable offence, the police can enter and search any premises in which the person was arrested or in immediately before the person was arrested for evidence relating to the offence.[78] The search must be reasonably required for the purpose of discovering any evidence relating to the suspected offence.[79]

6.62 The police may enter and search any premises occupied or controlled by a person who is under arrest for an indictable offence, if the officer has reasonable grounds for suspecting that there is on the premises evidence, other than items subject to legal privilege, that relate to the offence or to some other indictable offence which is connected with or similar to the offence.[80] The search must be reasonably required for the purpose of discovering such evidence.[81]

6.63 The police may seize and retain any evidence for which they are entitled to search.[82]

76 PACE s32(4).
77 PACE s32(8)–(9).
78 PACE s32(2)(b).
79 PACE s32(3).
80 PACE s18.
81 PACE s18(3).
82 PACE s18(2).

Detention at the police station

Authorising detention

6.64 The custody officer must first authorise a person's detention and then open a custody record which includes the grounds for arrest and detention.[83] A person can only be detained without charge where there is not sufficient evidence to charge him or her and the custody officer has reasonable grounds for believing that the suspect's detention without charge is *necessary* to secure, preserve or obtain evidence relating to the offence for which the suspect is under arrest by questioning him or her.[84]

All persons in custody must be dealt with expeditiously, and released as soon as the need for detention no longer applies.[85]

6.65 When authorising a person's initial detention, the person must be informed of his or her right to legal advice and to have someone informed of his or her arrest.[86] These rights apply to all people, but there are additional rights for children detained at the police station. PACE refers to children as 'arrested juveniles', which is defined as 'any person who appears to be under the age of 18'.[87] See para 1.8 for more on the term juvenile. A child can only be detained for six hours before the child's detention must be reviewed[88] subject to certain criteria.

6.66 Generally, a suspect cannot be detained without charge for more than 24 hours unless the detention is extended (see paras 6.67–6.172 below).[89]

Extended detention

6.67 A police officer of the rank of superintendent or above may authorise an extension of up to 36 hours if they have reasonable grounds to believe:

83 PACE Code C; paras 2.1 and Code C notes for guidance 3.4 and Code G 2.2 and 4.3.

84 PACE s37(3) as amended by PCA 2017 s54(6).

85 PACE Code C, para 1.1.

86 PACE Code C, para 3.1(i) and (ii).

87 PACE s37(15).

88 PACE s40(3)(a).

89 PACE s41.

- the detention of that person without charge is necessary to secure or preserve evidence relating to an offence for which he or she is under arrest or to obtain such evidence by questioning him;
- the offence for which he is under arrest is an indictable offence; and
- the investigation is being conducted diligently and expeditiously.[90]

6.68 Before authorising continued detention, the officer must give the detainee, appropriate adult and the defence lawyer (provided they are available at the time) the opportunity to make representations.[91]

6.69 Detention of a child or a vulnerable person for longer than 24 hours will be dependent on the circumstances of the case and with regard to:

- the person's special vulnerability;
- the legal obligation to provide an opportunity for representations to be made prior to a decision about extending detention;
- the need to consult and consider the views of any appropriate adult; and
- any alternatives to police custody.[92]

Warrant of further detention

6.70 In order to detain a suspect beyond 36 hours, a constable may make an application to court. On an application by a constable on oath supported by an information, the magistrates' court may issue a warrant of further detention, authorising the keeping of a detainee in police detention. The court must have reasonable grounds for believing:

- the detainee's detention without charge is necessary to secure or preserve evidence relating to an offence for which he or she is under arrest or to obtain such evidence by questioning him or her;
- an offence for which the detainee is under arrest is an indictable offence; and
- the investigation is being conducted diligently and expeditiously.[93]

6.71 The magistrates' court may issue a warrant authorising up to a further 36 hours' detention. Multiple applications can be made up to the maximum period of 96 hours detention.[94]

90 PACE s42.

91 PACE Code C, para 15.3.

92 PACE Code C, para 15.2A.

93 PACE s43.

94 PACE s44.

Terrorism

6.72 Under Terrorism Act 2000 s41, the normal maximum period which a suspect can be detained pre charge is 48 hours. The detention period can be extended by a warrant for further detention up to a maximum of 14 days.[95]

Conditions of detention for children

6.73 Code C states that:

> . . . a juvenile shall not be placed in a police cell unless no other secure accommodation is available and the custody officer considers it is not practicable to supervise them if they are not placed in a cell or that a cell provides more comfortable accommodation than other secure accommodation in the station. A juvenile may not be placed in a cell with a detained adult'[96]

6.74 Detainees should be visited at least every hour.[97] Whenever possible, children and mentally vulnerable detainees should be visited more frequently.[98]

Informing parents or person responsible for a child's welfare

6.75 When a child is arrested and detained at a police station, the child's parents, guardian or other person responsible for their welfare must be informed that the child has been arrested. This right is in addition to the general right a detainee has to have someone informed of their detention. The custody sergeant must take such steps as are practicable to find out the identity of the person who is responsible for the child's welfare.[99] If the child is a looked after child, it is the local authority who should be informed rather than the parent or guardian.[100] The person informed must be told what the child is being arrested for, why the child has been detained and where the child is being detained, unless it is impracticable to do so.[101] If the child is already subject to a court order, the custody officer must inform the

95 Terrorism Act 2000 Sch 8.
96 PACE Code C, para 8.8.
97 PACE Code C, para 9.3.
98 PACE Code C Note for Guidance 9B.
99 PACE Code C, para 3.13.
100 CYPA 1933 s34(8).
101 PACE s57.

person or organisation that is responsible for supervising or monitoring the child.[102]

Detention in a cell

6.76 A child should not be placed in a police cell unless there is no other secure accommodation available and the custody officer considers that it is not practicable to supervise the child unless the child is placed in a cell (see para 6.73 above).[103] Any period of detention in a police station should be no longer than necessary[104] and children must never be held in a police cell with a detained adult.[105]

6.77 Experiences of children and young people show that they find being detained in a police cell an extremely distressing:

> 'I don't know, the whole being in the cell thing makes you feel like an animal, you know, locked away in the cell.' (16 year old female) [106]
>
> 'Being arrested is horrible. I'd rather do time in prison cells than spend an hour in a police cell. They mess with your head.' (Tyler young person, UR Boss project)[107]

6.78 A lawyer representing a child at the police station should make representations to the police to ensure that wherever possible the child is not held in a cell and if that is unavoidable that it is for the shortest period of time possible.

Other entitlements

6.79 A detained child is also entitled to an appropriate adult. This person is not necessarily the same person as the person responsible for the child's welfare (see paras 6.108–6.131 on appropriate adult). The defence lawyer should check with the custody officer who has been informed of the child's detention and whether an appropriate adult is at the police station.

6.80 In addition, all detainees have rights to writing materials on request and to speak to someone on the telephone for a reasonable

102 PACE Code C, para 3.14.
103 PACE Code C, para 8.8.
104 PACE Code C, para 1.1.
105 PACE Code C, para 8.8.
106 Professor Neal Hazel, University of Salford, 2006.
107 APPG C 2013 p13: www.ncb.org.uk/sites/default/files/uploads/documents/Policy_docs/appgc_children_and_police_report_-_final.pdf.

amount of time.[108] These rights can only be limited where an officer of the rank of inspector or above has reasonable grounds to believe that sending a letter or making a telephone call will:

- lead to interference with, or harm to, evidence connected with an indictable offence; or interference with, or physical harm to, other people; or
- lead to alerting other people suspected of having committed an indictable offence but not yet arrested for it; or
- hinder the recovery of property obtained in consequence of the commission of such an offence.[109]

Taking fingerprints, DNA, photographs and samples

Consent

6.81 In order for the police to take fingerprints, photographs and samples from a detainee, the appropriate consent must be given. PACE defines this as:

a) in relation to a person who has attained the age of 18 years, the consent of that person;
b) in relation to a person who has not attained that age but has attained the age of 14 years, the consent of that person and his or her parent or guardian; and
c) in relation to a person who has not attained the age of 14 years, the consent of his or her parent or guardian.[110]

Fingerprints

6.82 Fingerprints may be taken *without* appropriate consent if detained in consequence of an arrest for a recordable offence or charged with a recordable offence and the fingerprints have not been taken in the course of the investigation by the police.[111]

Photographs

6.83 A person may be photographed with appropriate consent *or* if the appropriate consent is withheld *or* it is not practicable to obtain it.

108 PACE Code C, para 5.6.
109 PACE Code C, Annex B, para 1.
110 PACE s65 – supplementary.
111 PACE s61(3), (4).

Footwear impressions

6.84 An impression of footwear may be taken *without* appropriate consent if a person is under arrest for a recordable offence or has been charged with a recordable offence and the impressions have not been taken in the course of the investigation by the police.[112]

Non-intimate samples

6.85 Non-intimate samples include hair (not pubic), nails or under the nails, a swab from the body including the mouth (but not other orifices), saliva and skin impressions.[113]

6.86 A non-intimate sample can be taken from a person *without* appropriate consent if the person is arrested for a recordable offence and one hasn't been taken in the course of the investigation, if an officer of at least the rank of inspector authorises it or if the person has been charged with a recordable offence.[114]

6.87 An appropriate adult should be present for the taking of non-intimate samples[115] unless the child prefers the appropriate adult's absence and the adult agrees.[116]

Intimate samples

6.88 'Intimate sample' means a sample of blood, semen or any other tissue fluid, urine, pubic hair, a dental impression, a swab taken from genitals or orifice other than a mouth.[117]

6.89 Intimate samples can only be taken if appropriate consent is given.[118] Where the consent is withheld without good cause, an adverse inference may be drawn.[119]

6.90 When an intimate sample is taken from a child, an appropriate adult should be present.[120] Again, if involving the removal of clothes it may take place in the absence of the appropriate adult if the child doesn't want the adult to be present and the adult agrees.[121]

112 PACE s61A(3).
113 PACE s65(1).
114 PACE s63.
115 PACE Code D, para 2.15.
116 PACE Code D, para 6.9.
117 PACE s65(1).
118 PACE s62(1).
119 PACE s62(10).
120 PACE Code D, para 2.15.
121 PACE Code D, para 6.9.

Drug testing

6.91 Before charge, the police can only drug test suspects aged 18 and over (where the other requisite requirements are satisfied).[122] Post-charge drug testing is available for children aged 14–17 in certain police stations.[123]

Searches at the police station (including strip searches)

6.92 A custody officer must ascertain what property a detainee has on him or her when the detainee arrives at the police station. In order to achieve this, an officer may authorise a search to be carried out when an arrested child arrives at the police station.[124] There does not have to be an appropriate adult present during the search unless the search is a 'strip search' (see para 6.95–6.107 on strip searches and intimate searches).

Seizure of evidence and removal of property

6.93 The police may seize all of a detainee's personal property (personal belongings and clothing) if the custody officer believes that the person from whom they are seized may use them:

- to cause physical injury to himself or herself, or any other person;
- to damage property;
- to interfere with evidence;
- to assist him to escape; or
- has reasonable grounds for believing that they may be evidence relating to an offence.[125]

This will include mobile phones and belts.

6.94 The police have separate powers to seize clothes or possession as evidence (see paras 6.58–6.60 search and seizure on arrest and PACE s32(8) and (9)). Children may find having their possessions taken by the police particularly difficult and should be advised about when and how they will be returned.

122 PACE s63B.
123 PACE s63B(3)(a); and Code C, Notes for Guidance 17F.
124 PACE s54.
125 PACE s54(4).

Strip searches

6.95 A strip search is 'a search involving the removal of more than outer clothing'.[126] Outer clothing includes shoes and socks.[127] As a result, representatives should be aware that that any removal of more than a detainee's outer clothing during a search under PACE s54 search still amounts to a 'strip search'.

6.96 A strip search may take place only if it is considered necessary to remove an article which a detainee would not be allowed to keep and the officer reasonably considers the detainee might have concealed such an article. *Strip searches shall not be routinely carried out if there is no reason to consider that articles are concealed.*[128]

6.97 If a strip search is carried out, the reasons for it must be recorded on the custody record.[129]

6.98 If a strip search takes place on a child, an appropriate adult must be present unless the need for the strip search is urgent.[130] If a search involves exposure of intimate parts of the body, it must take place in the presence of an appropriate adult, unless the child asks, in the presence of the appropriate adult, for them not to be present and the appropriate adult agrees.[131]

6.99 Additionally, the police officers carrying out the strip search must be the same sex as the detainee[132] and the search shall take place in an area where the detained child cannot be seen by anyone who does not need to be present.[133] Strip searches should be carried out in a manner designed to minimise, not exacerbate, a detained person's embarrassment.[134] During a strip search, the police can request that the detained person hold his or her arms in the air and his or her legs apart and bend forward so a visual examination can be made of their genital and anal areas, but the officers cannot make physical contact.[135] Detainees who are searched shall not normally be required to remove all their clothes at the same time, for example a person should be

126 PACE Code C, Annex A, para 9.
127 PACE Code C, Annex A, para 9.
128 PACE Code C, Annex A, para 10.
129 PACE Code C, Annex A, para 12.
130 PACE Code C, Annex A, para 11(c).
131 PACE Code C, Annex A, para 11(c).
132 PACE Code C, Annex A, para 11(a).
133 PACE Code C, Annex A, para 11(b).
134 PACE Code C, Annex A, para 11(d).
135 PACE Code C, Annex A, para 11(e).

allowed to remove clothing above the waist and re-dress before removing further clothing.[136]

6.100 Police officers should observe particular care when carrying out strip searches of children, and they should only be conducted when absolutely necessary. Given what is known about the vulnerabilities and backgrounds of the majority of the children in contact with the criminal justice system, especially those who have historically been abused, police can be reminded that strip searching can be extremely traumatic (see paras 3.82–3.102 backgrounds of children in the criminal justice system).

6.101 The Court of Appeal found that removing the clothes of a detained person for the person's own protection (PACE 1984 s54) is a strip search for the purposes of attracting the protections found in Code C Annex A and that these protections apply whenever a detained person's clothing is removed.[137] The court went on to express concern:

> that it should have been thought appropriate immediately to remove the clothes of a distressed and vulnerable 14 year old girl without thought for alternative and less invasive measures to protect her from herself.[138]

6.102 The College of Policing's Authorised Professional Practice for detention and custody states:

> If a detainee is believed to be at risk of suicide or self-harm, the seizure and exchange of clothing may not remove the risk but may increase the distress caused to the detainee and, therefore, increase the risk of them self-harming. Leaving a detainee in their own clothing can help to normalise their situation. Constant observation or within close proximity (Level 3 or 4) may be a more appropriate control measure in these circumstances . . .[139]

6.103 A strip search has the potential to humiliate and shame children – Code C states: 'before authorising any intimate search the authorising officer must make every reasonable effort to persuade the detainee to hand over any article without a search'.[140]

Intimate searches

6.104 An intimate search goes further than a strip search and is defined as a physical examination of a person's body orifices, other than their

136 PACE Code C, Annex A, para 11(d).

137 *PD v Merseyside Police* [2015] EWCA Civ 114, para 35.

138 *PD v Merseyside Police* [2015] EWCA Civ 114, para 44.

139 www.app.college.police.uk/app-content/detention-and-custody-2/detainee-care/.

140 PACE Code C, Annex A, Note for Guidance A1.

mouth.[141] The intrusive nature of such searches means the risks associated with intimate searches must never be underestimated.[142]

6.105 An intimate search can only take place if authorised by a police officer of inspector rank or above who has reasonable grounds to believe that a person may have concealed on themselves:

- anything which could cause physical injury to themselves or others at the station; or
- a class A drug which they intend to supply to another or to export.

and the officer has reasonable grounds for believing that an intimate search is the only means of removing those items.[143]

6.106 An intimate search should be carried out by a registered medical practitioner or registered nurse, unless an officer (of at least inspector rank) considers that it is not practicable. This must only be considered as a last resort.[144]

6.107 An appropriate adult must be present for an intimate search, unless the child states in the appropriate adult's presence that they don't want them present and the appropriate adult agrees.[145] The appropriate adult must be the same sex as the child, unless the child specifically requests an appropriate adult of a different sex and an appropriate adult of that sex is present at the police station.[146]

Appropriate adult

Overview

6.108 All children are entitled to an appropriate adult at the police station. The custody officer must, as soon as is practicable, inform the appropriate adult, who may or may not be the person responsible for the child's welfare, the reason the child is being detained and the police station where the child is being detained.[147] The duty to contact the appropriate adult is in addition to the police duty to contact the child's parent or any other person who is responsible for the welfare of the child (see

141 PACE Code C, Annex A, para 1.
142 PACE Code C, Annex A, para 1.
143 PACE s55(1)–(2).
144 PACE Code C, Annex A para 3A.
145 PACE Code C, Annex A para 5.
146 PACE Code C, Annex A para 5.
147 PACE Code C, para 3.15.

para 6.75 on informing parents or person responsible). The police must secure the attendance of the appropriate adult to the police station.[148]

Selecting an appropriate adult

Generally

6.109 An appropriate adult can be a parent, guardian or any responsible adult over the age of 18 who is not a police officer or employed by the police.[149] PACE Code C provides a list of suitable adults who might act in the role of an appropriate adult for a child:

(i) the parent, guardian or, if the juvenile is in the care of a local authority or voluntary organisation, a person representing that authority or organisation (see Note 1B);
(ii) a social worker of a local authority (see Note 1C);
(iii) failing these, some other responsible adult aged 18 or over who is not:
- a police officer;
- employed by the police;
- under the direction or control of the chief officer of a police force; or
- a person who provides services under contractual arrangements (but without being employed by the chief officer of a police force), to assist that force in relation to the discharge of its chief officer's functions, whether or not they are on duty at the time.[150]

6.110 Helping a child and the child's family decide who is best placed to act as an appropriate adult is not always straight forward. The role of the appropriate adult requires an understanding of the duties owed to children at the police station as well as their rights and entitlements which are contained in the codes of practice and should be available at the police station (see para 6.5 for the outline of what is in each code of practice). Parents can be well placed to act as appropriate adult but in certain circumstances someone else may be the better choice. A parent who is cross with their child, or one who is distracted by something such as concern for other children waiting at home, may not be able to fulfil their duties as appropriate adult. The National Appropriate Adult Network, the national membership body supporting and representing organisations delivering appropriate adult

148 PACE Code C, para 3.15.
149 PACE Code C, para 1.7.
150 PACE Code C, para 1.7.

services in England and Wales offers guidance[151] for people undertaking the role of appropriate adults, it states:

> Family members are not always in a position to act as a person's appropriate adult. This might be because they are unavailable, unsuitable (for example if they may be a witness) or they simply don't feel they are the right person to take on the role.[152]

Parent or guardian

6.111 The role of the appropriate adult and the importance of the involvement of parents is encapsulated by Lord Justice Moses in the High Court judgment of *HC*:[153]

> It is difficult to imagine a more striking case where the rights of both child and parent under Article 8 are engaged than when a child is in custody on suspicion of committing a serious offence and needs help from someone with whom he is familiar and whom he trusts, in redressing the imbalance between child and authority. The wish of a 17-year-old in trouble to seek the support of a parent and of a parent to be available to give that help must surely lie at the heart of family life which, quite apart from Article 8, the government seeks to maintain and encourage.

Another responsible person

6.112 PACE Code C para 1.7 simply states that the appropriate adult can be some other responsible adult aged 18 or over who is not: a police officer; employed by the police; under the direction or control of the chief officer of a police force; or a person who provides services under contractual arrangements (but without being employed by the chief officer of a police force), to assist that force in relation to the discharge of its chief officer's functions.

6.113 This, therefore, could include an older sibling, a key worker, or any other 'responsible' adult that the child feels can support them through the police station process.

Professional appropriate adults and appropriate adult schemes

6.114 The local authority has a statutory duty under Crime and Disorder Act (CDA) 1998 s38, in conjunction with the police, probation and

151 www.appropriateadult.org.uk/index.php/information/guidance-aa.

152 www.appropriateadult.org.uk/index.php/information/guidance-aa.

153 *R (HC) v Secretary of State for the Home Department* [2013] EWHC 982 (Admin), para 85.

health authorities, to ensure that appropriate adult services are available in the local area to safeguard the interests of children detained by the police at the police station.[154]

6.115 The provision of appropriate adult services varies from each local authority. Sometimes it is a volunteer scheme run by the local authority, and in other areas, it is provided by children's services' staff or the youth offending service. Children do not have to use these professionals as their appropriate adult, and can request an appropriate adult who is a parent or carer or any responsible adult.

People unsuitable to act as an appropriate adult

6.116 There are certain adults, who while they may be available as appropriate adults are not appropriate for various reasons.

Suspect, witness or victim

6.117 A person, including a parent or guardian, should not act as appropriate adult if there is a suspicion that they may be involved in the offence. This includes if they are a potential victim, witness or involved in the investigation of the alleged offence.[155]

Estranged parents

6.118 Where a child is estranged from his or her parent and the child specifically objects to the parent's presence, the parent should not act as an appropriate adult.[156]

Previous admissions

6.119 Code C Note for Guidance 1C states:

> If a juvenile admits an offence to, or in the presence of, a social worker or member of a youth offending team other than during the time that person is acting as the juvenile's appropriate adult, another appropriate adult should be appointed in the interest of fairness.

6.120 Where a child has made admissions to an adult, that adult is no longer suitable to act in the role as an appropriate adult as this may place them in a difficult position (see paras 6.129–6.130 on appropriate adults and legal privilege). The appropriate adult should be

154 CDA 1998 s38(1), (4).
155 PACE Code C, Note for Guidance 1B.
156 PACE Code C, Note for Guidance 1B.

able to advise and assist the child fairly, without the interference of anything the child might have said outside of the police station.

Unable to speak English

6.121 There is nothing in the Codes that allows for an interpreter for a parent or guardian unable to speak English. To enable a non-English speaking parent or guardian to fulfil their duty as an appropriate adult they would need someone who could translate for them to allow them to look after the child's interests.

Solicitor or independent custody visitor

6.122 A solicitor or independent custody visitor who is present at the police station and acting in that capacity, is unable to be the appropriate adult.[157]

The role of the appropriate adult

6.123 The legislation and the Codes envisage that the appropriate adult plays an active role. Home Office Guidance for Appropriate Adults states they are there to 'ensure that the detained person for whom you are acting as appropriate adult understands what is happening to them and why'.[158]

6.124 The appropriate adult is entitled to be there when the child:

- is informed of their rights by the custody officer;
- is strip searched or is required to have an intimate search;
- is interviewed;
- takes part in identification procedures;
- is photographed;
- is cautioned or charged;
- has his or her detention reviewed.

6.125 Key roles and responsibilities are as follows:

- to support, advise and assist the detained person, particularly while they are being questioned;
- to observe whether the police are acting properly, fairly and with respect for the rights of the detained person. And to tell them if they think they are not;

157 PACE Code C, Note for Guidance 1F.
158 Home Office Guidance for Appropriate Adults Annex A.

- to assist with communication between the detained person and the police;
- to ensure that the detained person understands his or her rights and that to have a role in protecting his or her rights.[159]

6.126 The appropriate adult's role is not to provide the detained person with legal advice.[160] There is information, from government and the National Appropriate Adult Network available to support people taking on the role of an appropriate adult.[161] This information should be read by those acting as appropriate adults at the police station.

6.127 A child must not be interviewed or asked to provide a written statement in the absence of an appropriate adult,[162] unless an officer of superintendent rank or above considers delaying the interview could pose an immediate risk of harm to persons or serious loss or serious damage to property.[163] An interview must not continue once sufficient information has been obtained to prevent the immediate risks.[164]

6.128 For the procedure as it relates to voluntary interviews see paras 6.158–6.164 below.

Appropriate adults and legal privilege

6.129 Professionals should be aware that an appropriate adult is not covered by legal privilege or a duty of confidentiality[165] There is therefore a real danger that any privileged information revealed by the child to the child's lawyer, in the presence of the child's appropriate adult, could be used as evidence against the child, even potentially unwillingly on the part of the appropriate adult. See, for example, *R v Marcus Brown*[166] where a social worker passed on to the police evidence of a child's admission in relation to an additional offence, not the one under investigation, and was then obliged to be a witness against the child in the criminal proceedings.

159 Home Office Guidance for Appropriate Adults Annex A.

160 Home Office Guidance for Appropriate Adults Annex A.

161 www.gov.uk/government/uploads/system/uploads/attachment_data/file/117625/guidanceappadultscustody.pdf; and www.appropriateadult.org.uk/index.php/information/guidance-aa.

162 PACE Code C, para 11.15.

163 PACE Code C, para 11.18.

164 PACE Code C, para 11.19.

165 PACE Code C Notes for Guidance C1E and Home Office Guidance for Appropriate Adults Annex A.

166 [1999] (unreported).

6.130 Representatives are therefore advised that when taking instructions from the child regarding the allegations, it might be better for the appropriate adult not to be present. This can be explained in an initial meeting with the child and appropriate adult present. Appropriate adults, particularly parents, might be resistant to this approach, so it will need to be carefully explained that this is to protect the appropriate adult from being compelled to give evidence against the child or risk contempt of court or perjury charges themselves for failure to do so. There may be circumstances where it is not appropriate, or even possible, to have a consultation in the absence of the appropriate adult. For example, a child who wants their parent present may not be able to communicate effectively without their parent. While the starting point position is for the consultation to take place in the absence of the appropriate adult, defence lawyers will have to decide how to proceed on a case-by-case basis.

Rights of the appropriate adult

6.131 The appropriate adult should be given access to the custody record[167] and has the right to consult with the child in private at any time.[168] The appropriate adult can request free legal advice for the child. The appropriate adult has the right to ask for a lawyer to attend the police station without the child agreeing – although the child cannot be forced to see the lawyer.[169] If the appropriate adult decides that a lawyer is not necessary when he or she first arrives at the police station, the adult can change his or her mind about that at any time.[170]

Legal advice and assistance at the police station

Overview

6.132 A suspect involved in a police criminal investigation has a statutory right to legal advice.[171] A suspect must be entitled to consult a lawyer

167 Home Office Guidance for Appropriate Adults Annex B.

168 Home Office Guidance for Appropriate Adults Annex B.

169 PACE Code C, para 6.5A.

170 Home Office Guidance for Appropriate Adults Annex B/uploads/system/uploads/attachment_data/file/117625/guidanceappadultscustody.pdf at p4 of 7.

171 PACE s58(1).

as soon as is practicable.[172] Many children will have a limited understanding of what 'free legal advice' means when this is offered to them by the custody sergeant. It is the responsibility of the appropriate adult to ensure that children are given free legal advice (see para 6.131 above on appropriate adults rights to request free legal advice). It is the responsibility of the lawyer to explain to the child the lawyer's role and his or her independence from the police, particularly if the lawyer has been contacted as part of the duty solicitor scheme.

6.133 It is possible that there are occasions where the police discourage children from accessing legal advice, using the argument that it will delay a child's release from the police station. It has been identified that children, particularly 10–13 year olds, are least likely to request and receive legal advice.[173] In his review of the youth justice system Charlie Taylor recommended that there be a presumption that a lawyer is called and legal advice provided for all children.[174] There are many decisions that are made at the police station that can have life-long consequences for children. It is the view of the authors that the best interests of children are protected by accessing the free legal advice that is available from a legal representative.

6.134 Another reason that a child may refuse the assistance of legal advice is due to a misplaced understanding that 'duty solicitors' are either a) no good or b) work for the police. The trust deficit between BAME suspects and their lawyers was identified by the Lammy review as a barrier to better outcomes.[175] The government's website makes it clear that duty solicitors are independent from the police[176] and this can be shown to children in custody.

6.135 Once the arrested person tells the police that he or she would like legal advice, the police will either contact the Defence Solicitor Call Centre (DSCC) or the arrested person's named solicitor.

6.136 It is the duty of the interviewer (see paras 6.145–6.157 on police interviews with children), at the commencement of the interview or re-commencement if the interview is stopped and begins again,

172 PACE Code C, para 6.50.

173 Kemp, V, Pleasence, P, & Balmer, N J (2011) Children, young people and requests for police station legal advice: 25 years on from PACE. *Youth Justice*, 11(1), 28–46.

174 Review of the Youth Justice System in England and Wales, by Charlie Taylor (Ministry of Justice) published Dec 2016, para 69.

175 *The Lammy Review: An independent review into the treatment of, and outcomes for, Black, Asian and Minority Ethnic individuals in the Criminal Justice System* (published 8 September 2017) p 29.

176 www.gov.uk/arrested-your-rights/legal-advice-at-the-police-station.

to remind the child and the child's appropriate adult of their entitlement to free legal advice. This should be done on tape and recorded, and the interview should be delayed or halted to get legal advice if the person being interviewed expresses the desire to have legal advice.[177]

The role of the police station representative

6.137 A child, or a third party on the child's behalf (such as a member of the child's family), can instruct a lawyer of his or her choosing to act at the police station. In this case, the named lawyer must log the case with the DSCC within 48 hours of receiving instructions.[178] Alternatively, the police can contact the DSCC for the case to be allocated to a duty solicitor. The obligations of the legal representative to a person who is arrested and detained at the police station are set out in the standard crime contract.[179]

6.138 A duty solicitor who accepts a case from the DSCC must endeavour to contact the client (whether in person or on the telephone) within 45 minutes of the call.[180] If the person is asleep, drunk, violent or otherwise unable to coherently speak on the telephone, the police may postpone the initial advice.[181] In these situations the lawyer must make arrangements to provide initial advice as soon as the person arrested is capable of speaking to the lawyer.[182] The duty solicitor will then wait for the police to inform him or her that they are ready to interview the suspect. Except in certain circumstances, where the lawyer can justify non-attendance or the case is restricted to telephone-only advice, once a case has been accepted by the duty solicitor a legal representative must attend to advise the detainee in person.

6.139 The duty solicitor will be present for any interviews of the arrested person and for any identification procedures that may take place. A legal representative must also be present if there is an application to extend the detention of the arrested person and the lawyer should make representations about the warrant of further detention (see paras 6.67–6.71 on extended detention). To qualify for payment

177 PACE Code C, para 11.2.

178 Standard Crime Contract 2017, para 9.20.

179 www.gov.uk/government/publications/standard-crime-contract-2017.

180 Standard Crime Contract 2017, para 9.23.

181 Standard Crime Contract 2017, para 9.42(a).

182 Standard Crime Contract 2017, para 9.42(a).

under the legal aid scheme, the sufficient benefit test must be satisfied. The test requires there to be sufficient benefit to the client, having regard to the circumstances of the matter, including the personal circumstances of the client, to justify work or further work being carried out.[183] The sufficient benefit test is deemed satisfied where a person has a right to legal advice under PACE.[184] Attendance while the detainee gives fingerprints and swabs or in order to make representations about bail will need to be justified.[185] Given the particular vulnerability of children, the presence of a defence lawyer is always likely to be justifiable.

6.140 Legal advice at the police station can be given by qualified solicitors and 'accredited police station representatives' who may not be qualified lawyers but have undertaken training and are qualified to provide representation to people arrested at the police station. If the person assisting a child at the police station is an accredited representative rather than a duty solicitor, the arrested person or the person's appropriate adult should be informed of that status.[186]

Changing legal representation

6.141 The duty solicitor must inform every arrested person that they are not obliged to instruct a duty solicitor. If the arrested person wishes to instruct another lawyer, the duty solicitor must not act unless the named person is not available and then the duty solicitor may represent the person on that occasion only. A duty solicitor must make available to any other lawyer instructed any relevant information or papers.[187]

6.142 If a duty solicitor has been allocated a police station case by the DSCC and then the child decides they would like a different lawyer, the DSCC have the power to re-allocate the case to the named person. However, the duty solicitor who was originally given the case would have to agree to relinquish the case back to the DSCC.

6.143 This often happens when children have requested the duty solicitor but their parents decide they would like them to be represented by someone else. If the original duty solicitor won't relinquish the case the parent can be advised on the telephone that the child should

183 Standard Crime Contract 2017, para 3.10.
184 Standard Crime Contract 2017, para 9.14.
185 Standard Crime Contract 2017, para 9.16.
186 Standard Crime Contract 2017, para 9.45.
187 Standard Crime Contract 2017, paras 6.64–6.66.

not sign a legal aid application with the duty solicitor. If the child signs a legal aid application at the police station, this will enable them to apply for a legal aid certificate if the child is charged and matters proceed to court. By not signing the legal aid application, children and their family can make an informed choice of legal representative, should it be needed, at the youth court.

Representing potential prosecution witnesses

6.144 Children will sometimes be invited to speak to the police with a view to providing a statement and potentially acting as a prosecution witness (see chapter 5 for more on children as victims and witnesses). When the potential witness is at risk of self-incrimination, legal aid may be available for a defence lawyer to provide advice and assistance.[188]

Police interviews with children

6.145 A police interview is defined as 'the questioning of a suspect regarding their involvement or suspected involvement in a criminal offence'.[189] The term 'interview' includes in its definition any questioning of the suspect, not just the interview which takes place at the police station. The police interview process for a child suspect takes the same format as it would for an adult. The police station representative should ensure, as far as it is possible, that the 'interrogation process' is adapted to take into consideration the child's age and any communication difficulties they may have. The police station representative may wish to state clearly to the police and on the audio recording that the person being questioned is a child and therefore the interview process should take this into consideration.

6.146 Before a person is interviewed, they and their legal representative, if they are legally represented, must be given sufficient information to enable them to understand the nature of the offence alleged against them and why they are suspected of committing it.[190]

6.147 An interview must be carried out under caution.[191] Children should not be interviewed without the appropriate adult present

188 Standard Crime Contract 2017, para 9.3.

189 PACE Code C, para 11.1A.

190 PACE Code C, para 11.1A.

191 PACE Code C, para 10.1.

unless an urgent interview is necessary.[192] An interview under caution at the police station is recorded, usually this is simply an audio recording[193] but in some circumstances there may also be a video recording.[194]

6.148 Children have the same right to silence as adults. The Criminal Justice and Public Order Act (CJPOA) 1994 sets out the circumstances when an adverse inference can be drawn from a suspect's failure to answer questions:

- Section 34: where, before charge, the suspect fails to mention any fact relied on in their defence. (see paras 13.74–13.77 for more on how adverse inferences can be made in trial)
- Section 36: where the suspect fails to account for any object, mark or substance found on or near them at the time of arrest.
- Section 37: where the suspect fails to account for their presence at the place where the offence occurred.

6.149 In order for an adverse inference to be drawn under CJPOA 1994 s36 or s37 the interviewing officer must give the suspect a special warning.[195]

6.150 *Defending suspects in the police station* by Ed Cape lists as the criteria for representatives to consider when formulating advice:[196]

- the police case;
- the legality of arrest, detention and questioning;
- prior comments and silences of the client;
- the likely fairness of the interview;
- the state of the client;
- the client's case;
- specific reasons for not answering questions;
- advantages of admitting guilt.

6.151 When considering whether a child should answer questions in interview, make a prepared statement or exercise their right to silence, the child's age, maturity and ability to cope with police questioning are factors which will affect the advice given. A child's inability to manage in a police interview, and the impact this may have on their mental health, may be reason alone to advise them against answering questions or to make a prepared statement.

192 PACE Code C, para 11.15.
193 PACE Code E.
194 PACE Code F. Notes for Guidance 2E
195 PACE Code C, para 10.11.
196 Ed Cape, *Defending Suspects at Police Stations*, 7th edn, LAG, 2018, para 5.109.

6.152 Children are not on a level playing field with their interrogators, and legal representatives need to ensure, as far as possible, that children go in to interview well prepared. In order to do this effectively, legal representatives will need to spend time building rapport with their young clients and explaining things in a way that they are genuinely able to understand. (See para 3.6 textbox, 'Tips for talking with adolescents'.)

6.153 *Defending suspects in the police station* lists the defence lawyer's objective in interview as:

- to ensure that the police act fairly at all times and observe the requirements of PACE and the Codes of Practice;
- to ensure that the client does his or her best in interview, whether or not he or she is answering questions;
- to protect the client from unnecessary or inappropriate pressure and distress and, in particular, to protect vulnerable clients;
- to ensure that an accurate account is kept of the interview, and that the lawyer keeps his or her own record.[197]

6.154 An interview may be stopped at any time at the request of the child or the child's legal representative and the child may be given the opportunity to consult privately with them. Those representing children need to be especially robust in protecting their clients from unfair, inappropriate or oppressive questioning. In interview:

> . . . the solicitor may intervene in order to seek clarification, challenge an improper question to their client or the manner in which it is put, advise their client not to reply to particular questions, or if they wish to give their client further legal advice.[198]

At the re-commencement of any interview the same caution must be given as given at the beginning of an interview and for the purposes of the recording must identify any people that are present during the interview.[199]

197 7th edn, LAG, 2018, para 7.34.
198 PACE Code C, Note for Guidance 6D.
199 PACE Code C 10.1. and 12.7

Representing children during interviews at police station

6.155 Representing children during interviews at the police station can present particular difficulties that may not apply when representing adult suspects:

1) A child suspect needs to know that their legal representative is on their side and is not just another figure of authority.
2) A child may be particularly scared or nervous about his or her experience at the police station. Being held in a police station is a distressing experience.[200] Anxiety or fear may not be visible to an appropriate adult or to the police.
3) A child may not understand the seriousness of the situation that he or she is in, nor the importance of not telling the lawyer the truth or the repercussions that might occur.
4) A child may be inhibited to speak openly in front of their parent. There may be other pressures such as gang involvement or cultural and religious reasons why a child may withhold information from their lawyer. For these reasons It can be important for a legal representative to speak to a child, without the appropriate adult present and to spend time to allow their client to talk about difficult and sensitive issues. (See paras 6.129–6.130 for appropriate adults and legal privilege.)
5) Children in the criminal justice system are more likely to have neurological issues, learning difficulties or psychiatric issues (see paras 3.45–3.102 for more on the importance of background). Children may have learned to mask or hide these disabilities. The legal representative should try to ask relevant questions, sensitively and possibly indirectly, to the child and the appropriate adult
6) In theory, an intermediary (see para 5.32–5.35 on intermediaries) could assist a child at the police station. The Advocate's Gateway states:

> The use of an intermediary potentially includes assistance to a suspect in the police station, eg, during an interview under caution. It would be the responsibility of defence solicitors

200 See 'National strategy for the policing of children and young people', National Police Chiefs' Council, 2016, p11 and para 6.77. Children have taken their lives, or tried to take their lives, after an experience at the police station even when investigated for fairly minor offences.

> (or the duty solicitor) to source someone and having regard to the limits on the time in which a suspect may be detained in custody at the police station. The intermediary's assessment of the suspect would have to take place in the police station.[201]

> There is no available funding to instruct intermediaries in the police station, and the police would have to authorise payment.

6.156 The legal representative should remind the police that the Notes for Guidance in PACE Code C state:

> Although juveniles ... are often capable of providing reliable evidence, they may, without knowing or wishing to do so, be particularly prone in certain circumstances to provide information that may be unreliable, misleading or self-incriminating. Special care should always be taken when questioning such a person and the appropriate adult should be involved if there is any doubt about a person's age, mental state or capacity. Because of the risk of unreliable evidence it is also important to obtain corroboration of any facts whenever possible.[202]

6.157 In interview, the appropriate adult is not expected to act simply as an observer, and the purpose of the adult's presence is: to advise the person being interviewed; observe whether the interview is being conducted properly and fairly; and to facilitate communication with the person being interviewed.[203] The appropriate adult may intervene if he or she considers it is necessary to help the child or young person understand any question asked, and to help the child or young person to answer any question.[204] (See paras 6.123–6.127 on role of appropriate adult.)

Voluntary interviews

6.158 A voluntary police interview is when a person is interviewed by the police for the purpose of helping with an investigation without being

201 'How to Obtain The Services of An Intermediary: Defendants', The Advocates Gateway.

202 PACE Code C, Note for Guidance 11C.

203 PACE Code C, para 11.17.

204 PACE Code C, Note for Guidance 11F.

arrested.[205] A volunteer is entitled to leave at any time, unless the volunteer is told that he or she is being arrested – however, the police often invite people in for voluntary interviews and then arrest them if they fail to attend or leave before the interview is finished. The police must always consider whether an arrest is necessary in order to carry out an interview.[206]

6.159 The police may ask a person if they can have a conversation with him or her in order to help them with an investigation. Sometimes the police ask parents if they would be happy for their child to 'have a chat' about a particular matter. Alternatively, they may invite the child in to the police station for a 'voluntary interview'.

6.160 Despite the terminology being used by the police, these 'chats' and 'voluntary interviews' are the same as any other type of police interview and can result in the same outcomes. The rights, entitlements and safeguards that apply to the conduct and recording of interviews with suspects are not diminished simply because the interview is arranged on a voluntary basis. The duty of the interviewer is the same as the custody officer with regard to detained suspects.[207]

6.161 In 2018 the Home Office, Law Society and Legal Aid Agency issued guidance called *Remember your Rights – Voluntary Interviews*[208] which states:

- You are not under arrest and you do not have to consent to being interviewed.
- Before the police interviewer asks you to consent, you must be told about your rights, entitlements and safeguards that that will apply to the interview.
- You are free to leave at any time unless you are arrested, or if the interviewer needs consent from you or someone else to stay, the interviewer must leave if you or the other person withdraw your consent.[209]

6.162 It is likely that this guidance has been issued due to an increase in the use of voluntary interviews by the police and people not always being aware that they are suspects and so not exercising their right to

205 PACE s29.

206 PACE Code G, Note for Guidance 2F.

207 PACE Code C, para 3.21(b).

208 *Remember your Rights – Voluntary Interview (2018)* Home Office, Legal Aid Agency, Law Society.

209 *Remember your Rights – Voluntary Interview (2018)* Home Office, Legal Aid Agency, Law Society.

free legal representation as they would if interviewed after arrest and caution. The guidance aims to ensure people access their right to free legal advice even when the interview is voluntary.

6.163 If the police suspect the child has committed an offence, they must caution the child.[210] They will do this at the beginning of the interview, and this means that the interview can be used as evidence against the child at a later date.

6.164 Those attending for voluntary interviews are entitled to receive free legal advice and must be advised of this right by the interviewer in advance of the interview taking place.[211] A child attending a voluntary police interview will still need to have an appropriate adult even though the interview is voluntary[212] – the appropriate adult should still request legal advice for the child as in a non-voluntary interview (see para 6.131 on appropriate adults requesting legal advice).

Identification procedures

Overview

6.165 PACE Code D provides guidance on identification procedures by the police.

6.166 When a suspect is known to a witness, an identification procedure should not take place.[213] Where the identity of a suspect is not known, the police can ask an eye-witness to see if he or she can identify the suspect in the street or in photographs.[214]

6.167 An identification procedure must be held where:

- an eye-witness has identified a suspect or purported to have identified them; or
- there is an eye-witness available who expresses an ability to identify the suspect; or
- there is a reasonable chance of an eye-witness being able to identify the suspect;

and:

210 PACE Code C, para 10.1.
211 PACE Code C, para 3.21A(b)(i).
212 PACE Code C, para 3.21A(c)(i).
213 PACE Code C, para 3.12(c)(ii)
214 PACE Code D, paras 3.2 and 3.3.

- the witness has not been given an opportunity to identify the suspect already;

and:

- the suspect disputes being the person the eye-witness claims to have seen on a previous occasion;

unless:

- holding the procedure is not practicable or it would serve no useful purpose.[215]

6.168 The types of identification procedure available are:

- video identification;
- identification parade;
- group identification;
- confrontation.

6.169 The suspect shall initially be invited to take part in a video identification unless:

- a video identification is not practicable; or
- an identification parade is both practicable and more suitable than a video identification; or
- the officer in charge of the investigation considers a group identification more suitable than a video identification or an identification parade, and the identification officer considers it practicable to arrange.[216]

6.170 Before any identification procedure takes place, the suspect or the suspect's solicitor shall be provided with details of the first description of the suspect by any witnesses who are attending the identification parade.[217]

Identification procedures

Video identification

6.171 A video of the suspect will be taken by the police and shown together with videos of eight other people who resemble the suspect in age, general appearance and position in life.[218] The witness will be invited to view the compilation videos and make an identification. The

215 PACE Code D, para 3.12.

216 PACE Code D, para 3.14.

217 PACE Code D, Annex A para 8, Annex B para 3, Annex C para 11 and Annex D para 2.

218 PACE Code D, Annex A, para 2.

appropriate adult must be present when the police video a child suspect and choose the other videos to add to the compilation.[219] The suspect or the suspect's solicitor, friend or appropriate adult must be given a reasonable opportunity to see the complete set of images before it is shown to any eye-witness. If the suspect has a reasonable objection to the set of images or any of the participants, the suspect shall be asked to state the reasons for the objection. Steps shall, if practicable, be taken to remove the grounds for objection.[220]

6.172 The identification procedure must be video recorded with sound.[221]

Identification parade

6.173 An identification parade must consist of at least eight people (in addition to the suspect) who, so far as possible, resemble the suspect in age, height, general appearance and position in life.[222] The parade must take place in the presence of the appropriate adult.[223]

6.174 A video recording must normally be taken of the identification parade. If that is impracticable, a colour photograph must be taken.[224]

Group identification

6.175 Group identification is where a witness is asked to identify a suspect from a group. The place where the group identification is held should be one where other people are either passing by or waiting around informally, in groups such that the suspect is able to join them and be capable of being seen by the witness at the same time as others in the group.[225] Group identifications may take place either with the suspect's consent and co-operation, or covertly without the suspect's consent.[226] During the procedure witnesses will need to be able to see, from time to time, a number of others whose appearance is broadly similar to that of the suspect.[227] This presents a particular challenge for officers arranging a group identification for a child suspect, as they will need

219 PACE Code D, para 2.15.
220 PACE Code D, Annex A, para 7.
221 PACE Code D, Annex A, para 9.
222 PACE Code D, Annex B, para 9.
223 PACE Code D, para 2.15.
224 PACE Code D, Annex B, para 23.
225 PACE Code D, Annex C, para 4.
226 PACE Code D, Annex C, para 2.
227 PACE Code D, Annex C, para 6.

to ensure there are other children in the group. The procedure must take place in the presence of the appropriate adult.[228]

Confrontation

6.176 A confrontation is an identification procedure which involves the suspect being directly confronted by the eye witness. The procedure can take place without the suspect's consent, but force may not be used to make the suspect's face visible to the eye-witness.[229] The procedure must take place in the presence of the appropriate adult.[230]

Identification procedures and consent

6.177 Where consent is required for an identification procedure to take place, the consent must be given by both the child and the parent or guardian. If the child is under 14 years old, the police do not need the child's consent, just the consent of the parent or guardian.[231] If the consent is refused, the identification officer may still carry out a video identification procedure but using still images, eg the suspect's custody photograph.[232]

6.178 If the suspect is known to the police but not available, the police may make arrangements for a video identification procedure with any moving or still images that they have.[233]

6.179 Given the unreliability of identification evidence, the legal representative must be diligent in ensuring that the identification procedure complies with the Codes. The legal representative should keep notes of any concerns about the identification process in case the matter proceeds to court and arguments are made for exclusion of this evidence.

Ongoing investigation

6.180 If the police do not have sufficient evidence to charge a child with a criminal offence but they believe that they may have sufficient evidence in the future, then they can release a suspect unconditionally

228 PACE Code D, para 2.15.
229 PACE Code D, Annex D, para 3.
230 PACE Code D, para 2.15.
231 PACE Code D para 2.12.
232 PACE Code D, para 3.21.
233 PACE Code D, para 3.21.

(released under investigation (RUI)) or on police bail. This is usually for the collection of further evidence, including witness statements or identification procedures.

Release under investigation (RUI)

6.181 Since 3 April 2017, many suspects who are released from the police station without charge but not 'no further action'-ed are 'released under investigation' (RUI). This followed the introduction of strict limitations on the amount of time someone can be kept on police bail (see para 6.182–6.184 below). A person 'released under investigation' is informed that the police will continue with their investigation and that they will be informed of the outcome in due course.

Release on police bail

6.182 The police are entitled to grant bail to re-attend a police station at a later date under PACE s37(3)(c). The police have powers to impose conditions on the bail that the person is released under PACE s37(1A).

6.183 The Police and Criminal Justice Act 2017 introduced a limitation on the amount of time a person can be kept on police bail. Bail is limited to 28 days,[234] although it can be extended to three months if it is a serious case and is authorised by an officer who is a superintendent or above.[235]

6.184 When a person is released from police bail, he or she is given a notice specifying the date and time on which the person must surrender back to the police station, which may be a different police station. The police can change the date and time that is set out on the notice, so it is worthwhile checking before re-attending the police station that the date and time still applies. When attending the police station for a second time on the same charge, the amount of time spent detained is calculated cumulatively, over the two periods of detention. It is important that the lawyer keep track of the time that a child was detained on the earlier occasion to ensure that any subsequent detention does not go over the time limits (see para 6.64–6.67 on authorising police detention).

234 PACE s30B(8) (as amended by Police and Crime Act 2017).
235 PACE s47ZD (as amended by Police and Crime Act 2017).

Decision to divert, take no further action or charge

6.185 A police investigation will conclude in one of the following ways:

- no further action (NFA): The police will take no further action against a suspect where there is not enough evidence to charge them with an offence or where there is sufficient evidence but it is not in the public interest to prosecute them. This may include informal diversions such as youth restorative disposals, triage and community resolution (see paras 7.43–7.56).
- a formal diversion.
- Charge (see paras 7.106–107 on the police decision to prosecute; see paras 7.108–7.131 on the CPS decision to prosecute).

6.186 Formal diversions are:

- youth caution (see paras 7.57–7.75);
- youth conditional caution (see paras 7.76–7.105).

Children as suspect and victim

6.187 There are several situations in which a child can be both a suspect and a victim. Common examples include victims of child criminal exploitation, modern slavery, child sexual exploitation and trafficking, who are arrested for linked offences. Particularly prevalent over the last couple of years are children involved in county lines gangs who are arrested for possession with intent to supply drugs (see para 3.100–3.103 and paras 13.14–13.53 for defences for trafficked children).

6.188 It is vital that these issues are identified at the earliest possible opportunity (which is often at the police station) so that the correct referrals can be made and the appropriate safeguarding measures put in place. In practice, this requires a first responder (such as a local authority, youth offending team or the police) to refer the child to the National Referral Mechanism. Usually, if this referral results in a conclusive grounds decision (that it is more likely than not that they are a victim of human trafficking or modern slavery), the police will not charge the child or, if already taken to court, the prosecution will be discontinued. See paras 3.100–3.103 on children and trafficking and paras 13.14–13.53 for defences for trafficked children).

6.189 The Youth Justice Legal Centre have published a guide for lawyers representing children who have been trafficked and caught up in county lines criminality.[236]

Post-charge police bail

6.190 If a person is charged with a criminal offence at the police station, the person must either be released from the police station with or without bail pending a court appearance or detained by the police until they can be produced before a court. There are very few circumstances in which the police can detain children and the legal representative should be familiar with section 38 of PACE when making representations to the custody sergeant with regards to the detention or release of children from the police station following charge.

6.191 The decision whether to grant a child bail is based upon the same criteria that are applicable for adults, with an additional power to detain if it is the officer's belief 'that he ought to be detained in his own interests'[237] (see para 6.205). The custody officer can detain a person after charge where:

1) the person's name and address cannot be ascertained (PACE s38(1)(a)(i));
2) the custody officer has reasonable grounds for believing that the person arrested will fail to appear before the court (this will depend upon the seriousness of the offence, the character and antecedents of the person, community ties, record in respect of previous bail, the strength of the evidence and any other relevant consideration) (PACE s38(1)(a)(ii));
3) the person has been arrested for an imprisonable offence and the custody officer has reasonable grounds that the person needs to be detained to prevent the person from committing a further offence (PACE s38(1)(a)(iii));
4) the custody officer needs to detain someone to take a sample (PACE s63B);
5) the detained person is arrested for a non-imprisonable offence and the custody sergeant has reasonable grounds to believe that detention will prevent the detained person from causing physical

236 'Child criminal exploitation, county lines gangs, child trafficking & modern slavery defences for children', Youth Justice Legal Centre/Just for Kids Law, 2018.

237 PACE s38(1)(b)(ii).

injury to another person or loss or damage to property (PACE s38(1)(a)(iv));

6) the custody officer has reasonable grounds for believing that the detention is necessary to prevent the person from interfering with the administration of justice or with the investigation of offences (PACE s38(1)(a)(v));
7) the custody officer has reasonable grounds for believing that the detention is necessary for person's own protection (PACE s38(1)(a)(vi)).

6.192 Where a child is to be detained by the police after charge, it must be done in accordance with PACE s38(6) (see paras 6.195–6.204 for s.38(6) detention after charge).

6.193 If granted bail from the police station, a child is given a date that he or she should appear before the court. This is usually the first sitting of the relevant youth court.[238] It is important to note that due to recent closures of youth courts, the sittings might be only on certain days of the week and could be at courts that are a significant distance from the police station or where the child lives.

6.194 If a child is detained, PACE s38(6) arrangement to transfer child to local authority accommodation applies (see paras 6.195–6.204).

Police and Criminal Evidence Act 1984 s38(6) – detention after charge

6.195 PACE s38(6) states that if a child is to be detained after charge, the custody officer must arrange for the child to be transferred to local authority accommodation unless it is certified that:

1) it is impracticable for them to do so;
2) in the case of an arrested juvenile who has reached the age of 12, that there is no secure accommodation available and that keeping them in other local authority accommodation would not be adequate to protect the public from serious harm by them.[239]

6.196 Code C 16.6 states that chief officers should ensure that the operation of the provisions of PACE s38(6) at the police station in their areas is 'subject to supervision and monitoring by an officer of the rank of inspector or above'.[240]

238 PACE s47(3A).
239 PACE s38(6)(a)(b).
240 PACE Code C, Note for Guidance 16.7.

6.197 Impracticable is not clearly defined in the statute. A Home Office circular states that impracticable means circumstances where a transfer would be physically impossible by, for example, floods or blizzards or an impossibility, despite repeatedly trying, of getting in contact with the local authority. The Notes for Guidance to Code C state:

> Neither a juvenile's behaviour nor the nature of the offence provides grounds for the custody officer to decide it is impracticable to arrange the juvenile's transfer to local authority care. Impracticability concerns the transport and travel requirements and the lack of secure accommodation which is provided for the purpose of restricting liberty does not make it impracticable to transfer the juvenile. The availability of secure accommodation is only a factor in relation to a juvenile aged 12 or over when other local authority accommodation would not be adequate to protect the public from serious harm from them. *The obligation to transfer a juvenile to local authority accommodation applies as much to a juvenile charged during the daytime as to a juvenile to be held overnight.*[241] (Emphasis added)

6.198 'Secure accommodation' has a technical meaning, and the local authority can only keep a child or young person in approved secure accommodation.[242]

6.199 Therefore it appears that there are very limited circumstances in which a child should be detained at the police station after charge. However, in reality few children are transferred to local authority accommodation. For example, evidence from the London Borough of Islington shows that in 2015 no children charged with a criminal offence and detained were transferred to local authority accommodation. In 2011, over 40,000 children were detained at the police station overnight and were not moved to local authority accommodation.[243]

6.200 This issue has become a concern for government. In January 2015 a joint letter to all local authorities was sent by the then Home Secretary, Theresa May and the then Minister for Education, Nicky Morgan. The letter stated:

> When a local authority receives a request from the police to accommodate a child or young person they have an absolute duty, under the Children Act 1989 to do so. In particular section 21(2) (b) makes clear that 'every local authority must receive and provide accommodation

241 PACE Code C, Note for Guidance 16D.

242 PACE s38(6A).

243 Overnight detention of children in police cells Howard League for Penal Reform.

for children whom they are requested to receive under section 38(6) of the Police and Criminal Evidence Act 1984. Evidence suggests that the legal requirements are not being followed.[244]

6.201 Despite this letter to local authorities, it still appears that children are being detained at the police station rather than being transferred to local authority accommodation.[245] The government has therefore published a concordat entitled Children in Custody Guidance for police forces and local authorities in England on their responsibilities towards children in custody.[246] The concordat acknowledges that the law in PACE already recognises that police cells are not a suitable place for children.[247] Yet despite this failings have been identified by Her Majesty's Inspectorate of the Constabulary (2015) amongst others and that it is 'clear that in many cases, the law is not being followed and that children are not receiving the support to which the law entitles them'. In this concordat we recognise that we must work together to ensure that legal duties are met'.[248] The concordat has a list of national partners, both statutory and independent, who have signed the concordat and committed to working together to ensure that transfers always happen as they should. The national partners include the College of Policing and the Association of Directors of Children Services. Legal representatives of children and young people who may be detained at the police station should draw to the attention of the custody officer or the local authority team member the concordat.

6.202 If a child is detained at the police station, or moved to the local authority accommodation, he or she must be produced at court as soon as is practicable and no later than the day following the day that the person has been charged excluding Sundays or bank holidays.

6.203 A checking mechanism available to legal representatives of children and young people at the police station who have been detained at the police station is a certificate of detention. PACE s38(7) states that where a custody officer certifies that a child be detained at the police station, rather than being transferred to local authority accommodation:

244 www.yjlc.uk/wp-content/uploads/2014/05/Joint_letter_from_the_Home_Secretary__the_Education_Secretary.pdf.

245 http://thejusticegap.com/2016/07/nochildincells-campaign-islington-review-police-practice-holding-kids-cells/.

246 Home Office Concordat on Children in Custody (2017).

247 Home Office Concordat on Children in Custody (2017) p5.

248 Home Office Concordat on Children in Custody (2017) p5.

> A certificate made under subsection (6) above in respect of an arrested juvenile shall be produced to the court before which he is first brought thereafter.

This certificate of detention should enable scrutiny by the court of any failure to comply with the law in regards to transfer of children to local authority accommodation. A defence lawyer should ask for a certificate of detention from the police when at court a child is produced from the police station rather than from local authority accommodation. Similarly, magistrates with oversight of a case where a child is produced from the police station should challenge the detention and if necessary ask both the police or the local authority to set out the reason that it was 'impracticable' to transfer the child and robustly challenge the decision.

6.204 The decision whether to grant bail or detain a child is solely that of the custody sergeant or officer, however they can be thwarted in having a child moved into the care of the local authority if the local authority state that they cannot provide either suitable accommodation (if there is the requirement of a secure component) or any accommodation when there is not a secure requirement. It is important that a legal representative for a child makes all of the relevant representations to the custody sergeant with regards to the release of the child from the police station and if necessary to the local authority. Where the local authority refuse to take responsibility for accommodating a child who has been charged with a criminal offence the legal representative for the child should make a further application for bail to be granted in preference to a child rather than them being detained further at the police station.

Power to detain children in police custody

6.205 There is an additional criterion by which children can be detained at the police station, PACE s38(1)(b)(ii) states that a custody officer or sergeant may detain a juvenile where he or she has reasonable grounds for believing that they ought to be detained for their 'own interests'. 'Own interests' are not defined by PACE.

CHAPTER 7

Diversion, out of court disposals and alternatives to prosecution

continued

Key points

- It is widely recognised that contact with the criminal justice system tends to increase the likelihood of children offending.
- Diversion and out-of-court disposal (OOCD) are alternatives to prosecution.
- Children should be diverted from the formal criminal justice system wherever possible.
- Out of court disposals can require an admission of an offence.
- Diversion and OOCDs for children include informal diversion (such as triage and community resolution) to formal OOCDs – youth cautions and youth conditional cautions.
- There is no restriction on the number of informal or formal OOCDs a child can receive.
- Police officers can think creatively about how best to respond to offending by children. There are a number of options, however, the guidance can be unclear and conflicting.
- Decisions as to the correct disposal or decision to prosecute can be challenged by way of judicial review.

Introduction

Background

7.1 'Out-of-court disposal' (OOCD) is an umbrella term for outcomes given to children as alternatives to being charged with a criminal offence. The Legal Aid, Sentencing and Punishment of Offenders Act (LASPO) 2012[1] introduced a new framework for OOCDs for children enabling a far more individualised and proportionate decision-making approach:

> [T]he benefits of the new out-of-court framework are:
> 1. there are no restrictions on which disposal can be considered;
> 2. it encourages joint decision making between the police and youth offending teams (YOTs) to promote positive outcomes.[2]

1 LASPO 2012 ss132–138.

2 Youth out-of-court disposals: guide for police and YOTs, MOJ and YJB, April 2013, para 1.8.

7.2 OOCDs can also be described as pre-court disposals or diversion, because the process 'diverts' a child away from the formal youth justice system (see para 7.8 on diversion). Evidence suggests that contact with the justice system can have a tainting effect on children[3] – in other words, it makes them more, rather than less, likely to offend:

> This means that rather than a criminal justice response nipping their behaviour in the bud, children who are formally dealt with seem to get pulled further into the system.[4]

7.3 The National Police Chiefs' Council's (NPCC) '*National strategy for the policing of children & young people*' (2016) recognises that it is important that children are not criminalised for behaviour which can be dealt with more appropriately by other means:

> Policing must be sophisticated enough to look beyond the blanket negative labelling of young people to identify the small numbers who are serious and persistent offenders. Often for these offenders enforcement may be the most effective tool, but for many others it can be a blunt instrument. Evidence shows that highly punitive sanctions have little impact on recidivism, so enforcement should be considered appropriately and used only where necessary to prevent others from becoming victims. Getting it wrong, especially when it results in the unnecessary criminalisation of C&YP [children and young people], can mean heavy costs to the individual for life and the wider society.[5]

7.4 It is therefore widely acknowledged that approaches that divert children away from the formal criminal justice system are more likely to prevent them offending.[6] The police have the following disposals available for children:

- No further action informal diversion (see paras 7.43–7.55), including:
  - triage (see para 7.47–7.51); and
  - community resolution (see para 7.52–7.55);

3 National Protocol on Reducing Criminalisation of Looked After Children November 2018, para 1.5.

4 'Review of the youth justice system in England and Wales' by Charlie Taylor, December 2016.

5 The National Police Chiefs' Council's (NPCC) 'National strategy for the policing of children & young people' (2016) para 1.3.

6 See for example, National Protocol on Reducing Criminalisation of Looked After Children November 2018 para 1.5 and Reoffending Statistics produced quarterly by the Ministry of Justice and National Statistics, demonstrate lower reoffending rates for children diverted at the police station than receiving a custodial sentence.

- youth caution (see para 7.57–7.75);
- youth conditional caution (see para 7.76–7.105).

7.5 Youth cautions and youth conditional cautions are considered *formal* OOCDs. Where children undertake youth offending team (YOT) or external agency intervention, but the police take no further action, these are considered *informal* OOCDs. See paras 7.43–7.45.

7.6 Different police forces will use differing terminology for their informal diversion. For example, the Metropolitan Police use the term 'triage'; Surrey and Leicestershire 'youth restorative intervention' (YRI); and other police forces use 'community resolution'.

7.7 Police forces and YOTs should have a joint protocol setting out locally agreed practice with regards to the OOCD system and joint decision-making.[7]

Diversion

7.8 The United Nations Convention on the Rights of the Child (UNCRC) places a duty on domestic governments to promote measures for dealing with children who commit criminal offences 'without resorting to judicial proceedings'.[8] Informal diversion is the most effective method of reducing reoffending, and therefore achieving the purpose of the youth justice system[9] because children who are diverted away from the formal youth justice system are less likely to keep offending:

> It is crucial that in all encounters with the police those below the age of 18 should be treated as children first . . . Policing supports YJB's evidence-based practice by keeping C&YP out of the criminal justice process unless necessary.[10]

Gravity Score Matrix

7.9 Offence seriousness is determined by reference to the Association of Chief Police Officers (ACPO) Gravity Matrix, which sets out the

7 Youth out-of-court disposals: guide for police and YOTs, MOJ and YJB, April 2013, para 4.6.

8 UNCRC 1991 Article 40(3)(b).

9 The principal aim of the youth justice system is to prevent offending – Crime and Disorder Act 1998 s37.

10 'National strategy for the policing of children & young people', NPCC, 2015, p8.

most prevalent offences, and provides them with a score of 1, 2, 3 or 4. The score may be raised or lowered by one level according to aggravating and mitigating factors which are set out in the ACPO Gravity Matrix. The seriousness of the offence is one factor the police take into account when considering OOCDs. Offences with a gravity score of 3 or below should always be considered for diversion. Any offences that are not shown in the matrix should be dealt with in accordance with the general principles of the document. Discretion does exist to deviate from the normal response in the matrix, but only if the circumstances justify this, and the reasons for such action would need to be fully recorded by the decision-maker.

Restorative justice

7.10 The Ministry of Justice (MOJ) and Youth Justice Board (YJB) guidance says that restorative justice enables people directly affected by an offence, including offenders, victims and the wider community, to communicate, with the help of a trained facilitator in deciding how to deal with the offence and its consequences.[11]

7.11 The MOJ and YJB guidance on youth OOCDs states:

> Wherever appropriate, restorative processes should be used alongside the delivery of out-of-court disposals or as a way to determine the appropriate disposal. For example, restorative justice disposals are an informal diversion, restorative justice interventions could be used as part of a community resolution or as a condition of a youth conditional caution.[12]

British Transport Police

7.12 Where an offence falls under the remit of the British Transport Police (BTP) they are able to use the full range of OOCDs.[13] It is BTP policy to refer all children to the local YOT for 'joint and collaborative decision making to ensure a more consistent and appropriate response'.[14]

11 'Youth out-of-court disposals: guide for police and youth offending services', MOJ and YJB, 2013, para 3.23.

12 'Youth out-of-court disposals: guide for police and youth offending services', MOJ and YJB, 2013, para 3.24.

13 Para 11.9.

14 BTP letter to YOTs and YOSs dated 27 February 2015.

Guidance to police officers, youth offending teams and the Crown Prosecution Service

7.13 There is a plethora of guidance, some statutory, for police officers, YOTs and Crown Prosecution Service (CPS) youth offender specialists to navigate. The guidance includes:

- 'Youth cautions: guidance for police and youth offending teams', Ministry of Justice (MOJ) and Youth Justice Board (YJB), 2013;
- 'Code of Practice for youth conditional cautions Crime & Disorder Act 1998 (as amended by the Criminal Justice & Immigration Act 2008 and the Legal Aid, Sentencing and Punishment of Offenders Act 2012)', MOJ, 2013;
- 'Youth out-of-court disposals: guide for police and youth offending services', Ministry of Justice, Youth Justice Board (YJB) for England and Wales and CPS, 2013;
- 'Code of practice for victims of crime', Ministry of Justice 2015.

Additional police guidance:

- 'ACPO Youth Gravity Factor Matrix', 2009;
- 'ACPO community resolution guidance: Guidelines on the use of community resolutions (CR) incorporating restorative justice (RJ)', ACPO, 2012;
- 'National strategy for the policing of children & young people', NPCC, 2015.

Additional YOT guidance:

- 'YJB case management guidance: how to use out-of-court disposals', YJB.

Additional CPS guidance:

- Code for Crown Prosecutors, 26 October 2018 (including The Full Code Test);
- CPS Legal Guidance on Youth Offenders;
- CPS Legal Guidance on Cautioning and Diversion;
- Director of Public Prosecution's (DPP) guidance on youth conditional cautions (for original pilot sites);
- Director's Guidance on Conditional Cautioning (7th Edition: April 2013);
- 'DBS list of offences that will never be filtered for a criminal record check', Disclosure and Barring Service (DBS) and Home Office, 2013.

7.14 At times the guidance is inconsistent but the decision-maker should interpret any inconsistency taking into consideration the welfare of the child and the child's best interests. (See paras 1.68–1.74.)

7.15 A number of principles can be taken from the various guidance:

- It is not usually in the public interest to criminalise children.[15]
- 'It is important that young people are not criminalised for behaviour which can be dealt with more appropriately by other means.'[16]
- In a case involving a child, '[a] prosecution is less likely to be required if ... the seriousness and the consequences of the offending can be appropriately dealt with by an out-of-court disposal which the suspect accepts and with which he or she complies'.[17]
- 'This is a factor which will always carry a special weight in the case of youths who are at a very early stage of their offending, and can be traced back to historic police practice ... of starting from a presumption of diverting youths away from the courts where possible.'[18]
- "An out-of-court disposal may take the place of a prosecution in court if it is an appropriate response to the offender and/or the seriousness and consequences of the offending.'[19] Prosecutors must follow any relevant guidance when asked to advise on or authorise a simple caution; a conditional caution; any appropriate regulatory proceedings; a punitive or civil penalty; or other disposal.'[20]
- Prosecutors 'should ensure that the appropriate evidential standard for the specific out-of-court disposal is met including, where required, a clear admission of guilt, and that the public interest would be properly served by such a disposal'.[21]

15 CPS Legal Guidance on Youth Offender, Public Interest and Sensitive Issues: The Decision to Prosecute.

16 'National strategy for the policing of children & young people', NPCC, 2015, p11.

17 CPS Legal Guidance on Youth Offender, Public Interest and Sensitive Issues: The Decision to Prosecute.

18 CPS Legal Guidance on Youth Offender, Public Interest and Sensitive Issues: The Decision to Prosecute.

19 Code for Crown Prosecutors 2018 para 7.1.

20 Code for Crown Prosecutors 2018 para 7.2.

21 Code for Crown Prosecutors 2018 para 7.2.

- The police will take into account the offending history and the seriousness of the offence when deciding whether to issue a youth caution.

7.16 The Youth Out of Court Disposal Guide published by the MOJ/YJB says the following factors should be taken into consideration when deciding the most appropriate disposal to give a child:

- the seriousness and circumstances of the offence (gravity factors). Based on the ACPO Youth Gravity Factor Matrix, is the crime serious enough to go to court, or can this be dealt with outside of court?
- any views expressed by the victim. The views of the victim will be important, but cannot be conclusive. The decision as to whether to give an out-of-court disposal lies with the decision-maker
- the young person's offending history. Has the young person offended before? If so, what disposals have they received and for what offences?
- the frequency of the young person's offending. How often have they offended and over what time frame? Has the frequency increased recently? Has there been a significant period of non-offending since the last disposal?
- the willingness of the offender to comply with possible interventions the likely outcome if the offender was prosecuted
- the young person's compliance history. In cases where there has been a previous disposal, decision-makers should check:
  whether any intervention was offered
  whether the intervention was voluntary or compulsory
  whether the intervention was complied with.[22]

Home Office outcome codes and outcome 21

Outcome codes

7.17 The Home Office Counting Rules (HOCR) require each crime to be allocated an outcome from a menu of predefined codes on the Police National Database (PND).[23] For more information about HOCR, the Police National Computer (PNC) and the PND, see para 25.5–25.17 on what information is retained by the police.

22 'Youth out-of-court disposals: guide for police and youth offending services', MOJ and YJB, 2013, para 4.30.

23 Briefing Note: Police action in response to youth produced sexual imagery ('sexting') Version 1.0 published in November 2016, *College of Policing* para 19.

7.18 The Home Office introduced the outcomes framework in April 2013. Since then, the framework has developed to cover a broader range of outcome types for police forces to use. There are currently 21 outcome codes.[24]

Outcome 21

Overview

7.19 In 2016 a new outcome code was designated to address situations where the police are informed of a criminal offence but it is not in the public interest to investigate further:

> Outcome 21: Further investigation resulting from the crime report that could provide evidence sufficient to support formal action being taken against the suspect is not in the public interest – police decision.[25]

7.20 Outcome 21 was created primarily to deal with criminalising 'sexting' by children, also described as 'youth produced sexual imagery' and was intended to indicate to the disclosure officer that the crime record should usually not be disclosed (see chapter 25 on criminal records). Outcome 21 is recommended by the College of Policing where a child has sent a naked photo to another child,[26] 'where the making and sharing is considered non-abusive and there is *no evidence* of exploitation, grooming, profit motive, malicious intent (eg extensive or inappropriate sharing (eg uploading onto a pornographic website) or it being persistent behaviour'.[27]

7.21 Outcome 21 is not restricted to 'sexting' or 'youth-produced sexual imagery' offences – the police may use outcome 21 to record an offence where they believe a crime may have occurred but have decided not to pursue the matter further as it is considered in the public interest not to do so.

24 Home Office Crime outcomes in England and Wales: year ending March 2018, published in July 2018. See table A1.1: Detection types prior to April 2013 and the outcomes frameworks in place thereafter.

25 Home Office Crime outcomes in England and Wales: year ending March 2018, published in July 2018. See table A1.1: Detection types prior to April 2013 and the outcomes frameworks in place thereafter.

26 Briefing Note: Police action in response to youth produced sexual imagery ('sexting') Version 1.0 published in November 2016, College of Policing.

27 Briefing Note: Police action in response to youth produced sexual imagery ('sexting') Version 1.0 published in November 2016, College of Policing, para 22.

7.22 All decisions with regards to outcome 21 must be clearly communicated with all appropriate parties involved in the case.[28] Where an investigation has already begun, for example where the child has already been interviewed, then the police will send a letter informing the child that no further action will be taken. In cases where an allegation is made but the police have decided no investigation is needed, a letter should still sent.

Criminal record

7.23 Outcome 21 was created with the aim of enabling the police to record behaviour, such as 'sexting', without the allegation being disclosed on a DBS check. Enabling police officers to respond to an allegation in a proportionate way, which focuses on safeguarding children and avoids criminalising children when appropriate.[29]

7.24 Outcome 21 is not a formal diversion so will not automatically be disclosed on a basic or standard criminal record check. However, where a person applies for a position that requires an enhanced DBS check (an enhanced criminal record check), there can be no certainty as to whether or not an outcome 21 will be disclosed on an enhanced criminal record check. The decision whether to disclose 'non-conviction data' will depend on whether the chief officer of police considers the information to be both current and relevant to the application (see paras 25.57–25.61 on police intelligence and enhanced checks). The College of Policing guidance states:

> In the event that a future 'Enhanced Disclosure and Barring Service' (DBS) check is required it is unlikely that this record will be disclosed unless you/your child are investigated or have further action taken against you/them in the future which could suggest a relevant pattern of behaviour.[30]

7.25 However, the NPCC guidance also makes it clear there is no guarantee that an identity will be protected because it is recorded as outcome 21:

> The discretion on whether to disclose non-conviction information rests with each chief constable managing the process. Therefore, no

28 Briefing Note: Police action in response to youth produced sexual imagery ('sexting') Version 1.0 published in November 2016, College of Policing, para 22.

29 Sexting in schools and colleges: responding to incidents and safeguarding young people, UK Council for Child Internet Safety.

30 Briefing Note: Police action in response to youth produced sexual imagery ('sexting') Version 1.0 published in November 2016, College of Policing, para 22.

guarantee can or should be provided that this information would not be released.[31]

Availability of out-of-court disposals

7.26 The officer in the case should always think creatively about how to address offending by children. In all cases, officers should give consideration to whether the offence can appropriately be dealt with by an OOCD:

- Where admissions are made during the police investigation stage:
  Offences with a gravity score of 3 or below, or with a higher gravity score and mitigating factors, should always be considered for diversion.[32]
- Where the CPS are asked to make a decision whether to prosecute a case:
  An offence that attracts a gravity score of 2 or 3 will usually result in a youth being given a youth caution. If the offending behaviour cannot be satisfactorily addressed by a youth caution, the police will consider a youth conditional caution.[33]

7.27 It is worth noting that out-of-court disposals can still be given even after charge if it is the most appropriate outcome.

- The CPS should ensure those cases where an OOCD – in particular a youth caution or youth conditional caution – can be justified, consideration is given to that disposal even after the case has reached court:

  Where a case has proceeded to court, but the prosecutor decides that a youth caution or youth conditional caution can be justified, the matter should be adjourned for consideration of that disposal.[34]

Pre-requisites for out of court disposals

7.28 There are three pre-requisites for OOCDs:

> Prosecutors . . . should ensure that the appropriate evidential standard for the specific out-of-court disposal is met including, where

31 Briefing Note: Police action in response to youth produced sexual imagery ('sexting') Version 1.0 published in November 2016, College of Policing, para 22.

32 'Use out-of-court disposals: section 1 case management guidance', YJB, 15 October 2014, para 2.3.

33 CPS Legal Guidance on Youth Offender, Guidance: Youth Cautions.

34 CPS Legal Guidance on Youth Offender, Guidance: Youth Cautions.

required, a clear admission of guilt, and that the public interest would be properly served by such a disposal.[35]

Sufficient evidence

7.29 There must be sufficient, admissible evidence to charge the child with an offence before an OOCD should be considered.[36]

Admission of an offence

7.30 For all OOCDs, the child must make an admission. However, there is no requirement that an admission is made by the child before the decision maker determines whether an OOCD, including a youth conditional caution, is appropriate.[37] An admission should never be made simply to receive a youth conditional caution.[38] Admissions will usually need to be made during police interview, although there may be later opportunities to make admissions (see para 7.33–7.35 on admissions after the police interview).

7.31 The child must make an admission that he or she has committed the offence(s) in order for a child to receive:

- informal diversion (also called youth restorative disposal, triage, bureau and youth restorative intervention);[39]
- community resolution;[40]
- youth caution;[41]
- youth conditional caution.[42]

35 Code for Crown Prosecutors: out of court disposals, para 7.2.

36 CDA 1998 s66B.

37 See for example, Code of Practice for Youth Conditional Cautions: Crime & Disorder Act 1998 (as amended by the CJIA 2008 and LASPO 2012) March 2013, para 14.2.

38 Code of Practice for Youth Conditional Cautions: Crime & Disorder Act 1998 (as amended by the CJIA 2008 and LASPO 2012) March 2013, para 16.1

39 'Youth Restorative Disposal, administered by trained practitioners, as well as less formal community- based resolutions where the offender has made an admission' – taken from *Police recorded crime and outcomes: open data tables user guide* para restorative justice (RJ).

40 'Youth out-of-court disposals: guide for police and YOTs', MOJ and YJB, April 2013, paras 3.7–3.9.

41 CDA 1998 ss66ZA and 66ZB.

42 CDA 1998 s66A.

Admissions

7.32 Where an admission is needed to allow the police or CPS to consider an OOCD, the guidance is not consistent as to the extent of the admission needed. It appears that, provided the child has admitted the offence, this will be sufficient:

- 'A constable may give a child or young person ('Y') a caution under this section (a 'youth caution') if . . . Y *admits* to the constable that Y committed the offence'[43] (Crime and Disorder Act 1998 s66ZA).
- 'A Youth Caution may be given by the police for any offence where the child or young person makes a *full admission*'[44] ('Out of court disposals case management guidance').
- 'Prosecutors . . . should ensure that the appropriate evidential standard for the specific out-of-court disposal is met including, where required, a *clear admission* of guilt'[45] (Code for Crown Prosecutors).
- 'Prosecutors are reminded that an *admission of guilt* to the police is essential before a youth caution can be given'[46] ('CPS legal guidance on young offenders')

Admissions after the police interview (no comment interviews)

7.33 For children who do not make admissions in their police interview and are charged with an offence(s), the prosecutor at court may decide to adjourn the matter for consideration of an OOCD:

> Where a case has proceeded to court, but the prosecutor decides that a youth caution or youth conditional caution can be justified, the matter should be adjourned for consideration of that disposal. Prosecutors are reminded that an admission of guilt to the police is essential before a youth caution can be given. Once a young person has been correctly charged it is likely to be only in exceptional circumstances that a youth caution or youth conditional caution will be given.[47]

43 CDA 1998 s66ZA(1) and (1)(b).

44 Use out-of-court disposals: section 1 case management, YJB, October 2014, para 2.6.

45 Code for Crown Prosecutors, para 7.2.

46 CPS Legal guidance on young offenders: youth cautions.

47 CPS Legal guidance on young offenders: youth cautions.

and:

> There are occasions when a young person has been charged, but a prosecutor decides that the case should be adjourned for consideration of an out-of-court disposal. An admission of guilt is essential before a Youth Caution or Youth Conditional Caution can be given and it will only be in *exceptional circumstances* that a young person who has been correctly charged will receive such a disposal. The principles in this guide should be applied in such cases. Where an out-of-court disposal cannot be given, an explanation should be given to the CPS, who will decide whether the prosecution should proceed at the adjourned hearing date.[48]

7.34 In practical terms, if an admission wasn't made to the police but a child indicates that he or she wishes to admit an offence, an admission can be drawn up at court and handed to the YOT or the CPS to enable an OOCD to be considered.

7.35 The guidance set out above suggests that it is 'likely to be only in exceptional circumstances' that an OOCD will be considered at court where no admissions were made in police interview and the child has been 'correctly charged'.. In the authors' experience, this 'exceptional circumstances' test is able to accommodate a wide range of reasons for a child's failing to admit to the police – such as, inappropriate appropriate adult during police interview; presence of parent during police interview preventing child from making admissions; and no legal advice or poor legal advice prior to police interview or lack of adequate disclosure.

Not in the public interest

7.36 In order for the police or CPS to offer an OOCD, they must be satisfied 'that the public interest would be properly served by such a disposal'.[49] In cases where there is evidence to charge and the child suspect has made admissions, the decision to offer an OOCD will therefore be determined by whether it is not in the public interest to prosecute.

Disproportionality

7.37 The Lammy Review highlighted a disproportionately high number of suspects from black, Asian and minority ethnic (BAME) backgrounds

48 Youth out-of-court-disposals: guide for police and youth offending services, MOJ and YJB, 2013, para 3.22.

49 Code for Crown Prosecutors, CPS, 26 October 2018, para 7.2.

who give 'no comment' interviews.[50] The consequence is that BAME suspects are proportionately less likely to receive OOCDs. Both defence lawyers and prosecutors (as well as YOTs) should be alert to any cases where a BAME child gave a no comment interview and then indicates that he or she will admit at court. Arguably, with the exception of the most serious offences, these cases can be adjourned for consideration of an OOCD where the child is indicating at court a willingness to make an admission.

Deferred decision-making

7.38 In cases where children have not made admissions in police interview, the police may consider deferring making the decision to charge. This may involve offering voluntary attendance at the local YOT or a locally run intervention; Following a period of deferment and satisfactory engagement by the child, the decision may be to take 'no further action' (NFA).

Out of court disposals

Penalty notices for children and cannabis/khat warnings

7.39 A penalty notice for disorder or a cannabis/khat warning *cannot* be issued to under 18 year olds[51] – this power was removed when the approach to OOCDs was completely overhauled by LASPO 2012.

Fixed penalty notices from councils

7.40 Although there is no longer a power to issue fixed penalty notices for disorder to under 18 year olds (see para 7.34 above), councils (such as parish councils, district councils and London boroughs) and other authorities have the power to issue fixed penalty notices to anyone aged ten and over for a range of environmental offences, such as fly-tipping, graffiti and littering.[52]

50 'The Lammy Review: An independent review into the treatment of, and outcomes for, black, Asian and minority ethnic individuals in the criminal justice system', 2017, p6. See also para 3.96–3.98 on the Lammy Review in the importance of background.

51 LASPO 2012 s132.

52 Environmental Protection Act 1990 s88.

7.41 The council's enforcement strategy will include specific guidance on how to deal with children – for example, by suggesting that enforcement officers bring the situation to the attention of the parents before issuing a notice. Additional safeguards apply when dealing with children.[53] However, since financial penalties cannot be enforced against children, councils may well consider engaging with parents and YOTs to address issues around environmental crime committed by children as a more suitable and effective approach.

7.42 Fixed penalty notices can also be used for a range of road traffic offences, such as speeding. The procedure for issuing penalty notices for such offences is the same as in relation to adult offenders. For an explanation on when a FPN can be disclosed see paras 25.57–25.61.

Informal diversion (no further action)

7.43 Where a child admits an offence to the police, informal diversion enables the police to refer a child for intervention and following successful engagement by the child, the police disposal of the case is recorded as taking 'no further action' (NFA) as no further formal police action is appropriate or required. This minimises the criminalisation of children because informal diversions are not automatically disclosable on CRCs (see paras 25.57–25.61 on police intelligence/enhanced certificates.

7.44 The informal diversion options for children varies considerably depending on the police authority. Usually, more serious offences are excluded from informal diversion unless there are mitigating factors. Across England and Wales, there is a wide range of informal diversionary schemes for children – for example:

- 'youth restorative disposals' – Derby;
- 'triage' – Metropolitan Police;
- 'bureau' and 'youth restorative disposal' – Wales;
- 'youth restorative intervention' (YRI) – Surrey and Gloucestershire;
- 'community resolution' (CR) – Leeds

7.45 A number of areas are piloting the use of 'youth restorative disposals'.[54] Triage and YRIs are usually recorded as no further action

53 www.gov.uk/guidance/enforcement-officers-issuing-fixed-penalty-notices#children.

54 Avon & Somerset, Cumbria, Greater Manchester Police, Lancashire, Norfolk, North Wales and Nottinghamshire.

(NFA) – not in the public interest: outcome code 10. Some areas, such as Leeds, describe informal OOCD as 'community resolution' and are recorded as outcome code 8.

Local youth diversion panels

7.46 Some areas have a multi-disciplinary panel including representative of the police, YOT, CPS who review cases where children have admitted committing offences and decide whether a youth restorative disposal or other early intervention would be appropriate. Other agencies, such as Liaison and Diversion, are able to identify mental health, learning and other communication difficulties, substance misuse or other vulnerabilities affecting well-being.[55]

Triage

7.47 The term 'triage' describes a process by which children can be dealt with through informal measures and not through a formal diversion. Triage decisions are recorded by police as 'no further action' – outcome code 10.[56]

7.48 A key objective of triage is keeping children out of the formal youth justice system:

> The triage process can apply to first offences, and also to low gravity offending amongst children who have already received another formal disposal, if the assessment indicates that diversion is the most suitable outcome. If a child has been through the triage process before and re-offends, a formal out-of-court disposal or charge will usually apply.[57]

7.49 The model of the triage scheme is a key worker, usually from the YOT, working in partnership with police officers from the custody suite identify and engage children who have been arrested. In all triage assessments, individual circumstances should be assessed, and factors such as immediate admission of guilt, remorse and willingness to engage in preventative support should influence a decision to divert. Where an offence is eligible for consideration for triage, the decision must be taken jointly between the keyworker and the police.

7.50 There are circumstances when a triage diversion may be offered as a repeat option – these are:

55 See 'Liaison and diversion YOT information guide', YJB, July 2016.

56 See 'Liaison and diversion YOT information guide', YJB, July 2016.

57 Use of out-of-court disposals: section 1 case management guidance, para 2.3.

- if two low-gravity offences have been committed in a short timeframe, and diversionary support to the child has not yet been offered;
- if the second offence is a considerable time (over six months) after the initial offence;
- if the second offence, though also low-gravity, is of a different type than the first.[58]

7.51 How triage fits into the OOCD framework is to be determined locally and there is not a requirement to have a triage scheme.

Community resolution

7.52 CR[59] is the nationally recognised umbrella term for the resolution of a minor offence or anti-social behaviour incident through informal agreement between the parties involved, as opposed to through the traditional criminal justice process. CR is recorded as outcome 8: community resolution: a community resolution (with or without formal restorative justice) on the police recorded crime and outcomes.[60]

7.53 CR enables the police to deal with low-level crime. CR is primarily aimed at first-time offenders where there has been an admission of guilt, and where the victim's views have been taken into account.[61]

> The idea is based on the principle of devolving decision making to a local level and to enable local discretion on implementation on community resolutions.

7.54 A CR needs the agreement of the child in order that he or she is able to participate in and accept the CR that is available. The MOJ and YJB guidance states that it is considered best practice for the police to notify YOTs of all community resolutions.[62]

7.55 CR may be delivered either with or without the use of restorative justice elements (see paras 7.10–7.11 above on restorative justice).[63]

58 Use of out-of-court disposals: section 1 case management guidance, para 2.3.

59 Out of court disposal guide, para 3.7.

60 'Youth out-of-court disposals: guide for police and youth offending teams'.

61 'Youth out-of-court-disposals: guide for police and youth offending services', MOJ and YJB, 2013, para 3.8.

62 'Youth out-of-court disposals: guide for police and youth offending teams', para 3.1.

63 OOCD Guide para 3.9.

Criminal record: informal OOCD

7.56 If a child receives an informal OOCD – a triage or CR or another form of informal diversion – it will be recorded on the PND and on local police systems (see paras 25.5–25.17 for records that are kept by the police). Informal OOCDs do not come under the Rehabilitation of Offenders Act 1974 – they are not considered 'spent' or 'unspent'.[64] These offences will not ordinarily need to be disclosed, however there are circumstances when they could be disclosed on an Enhanced criminal record certificate (see paras 25.57–25.61 on police intelligence/enhanced certificates).

Youth caution

7.57 A youth caution is a formal OOCD given to children aged ten to 17. A youth caution is recorded as outcome code 2 on the Police Recorded Crime and Data Outcomes (see para 7.17 on outcome codes).[65]

Statutory framework

7.58 Youth cautions were introduced by LASPO 2012 s135, replacing reprimands and final warnings.[66] The statutory criteria for youth cautions are set out in Crime and Disorder Act 1998 ss66ZA and 66ZB:

> (1) A constable may give a child or young person ('Y') a caution under this section (a 'youth caution') if–
> (a) the constable decides that there is sufficient evidence to charge Y with an offence,
> (b) Y admits to the constable that Y committed the offence, and
> (c) the constable does not consider that Y should be prosecuted or given a youth conditional caution in respect of the offence.[67]

7.59 The statutory framework provides for guidance on youth cautions to include:

64 'Youth out-of-court disposals: guide for police and youth offending teams', para 7.5.

65 'Youth out-of-court disposals: guide for police and youth offending teams', MOJ and YJB, 2013.

66 Following the commencement of LASPO 2012 s135, reprimands and final warnings were abolished.

67 Crime and Disorder Act 1998 s66ZA.

- the circumstances in which it is appropriate to give youth cautions;
- the places where youth cautions may be given;
- the category of police constable who may give a youth caution;
- the form youth cautions are to be given and recorded;
- as well as guidance on any rehabilitation programme to be offered as part of a youth caution.[68]

This guidance has been published jointly by the MOJ and YJB and is endorsed by the Association of Chief Police Officers and the CPS: 'Youth cautions: guidance for police and youth offending teams'.[69]

7.60 The statutory guidance provides that the police may make the decision to authorise a youth caution for a first-time summary only or either way offence.[70] Any cases involving indictable-only offences should always be referred to the CPS for consideration.[71] The CPS may also instruct a youth caution be administered in any summary or either way case.[72] For second and subsequent cautions, the police should make a joint decision following an assessment by the YOT.[73] Police officers should follow the six-step decision-making process.[74]

1. What is the offence?
2. Is there sufficient evidence against the young person to give a realistic prospect of conviction if they were prosecuted?
3. Does the young person admit the offence?
4. How serious is the offence?
5. What is the young person's offending history?
6. Is it in the public interest for the young person not to be prosecuted?

68 CDA 1998 ss66ZA(5) and 66ZB (4).

69 Youth Cautions: Guidance for Police and Youth Offending Teams', MOJ and YJB, 2013 Effective from 8 April 2013.

70 'Youth Cautions: Guidance for Police and Youth Offending Teams', MOJ and YJB, 2013, para 4.3.

71 'Youth Cautions: Guidance for Police and Youth Offending Teams', MOJ and YJB, 2013, para 4.3.

72 'Youth Cautions: Guidance for Police and Youth Offending Teams', MOJ and YJB, 2013, para 4.3.

73 'Youth out-of-court disposals: guide for police and youth offending teams', MOJ and YJB, 2013, para 3.5.

74 'Youth cautions: guidance for police and youth offending teams', MOJ and YJB, 2013, paras 4.3–4.19.

7.61 The guidance indicates that a youth caution will usually be considered for an offence with a gravity score of 2 or 3, and more serious offences with mitigating factors (see para 7.9 above on gravity score matrix).[75] An Informal diversion may also be considered (see para 7.43–7.56 on informal diversion).

Involvement of the youth offending team

7.62 Police services and YOTs should have a joint protocol setting out locally agreed practice for youth cautions.[76]

7.63 The police must refer every child who receives a youth caution to the YOT as soon as practicable,[77] although in practice the YOT are often consulted before a youth caution is given. The police must notify the YOT within one working day of the arrest of all children who have been given a youth caution or are being bailed for assessment by the YOT.[78] In 'higher risk cases' or where children have previously been given a youth caution, 'the police should refer the case to the YOT for assessment to inform the decision whether or not a youth caution is in the public interest'.[79]

7.64 Where a child is referred by the police, the youth offending team may assess the child and may arrange for the child to participate in a rehabilitation programme.[80] If there is a second or subsequent youth caution, the YOT *must* assess the child and put in place a rehabilitation programme to prevent further offending, where it is appropriate.[81] Participation in the interventions attached to a youth caution are voluntary and there is no separate penalty for failing to comply with them. However, failure to comply with the interventions could be a consideration when choosing any future disposal options and could be cited in any future criminal proceedings.[82]

75 CPS legal guidance on young offenders: youth cautions.

76 'Youth cautions: guidance for police and youth offending teams', MOJ and YJB, 2013, para 6.1.

77 CDA 1998 s66ZB(1); and 'Youth cautions: guidance for police and youth offending teams', MOJ and YJB, 2013, para 3.2.

78 'Youth cautions: guidance for police and youth offending teams', MOJ and YJB, 2013, para 6.3.

79 'Youth cautions: guidance for police and youth offending teams', MOJ and YJB, 2013, para 8.1.

80 CDA 1998 s66ZB(3).

81 CDA 1998 s66ZB(2).

82 'Youth out-of-court disposals: guide for police and youth offending teams', MOJ and YJB, 2013, para 3.11.

Victim's views

7.65 The victim should be contacted by the YOT to establish their view about the offence and their willingness to participate in any restorative process.[83] However:

> Victims should not be involved in decisions on the correct disposals for young offenders. For instance they cannot demand that a young person be charged or given a Youth Caution . . .[84]

Repeat youth cautions

7.66 There is no statutory restriction on the number of youth cautions that a child can receive, and a child may receive a youth caution even if he or she has previous convictions, reprimands, warnings, youth cautions and youth conditional cautions.

7.67 A child who has received two or more youth cautions who is convicted of an offence within two years of the most recent youth caution, may not receive a conditional discharge unless there are exceptional circumstances relating to the offence or the person to justify doing so.[85]

Administering a youth caution

7.68 A youth caution must be given in the presence of an appropriate adult[86] and it is good practice for a member of the YOT to be present.[87] The person administering the caution must explain the effect of the youth caution in 'ordinary language'.[88] The child is entitled to free legal advice before accepting a youth caution.[89] However, unlike adult cautions, a child is not required to consent to the caution (see para 7.72 below on youth cautions and consent). The authors would encourage a child, the child's parents or carers or appropriate adult (if different) to seek legal advice before accepting a youth caution

83 'Youth cautions: guidance for police and youth offending teams', MOJ and YJB, 2013, para 8.8.

84 'Youth cautions: guidance for police and youth offending teams', MOJ and YJB, 2013, para 8.10.

85 CDA 1998 s66ZB(5) and (6).

86 CDA 1998 s66ZA(2).

87 'Youth out-of-court disposals: guide for police and youth offending teams', MOJ and YJB, 2013, para 5.15.

88 CDA 1998 s66ZA(3); and 'Youth cautions: guidance for police and youth offending teams', MOJ and YJB, 2013, paras 9.9–9.12.

89 'Youth out-of-court disposals: guide for police and youth offending teams', MOJ and YJB, 2013, para 5.22.

because of the lifelong consequences for a child's criminal record (see paras 25.31–25.56 on disclosure of criminal records).

7.69 Where a child has been bailed, the police and YOT should decide the most appropriate place to deliver a youth caution following the guidance.[90] Youth cautions must be given by a police officer, preferably in uniform, who has appropriate expertise and is appropriately trained.[91]

Sexual offences notification requirements (sex offenders' register)

7.70 Children who are given a youth caution or youth conditional caution for sexual offences listed in Sexual Offences Act 2003 are subject to notification requirements for 12 months (commonly described as being placed on the 'sex offenders' register').

7.71 The police officer must explain this to the child and the child's appropriate adult. If the child turns 18 before the caution is administered and therefore receives an adult caution the notification period is two years (see paras 25.76–25.81 on notification requirements).

Youth cautions and consent

7.72 Children are not required to explicitly consent to cautions. Under the statutory regime, it is a matter for the police to decide the appropriate disposal in accordance with the statutory criteria and the youth caution guidance.[92] A youth caution cannot be challenged on the grounds the child or the child's parent did not consent to it.[93]'The House of Lords in *R v Durham Constabulary*[94] determined that being administered a caution did not engage Article 6 (right to a fair trial) as a caution is a diversionary measure.

90 'Youth cautions: guidance for police and youth offending teams', MOJ and YJB, 2013, paras 9.3–9.6. Although see conflicting guidance at para 5.14 of the 'Youth out-of-court disposals: guide for police and youth offending teams', MOJ and YJB, 2013.

91 'Youth cautions: guidance for police and youth offending teams', MOJ and YJB, 2013, paras 9.7–9.8; and 'Youth out-of-court disposals: guide for police and youth offending teams', MOJ and YJB, 2013, paras 5.13, 5.16 and 5.20.

92 'Youth cautions: guidance for police and youth offending teams', MOJ and YJB, 2013, para 4.7.

93 Youth cautions: guidance for police and youth offending teams', MOJ and YJB, 2013, para 4.8

94 [2005] UKHL 21.

Turning 18

7.73 The statutory guidance provides that young adult suspects who were 17 (or under) when the offence was committed and would have been eligible for a youth caution but have turned 18 should be given an adult simple caution.[95]

Criminal record for youth caution

7.74 A youth caution is a formal admission of guilt, and a youth caution forms part of a child's criminal record. Under the Rehabilitation of Offenders Act 1974 the youth caution will be considered 'spent' immediately (see para 25.23 on spent convictions) but it will automatically appear on any standard or enhanced criminal record certificate unless it is filtered (see paras 25.49–25.56 on filtering). However, a recent case in the Supreme Court held that the current filtering rules of youth diversions are incompatible with Article 8 ECHR (right to private life). At the time of writing, the government has not responded to this judgment.[96] For this reason, youth informal diversion might be a more proportionate response to low-level or first-time offending. Children who are given a youth caution for sexual offences listed in Sexual Offences Act 2003 are subject to notification requirements for 12 months (see paras 7.70–7.71 on sexual offences notification requirements or paras 25.76–25.81).

7.75 A youth caution may be cited in any future criminal proceedings as well as any failure to participate in a rehabilitation programme.[97]

Youth conditional caution

7.76 The youth conditional caution is a formal OOCD that requires compulsory assessment and intervention, it is available for children aged ten to 17 years old if they admit a criminal offence. A youth conditional caution is a caution with conditions attached and consequences for non-compliance. A youth conditional caution is recorded as outcome code 2 on the Police Recorded Crime and Data Outcomes (see paras 7.17–7.18 on outcome codes).

95 Youth cautions: guidance for police and youth offending teams', MOJ and YJB, 2013, para 4.24.

96 *R (P, G and W) v Secretary of State for the Home Department* [2019] UKSC 3.

97 CDA 1998 s66ZB(7).

Statutory framework

7.77 The statutory criteria for a youth conditional caution are set out in Crime and Disorder Act (CDA) 1998 ss66A and 66B. Youth conditional cautions may be given by an authorised person (a police constable, an investigating officer or person authorised by a relevant prosecutor)[98] if each of the five requirements of a youth conditional caution is satisfied:

(1) The first requirement is that the authorised person has evidence that the offender has committed an offence.
(2) The second requirement is that a relevant prosecutor [or the authorised person] decides–
  (a) that there is sufficient evidence to charge the offender with the offence, and
  (b) that a youth conditional caution should be given to the offender in respect of the offence.
(3) The third requirement is that the offender admits to the authorised person that he committed the offence.
(4) The fourth requirement is that the authorised person explains the effect of the youth conditional caution to the offender and warns him that failure to comply with any of the conditions attached to the caution may result in his being prosecuted for the offence.
(5) [The] explanation and warning mentioned in subsection (4) must be given in the presence of an appropriate adult.
(6) The fifth requirement is that the offender signs a document which contains–
  (a) details of the offence,
  (b) an admission by him that he committed the offence,
  (c) his consent to being given the youth conditional caution, and
  (d) the conditions attached to the caution.[99]

7.78 The guidance on youth conditional cautions includes the Code of Practice for Youth Conditional Cautions[100] required by the statutory framework.[101] The Director of Public Prosecutions (DPP) has issued separate guidance to assist Authorised Persons and Relevant Prosecutors (the decision makers) to apply the Code of Practice on Youth Conditional Cautions.[102]

98 CDA 1998 ss66A(1)–(5).
99 CDA 1998 s66B(7).
100 Code of Practice for Youth Conditional Cautions: Crime & Disorder Act 1998 (as amended by the CJIA 2008 and LASPO 2012), MoJ, March 2013.
101 CDA 1998 s66G.
102 Youth Conditional Cautions (The Director's Guidance): Guidance to Police Officers and Crown Prosecutors Issued by the Director of Public Prosecutions under section 37A of the Police and Criminal Evidence Act 1984, CPS, 3rd edn, January 2015, para 1.2.

7.79 When considering a youth conditional caution, the CPS full code test must be applied to decide if there is sufficient evidence for a realistic prospect of conviction.[103] When deciding whether there is sufficient evidence, consideration should be made to all evidence including any admissions made. Once it is determined that there is sufficient evidence, consideration must then be given to whether it would be in the public interest to offer a youth conditional caution. This is called the public interest stage (see para 7.109 for specific public interest issues for children).[104] Additional consideration should be given to other factors listed in the Code of Practice including the seriousness of the offence, the circumstances of the offences and the age of the offender.[105]

7.80 All offences are eligible for a youth conditional caution disposal, but if the offence is an indictable-only offence, the CPS will need to be consulted and authorise the decision to offer a youth conditional caution.[106] The guidance states that '[o]nly in the most exceptional circumstances will a Youth Conditional Caution be an appropriate way of dealing with'[107] an indictable only offence; and that before considering referring any indictable only offence to a prosecutor, authorised persons must first determine that exceptional circumstances are present in the case.[108]

Involvement of the youth offending team

7.81 Police services and YOTs should have a joint protocol setting out locally agreed practice for youth conditional cautions.[109]

103 Code of Practice for Youth Conditional Cautions: Crime & Disorder Act 1998 (as amended by the CJIA 2008 and LASPO 2012) March 2013, para 5.2.

104 Code of Practice for Youth Conditional Cautions: Crime & Disorder Act 1998 (as amended by CJIA 2008 and LASPO 2012) March 2013, paras 5.3–5.5.

105 Code of Practice for Youth Conditional Cautions: Crime & Disorder Act 1998 (as amended by CJIA 2008 and LASPO 2012) March 2013, para 6.1.

106 Youth cautions: guidance for police and youth offending teams', MOJ and YJB, 2013 para 4.3.

107 Youth Conditional Cautions (The Director's Guidance): Guidance to Police Officers and Crown Prosecutors Issued by the Director of Public Prosecutions under S37A of the Police and Criminal Evidence Act 1984, CPS, 3rd edition January 2015, para 5.2.

108 Youth Conditional Cautions (The Director's Guidance): Guidance to Police Officers and Crown Prosecutors Issued by the Director of Public Prosecutions under S37A of the Police and Criminal Evidence Act 1984, CPS, 3rd edition January 2015, para 5.3.

109 'Youth cautions: guidance for police and youth offending teams', MOJ and YJB, 2013, para 6.1.

7.82 Whenever the authorised person is deciding whether a youth conditional caution is appropriate for a child, they should refer the matter to the YOT for an assessment. The YOT *must* assess the child and advise on appropriate conditions, an authorised person should not agree conditions that are to be delivered by the YOT without the YOT's prior agreement. The decision whether to issue a youth conditional caution should take into account any information or recommendations from YOT although the final decision lies with the decision-maker.[110]

Conditions of the youth conditional caution

7.83 The conditions attached to the youth conditional caution can be rehabilitative, reparative or punitive in nature.[111] Guidance for the management of youth conditional cautions states that interventions must be: appropriate, achievable and proportionate.[112] When considering appropriateness, consideration should be made to conditions aimed at changing the child's behaviour and providing redress to the victim. The conditions must be achievable in the time frame and take into consideration individual circumstances such as religious beliefs and attendance at school. Whether the conditions are proportionate should be looked at in their totality with few conditions as possible to achieve the aims of the youth conditional caution. [113]

7.84 Restorative justice processes can be used to inform decisions as to what conditions to impose to a youth conditional caution.[114]

7.85 The YOT will put in place processes for compliance. This may include agreements with:

1) organisations involved in delivering the conditions (such as drugs referral agencies);
2) police officers and other police staff;
3) Her Majesty's Courts & Tribunals Service (for collection of monies).[115]

110 Code of Practice for Youth Conditional Cautions: Crime & Disorder Act 1998 (as amended by CJIA 2008 and LASPO 2012) March 2013, para 15.5.

111 CDA 1998 s66A(3).

112 Code of Practice for Youth Conditional Cautions: Crime & Disorder Act 1998 (as amended by CJIA 2008 and LASPO 2012) March 2013, para 8.1.

113 Code of Practice for Youth Conditional Cautions: Crime & Disorder Act 1998 (as amended by CJIA 2008 and LASPO 2012) March 2013, paras 8.2–8.6.

114 Code of Practice for Youth Conditional Cautions: Crime & Disorder Act 1998 (as amended by CJIA 2008 and LASPO 2012) March 2013, para 12.2.

115 Code of Practice for Youth Conditional Cautions: Crime & Disorder Act 1998 (as amended by CJIA 2008 and LASPO 2012) March 2013, para 17.2.

Time-limits on completing the conditions

7.86 There are time limits of six months in bringing proceedings in summary cases, so conditions must be completed within 16 weeks. If the youth conditional caution relates to either way or indictable only offences in limited circumstances and depending on the facts of the case it can be extended to 20 weeks.[116]

Conditions with a financial element

7.87 Conditions can include compensation as part of a reparative condition or a financial penalty as part of a punitive condition. A financial penalty condition may not be attached to a youth conditional caution unless the offence is one that is prescribed, or of a description prescribed, in an order made by the Secretary of State.[117] An order must prescribe the maximum amount of the penalty and the amount must not exceed £100.[118]

7.88 There are no restrictions on the amount of compensation that can be paid but any financial condition must take into account the child's means and ability to pay, the seriousness of the offence and YOT assessment. The child is solely responsible for payment. Parents and carers are not responsible for payment so their means should not be taken into account. Failure to pay the financial element of a condition will not result in enforcement but if unpaid, without a reasonable excuse, it could lead to prosecution of the original offence for non-compliance with the terms.[119]

Involvement of the victim

7.89 Reasonable efforts must be made to gain the views of the victim in order to consider what conditions to impose and in particular considering the victims views as to whether any of the actions in the local 'community remedy document' should be carried out.[120] A community remedy document is prepared by each local police area and is a list of actions, which may be carried out by persons who engage in anti-social behaviour or are being dealt with for an offence by way of an

116 Code of Practice for Youth Conditional Cautions: Crime & Disorder Act 1998 (as amended by CJIA 2008 and LASPO 2012) March 2013, para 9.2.

117 CDA 1998 s66C.

118 CDA 1998 s66C(3).

119 Code of Practice for Youth Conditional Cautions: Crime & Disorder Act 1998 (as amended by CJIA 2008 and LASPO 2012) March 2013, para 11.1–11.10.

120 CDA 1998 s66BA(1).

out of court disposal. If a victim expresses a view that the person should carry out that action then this must be attached to the youth conditional caution unless it would be inappropriate to do so.[121]

Youth conditional cautions and consent

7.90 Unlike the youth caution, the child must consent to the youth conditional caution and the conditions attached. This is one of the five criteria in the legislation (see para 7.77).[122] The child may decide at any stage to withdraw from the youth conditional caution, whether before, during or after it has been administered.

Administering a youth conditional caution

7.91 As with a youth caution the child must have an appropriate adult present and they are entitled to free legal advice, which the authors would recommend they take up, before they sign a youth conditional caution.

7.92 When a youth conditional caution is made, the child must sign a document that contains:

1) Contain the details of the offence(s) for which the caution is administered;
2) Clearly set out all the conditions to be complied with;
3) Set out the arrangements for monitoring compliance;
4) Specify the effect of the youth conditional caution and the consequences of any failure to comply with the conditions, including the possibility of future prosecution for the offence(s);
5) Record the young person's clear admission to the offence(s), consent to being given the youth conditional caution and agreement to and undertaking to abide by the condition. This admission must be made at the time the youth conditional caution is administered;
6) Provide details of the person in the YOT who will supervise completion of the youth conditional caution that the young person should contact in the case of non-compliance, or if they are unable or unwilling to comply with the condition.[123]

121 CDA 1998 s66BA(2).
122 CDA 1998 66B(6)(c).
123 CDA 1998 66B(6) and Code of Practice for Youth Conditional Cautions: Crime & Disorder Act 1998 (as amended by CJIA 2008 and LASPO 2012) March 2013, para 16.4.

7.93 It must also also be explained that a youth conditional caution will form part of the child's criminal record (see chapter 25 on criminal records).[124]

Failure to comply with conditions of a youth conditional caution

7.94 Unlike youth cautions, failure to comply with the conditions in a youth conditional caution, without reasonable excuse, can result in criminal proceedings being instituted against the child for the offence in question.[125]

7.95 The implications of such action should be explained: if a child does not keep to the conditions he or she could be prosecuted for the original offence.

7.96 It should,, be borne in mind that the purpose of securing compliance with all out of court disposals including youth conditional cautions is to address the risk of reoffending and if an assessment by YOT identifies welfare-related matters these should be referred to children's services.[126]

7.97 The YOT may offer the child voluntary intervention(s) in addition to, or following, the formal part of the caution, and the child may agree to this. However, where the child fails to complete this voluntary involvement, this will not be citable if the child reoffends. These voluntary interventions are referred to as 'non-citable' components.[127]

Power of arrest

7.98 The police have the power to arrest and detain a child when they believe there to be reasonable grounds for believing that the child has failed, without reasonable excuse, to comply with any conditions attached to a youth conditional caution.[128] This power should only be exercised where considered necessary.

124 Code of Practice for Youth Conditional Cautions: Crime & Disorder Act 1998 (as amended by CJIA 2008 and LASPO 2012) March 2013, para 16.1.

125 CDA 1998 s66E

126 Youth Out of Court Disposals: Guide for Police and Youth Offending Services, MOJ and YJB (2013 para 4.32.

127 Youth Out of Court Disposals: Guide for Police and Youth Offending Services, MOJ and YJB (2013) para 8.15.

128 Code of Practice for Youth Conditional Cautions: Crime & Disorder Act 1998 (as amended by CJIA 2008 and LASPO 2012) March 2013, para 18.1.

Repeat youth conditional cautions

7.99 There are no statutory restrictions on the number of youth conditional cautions that a child can receive. Previous convictions, reprimands, warnings, cautions, youth conditional cautions or other OOCDs do not preclude the use of a further youth caution or youth conditional caution. However, the police officers and YOT staff involved in taking the decision should consider whether the new offence is part of a pattern of offending which requires a more serious response such as a prosecution.

7.100 In assessing the suitability for a youth conditional caution the child's previous offending history will be checked on a PNC check. The police may also check the offending history with the child's home area YOT to ensure that previous offences, particularly non-recordable offences, are not missed. A youth conditional caution is unlikely to be appropriate where the offence forms part of a pattern of offending.[129]

7.101 A second youth conditional caution should not generally be given for the same or similar offence unless there are exceptional circumstances or where there has been a failure to comply with the conditions of the previous youth conditional caution.[130]

7.102 Other factors which would influence a decision to impose a further OOCD include whether:

- there has been a sufficient lapse of time to suggest that a previous caution or conviction has had a significant deterrent effect;
- the current offence is not similar or is unrelated to any previous offence;
- it is the best outcome for the child person and for any victim, depending on the circumstances of the individual case;
- the child is willing to comply with any possible interventions and has previously complied with interventions including voluntary interventions as part of prior OOCDs;
- it is likely to be effective in preventing offending.

Advice to 'practitioners' by the MOJ is that they are advised to guard against inappropriate repeat cautioning, and the protection and confidence of the public must be maintained as the focus throughout decision-making.[131]

129 Code of Practice for Youth Conditional Cautions: Crime & Disorder Act 1998 (as amended by CJIA 2008 and LASPO 2012) March 2013, para 6.5.

130 Code of Practice for Youth Conditional Cautions: Crime & Disorder Act 1998 (as amended by CJIA 2008 and LASPO 2012) March 2013, para 6.6.

131 Youth Out of Court Disposals: Guide for Police and Youth Offending Services, MOJ and YJB (2013), para 3.5.

Criminal record

7.103 A youth conditional caution is a formal admission of guilt, and a youth conditional caution forms part of a child's criminal record. Under the Rehabilitation of Offenders Act 1974 the youth caution will be considered 'spent' three months after it is issued: see paras 25.21–25.30 on spent convictions. but it will automatically appear on any standard or enhanced DBS check unless it is filtered (see paras 25.49–25.56 on filtering). For this reason, youth informal diversion might be a more proportionate response to low-level or first-time offending (see para 7.74 and para 25.42 for discussion on recent Supreme Court case about disclosure of diversions for children).

7.104 A youth conditional caution may be cited in any future criminal proceedings.

Sexual offences notification requirement (sex offenders register)

7.105 Children who are given a youth conditional caution for sexual offences listed in Sexual Offences Act 2003 are subject to notification requirements for 12 months (see paras 7.70–7.71 and 25.76–25.81 on Sexual offences notification requirements).

Decision to prosecute

Police decision to prosecute

7.106 Where the police have decided not to offer a child an OOCD or an OOCD is not available, the police will then need to decide whether or not to charge the child or to refer the case to the CPS for a charging decision. The police may make the charging decision for most summary and some either way offences. With certain exceptions,[132] the police may charge:

- any summary only offence (including criminal damage where the value of the loss or damage is less than £5,000) irrespective of anticipated plea;

132 The police may not make the decision to charge in: a case requiring the consent to prosecute of the Director of Public Prosecutions (DPP) or law officer; a case involving a death; connected with terrorist activity or official secrets; classified as hate crime or domestic violence under CPS policies; an offence of violent disorder or affray; causing grievous bodily harm or wounding, or actual bodily harm; a Sexual Offences Act offence committed by or upon a person under 18; an offence under the Licensing Act 2003.

- any offence of retail theft (shoplifting) or attempted retail theft irrespective of anticipated plea provided it is suitable for sentence in the magistrates' court; and
- any either way offence anticipated as a guilty plea and suitable for sentence in an adult magistrates' court.[133]

7.107 The CPS will make charging decisions in all other cases.[134]

CPS decision to prosecute

7.108 Any CPS decision to prosecute a child or divert a child must be referred to a CPS youth offender specialist.[135] The decision to prosecute is a two-part process:

1) the evidential stage;
2) the public interest stage.

7.109 The Code for Crown Prosecutors sets out the public interest factors that must be taken into account when considering decisions to prosecute in relation to children:

> The criminal justice system treats children and young people differently from adults and significant weight must be attached to the age of the suspect if they are a child or young person under 18. The best interests and welfare of the child or young person must be considered including whether a prosecution is likely to have an adverse impact on his or her future prospects that is disproportionate to the seriousness of the offending. Prosecutors must have regard to the principal aim of the youth justice system which is to prevent offending by children and young people. Prosecutors must also have regard to the obligations arising under the United Nations 1989 Convention on the Rights of the Child.
>
> As a starting point, the younger the suspect, the less likely it is that a prosecution is required.[136]

7.110 The Code is clear that the decision-maker must consider whether a prosecution is 'likely to have an adverse impact on the child's future prospects that is disproportionate to the seriousness of the offence'. These considerations are also relevant when considering OOCDs.

133 Charging (The Director's Guidance) 2013, 5th edn, May 2013 (revised arrangements) para 15.

134 Charging (The Director's Guidance) 2013, 5th edn, May 2013 (revised arrangements) para 16.

135 CPS legal guidance, youth offenders – youth offender specialist (YOS); principles guiding the decision to prosecute

136 CPS Code for Crown Prosecutors.

Obtaining sufficient background information

7.111 It is essential that the prosecutor obtains sufficient information about the child's home circumstances and gathers background information from the police, youth offending service, children's services and other agencies before making the decision whether to prosecute.[137] Each case should be looked at individually, as individual aggravating or mitigating factors may lead the decision maker to reassess the ACPO gravity matrix score (see para 7.9 on the ACPO gravity matrix).

7.112 If the child has specific learning difficulties, mental health issues or indeed a psychical disability these factors should all be given appropriate weight as will any intervention, compensation or restoration the young person has or is willing to engage in voluntarily (see paras 3.37–3.81 on mental disorders and learning disabilities).

Suitability of an out-of-court disposal

7.113 The prosecutor must give full consideration to the suitability of an OOCD. When applying the public interest factors in the Full Code Test in a case involving a child particularly important is:

> A prosecution is less likely to be required if . . . the seriousness and the consequences of the offending can be appropriately dealt with by an out-of-court disposal which the suspect accepts and with which he or she complies.
>
> This is a factor which will always carry a special weight in the case of youths who are at a very early stage of their offending, and can be traced back to historic police practice (as set out, for example, in Home Office Circular 18/1994) of *starting from a presumption of diverting youths away from the courts where possible.* [Emphasis added.][138]

7.114 For children for whom formal diversion is not an option, the CPS legal guidance on youth crime states:

> [I]t is still important to ensure that a prosecution is only brought in circumstances where this is a proper and proportionate response. The separate Legal Guidance chapter on Minor Offences – Prosecution Guidance and its steer towards the taking of a common sense approach to less serious cases has direct application to a number of youth matters. Alternative options, including restorative interventions, Acceptable Behaviour Contracts and internal sanctions such as school disciplinary measures may be available, and sufficient to satisfy the public interest without a prosecution and the statutory duty to prevent offending (Crime and Disorder Act 1998 s37).[139]

137 CPS legal guidance Youth offenders.

138 CPS legal guidance Youth offenders.

139 CPS legal guidance Youth offenders.

Considering all relevant policy and guidance

7.115 The defence lawyer should alert the police and prosecution to any evidence that may be relevant to the child's case. Any policy or guidance, whether statutory or otherwise, may be highly relevant to the decision-maker. There is a huge amount of guidance and some provides conflicting recommendations. It will be important to highlight the guidance relevant in a particular case.

Looked-after children

7.116 The police are more likely to be called to a children's home than a domestic setting to deal with an incident of offending behaviour by a child. The evidence shows that children in children's homes are more likely to be prosecuted or criminalised for what is often common childhood/adolescent behaviour. Recent research has found that children living in residential care are at least 13 times more likely to be criminalised than all other children with broad systemic issues contributing to this criminalisation.[140] The CPS guidance on young offenders has recognised that looked after children are more likely to be criminalised for offending behaviour in homes than other children. The guidance assists youth offender specialists in considering whether it is in the public interest to prosecute a child in these circumstances.

7.117 The guidance states that although it is not intended to deal with all circumstances in which a looked after child commits an offence. It does state that some of the principles may be helpful when applying the public interest stage of the Full Code Test to offences committed outside the home.

7.118 The CPS guidance Youth offenders recognises factors that increase the risk of offending by children in children's home such as their behaviour which is likely to be more challenging and demanding because of their family experience, the breakdown of foster placements and frequent moves from other children's homes. Many looked after children display challenging behaviour, which may be a reaction to past experiences of abuse and neglect. They may also have been diagnosed as experiencing Attention Deficit and Hyperactivity Disorder and Oppositional Defiant Disorder (see paras 3.45–3.56 for more on these disorders).[141]

7.119 Alternatives to a criminal justice response, regardless of the child's offending history, should be considered in these cases including

140 Howard League for Penal Reform (2018) – Research briefing.

141 CPS legal guidance Youth offenders – offending behaviour in children's homes.

informal disposals such as restorative justice or reparation. Every children's home must have its own behaviour management policy and this should always be attached to advise the CPS. This document is required in order to comply with Children's Home Regulations 2001 and National Minimum Standards under Care Standards Act 2000 s23. There should also be in place separate procedures and guidance on police involvement in the home that all staff are aware of.

7.120 Police officers who deal with children from care homes are required to receive information in relation to the 10 questions, sometimes referred to as the 10-point plan, before any decision on charge will be made by CPS reviewing lawyers. This is set out in CPS legal guidance for young offenders:

1. Disciplinary policy of the children's home
2. Why have the Police been involved and is it agreed in the policy? There should be an explanation from the home regarding their decision to involve the Police which should refer to the procedures and guidance on police involvement
3. Any informal action/disciplinary action already taken?
4. Any apology/reparation?
5. Victim's views?
6. Social worker's views? The views of the key worker, social worker, counsellor or CAHMS worker on the effect of the criminal justice intervention on the youth, particularly where the youth suffers from an illness or disorder.
7. Care plan for looked after child? If the looked after child wishes it to be considered, information about the local authority's assessment of his/her needs and how the placement provided by the home is intended to address them. The local authority should be able to provide this information as it is an integral part of the care plan for the looked after child.
8. Recent behaviour/incidents re the looked after child? Information from the home about the recent behaviour of the youth, including similar incidents and any incidents in the youth's life that could have affected their behaviour, any history between the youth and the victim, history of the incident and any action under the disciplinary policy of the home.
9. Information about the incident from the looked after child (interview or other)?
10. Aggravating and mitigating factors.[142]

142 CPS legal guidance Youth offenders.

7.121 When dealing with offending behaviour in a children's home, the CPS are required to consider all the circumstances surrounding the offence and the circumstances of the child, including responses to the ten questions above, before reaching a decision and to apply all relevant CPS policies and documents. Failure to do so could lead to an application for judicial review.

7.122 The Home Office, Ministry of Justice and the Department of Education have published a national protocol on reducing unnecessary criminalisation of looked after children and care leavers.[143]

7.123 The protocol acknowledges the state's duty to safeguard and promote the welfare of children in their care and notes that the UNCRC includes preventing the criminalisation of children. The protocol sets out best practice for avoiding the criminalisation of looked after children and care leavers up to the age of 25. It reiterates the importance of restorative and diversionary approaches which it states should underpin responses, whether the behaviour occurs in a child's placement or the wider community.[144]

7.124 The protocol strongly dissuades authorities from involving the police in incidents which occur in residential care placements. It also states that a local authority responsible for a child who is charged with a criminal offence should ensure the child is represented by a lawyer with expertise in youth justice.

County lines

7.125 County lines is the exploitation of children, young people and vulnerable adults by gang members in their efforts to move and sell drugs across the country. The gangs recruit vulnerable people, often children, to act as couriers and to sell drugs and are sometimes referred to as 'runners'. Children involved in these activities are often exposed to potentially serious emotional and physical harm. For more information see paras 13.14–13.53 for defences to county lines trafficking.

7.126 There is much guidance available on children exploitation and county lines which encourage children to be safeguarded rather than prosecuted when they come to the attention of the police and prosecuting authorities. This should be borne in mind

143 The national protocol on reducing unnecessary criminalisation of looked after children and care leavers, Home Office, Ministry of Justice and Department of Education (November 2018).

144 The national protocol on reducing unnecessary criminalisation of looked after children and care leavers, Home Office, Ministry of Justice and Department of Education (November 2018), page 27 and Annex 2.

in any decision to prosecute and considering should be made by defence solicitors as to whether representations should be made to the CPS in these cases that it would not be in the public interest to prosecute.

7.127 The CPS legal guidance Youth offenders recognises that:

> ... children, often boys aged 14 to 17 years, who are groomed with money and gifts and forced to carry out day to day dealing. Runaway and missing children are also used by gangs to expand inner city drugs empires into county towns. Children as young as 11 years of age have been reported as being recruited into the highly sophisticated gangs.

Sexual offences

7.128 There are some children who may commit offences as they begin to explore their sexuality. Careful consideration of the public interest factors including the views of the victim and their family should be taken into consideration. It is important to determine whether or not a prosecution or formal out of court disposal such as a youth caution or youth conditional caution would provide a proportionate response given the long term implications of a caution or conviction for a sexual offence on your criminal record (see chapter 25 for more information about criminal records). Evidence suggests criminalising children for sexual exploration which may simply be a part of their development can have a stigmatising affect and risks labelling children as sex offenders. Children 'make mistakes as they start to understand their sexuality and experiment with it'. 'These children are unlikely to pose further risk to the public, given appropriate support, but unnecessarily criminalising or stigmatising them as a sex offender at such a young age makes it more likely that they will struggle to regain a normal life, and increases their propensity to re-offend'.[145]

7.129 The CPS legal guidance Youth offenders states:

> There is a fine line between sexual experimentation and offending and in general, children under the age of 13 should not be criminalised for sexual behaviour in the absence of coercion, exploitation or abuse of trust.[146]

145 Now I know it was wrong – Parliamentary inquiry into support and sanctions for children who display harmful sexual behaviour, Barnardo's.

146 CPS legal guidance Youth offenders – Sexual Offences and Child Abuse by Young Offenders.

Where there are children who engage in harmful sexual behaviour consideration should be made to therapeutic, supportive and rehabilitative approaches, away from criminalisation wherever possible.

Mental disorders and learning disabilities

7.130 Decision makers should give extra consideration to the decision whether to prosecute in cases where the child suffers from or may suffer from a specific mental disorder or learning disability. CPS guidance recognises that these children are 'doubly vulnerable'. The prosecutor should consider information including the circumstances of any previous offending; the nature of the youth offender's mental disability or disorder; the likelihood of repetition; and the availability of suitable alternatives to prosecution:

> Information may be obtained from a variety of sources, including criminal justice mental health teams, criminal justice liaison and diversion schemes and the youth offending team. A plea should not be accepted until the prosecutor has all the available information and has reviewed the file.[147]

BAME children

7.131 Despite a reduction in the overall numbers of children entering the youth justice system, children from BAME backgrounds account for 45% of the custodial population despite only making up 18% of the 10–17 year old general population.[148] Children from BAME background account for 28% of the children and young people arrested and they accounted for 25% of the total children and young people who received a caution or conviction, which is a 7 percentage point increase compared with 10 years ago.[149] Therefore, as was recognised by the sentencing council in its guidelines for children and young people, consideration should be given to the factors leading to these figures when deciding whether to prosecute (issue a youth caution or youth conditional caution) a child from a BAME background (see paras 3.96–3.99 for more on children from BAME background).

147 CPS legal guidance Youth offenders – youths with mental disorders, including learning disabilities.

148 For ethnicity, population is based on the 2011 census. The ethnic breakdown of the population will likely have changed from 2011, so these figures should be treated as an estimate.

149 Youth Justice Statistics 2016 / 17 England and Wales, Ministry of Justice.

CPS reviewing a decision to prosecute

7.132 Where a prosecutor is dealing with a case where a child has been charged with an offence, but it appears upon review by a prosecutor that a youth caution or a youth conditional caution is more appropriate, the reviewing Prosecutor should consult the YOT and if it is still considered appropriate should direct an authorised person to offer a youth caution or youth conditional caution.[150]

7.133 The prosecution should be adjourned whilst this action is taken. The police should then offer a youth caution or authorised person shall offer a youth conditional caution with conditions as specified by the prosecutor. Once a youth has been correctly charged, it is likely to be only in exceptional circumstances that a youth caution or youth conditional caution will be given.[151]

Challenging the police or CPS decision to prosecute

7.134 A decision whether to prosecute a child could be subject to judicial review if it can be demonstrated that the decision was made regardless of, or clearly contrary to, a clear policy or guidance.[152]

7.135 In *R v Chief Constable of Kent,* the court held that an application for judicial review could be successful if the decision to prosecute was made without any or sufficient inquiry into the circumstances and general character of the accused.[153]

7.136 In *R (E, S* and *R) v DPP,*[154] failure to show that the legal guidance has been followed and properly applied to all the information on the case may result in the decision to prosecute being quashed. In this case, the decision of a Crown prosecutor to prosecute a 14-year-old girl for the alleged sexual abuse of her two younger sisters had to be quashed where the decision-making process was flawed in that it was unclear whether the Crown prosecutor had properly taken into account the concern raised in a report by a multi-agency strategy group that prosecution was not in the best interests of any of the children.

150 CPS Youth Conditional Cautions – Director's Guidance para 8.1.

151 CPS legal guidance Youth offenders – youth cautions.

152 See, for example, *R v Chief Constable of Kent and another ex p L, R v DPP ex p B* [1991] 93 Cr App R 416; *R (E, S and R) v DPP* [2011] EWHC 1465 (Admin).

153 *R v Chief Constable of Kent and Another ex p L, R v DPP ex p B* [1991] 93 Cr App R 416.

154 [2011] EWHC 1465 (Admin).

7.137 As a practical first step, setting out the reasons why a different decision should have been made by the decision maker in written representation, or, setting out this reasoning in a letter before claim enables the decision maker to review their decision without resorting to legal proceedings.

Police or prosecution going back on a promise

7.138 Where a person has been induced to believe that he or she will not be prosecuted, this may be challengeable by way of judicial review or it could be argued that the prosecution should be stayed for abuse of process. However, it is not likely to succeed unless: i) there has been an unequivocal representation by those with conduct of the investigation or prosecution of a case that the defendant will not be prosecuted; and (ii) the defendant has acted on that representation to his detriment; even then, if facts come to light which were not known when the representation was made, these may justify proceeding with the prosecution despite the representation.[155]

7.139 However, in *H v Guildford Youth Court*[156] the prosecution should have been stayed where it had been indicated at the police station to the defendant and his solicitor by a police officer that the offence would be dealt with by way of a final warning.

155 *R v Hamza* [2007] 1 Cr App R 27, CA.

156 [2008] 4 *Archbold News* 1, QBD.

CHAPTER 8

The youth court and first appearance

continued

Key points

- The youth court is a specialist court, emphasising protection of the child's welfare with district judges, magistrates and advocates who should be specially trained.
- Children should normally be accompanied by their parent who should be specially trained or guardian (and must be accompanied if under 16).
- Where offences are committed outside of the child defendant's home jurisdiction, courts may decide to remit the proceedings to the child's home court.
- There is a presumption children will be tried in the youth court unless the child is charged with an adult co-defendant or the particular offence requires trial in the Crown Court.
- A child will typically appear in the youth court for first appearance unless the youth court is not available. The adult court will determine bail only and remit the case to the appropriate court.
- If a child is jointly charged with an adult, the first appearance will be in adult magistrate's court. The court may then determine if the child's trial should be severed from the adult's and tried in a separate court.
- For complex and/or serious cases for indictable offences, the defence lawyer may make a written application to the youth court for a certificate for an assigned advocate.

Introduction

8.1 Children should always have their first hearing in any criminal case in the youth court, unless they have an adult co-defendant when they will usually have their first hearing at the adult magistrates' court (see paras 8.104–8.117 on adult co-accused). This first hearing is called a 'first appearance'. Where a child appears at court in custody and no youth court is sitting, the child will appear in the adult magistrates' court which will usually deal with bail only, and remit the matter to the youth court for their first appearance (see further paras 8.72–8.73 below).

8.2 When children appear in court, the procedure, the layout and the feel of the proceedings should be fundamentally different to that when an adult appears before the court. Children are neurologically different from adults, and require a fundamentally different approach in all aspects of criminal proceedings. (See paras 3.30–3.36 on child and adolescent brain development.)

8.3 A youth court is a magistrates' court that sits for the purpose of hearing any charge against a child.[1] Therefore any procedure, rules and legislation that makes reference to the magistrates' court applies equally to the youth court. Trials in the youth court are summary trials and bear a great deal of similarity to those in the adult magistrates' court. Criminal Procedure Rules Part 24 applies to all summary trials in youth or adult magistrates' court. However, the youth court is designed as a specialist court for children, and there are a number of important and fundamental differences (see paras 8.5–8.44 below).

8.4 At all times, when making decisions and exercising its powers, the youth court will have regard to:

- the principal aim of the youth justice system – to prevent offending;[2] and
- the welfare of the child.[3] (see paras 1.68–1.71 for more on the welfare principle)

The youth court

Specialist court

8.5 The youth court is a specialist court designed to fulfil the distinct aims of the youth justice system, which is to prevent offending by children.[4] Youth courts are required to have specially trained magistrates[5] who have to be authorised to sit in the youth court.[6] Youth ticketed district judges are also required to undertake specialist training and the Bar Standards Board requires barristers practising in the youth court to register their competence to do so.[7]

1 Children and Young Persons Act (CYPA) 1933 s45.
2 Crime and Disorder Act (CDA) 1998 s37(1).
3 CYPA 1933 s44.
4 CDA 1998 s37(1).
5 Justices of the Peace Rules 2016 SI No 709 r30.
6 CYPA 1933 s45(3).
7 See para 4.30 above.

Youth Court Bench Book and Protocol

8.6 The Youth Court Bench Book[8] is published by the Judicial College and provides guidance on case management and procedure in the youth court. Included in the Youth Court Bench Book is the Magistrates Association's Youth Court Protocol 2017 (see appendix A). Courts are encouraged to adopt the protocol, which offers advice about procedure in the youth court.

8.7 It is noteworthy that the youth court protocol observes that it would be desirable for all advocates appearing in the youth court to have received specialist training.[9] At the very least, defence lawyers are expected to be familiar with the terms of the protocol.

Aims of the youth justice system

8.8 Fundamentally different considerations govern decision-making in the youth court as compared to the adult criminal justice system as set out in para 8.4 above. In addition, the Youth Justice Board (YJB) have identified six key objectives of the youth justice system:

1) swift administration of justice;
2) confronting young offenders with their offending behaviour;
3) intervention that tackles particular factors that lead youths to offend;
4) punishment proportionate to the offending;
5) encouraging reparation;
6) reinforcing the responsibility of parents/guardians.[10]

Jurisdiction

8.9 The youth court is considered part of the magistrates' court and therefore all procedural rules and legislation that provides powers to the magistrates' court apply equally in the youth court.[11] There is an automatic right of appeal from the youth court to the Crown Court against conviction or sentence. A matter can be appealed to the High Court by way of case stated. The procedure to appeal from the youth court is the same as appealing from the adult magistrates' court (see further chapter 15 on appeals).

8 Youth Court Bench Book, Judicial College (August 2017).

9 Youth Court Protocol, para 11 (found at Youth Court Bench Book, Judicial College (August 2017) p109).

10 Youth Court Bench Book, Judicial College (August 2017) para 2.

11 CYPA 1933 s45; and also Magistrates' Court Act (MCA) 1980 s152.

8.10 The adult magistrates' court has no jurisdiction to hear cases involving child defendants,[12] other than in particular circumstances, such as when the child has an adult co-defendant or to deal with bail when there is no youth court sitting (see further below paras 8.72–8.73). Where there has been a mistake as to whether the defendant is a child, the adult magistrates' court have the power to continue to hear the case[13] (see paras 2.16–2.18 on mistake as to age).

Layout

8.11 The courtroom layout should be less formal than an adult magistrates' court.[14] Magistrates should sit on the same level as the other parties, and the parent or guardian should sit next to the child. Not all courts adhere to this, and there is a lot of variation from court to court, including where everyone sits. Usually the child will sit next to his or her defence lawyer in order to allow them to take instructions easily. Ideally the child would also sit next to his or her parent or guardian, but this may depend on where there is room to sit. In most youth courts there is either a picture or a diagram of the court's layout displayed outside the courtroom.

8.12 It should be noted that there is no court list on display outside the court room given that the youth court is a closed court. Also, whenever a youth court case is being called, this is usually done by the usher by calling out the first name of the child only, not the surname, so that the child is not identified to others. Best practice is for the usher to be aware of who is in attendance at court and approach them discreetly when their case is called on. The tannoy system should not be used for calling youth court cases.

8.13 Children and adults need to be kept separate in cells at court and in being transported to and from court, and in the cells.[15] The youth court protocol recommends separate entrances for children and adults, and separate waiting areas with their own toilet facilities. In practice, many courts have one entrance and the child attending court would be searched in the usual way upon entry. In some courts the security officer at the entrance will cross-check the child's details against the court list, and the officer may only allow their parent or guardian to enter the court building with the child. Courts should have facilities to obtain instructions from the children in private, such an interview room.

12 CYPA 1933 s46.

13 CYPA 1933 s46(1)(c).

14 Youth Court Bench Book, Judicial College (August 2017) para 12.

15 CYPA 1933 s31.

8.14 During proceedings, the youth court protocol suggests that the child stand when being identified, having the charges put to him or her, and when being told the disposal of the case, but should remain seated at all other times. It suggests all other parties remain seated throughout. In reality, practice varies from court to court as to whether to stand or sit throughout proceedings and when making representations. In circumstances where a matter is heard over the video link, the usual practice is for all parties to be seated during the whole proceedings, including sentencing.

Secure docks

8.15 Since the youth court is a specialist court designed to consider the welfare of the children that appear before it, the child should ordinarily sit outside the dock and next to his or her parent or guardian. The court has a discretion to use a secure dock where appropriate.

8.16 The Youth Court Protocol recommends that the secure dock should not be used routinely, even for those held in custody. It will usually be used for a child who is charged with a particularly serious crime, or where that child presents a risk if allowed to sit in the body of the court. The protocol goes on to suggest that children should only be produced in a secure dock in the following circumstances:

1. They have attained the age of 15; and
2. They are produced to the court from custody; and
3. He or she is charged with an offence of:
   i. A violent nature (other than common assault but including witness interference and offences specified in Schedule 15 of the Criminal Justice Act (CJA) 2003), or
   ii. A sexual nature, or
   iii. Possession of a real or imitation firearm or other weapon

A young person will also be produced in the secure dock where the court so orders it of its own volition or upon representations.[16]

Language and understanding

8.17 The court will often speak directly to the child, and to the child's parent or guardian, especially during applications for bail or at sentence. The Youth Court Protocol encourages the chair of the bench to engage with the child before the court, and the child's parent. It encourages the bench to ensure the child speaks for himself or herself where appropriate, and states that the parent or guardian should directly address the court before any disposal.

16 Annex A to Youth Court Bench Book – Youth Court Protocol, see Appendix A.

8.18 Having confirmed his or her full name at the start of the hearing, the child should be addressed using his or her first name.[17]

8.19 The court is required to explain to the child the nature of the proceedings and the substance of the charge in simple language, suitable to their age and understanding,[18] and also to explain the nature of any disposal.[19]

8.20 The Youth Court Protocol states that the magistrates should ensure that both the child and the child's parent or guardian fully understand the proceedings. This involves:

- explaining the role of everyone in court at the outset;
- explaining the meaning of any decision the court makes, including disposal; and
- asking questions to ensure that the child has understood.

It also means that the court needs to ensure that the child can follow proceedings, and consider how long the court sits for and how often they take breaks, especially in trials.[20] (See further paras 4.31–4.53 on modifications and special measures).

8.21 Where a child gives evidence before any court, the form of words to be used is 'I promise' instead of 'I swear'. Where any witness, including an adult, gives evidence in a youth court, the form of words is also 'I promise'.[21]

8.22 When a child is found guilty before a youth court or adult magistrates' court, the matter is not said to be a conviction but a 'finding of guilt' and the disposal is 'an order' and not called a sentence.[22]

Closed court

8.23 Proceedings in the youth court are considered private, and there is no public gallery. The people who may be present in court are restricted to:

- officers of the court;
- parties, and their legal representatives, witness, those directly concerned with proceedings;

17 See Youth Court Protocol para 5.
18 Magistrates' Courts (Children and Young Persons) Rules 1992 r6.
19 Magistrates' Courts (Children and Young Persons) Rules 1992 r11.
20 See Youth Court Protocol, para 5.
21 CYPA 1963 s28(1).
22 CYPA 1933 s58.

- bonafide members of the press;
- anyone else the court authorises.[23]

8.24 The relevant section[24] does not specifically mention the presence of parents in court, however, as below, parents or guardians are expected to attend court with their children (see further paras 8.26–8.41). Criminal Procedure Rules 2015, as amended, r24.2(c) states that:

> (c) unless the court otherwise directs, only the following may attend a hearing in a youth court –
> (i) the parties and their legal representatives,
> (ii) a defendant's parents, guardian or other supporting adult,
> (iii) a witness,
> (iv) anyone else directly concerned in the case, and
> (v) a representative of a news-gathering or reporting organisation."

8.25 The Youth Court Protocol states that witnesses will usually be allowed to remain in court having given their evidence, but this is at the court's discretion.

Supporting adults, parents and guardians

Attendance of parent or guardian

8.26 A child aged 15 or under must have the child's parent or guardian with him or her at court unless the court decides it is unreasonable to require their attendance.[25] The court may order that the parent or guardian attend the court when the child is 16 or 17.[26] The Youth Court Protocol suggests that the court should ordinarily exercise its discretion to require a parent or guardian to attend the hearing for any child under 18, and that, where applicable, it is desirable that both parents attend. There is no guidance on the role parents, guardians and/or supporting adults should play in court, however the Youth Court Bench Book states the children as well as their parent or guardian should be actively involved in the proceedings, and that the bench may want to speak to them directly.

8.27 A 'guardian' is defined as any person, who in the opinion of the court has for the time being the care of the child.[27] A 'parent' is not defined.

23 CYPA 1933 s47(2).
24 CYPA 1933 s47(2).
25 CYPA 1933 s34A(1)(b).
26 CYPA 1933 s34A(1)(a).
27 CYPA 1933 s107.

8.28 It should be noted that the purpose of requiring a parent or guardian to attend court is different to that of the appropriate adult at police station. The role of the parent or guardian at court is different – it is to ensure both that the child's rights and welfare are protected, and also to ensure that the person with parental responsibility is at court. The Youth Court Bench Book states:

> This is to encourage parents/guardians to take responsibility. In addition, certain court orders and sentences may be made against the parent/guardian eg payment of financial penalties and parenting orders.[28]

See further para 23.13 on parenting orders.

Supporting adults

8.29 The purpose of requiring the attendance of a parent or guardian is to ensure that the adult with responsibility for the child:

- is present in court;
- is aware of the proceedings;
- can play a part in the proceedings;

and

- to allow the court to pass orders on them, such as parenting orders, where appropriate.

Therefore courts will usually insist on someone with parental responsibility being present in court, and will not allow another family member or supporting adult to stand in for the parent without good reason. Where a child attends without a parent or guardian, the court may adjourn proceedings to allow the parent to attend.

8.30 Children require support at court and during proceedings. The criminal practice direction on vulnerable defendants[29] states that a vulnerable defendant, especially if young, should be free to sit with members of his or her family or those in like relationship if the defendant wishes to do so *and* a supporting adult such as a social worker.

8.31 It is usual in the youth court for the defendant to sit next to his or her parent or guardian, who are usually expected to support the child as well as help the child follow proceedings. The youth court protocol suggests both parents should be allowed to be present in court. However, where it is appropriate for another adult to fulfil that supportive function, the court should ordinarily allow another adult to be in court, in addition to the parent or guardian, in accordance

28 Youth Court Bench Book, Judicial College, introduction, para 4.

29 CrimPD I, para 3G.8.

with the practice direction. It may be appropriate to ask the child whom they would like to sit with in order to receive maximum support. In practice, children may sit next to their defence lawyer in order to give instructions more easily and there may not be space to sit next to their parent as well. Seating arrangements vary from court to court.

Looked after children

8.32 Children who are in the care of the local authority (or who are provided accommodation by the local authority) and for whom the local authority have parental responsibility need to be accompanied to court by someone from the local authority or an adult whom they are living with.[30]

8.33 Criticism has been made of the practice of sending key workers or other members of staff with children rather the child's social worker.[31] Courts should consider requiring the child's allocated social worker to attend in person, particularly at the sentencing hearing. The social worker may have valuable information for the bench regarding the child's behaviour, engagement and progress which could make a difference to the type of sentence passed.

8.34 Even when the child's parents do attend court it is best practice for a social worker to attend when the child has looked after status. All children who are remanded to youth detention accommodation or local authority accommodation will acquire looked after status (see further paras 11.120–11.123 on bail and remand, looked after status).

8.35 The Children Act 1989 Guidance and Regulations Volume 2: Care Planning and case Review June 2015 states:

> It is good practice for the child's social worker to attend court with the child, particularly on the day of sentence. Where it is not possible for the child's social worker to be in court then then child must be accompanied by their foster carer or, if they are placed in a children's home, by the home's registered manager. This is to support the child and also to ensure that the child's best interests are represented . . .

Engaging parents and guardians

8.36 The youth court protocol states:

> Voluntary engagement with parents/guardians is preferable to a court order and the court would not be expected to give a Parenting Order

30 CYPA 1933 s34A(2).

31 See 'Review of the Youth Justice System in England and Wales' by Charlie Taylor, para 102.

where the parents/guardians are fully compliant with the support offered by the YOT on a voluntary basis.[32]

See further paras 23.3–23.16 on parenting orders.

8.37 A parent or guardian is not covered by legal privilege, and therefore any representative should be cautious about taking instructions in their presence (see further paras 6.129–6.130).[33]

8.38 Where a child is not legally represented, the child's parent or guardian may assist him or her in the conduct of the case,[34] or conduct the case on their behalf.[35] Rule 15 of the Magistrates' Court (Children and Young Persons) Rules 1992 states that the parent or guardian can make representations after the conclusion of the evidence.

8.39 Where appropriate, the court can ask the adult to withdraw while the child gives evidence.[36]

Compelling attendance of parents or guardian

8.40 Where the local authority has parental responsibility, it needs to attend court. The court will usually ask the youth offending team (YOT) to ensure that a parent or local authority attends,[37] but can summons the adult or local authority to court where necessary.[38]

8.41 The form to issue such a summons can be found in Magistrates' Court (Children and Young Persons) Rules 1992 Sch 2. Should the person summonsed to court fail to attend, a warrant may be issued for his or her arrest.[39]

Child's attendance at court

Arrest and charge

8.42 Most cases, start by a child being arrested and then charged with an offence. Following charge, the child will either be denied bail and therefore will arrive at court in custody and will be in the cells; or the child will have been bailed to attend court. (See further paras 6.190–6.204 on bail at the police station.)

32 Youth Court Protocol, para 6.
33 *R v Marcus Brown* 21 May 1999, CA, unreported.
34 Magistrates' Court (Children and Young Persons) Rules 1992 r5.
35 Magistrates' Court (Children and Young Persons) Rules 1992 r18.
36 Magistrates' Court (Children and Young Persons) Rules 1992 r19(2).
37 See Youth Court Protocol, para 6, in Youth Court Bench Book, p108.
38 Magistrates' Court (Children and Young Persons) Rules 1996 r26.
39 Magistrates' Court (Children and Young Persons) Rules 1996 r26.

Child in custody

8.43 Where a child is denied bail, the police have a duty to transfer the child to local authority accommodation under Police and Criminal Evidence Act 1984 s38(6). If the child has not been transferred for whatever reason, a certificate of impracticability should be presented to the court with the reasons why the child was not transferred.[40] The purpose of this provision is to allow the court to scrutinise the decision not to transfer the child and make appropriate enquiries of the local authority and police where appropriate. The defence lawyer should ask to see the certificate if the child is brought in custody from the police station. (See paras 6.195–6.204 on detention after charge.)

8.44 The defence lawyer should ensure that the relevant court usher is aware that the child is in custody and the case called on as a priority. Where there are issues with service of prosecution papers, the defence lawyer ought to consider making an application for bail so that the child could be released with a condition of remaining within the court building pending service of papers.

Failure to attend while on bail

8.45 If the child has been bailed to attend court and fails to attend the first appearance on time, then the child commits a criminal offence under the Bail Act (BA) 1976 unless the child has a reasonable excuse for the failure to attend.[41] Where the child has a reasonable excuse for not attending, the child will need to surrender to the court as soon as reasonably practicable, otherwise he or she will commit a criminal offence.[42]

8.46 If a child fails to attend, the court may issue a warrant for the child's arrest.[43] If there is no objection, the clerk may issue the warrant under delegated powers.[44] However, the court may also adjourn proceedings without issuing a warrant if they can be persuaded to do so.[45]

8.47 Any warrant may be 'backed for bail'.[46]

8.48 CrimPD III, para 14B.2 states that where an accused is too ill to attend, he or she must supply the court with a medical certificate in advance of the hearing.

40 Police and Criminal Evidence Act 1984 (PACE) s38(7).
41 BA 1976 s6(1).
42 BA 1976 s6(2).
43 BA 1976 s7(1).
44 Justices' Clerks' Rules 2005 Sch 1 para 3.
45 MCA 1980 s129.
46 MCA 1980 s117; or Senior Courts Act 1981 s81(4) (for Crown Court power).

Bail Act offence

8.49 Where the child is on bail granted by the police (police bail) and fails to attend court, the decision whether to lay a Bail Act 1976 charge is made by the prosecution.[47] When a child attends court for the first time he or she will be on police bail (as opposed to court bail), unless he or she has been summonsed or requisitioned and therefore not on bail at all, or is in custody. Hence, the defence lawyer should discuss the reason for the non-attendance with the prosecutor first. The Bail Act charge is a separate offence which will appear on the child's antecedent history if convicted, and could be crucial in future bail applications. In most cases the child will have been arrested on warrant[48] by the police and remanded in police custody overnight or over the weekend to appear at court. In those cases, the defence lawyer may want to use the fact that the child has already spent time in custody and seek to persuade the prosecutor not to proceed with the Bail Act charge.

8.50 If the child fails to attend following court bail, then the discretion as to whether to put the charge lies with the court.[49] It still may be possible to persuade the court not to formally put the charge using similar arguments that could be made to the prosecutor.

Summonsing and postal requisitioning

8.51 In addition to being arrested and charged with an offence any defendant can be brought before the court either by the prosecution laying an information at court and the court issuing a summons,[50] or by a prosecutor issuing a written charge and a requisition document which requires the defendant to attend court to answer that charge. A summons or requisition issued to a child may require that a parent or guardian attend or a separate summons or requisition may be issued to the parent or guardian for that purpose.[51]

8.52 The procedure for summonsing or requisitioning a defendant is the same for children and adult defendants. For further information about the procedure generally, see *Blackstone's Criminal Practice* 2019.[52]

47 CrimPD III, para 14C.1.
48 BA 1976 s7(1).
49 CrimPD III, para 14C.4
50 CrimPR r7.4; MCA 1980 s47; and CJA 2003 s30(5).
51 CrimPR r7.4(9); CYPA 1933 s34A.
52 *Blackstone's Criminal Practice* 2019 D5.9–D5.15.

Failure to attend following summons

8.53 A child attending court having been summonsed or requisitioned is not on bail, and therefore commits no criminal offence by failing to attend. However, a warrant may still be issued for the child's arrest if he or she fails to appear.[53] Before issuing the warrant, the court will need to be satisfied that the summons was properly served on the child. The prosecutor will usually provide a statement confirming proof of service at the last known address. If the child is represented, it is worth making an application for an adjournment rather than agreeing to a warrant. If the court is not prepared to adjourn, then the defence lawyer can ask for a warrant backed for bail,[54] which simply means that the police will inform the child to attend court on a given date rather than arresting the child and remanding the child in custody.

8.54 CrimPD III para 14B.2 states that if the accused is too ill to attend, he or she must supply the court with a medical certificate in advance of the hearing.

Appearance by video link

Live link procedure

8.55 Crime and Disorder Act (CDA) 1998 ss57A–57F allow for a defendant in custody to give a plea and/or be sentenced over a live link. In some circumstances, it is also possible for defendants not in custody to appear over live links. The Act does not allow for a trial for the defendant to take place over live link. However, there may be circumstances when a defendant may be allowed to observe the trial over live link and give evidence as a special measure (see para 4.53 on live link and special measures). See also CrimPD 3N.10 and 3N.11.

8.56 Arrangements must be made in advance of any live link hearing for the youth offending worker to be either at the secure establishment where the child is being held, or for them to have 'sufficient access to the youth via the live link booth before and after the hearing'.[55]

8.57 CrimPD I, para 3N deals with the use of live links and telephone facilities. CrimPR r3.5(2)(d) states that the court can receive applications by letter, email, phone and other electronic means. It also states that the court can conduct any hearing by the use of live link, telephone or other electronic means. The court is encouraged to use

53 MCA 1980 s1.

54 MCA 1980 s117.

55 CrimPD I, para 3N.15.

such facilities where it furthers the overriding objective.[56] However, it may not be appropriate in many cases involving children.

Suitability for children

8.58 There may be some advantages to a child to have a hearing over a live link – for example, if the child is living very far from court and it might involve a long journey. However, there are concerns about how well the child can effectively participate over a live link, especially if the child already has communication difficulties. It may be more difficult to establish rapport with a young client over a link; and the child may feel more comfortable and more involved if the child can see his or her lawyers and the magistrates face-to-face. There are often restrictions on the time that can be spent with the child's representatives in order to take instructions, and there is a concern that the child may not receive full legal advice. Further, there is a concern about unconscious bias against children who are only seen over a video link in a secure establishment.

8.59 While there is no prohibition on live link being used for any hearing, other than trial, it should be unusual for a live link to be used for any substantive hearing.

8.60 The YJB made it clear in its position statement published in April 2016[57] that they did not consider live links to be suitable for trial, sentencing or appeal hearings involving child defendants.

8.61 The Youth Court Protocol makes it clear that children should appear in court in person unless there are exceptional circumstances. If the court is satisfied that it is in the interests of justice for a child to appear by video link, the YOT must be able to make representations as to the suitability of this course of action in relation to the child's specific needs.

8.62 The criminal practice directions state that it will usually be appropriate for a child to be produced in person[58] to ensure proper engagement with the child. Hearings that may be appropriate for a live link for children include: onward remand hearings at which there is no bail application; and case management hearings, particularly if the child is already serving a custodial sentence.[59]

56 To deal with cases justly (CrimPR Part I).

57 http://youthjusticeboard.newsweaver.co.uk/icfiles/1/1861/11612/5475544/1edb16998b2fd5187bfea092/yjb%20position%20statement%20on%20video%20link%20hearings.pdf.

58 CrimPD I, para 3N.13.

59 CrimPD I, para 3N.13.

Sentencing over live link

8.63 Crim PD I, para 3N.14 states that while sentencing a child over the live link is rare, it might be appropriate in the following circumstances:

- where it is contrary to the welfare of the child to be produced before the court; or
- where the child is already serving a custodial sentence and the court is intending to pass a sentence that will either have no material impact upon that sentence or will result in a longer time in custody.

Pleading by post

8.64 Magistrates' Court Act (MCA) 1980 s12 allows for a defendant to plead guilty by post to certain summary only offences. This is usually used for road traffic offences. It can be used for any defendant who is 16 or over at the time the summons is issued sets out the procedure to be used in these occasions.[60]

Determining which court

Remittal to home court

8.65 Trials usually happen in the area where the alleged crime occurred. This is for the convenience of any victims and witnesses. The police force investigating will send the case to the court connected to that police station. In the case of adult defendants, it is usual for the case to remain at the court where the plea is taken or any trial takes place. In cases with child defendants, it is desirable that the child is sentenced in his or her home court (the court acting for the area where the defendant usually resides). This is so that the local YOT, who will be supervising any order, can write the relevant reports, and will be known to the sentencing court.

8.66 Upon convicting a child, a youth court or an adult magistrates' court may remit the case to the child's home youth court or another youth court in the same area as the remitting court to deal with sentence.[61] If the child is convicted in an adult magistrates' court, the

60 MCA 1980 s12(2).

61 PCC(S)A 2000 s8(1), (2).

court must exercise its power to remit to the youth court unless it wishes to pass one of the following sentences:

- referral order;
- fine;
- absolute or conditional discharge; or
- parenting order under Powers of Criminal Courts (Sentencing) Act (PCC(S)A) 2000 s150.[62]

8.67 Where a child is convicted in the Crown Court, the case must be remitted back to the youth court for sentence unless it is undesirable to do so.[63] Oddly, the power is to remit to a youth court acting for the place where the child was committed for trial, and not the home youth court. (See further paras 17.22–17.27 on remittal.)

Children with adult co-defendant

8.68 If jointly charged with an adult, children will have their first appearance in the adult magistrates' court – the youth court has no jurisdiction.[64] Children and Young Persons Act (CYPA) 1933 s46(1)(a) provides that:

> . . . a charge made jointly against a child or young person and a person who has attained the age of eighteen years shall be heard by a magistrates' court other than a youth court.

8.69 Where a child is charged as an aider or abettor to an offence committed by an adult,[65] or where an adult is charged with aiding or abetting an offence committed by a child,[66] or where an adult and child are charged with offences 'arising out of circumstances which are the same as or connected with' each other,[67] then the adult court has jurisdiction to hear the first appearance for the child and adult, and will usually do so, but the youth court also has jurisdiction to deal with the child's first appearance.[68]

8.70 CYPA 1933 s46(1)(b) provides that:

62 PCC(S)A 2000 s8(2), (6), (7) and (8).
63 PCC(S)A 2000 s8(2)(a).
64 CYPA 1933 s46(1)(a).
65 CYPA 1963 s18(a).
66 CYPA 1933 s46(1)(b).
67 CYPA 1963 s18(b).
68 CYPA 1963 s18; CYPA 1933 s46(1)(b).

> ... where a child or young person is charged with an offence, the charge may be heard by a magistrates' court which is not a youth court if a person who has attained the age of eighteen years is charged at the same time with aiding, abetting, causing, procuring, allowing or permitting that offence ...

And a similar provision is found in CYPA 1933 s18(1), which states:

> ... a magistrates' court which is not a youth court may hear an information against a child or young person if he is charged–
> (a) with aiding, abetting, causing, procuring, allowing or permitting an offence with which a person who has attained the age of eighteen is charged at the same time; or
> (b) with an offence arising out of circumstances which are the same as or connected with those giving rise to an offence with which a person who has attained the age of eighteen is charged at the same time."

8.71 See paras 8.104–8.119 on allocation; and children with adult co-defendant – to decide upon the appropriate court for the trial.

No available youth court sitting

8.72 The first appearance will usually happen at the youth court, unless the child appears in custody and there is no youth court available that day, or if the child has a joint first appearance with an adult co-defendant (see paras 8.68–8.71 above on children with adult co-defendant). Unless a child is jointly charged with an adult, the adult magistrates' court has no jurisdiction to hear a charge against a child,[69] other than to decide bail.[70] The adult magistrates' court will remit the case to the appropriate youth court and decide upon bail. The magistrates should consider an order for anonymity under Youth Justice and Criminal Evidence Act 1999 s45 (see paras 14.27–14.29 on anonymity) as there will be no automatic reporting restrictions in place. Further the court should consider any appropriate modifications (see chapter 4 on modifications).

8.73 It is often possible to constitute a youth bench on the day if the appropriate magistrates are available in other courts, or a district judge. This has the advantage that the public gallery would be cleared and automatic reporting restrictions would apply.

69 CYPA 1933 s46(1).
70 CYPA 1933 s46(2).

First appearance

Overview

8.74 At the first appearance, the court will usually take a plea and make any decision on allocation. The trial will take place in the youth court unless the child has an adult co-defendant or the child is charged with a grave crime and jurisdiction is declined (see paras 8.97–8.158 below on allocation). If the matter is further adjourned, the court will consider bail.

Duty to notify the local authority

8.75 It is the duty of whoever brings a prosecution against a child to notify both the local authority where the child lives[71] and the probation service local to the court.[72] However, failure to notify does not render the proceedings a nullity.[73] The local authority is then under a duty to provide background information about the child.[74] This is usually achieved by the YOT (who are part of the local authority) being notified and providing relevant information.

Taking instructions

8.76 At the first appearance, it will be necessary to take instructions from the child about the offence in order to advise on plea, and also about the child's background. See the first appearance checklist below at para 8.91 for relevant matters to consider. It is important that instructions are taken from the child, but that relevant information is also obtained from the YOT, and any adult that accompanies the child (see chapter 3 for relevance of background).

Parents and guardians

8.77 Parents, guardians or social workers are not subject to legal privilege.[75] Therefore, it may not be appropriate to take full instructions from the child in their presence. Further, provided the child is fit to plead, the defence lawyer is bound to act on the child's instructions, not those of

71 CYPA 1969 s5(8).

72 CYPA 1969 s34.

73 *R v Marsh* [1997] 1 WLR 649; *DPP v Cottier* [1996] 1 WLR 826.

74 CYPA 1969 s9.

75 *R v Marcus Brown*, 21 May 1999, CA, unreported.

the child's parent or guardian. This may be practically difficult, especially when dealing with very young children, however it will usually be appropriate for instructions to be taken from the child without the child's parent or guardian present. The defence lawyer may want to explain to the parent or guardian the need to speak to the child alone due to the issues with privilege. Each situation is different and ultimately the defence lawyer will have to decide how to best handle a situation with a young child who may be uncomfortable speaking to a defence lawyer without his or her parent or guardian present.

8.78 This does not, of course, preclude some discussions taking place with the parent or guardian. However, as the communications between the defence lawyer and child are subject to legal professional privilege, it will ultimately be up to the child what he or she wishes to disclose to his or her parent or guardian. (See also paras 6.129–6.130 on appropriate adults and legal privilege in the police station.)

Deciding on plea

8.79 Having taken instructions, the defence lawyer should consider whether it is appropriate for a plea to be taken immediately. The court will expect to take a plea at the first hearing. The Youth Court Bench Book states:[76]

> The court must take a plea from the child or young person. This obligation does not depend on the extent of initial details, disclosure of unused evidence or the grant of legal aid.

8.80 Further, the Youth Court Bench Book emphasises the need for matters to be dealt with:

> . . . as expeditiously as possible as is consistent with the interests of justice and the fair trial provisions in Article 6 of the European Convention on Human Rights.[77]

8.81 Therefore, defence lawyers should not cause undue delay, nor ask for the taking of the plea to be delayed without good reason, as they should expect to be carefully scrutinised. Equally it is not appropriate to take a plea at all costs. In particular, the defence lawyer should consider:

- whether there any issues at to the child's capacity which means it will be necessary to ascertain whether the child is fit to plead and effectively participate before proceeding with the case (see chapter 4 on effective participation);

76 Effective Case Management, para 19.

77 Essential Case Management, Youth Court Bench Book, para 1.

- whether the prosecution is necessary or whether there is a possibility of an alternative means of dealing with the offence, such as an out-of-court disposal. This may be particularly relevant if the defence lawyer is now aware of issues that might affect the decision to prosecute that the Crown Prosecution Service (CPS) were not aware of at the time. (See chapter 7 on out of court disposals and decisions to prosecute.)

8.82 In these scenarios it may be appropriate to ask the court to adjourn proceedings before plea, in order to allow further enquiries or representations to be made (see paras 7.29 and 7.119 on decisions to prosecute). See further discussion on adjournments below at paras 8.92–8.96. Where the court refuses such an application, the defence should consider entering no plea, in which scenario the court would enter a not guilty plea on the child's behalf and continue as if a not guilty plea had been entered. The defence lawyer should consider the impact on any credit for a guilty plea in that scenario (see paras 17.118–17.134 on credit for guilty plea and sentencing) and that referral orders are not available following a finding of guilt. The defence lawyer also discuss with the child and the child's parents the issue of costs if convicted after trial.

8.83 If a plea is entered, and it later transpires that it should not have been (for example, that the child is not fit to plead, or has a defence) then the defence should consider whether that plea could be vacated. See further paras 8.159–8.160 on vacating pleas.

Procedure at first appearance

Overview

8.84 The procedure of the first appearance in the youth court has many similarities to that of a first appearance in the adult court. The Criminal Procedure Rules apply equally to the youth court as they do in the adult magistrates' court and Crown Court. CrimPR Part 7 deals with starting a prosecution in the adult magistrates' court, and Part 8 with initial disclosure. However, the layout and formality of the court is different – for example, the court will usually speak directly to both the child and the child's parent or guardian. There are different considerations when deciding bail and allocation. As the court is obliged to consider the welfare of the child,[78] it is more likely that information as to the child's background may have a material effect on proceedings.

78 CYPA 1933 s44.

8.85 For a list of matters to consider at a child's first appearance, see the first appearance checklist at para 8.91 below.

Disclosure

8.86 CrimPR Part 8 sets out what the prosecution is required to disclose prior to the first hearing. In cases where the child has been held in custody prior to the hearing, this is just a summary of the case against the child, and a list of previous convictions. Where the child appears on bail, the prosecutor is required to provide more of the evidence in the case, including details of what was said in interview, and any available statements from witnesses or victims that may be relevant.[79]

8.87 Papers are usually served electronically and where the case has been identified as likely to result in a guilty plea, the prosecution will often serve the police summary only and not include any evidence. However, when advising children who may have communication needs or other difficulties, the defence lawyer may not be able to properly advise without a fuller understanding of the prosecution case. This may require the prosecution to provide futher evidence.

Guilty pleas

8.88 If the child pleads guilty the court will consider sentence, and the defence lawyer should be prepared to deal with sentence at the same hearing. The Youth Court Bench Book encourages the court to pass sentence on the same day if possible (see paras 17.67–17.68). A pre-sentence report is required before imposing a detention and training order (DTO) or youth rehabilitation order (see paras 17.65–17.66). If the court is proposing to use a previous report, careful thought should be given as to whether all relevant matters are covered by that report. (See paras 17.103–17.104 and 17.81–17.111 on pre-sentence reports generally.)

Not guilty pleas

8.89 If the plea is not guilty, the court will deal with venue if appropriate (see paras 8.97–8.117 on allocation below), and if the matter remains in the youth court then a preparation for effective trial form will need to be filled out[80].

8.90 Finally the court will consider bail. See chapter 11 on bail.

79 CrimPR Part 8.3.

80 www.justice.gov.uk/courts/procedure-rules/criminal/docs/october-2015/cm001england-eng.pdf.

First appearance checklists for defence lawyer

8.91 There are a number of considerations for a defence lawyer at the first appearance. The defence lawyer is likely to have a meeting with his or her client at court for the first time. Below are two checklists – the background checklist sets out considerations for any defence lawyer meeting the child for the first time, which will often be at the first appearance and includes issues that the defence lawyer should check with the child and/or their parent or guardian in order to advise on plea, procedure and other relevant considerations. The first appearance checklist is specific to the first appearance hearing including a list of potential questions for the youth offending team (YOT).

Background checklist (when meeting client for first time/ taking instructions)

Child's background

Family

- Child's personal circumstances: who is in the child's family?
- Who does the child live with?
- Parental occupations?
- Issues at home such as drugs, alcohol or violence?
- Does the child have siblings who have achieved/been in trouble with the police?

Health

- Doctor's name and contact details?
- Any medical conditions or diagnosis, including any mental illness?
- Is the child currently on any medication?
- Has the child ever experienced or witnessed any trauma?
- Has the child ever lost consciousness or suffered a traumatic brain injury?

Education

- Is the child at school or college? Does the child get any extra help at school? Does the child have an education, health and care plan (EHCP)?
- What is the child's educational history? Are they doing well at school, what achievements have there been? Have there been exclusions or issues over non-attendance?
- What other activities does the child engage in during his or her week? Sport? Music? Work?

Previous offending

- Has the child been in trouble with the police before? If so are the details (offence, date, disposal etc) available?

Social services

- Is the child or the family known to social services, have a social worker or any extra support? Or have they been in the past? If so:
  - Who is the current social worker, and what relationship do they have with him/her?
  - What is their care plan or pathway plan?
  - What is the history and number of placements? (if relevant)
  - What is the reason for them being looked after? (if relevant)

Exploitation

- Are there any reasons to be concerned about trafficking, gang or sexual exploitation?

Immigration

- What is the child's immigration status?

Other issues

- Does the child have a stable address?
- Any other questions the child or supporting adult may have.
- As a result of any these questions, should the child be referred to another agency (for example immigration solicitor, the National Referral Mechanism (see paras 13.48–13.51), or the local authority.

Things to consider about the offence:

- Was it necessary to prosecute or is this suitable for out of court disposal, especially if the child made full admissions in interview (or will accept guilt now) and has no previous convictions? (See chapter 7 on out of court disposals and on decisions to prosecute.)
- Are there factors that the CPS may not have been aware of, that should be considered in deciding whether to prosecute?
- What defences might be available? For information on how being a child may affect defences see paras 13.14–13.71 on defences.
- Was the offence committed in a residential children's home? If so see the ten-point checklist about prosecuting looked-after children (see paras 7.116–7.127).

First appearance checklist

- Consider the background checklist.
- How old is the child? Is there a dispute as to age? Is the child close to 18? (See further paras 2.24–2.55 on age-disputed defendants and paras 2.8–2.15 on turning a significant age threshold).
- Does the child or their parents or supporting adult need an interpreter?
- Does the child have an appropriate supporting adult? (See paras 8.26–8.41 above on supporting adults.)

Speak to YOT:

  - Does the YOT know the child? Do they have any relevant information to the above questions, or other relevant information?
  - Is the child currently on an order? If so, how is that going?
  - What is the YOT's position on bail/bail conditions/sentencing?

- Is the child charged with a serious offence such as murder or a grave crime? See paras 8.120–8.150 on serious offences and grave crimes
- Is the child charged with a specified offence? (The court may consider dangerousness see paras 8.145–8.146 on dangerousness.)
- Is the child jointly charged with an adult? If so, what is the anticipated plea of the adult? (See paras 8.104–8.119 on child with adult co-defendant.)
- Is the child already on bail or does he or she need a bail application? If he or she on bail, what are the bail conditions and are they appropriate? (See further chapter 11 on bail.)
- If the child requires a bail application, do they need to be housed outside of their usual area? If so confirm this is being adequately case managed by the 'home' and 'host' YOTs.

In court:

1) Anonymity is automatic in youth court. An application for reporting restrictions should be considered if:
   a) the case is in adult magistrates' court for first appearance;
   b) the matter is sent to the Crown Court;
   c) the proceedings are for a civil injunction.
   (See chapter 14 on anonymity.)

2) Does the child have appropriate support/modifications?
   a) Is the child in a secure dock, and is that appropriate?
   b) Is the child sitting next to a parent or guardian/supporting adult who will assist the child in court?
   c) If not what arrangement could facilitate the attendance of a supporting adult?
   d) What other arrangements could be made to facilitate the child's participation?
3) Case management:
   a) If there are concerns that the child may not be fit to plead – he or she should not enter a plea. Thought should be given to a Ground Rules Hearing and an intermediary if appropriate. (See chapter 4 on effective participation and fitness to plead.)
   b) If there are concerns the CPS should not have prosecuted – the defence should ask for an adjournment for them to reconsider (see paras 8.92–8.96 on adjournments).
   c) If extra reports are needed to ascertain fitness to plead/effective participation or the need for extra modifications it will usually be appropriate to alert the court especially if extra time is needed to obtain a report.
   d) If the child is charged with a grave crime (paras 8.126–8.144), a specified offence (paras 8.145–8.150) or has an adult co-defendant (paras 8.104–8.119) the court will need to consider where any trial is heard.
4) Are there any modifications or special measures that will be needed for trial – for the defendant or defence witnesses? These should be raised at the first appearance if possible. (See paras 4.31–4.55 on modifications and special measures.)

Adjournments

8.92 The principles for a court to consider an adjournment are set out in *CPS v Picton*,[81] which emphasises that an application to adjourn will be rigorously scrutinised, and that delays bring the law into disrepute. This is emphasised in *Visvaratnam v Brent Magistrates' Court*,[82]

81 [2006] EWHC 1108 (Admin).
82 [2009] EWHC 3017 (Admin).

which states that an application to adjourn will be dismissed unless necessary and just, and that the prosecution could not assume that the court would adjourn a trial when they were not trial ready, due to their own failings.

8.93 While both cases above concerned trials, the principles apply to any proceedings. These cases were also concerning adults, and do not deal with any separate considerations for children. The Youth Court Bench Book makes it clear that the need for speedy justice is particularly important for children.[83] However this may need to be balanced against the need to ensure the court has all relevant information and the decision to prosecute has been appropriately scrutinised.

8.94 At para 6 of Effective Case Management, the Youth Court Bench Book deals with adjournments:

> 6. When dealing with applications to adjourn, courts should consider the following:
>
> a. Unnecessary adjournments should be avoided.
> b. Every application should be examined and the party requesting it should be asked to justify it.
> c. Any adjournments granted should be for the shortest possible period to allow for progress.
> d. The reason for any adjournment should be made clear and noted on the court file so that all parties know what is expected next time.
> e. Justice delayed may be justice denied in respect of all parties, not just the child or young person.

8.95 However, as stated in *Picton*[84] the factors to consider will depend on the circumstances of each case. In dealing with any application relating to children, the court has extra duties over and above those of adults, to consider the welfare[85] and best interests of the child.[86]

8.96 Where the adjournment is necessary and agreed by both the prosecution and defence, and the defendant is on bail, then the application for adjournment can be dealt with by the legal adviser under delegated powers. Hence, if there is a busy court list, this application can be dealt with when the bench are in deliberation.[87]

83 See the Effective Case Management section of the Youth Court Bench Book.

84 Para 9(h).

85 CYPA 1933 s44.

86 United Nations Convention on the Rights of the Child (UNCRC) Article 3.

87 Justices' Clerks' Rules 2005 SI No 545 r2.

Allocation/mode of trial

Presumption for trial to be heard in the youth court

8.97 There is a presumption that any criminal case which has a child as a defendant should be heard in the youth court. This is established by MCA 1980 s4:

> Where a person under the age of 18 years appears or is brought before a magistrates' court on an information charging him with an indictable offence he shall, subject to sections 51 and 51A of the Crime and Disorder Act 1998 and to sections 24A and 24B be tried summarily.

This is emphasised by the Sentencing Guidelines Council, in their guidelines: *Sentencing children and young people: definitive guideline*, which states:[88]

> Subject to the exceptions noted below, cases involving children and young people should be tried in the youth court. It is the court which is best designed to meet their specific needs. A trial in the Crown Court with the inevitably greater formality and greatly increased number of people involved (including a jury and the public) should be reserved for the most serious cases.

8.98 This follows the case of *R (H, A and O) v Southampton Youth Court*,[89] which emphasises the need for children, especially those under 15, to be tried in the youth court where at all possible.

8.99 The case set out the following three principles:

> 1. The general policy of the legislature is that those who are under 18 years of age and in particular children of under 15 years of age should, wherever possible, be tried in the youth court. It is that court which is best designed to meet their specific needs. A trial in the Crown Court with the inevitably greater formality and greatly increased number of people involved (including a jury and the public) should be reserved for the most serious cases.
>
> 2. It is a further policy of the legislature that, generally speaking, first-time offenders aged 12 to 14 and all offenders under 12 should not be detained in custody and decisions as to jurisdiction should have regard to the fact that the exceptional power to detain for grave offences should not be used to water down the general principle. Those under 15 will rarely attract a period of detention and, even more rarely, those who are under 12.
>
> 3. In each case the court should ask itself whether there is a real prospect, having regard to his or her age, that this defendant whose

88 At para 2.1.

89 [2004] EWHC 2912 (Admin).

> case they are considering might require a sentence of, or in excess of, two years or, alternatively, whether although the sentence might be less than two years, there is some unusual feature of the case which justifies declining jurisdiction . . .

Allocation procedure

8.100 There are two situations where the court will have the discretion to try the child somewhere other than the youth court: where the child has an adult co-defendant; (see chapter 9 children in the adult magistrates court) and where the offence falls into one of those listed at CDA 1998 s51A(3).

8.101 The allocation decision can be decided by a single magistrate.[90] When dealing with a sexual offence, the procedure should be overseen by an authorised district judge.[91] Allocation procedures can take place in the defendant's absence if legally represented, and the defendant's disorderly conduct means that he or she is removed from court.[92]

8.102 In accordance with CrimPR r9.13, the court must first read and explain the allegation to the child, and the procedure that is about to take place. Then the child is asked what they intend to plead. If they plead guilty, that plea is recorded and the court makes a finding of guilt. The child can still be sent to the Crown Court for sentence under PCC(S)A 2000 s3B. Where the child enters no plea or pleads not guilty, the court will then hear representations and proceed to decide the appropriate venue.

8.103 There are three flowcharts in the *Sentencing children and young people: definitive guideline*, which set out the different procedures depending on whether the child has an adult co-defendant, or is charged with a serious offence such as a grave crime, or both, and whether the adult is charged with an indictable only offence or either way offence.

Child with adult co-defendant

8.104 A child may be jointly charged with an adult, or one may be charged as a principal and the other as an aider or abettor, or with an offence related to the offence with which the adult is charged. As to where the first appearance will be heard (see above paras 8.68–8.71 on determining which court – child with adult co-defendant).

90 MCA 1980 s24D(1).

91 Sexual Offences in the Youth Court, a protocol issued on 31 March 2010, paras 12 and 13.

92 CrimPR r9.2(3)(a).

8.105 Where the court decides that the adult's case will be heard in the Crown Court, the court may send the child to the Crown Court along with the adult if the child is charged with an indictable offence. CDA 1998 s51(7) provides that:

> Where–
> (a) the court sends an adult ('A') for trial under subsection (1), (3) or (5) above; and
> (b) a child or young person appears or is brought before the court on the same or a subsequent occasion charged jointly with A with an indictable offence for which A is sent for trial under subsection (1), (3) or (5) above, or an indictable offence which appears to the court to be related to that offence, the court shall, if it considers it necessary in the interests of justice to do so, send the child or young person forthwith to the Crown Court for trial for the indictable offence.

Interests of justice

8.106 The court will have to decide whether it is in the interests of justice for the child to have a joint trial with the adult or a separate trial in the youth court.

8.107 The Sentencing Council's Allocation Guidelines (2015) provides a non-exhaustive list of factors to consider whether it is in the interests of justice for a joint trial:

> 2. Examples of factors that should be considered when deciding whether it is in the interests of justice include:
> - whether separate trials will cause injustice to witnesses or to the case as a whole
> - the younger the youth, the greater the desirability that the youth be tried in the youth court;
> - a substantial gap in age militates in favour of the youth being tried in the youth court;
> - the lack of maturity of the youth;
> - the relative culpability of the youth compared with the adult;
> - the lack of previous convictions on the part of the youth.

8.108 Additionally, the court should consider the presumption that cases involving children will remain in the youth court (see paras 8.97–8.99). Some of the case-law concerning whether or not a case involving a grave crime should remain in the youth court or be allocated to the Crown Court, may also assist (see paras 8.126–8.144). Where the court decides that the case should be heard as a joint trial in a adult court, appropriate modifications should be made to accommodate the child (see paras 4.31–4.55 on modifications and special measures).

Procedure

8.109 If the offence is not a serious offence for the child under CDA 1998 s51A (see para 8.120 below) then the court will first deal with the allocation of the adult. The court will first deal with plea before venue for the adult, and where it is a triable either way offence, will make a decision as to venue for the adult. A plea will then be taken from the child.[93] Next, the court will consider which court will hear the child's case.[94]

8.110 If the child pleads guilty, the court will treat the child as if there has been a finding of guilt[95] and either proceed to sentence[96] or remit to the youth court for sentence, or commit the matter to the Crown Court for sentence if PCC(S)A 2000 s3B applies (see paras 17.11–17.13 on committal for sentence).

8.111 If the child pleads not guilty and the adult has pleaded guilty, then the child will be sent to the youth court for trial.

8.112 Where both the child and the adult plead not guilty, the court will go on to consider whether the trial will take place jointly with the adult – which will be either in the adult magistrates' court or in the Crown Court, depending on the venue decision for the adult. If the court decides upon separate trials, then the child will have his or her trial in the youth court. Whether the adult is having his or her trial in the adult magistrates' court or in the Crown Court, the above factors (at para 8.107) will determine whether a joint trial or separate trials are appropriate.

8.113 Where the offences are summary only, the same procedure and criteria apply – there will be no allocation decision for the adult, but pleas will be taken, and where both adult and child plead not guilty then a decision will be made as to separate trials or a joint trial.

8.114 If the offence does fall under CDA 1998 s51A for the child (see paras 8.120–8.125), then the court will first deal with the child's plea before venue procedure and go on to decide whether to send the child to the Crown Court under section 51A.[97] Where the court does so decide, then the adult will also be sent to the Crown Court if he or she pleads not guilty, and no mode of trial procedure will take place for the adult. Should the adult plead guilty, then the court will proceed

93 *Sentencing children and young people: definitive guideline*, flowcharts pp 12–13.
94 CrimPR r9.13.
95 CrimPR r9.13(5).
96 See para 9.20 above for magistrates' courts powers of sentence.
97 *Sentencing children and young people: definitive guideline*, flowcharts pp 12–13.

to sentence or commit the adult for sentence if their sentencing powers are insufficient.[98]

8.115 Where, however the court decides not to send the child to the Crown Court under section 51A, then they proceed as above as if it were not a serious offence, and consider the position of the adult before going on to consider the appropriate court for the child.

8.116 The child does not need to be in court at the same time as the adult with whom the child is jointly charged – if the child later appears at a youth court after the adult has been sent to the Crown Court for trial, the youth court still has the power to send the child for trial under section 51(7).[99]

8.117 If the first appearance is heard in the adult magistrates' court and the court sends the adult but not the child to the Crown Court, the adult magistrates' court must then either try the child in the magistrates' court or remit the child to the youth court for trial.[100]

Severance

8.118 The CrimPD I states:[101]

> . . . a vulnerable defendant, especially one who is young, is to be tried jointly with one who is not, the court should consider at the plea hearing, or at a case management hearing in a magistrates' court, whether the vulnerable defendant should be tried on his own.

The court should so order:

> . . . if satisfied that a fair trial cannot be achieved by use of appropriate special measures or other support for the defendant.

8.119 However, once the child has entered a plea in the Crown Court, a successful application for severance would only result in a separate trial for the child in the Crown Court, as there is no power to remit back to the youth court.[102] It may sometimes be appropriate to apply to sever the child's case to enable a separate trial. Particularly for example in cases where trafficking would appropriately be raised.

98 CrimPR r9.13.

99 *R v Coventry City Magistrates' Court ex p M* (1992) JP 809.

100 MCA 1980 s29(2).

101 Crim PD para 3G.1.

102 *R (W) v Leeds Crown Court* [2011] EWHC 2326 (Admin).

Serious offences

Overview

8.120 When a child is charged with certain serious offences, the youth court will need to decide whether the case should be sent to the Crown Court. CDA 1998 s51A provides that:

> (2) Where a child or young person appears or is brought before a magistrates' court ('the court') charged with an offence and any of the conditions mentioned in subsection (3) below is satisfied, the court shall send him forthwith to the Crown Court for trial for the offence.
>
> (3) Those conditions are–
>
> (a) that the offence falls within subsection (12) below;
>
> (b) that the offence is such as is mentioned in subsection (1) of section 91 of the Powers of Criminal Courts (Sentencing) Act 2000 (other than one mentioned in paragraph (d) below in relation to which it appears to the court as mentioned there) and the court considers that if he is found guilty of the offence it ought to be possible to sentence him in pursuance of subsection (3) of that section;
>
> (c) that notice is given to the court under section 51B or 51C below in respect of the offence;
>
> (d) that the offence is a specified offence (within the meaning of section 224 of the Criminal Justice Act 2003) and it appears to the court that if he is found guilty of the offence the criteria for the imposition of a sentence under [section 226B] of that Act would be met.

Offences where child must be sent to Crown Court

8.121 CDA 1998 s51A(12) provides that:

> (12) An offence falls within this subsection if–
>
> (a) it is an offence of homicide;
>
> (b) each of the requirements of section 51A(1) of the Firearms Act 1968 would be satisfied with respect to–
>
> (i) the offence; and
>
> (ii) the person charged with it,
>
> if he were convicted of the offence; or
>
> (c) section 29(3) of Violent Crime Reduction Act 2006 (minimum sentences in certain cases of using someone to mind a weapon) would apply if he were convicted of the offence.

Murder and offences of homicide

8.122 A child charged with murder must be sent to the Crown Court. However an 'Offence of homicide' is not defined in the Act. ' Attempted murder' is treated as murder (Criminal Attempts Act 1981 s2(2)(c)) for allocation for adults, and therefore arguably should fall into this category. Offences of causing or allowing the death of a child or vulnerable adult (contrary to Domestic Violence, Crime and Victims Act 2004 s5) are offences of homicide.[103]

8.123 A child must to be sent to the Crown Court if charged with a firearms offence where the child would be subject to the mandatory minimum sentence of three years. The mandatory minimum sentence applies to children who are 16 or 17 years old at the time when the offence was committed, provided it was committed after the relevant provision came into force. The mandatory minimum sentences are provided for under Firearms Act 1968 s51A or Violent Crime Reduction Act 2006 s29.

Notices in serious complex fraud cases

8.124 Notices can be given under Firearms Act 1968 s51B (serious and complex fraud cases), where a notice is given by a designated authority (Director of Public Prosecutions (DPP), secretary of state or Director of the Serious Fraud Office) in relation to an indictable offence.[104]

8.125 Where any of these provisions under CDA 1998 s51A (3)(a), (b) or (d) apply, the child must be sent to the Crown Court regardless of plea. Therefore, no plea is taken and the child is sent to the Crown Court.

Grave crimes

What is a grave crime?

8.126 CDA 1998 s51A(2) as set out above allows the court to allocate a case to the Crown Court where the offence charged is mentioned in PCC(S)A 2000 s91(1). These are:

(a) an offence punishable in the case of a person aged 21 or over with imprisonment for 14 years or more, not being an offence the sentence for which is fixed by law;

103 Domestic Violence, Crime and Victims Act 2004 s6(5).

104 See CrimPR r9.6.

(b) an offence under section 3 of the Sexual Offences Act 2003 (sexual assault); or
(c) an offence under section 13 of the 2003 Act (child sex offences committed by children or young persons); or
(d) an offence under section 25 of the 2003 Act (sexual activity with a child family member); or
(e) an offence under section 26 of the 2003 Act (inciting a child family member to engage in sexual activity).

8.127 PCC(S)A 2000 s91(1B) and (1C) also deal with firearms offences, however children charged with those offences will be sent to the Crown Court under CDA 1998 s51A(3)(a) and (12) – see para 8.123.

8.128 For children charged with any of the offences listed at (a)–(e), the court has a discretion as to whether to send the case to the Crown Court or retain jurisdiction in the youth court.

Grave crimes – procedure

8.129 As the court has a discretion as to whether or not to send the child to the Crown Court, a plea is taken first.

8.130 Where the child pleads guilty and the court nevertheless consider that there is a real prospect of a sentence in excess of two years, the court may commit to the Crown Court under PCC(S)A 2000 s3B for sentence.

8.131 Where the child pleads not guilty, the court will then go on to decide whether to allocate to the Crown Court under CDA 1998 s51A '*if there is a real prospect of a sentence in excess of two years*', or retain the matter in the youth court. The court will take in account of the new allocation guidelines and its powers to commit for sentence.[105] Hence, the court can retain cases even where the sentence *could* exceed two years.

8.132 The court should hear representations from both prosecution and defence.[106] The court is entitled to know about the child's previous convictions in determining the likely sentence,[107] but will not hear evidence about the offence.[108] Where the court retains jurisdiction, the child should be warned that the court may still commit the case to the Crown Court for sentence (called a s53 warning).

105 Criminal Justice and Courts Act 2015 s53.

106 Sentencing Council, *Sentencing children and young people: definitive guideline*, 2017, para 2.10.

107 *R (Tullet) v Medway Magistrates' Court* (2003) 167 JP 541.

108 *South Hackney Juvenile Court, ex p RB and CB* (1983) 77 Cr App R 294.

Grave crimes – Crown Court or youth court?

8.133 There is a presumption that children be tried in the youth court, even for serious crimes (see above paras 8.97–8.99).

8.134 The test for whether a matter should be sent to the Crown Court was set out in *R (H, A and O) v Southampton Youth Court*: (the three principles are set out in para 8.99)[109]

> In each case the court should ask itself whether there is a real prospect, having regard to his or her age, that this defendant whose case they are considering might require a sentence of, or in excess of, two years or, alternatively, whether although the sentence might be less than two years, there is some unusual feature of the case which justifies declining jurisdiction . . .

8.135 This was emphasised further in *R (B) v Norfolk Youth Court*[110] by Cox J:

> . . . a trial in the Crown Court should be reserved for those most serious and . . . exceptional cases, which truly merit the description 'grave crime.

8.136 The presumption of hearing cases involving child defendants in the youth court has been extended by the introduction of Criminal Justice and Courts Act 2015 s53 which inserted the power to commit a case after a trial in the youth court to the crown court for sentence (PCC(S) A 2000 ss3B and 3C). This enables the youth court to take a broader view at the early stage when they are deciding which court is appropriate. While previously it was necessary to take the prosecution case at its highest, this greater flexibility means that that is no longer appropriate in deciding venue.[111]

8.137 The *Sentencing children and young people: definitive guideline* states: [112]

> In most cases it is likely to be impossible to decide whether there is a real prospect that a sentence in excess of two years' detention will be imposed without knowing more about the facts of the case and the circumstances of the child or young person. In those circumstances the youth court should retain jurisdiction and commit for sentence if it is of the view, having heard more about the facts and the circumstances of the child or young person, that its powers of sentence are insufficient.

And further:

> Children and young people should only be sent for trial or committed for sentence to the Crown Court when charged with or found guilty of

109 [2004] EWHC 2912 (Admin).

110 [2013] EWHC 1459 (Admin).

111 *R (DPP) v South Tyneside Youth Court* [2015] EWHC 1455 (Admin).

112 Para 2.10.

an offence of such gravity that a custodial sentence substantially exceeding two years is a realistic possibility. For children aged 10 or 11, and children/young people aged 12–14 who are not persistent offenders, the court should take into account the normal prohibition on imposing custodial sentences.

8.138 It was suggested in *AM*[113] by Lord Bingham CJ that where a child is charged with more than one offence, but not all offences are ones to which PCC(S)A 2000 s91 applies, the court can consider the seriousness of the totality of the offending when considering whether jurisdiction should be retained. However, sentences under section 91 can only be passed in relation to those offences to which the section applies. Therefore, it is the authors' view that this approach should be treated with caution, as the court should be considering what sentence is realistically likely to be passed.

Grave crimes – children under 15

8.139 A child under 15 can only receive a detention and training order (DTO) if the child is a persistent offender, and it is not available for any children aged ten to 11. For such children, the youth court cannot pass a custodial sentence, and the only option to pass a sentence of detention is under PCC(S)A 2000 s91 in the Crown Court. The definition of persistent offender is addressed at paras 21.76–21.78 on persistent offenders.

8.140 While the Crown Court usually passes a sentence of detention under section 91 of two years or more, it can pass sentences of any length, including sentences under two years. However, it is unusual,[114] and as the case of *H, A and O* (see para 8.134) makes it clear, for those children for whom a DTO is not a possibility, the test for allocating cases there remains the same: whether there is a real prospect the child will receive a sentence of two years or more. It is not appropriate for the youth court to simply conclude that custody is appropriate and decline jurisdiction on that basis. They must form the view that the likely custodial sentence will be two or more years in length, taking into account their very young age. And therefore it is very rare that such children will be allocated to the Crown Court.

8.141 There is a presumption against custody for such children, and it will be rare that the Crown Court would exercise its powers to sentence them to detention of less than two years.

113 [1998] 1 All ER 874.

114 *R v Brown* [1999] 1 Cr App R(S) 132.

8.142 This is mirrored in the Youth Court Bench Book:[115] Jurisdiction and Grave Crimes – A structured approach, which states:[116]

> The court should determine whether, if convicted, a sentence beyond its powers should be available. (A sentence exceeding two years in the case of 10–11 year olds and 12–14 year old non-persistent offenders, and substantially more than two years in the case of 12–14 year old persistent offenders and 15–17 year olds).

8.143 The High Court has repeatedly reiterated that it is only the most serious cases where a committal to the Crown Court can be justified for children under 15. In *R (B) v Norfolk Youth Court*[117] the court quashed the decision of the youth court who had declined jurisdiction for the 13-year-old defendant, who was accused of holding a knife to the victim during a robbery, on the grounds that a sentence of over two years' detention would have been manifestly excessive and therefore the case should be heard in the youth court. This case follows *R (G) v Llanelli Magistrates Court*[118] and is cited with approval in *R (T) v Bromley Youth Court,*[119] both of which are further examples of children under 15 accused of robbery offences.

8.144 When dealing with the case of an 11-year-old whose case was allocated to the Crown Court in respect of a sexual offence, the Mrs Justice Andrews giving judgment in *R (BH) v Llandudno Youth Court*[120] went as far to say:

> The tariff that an adult offender might receive for an offence of this nature affords no guidance to the sentence that a child, especially a child who was 11 at the time of the offence, is likely to receive.

The judgement cited with approval a number of High Court authorities concerning children under 15 charged with sexual offences where the decision to send them to the Crown Court was quashed, including: *R v Southampton Youth Court ex p W*[121] and *R (W) v Thetford Youth Justices.*[122]

115 Youth Court Bench Book, published by the Judicial College (August 2017).
116 At para 17j.
117 [2013] EWHC 1459 (Admin).
118 [2006] EWHC 1413 (Admin).
119 [2014] EWHC 577 (Admin).
120 [2014] EWHC 1833 (Admin).
121 [2002] EWHC 1640 (Admin).
122 [2003] 1 Cr App R (S) 67.

Dangerousness

8.145 As provided by CDA 1998 s51A(3)(d), where the child is charged with a specified serious offence and the court considers that the dangerousness criteria under CJA 2003 s226B have been met, then the child will be sent to the Crown Court before taking a plea. However, should the court not be sure whether the criteria have been met, the youth court should not exercise this power, as the case can later be sent to the Crown Court if the court having learned more about the case considers it to be appropriate under PCC(S)A 2000 s3C (see paras 17.14–17.15). In most cases, an assessment of dangerousness will not be appropriate until after conviction. The child can then be committed for sentence if the conditions are met.[123]

8.146 This is dealt with at paras 2.3–2.7 of the sentencing guidelines, in particular para 2.7 which states:

> In anything but the most serious cases it may be impossible for the court to form a view as to whether the child or young person would meet the criteria of the dangerous offender provisions without greater knowledge of the circumstances of the offence and the child or young person. In those circumstances jurisdiction for the case should be retained in the youth court. If, following a guilty plea or a finding of guilt, the dangerousness criteria appear to be met then the child or young person should be committed for sentence.

Specified offences which are not grave crimes

8.147 Specified offences are defined in CJA 2003 s224(1) and are listed in full in CJA 2003 Sch 15, which includes all indictable only and either way offences of sex or violence. CJA 2003 s226B states that:

> (1) This section applies where–
> (a) a person aged under 18 is convicted of a specified offence (whether the offence was committed before or after this section comes into force),
> (b) the court considers that there is a significant risk to members of the public of serious harm occasioned by the commission by the offender of further specified offences,
> (c) the court is not required by section 226(2) to impose a sentence of detention for life under section 91 of the Sentencing Act, and
> (d) if the court were to impose an extended sentence of detention, the term that it would specify as the appropriate custodial term would be at least 4 years.

123 *CPS v South East Surrey Youth Court* [2005] EWHC 2929 (Admin).

And further:

> (4) The appropriate custodial term is the term of detention that would (apart from this section) be imposed in compliance with section 153(2).

8.148 Ordinarily the Crown Court can only pass sentences of four years or more if the offence is one listed in PCC(S)A 2000 s91, often referred to as a 'grave crime' (see paras 8.126–8.144). However, CJA 2003 s153 allows the court to pass a custodial term of any length as part of an extended sentence under CJA 2003 s226B, provided that it does not exceed the permitted maximum in the case of an adult, and further the sentence must be for the shortest period commensurate with the seriousness of the offence.

8.149 Therefore, an extended sentence is permissible for any specified offence, including those that are not grave crimes. However, the fact that the court would ordinarily be restricted to a sentence of a maximum of two years must be a strong argument against imposing such a sentence.

8.150 The Justice Clerks' Society in their paper on youth court jurisdiction[124] deal with the procedure to be used when dealing with allocation of an offence that is a specified offence but not a grave crime, and advises that the issue of dangerousness is dealt with at the outset before plea is taken, allowing the court to allocate the case to the Crown Court if it considers the child to meet the dangerousness criteria. However, given the power to commit, and the need to have a proper assessment from the YOT, it seems very unlikely that many courts will exercise their power to allocate the case to the Crown Court before trial on the basis that they consider the dangerousness criteria to be met.

Sex offences

8.151 Serious cases, including serious sexual offences, are often tried in the youth court. Following the case of *B v Richmond Youth Court*,[125] which clarified that it was appropriate to hear some rape cases in the youth court, the Rape Protocol 2007 was issued. This has been followed by the 'Sexual offences in the youth court: a protocol' issued

124 'Youth court jurisdiction: the modern approach', published by the Justices' Clerks' Society and the Senior District Judge (Chief Magistrate), July 2015.

125 [2006] EWHC 1413 (Admin).

by the Senior Presiding Judge in 2010.[126] If a serious sex offence is to be tried in the youth court it may be appropriate to apply for a certificate for assigned advocate, given that an adult charged with the same offence would have a senior advocate and litigator allocated to their case (see paras 8.167–8.173 for certificate for assigned advocate)

8.152 The protocol states that the allocation decisions concerning sexual offences should be listed before a district judge authorised to hear serious sexual offences wherever possible. This is also found at CrimPD XIII para G, annex 2, which further states that cases that are retained in the youth court will be tried by an authorised district judge if it is considered that the case is so complex or serious to require that, and in cases involving penetration or attempted penetration.

Linked offences

8.153 Where a child is being sent to the Crown Court in respect of one offence, it may be that other offences can also be dealt with at the Crown Court. Any offence that is related to the offence that has or is being sent to the Crown Court can also be sent to the Crown Court, provided that it is punishable with imprisonment (in the case of an adult) or disqualification from driving.[127] If the offence has already been sent to the Crown Court in respect of one offence, this does not prohibit the court later sending a linked offence to be joined.[128] See also Youth Court Bench Book on allocation paras 18–20.

8.154 Offences to which the child has pleaded guilty may also be sent there for sentence if the child is being sent there for other matters.[129] In respect of such offences, the Crown Court is limited to the sentence that the magistrates would have been able to impose, unless it is an offence to which PCC(S)A 2000 s91 applies and either when committing it the magistrates stated that they considered this is an offence which ought to be possible to be sentenced to section 91 detention, or the child is convicted of the linked matters he or she was sent to the Crown Court for.[130]

8.155 Where some offences are sent to the Crown Court and some are retained, there is no need to adjourn the hearing of the retained offences in the youth court.[131]

126 'Sexual offences in the youth court: a protocol', 2010.
127 CDA 1998 s51(8), s51A(4).
128 CDA 1998 s51A(5).
129 PCC(S)A 2000 s4A.
130 PCC(S)A 2000 s4A(4).
131 MCA 1980 s10(3A).

Challenges to mode of trial decisions

8.156 The decision to send (or not to send) the matter to the Crown Court for trial can be challenged by a judicial review to the administrative court.[132] The lower court should give reasons for its decision to send the matter to the Crown Court.[133]

8.157 The test applied by the High Court is whether the original decision of the lower court was 'wrong'.[134] This is not the same as allowing the High Court to consider whether it would have reached the same conclusion – it may only interfere if the original decision was wrong. However, it would appear that this is a lower threshold than the need to find the magistrates' decision to be unreasonable or perverse. For further discussion of judicial review see paras 15.46–15.50.

8.158 It is not open to the magistrates' or youth court to reopen a decision once it has been made.[135] Committal for sentence to the Crown Court after trial is permissible,[136] but the court does not have the power to reopen the matter once summary jurisdiction has been accepted in the case of children;[137] nor does the Crown Court have the power to remit the case back to the youth court for the matter to be tried in the youth court (see para 10.2 once the child has been arrainged).[138] The Crown Court can only remit back for sentence.[139]

Changing or vacating plea

8.159 A court can allow a change of plea any time prior to the court passing sentence,[140] although they have the discretion not to allow a change of plea even in the case of a defendant who was unrepresented at the time of entering the guilty plea.[141]

132 *AH* (2003) 167 JP 30; *R (DPP) v Camberwell Youth Court* [2005] 4 All ER 699.

133 *R (C) v Balham Youth Court* [2004] 1 Cr App R (S) 143, per Scott Baker LJ, at para 14.

134 *R (D) v Sheffield Youth Court* (2003) 167 JP 159, per Stanley Burnton J, at para 41.

135 MCA 1980 s25 allows for the decision to be revisited for adults only.

136 PCC(S)A 2000 s3B and s3C.

137 *R (D) v Sheffield Youth Court* (2008) 172 JP 576 per Richards LJ at para 18.

138 *R (W) v Leeds Crown Court* [2011] EWHC 2326 (Admin).

139 PCC(S)A 2000 s8(2)(a).

140 *S (an infant) v Recorder of Manchester* [1971] AC 481.

141 *R v South Tameside Magistrates' Court ex p Rowland* [1983] 3 All ER 689.

8.160 Criminal Procedure Rules 24.10 states that the defendant must serve any application on the prosecutor and court in writing as soon as possible, stating why it would be unjust not to allow the defendant to withdraw their plea and stating any evidence to be called and whether legal privilege is waived.

Case management

8.161 All cases will begin with a first appearance. The court will usually expect to take a plea, and deal with allocation at the first hearing. (See above paras 8.74–8.90 on first appearance.) If the plea is guilty, the court will usually proceed to sentence if the disposal is a referral order, fine, conditional discharge or absolute discharge. If not, the court will seek reports prior to sentence. Unlike in the adult courts, where a stand down or oral report could be prepared on the day, the practice in the youth courts is for the sentencing to be adjourned to allow the YOT time to prepare the report. In certain cases, where the defendant is on a newly imposed order which has not quite started, the YOT may ask the court to proceed with sentence by revoking the order and resentencing the defendant to a new order. The court would then be provided with the report prepared previously. (See paras 17.81–17.111 on pre-sentence reports.)

8.162 However, there will be situations where it is not possible to take a plea, and the first appearance will be adjourned and the plea and/or allocation procedure will be dealt with at a later hearing (see paras 8.92–8.96 on adjournments).

8.163 Where a not guilty plea is entered, the case will be adjourned for trial; where a guilty plea is entered, or a finding of guilt is made after trial and reports are necessary, then the matter will be adjourned for sentence.

8.164 The court also has the power to list the case for a case management hearing, where there are outstanding matters to deal with before the trial. Usually, however, the court will attempt to deal with all case management issues at the first appearance. If matters arise after the first appearance, the court will attempt to deal with them on the papers without the need for a further hearing unless the parties formally request for such a hearing.

8.165 In order to ensure effective case management, the parties are required to fill in a Preparation for Effective Trial form (PET)[142] at the

142 www.justice.gov.uk/courts/procedure-rules/criminal/docs/october-2015/cm001england-eng.pdf.

first appearance. These are required when there is to be a trial in the youth court or adult magistrates' court; they are not needed when there is a guilty plea or the matter is allocated to the Crown Court.

8.166 The Criminal Procedure Rules and criminal practice directions apply to all proceedings, including those involving children in all criminal courts. CrimPR Part 3 deals with case management.

Certificate for assigned advocates

Complex cases

8.167 If a child is being tried in the youth court in a serious and complex case, legal aid to cover the cost of two lawyers can be obtained by making an application for an assigned advocate.

8.168 Adults with serious and complex cases would usually be tried in the Crown Court and would be represented by a solicitor and an advocate (a barrister or a solicitor with higher rights), whereas even in very serious matters a child's case is often kept in the youth court. As a result, applications for Certificates for Assigned Advocates are much more common in the youth court than in the adult magistrates' court. Where the certificate is granted, legal aid will extend to the provision of an advocate in the case (this includes both barristers and solicitors with higher rights).

8.169 The legal aid regulations[143] cover applications for an assigned advocate rather than for an advocate with a particular level of expertise. The extra funding available once a Certificate for Assigned Advocate is granted should allow those representing children in relevant cases to instruct advocates with experience in youth justice and the particular area of law to which the case relates. In *R v Grant-Murray and Henry; R v McGill, Hewitt and Hewitt*[144] the Lord Chief Justice commented that:[145]

> . . . it would be difficult to conceive of an advocate being competent to act in a case involving young witnesses or defendants unless the advocate had undertaken specific training.

Cases involving sexual offences tried in the youth court are an example of the type of case in which a certificate for an assigned advocate is usually granted.

143 Criminal Legal Aid (Determinations by a Court and choice of Representative) Regulations 2013 para 16.

144 [2017] EWCA Civ 1228.

145 At para 226.

Making the application

8.170 Applications can only be made when a child is charged with an indictable offence. Applications will be granted where the relevant court determines that because there are circumstances which make the proceedings unusually grave or difficult, representation by an advocate would be desirable.

8.171 The application must be made to the court hearing the case, and the decision as to whether to grant the certificate is made by the magistrates or district judge. Applications must be:

- made in writing; and
- specify what the relevant court is being asked to determine; and
- set out the grounds for the application. This must contain information about why the case is 'unusually grave or difficult' in comparison to a 'usual case' of its type.

8.172 The court must give reasons for its decision following an application. If the application is successful, the legal aid order is amended to allow for a solicitor and an advocate to be instructed.

8.173 The Inns of Court College of Advocacy has produced a guide[146] on applying for a certificate of assigned advocate, which includes an example application.

146 https://www.icca.ac.uk/images/download/youth-justice-certificate-for-assigned-advocate-guidance-icca-guide_5.pdf.

CHAPTER 9

Children in adult magistrates' courts

Key points

- Children should rarely appear in the adult magistrates' court, and when they do their case will often be remitted to the youth court.
- When children do have their trials in the adult magistrates' court it will be because they are with an adult co-defendant.
- The court should be reminded of the practice direction for vulnerable defendants and make appropriate modifications where a child is in the adult magistrates' court.
- The court should also consider reporting restrictions, even where a child is there for a single hearing.

Introduction

9.1 Children should rarely appear in the adult magistrates' court. The court has limited jurisdiction to hear cases involving child defendants and will only do so in the two following situations:

1) where a child arrives at court in custody and there is no youth court sitting;
2) where a child is jointly charged with an adult defendant (or where their case is otherwise linked to an adult's case).

9.2 Further, the court may be asked to deal with breaches of an order that was passed by the youth court where the child has since turned 18 (see paras 20.133–20.134 on Youth Rehabilitation Orders, 'Turning a significant age threshold') or trials which started in the youth court, but where the defendant has turned 18 during proceedings. Where a defendant is a child at the start of the proceedings, but turns 18 during proceedings, the youth court has the discretion to continue with the case or to send it to the adult magistrates' court to be heard there (see paras 2.10–2.15 on turning 18 during proceedings).

9.3 Where a child is before the adult magistrates' court for any reason, consideration should be given to any modifications that should be made to allow for effective participation (see paras 4.14–4.61). Anonymity is not automatically granted, as it would be in the youth court, and therefore an application needs to be made under Youth Justice and Criminal Evidence Act (YJCEA) 1999 s45 (see further chapter 14 on anonymity).

First appearances at adult magistrates' court

9.4 A child will appear in the adult magistrates' court either because the child has an adult co-defendant, or because the child is in custody and there is no youth court sitting that day.

9.5 Where a child appears before an adult magistrates' court due to a mistaken belief that the child is an adult, the court can continue with the child's case[1] (see paras 2.16–2.18 on mistake as to age).

No youth court sitting

9.6 If a child appears in custody and there is no youth court sitting that day, then the child will appear before the adult magistrates' bench in order to decide on bail, before being adjourned to the next date that the youth court sits. See further paras 8.72–8.73. If possible, a youth bench should be constituted, for example if a district judge is sitting. Children and Young Persons Act (CYPA) 1933 s46(2) allows the adult court to hear a bail application for a child and any relevant information regarding that bail, however the court has no jurisdiction to deal with any other matters. However, there may be no youth offending team (YOT) at court to prepare a bail package. The defence lawyer should contact the YOT themselves. The court should consider reporting restrictions (paras 9.15–9.17) and modifications (paras 9.18–9.19).

Adult co-defendant

9.7 If a child appears before the adult magistrates' court with an adult co-defendant, the court must go on to decide allocation for both defendants. See paras 8.97–8.158 on allocation.

9.8 If the child is jointly charged with an adult, the child will have his or her first appearance in the adult magistrates' court – the youth court has no jurisdiction.[2] Where a child is charged as an aider or abettor to an offence committed by an adult,[3] or where an adult is charged with aiding or abetting an offence committed by a child,[4] or where an adult and child are charged with offences 'arising out of circumstances which are the same as or connected with' each other,[5]

1 CYPA 1933 s46(1)(c).
2 CYPA 1933 s46(1)(a).
3 CYPA 1963 s 18(a).
4 CYPA 1933 s46(1)(b).
5 CYPA 1933 s18(b).

then the adult court has jurisdiction to hear the first appearance for the child and adult, and will usually do so, but the youth court also has jurisdiction to deal with the child's first appearance.[6]

9.9 CYPA 1933 s46(1)(b) provides that:

> . . . where a child or young person is charged with an offence, the charge may be heard by a magistrates' court which is not a youth court if a person who has attained the age of eighteen years is charged at the same time with aiding, abetting, causing, procuring, allowing or permitting that offence . . .

And a similar provision is found in CYPA 1933 s18(1), which states:

> . . . a magistrates' court which is not a youth court may hear an information against a child or young person if he is charged–
>
> (a) with aiding, abetting, causing, procuring, allowing or permitting an offence with which a person who has attained the age of eighteen is charged at the same time; or
>
> (b) with an offence arising out of circumstances which are the same as or connected with those giving rise to an offence with which a person who has attained the age of eighteen is charged at the same time.

Trials with adults

9.10 In some circumstances where a child has an adult co-defendant, a joint trial will be heard in the adult magistrates' court. See paras 8.104–8.117 on children with adult co-defendants. .

9.11 Where a child has a trial in the adult court, the court should do its utmost to ensure that the proceedings are modified to be as much like the youth court proceedings as possible.

9.12 The court should consider its inherent powers and the criminal practice direction for vulnerable defendants in determining how to modify any procedure. (See paras 4.14–4.61 on effective participation and modifications.)

9.13 The court should consider at the first appearance, or the first hearing when a joint trial is ordered, what appropriate modifications should be made. The court may also order a Ground Rules Hearing (see paras 4.48–4.49 on Ground Rules Hearings and effective participation).

6 CYPA 1963 s18; CYPA 1933 s46(1)(b).

9.14 There are a number of ways that a trial of a child may be different from that of an adult. The age of the defendant will be relevant to some defences (see paras 13.54–13.71 on age as a relevant characteristic), and to some applications. Chapter 13 on trials of child defendants should be considered.

Reporting restrictions

9.15 Anonymity is not automatically granted as it would be in the youth court, and therefore an application needs to be made under YJCEA 1999 s45.

9.16 This is necessary even when the child only appears before the court for a bail application. Given the child will only be before the court because he or she is jointly charged with an adult or because there is no youth court sitting that day, and not because of the serious nature of the crime committed (as with the Crown Court), it is difficult to imagine why the court would not impose reporting restrictions, which would be imposed automatically were the child before the youth court.[7]

9.17 Arguments concerning anonymity and reporting restrictions are dealt with more fully in chapter 14.

Modifications

9.18 Modifications should be considered at all hearings in the adult magistrates' court, even a bail application or a case management hearing, although of course it may be appropriate to make more modifications for a trial than for a case management hearing.

9.19 The practice direction for vulnerable defendants[8] applies equally in the magistrates' court as the Crown Court. See further paras 4.20–4.30 on Criminal Practice Direction for vulnerable defendants.

Sentencing powers

9.20 The adult magistrates' court has limited sentencing powers when dealing with child defendants. When an adult magistrates' court

7 Under CYPA 1933 s49.

8 CrimPD I, para 3.G.

makes a finding of guilt the court should ordinarily remit the matter to the youth court for sentence (see paras 17.22–17.27 on remittal for sentence). This could be the youth court in the same area as the magistrates' court where the child is convicted, or the youth court that is local to the child's area, where different.[9]

9.21 The magistrates must remit to the youth court unless they pass one of the following sentences:[10]

- a referral order[11] (see chapter 19 on referral orders);
- an absolute or conditional discharge;
- a fine;
- a parenting order under Powers of Criminal Courts (Sentencing) Act (PCC(S)A) 2000 s150[12] (see chapter 23 on parenting orders).

Breaches of orders

9.22 Where a child has been sentenced in the youth court but has turned 18 during the course of his or her sentence, that person will be brought in front of the adult magistrates' court to be dealt with the breach of the order – see further para 20.134 on youth rehabilitation orders, turning a significant age threshold, which deals with breaches.

9 PCC(S)A 2000 s8(2)(b).
10 PCC(S)A 2000 s8(6).
11 PCC(S)A 2000 s8(7).
12 PCC(S)A 2000 s8(8).

CHAPTER 10

Crown Court procedure

Key points

- Children should rarely appear in the Crown Court.
- Where children are in the Crown Court and plead guilty, the court should consider remitting them for sentence in the youth court.
- Where a child has a trial in the Crown Court, substantial changes or modifications should be made to the trial process.
- Defence lawyers should remember to consider reporting restrictions as soon as the case is sent to the Crown Court, and consider the Plea and Trial Preparation Hearing (PTPH) checklist for a list of matters to consider when representing a child.

Introduction

10.1 Children rarely appear in the Crown Court. They may appear in the Crown Court for the following reasons:

- they have an adult co-defendant;[1]
- they are charged with murder or other serious offences;[2]
- they are charged with a grave crime and the youth court considers it has insufficient sentencing powers;[3] or
- they are charged with a specified offence and the youth court considered the dangerousness criteria have been met.[4]
- a notice is given to court under CDA 1998 s51B (complex fraud) or CDA 1998 s51C (child witnesses).[5]

The Crown Court also acts as an appeal court for cases appealed from the youth court.

Remittal to youth court

Remittal for trial

10.2 The power to remit to the youth court only applies to sentence (see para 10.3 on remittal for sentence), or where the main offence is

1 See paras 8.104–8.117 on children with adult co-defendants.
2 CDA 1998 s51A(3)(a) and further see paras 8.121–8.123.
3 CDA 1998 s51A(3)(b) and further see paras 8.126–8.144 on grave crimes.
4 CDA 1998 s51A(3)(d) and further see paras 8.145–8.150 on dangerousness.
5 See para 8.124.

discontinued prior to arraignment.[6] Where the prosecution is no longer proceeding with the offence that the child was sent to the Crown Court to face[7] and the child has not been arraigned, the court shall remit any other charges back to the magistrates' court (this may be the adult magistrates' or youth court). There is no power to remit the matter back to the youth court for trial once a child has been arraigned, even if the matter has been sent to the Crown Court in error. In the case of *R(W)* when a child was sent to the Crown Court jointly charged with an adult and the adult pleaded guilty, the child had a trial in the Crown Court alone even though the child would never have been there if not jointly charged with an adult, because the court had no power to remit.[8] Where the magistrates had erroneously found the defendant to be an adult and sent him or her to the Crown Court, even if the Crown Court disagreed with the adult magistrates' court decision and considered the defendant a child, they had no power to remit the case to the youth court, and therefore the only remedy for the defendant was a judicial review of the adult magistrates' court decision.[9] The only legal route for a defence lawyer to challenge erroneous decisions to send a child to the Crown Court for trial is by judicial review (see paras 8.156–8.158 on challenges to mode of trial decisions).

Remittal for sentence

10.3 If a child or young person is found guilty before the Crown Court of an offence other than homicide, the court must remit the case to the youth court for sentence, unless it would be undesirable to do so.[10] See fuller discussion at paras 17.22–17.27 on remittal, pre-sentence reports and procedure.

10.4 The Sentencing Council's *Sentencing children and young people: definitive guideline* states that:[11]

> In considering whether remittal is undesirable a court should balance the need for expertise in the sentencing of children and young people with the benefits of the sentence being imposed by the court which determined guilt.

6 CDA 1998 Sch 3 para 13.

7 CDA 1998, sch 3, para 13(b).

8 *R (W) v Leeds Crown Court* [2011] EWHC 2326 (Admin).

9 *R (M) v Hammersmith Magistrates' Court* [2017] EWHC 1359 (Admin).

10 Powers of Criminal Courts (Sentencing) Act 2000 s8.

11 Sentencing Council, *Sentencing children and young people: definitive guideline*, 2017, paras 2.15–2.16.

> Particular attention should be given to children and young people who are appearing before the Crown Court only because they have been charged with an adult offender; referral orders are generally not available in the Crown Court but may be the most appropriate sentence.

See further para in chapter 17 on pre-sentence reports and procedure.

Reporting restrictions

10.5 Anonymity is not automatically granted to a child in the Crown Court as it would be in the youth court,[12] and therefore an application needs to be made under Youth Justice and Criminal Evidence Act (YJCEA) 1999 s45.

10.6 This is necessary even when the child only appears before the court for a bail application. It is possible to apply for an order under YJCEA 1999 s45 at the youth or adult magistrates' court when the case is sent or allocated to the Crown Court. However, it should be checked at the Plea and Trial Preparation Hearing (PTPH) or first hearing in the Crown Court to avoid inadvertent reporting. The defence lawyer should contact the Crown Court in advance of the PTPH to check both that the order is in place, and that the list office are aware of it, so that the matter is not made public and the child's name is not published on the court list.

10.7 Where a child appears before the court for an appeal from the youth court, Children and Young Persons Act 1933 (CYPA) s49 still applies and the child has the benefit of automatic reporting restrictions.

10.8 Arguments concerning anonymity and reporting restrictions are dealt with more fully in chapter 14.

Crown Court checklist

10.9 Representing a child in the Crown Court should not be fundamentally different from representing a child in the youth court. When considering how to modify the Crown Court proceedings, the court should attempt to mirror proceedings in the youth court as far as possible.

10.10 The fact that the child is in the Crown Court is either due to the fact that the child is jointly charged with an adult, which is an

12 CYPA 1933 s49.

arbitrary distinction; or it is due to the serious nature of the crime the child is charged with.

10.11 There is no reason to believe that just because the child is charged with a serious crime that the child is any less vulnerable, or that the child's effective participation is any less important – quite the contrary, as the stakes are likely to be higher a fair trial is all the more important.

10.12 The fact the defendant is a child should influence all aspects of the case.

PTPH checklist

10.13 For defence lawyers – meeting their client for the first time, there are a number of considerations to consider when representing a child at the pre-trial and preparation hearing. There is considerable overlap between the considerations at this hearing and at the first appearance, see the background checklist and first appearance checklist at para 8.91.

10.14 Some of the main points to consider when first meeting the child:

- *Age*
- *Any additional vulnerabilities or participation issues (effective participation, fitness to plead, need for intermediary or modifications)*
- *Trafficking*
- *Looked after child*
- *BAME [black, Asian and minority ethnic]*
- *Immigration status*

10.15 In court:

1) *Age and maturity*. The court should consider the age and the maturity of the child in order to assist with making any the following decisions including those listed below.
2) *Reports or extra information*. The court and defence lawyer should consider whether any reports, such as psychiatric or psychological reports, are necessary to consider whether the child is fit to plead, able to effectively participate or to assist with modifications; or a possible defence or other application, such as whether adverse inferences should be drawn from silence in interview. For a full discussion about when it may be necessary to instruct an expert, see chapter 12 on instructing an expert.

3) *Modifications or special measures.* The court should consider what modifications are necessary for the trial to ensure effective participation and considering their welfare duty towards the child. For a list of modifications and discussion, see paras 4.31–4.55 and 10.16–10.22 on modifications and special measures. If further information is being sought on the child, it may be that decisions about modifications will be made at a later hearing.
4) *Ground Rules Hearing.* The court should consider whether a Ground Rules Hearing is necessary – see paras 4.48–4.49 on Ground Rules Hearings.
5) *Reporting restrictions.* If reporting restrictions are not already in place, they should be applied for (see chapter 14 on anonymity).

Crown Court trials

Modifications and effective participation

10.16 The principle that the right to a fair trial (Article 6) includes the right to effectively participate has been established by judgments of the European Court of Human Rights (ECtHR).[13] The right of a child to effectively participate means that due regard must be given to their vulnerabilities at all stages of contact with the criminal justice system and not just at trial.[14] In *V v UK* the court found that 'the full rigours of an adult, public trial deprived him of the opportunity to participate effectively . . . in breach of Article 6' of the European Convention on Human Rights (ECHR).[15] (For a fuller discussion of effective participation see paras 4.14–4.19.)

10.17 The criminal practice direction for vulnerable defendants was brought in following the *Venables* case. The practice direction provides that:

> . . . the court is required to take 'every reasonable step' to encourage and facilitate the attendance of witnesses and to facilitate the participation of any person, including the defendant.[16]

13 *V v UK* (2000) 30 EHRR 121, para 84; *SC v UK* (2005) 40 EHRR 10, para 33; *Martin v Estonia* (2013) EHRR 493, para 92.

14 *Martin v Estonia* (2013) EHRR 493, para 92.

15 *V v UK* (2000) 30 EHRR 121, para 84.

16 Criminal Practice Direction 2015, para 3D.2; and also Criminal Procedure Rules 2015, para 3.9(3)(a) and (b).

10.18 Modifications and effective participation should be considered for every trial involving in a child defendant, even in the youth court. However, it is in the Crown Court where the child is likely to face the most difficulties in participating, given the greater formality that is usually present. Therefore, in order to ensure a fair trial, far more may need to be done to ensure that the child is able to participate effectively.

10.19 Modifications and special measures are dealt with at paras 4.31–4.55, along with the practice direction at paras 4.20–4.30 and consideration of effective participation at paras 4.14–4.19 and paras 4.56–4.68.

10.20 Modifications can include, but are not limited to:

- referring to the child by first name;
- sitting out of the dock, close to a supporting adult and legal representative;[17]
- everyone sitting on the same level;[18]
- ensuring regular breaks;[19]
- ensuring that the child understands what is going on;[20]
- avoidance of complicated language;[21]
- housing a court familiarisation visit;[22]
- using an intermediary;[23]
- giving evidence via live link;[24]
- removing wigs and gowns; security staff should not wear uniform;[25]
- restricting attendance by members of the public in the courtroom to a small number;[26]
- implementing reporting restrictions.[27]

Criminal Practice Directions – *Treatment of Vulnerable Defendants* 3G

10.21 The Criminal Practice Direction (CrimPD) should always be considered for child defendants to determine what adaptations and modifications are required to enable them to effectively participate in

17 Para 3G.8.
18 Para 3G.7.
19 Para 3G.10.
20 Para 3G.9.
21 Para 3G.10.
22 Para 3G.2.
23 Para 3G.3 – special measure.
24 Para 3G.4, 3G.1 – special measure.
25 Para 3G.12.
26 Para 3G.13.
27 Para 3G.14; YJCEA 1999 s45 – see chapter 14 on anonymity.

their trial, but the court also has a duty to consider the welfare of any child before it, and the best interests of the child under Article 3 of the United Nations Convention on the Rights of the Child (UNCRC) (see paras 1.21–1.41 for a full discussion of UNCRC).

10.22 All defendants have a right to effectively participate in their trial, and the CrimPD on Vulnerable Defendants also applies to vulnerable adults. However, children are less likely to be able to effectively participate due to their age and developmental immaturity such that even children without any additional needs should expect modifications. The duty to have regard to[28] a child's welfare provides even stronger arguments in favour of adaptation of court procedures for children.

Relevance of age at trial

10.23 The Crown Court Benchbook states that:

> The age of a child (whether over or under 14 years) is likely to be a relevant factor where:
>
> (1) the offence in question requires a specific intent or subjective recklessness (e.g. foresight of consequences);
> (2) a possible defence has a subjective element;
> (3) a possible defence requires an assessment of reasonableness (e.g. loss of control, duress, self-defence);
> (4) it is shown that a child is not of normal development for his age (e.g. in a defence of diminished responsibility).

10.24 The relevance of age in certain defences is discussed in full at paras 13.14–13.71 on trials of child defendants.

10.25 However, age may also be relevant during certain applications at court, and when considering jury directions and sentence (see paras 17.29–17.60).

Appeals from the youth court

10.26 The Crown Court will hear appeals from the youth court, or adult magistrates' court. See paras 15.14–15.27 on appeals to the Crown Court.

10.27 The appeal hearing is a rehearing of the case[29] – the court usually consists of a panel of a Crown Court judge and two lay magistrates.

28 CYPA 1933 s44(1).

29 Senior Courts Act 1981 s79(3).

Criminal Procedure Rules Part 34.11 sets out the constitution the Crown Court must take. When the Crown Court is hearing an appeal from the youth court, automatic reporting restrictions under CYPA 1933 s49 apply to the proceedings. As it is a rehearing, the court may confirm, reverse of vary the sentence, under Senior Courts Act 1981 s48(2).[30] Unlike appeals to the Court of Appeal, the Crown Court has the power to sentence more severely than the lower court.[31]

30 Formerly called the Supreme Court Act 1981.

31 Senior Courts Act 1981 s48(4); *Dutta v Westcott* [1987] QB 291.

CHAPTER 11

Bail and remand

continued

Key points

- The youth offending team (YOT) is highly influential in bail proceedings. The YOT can provide bail support packages and will often make representations to the court as to whether bail should be granted.
- Defendants have a right to bail for most offences, but not a right to unconditional bail. For certain serious offences, such as murder, courts retain discretion to grant bail.
- Defendants can make bail applications at the first appearance and retain the right to make a second application at the next hearing if in custody. The courts may decide to consider further bail applications, and are likely to do so where the defendant is a child.
- If bail is denied, defendants may apply to Crown Court for reconsideration. If bail is granted, the prosecution may appeal against bail if the defendant is charged with particular offences.
- Courts are obliged to remand a child to the care of the designated local authority if bail is denied. The local authority assumes the duty for the child's welfare. This is true even for the most serious offences, including murder. It is only when the secure conditions are met that a custodial remand is possible.
- If a child breaches a bail support package created by the YOT, the YOT may decide whether or not it is appropriate to report the breach to the court.

Introduction

11.1 This chapter deals with bail and remand decisions made by the court. Bail may also be granted when a child is arrested by the police, before or after charge (see paras 6.182–6.186 on release on police bail).

11.2 Bail applications for children are essentially a two-stage process. The court must first decide whether or not to grant bail. There is a statutory right to bail for children, unless certain statutory exceptions apply. The possible objections to bail are similar to those for adults.

11.3 If bail is refused, the second stage is that the court must then go on to consider whether the conditions to remand to youth detention accommodation (YDA) are met:

- If the conditions are not met, the court must remand the child to local authority accommodation (RLAA).
- If the conditions *are* met, children aged 12–17 *may* be remanded to YDA.[1]

11.4 The YDA conditions apply to all children[2] and are governed by the Legal Aid, Sentencing and Punishment of Offenders Act (LASPO) 2012 ss98–102

11.5 This two-stage process applies whichever court the child is appearing before.

11.6 In addition to the provisions about remand to YDA, it is important that the courts treat children distinctly from adults. United Nations Convention on the Rights of the Child (UNCRC) Article 37(b) provides that children should only be deprived of their liberty as a measure of last resort. Courts also must always have regard to the child's welfare.[3]

First appearances at court[4]

Following charge

11.7 At the first court hearing, a child will arrive either: in custody, having been denied bail by the police (they may be brought directly from the police station or from local authority accommodation), or on bail.

11.8 If children arrive on police bail and the case is not concluded at the first appearance, the court has the power to grant bail (with or without conditions) or refuse bail and to decide upon any relevant bail conditions. If the court refuses bail, they must then remand to local authority accommodation unless the secure conditions are met (see paras 11.95–11.119 below). If the child fails to attend the first appearance on time (or at all), the child will commit a criminal offence under the Bail Act (BA) 1976 s6(1) unless he or she has a reasonable cause for the failure to attend.[5]

1 LASPO 2012 ss91(6) and 98(2) or 99(2).
2 LASPO 2012 s107 defines a child as a person under 18 years.
3 Children and Young Persons Act (CYPA) 1933 s44.
4 For more information on first appearances, see paras 8.75–8.91 on first appearance and youth court procedure.
5 BA 1976 s6(1).

Following summons or requisitioning

11.9 Any defendant who receives a summons or requisition requiring them to attend court will not be on police bail. There is therefore no offence committed should that person fail to attend, however the court will usually have the power to issue a warrant for their arrest.[6] Following the first appearance, the court can simply adjourn proceedings, without releasing the child on bail. It is more usual, however, for the child to be bailed if there is a further hearing.

Bail applications

Procedure

Overview

11.10 Criminal Procedure Rules (CrimPR) Part 14 applies to bail applications before the youth court, adult magistrates' court and Crown Court, and is equally applicable to the procedure for children as it is for adults, there are no distinct procedure rules for children. The questions for the court when considering a bail application for a child can be summarised as:

1) Does the child have a right to bail? If so:
2) Are there substantial grounds for believing an objection to bail exists?
3) Can those objections be met adequately by bail conditions (including bail support packages from a youth offending team (YOT))?
4) If bail is refused, and the child is 12 years or over and charged with an imprisonable offence, consider whether the remand to YDA conditions are met (under LASPO 2012 s98 or s99)?
   a) If not met, or don't apply, remand to local authority accommodation (with any conditions that are available for conditional bail).
   b) If met, the court may remand to a YDA or choose to remand to LAA.
5) Where the child does not have a right to bail, the court may still grant bail[7] with or without conditions. If bail is witheld the court

6 Magistrates' Court Act 1980 s1(b), as amended by Courts Act 2003 s43(1)(b).

7 Unless in the magistrates' courts and charged with murder: see paras 11.27–11.28.

must then go on to decide whether the secure conditions are met as set out in 4) above.

11.11 The objections to bail will depend on the nature of the offence (see paras 11.29–11.40 on objections to bail).

11.12 The strict rules of evidence do not apply to bail applications and hearsay evidence may be relied upon.[8] The hearing for a bail application may occur in public or in private.[9]

11.13 The prosecutor must provide all relevant information to both the defence lawyer and the court.[10] The prosecutor can object to bail being granted entirely, and in which case the prosecutor should specify which exceptions to the general right of bail apply. Or the prosecutor can object to bail unless certain conditions are imposed.

11.14 Bail will be decided at the first appearance and at each subsequent hearing. Where a defendant wishes the youth or adult magistrates' court to consider bail before the next hearing[11] or where a defendant wishes the Crown Court to hear a bail application[12] then a notice must be served on all parties and the court two business days before any hearing.[13] Equally the prosecution must serve a notice if they want the court to withdraw bail or impose a new condition of bail.[14]

11.15 The YOT play a large role in bail applications. They will often asses a child to decide whether the child is suitable for a bail package (see paras 11.66–11.73 below), and make representations to the court about whether the child is suitable for a bail package or not. Where the YOT do not offer a bail package, it can be extremely difficult to get bail – it is therefore essential to speak to the YOT prior to any bail application to ascertain their views, and if necessary to seek to persuade them to support bail. The local authority have a duty to provide 'support for children [on bail]'.[15] This duty is fulfilled through the YOT providing support packages for bail.

8 *Moles, Re* [1981] Crim LR 170 QBD; *R (DPP) v Havering Magistrates' Court* [2001] WLR 805.

9 CrimPR r14.2(2).

10 CrimPR r14.5(2).

11 CrimPR r14.7(1)(a)(ii).

12 CrimPR r14.7(1)(b)(i).

13 CrimPR r14.7(2).

14 CrimPR r14.7(1)(a)(i).

15 Crime and Disorder Act 1998 s38(4)(c).

Presence of the accused

11.16 If the defendant is in custody, he or she has a right to be present – either in person or via video link – at the first hearing for bail, but not on subsequent occasions.[16] Although the use of video link is often not appropriate for children (see paras 8.58–8.62 on video links) that does not prohibit the court agreeing to produce the defendant should he or she wish to attend, and while there are no different provisions for children, it may be appropriate, given the court's welfare duties[17] to allow children to attend their bail hearings should they wish to do so. Defendants may waive their rights to attend any bail hearing.[18] If the defendant is not present, he or she must be afforded the right to make representations[19] – this will usually be achieved by the defendant being legally represented at the hearing.

11.17 Where there is an appeal by the prosecutor against the grant of bail, this bail hearing may proceed in the defendant's absence if the court considers it just to do so.[20]

Right to bail

Background

11.18 The right to bail is governed by the BA 1976. BA 1976 s4 provides that there is a right to bail for almost all offences when any person accused of an offence is brought before the court, or when the person applies to the court for bail. Therefore the court must grant the defendant bail, unless one of the exceptions apply. These exceptions are listed in BA 1976 Sch 1. The court is not obliged to grant unconditional bail, and may impose any conditions on the defendant if the court considers conditions are necessary. If the court does not grant bail, it must provide reasons for not granting a defendant bail.

Convicted defendants

11.19 Once a defendant is convicted (pleads guilty or there is a finding of guilt), there is still a right to bail if the court adjourns the case for further inquiries to assist with sentencing.[21] There is also a right to

16 CrimPR r14.2(1)(b)(ii).
17 CYPA 1933 s44.
18 CrimPR r14.2(1)(b)(i).
19 CrimPR r14.2(1)(a)(ii).
20 CrimPR r14.2(1)(c)(ii).
21 BA 1976 s4(4).

bail if someone has been brought back to court for breaching certain court orders (referral order, reparation orders or youth rehabilitation orders).[22] In all other situations, there is no right to bail for an individual who has been convicted of the/an offence he or she is before the court for,[23] and therefore in such cases the court has a discretion as to whether to grant bail.

Breach of bail

11.20 The court also need not grant bail if the defendant has been brought back to court having been arrested under BA 1976 s7 for breach of bail or having failed to surrender to custody (see paras 11.124–11.129 on breach of bail).

Offences committed on bail

11.21 Where a child is charged with an indictable offence and was on bail in criminal proceedings on the date of the alleged offence, then the court 'need not' grant bail, and the court will consider whether to grant bail; objections need not apply.[24]

11.22 Where a child is charged with a summary only offence and has committed an offence on bail, in those proceedings the child still retains his or her right to bail. The court may only refuse bail if there are substantial grounds to believe the child will commit further offences.[25] This only applies to imprisonable offences, and is not a ground to refuse bail for non-imprisonable offences.[26]

Insufficient information

11.23 The defendant need not be granted bail where the court is satisfied that there has not been enough time to obtain sufficient information to consider bail.[27] This objection is only applicable when defendants are charged with imprisonable offences.[28]

22 BA 1976 s4(3).
23 BA 1976 s4(2).
24 BA 1976 Sch 1 Part 1 para 2A.
25 BA 1976 Sch 1 Part 1A para 3.
26 BA 1976 Sch 1 Part 2.
27 BA 1976 Sch 1 Part 1 para 5; and Part 1A para 8.
28 BA 1976 Sch1 Part 2.

Serious offences

Overview

11.24 When a defendant is charged with certain serious offences there is no right to bail, although bail may still be granted at the court's discretion. These offences are:

- treason,[29]
- murder,[30]
- certain serious offences if the defendant has a previous conviction for an equivalent offence.[31]

Serious offences

11.25 There is no presumption of bail where a person is charged with an offence listed in Criminal Justice and Public Order Act (CJPOA) 1994 s25(2), and has a previous conviction for any section 25(2) offence or a previous conviction in a 'member state' for an equivalent offence.[32] There is no definition of 'member state' in the Act – it is presumed that this refers to other EU countries. The offences listed in section 25(2) are:

- murder;
- manslaughter;
- rape; and
- offences under Sexual Offences Act 2003 ss2, 4, 5, 6, 8, 30 and 31, and the equivalent offences in Northern Ireland.

11.26 The court can still grant bail, but only if there are exceptional circumstances which justify it.[33]

Murder

11.27 When charged with murder, only a Crown Court judge may grant bail. This means there is no bail application in the youth court or adult magistrates' court.[34] This does not apply to attempted murder or conspiracy to murder. However, when dealing with a child charged with murder, the youth court or adult magistrates' court must consider whether the conditions to remand the child to YDA are met,

29 When charged with treason, bail may only be granted by a High Court judge or on the direction of the Home Secretary as per Magistrates' Courts Act 1980 s41.

30 BA 1976 Sch 1.

31 CJPOA 1994 s25.

32 CJPOA 1994 s25(3).

33 CJPOA 1994 s25(1).

34 Criminal Justice Act 2009 s115.

and if not, remand to local authority accommodation (see paras 11.83–11.94 on remand to local authority accommodation).[35]

11.28 The Crown Court must decide on bail by the second business day after the first hearing in the youth court or adult magistrates' court.[36] The Crown Court judge may only grant bail if the court is satisfied that there is no significant risk that, if released on bail, the child would commit an offence that would be likely to cause physical or mental injury to another person.[37] In coming to that decision, the court must have regard to the nature and seriousness of the offence, the child's character and antecedents and his record in relation to previous grants of bail.[38]

Objections to bail

11.29 If none of the statutory exemptions apply, the defendant will have a right to bail. The court must consider whether there is any objection to bail. Bail can only be withheld if there are substantial grounds for believing that an objection to bail exists, and that cannot be remedied by appropriate bail conditions. Objections to bail are the same for children as those as for an adult, except that the court may also refuse bail for the child's own welfare (see para 11.30). However, bearing in mind the court's welfare duty to the child[39] and that the custody threshold is higher for children than adults (it is not possible to pass a custodial sentence of less than 4 months in the youth court or adult magistrates' court – see paras 21.85–21.86 on non-imprisonable offences for children), the reasons for refusing bail should be narrower than for adults. The possible objections to bail depend on the offence the child is charged with.

Refusal of bail for a child's own welfare

11.30 The court has the power to refuse bail for the child's own welfare.[40] However, should this reason be raised by the YOT or the court, the defence lawyer should discuss with the YOT, any social worker, parent, guardian or other supporting adult how the child's welfare needs could be addressed on bail. If bail was refused on welfare grounds the child should be remanded to local authority accommodation (see para 11.83–11.94).

35 *R v A (Lewisham Youth Court)* [2011] EWHC 1193 (Admin).
36 CrimPR r14.10.
37 BA 1976, as amended by Coroners and Justice Act 2009 s114.
38 BA 1976 Sch 1 Part 1 para 9.
39 CYPA 1933 s44.
40 BA 1976 Sch 1 Part 1 para 3; Sch 1 Part 1A para 5; Sch 1 Part 2 para 3.

Indictable imprisonable offences

11.31 The court can withhold bail when a defendant is charged with indictable imprisonable offences only if there are *substantial* grounds for believing the defendant would:

- fail to surrender to custody; or
- commit an offence on bail; or
- interfere with witnesses or otherwise obstruct the course of justice.

11.32 Or bail can be withheld if:

- it is for the defendant's own welfare or protection (or welfare if a child);
- the defendant is already in custody serving a sentence;
- there is insufficient information (see para 11.23 above);
- the child has been on bail in these proceedings and is arrested for breach of bail of conditions (see paras 11.124–11.133 on breach of bail);
- it is impracticable to complete enquiries or to make the report unless in custody.[41]

Summary-only imprisonable offences

11.33 The court can withhold bail for such offences only if there are substantial grounds for believing that the defendant would:

- fail to surrender if granted bail *and* the defendant has previously failed to surrender;
- commit further offences *and* this offence was committed while on bail;
- cause mental or physical injury or fear of mental or physical injury to an associated person (family member) ie domestic violence.

11.34 Or bail can be withheld, if:

- it is for the defendant's own protection (or welfare if a child);
- the defendant is in custody serving a sentence;
- in relation to these proceedings, the defendant been arrested for breach of bail and substantial grounds for believing would fail to surrender, commit further offences, interfere with witnesses/obstruct justice;
- there is insufficient information.[42]

41 BA 1976 Sch 1 Part I paras 2–7.

42 BA 1976 Sch 1 Part 1A.

Definition of imprisonable offences for children

11.35 The fact that some offences are imprisonable for adults and not for children (see paras 21.85–21.86 on non-imprisonable offences for children) is not relevant for considering whether offences are imprisonable or not for the purposes of BA 1976. The definition of an imprisonable offence is governed by whether the offence is imprisonable for an adult.[43] However, this is relevant when considering whether the child will face a custodial sentence if convicted.

Non-imprisonable offences

11.36 Bail for non-imprisonable offences is governed by BA 1976 Sch 1 Part II and can only be withheld in the following circumstances:

- the defendant has previously failed to surrender and the court believes if granted bail would fail to surrender;
- for the defendant's own protection (or welfare if a child);
- the defendant is in custody serving a sentence;
- in relation to these proceedings, the child[44] has been arrested for breach of bail and substantial grounds for believing would fail to surrender; commit further offences; interfere with witnesses/ obstruct justice; or cause mental or physical injury or fear of mental or physical injury to an associated person (family member) ie domestic violence.[45]

Considerations

11.37 The prosecution will usually outline any objections to bail, which must fall into one of the above categories depending on the nature of the offence. The information the court should take into account in deciding whether one of the objections to bail exists is listed in BA 1976 Sch 1 Part 1 para 9:

a) the nature and seriousness of the offence (and likely sentence);
b) the character, antecedents (criminal record), associations and community ties of the defendant;
c) the defendant's previous bail record;
d) the strength of the evidence against the defendant (except if the case is adjourned for inquiries or a report);

43 BA 1976 Sch 1 Part 3 para 1.

44 These are specific conditions for a child defendant.

45 BA 1976 Sch 1 Part 2 para 5.

e) if substantial grounds for believing that the defendant, if released on bail (whether subject to conditions or not), would commit an offence while on bail, the risk that the defendant may do so by engaging in conduct that would, or would be likely to, cause physical or mental injury to any person other than the defendant;
f) any other relevant factor.

Support from youth offending team/local authority

11.38 The YOT will assess a child who is being considered for bail and may offer a bail support package (see paras 11.66–11.73 below). Where there are objections to bail, it is important to discuss with the YOT what support package they may be able to offer.

Duty to provide accommodation and support (Children Act 1989 s20)

11.39 It also may be relevant to find out what support the local authority is giving or may be able to give a child. This is particularly true where the child has no address or no stable address, or they cannot reside at their home address on bail, which may make a bail application difficult. The local authority has an obligation to provide children in its area with accommodation in certain circumstances such as if they are homeless, under Children Act 1989 s20. The local authority should assess any 'child in need' in its local area and provide accommodation and support where needed.[46] As the YOT are part of the local authority, then it should be possible for them to make a referral under Children Act 1989 s17 and to make enquiries if the local authority is not providing the support needed. However, in some circumstances it may be appropriate to contact the local authority directly or speak to a community care lawyer.

11.40 A child should not be denied bail due to problems with his or her accommodation.

Bail applications

11.41 Every defendant has the right to make a bail application at his or her first appearance, and, if the defendant is then remanded in custody, a second application at the next hearing. This means that if no bail

46 There is a duty to 'safeguard and promote the welfare of children within their area who are in need' by the provision of services. Children Act 1989 s17(1) and a duty to provide accommodation under Children Act 1989 s20.

application is made at the first hearing, then there is still a right to a bail application at a future hearing, but the defendant only has the right to one bail application after the first appearance; not two. The court still retains a discretion to hear further bail applications (see paras 11.44–11.47 on change in circumstances further bail applications).

11.42 BA 1976 Sch 1 Part IIA para 1 provides:

> 1 If the court decides not to grant the defendant bail, it is the court's duty to consider, at each subsequent hearing while the defendant is a person to whom section 4 above applies and remains in custody, whether he ought to be granted bail.
>
> 2 At the first hearing after that at which the court decided not to grant the defendant bail he may support an application for bail with any argument as to fact or law that he desires (whether or not he has advanced that argument previously).
>
> 3 At subsequent hearings the court need not hear arguments as to fact or law which it has heard previously.

11.43 Even when there is no bail application, it is the court's duty to consider whether the remand to YDA remains justified. This is particularly important for children, where the court has an additional duty to have regard to the child's welfare.[47]

Change in circumstances

11.44 Further bail applications can usually only be made in limited circumstances:

> At subsequent hearings the court need not hear arguments as to fact or law which it has heard previously.[48]

This is often interpreted as meaning there needs to have been a 'change of circumstances' for a further bail application to be made. The statutory test should, however, be interpreted a little wider than '"Has there been a change?", it is "Are there new considerations which were not before the court when the accused was last remanded in custody?"'[49]

11.45 The Youth Court Bench Book suggests that the passage of time may be considered a change of circumstance in certain cases.[50]

47 CYPA 1933 s44.

48 BA 1976 Sch 1 Part IIA para 3.

49 Lord Justice Donaldson in *R v Nottingham Justices ex p Davies* [1981] 1 QB 38.

50 Judicial College (2017) Youth Court Bench Book, para 35, p30.

Further bail applications

11.46 The wording of BA 1976 Sch 1 Part IIA para 3 states that the court 'need not hear further applications',[51] therefore the court retains a discretion whether to hear further applications.[52] When exercising its discretion, the court needs to consider its welfare duty under Children and Young Persons Act (CYPA) 1933 s44. In *R (B) v Brent Youth Court*,[53] the High Court found that the decision of the youth court not to hear what would have been a fourth bail application, was unlawful, because even if the bench had been right in saying there were no new circumstances, they had failed to consider whether they should have exercised their discretion to hear the application bearing in mind the court's welfare duty given the applicant was a child.

11.47 At the end of the hearing, the child will be either bailed or remanded until the next hearing. At the next hearing the court has to re-consider the bail decision if the child is remanded to custody by virtue of BA 1976 Sch 1 Part IIA.[54]

Remand in absence

11.48 In some circumstances, where a child fails to attend a hearing, the court has the power to remand the child in his or her absence to the subsequent hearing. Where the court does so, notice shall be given to the child of the next date he or she need attend court.[55]

Appeals

Defence application to Crown Court

11.49 Where the defendant has been denied bail by the youth court or adult magistrates' court, the defendant can apply to the Crown Court to reconsider an application for bail.[56] Where the defendant has been granted conditional bail in the youth court or adult magistrates' court, the defendant can appeal to the Crown Court against one of

51 BA 1976 Sch 1 Part IIA para 3.
52 *R (B) v Brent Youth Court* [2010] EWHC 1893 (Admin) at para 17.
53 [2010] EWHC 1893 (Admin).
54 BA 1976 Sch 1 Part IIA para 1.
55 Magistrates' Court (Children and Young Persons) Rules 1992 r12.
56 Senior Courts Act 1981 s81.

those conditions, provided there has been an application to vary that condition in the lower court.[57]

11.50 Only certain conditions can be appealed against – those are conditions to:

1) live and sleep at a specified place, or away from a specified place;
2) give a surety or a security;
3) stay indoors between specified hours;
4) comply with electronic monitoring requirements; or
5) make no contact with a specified person.

11.51 Where such an application is made to the Crown Court it must be made as soon as practicable and served on the Crown Court, the youth court or adult magistrates' court, the prosecutor and any surety.[58] It must include the copy of the certificate of full argument made in the lower court.[59] The Crown Court will determine when to list the matter, but it will usually be the next business day.[60]

Appeals by the prosecution to the Crown Court

11.52 The prosecutor may appeal to the Crown Court against the grant of bail to a defendant, only if the defendant is charged with an offence punishable by imprisonment.[61] Where the prosecutor does so, he or she must inform the court and the defendant of the intention to appeal at the end of the hearing and before the defendant is released[62] and then serve a notice to appeal on both the court and the defendant within two hours of having informed them of the intention to appeal.[63] Failure to serve the notice in time will result in the defendant being released from custody.[64] However, provided the notice is served the defendant will remain in custody until the appeal is heard,[65] which should be as soon as practicable and no later than the second business day.[66]

57 Criminal Justice Act 2003 s16.
58 CrimPR r14.8(2).
59 CrimPR rr14.8(3)(e) and 14.4(4).
60 CrimPR r14.8(6).
61 CrimPR r14.9(1)(a); Bail (Amendment) Act 1993 s1(1).
62 CrimPR r14.9(2); Bail (Amendment) Act 1993 s1(4) and (5).
63 CrimPR r14.9(4); Bail (Amendment) Act 1993 s1(5).
64 CrimPR r14.9(10).
65 CrimPR r14.9(3).
66 CrimPR r14.9(8).

High Court bail

11.53 The prosecution may appeal against a Crown Court judge's decision to grant bail to the High Court,[67] unless the Crown Court judge was hearing the application on appeal from the magistrates' or youth court.[68] In these circumstances there is no further right of appeal although they may apply for review (see para 11.57).

11.54 The High Court has the power to grant bail where the case is being appealed to the High Court by way of case stated or by judicial review.[69]

11.55 It is possible to challenge a court's bail decision by way of judicial review (see paras 15.46–15.52), but it is unlikely that the administrative court will interfere with the judge's decision.[70]

Review of bail

11.56 When the defendant has been granted bail, and is charged with an indictable offence, the prosecutor can apply to the court to review the decision to grant bail. Such an application can only be made if it is based upon new information which was not before the court or constable who granted bail.[71]

11.57 The application can be to review court bail or police bail.[72] The court can:

- impose new conditions;
- vary conditions; or
- deny bail.[73]

Bail conditions

Overview

11.58 When deciding whether an objection to bail exists, the court must consider whether the imposition of bail conditions will allay the

67 Bail (Amendment) Act 1993 s1B.
68 Bail (Amendment) Act 1993 s1C.
69 Criminal Justice Act 1967 s22(1); and Criminal Justice Act 1948 s37.
70 *R (M) v Isleworth CC* [2005] EWHC 363(Admin).
71 BA 1976 s5B(3).
72 BA 1976 s5B(1).
73 BA 1976 s5B(1).

court's fears. Bail may only be refused if there are no conditions that would meet the concern that leads the court to withhold bail.

11.59 Where a court grants bail, the following options are available, depending on the age of child:

- unconditional bail;
- conditional bail (which can include a bail support package provided by the YOT);
- conditional bail with tagging (this is only available for those aged 12 and over);
- conditional bail with intensive supervision and surveillance (ISS) – this includes up to 25 hours contact with YOT per week.

11.60 Conditions can be placed on bail regardless of what offence is charged. Therefore bail conditions can be placed on a defendant, even if the court would not be able to withhold bail (for example, if a defendant is charged with a non-imprisonable offence and does not meet any of the strict conditions necessary to withhold bail).

11.61 The court may only impose condition necessary to prevent the defendant from:

- failing to surrender to custody;
- committing an offence while on bail;
- interfering with witnesses/obstruct the course of justice.

Or for the purpose of:

- making the defendant available for the making of inquiries or a report to assist the court with sentencing;
- attending an interview with a legal representative;
- the defendant's own protections, or where the defendant is a child for his or her own welfare or in the child's own interests.[74]

Possible conditions

11.62 There is no exhaustive list of conditions that can be placed on a defendant for bail. Some conditions can be appealed against to the Crown Court (see paras 11.49–11.52 above). The YOT will often propose a bail package, where unconditional bail seems unlikely, that will include a list of conditions as proposed by the YOT. It is therefore vital for any defence lawyer to speak to the YOT prior to any bail application to discuss possible bail conditions and ensure that the conditions suggested by them are workable.

74 BA 1976 s3(6).

11.63 Possible conditions can include any of the following:

- residing at a certain address;
- reside as directed by the local authority;
- doorstep condition;
- curfew;
- electronic monitoring (this can only be imposed on those aged 12 and over, for an imprisonable offence – see paras 11.74–11.77 below);[75]
- not to contact specified persons;
- reporting to a police station at certain times;
- bail supervision and support – reporting to YOT a number of times per week;
- intensive supervision and support programme (ISSP);
- surrender passport or travel documents;
- security;
- surety.

Parental surety

11.64 Parents can provide a surety for a sum up to £50 for a child who is under 17 years of age, if that child will not reach 17 before he is due to surrender to custody.[76]

11.65 In the case of adult defendants a surety will only be used to ensure the defendant surrenders to custody. A parental surety may be taken to ensure compliance with any bail condition.

Bail support packages by youth offending team

11.66 The YOT have a duty to support children on bail.[77] Any defence lawyer should speak to the YOT prior to any bail application to ascertain whether there has there been a bail assessment, and if so what it says and what the YOT are proposing. The YOT will often support a bail application with a bail support package if appropriate, or they may support unconditional bail. Equally they may not be supporting bail, and that is important to consider prior to court.

11.67 The YOT may be able to verify information about the child, such as where the child is living, the school the child is at, or other personal

75 BA 1976 s3AA(2).

76 BA 1976 s3(7).

77 Crime and Disorder Act 1998 s38(4)(c).

information, especially if the child has already worked with the YOT, which they may have done even if they do not have a criminal record.

11.68 The YOT will often offer a bail package which often includes reporting to the YOT as part of the bail conditions. There are no equivalent bail conditions for adult defendants, and it essentially means that the child is subject to a community order as part of the bail conditions. While this may make bail conditions more onerous for children, it may also make it more likely that they will be granted bail as such bail packages are more likely to allay the court's fears over the possible commission of further offences.

11.69 The YOT can offer intense bail packages, often referred to as 'Bail ISS', which stands for intensive supervision and support. This is similar to receiving a sentnece of a youth rehabilitation order with ISS (see paras 20.86–20.106 on intensive youth rehabilitation orders). These bail packages are far more intensive and will include electronic monitoring (see paras 17.74–17.77) and usually 25 hours or more contact time with the child.

11.70 Bail ISS is not created by statute. The YOT assess suitability for any of the packages themselves, and in doing so use 'AssetPlus' (see further paras 17.98–17.101 on AssetPlus in sentencing). AssetPlus has a bail and remand section which is used to assess the risk posed by the child. If the risk is assessed as too high for safe management in the community, then the YOT will usually not support bail. Ultimately, whatever package is propsoed, it is a matter for the court whether to grant bail, and to decide which package, if any is appropriate.

11.71 When using AssetPlus to assess the child, the YOT will consider a detailed picture of the child's circumstances and needs. It is likely that the more needs the child has, the more intense a package the YOT will propose to meet those needs. In particular, AssetPlus looks at the accommodation needs of the child, and substance misuse, the child's lifestyle, peers and friends, family and other social networks. Therefore it may be appropriate to ensure that the YOT have accurate information about these areas. Further, it is important to ensure that the conditions are imposed for reasons that can be justified under the BA 1976 and are proportionate considering the nature of the offence.

11.72 The bail condition that the court usually imposes if the YOT propose a package is: 'to comply with the requirements of the bail supervision and support programme'.

11.73 The guidance to YOTs is to ask for this condition in order to give the YOT 'the scope to amend the programme content as the needs and risks presented by the child or young person vary'.[78] However, it may be appropriate to make a clearer condition to ensure that everyone is aware of precisely what will constitute a breach, and to ensure that proportionality is maintained.

Electronic monitored curfews or tagging

Conditions for curfew

11.74 There are two types of curfew:

1) an electronically monitored curfew, often known as a 'tag'; and
2) what is often referred to as a 'doorstep curfew'.

11.75 A 'doorstep curfew' can be imposed in the same manner any other bail condition can be imposed. This is usually defined as a condition that the defendant must remain within his or her home address between certain hours and also must present him- or herself if the police arrive to check that the defendant is at home. There is no reason that the court cannot impose a curfew without the doorstep condition if it considers appropriate. This would mean the defendant would be arrested for breach of bail if found outside his or her address during the hours of the curfew.

11.76 There are stricter conditions about when a court can impose an electronically monitored curfew or 'tag'. It can only be imposed on those 12 or over and for imprisonable offences. In order for the court to order electronic monitoring, there are five conditions set out in LASPO 2012 s94:

> (2) The first requirement is that the child has reached the age of twelve.
> (3) The second requirement is that the offence [the child is charged with or convicted of] or one or more of those offences, is an imprisonable offence.
> (4) The third requirement is that–
> (a) the offence [the child is charged with or convicted of] or one or more of those offences, is a violent or sexual offence or an offence punishable in the case of an adult with imprisonment for a term of 14 years or more, or
> (b) the offence or offences [. . .], together with any other imprisonable offences of which the child has been convicted in any proceed-

78 Youth Justice Board Guidance, 'Manage bail and remands, section 3 case management guidance', published October 2014: www.gov.uk/government/publications/manage-bail-and-remand/manage-bail-and-remands-section-3-case-management-guidance.

ings, amount or would, if the child were convicted of that offence or those offences, amount to a recent history of committing imprisonable offences while on bail or subject to a custodial remand.

(5) The fourth requirement is that the court is satisfied that the necessary provision for electronic monitoring can be made under arrangements currently available in each local justice area which is a relevant area.

(6) The fifth requirement is that a youth offending team has informed the court that, in its opinion, the imposition of an electronic monitoring condition will be suitable in the child's case.

Credit for time on curfew

11.77 For a child to receive credit for time spent on curfew the curfew must be a 'qualifying curfew'. This means it must be for nine hours or more and must be electronically monitored. Each day the child spends on such a curfew means that half-day must be deducted from any subsequent custodial sentence. The total will be rounded up if necessary.[79]

Detention under section 91

11.78 When the child is being sentenced under Powers of Criminal Courts (Sentencing) Act (PCC(S)A) 2000 s91, the judge must determine numbers of days to be deducted and order they be deducted.[80] This is the same as for adult defendants who receive a custodial sentence. (See paras 21.120–21.131 on s91 long-term detention.)

Detention and training orders

11.79 Where the child is being sentenced to a detention and training order (DTO), it is not possible to deduct days from the sentence, instead the court must consider the amount of time that should be deducted and use that to reduce the length of the DTO.[81]

11.80 PCC(S)A s101(8):

> In determining the term of a detention and training order for an offence, the court shall take account of any period for which the offender has been remanded in custody in connection with the offence, or any other offence the charge for which was founded on the same facts or evidence.

79 Criminal Justice Act 2003 s240A.

80 Criminal Justice Act 2003 s240A.

81 *R v Eagles* [2006] EWCA Crim 2368.

11.81 When the time is deducted from a sentence under PCC(S)A 2000 s91, or indeed an adult sentence, it is deducted from the custodial part of that sentence. Therefore if the sentence is two years under section 91, and the time to be deducted is six months, that reduces the custodial part of the sentence from one year to six months. However, when the court considers the appropriate length of a DTO, the court has no power to reduce just the custodial part of the sentence – the court can only reduce the whole sentence: if the sentence were reduced by six months, for example from a 24-month DTO to an 18-month DTO, that would have the effect of reducing the time spent in custody from one year to nine months, and therefore in order that children are not treated more harshly than adults, any time on remand, or time on an electronic curfew needs to be doubled, before being deducted from a detention and training order. So, for example six months on remand, or 12 months on a curfew, should result in 12 months being deducted from the sentence. Having calculated the appropriate reduction, the court will need to consider the nearest permissible period that can be given and should usually round down (see para 21.82).

Varying conditions

11.82 Bail conditions can be varied at a hearing, or without a hearing if agreed with the prosecution.[82]

Remand to local authority accommodation

Overview

11.83 Where a court refuses bail, the court must remand the child to local authority accommodation (RLAA),[83] unless the conditions under LASPO 2012 s91(4) have been met, in which case the court may remand the child to YDA – see paras 11.95–11.119 on remand to YDA.

11.84 Remand to local authority accommodation should be the first option for any child, even when charged with murder:[84]

82 CrimPR r14.2(3)(a).

83 LASPO 2012 s91(3).

84 *R v A (Lewisham Youth Court)* [2011] EWHC 1193 (Admin).

Even for a child or young person charged with an offence as grave as murder, remand in a prison establishment should be the final resort.[85]

11.85 Where a child is remanded to local authority accommodation, the local authority has the duty to find appropriate accommodation for the child.[86] This may be in a foster home, children's home or with living with a family member. A child may also be placed in a secure children's home if the local authority consider it appropriate and make an application for a child to be placed in 'secure accommodation' (see paras 11.91–11.94 below on secure accommodation).

11.86 The child will not usually get credit for time on remand if remanded to local authority accommodation but there may be circumstances where it is appropriate to give some credit if the conditions were very strict. It will not be taken into account automatically and therefore the judge will need to alter the sentence to give effect to any appropriate credit.[87] Unless it is a secure remand (see paras 11.91–11.94). Custody time limits will apply[88] (see paras 11.137–11.140 on custody time limits below).

Conditions on remands to local authority accommodation

11.87 The court can impose any conditions on a child on RLAA as it could if the child was given bail.[89] This includes electronic tagging, provided the conditions for electronic tagging are met[90] (see paras 11.74–11.77 above on electronic monitoring). The court can also 'impose requirements' on the designated authority to make sure these conditions are adhered to.[91] These can include requirements about where the child is placed, and can prohibit the child being placed with a named person.[92]

11.88 The designated authority must be consulted about any conditions on the child, or requirements placed on itself before they are imposed.[93] This is usually done via the youth offending team.[94]

85 Toulson LJ in *R v A (Lewisham Youth Court)* above, para 20.
86 Children Act 1989 s21.
87 *R v A* [2019] EWCA Crim 106.
88 Prosecution of Offenders Act 1985 s23(11)(b).
89 LASPO 2012 s93(1).
90 LASPO 2012 s93(2).
91 LASPO 2012 s93(3).
92 LASPO 2012 s93(3)(b).
93 LASPO 2012 s93(4).
94 Judicial College (2017), Youth Court Bench Book para 24, p27.

11.89 Any conditions may be later be revoked or varied by the court on application by either the designated authority, or the child.[95]

11.90 Reasons must be given for any decision to impose, vary or revoke RLAA conditions and entered on the court register.[96]

Secure accommodation

11.91 It is matter for the local authority where the child is placed once remanded to local authority accommodation, provided it complies with any conditions the court has imposed. Any local authority providing accommodation to the child may not place the child in secure accommodation, unless the circumstances as set out in Children Act 1989 s25 apply. The local authority has the power to make an application to place the child in secure accommodation if:

- the child is likely to abscond from such other accommodation; or
- the child is likely to injure himself or herself or other people if the child is kept in any such other accommodation.[97]

11.92 The local authority must make an application to court for a secure accommodation order. This application can be made to the youth court which remanded the child to local authority accommodation, otherwise it is made to the family court.

Interim secure accommodation

11.93 If the conditions set out in Children Act 1989 s25 are met (see para 11.91 above), then the local authority may hold the child for up to 72 hours in secure accommodation, and after that the local authority will have to apply to court for a secure accommodation order.[98]

11.94 This power exists for any child that the local authority is accommodating and is not particular to those who have been remanded to local authority accommodation while facing a criminal charge, although the criteria for secure accommodation is slightly different for those who are accommodated by the local authority on remand.[99] It will usually be appropriate to consult a community care lawyer if the local authority is applying for a secure accommodation order.

95 LASPO 2012 s93(6).

96 LASPO 2012 s93(7).

97 Children Act 1989 s25 as modified/amended by Children (Secure Accommodation) Regulations 1991 reg 6.

98 Children (Secure Accommodation) Regulations 1991 reg 10.

99 Children (Secure Accommodation) Regulations 1991 reg 6.

Remand to youth detention accommodation

Introduction

11.95 A child aged 12 or over[100] can be remanded to YDA if either of the sets of conditions provided in LASPO 2012 s98 or s99 are met:

- serious offences condition (LASPO 2012 s98);
- recent history/history condition (LASPO 2012 s99).

11.96 A child who is ten or 11 can only be remanded to local authority accommodation.

Conditions

Legal representation condition

11.97 The legal representation condition[101] states that in order for a child to be remanded to YDA, that child must be legally represented, or the reason that the child is not so represented is for one of the following reasons (set out in LASPO 2012 s98(6)):

- representation was withdrawn due to the child's conduct; or
- representation was withdrawn or refused because of the child's financial resources; or
- the child refused or failed to apply for representation having been informed of the right to do so and having had the opportunity.

Overview of conditions

11.98 Where the child is 12 or over and represented, the two following circumstances allow the court to remand to YDA.

11.99 The serious offences condition[102] applies when the child is charged with a violent or sexual offence, or one which is punishable with imprisonment of 14 years or more in the case of an adult. The recent history condition[103] applies when the child is charged with any other imprisonable offence, not one of those in section 98.

11.100 If the child is charged with one of the section 98 offences the court may remand the child to YDA if necessary (see para 11.102

100 LASPO 2012 ss98(1), 99(1).

101 LASPO 2012 ss98(5) and (6), 99(8) and (9).

102 LASPO 2012 s98(3).

103 LASPO 2012 s99(6).

below on necessity condition), if the child is charged with any other imprisonable offence, the child may only be remanded if the other conditions in section 99 are met, and then only if the court finds it necessary (see para 11.102 below on the necessity condition).

11.101 If a child is not charged with any imprisonable offence, then it is not possible to remand the child to YDA.

Necessity condition

11.102 Where the child is charged with an offence mentioned in LASPO 2012 s98, or the conditions in s99 apply, the court may only remand to YDA if, after considering all the remand options, YDA is necessary, which is defined as the only adequate means of either:

- protecting the public from death or serious personal injury (whether physical or psychological) occasioned by further offences by the child; or
- preventing the commission of imprisonable offences by the child.[104]

This is known as the necessity condition.

Serious offences condition (LASPO 2012 s98)

11.103 The first set of conditions apply to any child aged 12 or over, where the representation condition is met. They apply to a child charged with a violent or sexual offence, or one punishable with 14 years or more for an adult. For these offences, the court may remand to YDA where it is necessary to do so (see para 11.102 above).

11.104 There is no seriousness threshold, and therefore the court will only consider the category of offence charged – there is no need for the court to consider the facts of the case in order to ascertain whether the child has been charged with a 'violent or sexual offence', although of course the facts will be relevant to other decisions the court has to consider.

11.105 Offences punishable with 14 years or more for an adult will also be grave crimes, and thus for these offences the court will also need to consider allocation.

104 LASPO 2012 s98(1)(c).

Recent history/history condition (LASPO 2012 s99)

11.106 The second set of conditions apply to any child aged 12 or over, where the representation condition is met, and who is charged with an imprisonable offence.[105]

11.107 Where a child is charged with a violent or sexual offence or one which is punishable with 14 years or more imprisonment in the case of an adult, there is no need to consider the conditions in section 99, because section 98 will apply. The court only needs to decide whether the necessity condition is met.

11.108 Where a child is charged with any other imprisonable offence, YDA is only available in the following circumstances:

1) the court considers that there is a 'real prospect' of receiving a custodial sentence upon conviction;[106] *and*
2) either:
   a) the *first history condition* is met – the child has a recent history of absconding while subject to a custodial remand *and* one of the alleged offences and at least one of the offences the child is charged with was allegedly committed while the child was remanded to local authority accommodation or YDA;[107] *or*
   b) the *second history condition* is met – the child has a recent history of committing imprisonable offences while on bail or subject to custodial remand.[108]

11.109 If these two conditions are met, then the court may remand to YDA if the necessity condition is met (see para 11.102 above on the necessity condition).

11.110 When considering whether there is a real prospect of a custodial sentence, a custodial sentence is defined as a sentence or order mentioned in PCC(S)A s76(1).[109] This includes sentences of imprisonment, detention and detention and training orders. The Sentencing Council's *Sentencing children and young people: definitive guideline*

105 LASPO 2012 s99(1)(c).
106 LASPO 2012 s99(3).
107 LASPO 2012 s99(5)(a), (b).
108 LASPO 2012 s99(6): 'The second history condition is that the offence or offences mentioned in section 91(1), together with any other imprisonable offences of which the child has been convicted in any proceedings, amount or would, if the child were convicted of that offence or those offences, amount to a recent history of committing imprisonable offences while on bail or subject to a custodial remand.'
109 LASPO 2012 s99(10).

must be consulted in order to determine whether there is a real prospect of a custodial sentence.[110]

Designated authority

11.111 The court designates which local authority will receive the child. This local authority will bear the costs of the remand, and make the necessary travel arrangements for the child.[111]

Placement decisions

11.112 When a child is remanded to YDA, the child can be remanded to a secure children's home, secure training centre (STC) or youth offenders institute (YOI). Where the child is placed will depend on the child's age and any needs that the child may have (see paras 1.89–1.97 on the secure estate).

11.113 The Youth Justice Board (YJB) used to make the placement decision, but it is now part of the Ministry of Justice, which created the Youth Custody Service (YCS)[112] in April 2017. This is a distinct arm of HM Prison and Probation Service, responsible for the placement of children into custody and the delivery of secure services.

11.114 The placement decision is based on the information provided by YOTs. The YCS should contact the relevant YOT upon receiving a placement request to make sure the needs, risks and circumstances of a child has been taken into account.

11.115 If a child has any particular needs, it is important the defence lawyer makes the YOT aware of them. In particular, the YCS will consider the following (non-exhaustive) factors:

- previous history within the secure estate;
- risk of harm (to self and to/from others);
- welfare;
- post court presentation;
- medical history/needs including mental health issues;
- special educational needs (SEN) or learning, emotional and social needs;
- looked after child status;
- maturity and resilience.

110 Youth Court Bench Book, para 33, p30.

111 LASPO 2012 s103.

112 The Youth Custody Service Placement Team Overview of operational procedures, P HM Prison & Probation Service/Youth Custody Service, September 2017.

11.116 The *Youth custody service placement team overview of operational procedures*[113] guidance provides an overview of the key responsibilities and activities of the YCS Placements Service.

11.117 Guidance on the responsibilities of YOTs with regards to this and how this relates to the Placement Team are laid out in both the National Standards for Youth Justice Services 2013, particularly *National standard 6: work in courts* and the *National protocol for case responsibility 2014*, and the YCS's Case Management Guidance, particularly *Custody and resettlement: Section 7 case management guidance.*

Challenging a placement decision

11.118 A placement decision may be challenged, or there may an urgent need to transfer a child. The contact details for the YCP team are on the gov.uk website. Any concern about the initial placement decisions should be escalated to the Head of Placements, and complaints can be made through the website. It is a duty of those involved to ensure that the child has reasonable input into those decisions otherwise the process could be procedurally unfair.[114]

11.119 The YOT should be able to assist if an alternative placement is sought due to a change in circumstances, following their transfer guidance.

Looked after status

11.120 Every child remanded to YDA becomes looked after by his or her designated local authority.[115] Where a child is looked after the local authority will owe duties under Children Act 1989 s22.[116]

11.121 Where a child is remanded to local authority accommodation, that child is also deemed to be looked after, and the local authority will also owe duties under Children Act 1989 s22 as it is providing accommodation for the child.[117]

11.122 If the remand lasts for 13 weeks or longer, the child becomes eligible for leaving care services. This means that he or she will get

113 The Youth Custody Service Placement Team Overview of operational procedures, P HM Prison & Probation Service/Youth Custody Service, September 2017.

114 See *ML v YJB* [2013] EWHC 3083 (Admin), para 44, Irwin J.

115 LASPO 2012 s104.

116 LASPO 2012 s104(6).

117 Children Act 1989 s22(1)(b).

advice and support for particular needs, including accommodation and financial assistance (including for higher education) by the responsible local authority.

11.123 Once a child is looked after, the local authority has a duty to safeguard and promote that child's welfare,[118] and make services available to the child.[119] This includes plans for the child's health, care and educational needs. There is statutory guidance for local authorities about the care planning and placement of such children.[120]

Breach of bail

Breach of YOT bail support package

11.124 When a child breaches his or her support package with a YOT, it is a matter for the YOT whether to bring the matter back before the court. A YOT will usually not report the breach if they consider that the child has a reasonable excuse, and will often issue a warning letter for a non-serious breach and only bring the matter before the court once there have been two breaches, or one serious breach without a reasonable excuse.[121]

11.125 The YOT will usually summons the child to court to answer their breach of bail. Should the child fail to attend the hearing having been summonsed, the court will consider whether to issue a warrant for their arrest.[122]

Arrest for breach of bail conditions

11.126 Breach of bail is not a criminal offence, however, a police constable can arrest anyone who they have reasonable grounds to believe has breached conditions or will breach conditions or will fail to surrender or surety has notified in writing that they wish to be relieved of obligations of being a surety and believe the defendant will fail to surrender.[123]

118 Children Act 1989 s22(3)(a).

119 Children Act 1989 s22(3)(b).

120 The Children Act 1989 guidance and regulations Volume 2: care planning, placement and case review June 2015

121 www.gov.uk/government/publications/manage-bail-and-remand/manage-bail-and-remands-section-3-case-management-guidance.

122 MCA 1980 s1.

123 BA 1976 s7(3).

11.127 If a defendant is arrested for breach of bail the defendant must be brought before a justice of the peace as soon as practicable, and in any event within 24 hours of arrest (if arrested within 24 hours of a court date, the defendant should be brought before the court at which he or she was due to attend).[124] If the defendant is charged with murder then he or she must be brought before a Crown Court judge.

11.128 The 24-hour period does not include Sunday, Christmas Day or Good Friday[125] (or if charged with murder, Saturday or bank holidays).[126]

Court procedure

11.129 Once brought before the court, the justice of the peace must release the defendant on the same bail conditions as before unless it is of the opinion either that the defendant:

- is likely to fail to surrender to custody; or
- has breached or is likely to breach.[127]

11.130 If so, the court may refuse to grant the defendant bail, as the defendant no longer has a right to bail,[128] or grant bail on the same or different bail conditions. Where a child is not granted bail, the court must remand to local authority accommodation unless the remand to YDA conditions are met.[129]

Breach of remand to local authority conditions

11.131 A child can be arrested and brought to court for breaching the conditions of remand to local authority accommodation. The child may be arrested without warrant if a constable has reasonable grounds for suspecting that the child has broken any of the conditions imposed under LASPO 2012 s93 in respect of a remand to local authority accommodation.[130]

11.132 Once arrested, the child must be brought before a justice of the peace within 24 hours, and the same rules for calculating that 24-hour

124 BA 1976 s7(4).
125 BA 1976 s7(7).
126 BA 1976 s7(8)(c).
127 BA 1976 s7(5).
128 BA 1976 Sch 1 Part I para 6; Part II para 5.
129 BA 1976 s7(6).
130 LASPO 2012 s97(1)(c).

period apply as in breach of bail conditions (see paras 11.126–11.127 above).[131] The child must be remanded on the same conditions as before,[132] unless the magistrates find that the child has broken one of the conditions, in which case they can revisit the remand decision and conditions.[133]

11.133 It should be noted that unlike BA 1976 s7, a constable may not arrest for breach of remand conditions if he or she only suspects that the conditions will be broken.

Warrant (failure to surrender to custody)

11.134 A person granted bail is under a duty to surrender to custody[134] and it is a criminal offence not to surrender to custody at the place and time appointed by the court. The court can issue a warrant if the defendant fails to attend a hearing or absents himself or herself from the hearing without leave of the court.[135] Warrants can be backed for bail, and there should always be consideration given to adjourning the case without issuing a warrant to allow time for further enquiries to be made, or issuing a warrant backed for bail, as a warrant not backed for bail will usually mean that the child spends a night in police cells (for more detail on failing to attend and warrants see paras 8.45–8.50).

11.135 A warrant can only be issued for a child if the offence is one that is imprisonable in the case of an adult defendant, or one where the court intends to disqualify the child from driving.[136]

11.136 If the warrant was backed for bail, the defendant will be told to appear before the next sitting youth court. If the warrant is not backed for bail, the defendant will be arrested by the police and brought before the court. If there is no court sitting at the time of arrest, for example if the defendant is arrested in the evening, the defendant, even if a child, will be held overnight in police cells to be brought to court the next morning.

131 LASPO 2012 s97(2).
132 LASPO 2012 s97(7).
133 LASPO 2012 s97(6).
134 BA 1976 s3(1).
135 BA 1976 s7.
136 BA 1976 s3A.

Custody time limits

11.137 Custody time limits apply equally to children as to adults. Offences that would be indictable only for an adult but are tried in the youth court by virtue of Magistrates' Court Act 1980 s24 are treated like either way offences.[137]

11.138 Prosecution of Offenders (Custody Time Limits) Regulations 1987[138] provide the following time limits, however these allow for time between first appearance and committal proceedings, which no longer exist. The relevant time limits therefore are the maximum time that a defendant may remain in custody between first appearance and:

- trial in the magistrates or youth court: 56 days;
- Crown Court trial: 182 days

11.139 Where the time limits expire, without having been extended the defendant shall be granted bail. The prosecutor can apply to extend the custody time limits[139] by making an application to the court. Notice must be given to the defence and the court not less than five days before the application in the Crown Court, and not less than two days before the application in the adult magistrates' or youth court.[140]

137 *R v Stratford Youth Court ex p S (a minor)* [1998] 1 WLR 1758.

138 SI No 299.

139 Prosecution of Offences Act 1985 s22(3).

140 Prosecution of Offences (Custody Time Limit) Regulations 1987 reg 7.

CHAPTER 12

Instructing a mental health expert and instructing an intermediary

Key points

- In many criminal cases that involve children there may be a need to get an expert report. The Royal College of Psychiatrists recommends that there should be a mandatory assessment of every child under 14 in the criminal justice system.
- The expert that should be instructed will depend upon the difficulties and the needs of the child.
- In criminal proceedings, the court makes rulings as to fitness to plead based on the evidence of registered medical practitioners.
- A psychologist report may be needed for many children, particularly around modifications, mitigation, IQ testing for a learning disability or diagnosing other types of neurodisability or behavioural problem.
- An intermediary may be needed to help a child communicate with their legal team and/or the court, however in recent years access to this support has been cut back.
- Experts are independent, they do not work for one party. Check a draft of the expert report as it is harder to amend factual inaccuracies after the report is finalised.

Introduction

12.1 In many criminal cases involving children, there may be a need for an expert report. There are many different kinds of experts – for example, forensic scientists, cell site experts, and identification experts. This chapter focuses specifically on: experts who assist in assessing the impairments of child defendants in criminal proceedings:

- psychologists;
- psychiatrists; and
- intermediaries.

Their expert evidence can be used to support any applications the legal team may make regarding:

1) fitness to plead;
2) effective participation;
3) communication support;
4) exclusion of certain evidence/interviews;
5) expert evidence on a medical condition;
6) mitigation.

12.2 For more information on the issues an expert may be able to help with, see chapter 3 on the importance of background; and chapter 4 on effective participation.

Criminal Practice Direction

12.3 Children are recognised as vulnerable people by the Criminal Practice Direction (CrimPD) 3D.1: 'vulnerable include those under 18 years of age'; and the Criminal Procedure Rules (CrimPR) requires the court to take 'every reasonable step' to facilitate the participation of any person, including the defendant.[1] This includes enabling a defendant to:

1) give his or her best evidence;
2) comprehend proceedings;
3) engage fully with his or her defence.[2]

12.4 The pre-trial and trial process should, so far as is possible, be adapted to meet those ends[3] (see paras 4.31–4.55 for modifications and the special measures available to enable vulnerable people to participate in their trial).

12.5 A defence lawyer will need to present the evidence to the court as to what decision the court should make regarding fitness to plead or effective participation, or what adaptation a child defendant needs or what evidence needs to be presented to the decision-makers. In order to present this as evidence to the court, it is likely that a defence lawyer will need expert reports to explain their reasoning.

12.6 The Criminal Practice Directions now contain guidance on commissioning these medical expert reports at 3P.1 and 3P.2.[4] They set out the procedures to be followed in magistrates' courts and in the Crown Court where there is doubt about a defendant's mental health and, in the Crown Court, the defendant's capacity to participate in a trial. Rule 3P.2[5] states that there must be 'prompt commissioning of a report' by a party's representatives where expert medical opinion is material to that party's case which are wholly independent of the court. As the practice direction acknowledges, 'in

1 CrimPR r3.9(3)(b).
2 CrimPD 3D.2.
3 CrimPD 3D.2.
4 CrimPD 3P.1.
5 CrimPD 3P.2.

some circumstances a second such assessment, by another medical practitioner, may be required'.[6] Medical experts are often busy and the rates paid by the legal aid agency may not be competitive but the practice directions set the expectation that the case must progress according to timetables, 'no more than 6–8 weeks after the court makes its request in a magistrates' court, and no more than 10–12 weeks after the request in the Crown Court'.[7]

12.7 There is guidance published by the Ministry of Justice and HM Courts and Tribunals Service[8] called *Good practice guidance: commissioning, administering and producing psychiatric reports for sentencing.* The guidance includes standard forms of letters of instruction and other documents. (Note: it appears some of the references in the appendices of the *Good practice guidance* refer to earlier manifestations of the criminal procedure rules – see, for example, appendix 4 which refers to Part 33.3 – Contents of expert's report. The 2015 Criminal Procedure Rules replaces this at 19.4.)

12.8 Where a medical report has been, or is to be, commissioned by a party then that party is responsible for arranging payment of the fees incurred, even though the report is intended for the court's use.[9]

12.9 A legally aided party can apply to the legal aid agency to cover the costs of the expert report. In order to do this prior authority can be obtained from the legal aid agency. It is often useful to have a written advice explaining the need for the report, where the court has requested it, this should be clearly explained.

Instructing mental health experts

Which expert?

12.10 When deciding which kind of expert to instruct, there are a number of factors to be considered. It is important to know what historic information is already available; and any historic reports, diagnoses and assessments which already exist in relation to a child. There are some children who enter the criminal justice system with no diagnosis of any disorder, even though it may appear to the defence lawyer that there are issues that should be investigated. However,

6 CrimPD 3P.4.

7 CrimPD 3P.7.

8 Good Practice Guide Psychiatric Reports (2010) (NB the report states it is for sentencing purposes only).

9 CrimPD 3P.15.

there are also other children who will have spent many years going through assessments that will be well documented.

12.11 The Royal College of Psychiatrists recommended in their 2006 Occasional Paper 56 that assessments be undertaken:

> . . . by a clinical psychologist and a child psychiatrist of all child defendants facing serious criminal charges, based on an assessment procedure jointly agreed by the Royal College of Psychiatrists and the British Psychological Society.[10]

'Serious criminal charges' are defined in Occasional Paper 56 as including murder, manslaughter, abduction, rape, arson or grievous bodily harm.

12.12 For some children, it may be that they simply have a communication difficulty and what will assist them through the criminal process and enable them to effectively participate is the support of an intermediary. A defence lawyer may need a psychological report first to identify a learning difficulty or a communication difficulty.

12.13 It may be that reports are needed only for mitigation or at sentencing, and an expert will be able to explain a condition or behavior to the court to enable the decision maker to take that into account when deciding what is the appropriate sentence.

12.14 However, if it is suspected that a child is unfit to plead or cannot effectively participate the court will need to go through the legislative process to get a determination (see chapter 4 for the differing processes for unfitness and effective participation in youth court and Crown Court).

Psychologists

12.15 A psychologist is not a registered medical practitioner as defined by the legislation. They may be doctors through a PhD, not a medical practicing certificate. They are able to diagnose and treat conditions but they are not able to prescribe medication. To be able to get medication requires a psychiatrist, who is medically qualified.

12.16 In cases where a child may be unfit to plead or unable to effectively participate, the youth court requires the evidence of two registered medical practitioners; this could be a psychiatrist and a GP, or two psychiatrists.

10 Child Defendants Occasional Paper OP56 March 2006 – Royal College of Psychiatrists

12.17 The Crown Court can only make a finding of unfitness, 'on the written or oral evidence of two or more registered medical practitioners at least one of whom is duly approved' (an approved psychiatrist under Mental Health Act (MHA) 1983 s12)[11] (see chapter 4 for the procedure for effective participation and fitness to plead in the Crown Court). There is nothing to say that both reports need to be commissioned by the defence. It is common, once one report has been written for the defence that finds a defendant is not fit to plead, for the prosecution to obtain their own report. If both reports agree, then the Criminal Procedure (Insanity) Act (CP(I)A) 1964 s4(6) is fulfilled and the court can make a determination (which may be different from the expert's findings). If not, then the defence will usually obtain their own second report, so that the court has the evidence of two or more registered medical practitioners before it.

12.18 However, there may be the need for psychological reports before instructing a psychiatrist if the child has a learning difficulty. Psychologists are often best placed to diagnose conditions, undertake IQ tests for learning difficulties (see paras 3.63–3.65 for more information on IQ tests and learning disabilities) or diagnose autism spectrum disorders (ASD) (see paras 3.57–3.62 for autism spectrum disorders).

12.19 The legal framework for experts and procedure was drafted some time ago (Criminal Procedure and Insanity Act 1964 and Mental Health Act 1983). Since those times there have been many advances in how we treat and handle various conditions and the law has not kept apace. There have been criticisms of how well the current legal framework is suited (see para 4.117 below for the Law Commission's report). For some children, a psychologist's reports will be of more assistance to the court in actually understanding the child's condition and making an assessment as to the child's fitness to plead or ability to effectively participate. However, if arguing that the child is unfit, then there will still be a need for two further reports from medical practitioners (as the psychologist is usually not a medical practitioner) to fulfill the legal requirements of CP(I)A 1964 s4.

12.20 As the Royal College of Psychiatrists identified:

> . . . many child defendants suffer from a degree of learning disability, which in some cases may be sufficiently severe for the child or young person to fail a psychiatric test of fitness to plead.[12]

11 Criminal Procedure (Insanity) Act (CP(I)A) 1964 s4(5).

12 Child Defendants Occasional Paper OP56 March 2006 – Royal College of Psychiatrists at p52.

A registered medical practitioner will not be able to give the court his or her opinion on fitness to plead until an appropriate IQ test has been undertaken, and this will usually be undertaken by a psychologist. Even when there is an identifiable mental illness, the Royal College of Psychiatrists Occasional Paper 56 states:

> . . . it would still be useful to have a report prepared by a clinical psychologist, given the correlation between psychiatric disturbance and learning disability, it would clearly be of assistance to the assessing forensic child psychiatrist (Hall, 2000) to be able to see the clinical psychology report on the child defendant before undertaking any assessment fitness to plead.[13]

12.21 For more on the difficulties with the current system relating to fitness to plead and effective participation see paras 4.127–4.130 and the Law Commission's review and recommendations in this aspect of criminal justice.

Psychiatrists

12.22 A psychiatrist is a medical practitioner with a specialisation in psychiatry, which he or she has completed in addition to his or her general medical practice. A psychiatrist is able to prescribe medication, which a psychologist is not. However, many psychiatrists and psychologists work together, one prescribing medication while referring to the psychologist who may provide therapeutic support.

12.23 In criminal proceedings in either the youth court or the Crown Court, a child will need an expert report prepared by a psychiatrist if the court is to consider fitness to plead or an ability to effectively participate. In the Crown Court, there is a requirement in a finding of fitness to plead (CP(I)A 1964 s4(6)) that one of the expert witnesses must be 'duly approved', which means approved for the purposes of Mental Health Act 1983 s12 by the secretary of state.[14] This is not a requirement in the youth court or adult magistrates court.

When to instruct a mental health expert

12.24 A defence lawyer should always consider instructing an expert, especially when a child defendant is very young and/or has any learning difficulties or behavioural problems. For a defence lawyer to be able

13 Child Defendants Occasional Paper OP56 March 2006 – Royal College of Psychiatrists at p54.

14 CP(I)A 1964 s8(2).

to effectively identify and develop relevant information about a child's vulnerabilities (see chapter 3 on the importance of background). It is better to do this earlier in the trial process, even if it is thought it may only be relevant for sentencing. If the child has any additional needs that the defence lawyer has not picked up on, it may affect how the trial is conducted.

12.25 A defence lawyer will need to write a letter of instruction asking the expert specific questions in relation to each child defendant the letter may need to ask an expert whether a child defendant is:

1) fit to plead;
2) able to effectively participate;
3) what possible adaptations to the trial process might be needed to enable a child to effectively participate in the proceedings;
4) anything relevant to argue for excluding interviews;
5) anything that would be relevant to preventing an adverse inference if a child does not give evidence;
6) anything relevant to a possible defence (suggestibility, compliance, ability to form mens rea);
7) anything that may be used as mitigation.

12.26 The expert, having considered all of matters in the letter of instruction and considering all the possible modifications and special measures available may conclude that effective participation is not possible or that a defendant is not fit to plead.

12.27 Due to the legal requirement of medical experts and the requirement that certain assessments are undertaken by psychologists, there may be the need for a defendant to be seen by up to three experts before any decisions can be made.

12.28 Funding for an expert should be available if the child has legal aid and the Legal Aid Agency (LAA) believe that funding is appropriate. Funding of experts for legal aid reports is paid at an hourly rate fixed by the LAA.[15]

12.29 The report needs to be specifically prepared for the criminal proceedings. Experts should set out in their reports the criteria by which they have decided that a child either is or is not fit to plead and is or is not able to effectively participate going through the legal requirements (see chapter 4) which should be set out in the letter of instruction. The steps should be compared with the information they

15 www.gov.uk/guidance/expert-witnesses-in-legal-aid-cases.

have from the lawyer and background materials, where relevant another expert's assessment and findings from the individual child and carer.

12.30 The courts are not readily willing to find a defendant unfit to plead or unable to effectively participate. In a 2011 appeal against conviction the experts, who had not been involved at the trial stage, presented evidence that the appellant would not have been fit to plead in his trial, fitness to plead had not raised by the trial lawyers, the Court of Appeal decided that:

> . . . a court must rigorously examine evidence of psychiatrists adduced before them and then subject that evidence to careful analysis against the Pritchard criteria as interpreted in Podola . . . a court would be failing in its duty to both the public and a defendant if it did not rigorously examine the evidence and reach its own conclusion.[16]

12.31 It may be that the Court of Appeal is less willing to consider retrospective findings by psychiatrists or psychologists when cases are on appeal. See also *R v Grant-Murray and another*,[17] where the Court of Appeal discusses why it dismissed the expert findings.

12.32 Expert evidence, presented to the trial court, should be considered carefully as mental health practitioners have expertise in assessing children's needs and conditions. In a case where the youth court ruled that a child defendant could not have the help of an intermediary because: 'This report does not show [the claimant] to have any greater difficulties in this than many other youths who appear before the court.'[18] The High Court ruled on a judicial review of the decision by the magistrates that:

> I have some difficulty in understanding how the justices were able to reach that view. . . . A registered intermediary could help him to overcome those difficulties, could ensure that the questions asked of him were simple and that he had adequate time to respond, and could alert the court to the difficulties which he faced in answering them. It seems to me that without those precautions being taken, the risk that this claimant would not receive a fair trial would be real.[19]

16 *R v Walls* [2011] EWCA Crim 443, para 38.

17 [2017] EWCA Crim 1228.

18 *R (AS) v Great Yarmouth Youth Court* [2011] EWHC 2059 (Admin), para 7.

19 *R (AS) v Great Yarmouth Youth Court* [2011] EWHC 2059 (Admin), paras 8–9.

12.33 The prosecution may instruct its own expert to examine the child and may not accept the report of the defence expert, especially if a defence expert finds a child not able to effectively participate or unfit to plead. The prosecution may be less likely to instruct their own expert if the child needs modifications or intermediary support only. It is a normal part of the procedure for a child to be seen by a prosecution expert.

12.34 Where the prosecution do choose to instruct their own expert the child will have an appointment with the prosecution expert. It is important to note that, while the expert is instructed by the prosecution, all experts are impartial and are preparing the report for use by the court. However, any admissions made or suggestions of offending behaviour to the experts will not be covered by legal privilege and/or confidentiality.

Content of expert's report

12.35 CrimPR r19.4 sets out what should be contained in an expert report:

(1) An expert's report must:
- (a) give details of the expert's qualifications, relevant experience and accreditation;
- (b) give details of any literature or other information which the expert has relied on in making the report;
- (c) contain a statement setting out the substance of all facts given to the expert which are material to the opinions expressed in the report or upon which those opinions are based;
- (d) make clear which of the facts stated in the report are within the expert's own knowledge;
- (e) say who carried out any examination, measurement, test or experiment which the expert has used for the report and–
  - (i) give the qualifications, relevant experience and accreditation of that person;
  - (ii) say whether or not the examination, measurement, test or experiment was carried out under the expert's supervision; and
  - (iii) summarise the findings on which the expert relies.
- (f) where there is a range of opinion on the matters dealt with in the report–
  - (i) summarise the range of opinion, and
  - (ii) give reasons for his/her own opinion.

(g) if the expert is not able to give his/her opinion without qualification, state the qualification;
(h) contain a summary of the conclusions reached;
(i) contain a statement that the expert understands his duty to the court, and has complied and will continue to comply with that duty; and
(j) contain the same declaration of truth as a witness statement.

(2) Only sub-paragraphs (i) and (j) of rule 33.3(1) apply to a summary by an expert of his conclusions served in advance of that expert's report.

Instructing an intermediary

Introduction

12.36 The role of an intermediary is set out in Youth Justice and Criminal Evidence Act 1999 s29. Section 29(1) states:

> The function of an intermediary is to communicate–
> (a) to the witness, questions put to the witness, and
> (b) to any person asking such questions, the answers given by the witness in reply to them,
> and to explain such questions or answers so far as necessary to enable them to be understood by the witness or person in question. [20]

12.37 CrimPD 3F.1 states that intermediaries facilitate communication with witnesses and defendants who have communication needs. Their primary function is to improve the quality of evidence and aid understanding between the court, the advocates and the witness or defendant.

> 3F.11 Statutory provisions providing for defendants to be assisted by an intermediary when giving evidence (where necessary to ensure a fair trial) are not in force . . .
>
> 3F.12 The court may direct the appointment of an intermediary to assist a defendant in reliance on its inherent powers . . .

12.38 An intermediary is often a speech and language therapist who has been trained to assist with communication with vulnerable people in criminal proceedings.

12.39 For more about the limitations on when intermediaries can be used in court, see paras 4.35–4.42.

20 Section 29(2).

Registered Intermediaries

12.40 Registered Intermediaries (RIs) are trained and accredited by the Ministry of Justice (MOJ) to assist victims and witnesses (including children) in giving evidence. Registered intermediaries are available and should be used for vulnerable witnesses and victims, they can be used both when a witness is being interviewed at the police station and when giving evidence at court. Child defendants are unable to access RIs through the MOJ for support in court. The MOJ oversees the RI scheme, providing training and best practice.

Non-Registered Intermediaries

12.41 When the RI scheme was developed, RIs were considered only for witnesses. The use of intermediaries for vulnerable defendants has been developed through common law, under 'equality of arms' and the court's inherent powers. In 2005, in a judicial review the High Court stated that although:

> . . . there is no statutory power permitting the appointment of an intermediary for a defendant, but there may be some procedural power in the Criminal Procedure Rules. Criminal Procedure Rule 1.11 sets out the overriding objective to deal with criminal cases justly, which includes at (c) recognising the rights of a defendant, particularly under Article 6 of the European Convention on Human Rights. Furthermore, the court's case management powers at Rule 3.10(b)(v) require the court to consider what arrangements are necessary to facilitate the participation of any person in the trial, including the defendant.[21]

12.42 A vulnerable defendant must be able to effectively participate in all parts of their trial, not just the giving of evidence, (see chapter 4 on effective participation). For a number of years the use of intermediaries to support defendants, throughout their trials, was the recommended to enable effective participation. See *R v Walls*[22] which makes it plain that the appointment of an intermediary is one mechanism which enables defendants to stand trial in circumstances where they may otherwise be unable to effectively participate and where the jury may not otherwise understand the defendant's limitations. In 2016 in its review of unfitness to plead, the Law Commission stated:

21 *C v Sevenoaks Youth Court* [2005] EWHC 2583 (Admin), para 16.
22 [2011] EWCA Crim 443.

> Although intermediary assistance is not a remedy for all participation difficulties, we consider that for many defendants with significant difficulties it offers the best mechanism for facilitating their effective participation in trial.[23]

12.43 In recent years the courts have become more reluctant to grant applications for defendants to have intermediaries for the whole trial. Defence lawyers should be aware that the Criminal Practice Directions 2015 (amended most recently in November 2018) states that although the court may exercise its inherent powers to appoint an intermediary to assist a defendant in giving evidence or for the entire trial, it will be '*extremely rare*' for directions to be given to appoint an intermediary for the entire trial (CrimPD 3F.13). Instead of an intermediary the Criminal Practice Direction states that 'the court should consider sympathetically any application for the defendant to be accompanied throughout the trial by a support worker or other appropriate companion who can provide that assistance'.[24] See paras 4.40–4.42 for more on special measures and intermediaries for defendants.

12.44 However, if a child needs the communication support for the whole of the trial, then the application should be made, with the support of a report written by a mental health expert and/or an intermediary. The report should specifically address whether the expert believes an intermediary should assist for the whole trial or evidence. An independent organisation that matches intermediaries, called Intermediaries for Justice has issued a policy on supporting defendants for the whole trial or just for the giving of evidence. The guidance states: 'Members consider that it is necessary to assess the individual defendant's communication needs and level of understanding, and then recommend accordingly.' They suggest that an intermediary for the giving of evidence only will only be appropriate in 'a minority of cases'.[25] The concern is that it may be difficult to support an individual giving evidence if the intermediary does not have the context of having heard the evidence in the case. Recently a conviction was upheld where an intermediary service refused to attend for the giving of evidence.[26]

23 Law Commission – Unfitness to Plead; at: https://s3-eu-west-2.amazonaws.com/lawcom-prod-storage 11jsxou24uy7q/uploads/2016/01/lc364_unfitness_vol-1.pdf.

24 CrimPD 3F.12.

25 Evidence Only Guidance, Intermediaries for Justice p3.

26 *R v Biddle* [2019] EWCA Crim 86.

12.45 The Law Commission review on unfitness to plead states:

> ... examples given by intermediaries and representatives of those who require an intermediary throughout trial are most often defendants who have: autism spectrum conditions, dissociative identity disorder (multiple personality disorder), or a significant learning disability combined with, for example, extremely limited working memory or Attention Deficit Hyperactivity Disorder ('ADHD').

It went on to conclude that:

> So as well as facilitating the giving of oral evidence by the defendant, the intermediary ensures that during the rest of the trial process the defendant is able to follow and engage with the proceedings as a whole as far as he or she can. In order to facilitate that, the intermediary also assists the court and other participants to adjust proceedings throughout the trial. An unqualified supporter would neither have the skills nor the standing to take on such a role. Nor could an intermediary attending only for the defendant's oral evidence achieve this wider communication role.[27]

12.46 In *R v Yahya Rashid*[28] the Court of Appeal made it clear that the courts do not have to defer to the experts opinions as to the best use of an intermediary, even when there is a consensus of opinion, in that case against the recommendation of two psychologists and an intermediary. The trial judge ruled that the defendant was only entitled to have the support of an intermediary when giving evidence. The Court of Appeal upheld this stating:

> The judge was in our view correct in analysing the need for an intermediary at the different stages of a trial and was right in his decision that an intermediary was only required during the time the applicant was giving evidence, overgenerous though (as the judge recognised) that might be.[29]

Rashid was a case concerning an adult vulnerable defendant. Therefore, while the court considered the need for the defendant to effectively participate, there was no assessment of the defendant's welfare. Courts dealing with child defendants need to ensure that they can effectively participate but are also obliged to consider their welfare[30] and bests interests.[31] Therefore, there may be stronger

27 *Unfitness to Plead*, Law Commission, para 2.53.

28 [2017] EWCA Crim 2.

29 Para 70.

30 Children and Young Persons Act 1933 s44.

31 United Nations Convention on the Rights of the Child s3.

arguments in favour of supportive measures, such as intermediaries for the whole of the trial in the cases of children in courts.

12.47 Some intermediaries may refuse to act for a defendant if the court does not direct attendance for the full duration of the trial. If the intermediary is required to facilitate more than a child's giving of evidence and is needed to ensure a child's effective participation in the trial, this should be explained in any expert or intermediary report.

Intermediaries for defendants

12.48 Since the Ministry of Justice do not provide RIs for vulnerable defendants, a number of independent intermediary organisations have been set up. Three of those are:

- Triangle;[32]
- Communicourt;[33]
- Intermediaries for Justice.[34]

12.49 Some courts may be unwilling to pay the rates charged by these organisations and may provide the defence with a list of intermediaries who are prepared to work at rates that are more acceptable to the courts.

12.50 Many of the intermediaries associated with the independent organisations may also be RIs, who act through the WIS scheme for witnesses and victims and through a separate organisation for defendants.

12.51 For more disturbed/impaired young defendants with co-morbid psychiatric disorders, it may be necessary for an Expert Mental Health professional to be present to communicate with the child defendant.[35] This can be in addition to or instead of an intermediary and can be authorised under the court's inherent powers (see para 4.38 for more about inherent powers).

Funding for an intermediary

12.52 Prior authority may need to be sought from the LAA for legal aid if needed to cover attendance of the intermediary for taking instructions, conferences with counsel, pre-trial hearings and familiarisation visit.

32 https://triangle.org.uk/service/intermediaries.

33 www.communicourt.co.uk/.

34 www.intermediaries-for-justice.org/.

35 Eileen Vizard – CBA 214.

If the court grants the application for an intermediary for the defendant during the trial, the funding of the intermediary is covered by the court paid from central funds.[36]

Quick guide to experts

Checklist of experts

12.53 *Intermediaries*

- Professional service
- Communications expert
- Often speech and language therapist
- Special knowledge of the communications difficulty faced by a defendant or witness
- Trained and accredited
- Impartial and independent (distinct role from parent, guardian or supporting adult)

Psychologist

- Undergraduate degree and postgraduate qualification – if they have completed a PhD they will have the title of Doctor
- *Not* a medical doctor
- May work for a hospital or NHS
- Functioning, personality, development
- Undertakes standardised and qualitative assessments
- Identifies learning difficulties
- Only psychologist can perform and IQ test
- Child and adolescent specialism and/or forensic specialism
- Specific IQ test for children (Weschler Intelligence Scale for Childrend (WISC)) (if an expert is not using WISC for a child defendant aged up to 16, he or she is probably not a specialist and test is subject to being invalid)
- Diagnoses Autistic Spectrum Disorders including Aspergers (now part of high functioning autism) – issues around giving evidence or actual offences

36 Internal guidance for court staff is in 'Guidance for HMCTS Staff: Registered and non registered intermediaries for vulnerable defendants and vulnerable defence and prosecution witnesses', HM Courts and Tribunals Service (HMCTS).

- Diagnoses Attention Deficit Hyperactivity Disorder – although medication for this would need to be prescribed by a psychiatrist (see below)
- Diagnoses post-traumatic stress disorder (PTSD) – can be used in mitigation, and to explain events can trigger reactions

Psychiatrist

- Medically trained – a qualified doctor with further specialism
- Registered medical practitioner – as required by legislation for finding of unfitness to plead in youth court and crown court Mental Health Act 1983 s37(3) and CP(I)A 1964 s4 (see paras 4.98–4.99)
- Section 12 approved under Mental Health Act 1983
- Should be a forensic specialist with child and adolescent specialism
- Forensic specialism is specialism in people in the criminal justice system
- Undertakes mental state examination, interview and observation
- Biological, medical and medication
- Diagnoses of mental disorder
- Mental Illness as defined by DSM-V or ICD-10 (DSM-V tends to be used more by American psychiatrists; UK psychiatrists tend to refer to ICD-10) (see paras 3.38–3.39)
- Schizophrenia
- Bi-polar (manic depressive)
- Drug induced psychosis
- Psychosis
- Personality disorders
- Can prescribe medication
- Can facilitate a hospital order (Mental Health Act 1983) (see chapter 22)

Suggestions for content for a letter of instruction

Psychologist/psychiatrist

- Personal details of client (name, date of birth, address, parent or carer, address)
- Background of client (parents/carers, family circumstances, education, any earlier reports, relevant medical records, details of adult to speak with)
- Details of court proceedings (offences, court, dates of hearings)
- Court process (trial/sentence, nature of the evidence, co-defendants)
- Setting out the legal framework for the expert. Their expertise is in their area, yours is the law: fitness to plead, effective participation, special measures, intermediary (for giving of evidence or whole trial), exclusion of evidence, mitigation
- Additional matters you might ask them to look into – IQ, suggestibility or compliance, as defined by Gudjonsson: Suggestibility – likelihood of yielding to investigative pressure. Is there a case for the interview to be excluded? Compliance – likelihood of acting under duress, vulnerability to custodial setting, specific issues to your client)
- Set out that the report is a privileged document for the purposes of the case only and as instructed by the client's lawyer
- Request a conversation with the expert before the report is finalised, in case there are errors or things that are factually wrong. (It is not ethical to exclude parts of the report when serving it on the other party or the court. It is possible to make amendments but it is better to get it right before it is served, hence why it is important to discuss while still in draft form)
- State if there are things that you do not want discussed or the client doesn't want to discuss
- Ask for the elements of an offence to be discussed in hypothetical, rather than getting into specifics of the offence charged. The client's instructions about the allegation may not be best placed in an expert report
- Remember – an expert witness works for the court not for you and has a duty to disclose all information favourable or not in a report
- Include the quotation for the costs and what the lawyer covers, any court attendance will be paid for by the court – check legal aid rates, confirm the limitation set by the legal aid agency

CHAPTER 13

Trials of child defendants

Key points

- Throughout proceedings, defence lawyers and the court should consider what adjustments must be made to allow children to effectively participate at trial, even where the child presents no additional difficulties.
- Children may have a defence to charges if they are victims of trafficking – trafficking can take many forms, including 'county lines' and trafficking from abroad.
- Prosecutors must consider whether it is in the public interest for victims of trafficking to be charged.
- Many defences which are also available to adults are adapted to the vulnerability of children, often through a modification of the mens rea requirement or the reasonable person test.
- Youth is a relevant factor when judges consider making an adverse inference direction and when juries decide whether to draw such inferences.
- When directing the jury, judges should consider whether directions should be modified to reflect a child's age, development and maturity.
- Trials may proceed in the absence of child defendants, unless there is a good reason for the absence.

Introduction

13.1 A defendant's age – both chronological age, and his or her maturity and mental capacity – should influence many aspects of any trial in whichever court it takes place.

13.2 The defendant's age is relevant in many legal applications. For example, when considering a bad character application by the Crown under the limb of propensity (Criminal Justice Act (CJA) 2003 s101(1)(d)), when deciding whether or not past behaviour will indeed provide any real evidence useful to the jury, one consideration should be how quickly children change and mature.

13.3 Age may be a relevant factor for a number of defendants, not just those who are children – for example, it may be appropriate in some cases to treat young adults differently from those over the age of 25.

13.4 Age and maturity are important factors when considering subjective tests – for example, self-defence or recklessness.

13.5 Age may even be relevant for objective tests – for example, age is a relevant characteristic in a reasonable person test.

13.6 The usual criminal procedure rules and rules of evidence apply to trials of children as much as they do to trials of adult defendants. This chapter covers those areas that are specific to child defendants and are relevant to children tried in the adult magistrates' court, Crown Court or youth court.

13.7 While legal directions are often referred to as 'jury directions', we have referred to them as 'legal directions', as magistrates will have to be directed by the legal adviser and district judges should also have regard to the relevant legal directions when trying a case. Thus, when it might be relevant to tailor a direction to a jury, it is just as important, if in the youth or adult magistrates' court, for the court to consider how a legal direction might be modified to be appropriately considered by the bench.

Effective participation, special measures and modifications

13.8 When considering a trial for a child, special care must be given to ensuring that the child can effectively participate. That is true, even when the trial is taking place in the youth court, and even when the child has no additional difficulties. Each child is different and will have different barriers to allowing him or her to participate in the trial process. It is incumbent on the court and the defence lawyer to ensure that the child has a fair trial, and that the child's welfare is considered. These considerations are important at all stages of the proceedings, including the initial hearings, such as the Plea and Trial Preparation Hearing (PTPH), and in conferences with the child defendant (see further chapter 4 on capacity, effective participation and fitness to plead).

13.9 The difficulties that are often faced by children are dealt with in the section on the importance of background (see paras 3.40–3.102). What is also important is the evidence about adolescent brain development and how all children face different challenges to adults when going through a trial process (see paras 3.30–3.36 on the adolescent brain development).

13.10 For many children it will be helpful to instruct an expert to consider their ability to effectively participate, as well as other matters relevant to their case (see chapter 12 on instructing an expert). This should be done early on, so the relevance of any report can be fully considered. Even where it is not done, the defence lawyer should ensure that he or she is fully aware of the child's needs.

13.11 The defence lawyer should then consider what applications to make to court concerning the child. This may be under the criminal practice direction for vulnerable defendants, or under a special measure. It should always be noted that the list of modifications set out in the Crim PD is not exhaustive.

13.12 In the Crown Court the court should raise the fact the defendant is a child at the PTPH and consider what modifications should be made for the trial. It may be appropriate to make directions later, for example, after a report has been written, but it is important that these matters are considered ahead of trial so that the appropriate steps can be taken to ensure that all facilities are available, and also so that this can be explained to the child so that the child is aware of what will happen at the trial.

13.13 The importance of effective participation is discussed at paras 4.14–4.19. An explanation of the criminal practice direction, is at paras 4.20–4.30. Modifications and special measures for child defendants are dealt with at paras 4.31–4.55. Child witnesses (other than the defendant) are automatically entitled to special measures.

Defences

Trafficked children

Overview

13.14 Child trafficking takes several forms. County lines is one form; children may also be trafficked from abroad, or within the country by other gangs.

County lines

13.15 'County lines' is the police term for gangs supplying drugs, mainly heroin and crack cocaine, to suburban areas, market towns and coastal towns.[1] Children are often used by these gangs to deliver drugs around the country. Many of these children may not consider

1 Home Office, 'Criminal exploitation of children and vulnerable adults: County lines guidance' (2017).

themselves to be trafficked. County lines is one of the main generators of gang-related exploitation of children.[2]

13.16 Those children who have been trafficked under county lines may have a defence to the crimes that they commit, either under the Modern Slavery Act (MSA) 2015 or under common law (see further paras 13.30–13.32 below on the MSA 2015 and common law). Further, any lawyer – defence or prosecution – who is concerned that a child may be being exploited by county lines gangs should consider referring the child to the police or local authority, who can in turn make a referral to the National Referral Mechanism (NRM). See further paras 13.40–13.44 on support for trafficked children.

Modern Slavery Act 2015

13.17 The MSA 2015 provides a statutory defence for victims of child trafficking and slavery accused of certain offences.

13.18 Where a child commits an offence and the child does so as a direct consequence of being or having been a victim of slavery or trafficking, there is a defence under MSA 2015 s45. It states that a child will be not guilty of an offence if:

> (a) the person is under the age of 18 when the person does the act which constitutes the offence,
> (b) the person does that act as a direct consequence of the person being, or having been, a victim of slavery or a victim of relevant exploitation, and
> (c) a reasonable person in the same situation as the person and having the person's relevant characteristics would do that act.[3]

'Relevant characteristics' means age, sex and any physical or mental illness or disability. 'Relevant exploitation' is exploitation that is attributable to the exploited person being, or having been, a victim of human trafficking.[4]

13.19 Offences subject to this defence include some forms of theft including pickpocketing, cultivation of cannabis, offences related to prostitution and immigration offences. There are 140 offences which are exempt from the statutory defence,[5] many of which are common in child trafficking cases – for example, arson. Other offences that are excluded include murder, kidnap and false imprisonment.

2 Detective Inspector Brittany Clarke, Trident, Metropolitan Police at Westminster Briefing on 29 June 2017.

3 MSA 2015 s45(4).

4 MSA 2015 s45(5).

5 MSA 2015 s45(7) and Sch 4.

13.20 Once it is established that a child is a victim of trafficking for the purposes of exploitation, the relevant consideration is whether there is a sufficient nexus between the trafficking for the purposes of exploitation and the offence. It is not necessary to go so far as to show that there was compulsion to commit the offences, as would be required in the case of an adult.[6]

Definition of trafficking

13.21 MSA 2015 s2 creates an offence of 'human trafficking'. This definition is set out below as the relevant definition for the defence under section 45 of the same Act. Other definitions are used in international law (see paras 13.33–13.35 on international obligations).

13.22 Under the MSA 2015, a person commits the offence of human trafficking if the person arranges or facilitates the travel of another person ('V') with a view to V being exploited.[7] It is irrelevant whether V consents to the travel (whether V is an adult or a child).[8] A person may in particular arrange or facilitate V's travel by recruiting V, transporting or transferring V, harbouring or receiving V, or transferring or exchanging control over V.[9]

13.23 A person 'arranges or facilitates' V's travel with a view to V being exploited if the person intends to exploit V (in any part of the world) during or after the travel, or the person knows or ought to know that another person is likely to exploit V (in any part of the world) during or after the travel.[10]

13.24 'Travel' means arriving in, or entering, any country; departing from any country; or travelling within any country.[11]

13.25 'Exploitation' is defined by MSA 2015 s3, which provides a wide definition covering a wide range of circumstances including organ removal and sexual exploitation. It also covers circumstances where an individual is subjected to 'force, threats or deception designed to induce' the individual into providing services of any kind.[12]

6 *R v VS and others* [2017] EWCA Crim 36, para 35.
7 MSA 2015 s2.
8 MSA 2015 s2(2).
9 MSA 2015 s2(3).
10 MSA 2015 s2(4).
11 MSA 2015 s2(5).
12 MSA 2015 s3(5).

Decision to prosecute

13.26 Where it is clear that the child has been a victim of trafficking, the Crown Prosecution Service (CPS) should review their decision to prosecute. It may be that it is not in the public interest to prosecute such cases.

13.27 Even where a defence may not be made out – for example, if the child is charged with an offence that is one of the exceptions under the MSA 2015 – there should be consideration as to whether it is in the public interest to prosecute (see paras 7.108–7.139 onwards on decisions to prosecute). The Home Office produced a factsheet about the Modern Slavery Bill in November 2014,[13] which stated:

> Where an offence is not covered by the defence, the CPS should still consider whether it is in the public interest to prosecute or not, considering the Director of Public Prosecutions guidance on modern slavery cases. In serious cases (such as rape or where someone had been killed), it is essential that prosecutors can look at all the circumstances of the case and consider both the victim of the offence and position of the modern slavery victim when determining whether it is in the interests of justice, that a prosecution should proceed.

13.28 The CPS legal guidance on human trafficking, smuggling and slavery states:

> Where there may be consideration of charge and prosecution of vulnerable children or adults, prosecutors should consider applying the statutory defence or CPS policy on the non-prosecution of suspects who may be victims of trafficking.

And:

> When considering whether to prosecute a child victim of trafficking/slavery, prosecutors will only need to consider whether or not the offence is committed as a direct consequence of, or in the course of trafficking/slavery.

13.29 The CPS will want to consider whether the child is a victim, and that may be done through the Conclusive Grounds from the NRM (see paras 13.48–13.51 below). However, they will also need to consider any evidence about the relevant characteristics of the child that might be important to consider the 'relevant person' test under the statutory defence, such as age and vulnerability.[14]

13 Modern Slavery Bill, Factsheet: Defence for victims (Clause 45) Home Office, November 2014.

14 MSA 2015 s45(c).

Abuse of process under common law

13.30 The prosecution of victims of trafficking for offences they committed as a result of being trafficked was held to be an abuse of process in the case of *R v L, HVN, THN and T*[15] in 2013. This case was heard before the defence under the MSA 2015 came into force, and it may well be that the defendants in those appeals would now benefit from a defence under MSA 2015 s45. However, there will be situations where the statutory defence does not apply, and the defence may wish to argue that the case is an abuse of process. In such circumstances, thought should be given to writing representations to the CPS to argue that the case should not be prosecuted.

13.31 In the case of *L*, the Court of Appeal made it clear that the culpability of any victim of trafficking may be 'diminished, and in some cases effectively extinguished . . . because not realistic alternative was available'.[16] The protection provided against prosecution or punishment is the 'abuse of process' jurisdiction.[17] The case also makes it clear that age is a relevant factor in deciding culpability, and deciding whether there has been an abuse of process is fact-specific, depending both on whether the defendant is a victim of trafficking, and whether the circumstances meant that there was no culpability in the offence. Further, in circumstances where it is not an abuse of process it may still be strong mitigation.

13.32 The court has previously emphasised the importance of the parties being aware as to whether a child has been trafficked.[18]

International obligations

13.33 The defence under MSA 2015 s45 was intended to reflect the international principle of non-prosecution of trafficked children arising in a number of international instruments and the UK's obligations under:

- the Council of Europe Convention on Action against Trafficking in Human Beings 2005;[19] and
- the EU Directive on preventing and combating trafficking in human beings and protecting its victims.[20]

15 [2013] EWCA Crim 991.
16 Para 13 of the judgment.
17 Para 14 of the judgment.
18 *LM and others* [2010] EWCA Crim 2327; *R v O* [2008] EWCA Crim 2835.
19 CETS No 197.
20 Directive 2011/36/EU of the European Parliament and of the Council of 5 April 2011 on preventing and combating trafficking in human beings and protecting its victims.

13.34 The UK ratified the Council of Europe Convention against Trafficking in Human Beings in 2008. The convention states:

> ... each party shall, in accordance with the basic principles of its legal system provide for the possibility of not imposing penalties on victims for their involvement in unlawful activities, to the extent that they have been compelled to do so.[21]

'Child trafficking' is defined as the 'recruitment, transportation, transfer, harbouring or receipt' of a child for the purposes of exploitation (by Article 3 Protocol to Prevent, Suppress and Punish Trafficking in Persons Especially Women and Children, supplementing the United Nations Convention against Transnational Organised Crime).

13.35 The EU Directive on preventing and combating trafficking in human beings and protecting its victims, came into effect on 6 April 2013. Recital 8 of the EU Directive underlines:

> Children are more vulnerable than adults and therefore at greater risk of becoming victims of trafficking in human beings. In the application of this Directive, the child's best interest must be of primary consideration, in accordance with the Charter of Fundamental Rights of the European Union and the 1989 United Nations Convention on the Rights of the Child.

Identifying trafficked victims

13.36 It may be that a child arrested for a criminal offence has not yet been identified as a victim of trafficking. There is too little awareness of the extent of child criminal exploitation (CCE), and it may be that the defence lawyer is the first to realise the true situation. While the defence lawyer may be best placed to ascertain that the child is being exploited, it is also important for prosecutors, police and especially the youth offending team (YOT) to be aware of the issues, and to ask appropriate questions if they are concerned.

13.37 The following factors should be considered as a possible sign of county lines exploitation:

- The child has been arrested for possession and intent to supply significant quantities of drugs, particularly heroin and crack cocaine.
- The child has been arrested far from where the child usually lives.
- The child was arrested on public transport, in particular a train.
- The child was arrested in the address of a vulnerable person (who may be being exploited for use of his or her address).

21 Council of Europe Convention on Action against Trafficking in Human Beings 2005, Article 26.

- The child is in care.
- The child was carrying a weapon when arrested.
- The child has unexplained injuries.
- The child was arrested with, or seen with, older people.

13.38 The Home Office has issued guidance setting out the kind of indicators that might signal that a child is vulnerable to exploitation or currently being exploited by a gang.

13.39 There are obviously other factors that might be relevant to suggest other forms of exploitation. Particular care should also be taken when dealing with children who have travelled to this country unaccompanied from a different country and who are arrested for criminal activity.

Support for trafficked victims

13.40 Once a victim of CCE is identified, the following steps should be taken:

- a report should be made to the police;
- the child should be referred to children's social care;
- a referral should be made to the NRM – done by police or local authority;
- a strategy meeting should be convened.

13.41 A defence lawyer may need to consider his or her ethical duties when considering whether to report the matter to the police or the NRM, as in many cases the child may not support such action. Any lawyer should consult the relevant code of conduct.[22] While lawyers are bound by rules of client confidentiality, there are circumstances when this comes into conflict with other rules in the code of conduct.[23] There are no specific exceptions to the rules on confidentiality when dealing with trafficked victims, the general principles apply. However, The Law Society have published a practice note on criminal prosecutions of victims of trafficking, which states that there may be a conflict between duties of confidentiality and the solicitor's ability to act in the client's best interest if a child refuses to allow the solicitor to disclose information about ongoing abuse:[24]

22 For barristers: Bar Standards Board Handbook, 3rd edn, November 2018, Part Two: The Code of Conduct (BSB Code). For solicitors: Solicitors Regulation Authority Code of Conduct 2011 (SRA Code), version 20, October 2018.

23 Such as the duty to act in the best interests of your client (Principle 4 SRA Code; and Core Duty 2 of the BSB Code).

24 Para 6.6.

You must consider whether the threat to the child's life or health, both mental and physical, is sufficiently serious to justify a breach of the duty of confidentiality.

13.42 The Code of Conduct for barristers will create similar tensions – see the Bar Standards Board Handbook. Any lawyer who is concerned about a case should contact the Law Society's Practice Advice Service, or the Bar Council Ethics Line.

13.43 Further, if the child is still under the control of exploiters at the time, any co-operation with authorities might put the child in further danger.

13.44 Children who are not UK nationals may need immigration and asylum advice.

Children's Society guide

13.45 The Children's Society – as part of the National Child Sexual Abuse and Exploitation (CSAE) Prevention Programme for England and Wales, in partnership with Victim Support and the National Police Chiefs' Council (NPCC) – have published a guide to share knowledge on county lines and to offer suggestions on how to support the children involved.

13.46 The guide gives examples of how gangs threaten or coerce children into committing offences; examples of indicators that a child is being exploited; and examples of the types of vulnerabilities that may increase a child's risk of become a victim. It then goes on to explain some of the barriers which prevent victims engaging with professional networks – for example, not identifying as victims.

13.47 A directory which suggests ways language can be used to underline the fact that the victims of CCE are victims rather than suspects is included along with lists of relevant services and resources.

National Referral Mechanism

13.48 The NRM is a framework for identifying victims of human trafficking or modern slavery. The child does not need to consent for a referral to be made.

13.49 The police and local authority are competent authorities to make a referral.

13.50 Once referred, there are two stages of the investigation. The first stage is 'reasonable grounds'. The NRM team has a target date of five working days from receipt of referral in which to decide whether there are reasonable grounds to believe that the individual is a potential victim of human trafficking or modern slavery. The test is 'from the information available so far I believe, but cannot prove' that the individual is a potential victim of trafficking or modern slavery.

13.51 The second stage is a 45-day reflection and recovery period during which the competent authority gathers further information. This additional information is used to make a conclusive decision on whether the referred person is a victim of human trafficking or modern slavery. The decision should be made as soon as possible after the 45-day period, but there is no target, as the amount of time taken to reach a conclusive decision will depend on the circumstances of the case. The test for this decision is the balance of probabilities: 'it is more likely than not' that the individual is a victim of human trafficking or modern slavery.

Age disputes

13.52 Where a trafficked child has arrived from another country, it is not unusual for the child to have arrived without clear proof of age. MSA 2015 s51 provides a presumption that where a public authority has reasonable grounds to believe that a person may be a victim of human trafficking and there is some uncertainty as to the person's age but the person may be a child, then the person should be presumed to be a child until there has been an assessment and determination of the person's age. Age disputes are covered in paras 2.24–2.55.

Other guidance

13.53 For further guidance, see the following:

- *Modern Slavery Bill. Factsheet: Defence for victims* (Clause 45) (Home Office, November 2014);
- *Legal guidance: Human trafficking, smuggling and slavery* (CPS, June 2018);
- *Human trafficking: practical guidance* (Home Office, 2013) – for guidance on indicators of trafficking;
- *Safeguarding children and young people from sexual exploitation. Supplementary guidance to Working Together to Safeguard Children* (Department for Children, Schools and Families, 2009);
- Law Society's *Practice Note – Criminal prosecutions of victims of trafficking* (2 November 2016);
- *Child criminal exploitation: county lines gangs, child trafficking & modern slavery defences for children* (Youth Justice Legal Centre (YJLC), updated January 2018).

Age as a relevant characteristic

Overview

13.54 There are a number of defences where the objective test is defined as the reasonable actions of someone of the same age as the defendant – see further paras 13.56–13.60.

13.55 The Crown Court Bench Book states:[25]

> The age of a child (whether over or under 14 years) is likely to be a relevant factor where:
>
> (1) the offence in question requires a specific intent or subjective recklessness (eg foresight of consequences);
> (2) a possible defence has a subjective element;
> (3) a possible defence requires an assessment of reasonableness (eg loss of control, duress, self-defence);
> (4) it is shown that a child is not of normal development for his age (eg in a defence of diminished responsibility).

Reasonable person tests

13.56 A number of defences involve a 'reasonable person test'. These include self-defence; duress; and the partial defence to murder of loss of control.

13.57 The common law defence of self-defence is now partially codified in the Criminal Justice and Immigration Act 2008 s76. It is a two-part test: first, whether the defendant genuinely believed that he or she or another were in danger; and second, whether the defendant acted reasonably upon that genuine belief. The defendant's age may be relevant in assisting the jury to decide what the defendant genuinely believed, as well as assessing whether the defendant's actions were reasonable.

13.58 Duress is a defence to crimes other than murder, one element of which is whether a person of reasonable firmness would have acted in the same manner. Only certain characteristics inform the person of reasonable firmness test, but age is one of them.[26] The Law Commission report on homicide[27] recommended a the different approach that should be taken with children, and also argues that it should be a defence to murder, although this has not been adopted:

25 At para 7.

26 *R v Bowen* [1997] 1 WLR 372.

27 LCCP 177, *A new Homicide Act for England and Wales?* (2005), para 7.72.

Capacity to withstand duress is increased with maturity and it would be unjust to expect the same level of maturity from a twelve-year-old as from an adult. *Bowen* [1997] 1 WLR 372 also states that youth is a relevant characteristic for the purpose of whether or not the defendant could have been expected to resist the pressure of a threat in cases other than murder. A ten-year-old whose moral character is not fully formed should not be expected in all the circumstances to resist the temptation to kill in order to avert a threat to himself.

13.59 The partial defence of loss of control under Coroners Act 2009 ss54 and 55 has three elements, the third being:

(c) a person of the defendant's sex and age, with a normal degree of tolerance and self-restraint and in the circumstances of the defendant might have reacted in a similar way.

13.60 When dealing with a child who is running a defence that involves an assessment of what a 'reasonable child' may have done, then it is important to consider paras 3.30–3.36 on the importance of background and adolescent brain development in order to consider what is reasonable for a child of the defendant's age and maturity to have done. It will be especially important to consider maturity as well as chronological age, and it may be necessary to instruct an expert to consider any additional needs or vulnerabilities the child may have as this may also be relevant to the reasonable person test (see further instructing an expert chapter 12).

Recklessness and mens rea

13.61 In the leading authority of *G*,[28] in the context of criminal damage, Lord Bingham based his definition of 'recklessness' on the Draft Criminal Code, cl 18(c) and stated:

A person acts recklessly within the meaning of section 1 of the Criminal Damage Act 1971 with respect to – (i) a circumstance when he is aware of a risk that it exists or will exist; (ii) a result when he is aware of a risk that it will occur; and it is, in the circumstances known to him, unreasonable to take the risk.

13.62 The court confirmed that the age of the defendant is material to assisting the court and the jury in determining what the defendant was aware of, and what was reasonable for the defendant to do. In particular, Lord Steyn dealt with the special position of children in the criminal justice system:[29]

28 *R v G* [2003] UKHL 50.

29 At para 53.

> Ignoring the special position of children in the criminal justice system is not acceptable in a modern civil society. In 1990 the United Kingdom ratified the Convention on the Rights of the Child which entered into force on 15 January 1992. Article 40.1 provides:
>
> 'States Parties recognise the right of every child alleged as, accused of, or recognised as having infringed the penal law to be treated in a manner consistent with the promotion of the child's sense of dignity and worth, which reinforces the child's respect for the human rights and fundamental freedoms of others and *which takes into account the child's age* and the desirability of promoting the child's reintegration and the child's assuming a constructive role in society.' (Emphasis added)
>
> This provision imposes both procedural and substantive obligations on state parties to protect the special position of children in the criminal justice system.

This is useful for the court to keep in mind when trying children for any offence.

13.63 When it is under dispute what a child intended or foresaw in any given situation, it is important that the court is aware of the age and maturity of the child, as it is likely that inferences that may be drawn in respect of adults may not be appropriate for children. For more information about adolescent brain development when considering these points, see paras 3.30–3.36.

Joint enterprise

13.64 A defendant may be guilty of an offence where the defendant has acted with others, and where the defendant intended that the offence be committed. However, such intent may be conditional – for example, where the defendant intended that the perpetrator carry out an offence, only if certain conditions applied. Further, the defendant may join in a joint enterprise at the last minute – for example, in cases of spontaneous violence. In reality, such prosecutions rely on the actions of the defendant to draw inferences as to what he or she must have intended would occur. It is particularly important in such scenarios that the age of the defendant is taken into account. Children use different parts of their brain than adults when making decisions and it is possible that they are less likely to intend or foresee the consequences of their actions (see paras 3.30–3.36 for greater understanding of adolescent brain development). Events that may seem inevitable to a jury of adults with the benefit of hindsight may not have occurred to a child at the time.

13.65 The CPS guidance on joint enterprise draws attention to the difficulty of drawing such inferences against children in cases of spontaneous violence. At the time of writing, the guidance is in draft form and being consulted on, but reads:

> Spontaneous Violence and Children, young people and persons with learning disabilities, autism and mental health issues.
>
> In such situations or in respect of such suspects, it remains permissible to consider what the suspect foresaw and to use that as one part of the evidence in considering whether the evidence of intentional assistance or encouragement is made out (see the section on 'Conditional intent cases' below). However, that inference must be approached with particular care because of the real possibility that the spontaneous situation, or the mental capacity of the person, might mean that they did not have such foresight which will contribute to the decision about their intention. A fast moving situation, the lesser developed thinking or experience of a child or young person, the impaired or different thinking of a person with a learning disability, autism or other mental health issue – may mean a suspect is less able to appreciate what may follow.
>
> Further, it may be determined that the evidence that these persons intended to assist or encourage D1 to commit a particular crime may not be sufficiently strong and reliable to make D2 liable, once careful thought has been given to the situation in which they found themselves, or to their mental capacity due to age or condition.
>
> Prosecutors should consider the available evidence concerning the situation or the suspect, identifying and seeking further evidence where necessary, asking themselves how that evidence should be taken into account in reaching safe inferences about the suspect's intention.

13.66 In the authors' view, the issues highlighted here for children, young adults and those with specific difficulties is not confined to fast-moving situations where there are outbreaks of spontaneous violence. There should be a cautious approach when considering any case relying on the doctrine of joint enterprise.

Expert evidence

13.67 When dealing with a child facing a charge where the defence is a lack of *mens rea* or involves a test of reasonableness, the child's age and maturity may be of particular relevance to the defence. In such cases, it may be useful to instruct a psychologist or psychiatrist to consider whether the child is suffering from any particular disability that may be *relevant* to that test, bearing in mind the high percentage of children in the criminal justice system that have some communication or other difficulty, often undiagnosed. That expert should consider the relevance of any issue to the ability to form intent, or how that affects the reasonable person test.

13.68 Expert evidence in these cases is usually limited to evidence about any particular diagnosis or difficulty the child faces.

13.69 The general rule is that it is only appropriate to call expert evidence when the subject would be outside the knowledge and experience of the jury and would serve to assist the jury in evaluating the established facts of the case.[30] The test for expert evidence was established in *R v Bonython*,[31] which provides three questions:

1) Is the subject matter of the evidence one in which a person without specific experience in the area would be able to formulate sound opinions and judgments?
2) Is the subject matter part of a sufficiently recognised body of knowledge/experience reasonably accepted as reliable to the point where the expert's information would assist the court?
3) Does the expert have enough knowledge/experience to justify putting his or her opinion forth as 'expert'?[32]

13.70 In *R v Turner*,[33] this was expressed as:

> If on the proven facts a judge or jury can form their own conclusions without help, then the opinion of an expert is unnecessary.

13.71 However, there is a growing body of medical evidence about the adolescent brain and how it develops (see, for example, in the US, the MacArthur Foundation Research Network on adolescent brain development and the juvenile justice system). Some of this may be considered to be within the knowledge and experience of the jury, but much of it is not. Defence lawyers are encouraged to consider the information at paras 3.30–3.36, which deals with adolescent brain development, as it may be relevant to considering how to address the jury about the behaviour that can be expected of a reasonable child.

30 *R v H* [2014] EWCA Crim 1555.

31 [1984] SASR 45.

32 This has been approved in *R v Hodges* [2003] EWCA Crim 290 and *R v Dallagher* [2003] 1 Cr App R 12 at 195.

33 [1975] QB 834.

Adverse inferences

Introduction

13.72 When a defendant fails to answer questions in police interview or fails to give evidence in his or her own defence, the judge may in certain circumstances direct the jury that they may draw adverse inferences from such a silence. Criminal Justice and Public Order Act (CJPOA) 1984 ss34 and 35 respectively deal with the directions the judge should give to the jury in these circumstances. These sections apply equally in the youth court or adult magistrates' court, where the bench should decide whether to draw adverse inferences from a defendant's silence or failure to answer questions.

13.73 A defendant's youth may be relevant both to whether an adverse inference direction should be given at all; and second, to whether or not the jury or the bench should choose to draw such an inference.

Section 34 – failure to mention facts when questioned

13.74 CJPOA 1984 s34 provides that when questioned under caution if the defendant fails to mention any fact he later relies on in his defence in those proceedings, a court or a jury can draw an adverse inference when deciding upon the guilty of the defendant or determining whether there is a case to answer if it is a fact that the accused could reasonably have been expected to mention when questioned.

13.75 The court will therefore need to identify which facts the defendant has relied upon in his or her defence which were not mentioned during interview, and then decide whether the defendant could have reasonably been expected to mention them at the time of interview.

13.76 In *T v DPP*[34] the High Court criticised the justices for misunderstanding the test, failing to identify the fresh facts relied upon, and falling to address:

> . . . their minds to the particular situation of a 13 year old boy, acting on legal advice, providing a prepared account and thereafter making no comment, and then asking themselves the question whether that defendant could reasonably have been expected to mention any particular matter which he relied on later.[35]

13.77 The Taylor Review of the Youth Justice system commented on the tendency for children from black, Asian and minority ethnic (BAME)

34 [2007] EWHC 1793 (Admin).

35 Para 21 of the judgment.

groups to answer 'no comment' when interviewed by the police. It was suggested that this may be the result of a mistrust of the police by children from these communities.[36]

Section 35 – failure to give evidence

13.78 CJPOA 1984 s35 provides that it is permissible for the court or jury to draw an adverse inference from the defendant's failure to give evidence at trial unless:

> . . . it appears to the court that the physical or mental condition of the accused makes it undesirable for him to give evidence.[37]

13.79 In *R v Friend (Billy-Joe) (appeal against conviction) (No 2)*[38] the Court of Appeal accepted the evidence of Dr Susan Young, a Chartered Clinical Psychologist,[39] that the defendant was hampered by a number of problems at his trial, including attention deficit hyperactivity disorder (ADHD) as well as his young age and that no concessions were made at trial. The combination of factors led her to conclude that it was undesirable for him to give evidence, and the Court of Appeal, accepting that, found that had Dr Young's evidence been before the judge, the judge would not have ruled in favour of drawing any adverse inference, and therefore the conviction could not be regarded as safe.

13.80 In deciding whether it is undesirable for the defendant to give evidence, the court may consider a range of factors, and not just whether giving evidence may have an adverse effect on the health of the defendant.[40] Section 35 gives a wide discretion to the judge – it is not sufficient that the defendant suffers from *some* physical or mental condition; it must be a mental condition which is such as to make it undesirable for the defendant to give evidence. The fact that the defendant may have some difficulty in giving evidence is insufficient to justify the conclusion that it is undesirable that he or she should do so.[41]

36 Para 60 of the Review.
37 CJPOA 1984 s35(1)(b).
38 [2004] EWCA Crim 2661.
39 Para 25 of judgment.
40 *R v D* [2013] EWCA Crim 465.
41 *R v D* [2013] EWCA Crim 465 at para 11 onwards.

Admissibility of interviews conducted without appropriate adult

13.81 Police and Criminal Evidence Act 1984 (PACE) Code C para 11.15 requires that any interview of a child must be conducted in the presence of an appropriate adult unless it is an emergency covered by codes. It is unusual for an interview to be conducted without an appropriate adult.

13.82 Any breach of a PACE code may lead to the evidence being held to be inadmissible. There is no automatic exclusion, and the defence lawyer will have to show that the breach of PACE code leads to a reason to exclude the evidence under PACE s78 or s76. It is likely that an interview conducted without an appropriate adult will be found to be inadmissible.

13.83 The denial of the right to an appropriate adult might lead to a defendant failing to recognise the need for legal advice which has a fundamental effect on the fairness of the proceedings[42] (see paras 6.108–6.131 for role of appropriate adult).

Jury directions

13.84 When directing a jury, the judge needs to consider the defendant's age and maturity and any relevance that may have to the trial. It is likely to be relevant to any argument as to *mens rea*, and any defence where age is a relevant characteristic.

13.85 However it may also be relevant to directions, such as an adverse inference direction about the child's silence at interview or failure to give evidence in trial. Further it may be relevant to the child's behaviour in court or the manner in which they gave evidence. The judge should consider what directions need to be given to the jury, and whether they should be tailored in light of the child's age.

13.86 The Crown Court Bench Book provides as follows:

> 5. The need for and form of any directions to the jury relating to D's age should be discussed with the advocates in the absence of the jury before closing speeches.
>
> 6. Should a direction be thought appropriate, its exact terms will have to be tailored to the circumstances of the individual case. It will have to include an identification of the issue to which D's age is relevant and a direction that the jury should consider that issue in the light of

42 *R v Aspinall* [1999] 2 Cr App R 115.

what they know of D's age, development and maturity at the time of the alleged offence.

Example: D is charged with wounding with intent NOTE: The following example relates only to the age of the defendant. It does not incorporate a direction on Intention [Chapter 8–1] or Self-defence [Chapter 18–1]. D admits that he stabbed V with a pen-knife but says that he was acting in lawful self-defence because he believed that V was about to attack him with a metal bar. D also says that the knife was only a small one, that he did not realise that it might cause really serious injury and that he did not intend to do so. How relevant is it that D was 11 years old when this incident happened? His class teacher told you that D is a slow learner who can find some things difficult to understand, although he has not been formally diagnosed with a learning difficulty. You may take this into account when you are deciding whether D believed, or may have believed, that V was about to attack him with the bar; and, if the question arises, when you are deciding whether D intended to cause V really serious injury.

Proceeding in absence

Overview

13.87 Where a child fails to attend for his or her trial, the court may adjourn the trial and consider whether to issue a warrant for the child's arrest. The procedure for dealing with failure to attend is the same as failing to attend other court appearances in that it is a criminal offence under the Bail Act 1976 and the court has the power to issue a warrant. (As to failing to attend and issuing warrants, see paras 8.45–8.50 on failure to appear.)

13.88 However, the court may also proceed in the absence of the child.

Magistrates' or youth court

13.89 The court is more likely to proceed in the absence of the child if the trial is in the adult magistrates' court or youth court, as there is an emphasis that summary justice should be speedy. Magistrates' Court Act (MCA) 1980 s11 provides that the court may proceed in absence of the child if the child fails to attend their trial. This should be contrasted with the provisions for adult defendants which states that the court shall proceed, unless it is contrary to the interests of justice.

13.90 The court cannot proceed if it considers that there is good reason for his or her failure to appear,[43] or if he or she has been summonsed to court, unless there is evidence that the summons was served upon him or her.[44]

13.91 Where a trial has been heard in the absence of the defendant, the defendant can apply for the conviction to be set aside, and a retrial to be heard.[45] Failing that there is an automatic right of appeal to the Crown Court (see chapter 15 on appeals).

13.92 In *R (R) v Thames Youth Court*[46] the administrative court held that the youth court had been wrong to proceed to hear the prosecution evidence in the absence of the child when he had no control over his absence, having been arrested on another matter. In so deciding, the court referred to the Beijing Rules, and the United Nations Convention on the Rights of the Child (UNCRC), and held that:

> . . . what they do is to demonstrate the importance of the consideration that a juvenile may not have the same development and understanding as an adult. A juvenile who is absent but not deliberately absent from his trial will not have the opportunity of responding to prosecution evidence as it is given at his trial and to provide instructions to those who represent him.

Crown Court

13.93 The Crown Court may also allow a trial to proceed in the absence of the child. This was considered by the House of Lords in *R v Jones (Anthony)*,[47] whose principles still apply. The following passage from Lord Bingham summarises the common law position:

> If a criminal defendant of full age and sound mind, with full knowledge of a forthcoming trial, voluntarily absents himself, there is no reason in principle why his decision to violate his obligation to appear and not to exercise his right to appear should have the automatic effect of suspending the criminal proceedings against him until such time, if ever, that he chooses to surrender himself or is apprehended.

Note that Lord Bingham referred to a defendant of 'full age' – it is therefore arguable that the Crown Court is far less likely to proceed to trial in the absence of a child defendant.

43 MCA 1980 s11(3).
44 MCA 1980 s11(2).
45 MCA 1980, s142(1).
46 (2002) 166 JP 613.
47 [2002] UKHL 5, [2002] 2 WLR 524.

13.94 Criminal Practice Direction 14E deals with trials in absence in both the Crown Court and the adult magistrates' court. While reference is made to the case of *R v Jones* above, no mention is made of children and the appropriate approach to be taken in regard to the non-attendance of a child.

13.95 Nevertheless, the court is bound by its statutory duty to consider the welfare of the child,[48] as well as the other international instruments, such as the Beijing Rules and the UNCRC which mean that a distinct approach must be taken regarding defendants who are children. Further, given the different tests for proceeding in absence in the adult magistrates' court depending on whether the defendant is a child or an adult, it is clearly parliament's intention that the court be slower to proceed in absence in the case of a child.

48 Children and Young Persons Act 1933 s44.

CHAPTER 14

Anonymity

continued

Key points

- A court should hear from all relevant parties about the potential impact on the child, in particular from those who are best placed to assess that impact – such as the youth offending team, or the child's parents or guardians.
- Children are only protected by reporting restrictions once proceedings have begun in the youth court, and child defendants only until they turn 18. Where there is concern that a child may be named in the press after his or her 18th birthday or before proceedings have begun, a civil injunction can be sought.
- Reporting restrictions are only granted automatically when the child appears before the youth court – where the child appears before either an adult magistrates' court or a crown court, or where a child is before the court for a civil matter such as a civil injunction, it is necessary to apply for reporting restrictions at the outset of proceedings.
- Anyone affected by the reporting restrictions can make representations to the court. This will often come from representatives of the media, but can also include the police, the local authority and representatives from the establishment where the child is detained.

Introduction

14.1 Children appearing before the court – whether as defendant, victim or witness – are usually granted anonymity. In the youth court, this is granted automatically.[1] When representing a child who appears before adult courts, including a first appearance at the adult magistrates' court, reporting restrictions will need to be applied for. It is therefore important to be aware when it is necessary to apply for reporting restrictions in order to avoid children being accidentally named when they need not be.

14.2 While most children do retain anonymity, there are cases where other parties successfully apply to lift the reporting restrictions and allow the child to be named. This is especially common in cases involving civil injunctions for anti-social behaviour, and in cases of more serious offending. As every court has a duty to consider the

1 Children and Young Persons Act (CYPA) 1933 s49.

welfare of any child appearing before it,[2] it is important for defence lawyers to consider, and gather evidence of, any harm that may be done to the child by being publicly named, and to be ready to place that evidence before the court.

14.3 The Criminal Procedure Rules 2015 (CrimPR), as amended, Part 6 deals with reporting restrictions. This sets out the procedure to be followed when applying to make, lift or vary reporting restrictions in the criminal courts and should be consulted before making or responding to any application.

Harm of being named

Standing Committee for Youth Justice

14.4 The Standing Committee for Youth Justice's 2014 report by Dr Di Hart *What's in a name? The identification of children in trouble with the law*[3] deals with some of the problems that are caused by naming a child. The report[4] argues that 'naming and shaming' puts children at risk of harm and increases the likelihood of them reoffending in the future.

Court's welfare duties

14.5 Any court has a duty to consider both the welfare of the child[5] and to consider the child's best interests.[6] Therefore if the court is considering allowing the child before it to be named, that court should consider carefully the impact on the child's welfare.

14.6 To this end, the court should be in possession of relevant information on the impact of naming that child before making its decision. At the very least, it should ask the Youth Offending Team (YOT) to consider the impact of being named in any report that they write. The court may direct that any other party is notified of any application to lift reporting restrictions[7]. The Crown Prosecution Service

2 CYPA 1933 s44.

3 http://scyj.org.uk/wp-content/uploads/2014/05/Whats-in-a-Name-FINAL-WEB_VERSION_V3.pdf.

4 At p6.

5 CYPA 1933 s44.

6 United Nations Convention on the Rights of the Child (UNCRC) Article 3(1) – see further para 1.21.

7 CrimPR r6.4(3)(b)(ii).

(CPS) guidance on reporting restrictions[8] suggests that the governor of the secure establishment where the young person is being held and the police should be notified to gain their views on publicly naming the child.

Potential considerations

14.7 The potential harm done to any child by naming the child will of course be case-specific and depend on the facts and circumstances of the particular child in a particular case. However, the following are potential factors that may be relevant:

1) *The rehabilitation of the child.* The UN committee of the rights of the child makes it clear that rehabilitation is necessary to protect the child's best interests:

   > . . . the protection of the best interests of the child means, for instance, that the traditional objectives of criminal justice, such as repression/retribution, must give way to rehabilitation and restorative justice objectives in dealing with child offenders.[9]

   For example: Even after the conviction becomes spent, will information be known to future employers, for example by googling the child's name? The media attention and comments made in the media may affect both how the child views himself or herself, and how the child is viewed by his or her peers, which can in turn affect the child's future conduct. The CPS guidance states:

   > Identification of a youth may be detrimental to his own rehabilitation and that of other young people related to him or detained with him.

2) *The impact on the child's mental health and well-being by being exposed to press reports about the child.* It cannot be ignored that the press reports may include comments from members of the public and indeed commentary from journalists which may be distressing to the child. In high-profile cases, the level of press exposure may be extremely distressing to anyone involved. It may be appropriate in high-profile cases that this be addressed by a psychologist, especially in cases in which a psychologist is already involved in writing reports about the child.
3) *Will being named put the child in any danger of retribution from members of the public?* This will be of particular concern in cases

8 www.cps.gov.uk/legal/p_to_r/reporting_restrictions/.

9 United Nations Committee on the Rights of the Child, General Comment 10 (2007), para 10.

involving serious crimes, but may also be relevant in cases of less serious offending where there is a particular local interest. If the child is in the custodial estate, this may cause practical problems – for example, if the child needs to be separated from other children within the estate for the child's own safety.

4) *Is there a possibility of other effects of naming the child within the local community?* For example, children given anti-social behaviour orders (ASBOs) have sometimes been barred from local shops on the strength of the fact they have an ASBO. Will being named in their local community cause real disadvantage and stigma?
5) *Will there be an effect on other children?* For example, all children in the same family, in the same peer group, or in the same custodial establishment? The UN Committee on the Rights of Child general comment 14 (2013) when clarifying United Nations Convention on the Rights of the Child (UNCRC) Article 3, states that this includes:

   > The obligation to ensure that the child's best interests are appropriately integrated and consistently applied in every action taken by a public institution, especially in all implementation measures, administrative and judicial proceedings which directly or indirectly impact on children.[10]

   However, in *R v Will Cornick*[11] the judge expressly refused to consider the impact on any other children affected.[12] In the authors' view, the court should consider the wider implications of any reporting restrictions on other children, in line with the UNCRC.
6) *Is the child particularly vulnerable for other reasons?* The CPS guidance states:[13]

   > . . . some young people, for example looked after children, may be particularly vulnerable if their identity is published.
7) *Are there other proceedings or issues that may cause the child further issues if these proceedings are published?* For example, what impact may this have on immigration or family law issues that the child is facing?

10 UNCRC, General Comment 14 (2013), para 14(a).

11 [2014] EWHC 3623 (Admin).

12 Para 14.

13 www.cps.gov.uk/legal/p_to_r/reporting_restrictions/.

Pre-charge anonymity

Overview

14.8 Children and Young Persons Act (CYPA) 1933 s49 automatically provides anonymity to a child once proceedings have begun in the youth court. Prior to the proceedings in the youth court, there is no power to grant anonymity to a child who has been arrested for an offence other than getting a civil injunction. Criminal proceedings commence once a person is charged with an offence.[14]

14.9 Youth Justice and Criminal Evidence Act (YJCEA) 1999 s44 provides that children are granted anonymity pre-charge, however this section has not yet been brought into force.

14.10 In reality, most children are not named in the press before they are charged, not least because the police do not routinely release the names and details of those they arrest to the press. However, in a number of high-profile cases national newspapers have published names, photographs and details of children who have been arrested in connection with offences before the police charge. For example, Will Cornick, the teenager who murdered his teacher Ann McGuire in Leeds, was named prior to being charged with her murder. Once charged, he was then granted anonymity under CYPA 1933 s49. He was named again having been convicted of Ann Maguire's murder. In deciding to lift the reporting restrictions, the judge said the following:

> William Cornick had already been publicly identified in the Press, and is named on the internet, so the court has to avoid slipping into playing the role of King Canute.[15]

14.11 In another case, a 15-year-old boy in Northern Ireland was named by a number of national newspapers after he was arrested in connection with the 'TalkTalk' fraud. 'TalkTalk' made national headlines in 2015 after hackers accessed customers' personal and financial data, affecting up to four million people. He was successful in getting civil injunctions to prevent him being named further and to have his name removed from relevant websites. However, the damage had already been done and his family forced to leave their home due to fear of reprisals. He is now taking a case against the Department of Justice in Northern Ireland, arguing the failure of the Department to

14 See Judicial College, 'Reporting restrictions in the criminal courts', April 2015 (revised May 2016), p40.

15 *R v William Cornick* [2014] EWHC 3623 (Admin), para 28.

protect his rights under European Convention on Human Rights (ECHR) Article 8 rights puts them in breach of the Convention. His case failed in the High Court, and at the time of writing has been sent back to the High Court for a determination as to whether his claim will succeed under Article 14 ECHR (discrimination).[16]

Press codes

14.12 When the matter was last debated in parliament during the passage of the Crime and Criminal Courts Bill in 2014,[17] it was suggested by a government spokesperson that YJCEA 1999 s44 should not be enacted because the press were being encouraged to regulate themselves.

14.13 By contrast, the Editors' Code of Practice, which is monitored by Independent Press Standards Organisation (IPSO), is silent about whether or not children should be named prior to them receiving the protections of CYPA 1933 s49 in the youth court. Although the Editors' Code does provide some guidance about considering the welfare of children, it does not deal with this issue – and when the press have chosen to name children in the examples cited above, as well as on other occasions, no action has been taken against them by the regulators, as to do so does not appear to be in breach of the code.

14.14 Therefore, where there is press interest, the only way to protect the child's identity upon arrest prior to them having been charged with an offence is to apply for a civil injunction. This would involve an application to the administrative court. It would be necessary to apply for legal aid, as this would not be covered by the criminal legal aid at the police station, and there would be a risk of adverse costs if the application was unsuccessful.

Procedure for making, lifting or varying reporting restrictions

Automatic restrictions

14.15 In the youth court, CYPA 1933 s49 provides automatic reporting restrictions for any child appearing before it. In other court proceedings, the court has a discretion to make reporting restrictions under

16 *JKL's Application* [2016] NIQB 99

17 See, for example, Hansard for debate in House of Lords, 22 October 2014.

CYPA 1933 s39 (for civil proceedings, including criminal behaviour orders, injunctions for anti-social behaviour) and under YJCEA 1999 s45 (for the Crown Court or adult magistrates' court) and YJCEA 1999 s45A (for victims and witnesses only in any criminal court).

Criminal Procedure Rules

14.16 Orders under these sections can be made with or without a hearing, but any party directly affected should be afforded the opportunity to make representations.[18] The court can make, vary or lift an order on application, or on its own initiative.[19] Parties seeking to make, vary or lift an order to restrict reporting should notify the other parties in advance, and otherwise comply with the directions set out in Criminal Procedure Rules 2015 (CrimPR), as amended, r6.4 (making a reporting restriction) or r6.5 (lifting or varying a reporting restriction). Anyone directly affected by the making, varying or lifting of reporting restrictions can make representations and should comply with the directions in rule 6.7.

Parties to the proceedings

14.17 The court may direct any other party is notified of any application to lift reporting restrictions.[20] The CPS guidance suggests that the governor of the secure establishment where the child is being held and the police should be notified to gain their views on naming the child.

Local authority

14.18 In certain cases, the local authority has instructed their own counsel to make representations on their behalf about the welfare and the best interests of the child. In *R v F and D* at Leeds Crown Court, 7 April 2016, the local authority instructed counsel who appeared at the sentencing hearing, at which the court heard representations from the prosecution, the defence, the local authority and the media as to whether to lift reporting restrictions to name the two child defendants following the trial.[21]

18 CrimPR r6.2.

19 CrimPR rr6.4(2), 6.5(2).

20 CrimPR r6.4(3)(b)(ii).

21 *R v F and D*, Leeds Crown Court, 7 April 2016: www.yjlc.uk/wp-content/uploads/2016/04/R-v-F-and-D-sentence.pdf.

14.19 Where a child is looked after by the local authority, the local authority has specific duties to the child and the local authority will need to consider how best to protect the child's welfare if an application is made to publicly name the child. In any case where a child has been remanded, the child will acquire looked after status regardless of whether or not the child was 'looked after' prior to the offence.[22]

Youth offending team

14.20 YOTs should play an active role in assisting the court when there is consideration of naming a child. The Standing Committee for Youth Justice have produced guidance specific to YOTs.[23]

14.21 The CPS have issued guidance on reporting restrictions.[24] This guidance states that prosecutors should be aware when automatic reporting restrictions or discretionary reporting restrictions apply; seek reporting restrictions when appropriate to do so, and only apply to lift reporting restrictions in narrowly defined circumstances.

Anonymity for child defendants

Children and Young Persons Act 1933 s49: youth court

14.22 CYPA 1933 s49 applies in the youth court, where reporting restrictions automatically apply, unless the child is before the court for an application made under the Anti-social Behaviour, Crime and Policing Act (ASBCPA) 2014[25] for criminal behaviour orders (CBOs) or an Anti-social Behaviour Injunction (ASBI) (see further paras 24.35–24.38 on CBOs reporting restrictions (anonymity) and para 24.82 on ASBIs reporting restrictions (anonymity).

14.23 Section 49 applies once a child is charged with an offence, and it prevents the publication of anything:

> . . . which reveals the name, address or school of any child or young person concerned in the proceedings or includes any particulars likely to lead to the identification of any child or young person concerned in the proceedings.[26]

22 Legal Aid, Sentencing and Punishment of Offenders Act (LASPO) 2012 s104.

23 http://scyj.org.uk/wp-content/uploads/2015/10/1926-SCYJ-Guidance-for-YOTs-4-page-A4_FINAL_WEB_ONLY.pdf.

24 www.cps.gov.uk/legal/p_to_r/reporting_restrictions/.

25 ASBCPA 2014 s17.

26 CYPA 1933 s49(1)(a).

14.24 A child 'concerned in the proceedings' is any child who is a defendant, victim or witness in the case. It applies to any proceedings in the youth court (except where it is disapplied for CBOs or injunctions as stated above), and in proceedings heard in the adult magistrates' court which are dealing with breach of a youth rehabilitation order, and in appeals to the Crown Court against any such proceedings.[27]

14.25 Section 49(5) allows the court to lift the restrictions if it will avoid injustice to the child, or to assist with finding a child defendant who is at large, provided they are charged with/convicted of a serious violent or sexual offence (one punishable by 14 years or more for an adult).

14.26 Section 49(4A) allows the court a more general power to lift the reporting restriction against a convicted child if it is in the public interest to do so, and only after considering any representations on the matter.

Youth Justice and Criminal Evidence Act 1999 s45: adult courts

14.27 YJCEA 1999 s45 applies in both the Crown Court and adult magistrates' court. Section 45(3) provides that:

> The court may direct that no matter relating to any person concerned in the proceedings shall while he is under the age of 18 be included in any publication if it is likely to lead members of the public to identify him as a person concerned in the proceedings.

14.28 Having made such a direction, the court can dispense with it, if it considers it is in the interests of justice to do so.[28] In making such a decision, the court must have regard to the welfare of the child.[29]

14.29 Previously reporting restrictions for children were made under CYPA 1933 s39 in the Crown Court and adult magistrates' court. While that section no longer applies the case-law under section 39 is still relevant when considering the application of the new section 45 (see paras 14.37–14.51).

27 CYPA 1933 s49(2).
28 YJCEA 1999 s45(4).
29 YJCEA 1999 s45(6).

Youth Justice and Criminal Evidence Act 1999 s45A: victims and witnesses

14.30 YJCEA 1999 s45A applies to victims and witnesses only. It applies in all criminal courts, including the youth court, and provides child witnesses and victims lifelong anonymity, whereas the other orders all expire once the child turns 18.

14.31 An order under section 45A should only be made if the court is satisfied that the quality of the evidence or the level of co-operation from that child will be diminished as a result of the fear or distress at the prospect of being identified.[30]

Children and Young Persons Act 1933 s39: civil cases and criminal behaviour orders

14.32 Applications for Anti-Social Behaviour Injunctions (ASBIs) and Criminal Behaviour Orders (CBOs) are not covered by section 49[31] even though they might take place in the youth court. In these cases, CYPA 1933 s39 still applies. This is a discretionary power which allows any court to impose reporting restrictions, other than in criminal proceedings. This includes applications for criminal behaviour orders.[32] Breaches of a civil injunction are not a criminal offence, and reporting of those breaches will also be covered by section 39. However, breaches of a CBO are a criminal offence, and while section 49 does not apply to reporting of those breaches, YJCEA 1999 s45 does.[33] For further information on the injunctions and CBOs, see paras 24.35–24.38 on CBOs – reporting restrictions (anonymity) and paras 24.84–24.85 on ASBIs – reporting restrictions (anonymity).

14.33 In *R (T) v St Alban's Crown Court*[34] Elias J considered the correct approach when dealing with an application for reporting restrictions under section 39 when a child is subject to an ASBO. In the authors' view, case-law considering reporting restrictions and ASBOs remains relevant to the principles for reporting restrictions for ASBIs and CBOs. The administrative court found that in such cases, the usual balancing exercise between the welfare of the child and the principle

30 YJCEA 1999 s45A(5).
31 ASBCPA 2014 s17.
32 ASBCPA 2014 s23(8).
33 ASBCPA 2014 s30(5).
34 [2002] EWHC 1129 (Admin).

of open justice still needs to be carried out (as to which, see para 14.37 below). However, Elias J held that there is a greater public interest in revealing the identities of those who received anti-social behaviour orders for two reasons. First, the court considered that breaches of such order were more likely to be reported if the identity of the child was known. Second, the court held the public had a particular interest in knowing that the identity of those who committed anti-social behaviour in their neighbourhood. However, there is no presumption in favour of refusal to make section 39 order, each case turns on its own facts.

14.34 In *Keating v Knowsley MBC*[35] the court considered an application for anonymity in relation to an interim ASBO. It held that there was no presumption for or against granting anonymity even for an interim ASBO, but that a court considering such an application should take into account that the allegations against the child at that point are unproven.

Other reporting restrictions

14.35 The court can order that a name or any other matter that has been withheld from being mentioned in open court should not be published by the media, under Contempt of Court Act 1981 s11. However, this only applies in instances where the court already has the power to prevent the name or other matter from being mentioned in open court. It therefore will not apply to the name of the defendant. It may apply to other matters concerning the defendant, such as the defendant's address, where the court has already ruled that it should not be given in open court. It may also be used to protect the publication of the name of a witness who has been allowed to give evidence anonymously.

14.36 The court can also make an order under the Contempt of Court Act 1981 s4(2) to postpone the publication of any matter if it is necessary to avoid risking substantial prejudice to the administration of justice in those proceedings. This is often used in trials to prevent certain matters being reported which the jury might not be aware of, and is used whether the defendants are adults or children.

35 [2004] EWHC 1933 (Admin).

Welfare vs open justice

Balancing exercise

14.37 When considering whether to lift reporting restrictions or whether to impose them under any of the provisions outlined above, the court has to conduct a balancing exercise between the welfare of the child and the public interest in knowing the identity of the offender. This was set out by Lord Steyn in *Re S (FC) (a child) (appellant)*,[36] where he applied the test as set out in *Campbell v MGN Ltd*[37] namely that: neither Article 8 (right to privacy) or Article 10 (right to freedom of expression) of the European Convention on Human Rights (ECHR) has precedence over the other as such. Where the values of the two are in conflict, there needs to be an intense focus on the comparative importance of specific rights being claimed in the case.

Children and Young Persons Act 1933 s49 orders

14.38 Where automatic reporting restrictions apply, there is a greater likelihood that the balance will weigh in favour of granting anonymity:

> It is very difficult to see any place for 'naming and shaming' . . . This will rarely be the case, and the justices making an order under s49(4A) must be clear in their minds why it is in the public interest to dispense with the restrictions.[38]

Prior to conviction

14.39 When a child's case is being heard in the adult magistrates' court or the Crown Court, anonymity is usually granted until the proceedings have been concluded, with consideration being given to lifting them at the point of sentence.

14.40 In *R (Y) v Aylesbury Crown Court*, Hooper LJ stated:

> . . . prior to conviction, the accused's welfare is likely to take precedence over the public interest, but after conviction, the age of the accused and the seriousness of the crime of which he has been convicted will be particularly relevant.

36 [2004] UKHL 47 (SC).

37 [2004] 2 WLR 1232.

38 *McKerry v Teesdale and Wear Valley Justices* [2000] EWCA Crim 3553.

Open justice/Article 10 ECHR (right to freedom of expression)

14.41 English authorities have long emphasised the need for open justice – see, for example, *Scott v Scott*[39] and *AG v Leveller Magazine Ltd.*[40] The need for open justice was emphasised by Lady Hale in *R (C) v Secretary of State for Justice*:[41]

> The principle of open justice is one of the most precious in our law. It is there to reassure the public and the parties that our courts are indeed doing justice according to law.

She went on to consider this more fully:[42]

> However, in many, perhaps most cases, the important safeguards secured by a public hearing can be secured without the press publishing or the public knowing the identities of the people involved.

14.42 A similar point was made in *C v Winchester Crown Court*:[43]

> The public know that the prosecution has been successful. The public know that a young man has been convicted of these two very serious offences. The benefit of knowing the identity of the young man who has been so convicted is modest.[44]

Relevance of welfare

14.43 Lord Bingham argued that protecting the identity of children will usually supersede this principle of open justice in *McKerry*:[45]

> It is a hallowed principle that justice is administered in public, open to full and fair reporting of the proceedings in court, so that the public may be informed about the justice administered in their name. That principle comes into collision with another important principle, also of great importance and reflected in the international instruments . . . that the privacy of a child or young person involved in legal proceedings must be carefully protected, and very great weight must be given to the welfare of such child or young person.

39 [1913] AC 417.

40 [1979] AC 440.

41 [2016] UKSC 2, para 1.

42 At para 18.

43 [2014] EWCA Crim 339.

44 Para 12.

45 *McKerry v Teesdale and Wear Valley Justices* [2000] EWCA Crim 3553.

Lord Bingham went on to say that the court's power to dispense with anonymity under CYPA 1933 s49(4A):

> . . . must be exercised with very great care, caution and circumspection' and it would be wholly wrong to use this power as an additional punishment or as a 'naming and shaming' exercise.

14.44 However, *McKerry* concerned section 49 orders in the youth court, and subsequent case-law suggests that the test for discretionary orders is more balanced, and have distinguished *McKerry* from cases involving section 39 orders.[46]

14.45 In the case of *R v Leicester Crown Court ex p S (a minor)*,[47] Watkins LJ suggested that it will only be in rare and exceptional circumstances that a section 39 order is not given to a child defendant. Subsequent cases[48] have questioned this analysis and suggested that it is for the defendant to show good reason for reporting restrictions. In *R v Markham and Edwards*[49], in relation to the new section 45 orders, Leveson LJ quoted the passage of Watkins LJ:[50]

> In our judgment, the correct approach to the exercise of the power given by section 39 is that reports of proceedings should not be restricted unless there are reasons to do so which outweigh the legitimate interest of the public in receiving fair and accurate reports of criminal proceedings and knowing the identity of those in the community who have been guilty of criminal conduct and who may, therefore, present a danger or threat to the community in which they live. *The mere fact that the person before the court is a child or young person will normally be a good reason for restricting reports of the proceedings in the ways permitted by section 39 and it will, in our opinion, only be in rare and exceptional cases that directions under section 39 will not be given or having been given will be discharged* [emphasis added].

Relevant factors when considering reporting restrictions

Case-law

14.46 In *R (Y) v Aylesbury Crown Court*,[51] Hooper LJ considered the approach that should be taken when deciding whether to make a section 39 order and elucidated the following, having analysed the

46 *R v Central Criminal Court ex p W, B and C* [2001] 1 Cr App R 2.

47 [1993] 1 WLR 111, (1992) 94 Cr App R 153.

48 *R v Lee* [1993] 2 All ER 170; *R v Central Criminal Court ex p W, B and C* [2001] 1 Cr App R 2.

49 *R v Markham and Edwards* [2017] EWCA Crim 739.

50 At para 80.

51 [2012] EWHC 1140 (Admin).

preceding case-law (including the principles set out in the previous case of *R v Winchester Crown Court ex p B*[52] where Simon Brown LJ distilled case-law up until that point)[53]:

1) The defendant must satisfy court that there is good reason to impose the order, though not to any particular burden or standard of proof.
2) The court must have regard to child or young person's welfare in accordance with mandatory requirement of CYPA 1933 s44.
3) The future progress of child or young person may well be assisted by restricting publication:[54]

    Publication could well have a significant effect on the prospects and opportunities of the young person, and therefore, on the likelihood of effective integration into society. Identifying a defendant in the media may constitute an additional and disproportionate punishment on the child or young person. In rare cases (and not in this case) the child or young person may be at serious personal risk if identified.

4) The court should consider the public interest in knowing the outcome of court proceedings and the valuable deterrent effect that identification of those guilty of at least serious crimes may have on others.
5) Any order restricting publication must be necessary, proportionate and there must be a pressing social need for it.
6) The court must balance the welfare of child (likely to favour restriction on publication) with public interests and requirements of Article 10 ECHR (likely to favour no restriction on publication):
7) Prior to conviction, welfare of child is likely to take precedence over the public interest. After conviction, the age of the defendant and the seriousness of the crime will be particularly relevant.
8) Where the competing interests are evenly balanced, the court should make an order restricting publication.
9) The judge may decide to permit the publication of some details, but not all.

14.47 Further, the court stated:[55]

> Identifying a defendant in the media may constitute an additional and disproportionate punishment on the child or young person. In rare

52 [1999] 1 WLR 788.

53 See para 26.

54 At para 42.

55 At para 42.

> cases . . . the child or young person may be at serious personal risk if identified.

14.48 Many cases, for example *Aylesbury* above, cite deterrence as a factor in favour of publication. This has been criticised by some commentators (see, for example, Dr Di Hart's report *What's in a name?*) who argue that there is no evidence to suggest that publicising the name of the child has any deterrent effect on others, over and above reporting the details of the case without naming the child involved.

14.49 Young people are less well placed to deal with the consequences of media intrusion, so even though they may be named at 18, it is submitted that should not be a factor in favour of naming. In *Inner London Crown Court ex p Barnes*[56] it was held that the court should give considerable weight to the age of the offender and to the potential damage of public identification as a criminal before having the burden or benefit of adulthood. In *C v Winchester Crown Court* (above at para 14.42) the child's lengthy record was a factor the court considered in favour of restricting publication, as it held that the public had a strong interest in seeing him rehabilitated.

14.50 While increasingly names are made public in social media despite reporting restrictions, the court stated in *R (Y) v Aylesbury Crown Court* that the fact that the defendant's identity is already known to some people in the community is not necessarily a good reason for allowing much wider publication.

Judicial College guidelines

14.51 The Judicial College guidelines: *Reporting restrictions in criminal courts April 2015* (revised May 2016) set out the following considerations that are specific to dealing with applications of this nature involving children:

> The particular considerations relevant to offenders under 18 include the:
>
> - Duty to have regard to the principle aim of the youth justice system to prevent offending by children and young persons as required by Crime and Disorder Act 1998 s37;
> - Obligation to have regard to the welfare of the child or young person as required by Children and Young Persons Act 1933 s44;
> - Right to privacy under Article 8 ECHR (as interpreted through international instruments such as the UN Convention on the Rights of the Child and the Beijing Rules); and

56 *R v Inner London Crown Court ex p Barnes* [1995] 7 WLUK 7.

- Jurisprudence requiring the 'best interests of the child' to be 'a primary consideration' (though not necessarily one that prevails over all other considerations) in accordance with Article 3 of the UN Convention on the Rights of the Child.

Adult defendants

14.52 Courts have thus far rejected claims in adult cases that an adult defendant should be granted anonymity to protect the identity of related children. In *Croydon CC ex p Trinity Mirror*,[57] the court found that the Article 8 ECHR (privacy) rights of the defendant's children were not sufficient to trump the principle of open justice and justify the defendant's anonymity. There were similar findings in *S (FC)* about the interaction between Articles 8 (privacy) and 10 (freedom of expression) ECHR when children were involved in case but not a 'party'.

14.53 However, UN General Comment 14 states:

> Article 3, paragraph 1, establishes a framework with three different types of obligations for States parties:
>
> (a) The obligation to ensure that the child's best interests are *appropriately integrated and consistently applied* in every action taken by a public institution, especially in all implementation measures, administrative and judicial proceedings which directly or indirectly impact on children . . .

Turning 18

14.54 Orders made under CYPA 1933 ss39 and 49 expire once the child turns 18. This was established in the case of *R (JC and RT) v Central Criminal Court*.[58] Similarly, orders made under the new YJCEA 1999 s45 only last until the defendant turns 18.

14.55 The only way, therefore, to protect the identity of a defendant becoming known once the defendant turns 18 is to obtain a civil injunction granting the defendant anonymity for life. The civil courts granted such anonymity to the two boys in *A, B*[59] due to fear of reprisals should their identities become known. So far, such injunctions

57 [2008] EWCA Crim 50.

58 [2014] EWCA Civ 1777.

59 *A (a protected party by his litigation friend, the Official Solicitor), B (a child by his litigation friend, the Official Solicitor) v persons unknown* [2016] EWHC 3295 (Admin).

have been rare and only granted in high-profile cases. However, it is only relatively recently that it has been clarified that these orders expire upon a defendant's 18th birthday – it is therefore to be expected that there will be an increase in applications of this nature, and it is yet to be seen how willing the civil courts will be to grant lifelong anonymity to those convicted of offences when children.

14.56 YJCEA 1999 ss45 and 45A were enacted by parliament, following the case of *R (JC and RT) v Central Criminal Court*,[60] which clarified that orders made under CYPA 1933 s39 expire once the child turns 18. Orders made under YJCEA 1999 s45 can be made by any criminal court other than the youth court (where CYPA 1933 s49 applies) in respect of defendants, victims or witnesses. These orders will expire once the child turns 18. All criminal courts, including the youth court, can use YJCEA 1999 s45A to grant lifelong anonymity to any victim or witness involved in the proceedings, but not the defendant.

Appeals

14.57 In any case where an appeal is considered against the order of the court, it will first be necessary to inform the court of the intention to appeal as soon as possible and ask that the court stays the reporting restriction order until such an appeal has been made.

Crown Court

14.58 If a child seeks to appeal a decision about a reporting restriction order made in the Crown Court, the matter is not one that relates to a trial on indictment and therefore the Court of Appeal has no jurisdiction to hear the matter.[61] The only route of appeal, therefore, is by way of judicial review to the High Court[62] (see paras 15.46–15.50 on judicial review). A member of the press who wishes to appeal against the granting of anonymity can, however, appeal to the Court of Appeal under Criminal Justice Act 1988 s159.

14.59 It should be noted, however, that if there is an appeal to the Court of Appeal against conviction or sentence, then that is a new matter, and the Court of Appeal will have to consider anew whether to grant

60 [2014] EWCA Civ 1777.

61 *R v Lee* [1993] 2 All ER 170.

62 *R v Leicester Crown Court ex p S* [1993] 1 WLR 111, (1992) 94 Cr App R 153.

anonymity for the appeal. The Court of Appeal can reconstitute itself as a Divisional Court, which it did in the case of *C v Winchester Crown Court* (above). In *R v Markham and Edwards* the decision to name the defendants was appealed by way of judicial review to the administrative court, and simultaneously the sentences were appealed in the usual way to the Court of Appeal Criminal Division. The defendants appeared before the Court of Appeal in advance of the judicial review proceedings before the High Court. Leveson LJ in the Court of Appeal had to make a fresh decision on whether the defendants should be named in the appeal proceedings, and ruled that they should be named, rendering the judicial review proceedings superfluous.[63]

Youth court and adult magistrates' court

14.60 If appealing a reporting restriction decision made by the youth court or adult magistrates' court, it is arguable that Magistrates' Court Act 1980 s108 applies, which allows an appeal against sentence, which is defined under section 108(3) as 'any order made on conviction' with some particular exceptions, none of which relate to reporting restrictions. This would allow an appeal to the Crown Court. However, in *R (A) v Lowestoft Magistrates' Court v Crown Prosecution Service, Archant Community Media Limited*[64] the failure of the court to grant a section 39 (CYPA 1933) order was appealed by way of judicial review.

63 [2017] EWCA Crim 739.
64 [2013] EWHC 659 (Admin).

CHAPTER 15

Appeals

continued

Key points

- Trial errors and decisions of the youth court, adult magistrates' and Crown Court can sometimes be reopened in the same court.
- A conviction or sentence in the youth court or adult magistrates' court can be appealed to the Crown Court or to the High Court by way of case stated or by judicial review. Careful consideration should be given to the most appropriate way of proceeding.
- Cases in the Crown Court can be appealed to the Court of Appeal Criminal Division.
- Certain matters such as the decisions to charge and urgent matters arising in the course of a case can be challenged by way of judicial review, but time limits and the Civil Procedure Rules must be strictly followed.
- Remedies vary depending on the procedure followed: decisions may be affirmed, amended, sent for retrial or quashed altogether. Appealing may carry risks – eg appealing to the Crown Court may result in a more severe sentence.

Introduction

15.1 The procedure for appealing against conviction or sentence is the same for a child as for an adult. Criminal Procedure Rules 2015 (CrimPR) Parts 34–43 and the corresponding practice directions deal with appeals, and should be followed when dealing with any appeal. For many appeals, there is a form that should be filled out to lodge an appeal. Appeals to the Court of Appeal Criminal Division are now electronically lodged directly with the Court of Appeal.

15.2 When appealing from either the youth court or the adult magistrates' court, there is an automatic right of appeal to the Crown Court. The Court of Appeal will hear any appeal against conviction or sentence from the Crown Court. The Court of Appeal will only hear appeals relating to matter of trial on indictment, therefore there are some matters arising in the Crown Court that can only be challenged by way of judicial review, for example appealing against lifting a reporting restriction.

15.3 Appealing orders concerning reporting restrictions are covered more fully at paras 14.57–14.60. Appealing against bail decisions is covered at paras 11.49–11.55.

15.4 Courts have some powers to rectify mistakes – it may be worth considering whether the matter can be reopened in the court before appealing a decision.

15.5 For further information on appeals Criminal Procedure Rules Part 34.

Where to appeal?

Re-opening case in lower court

Adult magistrates' court and youth court

15.6 The youth court and adult magistrates' court has quite wide powers to rectify errors – Magistrates' Court Act (MCA) 1980 s142 allows the youth court or adult magistrates' court to quash a conviction, and order a re-trial, where it considers that it is in the interests of justice to do so.[1] It also allows the court to vary the sentence or order received, where it is in the interests of justice to do so. There is no time limit on this power, although it is not exercisable where the conviction or sentence complained of has been appealed to another court. This power also applies in the youth court – the procedure is no different whether the defendant is a child or an adult. This power is usually used to rectify an error – where, for example, the sentence that was given was unlawful. Where it is clear that the court made an error or acted unlawfully, then the matter being appealed should be first brought back to the adult magistrates' court or youth court before lodging an appeal.

15.7 The power under MCA 1980 s142 is often used to apply to re-open a case where the court has proceeded in absence against a defendant. See further paras 13.87–13.95 on proceeding in absence.

Crown Court

15.8 The discretion in the Crown Court to deal with errors is much narrower. The 'slip rule' allows the Crown Court to alter a sentence or other order within 56 days of the date on which it was made, under Powers of Criminal Courts (Sentencing) Act 2000 s155. The matter needs to be brought before the same judge who made the order. This should not be used as a means to re-argue the sentence, but

1 A youth court is a magistrates' court, and therefore the same procedure applies to the youth court: Children and Young Persons Act 1933 s45.

an opportunity to alert the court to a sentence that was unlawful or that was passed based on erroneous information. This allows the court to rectify the error without the need for appeal.

Case stated v Crown Court appeal

15.9 Having applied to appeal by way of case stated from the adult magistrates' court or youth court, the defendant loses their right to appeal to the Crown Court.[2] Careful consideration will therefore need to be given to whether a Crown Court appeal or appeal by way of case stated is preferable. If the child appeals by way of case stated and the matter is remitted back to the youth court for a retrial, the child can still appeal to the Crown Court after that retrial if convicted following the second trial.

15.10 Where there is a concern that there has been an error of law, it might be that the High Court is better placed to deal with that error. However, there is an automatic right of appeal to the Crown Court, and therefore, if appealed in time, the appeal will be heard, and the Crown Court will remake any decisions on law, and therefore the point can be argued there, along with an opportunity to re argue any other issues in the trial. There is no automatic right for the matter to be case stated, and if the appeal is unsuccessful in the High Court then there will be no opportunity to relitigate any of the other issues.

15.11 There are very strict deadlines for case stated and for judicial review (see paras 15.31 and 15.37 below). This may also be a relevant factor.

Case stated v judicial review

15.12 The case stated procedure (see paras 15.28–15.33 below) can only be used at the conclusion of proceedings. Similarly it is only possible to appeal to the Crown Court once matters have concluded. Therefore, if a matter needs to be urgently resolved during proceedings, then it will be necessary to challenge the matter by way of judicial review – for example, if there is a challenge to the magistrates' decision as to the age of the defendant during the proceedings.[3]

15.13 If proceedings are concluded and there is a point of law to be challenged in the adult magistrates' court, the appropriate way to challenge is usually by way of case stated, particularly where the facts

2 MCA 1980 s111(4).

3 *R (M) v Hammersmith Youth Court* [2017] EWHC 1359 (Admin).

are complicated.[4] Where the application is by way of case stated, the High Court has the benefit of the reasoning of the lower court when they state a case, which may assist in the application. This should be considered where both judicial review and case stated are available remedies.

Appeals to the Crown Court

Introduction

15.14 A defendant has an automatic right to appeal against conviction or sentence if dealt with in the adult magistrates' court or youth court. The procedure for appealing from the youth court to the Crown Court is the same as appealing from the adult magistrates' court to the Crown Court. It is governed by the MCA 1980, and CrimPR Part 34 applies. Whether the child is convicted by the youth court or the adult magistrates' court, the child may appeal to the Crown Court against conviction[5] (if the child pleaded not guilty) and/or against sentence.[6]

15.15 Having applied to appeal by way of case stated from the magistrates' or youth court, the defendant loses his or her right to appeal to the Crown Court.[7]

Notice of appeal

Time limits

15.16 A notice needs to be lodged within 21 days of the sentence.[8] The time limit runs from the date of the sentence even when the appeal is against conviction only. When appealing against conviction in the case of a deferred sentence, the time limit runs from the date of the decision to defer, not the deferred sentence.[9] It is possible to apply to appeal out of time – reasons for the late application must be given on

4 *R v Ipswich Crown Court ex p Baldwin* [1981] 1 All ER 596; *R v Morpeth Ward Justices* [1992] 95 Cr App R 215.
5 MCA 1980 s108(1)(b).
6 MCA 1980 s108(1).
7 MCA 1980 s111(4).
8 CrimPR r34.2(2).
9 CrimPR r34.2(2).

the form, and the Crown Court will decide whether or not to grant permission to apply out of time.

Service of notice

15.17 The notice should be served on both the magistrates' court officer and any other parties.[10] Other parties will usually be the Crown Prosecution Service (CPS), or other prosecuting authority. All criminal appeal forms can be accessed online.[11] This is in accordance with CrimPR r34.3, which sets out the necessary information to be put in the notice. It also asks whether the defendant wishes to apply for bail pending appeal, or for a suspension of any other order, such as disqualification from driving.

15.18 Once the notice is lodged, it is possible to apply for bail or for an order to be suspended pending appeal. Such an application can be heard by the adult magistrates' court (or youth court) or by the Crown Court.

Appeals by the prosecution

15.19 The prosecution cannot appeal sentence or conviction to the Crown Court. While the prosecution can appeal against terminatory rulings and unduly lenient sentences from the Crown Court to the Court of Appeal, no such equivalent power exists to appeal a decision made by the adult magistrates' or youth court. The prosecution can use the case stated procedure or judicial review in some circumstances, and can appeal against the adult magistrates' court refusal to impose some specific orders to the Crown Court, such as football banning orders. For a full list of which orders can be appealed to the Crown Court by the prosecution, see CrimPR r34.1.

Abandoning an appeal

15.20 An appeal may be abandoned prior to the hearing in accordance with CrimPR r34.9, which must be in writing and signed. As an appeal is a full re-hearing of the case (see below), there are risks of appealing which may result in an increased sentence. Therefore, a defendant who no longer wishes to pursue the appeal should consider formally abandoning it.

10 CrimPR r34.2(1).

11 www.justice.gov.uk/courts/procedure-rules/criminal/forms.

Appealing against a guilty plea

15.21 It is not possible to appeal against conviction if the defendant pleaded guilty under the MCA 1980. In order to challenge conviction following a guilty plea, it is possible to appeal to the Crown Court through a referral to the Criminal Cases Review Commission (CCRC), who have the power to refer the case to the Crown Court under Criminal Appeal Act (CAA) 1995 s11. A referral to the CCRC is made through submitting the relevant form, which can be found on the CCRC website, and one of the questions is whether the defendant wishes to challenge a conviction from the adult magistrates' court or youth court, where the defendant pleaded guilty.

15.22 A referral to the CCRC can be a lengthy process, and thought should also be given to whether the decision to prosecute the case could be challenged by way of a judicial review.

Bail pending appeal

15.23 Under MCA 1980 s113, the adult magistrates' court may grant an appellant bail pending appeal. The notice of appeal needs to be lodged before they have the power to do so, but it can be lodged on the court immediately.

15.24 The Crown Court also has the power to grant bail pending the appeal under Senior Courts Act (SCA) 1981 s81(1)(d).

15.25 CrimPR r14.7 applies whether the application for bail is in the Crown Court or in the adult magistrates' court. This specifies the procedure for the application. It specifies that the application will have to be served two business days before the application,[12] but it also allows the court to vary that time limit.[13]

Suspending a driving disqualification

15.26 Under Road Traffic Offenders Act 1988 s39, a court which has made an order disqualifying a person from driving may suspend the disqualification pending appeal. For such an application, CrimPR r29.2 applies.

12 CrimPR r14.7(2)(c).

13 CrimPR r14.7(7)(a).

The appeal hearing

15.27 The appeal hearing is a rehearing of the case;[14] the court usually consists of a panel of a Crown Court judge and two lay magistrates. CrimPR r34.11 sets out the constitution the court must take. When the Crown Court is hearing an appeal from the youth court, automatic reporting restrictions under Children and Young Persons Act 1933 s49 apply to the proceedings. As it is a rehearing, the court may confirm, reverse of vary the sentence, under SCA 1981 s48(2).[15] Unlike appeals to the Court of Appeal, the Crown Court has the power to sentence more severely than the lower court.[16]

Appeals to High Court – case stated

Overview

15.28 An adult magistrates' court, youth court or Crown Court may be asked to state a case. This involves asking the court against whom the appeal is being made to formulate a question or questions for the High Court to consider. Such an appeal is made to the administrative division of the High Court and can only be made once proceedings have concluded in the lower court. An appeal to the administrative court against the decision of a youth court is governed by MCA 1980 s111 and CrimPR Part 35. The Crown Court can also be asked to state a case, under SCA 1981 s28, for such proceedings Part 35 also applies.

15.29 Such an appeal may be brought by any party to the proceedings, against any order made by the adult magistrates' court, youth court or Crown Court if it is wrong in law or in excess of jurisdiction. For appeals brought against an adult magistrates' court or youth court, they may also be brought by any person 'aggrieved by the decision of the court'.

15.30 The court may refuse to state a case if it considers it to be frivolous.[17] If the magistrates refuse to state a case, that decision can be appealed to the High Court who can order the court state a case.[18]

14 SCA 1981 s79(3).

15 Formerly called the Supreme Court Act 1981.

16 SCA 1981 s48(4); *Dutta v Westcott* [1987] QB 291.

17 MCA 1980 s111(5).

18 MCA 1980 s111(6).

Time limits

15.31 Any application must be made in writing not more than 21 days after the decision complained of, and must be served on the court and all parties.[19] In the youth court or adult magistrates' court, the court has no power to extend the time limit, and therefore it is vital that a notice is lodged in time. If the time limit has been missed, the applicant should consider appealing to the Crown Court instead.

High Court hearing

15.32 The High Court may affirm, reverse or amend any order, or remit the matter back to the original court to make a fresh decision.[20]

15.33 Appeals to the administrative court are governed by the Civil Procedure Rules, in particular Part 52, which should be consulted in addition to Part 35 of the Criminal Procedure Rules. Civil proceedings are usually conducted on behalf of children through a 'litigation friend', who may be a parent or guardian, and unlike in criminal proceedings, instructions are taken from the litigation friend rather than from the child.

Appeals to the Court of Appeal

Overview

15.34 Following a trial on indictment, where a conviction in the Crown Court is unsafe,[21] or a sentence is manifestly excessive,[22] an appeal can be made to the criminal division of the Court of Appeal. Appeals can only be made against conviction or sentence, therefore if there is a challenge to another matter, such as, for example the Crown Court judge allowing a child to be named in the press, then the matter can only be challenged by way of judicial review.

15.35 Appeals can only be made against convictions or sentences following a trial on indictment.[23] It is not therefore possible to appeal a finding of guilt or sentence following a Crown Court appeal of a matter that was originally in the youth court or adult magistrates'

19 CrimPR r35.2(1).
20 SCA 1981 s28A.
21 Criminal Appeal Act (CAA) 1968 s1.
22 CAA 1968 s9.
23 CAA 1968 ss1 and 9.

court. The only route of appeal from there would be to case state or judicially review the Crown Court's decision.

15.36 The Attorney General can refer a sentence to the Court of Appeal that is unduly lenient, and the prosecution can appeal terminatory rulings: see CrimPR Part 41.

Application for leave to appeal

Time limits

15.37 An application for leave to appeal must be received by the Crown Court within 28 days of the conviction or sentence, whichever is being appealed. It is important to note that if appealing conviction, time runs from the date of the conviction and not the conclusion of the case, eg sentence. The notice of appeal must be sent to the Court of Appeal. An application to have the appeal heard out of time must accompany the notice where appropriate, along with any other application, such as for bail or expediency.

Notice of appeal

15.38 The application must include the notice of appeal, which should be signed by the applicant, who confirms that he or she has been advised that the Court of Appeal may order that the time spent awaiting the appeal hearing should not count towards sentence. It should also include grounds of appeal, signed by the lawyer who drafted them. There are separate notices of appeal for sentence and conviction (Form NG conviction and Form NG Sentence[24]).

Leave to appeal

15.39 Usually the application is considered by a single judge who considers the application on the papers, who will then either grant leave and the matter will be heard by the full court, or refuse leave. In some cases, for example where the matter is complex, the matter can be referred to the full court to decide upon leave. Where the single judge refuses leave to appeal, the applicant has the right to renew the matter before the full court at an oral hearing. However the applicant should consider the provisions on loss of time (see para 15.40). There is no legal aid available unless leave is granted, and therefore it may

24 www.justice.gov.uk/courts/procedure-rules/criminal/forms.

be that any defence lawyer who pursues such an appeal will be acting for free, or at risk of not being paid.

Loss of time

15.40 CAA 1968 s29(1) allows the Court of Appeal to direct that the time spent in custody pending the outcome of the appeal will not count towards the custodial sentence. Such an order is usually made after a matter which was refused leave is orally renewed before the full court, who consider it has no merit. Reasons need to be given if such a direction is made. The single judge does have the power to make such a direction, but would not normally do so when it is clear that the applicant has been advised by his or her legal team to pursue an appeal. The court has no power to so direct once leave has been granted. It is therefore something to consider when deciding whether to orally renew an application to the full court.

Powers of the court

15.41 If the Court of Appeal finds that the conviction is unsafe, they will quash the conviction.[25] They can then substitute the conviction for a different offence,[26] or order a retrial,[27] or simply quash the conviction and order the verdict be an acquittal.

15.42 The procedure for appealing to the Court of Appeal against conviction or sentence is set out in CrimPR Part 39, and is no different for children and adults. Parts 36–38 deal with other appeals to the Court of Appeal, including appeals brought by the prosecution.

Legal aid

15.43 The legal aid certificate for representing a defendant at trial covers providing the defendant with advice on appeal in the event of a conviction. Where the solicitors who represented the defendant at trial continue to act at appeal, the advice on appeal and drafting any grounds is covered by the legal aid certificate.

15.44 Where the defendant approaches different solicitors, it may be possible to apply for funding to consider an appeal and draft grounds.

15.45 Once an appeal has been lodged with the Court of Appeal, the Court of Appeal issue the relevant representation orders. If leave is

25 CAA 1968 s2.
26 CAA 1968 s3.
27 CAA 1968 s7.

granted, or the matter referred to the full court, then a representation order will usually be issued for an advocate to attend the hearing and prepare for that hearing. The court has the power to grant a representation order for the solicitors to undertake preparatory work for the appeal, but this is unusual. Any applications for two counsel or for silk will also need to be made to the court. Where leave is not granted and the applicant wishes to orally renew the application, there will be no legal aid to cover the hearing if the application is unsuccessful, therefore any advocate attending such a hearing will do so at the risk of not being paid.

Judicial review

15.46 Police charging decisions (or a failure to offer an out-of-court disposal) and the Crown Prosecution Service (CPS) decisions to prosecute may be challenged by/susceptible to judicial review (see paras 7.134–7.139). Decisions of the youth court, adult magistrates' court or Crown Court are subject to judicial review. However, a decision relating to trial on indictment is not subject to judicial review.[28] Unlike the case stated procedure, there is no requirement that proceedings be finished, and therefore interlocutory appeals will need to be made by judicial review.

15.47 Judicial review proceedings are made to the administrative court and Civil Procedure Rules Part 54 need to be closely adhered to, this includes following the pre-action protocol, even when the defendant is a court. There are strict time limits for judicial review, and any proceedings will need to be issued promptly, and in any event within three months of the date of decision. If proceedings are ongoing in the criminal court, the court will expect proceedings to be brought very quickly. In *Crown Prosecution Service v Newcastle-upon-Tyne Youth Court*[29] relief was refused on the basis that the case had been brought five weeks after the decision and that to overturn the decision would cause undue prejudice.

15.48 As with the procedure for case stated, the Civil Procedure Rules apply, and a litigation friend will need to be appointed.

15.49 Where there is a point of law to be challenged in the youth court or adult magistrates' court, the more appropriate way to challenge is

28 SCA 1981 s29(3).

29 [2010] EWHC 2773 (Admin).

by way of case stated, particularly where the facts are complicated.[30] This is because where the application is by way of case stated, the High Court has the benefit of the reasoning of the lower court when they state a case, which may assist in the application. This should be considered where both judicial review and case stated are available remedies.

15.50 For further information on judicial review, see *Judicial review: a practitioner's guide.*[31]

Legal aid

15.51 Crime contracts include the provision to allow firms to take judicial reviews that arise from criminal matters. Therefore there is no need for a firm to have a public law contract to take a judicial review that arises from a criminal matter. A legal aid certificate must still be obtained

15.52 Judicial review will be paid at civil legal aid rates. It is important to have legal aid in place before issuing a judicial review, as the applicant may be ordered to pay the costs of the other side if the challenge is unsuccessful. Where legal aid is in place, then any such costs will usually be borne by the Legal Aid Agency. All such applications now need to be made online, and given the tight timescales that will usually apply in criminal matters, it is likely that an emergency application will need to be made.

30 *R v Ipswich Crown Court ex p Baldwin* [1981] 1 All ER 596; *R v Morpeth Ward Justices* [1992] 95 Cr App R 215.

31 Manning, Brown and Salmon, *Judical Review: a practitioner's guide*, 3rd edn, LAG, 2014.

PART 3

Sentencing and criminal records

CHAPTER 16

Overview of youth sentencing

Key points

- The Sentencing Council's *Sentencing children and young people: definitive guideline* applies to all under 18-year-olds and the court must follow the guideline unless it would be contrary to the interests of justice to do so.
- Courts must have regard to the principal aim of the youth justice system (to prevent offending by children and young people), and the welfare of the child.
- The only available sentences will be those that can be lawfully passed based upon the defendant's age at the date of conviction.
- The principal aim of the youth justice system is to prevent offending by children and young people. It is important to avoid criminalising children unnecessarily.
- Sentencing should be individualistic and focused on the child, as opposed to offence focused (see para 16.9).
- Custody should always be a measure of last resort for children.
- Sentencers should take into consideration the over criminalisation of children from BAME backgrounds and looked after children.
- Children are less culpable than adults they are still developing, can act impulsively and may not fully appreciate the effect of their actions on others. They have the have greater capacity for change, particularly as offending is often a phase which passes fairly rapidly.
- When considering a child's age their emotional and developmental age is of at least equal importance to their chronological age (if not greater) (see paras 16.21–16.23).

Introduction

16.1 The approach courts take to sentencing children is fundamentally different to sentencing adults:

> If children are tried and convicted, they then have to be sentenced; but it will not be appropriate to sentence them in the same way as an adult, if their immaturity has the consequence that they were less culpable or that reformative measures are more likely to be effective.[1]

1 *V v UK* (2000) 30 EHRR 121, Lord Reed 191.

16.2 Sentencing of children should be individualistic, child-focused and courts must have regard to the principal aim of the youth justice system (to prevent offending by children and young people),[2] and the welfare of the child.[3] The best interests of the child should always be a primary consideration[4] (see paras 1.68–1.71 on the welfare principle and paras 1.72–1.74 on the best interests principle). The Sentencing Council's *Sentencing children and young people: definitive guideline,* provides thorough and practical guidance on the approach to sentencing all under 18-year-olds.[5]

16.3 The only available sentences will be those that can be lawfully passed based upon the defendant's age at the date of conviction (see paras 17.29–17.39 on relevant age for sentencing).[6]

The statutory purpose of sentencing children

16.4 The statutory purpose of sentencing does not apply to anyone aged under 18 at the date of conviction.[7]

16.5 The statutory purpose of sentencing under 18 year olds[8] has never been implemented. The difference between the proposed statutory purpose of sentencing for children and the statutory purpose of sentencing for adults is that it omits 'the reduction of crime (including its reduction by deterrence)'. Parliament's intention in passing this statutory provision is that children should not receive deterrent sentences for most offences.[9] However, until this provision is brought into force, courts are theoretically not precluded from imposing

2 Crime and Disorder Act 1998 (CDA) s37(1) and *Sentencing children and young people: definitive guideline* para 1.1.

3 Children and Young Persons Act (CYPA) 1933 s44(1) and *Sentencing children and young people: definitive guideline* para 1.1.

4 United Nations Convention on the Rights of the Child 1989 (UNCRC) Article 3(1).

5 Sentencing Council, *Sentencing children and young people: definitive guideline,* March 2017. Applicable to all children sentenced on or after 1 June 2017.

6 *R v Danga (Harbeer Singh)* [1992] QB 476, [1992] 2 WLR 277. See fuller discussion at paras 17.29–17.39 on the relevance of age.

7 Criminal Justice Act (CJA) 2003 s142(2)(a).

8 CJA 2003 s142A, added by Criminal Justice and Immigration Act 2008 s9(1) – date to be appointed.

9 CJA 2003 s142A(4) specifically excludes from the statutory purpose of sentencing under 18 year olds – sentences fixed by law minimum sentences for firearm offences and using someone to mind a weapon, detention for life for certain dangerous offenders or hospital orders.

deterrent sentences on children (see paras 21.6–21.7 on deterrent sentencing).

The Sentencing Council's *Sentencing children and young people: definitive guideline*

The status of the *Sentencing children and young people: definitive guideline*

16.6 The court must follow any sentencing guidelines unless it would be contrary to the interests of justice to do so.[10] The Sentencing Council's *Sentencing children and young people: definitive guideline*, applies to all children sentenced on or after 1 June 2017, regardless of the date of the offence.[11]

Key principles

Overview

16.7 The *Sentencing children and young people: definitive guideline* provides a framework for any youth sentencing exercise:

> It is important to avoid "criminalising" children and young people unnecessarily; the primary purpose of the youth justice system is to encourage children and young people to take responsibility for their own actions and promote re-integration into society rather than to punish.[12]

When sentencing a child, the court must have regard[13] to:

- the principal aim of the youth justice system – to prevent offending by children and young people;[14] and
- the welfare of the child.[15]

16.8 *Sentencing children and young people: definitive guideline* sets out the key elements to consider when determining a child's sentence:[16]

10 Coroners and Justice Act 2009 s125(1). This applies to all offences committed after 6 April 2010.

11 *Sentencing children and young people: definitive guideline*, p2.

12 *Sentencing children and young people: definitive guideline*, para 1.4.

13 *Sentencing children and young people: definitive guideline*, para 1.1. See exceptions.

14 CDA 1998 s37(1).

15 CYPA 1933 s44(1).

16 *Sentencing children and young people: definitive guideline*, para 4.1.

- the principal aim of the youth justice system – to prevent re-offending by children and young people;
- the welfare of the child or young person;
- the age of the child or young person (chronological, developmental and emotional);
- the seriousness of the offence;
- the likelihood of further offences being committed; and
- the extent of harm likely to result from those further offences.

16.9 *Sentencing children and young people: definitive guideline* provides the court with some broad principles when approaching the sentencing of a child. Sentencing should be child-focused rather than offence-focused, because children are less culpable and more susceptible to change. The following key principles emerge:

- Sentencing should be individualistic and focused on the child, as opposed to offence focused.[17]
- A custodial sentence should always be a measure of last resort for children (see paras 16.19–16.20).[18]
- Children are likely to be more receptive to change and should be given the opportunity to learn from their mistakes without undue penalisation or stigma that might hinder their prospects or opportunities in the future[19] – particularly as offending is often a phase which passes fairly rapidly.[20]
- It is important to avoid 'criminalising' children unnecessarily – sentences should encourage children to take responsibility for their own actions and address the underlying causes of their offending.[21] The focus should be on rehabilitation – restorative justice disposals may be of particular value for children.[22]

17 *Sentencing children and young people: definitive guideline*, para 1.2.

18 *Sentencing children and young people: definitive guideline*, para 1.3. This reflects the UK's obligations under UNCRC, Article 37(b). The arrest, detention or imprisonment of a child shall be in conformity with the law and *shall be used only as a measure of last resort* and for the shortest appropriate period of time' (emphasis added).

19 *Sentencing children and young people: definitive guideline*, para 1.6.

20 *Sentencing children and young people: definitive guideline*, para 1.7.

21 *Sentencing children and young people: definitive guideline*, para 1.4. This reflects the UK's obligations under UNCRC, Article 40(1) – The right of every child accused of infringing the law to be 'treated in a manner consistent with the promotion of the child's sense of dignity and worth . . . which takes into account the child's age and the *desirability of promoting the child's reintegration* and the child's assuming a constructive role in society' (emphasis added).

22 *Sentencing children and young people: definitive guideline*, paras 1.2 and 1.4.

- Courts should take into consideration any factors that diminish a child's culpability. Children are still developing; they are likely to be impulsive and fail to appreciate the effect of their actions on others, and are more susceptible to peer pressure and other external influences including changes taking place during adolescence that can lead to experimentation, resulting in criminal behaviour.[23]
- A child's emotional and developmental age is of at least equal importance to the child's chronological age (if not greater) – see paras 16.21–16.23.[24]

Welfare

16.10 Welfare considerations are the principles to be observed by all courts in dealing with children.[25] Having regard to a child's welfare will include the court taking into account:

- the wishes and feelings of the child concerned;
- the child's physical, emotional and educational needs;
- the likely effect on the child if circumstances changed as a result of the court's decision;
- the child's age, sex, backgrounds and any other characteristics which will be relevant to the court's decision;
- any harm the child has suffered or maybe at risk of suffering;
- capability of the child's parents (or any other person the courts find relevant) at meeting the child's needs;
- the powers available to the court in the given proceedings.[26]

16.11 Having regard to the welfare of the child requires the court to take into consideration both the positive and negative effect the sentence is likely to have on the child, as well as any underlying factors contributing to the offending behaviour.[27] Specifically, courts should be alert to whether a particular sentence will interfere with a child's education.[28]

23 *Sentencing children and young people: definitive guideline*, para 1.5.
24 *Sentencing children and young people: definitive guideline*, para 1.5.
25 CYPA 1933 s44(1).
26 This list is taken from Children Act 1989 s1(3), the welfare considerations a court should have particular regard to care proceedings.
27 *Sentencing children and young people: definitive guideline*, para 1.2.
28 CYPA 1933 s44(1) – 'Every court in dealing with a child or young person who is brought before it . . . shall have regard to the welfare of the child or young person and shall in a proper case take steps . . . for *securing that proper provision is made for his education and training*' (emphasis added).

16.12 In relation to the child's background and characteristics, courts should to be alert to:[29]

- any mental health problems;
- learning difficulties/disabilities;
- any experiences of brain injury or traumatic life experience (including exposure to drug and alcohol abuse) and the developmental impact this may have had (see paras 3.40–3.44 on neurodevelopment disorders);
- any speech and language difficulties and the effect this may have on the ability of the child (or any accompanying adult) to communicate with the court, to understand the sanction imposed or to fulfil the obligations resulting from that sanction (see paras 3.66–3.70 on communication difficulties);
- the vulnerability of children to self harm, particularly within a custodial environment; and
- the effect on children of experiences of loss and neglect and/or abuse (see paras 3.82–3.86 on deprivation and neglect).

16.13 Having regard to a child's welfare may also require the court to consider the impact of any sentence on the child's likely rehabilitation and re-integration into society. For example, a court might take into consideration how long a particular disposal will remain on a child's criminal record as a relevant consideration.[30]

16.14 Courts may also consider how a custodial sentence will be managed within the secure estate. For example, imposing a slightly shorter sentence to enable the child to be released before their 18th birthday and not be transferred to the adult secure estate or to enable the child to be released so that the full package of leaving care support is available on their release.

Duty to consider background

16.15 Children in the criminal justice system are more likely to come from deprived, chaotic backgrounds and have been exposed to neglect and negative peer influences including the misuse of drugs and alcohol.[31] The approach of the sentencer should be to consider the effect of these experiences, and how best to respond to these factors to 'promote re-integration into society rather than to punish.'[32]

29 *Sentencing children and young people: definitive guideline*, para 1.12.

30 See, for example, *R v Reyon Menelek Dillon* [2017] EWCA Crim 2642 at para 14.

31 *Sentencing children and young people: definitive guideline*, para 1.13.

32 *Sentencing children and young people: definitive guideline*, paras 1.4 and 1.14.

16.16 For these reasons, courts have a duty to consider background information about children who they are sentencing.[33] Courts should always ensure they have as much information as possible about a child's background and where necessary a proper assessment has taken place.[34] Courts have the power to request a 'section 9 report' from the local authority. Children and Young Persons Act 1969 s9 enables criminal courts to request the relevant local authority to make investigations and provide information about a child's home situation, school record, health and character. This can be used an opportunity for the criminal court to ensure the relevant welfare duties owed to the child are being met (see paras 17.73–17.74 on section 9 reports; and paras 17.81–17.88 on pre-sentence reports).

Black, Asian and minority ethnic children

16.17 The *Sentencing children and young people: definitive guideline* reminds courts that they must consider the over-representation of black, Asian and minority ethnic (BAME) children in the youth justice system and to take into account particular factors which arise in the case of children in this group.[35] Since the publication of the guideline, the Lammy Report findings[36] have highlighted this issue and all advocates should be alert to the risk of bias in the sentencing of BAME children (see paras 3.95–3.98 for more on racial disparity in the criminal justice system).

Looked after children

16.18 Looked after children are six times more likely than other children to be cautioned or convicted of a crime.[37] Courts are encouraged to take into consideration the issues facing looked after children,[38] including:

33 Magistrates' Court (Children and Young Persons) Rules 1992 r10.

34 *Sentencing children and young people: definitive guideline*, para 1.14.

35 *Sentencing children and young people: definitive guideline*, para 1.18.

36 The Lammy Review: An independent review into the treatment of, and outcomes for black, Asian and minority ethnic individuals in the Criminal Justice System, 2017.

37 'In care, out of trouble: how the life chances of children in care can be transformed by protecting them from unnecessary involvement in the criminal justice system', an independent review chaired by Lord Laming, Prison Reform Trust, 2016 (the 'Laming Review').

38 *Sentencing children and young people: definitive guideline*, paras 1.16, 1.17.

- the fact that looked after children may appear in court for low level offences that the police would not have been involved in if they had taken place in an ordinary family setting;
- a requirement to consider the impact a custodial sentence could have on leaving care rights; and
- instruction to consider the effect leaving care transitions might have had on a young person's behaviour (see paras 3.87–3.95 on looked after children).

Custody as a measure of last resort

16.19 Custody should always be used as a last resort.[39] International law underlines the importance of custody as both a last resort for children and for the shortest appropriate period of time.[40] Welfare considerations are likely to be particularly relevant when a court is considering a custodial sentence and, if relevant, its length. Children are likely to feel the impact of a custodial sentence more heavily than an adult and any sentence will seem longer proportionately longer due to their young age.[41] In addition, custodial sentences are more likely to interfere with a child education and this should be considered by a court at sentencing.[42] Courts should consider the effect of closed conditions on vulnerable children with significant risks of self-harm, including suicide.[43]

16.20 Welfare considerations are also relevant when considering mandatory minimum sentences or life sentences for murder (detention at her majesty's pleasure). The guideline requires sentencing of children to be individualistic.[44] In determining whether there are exceptional circumstances or whether a mandatory term would be 'unjust', a court will have regard to welfare considerations:

> . . . deterrence can be a factor in sentencing children and young people although normally it should be restricted to serious offences and can, and often will, be outweighed by considerations of the child or young person's welfare.[45]

39 CJA 2003 s152(2), *Sentencing children and young people: definitive guideline*, paras 1.3, 6.42.

40 UNCRC Article 37; *Sentencing children and young people: definitive guideline*, para 6.43.

41 *Sentencing children and young people: definitive guideline*, para 1.8.

42 *Sentencing children and young people: definitive guideline*, para 1.8.

43 *Sentencing children and young people: definitive guideline*, para 1.20.

44 *Sentencing children and young people: definitive guideline*, para 1.2.

45 *Sentencing children and young people: definitive guideline*, para 1.10.

(See paras 17.49–17.50 on turning 18 and deterrence and in custodial sentences and paras 21.1–21.11 for a fuller discussion of custodial sentences for children).

Age and maturity

16.21 Children's age and lack of maturity means they should receive lower sentences because they are considered less culpable than adults. This requires courts to assess a child's age with reference to the child's emotional and developmental maturity alongside the child's chronological age (see paras 17.114–17.115 on assessing culpability).

16.22 Children are less likely to have the experience and capacity to understand the effect of their actions or appreciate the pain and distress they may cause. They are inherently more vulnerable, less able to resist temptation and more susceptible to peer influences. When preparing for a sentencing hearing, practitioners should always consider what to present to the court about a child's emotional and developmental age, this includes any mental health problems and learning disabilities, as this may have greater weight and relevance than the child's chronological age[46] (see paras 3.30–3.36 on child and adolescent brain development).

16.23 There will be some circumstances where the child's age is in dispute, for example, unaccompanied minors or trafficked children who have no formal identification documents (see paras 2.24–2.30 on age disputed children and paras 2.31–2.55 on determining age).

46 *Sentencing children and young people: definitive guideline*, paras 1.5, 4.5 and 4.10.

CHAPTER 17

Procedure and reports

continued

Key points

- Sentencers must decide what information is needed before sentencing a child; the welfare principle makes it more likely that further background information will be needed when sentencing a child.
- Different sentencing options are available depending on the child's age and the sentencing court.
- Defence lawyers should provide the court with information about the sentence available on the date of the offence when children are crossing a significant age threshold during proceedings. This particularly concerns children turning 12, 15 or 18 years old.
- The starting point is the sentence that would have been imposed on the date the offence was committed.
- The youth court has the power to continue to deal with children who turn 18 during proceedings – they can continue to be sentenced in the youth court and receive youth sentences.
- Specific guilty plea guidance is applicable for children.
- A pre-sentence report (PSR) for a child will be prepared by the local youth offending team.
- A copy of the PSR should be provided to the child and the child's parents, guardian or other supporting adult.
- Parents should be able to make representations during the sentencing hearing and the sentence should be explained to the child in ordinary language.

Introduction

17.1 Before proceeding to embark on a sentencing exercise, the sentencer should ensure that he or she has sufficient information to make the sentencing decision. This includes understanding the available powers, sentencing options and, where appropriate, obtaining reports. This chapter explores sentencing procedure, pre-sentence reports (PSRs) and other reports that might be prepared for the sentencing hearing.

Sentencing procedure

Overview

17.2 When a child pleads guilty, or there is a finding of guilt, the court is encouraged to pass sentence on the same day if at all possible[1] or at the earliest opportunity.[2] The court must first decide whether further information is needed, this is more likely for children because the court has a duty to consider their welfare (see paras 17.61–17.66 on duty to consider background). The court will then decide whether to adjourn for a pre-sentence report, other report or further information.

The sentencing hearing

17.3 Before sentencing, if a pre-sentence report has been prepared, the youth offending team (YOT) should provide a copy of the pre-sentence report to the child and the child's parent or guardian[3] (also see para 17.102 on correcting errors in pre-sentence reports).

17.4 The prosecution will usually begin the sentencing hearing by summarising the facts of the case (if the sentencing court has not heard evidence).[4] If a stand down or oral report has been requested, the YOT's court officer will present their report. The defence advocate will then make submissions, setting out the mitigation and referring the court to relevant sections of any written pre-sentence report or other reports available for the court.

Opportunity for parents to make representations

17.5 Although this is not always common practice, in the youth court and adult magistrates' court the child and the child's parent or guardian, if present, must be given an opportunity to make representations and introduce evidence relevant to sentence (there is a discretion to do so

1 *Youth Court Bench Book*, Judicial College, August 2017, 'Effective Case Management', p18, para 22.

2 Criminal Procedure Rules (CrimPR) rr24.11(9)(a) (youth court and adult magistrates' court) and 25.16(7)(a) (the Crown Court).

3 Criminal Justice Act (CJA) 2003 s159(2)(b); and Youth Justice Board National Standards for Youth Justice Services April 2013, Youth Justice Board for England and Wales, para 5.4.

4 CrimPR rr24.11(3) (youth court and adult magistrates' court) and 25.16(3) (the Crown Court).

in the Crown Court).[5] Before imposing any sentence or disposal, the court should explain to the child and the child's parent or guardian, if present, or any person assisting the child in the case, of the manner in which it proposes to deal with the case and allow any of those persons to make representations, unless the court considers it undesirable so to do.[6]

Duty to explain the sentence in ordinary language and to give reasons

17.6 When passing sentence the court *must* state in open court, in ordinary language and in general terms, the court's reasons for deciding on the sentence; and explain to the child in ordinary language the effect of the sentence, the consequences of non-compliance and the court's power to vary or review the order (including the effects of a failure to pay a fine, if relevant).[7]

17.7 Where the defendant is under 18 and the court imposes a:

- youth rehabilitation order (YRO) with intensive supervision and surveillance or with fostering; or
- a discretionary custodial sentence,

the court must state the reasons why it made that decision.[8]

The court's approach to sentencing

17.8 The court's overall approach to sentencing children is as follows:

1) Obtain background information about the child and the offence.
2) Use the information about the child to assess the child's maturity and consider the child's welfare (and other needs) and how to prevent further offending (see paras 16.7–16.23).
3) Use the information about the offence to assess seriousness, culpability and harm.
4) Consider any relevant sentencing guidelines, in particular, the Sentencing Council's *Sentencing children and young people: definitive guideline* (2017), and any offence-specific guidelines:

5 CrimPR rr24.11(7) (youth court and adult magistrates' court) and 25.16(6)(b) (the Crown Court).

6 Magistrates' Court (Children and Young Persons) Rules 1992 SI No 2071 r11.

7 CJA 2003 s174(2) and (3).

8 CJA 2003 s174(8).

a. *Sexual offences guideline for children and young people* (2017);
b. *Robbery guideline for children and young people* (2017);
c. *Bladed articles and offensive weapons: definitive guideline for children and young people* (2018).

In the absence of any child-specific guideline in relation to the offence, the relevant adult guideline may be consulted as a preliminary consideration, and a sentence broadly within half to two-thirds *may* be appropriate for 15 to 17-year-olds and a greater reduction for those aged under 15.[9] Welfare considerations may require departing from the guidelines. Where the court decides it would be contrary to the interests of justice to follow the guidelines, the court must explain why.[10]

5) Apply any reduction for guilty plea. If this results in imposing a punishment which is less severe than the punishment it would otherwise have imposed, the court must state the fact.[11]
6) Deduct time served or time spent on a qualifying curfew.
7) Explain the sentence and any requirements in language a child understands.
8) Give reasons for sentencing decision. If appropriate, give reasons for not imposing a parenting order (see paras 23.3–23.16) or reparation order (see paras 18.30–18.38) or compensation order (see paras 18.61–18.65).

Sentencing in different jurisdictions and courts

Overview

17.9 The criminal courts have different powers when sentencing children, as summarised below.

9 Sentencing Council, *Sentencing children and young people: definitive guideline*, 2017, para 6.45–6.46.
10 CJA 2003 s174(6)(b).
11 CJA 2003 s174(7).

Sentence	Youth court	Adult magistrates' court	Crown Court
Absolute or conditional discharge or reparation order[i]	✓	✓	✓
Fine or compensation order[i]	✓	✓	✓
Mandatory referral order	✓	✓	✓
Discretionary referral order[ii]	✓	✓	✓ If exercising powers to sit as a district judge under Courts Act s66
Youth rehabilitation order	✓		✓
Youth rehabilitation order with intensive supervision and surveillance or fostering	✓ 15-year-olds and over (12–14-year-old persistent offenders *only*)		✓ 15-year-olds and over (12–14-year-old persistent offenders *only*)
Detention and training order	✓ 15-year-olds and over (12–14-year-old persistent offenders *only*)		✓ 15-year-olds and over (12–14-year-old persistent offenders *only*)
Committal for sentence – grave crimes	✓		
Committal for sentence – dangerousness	✓		
Section 91 long-term detention[12]			✓
Extended detention[13]			✓
Detention for life[14]			✓

12 Powers of Criminal Courts (Sentencing) Act 2000 s91.

13 CJA 2003 s226B.

14 CJA 2003 s226.

Sentence	Youth court	Adult magistrates' court	Crown Court
Detention at Her Majesty's Pleasure (mandatory sentence for murder)			✓
Hospital order	✓		✓
Hospital order with restriction	14 year olds and over can be committed to Crown Court to enable a restriction order to be imposed	14 year olds and over can be committed to Crown Court to enable a restriction order to be imposed	✓
Guardianship order	✓		
Supervision order			✓
Remittal to (home) youth court for sentence	✓	✓	✓
Deferred sentence	✓		✓

i For 10–15 year olds, financial orders must be made in the parent or guardian's name; for 16 and 17 year olds this is discretionary (see paras 18.52–1856).

ii 14 year olds and over can be committed to the Crown Court to enable a restriction order to be imposed (see para 22.41).

Sentencing in the youth court

Overview

17.10 A youth court has the following sentencing options:

- absolute discharge;
- conditional discharge;
- reparation order;
- fine;
- compensation order;
- referral order;
- YRO;
- YRO with intensive supervision and surveillance or fostering;
- detention and training order (DTO);
- hospital order;
- guardianship order;

- committal for sentence (grave crime or dangerousness or hospital order with restriction[15]).

Committal for sentence – grave crimes

17.11 The youth court has the power to commit children charged with 'grave crimes' as defined by Powers of Criminal Courts (Sentencing) Act (PCC(S)A) 2000 s91[16] to the Crown Court for sentence after pleading guilty or a finding of guilt.[17] The power exists in relation to defendants who are aged under 18 on the date of conviction. The youth court has the power to commit the case to the Crown Court if the offence or combination of offences is such that the Crown Court should, in the court's opinion, have power to deal with the child.

17.12 The youth court should only use this power to commit for sentence in cases where it subsequently transpires 'that the offending was more serious than it first appeared when the Youth Court accepted the case'.[18]

17.13 The child may be committed to the Crown Court for sentence on bail or in custody.[19] The Crown Court has all the sentencing options as if the child had been convicted of the offence on indictment before the Crown Court.[20] The committing youth court may also commit any other offence the child has been convicted of (by that or any other court) which the committing court has the power to deal with.[21]

Committal for sentence – dangerousness

17.14 The youth court has the power to commit children to the Crown Court for sentence if it appears to the court the criteria for the imposition of a sentence under Criminal Justice Act (CJA) 2003 s226B would be met (see paras 21.135–21.137 on assessment of dangerousness).[22]

15 The defendant must be aged 14 or over for the youth court or adult magistrates' court to have the power to commit to the Crown Court with a view to a restriction order being made – MHA 1983 s43(1) – also see paras 22.38–22.45 on hospital orders with a restriction order.

16 PCC(S)A 2000 s91(1).

17 PCC(S)A 2000 s3B (created by Criminal Justice and Courts Act 2015 s53).

18 Ministry of Justice Circular No 2015/01.

19 PCC(S)A 2000 s3B(2)(b).

20 PCC(S)A 2000 s5A.

21 PCC(S)A 2000 s6(2).

22 PCC(S)A 2000 s3C.

17.15 The defendant may be committed to the Crown Court for sentence on bail or in custody.[23] The committing youth court or adult magistrates' court may also commit any other offence the defendant has been convicted of (by that or any other court) which the committing court has the power to deal with.[24]

Sentencing in the adult magistrates' court

17.16 An adult magistrates' court has the following sentencing options:

- absolute discharge;
- conditional discharge;
- fine;
- referral order;
- remittal for sentence.

17.17 The adult magistrates' court must remit children to the youth court for sentence unless it would be undesirable to do so[25] (see paras 17.22–17.27 on remittal for sentence). However, the court may, but need not remit under PCC(S)A 2000 s8(2), if the compulsory referral order conditions are met[26] or the case may be dealt with by making an absolute or conditional discharge order, imposing a fine or a parental recognizance order.[27]

17.18 Where a child is being sentenced by an adult magistrates' court, particularly where a referral order is potentially under consideration, it is recommended that a youth court magistrate is included on the bench if the case is not remitted to the youth court.[28]

Sentencing in the Crown Court

Overview

17.19 The Crown Court has the following sentencing options:

- absolute or conditional discharge or reparation order;
- fine or compensation order;
- referral order;
- YRO;

23 PCC(S)A 2000 s3B(2)(b).
24 PCC(S)A 2000 s6(2).
25 PCC(S)A 2000 s8(2).
26 PCC(S)A 2000 s8(6) and (7).
27 PCC(S)A 2000 s8(6) and (8).
28 'Referral Order Guidance', Ministry of Justice and Youth Justice Board, 2018, para 3.11.

- YRO with intensive supervision and surveillance or fostering;
- DTO;
- section 91 long-term detention (PCC(S)A 2000 s91(1));
- extended detention (CJA 2003 s226B);
- detention for life (CJA 2003 s226);
- detention during her Majesty's Pleasure ((PCC(S)A) 2000 s90);
- hospital order (MHA s37);
- hospital order with restriction order (s41);
- guardianship order;
- supervision order;
- remittal for sentence.

17.20 The Crown Court has a duty to remit children to the youth court for sentence[29] (see paras 17.22–17.27 on remittal for sentence).

17.21 The compulsory referral order conditions do not bind the Crown Court. Therefore where a child is sentenced by the Crown Court following a plea of guilty in circumstances where the youth court would be bound to impose a referral order, the Crown Court judge is free to impose a YRO, or any other sentence that the judge could ordinarily impose on a child. This means the Crown Court judge has greater sentencing options than the youth court. However, the most appropriate course will usually be to remit the matter to the youth court in order for them to consider a referral order.

Remittal for sentence to (home) youth court

17.22 The Crown Court or adult magistrates' court dealing with a child who has pleaded guilty or where there has been a finding of guilt in relation to any offence other than homicide, must remit the case to the youth court 'unless satisfied it would be undesirable to do so'.[30] The Crown Court may only remit a case back to the youth court acting for the place where he or she was sent to the Crown Court for trial.[31]

17.23 A youth court that is not the 'home' youth court of the child being sentenced should also remit to the court where the defendant habitually resides.[32] Remittal is usually desirable because the youth court is a specialist court and will have expertise in sentencing children. Remitting to the home youth court will mean the YOT who will be overseeing any order will be able to provide input, advice and guid-

29 PCC(S)A 2000 s8(6).
30 PCC(S)A 2000 s8(2).
31 PCC(S)A 2000 s8(2)(a).
32 PCC(S)A 2000 s8(2)(b).

ance during the sentencing hearing, and will be able to be more involved in the sentencing process.

17.24 The *Sentencing children and young people: definitive guideline* states that:

> In considering whether remittal is undesirable a court should balance the need for expertise in the sentencing of children and young people with the benefits of the sentence being imposed by the court which determined guilt.[33]

17.25 Reasons that it might not be desirable to remit the case to the relevant youth court are:

- the trial judge would be better informed of the facts and circumstances;
- there was the risk of disparity of co-defendants being sentenced in separate courts; and
- remittal might result in delay, a duplication of procedures and fruitless expense.[34]

17.26 Where children plead guilty to offences in the Crown Court because they are jointly charged with adults and there will be further delay because some co-defendants have pleaded not guilty, it will usually be appropriate to remit any child to the youth court for sentence to avoid any further delay.[35]

Remittal for sentence and referral orders

17.27 In the adult magistrates' court and the Crown Court, the court must consider its duty to remit (see paras 17.22–17.26 above). As was highlighted in the case of *R v Reyon Menelek Dillon*, where a child pleads guilty and the compulsory referral order conditions are met, the youth court would be bound to make a referral order (see paras 19.8–19.10 on mandatory referral order conditions). In these circumstances, particularly where there has been no trial or examination of culpability, there could be no unjust disparity and no delay would be caused by the case being promptly remitted to the youth court – a remittal order must be made.[36] The *Sentencing children and young people: definitive guideline* states that:

> Particular attention should be given to children and young people who are appearing before the Crown Court only because they have

33 Sentencing Council, *Sentencing children and young people: definitive guideline*, 2017, para 2.15.

34 *R v Lewis* (1984) 79 Cr App R 94 at 99.

35 *R v Reyon Menelek Dillon* [2017] EWCA Crim 2642, para 11.

36 *R v Reyon Menelek Dillon* [2017] EWCA Crim 2642, para 13.

been charged with an adult offender; referral orders are generally not available in the Crown Court but may be the most appropriate sentence.[37]

Deferred sentencing

17.28 The power to defer sentence, on one occasion, for up to six months[38] applies to under 18-year-olds as it does to adults. The purpose of deferring sentence is to enable the court to assess the defendant's conduct, including where appropriate the making of reparation, or their capacity to change their behaviour.[39] The defendant must consent, undertake to comply with any requirements (this may include a residence requirement) and the court must be satisfied it would be in the interests of justice to exercise the power.[40] The court may appoint a supervisor, this is likely to be a member of the youth offending team (YOT).[41]

The relevance of age and available sentences

Determining age

17.29 In the vast majority of cases, the defendant's age will not be in dispute. There will, however, be a number of cases where a child asserts herself or himself to be an age that is either disputed or the child cannot verify because the child has no paperwork or documentation.

17.30 This most commonly arises for unaccompanied minors and victims of trafficking and exploitation. In this context, any person who asserts herself or himself to be a child before the criminal courts should be treated with sensitivity and with care (see paras 2.31–2.51 on procedure for age disputed defendants).

Available sentences

17.31 The defendant's age *on the date of conviction* (the date the defendant pleads guilty or there is a finding of guilt) determines what senten-

37 *Sentencing children and young people: definitive guideline*, 2017, para 2.16.
38 PCC(S)A 2000 ss1–1D.
39 PCC(S)A 2000 s1(1).
40 PCC(S)A 2000 s1(3).
41 PCC(S)A 2000 s1A.

cing disposals are available.[42] This may be of importance where a particular sentence only becomes available when a child reaches a certain age.

Sentences available by age

Sentence	**Age on date of conviction**		
	10–11	**12–14**	**15–17**
Absolute or conditional discharge	✓	✓	✓
Reparation order*	✓	✓	✓
Fine or compensation order*	(✓)	(✓)	(✓)
Referral order	✓	✓	✓
YRO	✓	✓	✓
YRO with intensive supervision and surveillance or fostering		✓ For persistent offenders *only*	✓
DTO		✓ For persistent offenders *only*	✓
Section 91 (long-term detention)[43]	✓	✓	✓
Extended detention	✓	✓	✓

42 *R v Dennis Obasi* [2014] EWCA 581; *R v Ghafoor (Imran Hussain)* [2002] EWCA Crim 1857; *R v Danga (Harbeer Singh)* [1992] QB 1996; *R v Robson* [2007] 1 Cr App (S) 54; *R v CB* [2013] EWCA Crim 2494. Also see *R v Cassidy* (2000) *Times* 13 October, CA on detention and training orders; *R v Robinson* (1993) 14 Cr App R (S) 448 on PCC(S)A 2000 s91.

43 PCC(S)A 2000 s91.

Detention for life	✓	✓	✓
Detention at Her Majesty's Pleasure	✓	✓	✓
Hospital order	✓	✓	✓
Hospital order with restriction	✓	✓	✓
Guardianship order			Available for 16- and 17-year-olds only
Supervision order	✓	✓	✓

* For children aged under 16, any financial order must be made in the parent or guardian's name.[44] For 16- and 17-year-olds, the financial order may be made in the parent/carer's name[45] (see paras 18.52–18.56 on power to order a parents, guardian or local authority to pay).

Crossing a significant age threshold between offence and sentence

Overview

17.32 Crossing a significant age threshold during proceedings can mean the maximum sentence available to the court is greater than that which was available on the date the offence was committed. This particularly concerns children turning 12, 15 or 18 years old.

17.33 The *Sentencing children and young people: definitive guideline* states the court should take as its starting point the sentence that would have been likely to have been imposed on the date the offence was committed.[46]

17.34 The *Sentencing children and young people: definitive guideline* also states that it will rarely be appropriate for a court to impose a more

44 PCC(S)A 2000 ss137(1)–(1A).

45 PCC(S)A 2000 ss137(3).

46 *Sentencing children and young people: definitive guideline*, para 6.2; *R v Ghafoor* [2002] EWCA Crim 1857, [2003] 1 Cr App R (S) 428.

severe sentence than the maximum sentence the court could have imposed at the time the offence was committed. However, when a significant age threshold is passed, a sentence at, or close to, that maximum may be appropriate.[47] It is therefore extremely important in cases involving children who have crossed a significant age threshold, that the sentencing court is provided with information regarding the defendant's age at the date of the offence and the available sentencing options at that time given the defendant's age.

17.35 In *R v Ghafoor*[48] the Court of Appeal outlined the approach to be taken where a defendant crosses a significant age threshold between the date of the offence and the date of conviction:

1) The starting point is the sentence that would have been passed at the date of the commission of the offence.
2) Justice requires there to be good reason to depart from the starting point and pass a sentence higher than would have been passed at the date of the commission of the offence.
3) That is not to say that the starting point may not be tempered somewhat in particular cases where there is a long interval between the date of commission of the offence and the date of conviction if circumstances have changed significantly.
4) In a case where the date of conviction is only a few months after the date of the offence, it would rarely be appropriate to pass a longer sentence than that which would have been passed at the date of the offence.

17.36 *Ghafoor* and been considered by the Court of Appeal in a number of subsequent decisions. The fact that a defendant may be sentenced under a different regime from that applicable given the defendant's age at the time the offence was committed is not unlawful,[49] provided the approach in *Ghafoor* is followed. A number of important principles have emerged:

- The court must not exceed the maximum sentence applicable to the *offence* at the time the offence was committed.[50]
- Where no custodial sentence of any kind could have been imposed given the age of the child at the time the child committed the offence, the court must not impose a custodial sentence.[51]

47 *Sentencing children and young people: definitive guideline*, para 6.3.
48 *R v Ghafoor* [2002] EWCA Crim 1857, paras 31–34.
49 *R v Bowker* [2007] EWCA Crim 1608.
50 *R v H* [2011] EWCA Crim 2753; *R v L* [2017] EWCA Crim 43.
51 *R v Forbes* [2016] EWCA Crim 1388, paras 117–120.

- It will rarely be appropriate for the court to exceed the maximum sentence applicable to the defendant, given the defendant's age on the date the offence was committed.[52]
- The child's chronological age at the time the offence was committed, as well as the child's emotional and developmental age, remain important factors in assessing culpability and maturity.[53]

17.37 In *Ghafoor*,[54] G was 17 and was charged with riot. He was committed for trial at the Crown Court as he was jointly charged with adults. At the Crown Court he pleaded guilty and, having attained 18, was sentenced to 54 months' detention in a young offender institution (YOI). On appeal, a sentence of 18 months was substituted on the basis the maximum sentence he could have received was a two-year detention and training order. Section 91 detention was not available, as the offence was not a grave crime[55] because the maximum penalty in the case of a person who has attained 21 is ten years' imprisonment. Bearing in mind his guilty pleas, the likely sentence he could have received at the time of the commission of the offence was 18 months.

17.38 In *Britton*,[56] B and his co-defendant had stolen two cars and had used them in a ram-raid on a city-centre shop, stealing goods to the value of some £7,000. B was 17 when he committed the offences, and he had turned 18 by the time he pleaded guilty. The Court of Appeal quashed a sentence of two-and-a-half years' detention and substituted 18 months' detention, as there had been no good reason for departing from the length of sentence that a 17-year-old would have received.

17.39 DM[57] was 17 when he committed an offence of inflicting grievous bodily harm. He had just turned 18 when he pleaded guilty and he was sentenced. The starting point for the sentencing court should have been the likely sentence DM would have received if he had been sentenced before he reached 18. In this case, the Court of Appeal reduced a 12-month sentence of detention to four months' detention and ruled that the starting point would have been a referral order on the basis DM had no previous convictions.

52 *R v Ghafoor* [2002] EWCA Crim 1857.

53 *Sentencing children and young people: definitive guideline*, para 4.10.

54 *R v Ghafoor* [2002] EWCA Crim 1857.

55 PCC(S)A 2000 s91(1)(a).

56 *R v Britton (Stephen Kade)* (2007) 1 Cr App R (S) 121.

57 *R v DM* [2012] EWCA Crim 1649.

Children who turn 18 between the offence and sentence

Introduction

17.40 Children who have their hearings in the youth court who turn 18 during proceedings may be able to continue to have their case heard in a youth court.[58] If the youth court continues to hear the case, the 18 year old can receive youth sentences (see para 17.42). Alternatively, the youth court may remit the case to an adult magistrates' court for sentence.[59] This creates an anomaly that 18-year-olds may be sentenced as children or as adults.[60]

Turning 18 between the offence and conviction

17.41 If a child turns 18 before he or she is convicted (pleads guilty or there is a finding of guilt), the child can generally no longer receive youth sentences and will be sentenced as an adult. Even though the court's sentencing powers will be governed by the adult sentencing regime, the starting point is the sentence the court would have been likely to have imposed on the date of the offence (see paras 2.10–2.15).

17.42 The exception to this general rule is where a defendant has turned 18 during proceedings in the youth court. CYPA 1963 s29(1) provides:

> Where proceedings in respect of a young person are begun for an offence and he attains the age of eighteen before the conclusion of the proceedings, the court may deal with the case and make any order which it could have made if he had not attained that age.

17.43 CYPA 1963 s29(1) gives the youth court a discretion to make any order as though the defendant had not attained the age of 18 and therefore impose youth sentences on 18-year-olds.

17.44 Where the court is sentencing a defendant as an adult for offences committed as a child, the court may have to impose an alternative penalty that most closely reflects the disposal that would have been imposed on the day the offence was committed. For example, a defendant who would have received a referral order should receive a community penalty or a discharge.[61]

58 CYPA 1963 s29(1) – for a fuller discussion see paras 2.10–2.15.

59 PCC(S)A 2000 s9(1) also see paras 2.10–2.15.

60 CYPA 1963 s29(1) – for a fuller discussion see paras 2.10–2.15.

61 *R v Reyon Menelek Dillon* [2017] EWCA Crim 2642.

Turning 18 between conviction and sentence

17.45 Children who turn 18 after they are convicted (plead guilty or there is a finding of guilt) but before they are sentenced, will continue to receive youth sentences. The available sentencing disposals are determined by a defendant's age on the day of conviction (see para 17.31 on available sentences).

Young adults

17.46 When sentencing young people who offend in early adulthood it is important to examine developmental age and maturity and other factors that could diminish culpability.[62] The Court of Appeal has recognised that children who turn 18 should be sentenced more leniently than older adults:

> [R]eaching the age of 18 has many legal consequences, but it does not present a cliff edge for the purposes of sentencing. So much has long been clear . . . Full maturity and all the attributes of adulthood are not magically conferred on young people on their 18th birthdays . . . The youth and maturity of an offender will be factors that inform any sentencing decision, even if an offender has passed his or her 18th birthday.[63]

17.47 Many of the factors that apply to sentencing children will apply equally to young adults aged 18–25, such as immaturity, lack of self-control and inability to appreciate the seriousness and consequences of their actions.[64] In *R v Balogun*,[65] the Court of Appeal stated 'the fact that the appellant had attained the age of 18 before he committed the offences does not of itself mean that the factors relevant to the sentencing of a young offender had necessarily ceased to have any relevance. He had not been invested overnight with all the understanding and self control of a fully mature adult'.[66]

62 See fuller discussion at para 1.9 on young adults and paras 3.30–3.36 on child and adolescent brain development.

63 *R v Clarke, Andres and Thompson* [2018] EWCA Crim 185, para 5. Also see *R v Peters* [2005] EWCA Crim 605.

64 See fuller discussion at para 1.9 on young adults. Also see *Howard League for Penal Reform: Sentencing Principles for young adults (2019)* at www.howardleague.org.

65 [2018] EWCA Crim 2933.

66 *R v Balogun* [2018] EWCA Crim 2933, para 41.

Sentencing guidelines

17.48 Where a defendant turns 18, but was a child when the offence was committed, the *Sentencing children and young people: definitive guideline* is a relevant guideline[67] with specific guidance at paras 6.1–6.3. The guideline may also be relevant where the defendant has committed offences in early adulthood having turned 18.[68]

Statutory purpose of sentencing

17.49 If defendants are aged under 18 at the date of conviction then there is currently no statutory purpose of sentencing. The relevant provision, CJA 2003 s142A that set out the statutory purpose of sentencing, has never been implemented.[69]

17.50 This raises the possibility that when a court sentences those over the age of 18 who committed the relevant offence(s) when they were a child, 'more general public policy considerations, in particular deterrence, can play a greater part'.[70] The *Sentencing children and young people: definitive guideline* says, 'the purpose of sentencing adult offenders has to be taken into account'.[71] This does not detract from the starting point which to determine the likely sentence at the date of the offence.

Adults sentenced for historic offences committed when a child

17.51 There are situations when adults are sentenced for offences committed when they were children. The principles in *Ghafoor* govern the sentencing exercise, and the court's sentencing powers are determined by the sentencing regime applicable at the date of sentence. Although the sentence has to be limited to the maximum sentence at the date when the offence was committed.[72]

Children who turn 15 between commission of the offence and conviction

17.52 Children who turn 15 during criminal proceedings may become liable to receive a more severe sentence than would have been available on the date of the offence(s). This is because children aged under

67 For example *R v Hobbs* [2018] EWCA Crim 1003, para 22.

68 *R v Balogun* [2018] EWCA Crim 2933, paras 37 and 41.

69 CJA 2003 s142A has not yet been brought into force.

70 *R v Bowker* [2007] EWCA Crim 1608, para 22.

71 *Sentencing children and young people: definitive guideline*, para 6.2.

72 *R v H* [2011] EWCA Crim 2753; *R v Forbes* [2016] EWCA Crim 1388.

15 who are not deemed to be a persistent offender *cannot* receive detention and training orders or intensive youth rehabilitation orders in the youth court.

17.53 In a youth court, if a child who is not a persistent offender turns 15 between the offence and conviction, the court should follow the principles in *Ghafoor*[73] (see paras 17.32–17.39). The youth court should not impose a detention and training order or intensive youth rehabilitation order (YRO) when no custodial sentence of any kind could have been imposed given the age of the child at the time the child committed the offence.[74]

17.54 The same principle does not apply in the Crown Court. Depending on the seriousness of the offence, custodial sentences can be available for a child aged under 15 and in these circumstances.[75]

17.55 A child turning 15 after conviction must be sentenced to any applicable sentence available to a child of their age on the date of conviction (see para 17.31 on available sentences).

Children who turn 12 between commission of the offence and conviction

17.56 Children who turn 12 during criminal proceedings may become liable to receive a more severe sentence than would have been available on the date of the offence(s).

17.57 Children aged 12 and under *cannot* receive detention and training orders, youth rehabilitation orders with intensive supervision and surveillance or youth rehabilitation orders with intensive fostering. Children aged 12–14 years only receive these sentences if they are deemed to be a persistent offender (see paras 21.50–21.55). Therefore children turning 12 who meet the criteria of a persistent offender become liable to more severe sentences.

17.58 If a child who is deemed to be a persistent offender turns 12 between the commission of the offence and conviction, the court should follow the principles in *Ghafoor*[76] and Forbes[77] (see paras 17.34–17.36) and the court should not impose a detention and training order when no custodial sentence of any kind could have been

73 *R v Ghafoor* [2002] EWCA Crim 1857.

74 *R v Forbes* [2016] EWCA Crim 1388.

75 *R v Thomas (Jahmarl)* [2004] EWCA Crim 2199.

76 *R v Ghafoor* [2002] EWCA Crim 1857.

77 *R v Forbes* [2016] EWCA Crim 1388.

imposed given the age of the child at the time they committed the offence.[78]

17.59 Similarly, the court should not impose a youth rehabilitation order with intensive supervision and surveillance or fostering because a sentencing disposal of this type could not have been imposed on the date at which the offence was committed.

17.60 A court sentencing a child who has turned 12 after conviction and before sentence, is restricted to sentencing provisions that apply on the date of conviction (see para 17.31 on available sentences).

Duty to consider background

Introduction

17.61 The court's duty to have regard to a child's welfare[79] requires the court to find out background information about the child and where necessary that a proper assessment has been made (see paras 16.10–16.16). The court is also under a duty to consider all available information about the child's general conduct, home surroundings, school record and medical history.[80] In addition to a pre-sentence report, the court may order a section 9 local authority report[81] (see paras 17.73–17.74) or other expert report. Other expert reports may also assist the court.

Children's demeanour and behaviour in court

17.62 Any court sentencing a child should be mindful that children may not always conduct themselves appropriately in court.[82] Courts should take into account the fact that many factors – including a child's nervousness, lack of understanding of court processes, perception of bias or discrimination, the presence of their peers and the child's lack of maturity – can affect how a child presents himself or herself in court.

17.63 When the judge or bench asks the child questions, the court should also take into account any communication difficulties, learning disabilities and mental health needs.

78 *R v Forbes* [2016] EWCA Crim 1388.

79 CYPA 1933 s44.

80 Magistrates' Court (Children and Young Persons) Rules 1992 r10(2).

81 CYPA 1969 s9.

82 *Sentencing children and young people: definitive guideline*, para 1.15.

Requesting pre-sentence reports and other background information

17.64 There are a number of different reports that might assist the court when sentencing a child:

- section 9 local authority reports (see paras 17.73–17.74);
- expert reports; education reports; reports from secure training centre (STC) or YOI; psychologist and psychiatric reports (see paras 17.75–17.80);
- pre-sentence reports – including stand down, specific, fast delivery reports (see paras 17.81 17.111).

Sentencing with or without a report

17.65 The court *must* obtain and consider a pre-sentence report before imposing a custodial sentence or a YRO.[83] The court can rely on a recent report if one is available (see paras 17.103–17.104 on using an existing report).[84] A specific sentence report is required before imposing a reparation order (see paras 17.109–17.110).

17.66 The court may impose the following sentences *without* a pre-sentence report:

- absolute discharge;
- conditional discharge;
- bind over;
- fine;
- referral order.

Power to adjourn for reports

Adjournment

17.67 The youth court and adult magistrates' court have the power to adjourn the case to enable inquiries to be made or to determine the most suitable method of dealing with the case. The adjournment can be for up to four weeks at a time, or three weeks if the child is in custody. This allows for repeated adjournments if necessary.

83 CJA 2003 s156(3).
84 CJA 2003 s156(5).

17.68 Courts are encouraged to pass to sentence on the same day following a plea of guilty or a finding of guilt.[85] Defence lawyers will have to consider what information the court will need to properly explore different sentencing options. Whether adjourning for reports might provide a court with additional background information that could not be provided in oral mitigation or whether an existing report, a stand down or oral report, could avoid unnecessary delay (see paras 17.103–17.104 on using an existing report).

Granting bail

17.69 Where the court adjourns for the preparation of a pre-sentence report, it is not unusual for the court to add a bail condition requiring the child to attend appointments with the YOT and to co-operate with the preparation of the pre-sentence report. This is to encourage co-operation, but also means the child can be arrested if the child fails to attend their appointment (see paras 11.126–11.128 on arrest for breach of on bail conditions; and paras 17.94–17.96 below on failure to co-operate with preparation of reports).

Warning the child

17.70 If the court adjourns the case before sentence, it is important to tell the child in plain and simple language the sentencing options the court is considering. The sentencing options should reflect the court's view of the seriousness of the offence (see paras 17.82–17.83 on the court's view on seriousness). When a case is adjourned for a pre-sentence report and the court's view is that the custody threshold has been passed, this should be explained clearly and simply to a child. Courts may indicate that 'all options are open', however children (and their parents or supporting adults) may not understand what this means. If necessary, the defence lawyers should explain that 'all options open' means the court thinks the offence(s) are so serious that they are considering a custodial sentence.

Section 53 warning[86]

17.71 Youth courts now have the power to commit children to the Crown Court for sentence if the child is charged with a grave crime.[87] In

85 Youth Court Bench Book, Judicial College, August 2017, 'Effective case management', p18, para 22 and CrimPR rr24.11(9)(a) (youth court and adult magistrates' court) and 25.16(7)(a) (the Crown Court).

86 Criminal Justice and Courts Act 2015 s53.

87 PCC(S)A 2000 s3B as inserted by Criminal Justice and Courts Act 2015 s53.

cases where jurisdiction has been retained for trial, the youth court should already have warned the child that he or she could still be committed to the Crown Court for sentence (see para 8.132 on warning the child and first appearance). This warning should be *repeated* if the case is adjourned for a pre-sentence report or further information and the court is considering committal for sentence.

Raising expectations of non-custodial sentences

17.72 If a court adjourns a case for a specific sentencing option to be considered, a legitimate expectation may be raised that if the report is favourable, that sentence or disposal will be imposed.[88] If, for example, the court adjourns so that an alternative to custody can be considered and the alternative is satisfactory, the court should follow the report's recommendation.[89] For this reason, a careful note should be made of the court's remarks when the case is adjourned for reports.

Section 9 local authority reports[90]

17.73 Children and Young Persons Act 1969 s9 enables criminal courts to request the relevant local authority to make inquiries and provide relevant background information There is a corresponding duty on the local authority to comply with a section 9 request, to make any necessary investigations, to provide information and to assist the court. The court shall consider the desirability of adjourning the case if necessary.[91] In certain cases, a court may want to make enquiries to find out additional background information about a child beyond the information that might be contained in a pre-sentence report. This may relate to the child's education (or the fact that the child is not currently receiving any), or the unsatisfactory nature of the child's housing or living arrangements.

17.74 While this power is exercised infrequently, requesting a section 9 report may create an opportunity in cases where the court has concerns about whether a local authority is adequately fulfilling its legal duties to a child, to address any shortcomings and hold the local authority education or children's services department to account. A multi-disciplinary approach is likely to be most effective

88 *R v Stokes* (1983) 5 Cr App R (S) 449, CA.

89 *R v Gillam* (1980) 2 Cr App R (S) 267, CA.

90 CYPA 1969 s9.

91 Magistrates' Court (Children and Young Persons) Rules 1992 r10(2)(c).

in addressing the principal aim of the youth justice system, the prevention of offending.[92]

Expert and medical reports

17.75 In some circumstances it will be appropriate to obtain expert reports – for example, a psychological, psychiatric or medical report on the mental or physical health of the child. In some cases, a report will have been obtained earlier in the proceedings, for example to deal with an issue as to fitness to plead or effective participation (see paras 4.56–4.102) or the need for extra assistance with proceedings (see paras 4.31–4.55 on special measures).

17.76 Where a report has already been obtained, it may be useful for the court to consider it at the sentencing hearing as it may provide useful information about the child that is relevant to sentence. However, if the report does not address sentencing, it may be necessary to get a further report, possibly from the same author, to specifically address the impact of different sentences on the child's mental or physical condition.

17.77 Where there has not been a report, but the court or the defence consider a report will be useful for sentencing, then it can be obtained either by the court ordering the YOT to obtain a report, or by the defence solicitors. It should be clear at the hearing who is obtaining the report.

17.78 Where it is clear that the defence should obtain the report, they will need to apply for prior authority through the Legal Aid Agency (LAA) and it will be useful to inform the LAA that the report has been requested by the court. The process in instructing an expert and deciding which expert to instruct is dealt with at paras 12.10–12.23 on instructing an expert.

17.79 It will usually be helpful for the YOT to see the report prior to writing the pre-sentencing report, and therefore any such report should be served on the YOT once received.

17.80 Where a mental health disposal is being considered, it will be helpful to obtain an expert report from a registered medical practitioner or a registered psychologist who will be able to supervise any treatment (see para 22.12 on available disposals where the child is fit to plead). Where a hospital order is being considered, the written or oral evidence of two registered medical practitioners will be required[93] (see paras 22.28–22.37).

92 Crime and Disorder Act 1998 s37(1).

93 MHA 1983 s37(2).

Pre-sentence reports

The purpose of the report

17.81 Pre-sentence reports assist the court to determine the most appropriate way to deal with a child. Pre-sentence reports are prepared and written according to the National Standards for Youth Justice Services.

Court's view on seriousness

17.82 When the court requests a pre-sentence report, the court will give an indication of their preliminary view of the seriousness of the offending and the range of sentences or requirements it wishes to consider. The court will give an indication of whether the offence(s) are either:

- serious enough to warrant a community penalty; or
- so serious that neither a fine alone, nor a community penalty, can be justified.

This indication might be important for the report writer in assessing the different sentencing options. A careful note should be made by all parties of any indication of seriousness (see para 17.72 on raising a legitimate expectation of a non-custodial sentence).

17.83 Where the court requests an 'all options' pre-sentence report, the YOT's court officer should ask the court to clarify their view of the seriousness to take this into account when preparing the report (see also para 17.70 on warning the child).[94]

Format

17.84 Pre-sentence reports for children are usually prepared by a member of a YOT.[95] Pre-sentence reports are generally written, although they can be given orally in court,[96] unless the court is considering imposing a custodial sentence, in which case the pre-sentence report must be in writing.[97]

94 Youth Justice Board (October 2014) Case Management Guidance, section 5: How to use reports, para 2.6.

95 They can also be prepared by an officer of a local probation board, an officer of a provider of probation services or a social worker of a local authority – CJA 2003 s158(2).

96 Youth Justice Board National Standards for Youth Justice Services April 2013, Youth Justice Board for England and Wales, para 5.3.

97 CJA 2003 ss158(1B) and 156(3)(a).

17.85 A pre-sentence report follows the following standard format:

- front sheet;
- sources of information;
- offence analysis;
- assessment of the child;
- assessment of the need for parenting support, including suitability for a parenting order;
- assessment of risk to the community, including the likelihood of reoffending, risk of serious harm to others, and risks to the child's safety or wellbeing;
- conclusion and proposal for sentencing.

Pre-sentence reports are intended to be brief and clear and – except in very complex cases, such as multiple offences or dangerousness assessments – should not exceed four pages.[98]

17.86 The preparation of a pre-sentence report must be based on:

- at least one interview with the child;
- where possible, an interview with the parents/carers;
- a home visit where appropriate;
- an assessment using the Youth Justice Board-approved assessment tools (Asset or AssetPlus);
- confirmation from relevant services that relevant provision exists and is forthcoming in support of proposals, particularly for certain YRO requirements.[99]

17.87 Children and their parent or guardian should be given a copy of the pre-sentence report, and have an opportunity to discuss the content and conclusions of the report prior to the sentencing hearing.[100]

17.88 The pre-sentence report will include the report writer's assessment of the child's risk of reoffending and risk of harm (see paras 17.98–17.101 on AssetPlus assessments and the scaled approach).

Dangerousness assessment

17.89 If a child is convicted of a specified offence (CJA 2003 Sch 15), the pre-sentence report will address the question of dangerousness, and

98 Youth Justice Board (October 2014) Case Management Guidance, section 5: How to use reports, para 2.2.

99 Youth Justice Board National Standards for Youth Justice Services April 2013, Youth Justice Board for England and Wales, para 5.3.

100 Youth Justice Board National Standards for Youth Justice Services April 2013, Youth Justice Board for England and Wales, para 5.4.

where appropriate include a dangerousness assessment. This will assist the court in deciding whether to:

a) commit the case to the Crown Court;
b) impose an extended sentence; or
c) impose detention for life.

17.90 The assessment of dangerousness[101] requires the court to assess whether there is a significant risk to members of the public of serious harm (meaning death or serious personal injury) occasioned by the child committing further specified offences. In light of the increased understanding of child and adolescent brain development and the fact that children continue to mature into their mid-twenties, assessing past behaviour of children may be a poor indicator of future conduct.

17.91 The report should not make a recommendation about the dangerousness of the child – it should provide information to inform the court in making its decision.[102] For example, the report may include any past harmful behaviour, whether convicted or not; the child's risk of committing further offences; and the child's risk of harm.

17.92 It is a matter for the court whether or not to make a finding of dangerousness – it is not a decision for the YOT. However, the report will address the risk the child poses of causing serious harm. While this may be useful information to the court in coming to a decision on dangerousness, the court is not bound by this assessment and may choose to reject or accept it.

17.93 If the report writer believes that a robust and appropriate risk management plan could be put in place to control and reduce the level of risk of serious harm to others, this should be outlined in the report.[103]

Failure to co-operate with preparation of pre-sentence reports

17.94 Children should be encouraged to engage with the preparation of the pre-sentence report. Where children do not comply, the report

101 CJA 2003 s229.

102 Youth Justice Board National Standards for Youth Justice Services April 2013, Youth Justice Board for England and Wales, para 2.12.

103 Youth Justice Board National Standards for Youth Justice Services April 2013, Youth Justice Board for England and Wales, para 2.12.

writer is required to inform the court in writing.[104] The use of bail conditions, requiring the child or young person to co-operate in the preparation of reports, should be requested in these circumstances.

Children who fail to attend an appointment

17.95 Children who have a bail condition to co-operate with the preparation of the pre-sentence report and who fail to attend an appointment with YOT are liable to be arrested (see paras 11.124–11.125 on breach of bail).

17.96 It is a matter for the YOT initially if they wish to offer another appointment prior to the next hearing date. It is then a matter for the court what action to take. Ultimately the court is likely to impose very strict bail conditions or withdraw bail for the report to be written (see paras 11.124–11.125 on breach of bail).

Mentioning previous convictions

17.97 The court will be informed of all previous convictions, youth conditional cautions or youth cautions, including spent convictions, and may be told about out of court disposals or other matters dealt with by diversion. This may include a report on a child's failure to participate in a rehabilitation programme as part of a youth caution.[105]

AssetPlus assessments and the scaled approach

17.98 The pre-sentence report is based primarily on the YJB's AssetPlus[106] assessment – this includes background information about the child and a risk assessment (likelihood of reoffending, risk of harm to others, risks to the child's safety or wellbeing). The level of intervention will be determined by the risk assessment and the 'scaled approach' principle, which means children with the greatest risk of reoffending and harm will require the greatest intervention. Defence lawyers should have regard to parity with co-accused and the risk that proposed sentences for children will be based upon perceived future risk rather than the offence.

104 Youth Justice Board (October 2014) Case Management Guidance, section 5: How to Use Reports, para 2.1.

105 Crime and Disorder Act 1998 s66ZB.

106 www.gov.uk/government/publications/assetplus-assessment-and-planning-in-the-youth-justice-system.

17.99 The scaled approach increases or decreases the level of intervention depending on the assessed likelihood of reoffending and risk of serious harm:

- Matches intensity of a YOT's work to a young person's assessed likelihood of reoffending and risk of serious harm to public.
- Three levels of intervention – standard, enhanced, intensive.
- Applies to referral orders, YROs and DTO licence.

Level of intervention	**Likelihood of reoffending or risk of harm**	**Asset score (inclusive)**	**Function of intervention**	**Possible sentence requirement**	**Contact requirement (min no per month in first 3 months)**
Standard	Low likelihood of offending AND Low risk of serious harm (No ROSHA)	1–14	Enabling compliance and repairing harm	Reparation Standalone unpaid work Standalone attendance centre	2 Reducing to 1
Enhanced	Medium likelihood of reoffending OR Medium risk of serious harm (indicated by ROSHA)	15–32	Enabling compliance and repairing harm AND Enabling help/change	Supervision Reparation Requirement to help/change behaviour	4 Reducing to 2
Intensive	High likelihood of reoffending OR High or very high risk of serious harm (indicated by ROSHA)	33–64	Enabling compliance and repairing harm AND Enabling help/change AND Enabling control	Supervision Reparation PLUS Requirement to help/change behaviour Requirement to monitor restrict movement	12 Reducing to 4

17.100 ROSHA is the risk of serious harm of assessment. The AssetPlus assessment tool considers the offence and identifies factors that may have contributed to the offending behaviour.

17.101 The AssetPlus assessment requires greater intervention depending on the vulnerability of the child. This risks more onerous sentences being imposed on more vulnerable defendants (see, for example, table of interventions for YROs at para 20.18).

Correcting errors in pre-sentence reports

17.102 A child being sentenced (and the child's parent, guardian or supporting adult) should have the opportunity to read the pre-sentence report before the sentencing hearing.[107] It is important to check for errors often information is taken from previous reports or other information so inaccuracies occur. Defence lawyers should spend time with the child (and their parent or guardian) going through the PSR and potentially challenge the YOT about the content. (Also see para 17.3 on providing a copy of the PSR to the child, and parent or guardian.)

Using an existing pre-sentence report

17.103 The pressure on courts to sentence children on the day of conviction will mean that courts will be reluctant to adjourn cases unnecessarily for new reports. Courts are not required to order a new report if the court forms the opinion it is unnecessary to do so.[108] Guidance for YOTs states that a court may sentence on the basis of an existing report written within the last three months, provided there has not been any significant change in the child's circumstances since the last AssetPlus assessment.[109] In this situation, the court officer must provide a written or verbal addendum, to cover the new offence.

17.104 A child may be disadvantaged by a sentencing hearing proceeding without the benefit of a new report if certain sentencing options have not been considered. This may be addressed by a specific sentence report, an addendum or stand down report. A different situation arises if there has been any significant change of circumstances for the child or that the office is so different from the previous offending that a new report is required – in these circumstances, defence lawyers should discuss these issues with the YOT before seeking an adjournment for a new report.

107 Youth Justice Board National Standards for Youth Justice Services April 2013, Youth Justice Board for England and Wales, para 5.4.

108 CJA 2003 s156(4) and (5).

109 Youth Justice Board Case Management Guidance, How to Use Reports: Section 5 case management guidance, para 2.1.

Draft intensive referral order contract

17.105 In custody threshold cases, an intensive referral order might be proposed in the PSR. In preparation for the sentencing hearing, the YOT should ensure the pre-sentence report presents a referral order as a 'robust and credible sentencing option' and consider convening a 'pre-sentence panel'.[110] The pre-sentence referral panel meeting should be used to consider a draft intensive referral order contract.

17.106 The pre-sentence panel meeting will consider a draft intensive referral order contract which should include a weekly timetable of structured activity.[111] The YOT should devise a programme for intensive support and supervision and this may include non-electronic curfew and monitoring.[112] The level of intervention and number of hours of reparation should be proportionate to the offence and scaled approach level (see paras 17.98–17.101).

17.107 The draft intensive referral order contract will then be included in the pre sentence report.

Stand down reports

17.108 A stand-down report is prepared on the day at court. It will be prepared at the request of the court and may be given either verbally or in writing. The report should be based on information about the child from the previous three months, and it must be based upon at least one interview with the child and, where relevant, his or her parent or guardian. A stand-down report will usually be used where there is an existing pre sentence report to deal with a new offence. A stand-down report is *not* suitable where custody is being considered.[113]

Specific sentence reports

17.109 A specific sentence report must be in writing and be based on a recent YOT assessment.[114] A specific sentence report may be reques-

110 Referral Order Guidance, Ministry of Justice and Youth Justice Board, October 2018, para 3.22. See paras 19.24–19.26.

111 Referral Order Guidance, Ministry of Justice and Youth Justice Board, October 2018, para 3.24.

112 Youth Justice Board Case Management Guidance, October 2014, How to use reports: section 5 case management guidance, para 2.1. Case management guidance, para 2.20.

113 Youth Justice Board National Standards for Youth Justice Services, April 2013, YJB, para 5.9.

114 Youth Justice Board National Standards for Youth Justice Services April 2013, Youth Justice Board for England and Wales, para 5.6.

ted if the court is considering the child's suitability for a reparation order, a particular disposal or YRO requirement.

17.110 A specific sentence report *must* be prepared before imposing a reparation order (see paras 18.30–18.34 on reparation orders). The report assessing a child's suitability for a reparation order must indicate the type of work or proposed requirements and outline the attitude of the victim(s).[115] The court must give reasons if it does not make a reparation order in a case where it has power to do so.[116]

Fast delivery reports

17.111 A fast delivery report requires a one-week adjournment and is typically shorter and less detailed than a pre-sentence report. They are not usually suitable for children as the shorter adjournment does not provide YOTs with adequate time to complete the requirements of an AssetPlus assessment. A specific sentence report will usually be more appropriate.

Assessing the seriousness of the offence

Overview

17.112 Even though sentencing of children should be individualistic and child-focused, the starting point will be the seriousness of the offence. In assessing seriousness, the court should consider:

- any aggravating or mitigating factors – 'If any of these factors is included in the definition of the offence they should not be taken into account when considering the relative seriousness of the offence before the court.'[117]
- culpability;[118]
- the harm caused;[119]

115 PCC(S)A 2000 s73(5).
116 PCC(S)A 2000 s73(8).
117 *Sentencing children and young people: definitive guideline*, para 4.7.
118 *Sentencing children and young people: definitive guideline*, para 4.5.
119 *Sentencing children and young people: definitive guideline*, para 4.6.

Assessing aggravating or mitigating factors

17.113 The *Sentencing children and young people: definitive guideline* summarises the aggravating and mitigating factors the court should consider.[120]

Assessing culpability

17.114 In assessing culpability, the court should have regard to the child's emotional, developmental and chronological age (see paras 16.21–16.23) and the court should consider the extent to which:

- the child is able to appreciate fully the consequences of their conduct;
- the child's actions were impulsive;
- the child's conduct has been affected by inexperience, emotional volatility or negative influences.[121]

17.115 In assessing culpability, the court will have regard to whether the offence was planned, the role played by the child and the level of force.[122] The child's emotional and developmental age will be relevant to assessing the extent of the child's awareness of the possible consequences of his or her actions (see paras 3.30–3.36 on child and adolescent brain development). Children often lack the maturity to foresee the consequences of their behaviour:

> [T]his is because children and young people are unlikely to have the same experience and capacity as an adult to understand the effect of their actions on other people or to appreciate the pain and distress caused and because a child or young person may be less able to resist temptation, especially where peer pressure is exerted.[123]

Assessing harm

17.116 In assessing harm, the court should consider:

- the level of physical and psychological harm caused to the victim;
- the degree of loss caused to the victim;
- the extent of any damage caused to property.[124]

15.117 This includes the extent of the harm intended to be caused or could foreseeably have been caused.[125]

120 *Sentencing children and young people: definitive guideline*, para 4.7.
121 *Sentencing children and young people: definitive guideline*, para 4.10.
122 *Sentencing children and young people: definitive guideline*, para 4.5.
123 *Sentencing children and young people: definitive guideline*, para 4.5.
124 *Sentencing children and young people: definitive guideline*, para 4.6.
125 *Sentencing children and young people: definitive guideline*, para 4.6.

Reduction in sentence for pleading guilty

Overview

17.118 All defendants who are going to plead guilty are encouraged to do so as early in the court process as possible. Defendants who plead guilty are entitled to a reduction in their sentence. The *Sentencing children and young people: definitive guideline* provides guilty plea guidance.[126] The maximum level of reduction for a guilty plea is one-third.

17.119 Children who plead guilty at the first stage of proceedings are entitled to a reduction of one-third in their sentence.[127] The fact that a child failed to make admissions in his or her police interview, or the fact that there is strong or overwhelming evidence, are factors that should *not* be taken into account when determining the level of reduction for pleading guilty for a child.[128] The 'first stage of proceedings' is not defined in the guidance – it will normally be the first hearing in the youth court, or adult magistrates' court.[129] Alternatively, children who do not have a 'first appearance' at court should indicate their guilty plea within the timeframes provided for online guilty pleas and pleading guilty by post.

17.120 The credit for pleading guilty after the first stage of proceedings is a maximum of one-quarter, and there is a sliding scale reducing to one-tenth for pleading guilty on the day of trial.[130] However, practitioners will note that the court may continue to give children the full credit for pleas of guilty after the first stage of proceedings (see para 17.121).

Further information, assistance or advice necessary before indicating plea

17.121 There is a specific exception to the requirement to plead guilty at the earliest opportunity:

> . . . where there are particular circumstances which significantly reduced the child or young person's ability to understand what was

126 *Sentencing children and young people: definitive guideline*, pp17–21. This applies to all cases where the first hearing was on or after 1 June 2017.

127 *Sentencing children and young people: definitive guideline*, para 5.5.

128 *Sentencing children and young people: definitive guideline*, para 5.4.

129 *Sentencing children and young people: definitive guideline*, para 5.5.

130 *Sentencing children and young people: definitive guideline*, para 5.6.

alleged, or otherwise made it unreasonable to expect the child or young person to indicate a guilty plea sooner than was done.[131]

Full credit for a guilty plea should be preserved where expert advice or sight of the evidence is necessary for the defence lawyer to advise the child. For example, where a solicitor has requested an adjournment at the first appearance to instruct an expert to assess the child's fitness to plead.[132] Also see *R v Markham and Edwards*[133] on full credit even where a child has pleaded not guilty.

Applying credit: the reduction for pleading guilty

17.122 The court should consider any reduction in sentence for pleading guilty after it has determined the appropriate sentence for the offence(s) following any offence specific sentencing guideline and using the *Sentencing children and young people: definitive guideline*.[134] Depending on the sentencing disposal, specific considerations apply.

Referral order

17.123 The reduction in sentence for pleading guilty does not apply in relation to referral orders as 'a referral order is a sentence that is only available upon pleading guilty'.[135] A child who changes his or her plea to guilty at any stage in proceedings does not affect his or her eligibility for a mandatory or discretionary referral order.

Youth rehabilitation order

17.124 The reduction in sentence for guilty plea can be taken into account by imposing one type of sentence rather than another. A YRO may be reduced to a different means of disposal. Alternatively the court can reduce the length or severity of any punitive requirements.[136]

Detention and training order

17.125 Since a DTO can only be imposed for 4, 6, 8, 10, 12, 18 or 24 months, the reduction in sentence for a guilty plea may result in a sentence

131 *Sentencing children and young people: definitive guideline*, para 5.16.
132 *Sentencing children and young people: definitive guideline*, para 5.17.
133 [2017] EWCA Crim 739.
134 *Sentencing children and young people: definitive guideline*, p18.
135 *Sentencing children and young people: definitive guideline*, para 5.15.
136 *Sentencing children and young people: definitive guideline*, para 5.10.

that falls between two prescribed periods. The court must impose the lesser of those two periods even though it may result in a reduction greater than a third.[137]

17.126 For DTOs, the reduction in sentence for pleading guilty may result in reducing a custodial sentence to a youth rehabilitation order with or without intensive supervision and surveillance or fostering.[138]

17.127 Practitioners will note that a child may receive a DTO of up to 24 months having pleaded guilty if the offence is one which, but for the plea, would have attracted a sentence of detention in excess of 24 months under PCC(S)A 2000 s91.[139]

17.128 When dealing with more than one summary offence, the total maximum sentence is six months.[140] Allowing for a reduction for each guilty plea, consecutive sentences might result in the imposition of the maximum six-month sentence. In these circumstances, 'the court *may* make a modest *additional* reduction to the *overall* sentence to reflect the benefits derived from the guilty plea.'[141]

Newton hearings and special reasons hearings

17.129 Where a Newton hearing or special reasons hearing has taken place and the child's version of events is rejected, the reduction in sentence for pleading guilty is normally halved (the reduction may be further reduced if witnesses were called during the hearing).[142] This applies to all cases, including murder.[143] As with any case involving a child defendant, an individualistic approach is required and specific features of the case or the child's background may merit full credit being given for their guilty plea.

137 *Sentencing children and young people: definitive guideline*, para 5.9; *R v Eagles* [2006] EWCA Crim 2368.

138 *Sentencing children and young people: definitive guideline*, para 5.10.

139 *Sentencing children and young people: definitive guideline*, para 5.14.

140 *Sentencing children and young people: definitive guideline*, para 5.13. Also see fuller discussion at para 21.62.

141 *Sentencing children and young people: definitive guideline*, para 5.13.

142 *Sentencing children and young people: definitive guideline*, para 5.19.

143 *Sentencing children and young people: definitive guideline*, para 5.25.

Mandatory minimum sentences

Firearms

17.130 In the case of a 16- or 17-year-old, there can be no reduction for a guilty plea if the effect of doing so would be to reduce the length of sentence below the three year mandatory minimum term (Firearms Act 1968 s51A).[144]

Knife offences

17.131 Courts sentencing children for knife and offensive weapon offences that require a mandatory minimum four-month DTO for a 16- or 17-year-old (possession of a knife or offensive weapon in a school or public place;[145] or convictions for a second knife offence[146]) may impose any sentence having taken into consideration the guidance on reduction in sentence for guilty pleas. This may result in only a non-custodial sentencing option being available if the credit reduces the length of custodial sentence below four months.[147]

Mandatory life sentences for murder

17.132 Children convicted of murder must receive detention for life, and will remain subject to the sentence for the rest of their life. There are statutory starting points for the minimum term to be served, the minimum term for children who commit murder is 12 years.[148] Any reduction for a guilty plea will need to ensure the minimum term reflects the seriousness of the cases and there is a different process to determine the level of reduction.

17.133 The *Sentencing children and young people: definitive guideline* provides the following guidance:

- the court will weigh carefully the overall length of the minimum term taking into account other reductions for which the child or young person may be eligible so as to avoid a combination leading to an inappropriately short sentence;
- where it is appropriate to reduce the minimum term having regard to a plea of guilty, the reduction will not exceed one-sixth and will never exceed five years; and

144 *Sentencing children and young people: definitive guideline* para 5.20.
145 Prevention of Crime Act 1953 s1 or 1A.
146 CJA 1988 ss139, 139AA, 139A.
147 *Sentencing children and young people: definitive guideline,* para 5.21.
148 CJA 2003 Sch 21.

- the maximum reduction of one-sixth or five years (whichever is less) should only be given when a guilty plea has been indicated at the first stage of the proceedings.[149] Lesser reductions should be given for guilty pleas after that point, with a maximum of one-twentieth being given for a guilty plea on the day of trial.[150]

Ancillary orders

17.134 The guilty plea guideline does not apply to ancillary orders, including disqualification from driving.[151]

149 See discussion of the definition of 'first stage of proceedings' at para 17.121.
150 *Sentencing children and young people: definitive guideline*, para 5.25.
151 *Sentencing children and young people: definitive guideline*, para 5.4.

CHAPTER 18

Discharges, bind overs and financial orders

continued

Key points

- Discharges are available for children, although most low-level offending will have been diverted before charge.
- Binding over orders are an available sentencing option for children.
- Financial orders are not generally the most effective disposal for children, as children will usually have limited financial resources.
- When the court makes a financial order on a defendant aged under 16, the court is required to order the parents or guardian to pay (the local authority for 'looked after children'); the duty is discretionary for 16- and 17-year-olds.

Introduction

18.1 This chapter will discuss the availability of the following disposals for children:

- discharges – absolute discharges, conditional discharges and reparation orders;
- bind overs – binding over orders; and
- financial orders – fines, compensation orders, costs and victim surcharges.

Discharges: absolute discharges, conditional discharges and reparation orders

Overview

18.2 An absolute or conditional discharge is available where the particular background facts about the child or the offence make immediate punishment inappropriate. For example, the offence is not serious enough (and an out of court disposal is not available), the defendant is about to move abroad or has become seriously ill. Alternatively, a discharge might be considered for a more serious offence where there is strong mitigation explaining the child's conduct.

Effect of an absolute or conditional discharge

18.3 Discharges are not deemed to be a conviction for the purposes of court proceedings, with the exception of procedures for dealing with a breach of a conditional discharge.[1]

18.4 There are a number of exceptions to this general rule. A discharge is deemed to be a conviction for the purposes of triggering the notification requirements to register as a sex offender[2] (see paras 25.76–25.81 on the sex offenders register). An absolute discharge and conditional discharge form part of a criminal record (see paras 18.11 and 18.29 on criminal records).

Absolute discharge

Meaning

18.5 An absolute discharge means a person doesn't receive any punishment.

Availability

18.6 An absolute discharge is available, provided the offence is not fixed by law or subject to a mandatory minimum sentence[3] and the court considers no punishment should be imposed.[4] An absolute discharge is also available in the Crown Court when a defendant is found not guilty by reason of insanity or unfitness to plead (see para 22.47 on disposals where the defendant is unfit to plead).[5]

Court's duties

18.7 A court can make an order discharging the defendant absolutely, if:

> . . . the court is of the opinion, having regard to the circumstances including the nature of the offence and the character of the offender, that it is inexpedient to inflict punishment.[6]

18.8 A court making an absolute discharge is not prevented from imposing costs.[7]

1 PCC(S)A 2000 s14(1).
2 Sexual Offences Act 2003 s134(1).
3 PCC(S)A 2000 s12(1)(a).
4 *Sentencing children and young people: definitive guideline*, 2017, para 6.13.
5 Criminal Procedure (Insanity) Act 1964 s5(2).
6 PCC(S)A 2000 s12(1)(a).
7 PCC(S)A 2000 s12(8).

18.9 Some courts use an absolute discharge to deal with additional offences alongside a custodial sentence, but it has been noted that imposing 'no separate penalty' could achieve the same outcome.[8]

18.10 Given that all low-level offending (and more serious offences where there is relevant mitigation) should always be considered for out of court disposals (see paras 7.26–7.27 on the availability of out of court disposals) it is becoming increasingly rare for there to be situations where an absolute discharge is made. Where a court indicates that it is considering an absolute discharge but the child has not yet entered a plea, defence lawyers should consider making representations to the Crown Prosecution Service (CPS) or prosecution that the case is suitable for diversion or that it is not in the public interest to pursue a prosecution (see paras 7.108–7.131 on the CPS decision to prosecute).

Criminal record

18.11 A person who is given an absolute discharge will have a criminal record, but the conviction becomes a spent conviction immediately (see paras 25.21–25.30 on spent convictions). A discharge triggers the notification requirements to register as a sex offender[9] (see paras 25.76–25.81 on the sex offenders register).

Conditional discharge

Meaning

18.12 A conditional discharge means a person doesn't receive any punishment on condition that the person does not commit an offence during a fixed period. Conditional discharges enable the court to re-visit the sentencing exercise should the person reoffend.

Availability

18.13 A conditional discharge is available provided the offence is not fixed by law, when the offence is not serious enough to warrant an immediate punishment.[10]

18.14 A conditional discharge is only available in exceptional circumstances for a defendant who, in the previous 24 months, has received two or

8 Ashford, Chard and Redhouse, *Defending Young People*, 2006, LAG, para 22.3.

9 Sexual Offences Act 2003 s134(1).

10 *Sentencing children and young people: definitive guideline*, para 6.14.

more youth cautions or a youth conditional caution followed by a youth caution (see para 18.22).

18.15 Conditional discharges may now be given to a child who has already received a referral order, whether or not the new offence pre-dates or post-dates the referral order (see paras 19.50–19.51 on referral orders and convictions for further offences). Similarly, a child who has received a conditional discharge is still eligible for a mandatory or discretionary referral order if, after receiving the conditional discharge, the child pleads guilty to an offence (see paras 19.28–19.32 on eligibility for referral orders).

18.16 A child convicted of breaching the requirements of a criminal behaviour order may not receive a conditional discharge.[11]

Court's duties

18.17 A court can make an order discharging the defendant conditionally – on the condition that the defendant does not commit an offence during the period of the order – if:

> . . . the court is of the opinion, having regard to the circumstances including the nature of the offence and the character of the offender, that it is inexpedient to inflict punishment.[12]

18.18 The length of the conditional discharge can be up to three years,[13] although for children the period of the conditional discharge is likely to be considerably shorter.[14]

18.19 When the court makes a conditional discharge, it should explain in plain and simple language to the child that if he or she commits another offence during the period of the conditional discharge, he or she will be liable to be re-sentenced for the original offence.[15]

18.20 When making a conditional discharge, the court may also allow 'any person to give a security for the good behaviour of the offender' if the court thinks it expedient for the purpose of the defendant's reformation and if he or she consents.[16] This power is rarely used, and is unlikely to be appropriate for children given the availability of

11 Anti-social Behaviour, Crime and Policing Act 2014 s30(6).

12 PCC(S)A 2000 s12(1)(b).

13 PCC(S)A 2000 s12(1)(b).

14 *Sentencing children and young people: definitive guideline*, para 4.5 – 'There is an expectation that in general a child or young person will be dealt with less severely than an adult offender.'

15 Criminal Justice Act (CJA) 2003 s174(3).

16 PCC(S)A 2000 s12(6).

a parental bind over order (see paras 23.17–23.25 on parental bind over).

18.21 A conditional discharge can be combined with a compensation order, deprivation order, restitution order and any disqualification.[17] The court is not prevented from imposing costs.[18]

Restrictions on use of a conditional discharge

18.22 A court must not impose a conditional discharge if a child has received two or more youth cautions, or a youth conditional caution followed by a youth caution, in the previous two years, unless there are exceptional circumstances relating to the offence or the offender to justify doing so.[19] The two-year period starts with the date of the most recent youth caution.[20] If the court is of the opinion that there are exceptional circumstances and makes an order conditionally discharging the child, it must state its reasons in open court.[21]

Breach of a conditional discharge

18.23 A child will breach a conditional discharge if the child is convicted of a further offence[22] during the period of the conditional discharge. The child is then liable to be re-sentenced for the original offence and the court re-sentencing them will have the sentencing powers available as if the child had just been convicted of that offence.[23]

18.24 In practical terms, the court re-sentencing the child will usually be the court dealing with them for the new offence. The youth court (or magistrates' court) must first obtain the consent of the original youth court or adult magistrates' court before dealing with the breach.[24] A Crown Court may deal with re-sentencing without seeking consent of the original sentencing court.[25] When a person is convicted before a youth court (or adult magistrates' court) in breach of a conditional discharge imposed by a Crown Court, the child may be committed on bail or in custody to appear at the Crown

17 PCC(S)A 2000 s12(7).
18 PCC(S)A 2000 s12(8).
19 Crime and Disorder Act 1998 s66ZB(5), (6)(a).
20 Crime and Disorder Act 1998 s66ZB(5).
21 Crime and Disorder Act 1998 s66ZB(6)(b).
22 They must be convicted by a court in Great Britain – PCC(S)A 2000 s13(10).
23 PCC(S)A 2000 s13(6), (7), (8).
24 PCC(S)A 2000 s13(8).
25 PCC(S)A 2000 s13(7).

Court.[26] A person may also be summonsed or a warrant issued for the person's arrest if it appears the person has been convicted by a court for an offence committed during the period of a conditional discharge.[27]

Sentencing powers on breach of a conditional discharge

18.25 The court dealing with a child for breach of a conditional discharge will have the sentencing powers available to deal with the original offence as if the child 'had just been convicted by or before that court of that offence'.[28] In some cases, this means a child turning 12, 15 or 18 after they received the conditional discharge and before being convicted of the new offence might become liable to a more severe sentence than would have been available at the time of the offence. However, the starting point for the court (re-)sentencing a child is the appropriate sentence at the date of the offence and it will rarely be appropriate to impose a more severe sentence than the maximum available at that time of the offence (see paras 17.32–17.60 on turning a significant age threshold age and available sentences).[29]

18.26 There is no requirement for a court dealing with an offence committed during the period of a conditional discharge to re-sentence for the original offence. A court sentencing a child for the new offences has the option to leave the conditional discharge in place or make no further order.

Breach of a conditional discharge where a child turns 18

18.27 Where a defendant receives a conditional discharge as a child, but breaches it after turning 18, the breach will be heard in the adult magistrates' court (or Crown Court) and the defendant will receive an adult sentence.

18.28 If the defendant had received a conditional discharge as a child for an offence that would have been indictable only in the case of an adult, the adult magistrates' court has the following sentencing powers when dealing with a defendant who has breached the order after turning 18:

26 PCC(S)A 2000 s13(5).
27 PCC(S)A 2000 s13(1), (3), (4).
28 PCC(S)A 2000 s13(6), (7), (8).
29 *Sentencing children and young people: definitive guideline*, paras 6.1–6.3.

- a fine (maximum £5,000);
- all other sentencing options up to a maximum six months' imprisonment.[30]

Criminal record

18.29 A person who is given a conditional discharge will have a criminal record, but the conviction becomes a spent conviction on the last day of the order (see paras 25.21–25.30 on spent convictions). A discharge triggers the notification requirements to register as a sex offender[31] (see paras 25.76–25.81 on the sex offenders register).

Reparation orders

Meaning

18.30 Children can receive a stand-alone reparation order. A reparation order requires a child to make reparation to the victim or to the community as a whole.

Availability

18.31 Reparation orders are available for all children convicted of an offence other than one for which the sentence is fixed by law.[32] Reparation orders require the child to perform direct or indirect reparation work for up to 24 hours[33] and should be completed within three months.[34] The requirements of the reparation order cannot include the payment of compensation.[35]

Court's duties

18.32 Courts wishing to make a reparation order should request a specific sentence report before making an order (see paras 17.109–17.110 on specific sentence reports). The report should include what work would be suitable and the views of the victim(s) in relation to the proposed requirements. The court must consider the report before

30 PCC(S)A 2000 s13(9).

31 Sexual Offences Act 2003 s134(1).

32 PCC(S)A 2000 s73(1).

33 PCC(S)A 2000 s74(1).

34 PCC(S)A 2000 s74(8)(b).

35 PCC(S)A 2000 s73(3).

making a reparation order.[36] The requirements must be commensurate with the seriousness of the offence(s)[37] and not conflict with the child's religious beliefs or interfere with the times the child normally works or attends school or any other educational establishment.[38]

18.33 In cases where the court has the power to make a reparation order but chooses not to, it must give reasons for its decision.[39]

18.34 Reparation orders cannot be combined with a referral order, youth rehabilitation order[40] or a custodial sentence.[41]

Breach of reparation order

18.35 A child who fails to comply with any requirement of a reparation order can be returned to court. In the youth court, the reparation order can be revoked or amended and the child can be ordered to pay a fine up to £1,000.[42] If the reparation order was made by an adult magistrates' court, the youth court may revoke the order and deal with the offender in any way in which the child could have been dealt with for the original offence.[43]

18.36 If the reparation order was made by the Crown Court, the youth court may commit the child in custody or release the child on bail until he or she can be brought or appear before the Crown Court.[44] The Crown Court may revoke the order and deal with the offender in any way in which the child could have been dealt with for the original offence.[45] It would also be open to the Crown Court to leave the reparation order in place, or amend the order (see para 18.37).

36 PCC(S)A 2000 s73(5).
37 PCC(S)A 2000 s74(2).
38 PCC(S)A 2000 s74(3).
39 PCC(S)A 2000 s73(8).
40 If the court wishes to impose a reparation order when a child is currently subject to a youth rehabilitation order, the court would first need to revoke the order under Criminal Justice and Immigration Act 2008 Sch 2 para 24.
41 PCC(S)A 2000 s73(4).
42 PCC(S)A 2000 Sch 8 para 2(a).
43 PCC(S)A 2000 Sch 8 para 2(b).
44 PCC(S)A 2000 Sch 8 para 2(c).
45 PCC(S)A 2000 Sch 8 paras 4 and 5.

Revoking, varying and amending a reparation order

18.37 The responsible officer[46] can apply to the relevant youth court[47] to have the reparation order varied. The order can be revoked or amended by removing, adding or substituting any provision.[48] The child must be present at court for the hearing.[49]

Criminal record

18.38 A person who is given a reparation order will have a criminal record, but the conviction becomes a spent conviction immediately (see paras 25.21–25.30 on spent convictions).

Bind over (binding over order)

Introduction

18.39 Bind overs or binding over orders may be imposed on children either as an alternative to prosecution or as a sentencing disposal. Any person before the court can be bound over including witnesses.

Purpose

18.40 The common law power to make binding over order is designed to prevent future misconduct. A binding over order is an agreement with the court to refrain from a specific activity or conduct and to forfeit a sum of money if the agreement (binding over order) is breached. A bind over may be used by a court as a sentencing disposal, and it can also be imposed as an alternative to prosecution or following an acquittal. Bind overs or binding over orders are no longer commonly used, but courts retain the power to make them.

46 The person specified in the reparation order – PCC(S)A 2000 s74(5).

47 The relevant court is a youth court in the local justice area in which the offender resides, or if it is not known where the offender resides, a youth court in the local justice area being named in reparation order made under PCC(S)A 2000 s74(4).

48 PCC(S)A 2000 Sch 8 para 5.

49 PCC(S)A 2000 Sch 8 para 6.

Where the defendant is not convicted

18.41 Courts have a common law power to bind a person over whether or not the person is convicted. In others words, a child (or adult) can receive a bind over without pleading guilty or there being a finding of guilt.

Alternative to prosecution

18.42 The bind over can potentially be a useful disposal in cases where a bind over might be an alternative to prosecution (see para 7.4 on alternatives to prosecution). In certain cases, prosecutors and defence lawyers may wish to discuss the possibility of the prosecution being discontinued if the child consents to being bound over. This might be a relevant consideration if a child is charged with low-level offending, such as a minor assault or public order offence where there is no possibility of an out of court disposal. It is not necessary for the child accepting a bind over to admit past use of violence in order to justify a court making a binding over order.[50]

Bind over following an acquittal

18.43 Bind overs can be used when a defendant has been acquitted. However, unlike adults, children cannot be imprisoned and there is no other sanction if a child refuses to be bound over.[51] A child can consent to be bound over,[52] but it is unlikely a child would consent following an acquittal or where the criminal case has come to an end.

Availability as a sentence

18.44 Bind overs or binding over orders are available where there is a real risk that a breach of the peace involving violence will occur in the future.[53]

50 *Hourihane and another v Commissioner of Police of the Metropolis* (1994) Times, 27 December.

51 *Veater v Glennon* [1981] 1 WLR 567.

52 *Conlan v Oxford* (1983) 5 Cr App R (S) 237.

53 Justices of the Peace Act 1361 s1; Justices of the Peace Act 1968 s1(7); Magistrates' Courts Act 1980 s115.

Court's duties

18.45 The Magistrates' Court Sentencing Guidelines[54] and the Criminal Practice Directions[55] provide guidance on the making of binding over orders as a sentencing disposal. The court making the binding over order must be satisfied so that it is sure that a breach of the peace involving violence, or an imminent threat of violence, has occurred or that there is a real risk of violence in the future.[56] Where admissions are made, the court should hear submissions and, if appropriate, evidence. If the order is contested, the court should hear evidence and the parties before making any order.[57]

18.46 As part of the agreement, the defendant agrees to forfeit a sum of money if the person 'breaches the peace' by failing to desist from the specific activity or conduct during this period. The court should bind a person over to 'be of good behaviour'[58] but must also identify the specific conduct or activity from which the person must refrain,[59] the length of the bind over (usually no longer than 12 months[60]) and the specified sum of money (this is called a 'recognisance'). This should all be set out in a written order.[61] In the case of a child, a bind over is likely to be far shorter than 12 months.

Criminal record

18.47 A binding over order made on conviction is spent on the last day of the order (see paras 25.21–25.30 on spent convictions). Where the order is made without a conviction, it *may* still be disclosed on an enhanced disclosure and barring service check as part of non conviction data (see paras 25.57–25.63 on non conviction data).

54 Magistrates' Court Sentencing Guidelines – Definitive Guideline, May 2008, p167.

55 CrimPD Part J.

56 CrimPD para J.2.

57 CrimPD paras J.5–J.7 and Magistrates' Courts Act 1980 ss51–57 set out the procedural requirements.

58 This was considered too imprecise to be enforceable – *Hashman and Harrup v UK* [2000] Crim LR 185.

59 CrimPD para J.3.

60 The maximum period is three years but courts are discouraged form exceeding a period of 12 months – see Magistrates' Court Sentencing Guidelines, p167 – key principles 4.

61 CrimPD para J.3.

Financial orders – fines, compensation orders, costs and victim surcharges

Overview

General principles when considering financial orders against children

18.48 Generally, courts are cautious before imposing financial penalties on children. The Sentencing Council's *Sentencing children and young people: definitive guideline* provide the following guidance:

> In practice, many children and young people will have limited financial resources and the court will need to determine whether imposing a fine will be the most effective disposal.[62]

Any fine is likely to place a financial burden on the child's parents, guardians or the local authority rather than the child. Courts have other sanctions, such as parenting orders and parenting bind over orders, should they feel these would be appropriate.

18.49 When the court imposes any financial order (fine, compensation order, costs or victim surcharge) on a child aged under 16, the court is required to order parents or guardians to pay and if the young person is aged 16 or 17, the duty is discretionary; local authorities with parental responsibility can similarly be ordered to pay financial orders in criminal cases (see paras 18.52–18.57 on power to order a parents, guardian or local authority to pay).

18.50 Sentencers should also take into consideration that financial orders may remain on the child's criminal record longer than other orders (see para 25.28 for a table of rehabilitation periods).

18.51 Where the child (or the child's parent or guardian) does not have sufficient means to pay the total financial penalty considered appropriate by the court, the order of priority is:

- compensation;
- victim surcharge;
- fine;
- costs.[63]

62 *Sentencing children and young people: definitive guideline*, para 6.17.

63 *Magistrates Sentencing Guidelines:* Prosecution costs: www.sentencingcouncil.org.uk/the-magistrates-court-sentencing-guidelines/.

Power to order a parent, guardian or the local authority to pay[64]

18.52 In the majority of cases the parent or guardian will be ordered to pay a financial penalty in relation to their child.

- If the defendant is aged ten to 15, the court *must* order the parent or guardian of a child defendant aged ten to 15 to pay a fine, costs, compensation order or victim surcharge.[65]
- If the defendant is aged 16 or 17 years old, the court *may* order a parent or guardian to pay.[66]

In both cases, the parent or guardian will not be ordered to pay if the court is satisfied

- the parent or guardian cannot be found; or
- it would be unreasonable to make an order for payment, having regard to the circumstances of the case.[67]

18.53 Where a local authority has parental authority and a child defendant is 'looked after' or provided with accommodation by the local authority, these powers apply to the local authority as they would to the parent or guardian (an order remanding a child to local authority accommodation does not confer parental responsibility to the local authority, parental responsibility is only acquired with a full care order).[68]

18.54 The court should not make an order without giving the parent, guardian or local authority an opportunity of being heard (unless the parent or guardian has been required to attend and has failed to do so).[69] Case-law suggests it would be 'unreasonable' to order a parent, guardian or local authority to pay a financial order where no fault had been identified or attributed to the parent, guardian or local authority to cause the child to commit the offence.[70]

18.55 Where the child defendant is aged 15 or under, and it would be unreasonable to order a parent, guardian (or local authority with parental responsibility) to pay a fine, costs or compensation order, the court should not make the financial order.

64 A fine, costs, compensation or victim surcharge.

65 PCC(S)A 2000 s137(1).

66 PCC(S)A 2000 s137(3).

67 PCC(S)A 2000 s137(1A).

68 PCC(S)A 2000 s137(8).

69 PCC(S)A 2000 s137(4), (5).

70 *R v JJB* [2004] EWCA Crim 14; *Bedfordshire CC v DPP* [1996] 1 Cr App R (S) 322; *R v Sheffield Crown Court ex p Clarkson* (1986) 8 Cr App R (S) 454.

18.56 For all children, including 16 and 17 year olds, the starting will usually be that the parent or guardian should be made liable, unless the child is in employment or otherwise able to pay from his or her own means. This protects the child from the enforcement provisions (see paras 18.90–18.92).

Financial (means) enquiry

18.57 Defendants must provide details of financial circumstances as required by the court,[71] this may be called a 'means enquiry'. In practice, courts often have a standard means form or financial circumstances questionnaire. If a child is ordered to pay a financial penalty then it is the child's means which are taken into account.

18.58 In most cases, however, the parent or guardian will be ordered to pay. Where the court is considering making the order against a parent or guardian to pay a fine, costs, compensation or victim surcharge, the court may make a financial circumstances order.[72] A financial circumstances order requires the parent or guardian to make a statement about their financial circumstances.[73] Parents or guardians who fail to comply or provide false information may be liable on summary conviction to a fine not exceeding level 3 on the standard scale.[74]

18.59 If a parent or guardian fails to co-operate with the court in relation to its financial enquiry, and the court considers that it has insufficient information to make a proper determination of the parent's or guardian's financial circumstances, it may make such determination as it thinks fit.[75]

Right of appeal

18.60 A parent or guardian can appeal an order made by a youth court or adult magistrates' court to the Crown Court,[76] or appeal an order made by the Crown Court to the Court of Appeal.[77]

71 CrimPR 2015 r24.11(4).
72 PCC(S)A 2000 s136(1).
73 CJA 2003 s162(3).
74 CJA 2003 s162(4), (5).
75 CJA 2003 s138(3).
76 CJA 2003 s136(6).
77 CJA 2003 s136(7).

Compensation orders

Availability

18.61 The court must consider making a compensation order when a person is convicted of an offence where personal injury, loss or damage has resulted from the offence. The compensation order may be made in addition to any another sentencing option, or as a stand-alone sentencing option (unless the sentence is fixed by law or the court imposes a mandatory minimum custodial term).[78] When a compensation order is made as a sentence in its own right, no victim surcharge is payable.

18.62 The compensation order may require the defendant:

a) to pay compensation for any personal injury, loss or damage resulting from that offence or any other offence which is taken into consideration by the court in determining sentence; or
b) to make payments for funeral expenses or bereavement in respect of a death resulting from any such offence, other than a death due to an accident arising out of the presence of a motor vehicle on a road.

Court's duties

18.63 In determining whether to make a compensation order against a person, and the amount to be paid, the court shall have regard to his or her means so far as they are known to the court.[79] An order made in the absence of a means enquiry may be unlawful.[80] When dealing with a defendant aged under 18, the maximum compensation order in the youth court and adult magistrates' court is £5,000.[81] The scales for a compensation order are set out in the *Magistrates' Court Sentencing Guidelines*. Where a court is considering making a compensation order and a fine and the defendant has insufficient means to pay, preference is given to the compensation order.[82]

18.64 The court must give reasons if it does not make a compensation order when it has the power to do so.[83]

78 PCC(S)A 2000 s130(1).
79 PCC(S)A 2000 s131(1).
80 *R v Gray* (2011) EWCA 225.
81 PCC(S)A 2000 s131(1).
82 PCC(S)A 2000 s130(12).
83 PCC(S)A 2000 s130(3).

Criminal record

18.65 A compensation order will remain on the defendant's criminal record until paid (see the table of rehabilitation periods at para 25.28).

Fines

18.66 Fines are less commonly used by sentencers dealing with children (see paras 18.48–18.51 on financial orders against children).

Availability

18.67 Courts may impose a fine for any offence (except when imposing a mandatory referral order – see para 19.39 or any other sentence fixed by law). The level of fines are generally lower for children than for adults. In the youth court and adult magistrates' court, the maximum fine for a defendant aged ten to 13 years is £250 and the maximum fine for a defendant aged 14–17 is £1,000.[84]

Age	Maximum fine
10–13 years	£250
14–17 years	£1,000

18.68 The court's powers are also limited to the statutory maximum for summary only offences based on the standard scale (set out below).

The standard scale of fines for summary offences[85]

Level on the scale	Amount of fine
1	£200
2	£500
3	£1,000
4	£2,500
5	£5,000

18.69 In the Crown Court there is no statutory maximum. As no adjustment is made for age, it may be helpful to make the Crown Court

84 PCC(S)A 2000 s135.
85 CJA 1982 s37(2).

aware of the maximum limits that apply in the youth court and adult magistrates' court. The Crown Court is required to fix a term of imprisonment in default (or a term of detention for a person aged 18–20)[86] even though it is unenforceable against under 18 year olds.[87]

Court's duties

18.70 Where financial orders are being considered, priority must be given to compensation orders and victim surcharge (see para 18.51 on priority of financial orders). Where the court also imposes an order for costs, the costs must not exceed the fine.[88]

Payment by parent or guardian

18.71 When the court imposes a fine on a child aged under 16, the court has a duty to order parents or guardians to pay the fine unless they cannot be found or it would be unreasonable; and if the child is aged 16 or 17, this duty is discretionary. If the local authority has parental responsibility, it may also be ordered to pay (see para 18.52–18.56 on power to order the local authority to pay).

Determining the level of fine

18.72 When the court is considering the appropriate amount of any fine:

- A court *must* first inquire into the defendant's (or their parents' or guardian's) financial circumstances.[89]
- The amount of any fine must reflect the seriousness of the offence.[90]
- In fixing the amount of any fine, a court must take into account the circumstances of the case including, among other things, the financial circumstances of the offender so far as they are known, or appear, to the court.[91] This may have the effect of increasing or reducing the amount of the fine.[92]

86 PCC(S)A 2000 s139(2).
87 PCC(S)A 2000 s108(1); and *R v Basid* [1996] 1 Cr App R (S) 421, CA.
88 Prosecution of Offences Act 1985, 18(5).
89 CJA 2003 s164(1).
90 CJA 2003 s164(2).
91 CJA 2003 s164(3).
92 CJA 2003 s164(4).

- Account should be taken of any guilty plea(s).[93]
- Normally a fine should be capable of being paid within 12 months.[94]

Assessment of means

18.73 Courts should consider the child's and the child's parents' or guardian's financial circumstances. Standard means forms or a financial circumstances questionnaire are often less applicable to children because they are likely to have limited income and financial commitments. For children living independently, the defence lawyer should help the child make a note of his or her outgoings, including any payable rent, water, electricity and gas bills or key meter, phone contract, council tax, food as well as travel and lunch costs if accessing education or training opportunities.

18.74 The defence lawyer should check whether any of the child's weekly income is for travel and lunch costs to enable them to attend school, college or an apprenticeship.[95]

Children who have spent overnight in police custody

18.75 Practitioners should be alert to the fact that in the adult magistrates' court, the practice of imposing a fine with a term of imprisonment in default which is 'deemed served' where defendants have spent overnight in custody is not available for child defendants (see paras 18.90–18.92 on enforcement against children). Theoretically, for defendants who have turned 18 during proceedings, a court could impose a default term. For all other child defendants, the defence lawyer may want to raise with the court the possibility a child who has spent a night in police custody could be treated less favourably than their adult equivalent and therefore the court should consider imposing no further sanction.

Criminal record

18.76 Fines remain on the child's criminal record for six months from the date of conviction (it is irrelevant whether the fine is paid – see the table of rehabilitation periods at para 25.28). This may be a

93 CJA 2003 s144(1).

94 Magistrates' Court Sentencing Guidelines – Approach to the assessment of fines.

95 *Sentencing children and young people: definitive guideline*, para 6.18.

relevant consideration for a court when deciding whether to impose a fine.

Victim surcharge

18.77 When a court passes a sentence it *must* also order that the relevant victim surcharge is paid.[96] Revenue raised from the victim surcharge is used to fund victim services through the Victim and Witness General Fund. The amount of the surcharge depends on the defendant's age on the date of the offence (*not* date of conviction) and the sentence. There are different amounts payable by adult defendants or organisations.

18.78 The court *must* order the parent or guardian of a child defendant aged ten to 15 to pay the victim surcharge,[97] and in relation to 16- and 17-year-olds the court has a discretion to order a parent or guardian to pay,[98] unless the parent or guardian cannot be found or it would be unreasonable to make an order for payment, having regard to the circumstances of the case.[99] Where a local authority has parental authority and a child defendant is looked after or provided with accommodation by the local authority, these powers apply to the local authority as they would to the parent or guardian.[100] (See fuller discussion at paras 18.52–18.56 on ordering parent, guardian or local authority to pay.)

Victim surcharge for offences committed on or after 8 April 2016[101]

Victim surcharge for defendants aged under 18 years old (at the date of the offence)

A conditional discharge	£15
A fine, a youth rehabilitation order or referral order	£20
A custodial sentence (all lengths)	£30

96 CJA 2003 s161A.
97 PCC(S)A 2000 s137(1).
98 PCC(S)A 2000 s137(3).
99 PCC(S)A 2000 s137(1A).
100 PCC(S)A 2000 s137(8).
101 Criminal Justice Act 2003 (Surcharge) (Amendment) Order 2016.

Victim surcharge for offences committed before 8 April 2016:[102]

Victim surcharge for defendants aged under 18 years old (at the date of the offence)

A conditional discharge	£10
A fine, a youth rehabilitation order or referral order	£15
A custodial sentence (all lengths)[103]	£20

18.79 If the court makes a suspended sentence order on a defendant (only available where the defendant is an adult on the date of conviction), the custodial sentence amount is applicable.

18.80 When sentencing for one or more offence(s) any one of which was committed after 1 April 2007 but before 1 October 2012, a surcharge is payable only if the offender is dealt with by way of a fine, at a flat rate of £15.[104] Where an offender is dealt with in different ways only one surcharge (whichever attracts the higher sum) will be paid.

18.81 Where the court is dealing with a defendant for more than one offence and at least one offence was committed when the defendant was a child, the surcharge should be ordered at the rate for children.[105]

18.82 There is no victim surcharge payable when compensation is ordered as a sentence.

Court's duties

18.83 When a person is sentenced, the court *must* order the person to pay the victim surcharge.[106] The court has a discretion as to whether they ask the child or the parent to pay it.

102 Criminal Justice Act 2003 (Surcharge) Order 2012.

103 When sentencing to immediate custody, if one or more of the offences was committed before 1 September 2014, no surcharge is payable – Criminal Justice Act 2003 (Surcharge) Order 2012 as amended by Criminal Justice Act 2003 (Surcharge) (Amendment) Order 2014.

104 Criminal Justice Act 2003 (Surcharge) Order 2012 art 7(2).

105 Criminal Justice Act 2003 (Surcharge) Order 2012 art 5(3).

106 CJA 2003 s161A; Criminal Justice Act 2003 (Surcharge) Order 2012; and Criminal Justice Act 2003 (Surcharge) (Amendment) Order 2016.

18.84 Where the child is under 16, the court must order the parent or guardian to pay the surcharge unless they can't be found or it would be unreasonable in the circumstances.[107] Where the child is 16 or 17, the court may order the parent or guardian to pay the surcharge duty.[108] For determining whether a parent or guardian should pay, the relevant age is the child's age on the date on conviction.

18.85 An example of where it may be unreasonable to order the parents to pay the victim surcharge is that they are the 'victim' of the offence, have limited financial resources or have demonstrated all efforts to prevent the child from offending (see paras 18.52–18.56 on ordering parent, guardian or local authority to pay).

18.86 Where the court makes an order for compensation, and the defendant has insufficient means to pay both the surcharge and the compensation, the court must reduce the surcharge accordingly (if necessary to nil).[109] There is no victim surcharge payable when compensation is ordered as a stand alone sentence.

Costs order

18.87 Where a defendant is convicted of an offence, the court has discretion to make such order as to costs as it considers just and reasonable.[110]

18.88 The court *must* order the parent or guardian of a child defendant aged ten to 15 to pay costs,[111] and in relation to 16- and 17-year-olds, the court has a discretion to order a parent or guardian to pay,[112] unless the parent or guardian cannot be found or it would be unreasonable to make an order for payment, having regard to the circumstances of the case.[113] Where a local authority has parental authority and a child defendant is looked after or provided with accommodation by the local authority, these powers apply to the local authority as they would to the parent or guardian.[114] (See fuller discussion at paras 18.52–18.56 on ordering parent, guardian or local authority to pay).

107 PCC(S)A 2000 s137(1A).
108 PCC(S)A 2000 s137(3).
109 CJA 2003 s161A(3)(b).
110 Prosecution of Offences Act 1985 s18(1).
111 PCC(S)A 2000 s137(1).
112 PCC(S)A 2000 s137(3).
113 PCC(S)A 2000 s137(1), (1A).
114 PCC(S)A 2000 s137(8).

18.89 When an order for costs is made alongside a fine, the order for costs must not exceed the amount of the fine[115] (also see para 18.51 on order of priority of financial orders where the defendant has insufficient resources).

Breach, failure to pay and enforcement of financial orders

Enforcement against children

18.90 There is no sanction available for non-payment of fines by children because there is no power to commit a child to prison[116] or detention[117] for default. Similarly, there is no power for the court to make a collection order against a child as this applies to a person aged 18 or over.[118] This creates an anomalous situation in the Crown Court, as the judge is required to fix a term of imprisonment or detention in default,[119] even though it is unenforceable against children.[120]

18.91 Some youth courts have sought to issue summons to secure the attendance of a child before the court for a means enquiry for non-payment of fines.[121] The legality of this has been challenged, and the Justices' Clerks Society's advice is that 'a warrant with bail should first be considered, . . . [a] warrant without bail would therefore be a last resort'.[122] Before issuing a warrant, all other options available to secure payment or attendance before the court should be considered. It is hard to conceive of any real benefit being achieved by pursuing children for non-payment through issuing court summons whether or not backed for bail. Other options for the court that do not require the attendance of the child at court: allowing further time to pay; or making a money payment supervision order (if local arrangements have been made with the local youth offending team (YOT) to supervise these orders).

115 Prosecution of Offences Act 1985 s18(5).
116 PCC(S)A 2000 s89(1).
117 PCC(S)A 2000 s108(1).
118 Courts Act 2003 Sch 5 para 1(1).
119 PCC(S)A 2000 s139(2).
120 PCC(S)A s108(1); and *R v Basid* [1996] 1 Cr App R (S) 421, CA.
121 Pursuant to Magistrates' Courts Act 1980 s83(1).
122 Justices' Clerks' Society News Sheet No: 01/2018, dated 13 December 2018. Also see the Howard League for Penal Reform campaign.

18.92 Defence lawyers representing 16 and 17 year-olds may wish to ask the court to exercise its discretion to have the fine or other financial penalty recorded in the parent or guardian's name, to protect against the child being arrested for non-payment and the risk that they will spend overnight in a police cell.

CHAPTER 19

Referral orders

continued

Key points

- Referral orders (ROs) are only available when a child pleads guilty to at least one offence.
- A RO can last from three to 12 months.
- There are two types of ROs: mandatory and discretionary.
- Mandatory ROs are available when a child pleads guilty to an imprisonable offence for the first time (with certain exceptions).[1]
- Discretionary ROs are available if a child has pleaded guilty to an offence regardless of previous offending history.
- If a child is eligible for a mandatory RO and pleads guilty to an offence that crosses the custody threshold, the youth court will have to decide between a RO and custody (youth rehabilitation orders (YROs) are not available). It is recommended that the pre-sentence report (PSR) proposes an intensive RO contract as a 'robust and credible sentencing option'.
- A RO is not automatically revoked following a new conviction. A RO can be extended (up to a maximum of 12 months) and a child can have multiple ROs that can be concurrent or consecutive.
- A RO can be imposed if the child hasn't pleaded guilty at the earliest opportunity.
- A court making a RO cannot impose other sentencing disposals except an absolute discharge for connected offence and ancillary orders, including costs and compensation orders.[2]

Introduction

19.1 Referral orders (ROs) are a unique community-based order for children, the court 'refers' the child to attend a community-led 'youth offender panel' convened by volunteer members of the community and held at an informal venue. A 'referral order contract' (also called a youth offender contract) is then agreed between the child and the panel:

> It should be remembered they are not community orders and in general terms may be regarded as orders which fall between community disposals and fines.[3]

1 See paras 19.2, 19.8–19.14 and 19.28.

2 See para 19.39.

3 *Sentencing children and young people: definitive guideline*, para 6.20.

19.2 ROs were designed to be the mandatory sentencing option[4] for children pleading guilty to their first offence before a youth court (or an adult magistrates' court). Owing to their success at reducing reoffending, the availability of ROs is now considerably wider than when they were first introduced. Mandatory orders are available when a child pleads guilty for the first time[5] to an imprisonable offence unless the court imposes a discharge, hospital order or custody. Discretionary ROs are available whenever a child pleads guilty – they can be given to children who have previous convictions and who have received previous ROs; they are available where a child has mixed pleas. ROs can be extended and multiple ROs (both consecutive and/or concurrent) can be imposed.

Referral order process

19.3 When the court makes a RO, the child is referred to a youth offender panel. The youth offender panel is made up of two members of the local community, one of whom will be chair, and an advisor from a youth offending team (YOT). At the initial panel meeting, the child, supported by their parent or guardian, will be invited to review the offence and its consequences and agree a contract with the panel. There is a strong focus on restorative justice. The referral order contract includes two core elements:

1) reparation/restoration to the victim or wider community; and
2) a programme of interventions/activities to address offending risk.

19.4 The purpose of the referral order contract is to enable the child to understand the harm they have caused and address their offending behaviour. Where there is an identifiable victim, the victim will be invited to attend the panel meeting.

19.5 The youth offender panel monitor a child's compliance with the contract. If the child is unwilling to agree a contract, or fails to comply with the order, they will be referred back to court (see paras 19.58–19.70 on breach of the RO). The court can also order a responsible

4 This chapter uses the terminology discretionary and mandatory referral orders; discretionary and mandatory referral orders conditions. PCC(S)A 2000 refers to compulsory referral order conditions rather than mandatory referral order conditions. This terminology is not used by the authors to avoid the confusion it may cause.

5 Children will still meet the mandatory referral order conditions if they have previously been given a bind over, absolute or conditional discharge (see para 19.28).

person to attend with the child (see para 19.48 on parental attendance) and a responsible person can be breached if they fail to comply with the order (see paras 19.82–19.84 on breach of parental attendance order).

Use of referral orders

Overview

19.6 A RO is the main sentencing disposal in cases when a child pleads guilty to at least one offence. ROs are available in the youth court and adult magistrates' court. ROs are also available in the Crown Court, where the judge exercises the power to sit as a district judge (see para 19.13).[6] A RO can be imposed if the child hasn't pleaded guilty at the earliest opportunity, and ROs are excluded from guidance on determining the level of reduction for a guilty plea.[7]

19.7 The revised *Referral Order Guidance* 2018 provides information and guidance to youth offending teams (YOTs) and youth offender panels.[8]

Mandatory referral orders

19.8 A RO is the mandatory sentence in a youth court or adult magistrates' court where a child pleads guilty for the first time to an imprisonable offence and has no previous convictions (bind overs, absolute or conditional discharges are disregarded[9]) provided the sentence is not fixed by law and the court does not wish to impose an absolute or conditional discharge,[10] a hospital order or a detention and training order (DTO) (see para 19.28 on availability of mandatory referral orders).[11]

6 Where the Crown Court judge exercises the power to sit as a district judge – Courts Act 2003 s66.

7 *Sentencing children and young people: definitive guideline*, para 5.15.

8 Referral Order Guidance, Ministry of Justice and Youth Justice Board, October 2018.

9 Where a court makes an absolute discharge or conditional discharge it is not considered a conviction for any other purpose by virtue of PCC(S)A 2000 s14(1). Bind overs or binding over orders are made without the defendant being convicted of an offence.

10 A conditional discharge is not available for offences committed before 3 December 2012.

11 PCC(S)A 2000 ss16(2), 17(1).

19.9 If the mandatory RO conditions are met, there is no requirement for a pre-sentence report. Therefore defence lawyers should not ask for a pre-sentence report to be prepared *unless* the court indicates it may consider imposing a custodial sentence. If the court considers the custody threshold has been met, then the pre-sentence report should consider an intensive RO (see paras 19.11–19.13 on custody threshold cases).

19.10 The mandatory RO conditions only apply in the youth court and adult magistrates' court[12] but are not applicable in the Crown Court (see para 19.13 below).

Referral orders in custody threshold cases

19.11 In custody threshold cases, where a child has offended for the first time and the mandatory RO conditions are met, it is important that the youth or adult magistrates' court can be persuaded that a RO can be sufficiently onerous to meet their concerns.

19.12 In custody threshold cases, particularly where the mandatory RO conditions are met, and the only available sentencing options are a RO or custody,[13] an intensive RO contract should be considered (see paras 19.22–19.23 on intensive ROs). The YOT may also arrange a pre-sentence panel meeting (see paras 19.24–19.26).[14]

19.13 The Crown Court is not bound by the mandatory RO conditions, therefore children pleading guilty for the first time in the Crown Court to imprisonable offences can receive a youth rehabilitation order (suspended sentences are not available for children – see para 17.9 on available sentences). The Crown Court can impose ROs where it exercises the power to sit as a district judge,[15] however, the Crown Court and the adult magistrates' court must remit the case to the youth court 'unless satisfied it would be undesirable to do so'.[16] So where the court is considering a RO it will usually be required to remit the case to the youth court[17] (see para 17.27 on remittal for sentence and referral orders).

12 PCC(S)A 2000 s16(1), (2).

13 Referral Order Guidance, Ministry of Justice and Youth Justice Board, October 2018, para 3.18.

14 Referral Order Guidance, Ministry of Justice and Youth Justice Board, October 2018, paras 3.23.

15 Courts Act 2003 s66.

16 PCC(S)A 2000 s8(2).

17 See *R v Reyon Menelek Dillon* [2017] EWCA Crim 2642.

Low-level offences

19.14 Children at court for the first time who plead guilty, or who have previously been in court and received an absolute discharge and/or conditional discharge, who intend to plead guilty will be eligible for a mandatory RO – but the court may also consider an absolute or conditional discharge or bind over. In these circumstances, practitioners should always review why the case wasn't considered for an out of court disposal, and in appropriate cases where admissions weren't made at the police station, defence lawyers should consider making representations for the prosecution to be reviewed as it is not in the public interest, or to be sent back to the police station for an out of court disposal (see paras 7.33–7.35 on admissions after interview).

Discretionary referral orders

19.15 Discretionary ROs are available where a child has pleaded guilty to the offence, or, if a child is being sentenced for a number of connected offences (see paras 19.19–19.21 on connected offences below), the child has pleaded guilty to at least one offence.[18]

19.16 The discretionary RO conditions apply in the youth court and adult magistrates' court where the child has pleaded guilty regardless of previous offending history[19] provided the compulsory RO conditions do not apply (see paras 19.8–19.10 on mandatory ROs).[20]

19.17 Although a Crown Court judge can impose a discretionary RO by exercising the power to sit as a district judge,[21] the Crown Court will usually remit the case to the youth court[22] (see paras 19.13 and 17.27 on remittal for sentence and referral orders).

19.18 As stated in the Sentencing Council's Sentencing children and young people: definitive guideline:

> Referral orders are the main sentence for delivering restorative justice and all panel members are trained Restorative Conference Facilitators; as such they can be an effective sentence in encouraging children and

18 PCC(S)A 2000 s17(2).

19 PCC(S)A 2000 s16(3); and *Sentencing children and young people: definitive guideline*, para 6.22.

20 PCC(S)A 2000 ss16(3), 17(2).

21 Courts Act 2003 s66.

22 Under PCC(S)A 2000 s8(2); and see *R v Reyon Menelek Dillon* [2017] EWCA Crim 2642.

> young people to take responsibility for their actions and understand the effect their offence may have had on their victim.[23]

The use of discretionary ROs is therefore an important sentencing disposal that can be used to successively prevent re-offending.

Connected offences

19.19 Connected offences are any offence(s) being dealt with by the court at the same time as the child is being dealt with for the offence to which he or she pleaded guilty.

> [A]n offence is connected with another if the offender falls to be dealt with for it at the same time as he is dealt with for the other offence (whether or not he is convicted of the offences at the same time or by or before the same court).[24]

This means a child who has pleaded guilty to an offence(s) and also falls to be sentenced after pleading not guilty but having a finding of guilt, will still be eligible for a discretionary RO if the child is being sentenced at the same time for at least one offence where he or she pleaded guilty.

19.20 There is no requirement for the two (or more) connected offences to relate to the same incident or be factually connected. For example, a child may fall to be sentenced for a number of 'connected offences' just because or by virtue of the fact a number of different charges have been adjourned to the same sentencing hearing.

19.21 As set out in the Referral Order Guidance 2018, discretionary RO conditions are met:

> ... where compulsory referral order conditions are not met but the child pleads guilty to an offence **or** at least one of any connected offence being dealt with.[25]

Intensive referral order contract (serious offences)

19.22 In 'custody threshold' cases, for example, a child who has offended for the first time and has pleaded guilty to a serious offence – it is recommended that the pre-sentence report proposes an intensive RO

23 *Sentencing children and young people: definitive guideline*, para 6.20.

24 PCC(S)A 2000 s16(4).

25 Referral Order Guidance 2018, Youth Justice Board, October 2018, para 3.15.

contract as a 'robust and credible sentencing option'.[26] The intensive RO contract is based upon the level of support and supervision available on an Intensive Supervision and Surveillance programme.

19.23 Where a court makes an intensive RO, the YOT should ensure that the panel is convened at the earliest opportunity following sentence to ensure 'the contract should subsequently start with minimum delay'.[27] The YOT panel report:

> . . . should fully reflect any comments made by the court when making the Referral Order, including any references to what might be included in the panel contract. The youth offender panel however retains the right to determine the content of the contract with the child and their parent/carer post sentence. In theory, this may vary from the contract included in the PSR to the court.[28]

Pre-sentence panel meeting

19.24 The RO guidance encourages YOTs to convene an informal 'pre-sentence panel' prior to the sentencing hearing (also referred to as a 'pseudo-panel' or 'pre-panel').[29] The child and their parents or guardians are asked to attend a youth offender panel and agree. The full range of intensive community intervention options, including non-electronic curfews and restrictions, should be considered.

> An intensive Referral Order contract should involve a timetable of structured activity each week, reflective of the serious nature of the offence.[30]

19.25 If it is not possible to convene a 'pre-sentence panel', the YOT should consider what range of options would be available to the RO panel, based upon the AssetPlus assessment and the scaled approach (see paras 17.98–17.101), and they should be set out in the PSR. This provides the sentencing court with sufficient information to assess an intensive RO as an alternative to custody.

26 Referral Order Guidance, Ministry of Justice and Youth Justice Board, October 2018, para 3.22.

27 Referral Order Guidance, Ministry of Justice and Youth Justice Board, October 2018, para 3.26

28 Referral Order Guidance, Ministry of Justice and Youth Justice Board, October 2018, para, 3.25.

29 Referral Order Guidance, Ministry of Justice and Youth Justice Board, October 2018, para 3.23; and *Sentencing children and young people: definitive guideline*, para 6.21.

30 Referral Order Guidance, Ministry of Justice and Youth Justice Board, October 2018, para 3.24.

19.26 If a proposed contract has been drafted, it is not open to the court to alter it in any way; the court will have to make a decision between RO and custody based upon the proposed intensive contract. It is open to the court to make comments on the draft contract, and these will be provided to the youth offender panel (see para 19.23 above).

Referral orders and turning 18

19.27 ROs are a sentencing disposal for children.[31] A defendant remains eligible for a RO provided they were under 18 years old when he or she pleaded guilty or there was a finding of guilt (the date of conviction), even if they have turned 18 by the sentencing hearing (see paras 17.45 and 17.32–17.39 on turning 18, relevance of age and available sentences).[32]

Availability

Mandatory referral orders[33]

19.28 A youth court or adult magistrates' court *must* make a RO if:

- the defendant is aged under 18 at the time of conviction;
- the offence is an imprisonable offence;
- the defendant has pleaded guilty to the offence, and to any connected offence(s);
- the defendant has no previous convictions (bind overs, absolute or conditional discharges are disregarded[34]);

unless:

- the sentence is fixed by law or the court is proposing to give the defendant an absolute or conditional discharge,[35] a hospital order or a custodial sentence (DTO).

31 PCC(S)A 2000 s16(1).

32 The relevant date for the court determining the defendant's eligibility for sentences is his or her age on the date of conviction, as established in *R v Danga* [1992] 2 WLR 277, CA. See also para 17.31.

33 PCC(S)A 2000 s16(1), (2) and s17(1).

34 Where a court makes an absolute discharge or conditional discharge, it is not considered a conviction for any other purpose by virtue of PCC(S)A 2000 s14(1). Bind overs or binding over orders are made without the defendant being convicted of an offence.

35 A conditional discharge is not available for offences committed before 3 December 2012.

Discretionary referral order[36]

19.29 A youth court or adult magistrates' court *may* make a RO if:

- the defendant is aged under 18 at the date of conviction;
- the defendant has pleaded guilty to an offence; and
- the compulsory RO conditions are not met.

19.30 If the defendant is being dealt with by the court for more than one offence, he or she must have pleaded guilty to at least one of those offences (see paras 19.19–19.21 on for connected offences).[37]

19.31 There is no limit on the number of ROs a child can receive (see para 19.38 on second or subsequent ROs below).

19.32 The Crown Court can impose ROs where it exercises the power to sit as a district judge,[38] although the court will usually be required to remit the case to the youth court[39] (see para 17.27 on remittal for sentence).

Court's duties

Overview

19.33 A court making a RO must:

- specify the YOT responsible for implementing the order;
- require the child to attend meetings with a youth offender panel; and
- specify the length of any youth offender contract (between three and 12 months).[40]

19.34 The court must also make an order requiring a parent, guardian or, in the case of a looked after child, a representative of the local authority to attend the youth offender panel meetings if the child is aged under 16, unless it would be unreasonable to do so.[41] The court has a discretion to make such an order for children aged 16 and over (see para 19.48 on parental attendance).

36 PCC(S)A 2000 s16(1), (2) and s17(2).
37 PCC(S)A 2000 s16(1), (3) and s17(2)(b)(ii).
38 Courts Act 2003 s66.
39 PCC(S)A 2000 s8(2); *R v Reyon Menelek Dillon* [2017] EWCA Crim 2642.
40 PCC(S)A 2000 s18(1).
41 PCC(S)A 2000 s20.

19.35 If a child is being sentenced in the adult magistrates' court and a referral order is under consideration, it is recommended that a youth court magistrate is included on the bench.[42] If the court is considering imposing a custodial sentence in a 'custody threshold case' (see paras 19.11–19.13 on custody threshold cases), a pre-sentence report is required.[43] The YOT should consider recommending an intensive contract (see paras 19.22–19.23 on intensive ROs) convening a pre-panel meeting (see paras 19.24–19.25 on pre-panel).

19.36 When the court makes a RO it should explain in ordinary language the effect of the order; and the consequences of no youth offender contract being agreed between the panel and the child, or, the effect of the child breaching the terms of the youth offender contract.[44]

Two or more connected offences

19.37 When a court makes a RO for two or more connected offences, the child is referred to a single young offender panel, but the lengths of the youth offender contract may be different for each offence and may be ordered to run consecutively or concurrently, but the total period must not exceed 12 months.[45] Additionally, courts can make more than one RO (see para 19.38 on second or subsequent ROs).

Second or subsequent referral orders

19.38 Children may receive more than one RO. The discretionary RO conditions enable courts to impose second or subsequent ROs:

> [S]econd or subsequent referral orders should be considered in those cases where:
>
> (a) the offence is not serious enough for a YRO but the child or young person does appear to require some intervention
>
> OR
>
> (b) the offence is serious enough for a YRO but it is felt that a referral order would be the best way to prevent further offending (as an example, this may be because the child or young person has responded well in the past to such an order and the

42 Referral Order Guidance, Ministry of Justice and Youth Justice Board, October 2018, para 3.11.

43 Referral Order Guidance, Ministry of Justice and Youth Justice Board, October 2018, para 3.18.

44 PCC(S)A 2000 s18(3).

45 PCC(S)A 2000 s18(5).

offence now before the court is dissimilar to that for which a referral order was previously imposed).[46]

Restrictions on courts' other sentencing powers

19.39 A court making a RO is prohibited from imposing any other sentencing disposal (YRO, fine, reparation order, conditional discharge or binding over order) other than an absolute discharge for an associated offence.[47] The court is also prohibited from making a parental bind over order.[48] The court may make a costs order and compensation order[49] and a parenting order (see para 23.10), restraining order and sexual harm prevention order.

Responsible youth offending team

19.40 The YOT specified in the RO is responsible for convening the youth offender panel and implementing the RO.[50] Where a child has been convicted by a court away from the child's home area, or is moving to a new area, the court must specify the YOT in the area it appears to the court that the child resides or will reside.[51] It is advisable the responsible YOT is contacted by the court to ensure the child is given instructions prior to leaving court.[52]

Setting the length of orders

19.41 When a RO is made, the court specifies the length of the youth offender contract. The contract can last between three and 12 months.[53] The length of the contract is based on the seriousness of the offence and is determined by the court. The court cannot decide the terms of the youth offender contract – that will be for the RO panel and the child to agree.

46 *Sentencing children and young people: definitive guideline*, para 6.20.

47 PCC(S)A 2000 s19.

48 PCC(S)A 2000 s19(5).

49 Referral Order Guidance, Ministry of Justice and Youth Justice Board, October 2018, para 3.11.

50 PCC(S)A 2000 s18(2).

51 PCC(S)A 2000 s18(2).

52 Referral Order Guidance, Ministry of Justice and Youth Justice Board, October 2018, para 3.10.

53 PCC(S)A 2000 s18(1).

19.42 Defence lawyers should seek to ensure that the court imposes a RO for the shortest possible period commensurate with the court's duties; provided the RO is for less than 12 months the court will have the power to extend the order in certain circumstances (see paras 19.50–19.57 on convictions for further offences; and paras 19.60–19.70 on breach).

Offence seriousness	Suggested length of referral order
Low	3–5 months
Medium	5–7 months
High	7–9 months
Very High	10–12 months

Source: Sentencing children and young people: definitive guideline, p25.

The referral order contract

19.43 The initial youth offender panel meeting should be held 'in a timely fashion' after the sentencing hearing as the period of the order does not begin until the contract is agreed and signed,[54] or, 'at the earliest opportunity' for an intensive RO (see paras 19.22–19.23).[55]

19.44 At the first meeting, the youth offender panel will seek to agree with the child a programme of behaviour with the aim of preventing the child from reoffending.[56] The youth offender panel will assess the level of intervention necessary to prevent the child from reoffending.

19.45 The programme may include any of the following:

- financial or other reparation to any person who appears to the panel to be a victim of, or otherwise affected by, the offence, or any of the offences, for which the child was referred to the panel;
- mediation sessions with any such victim or other person;
- unpaid work or service in or for the community;
- to be at home at times specified in or determined under the programme;
- attendance at a school or other educational establishment or at a place of work;

54 Referral Order Guidance, Ministry of Justice and Youth Justice Board, October 2018, para 8.1.

55 Referral Order Guidance, Ministry of Justice and Youth Justice Board, October 2018, para 3.26.

56 PCC(S)A 2000 s23(1).

- specified activities (such as those designed to address offending behaviour, those offering education or training or those assisting with the rehabilitation of persons dependent on, or having a propensity to misuse, alcohol or drugs);
- a requirement to present herself or himself to specified persons at times and places specified in or determined under the programme;
- to stay away from specified places or persons (or both);
- a provision enabling the child's compliance with the programme to be supervised and recorded.[57]

19.46 The programme may *not* include:

- the electronic monitoring of the child's whereabouts; or
- the child to have imposed on her or him any physical restriction on his or her movements.[58]

19.47 When agreed, the programme should be confirmed in writing and signed – this becomes the youth offender contract.[59] The period of the RO (the 'compliance period') starts on the date when the contract is agreed with the youth offender panel (*not* the sentencing hearing date).[60]

Parental attendance (responsible person)

19.48 Parental involvement and constructive engagement with the youth offender panel is an important aspect of the youth offender panel process. Courts *must* make an order requiring a responsible person, usually a parent or guardian (or in the case of a looked after child a representative of the local authority), to attend the meetings of the youth offender panel if the child is aged under 16, unless it would be unreasonable to do so.[61] The court may to require the attendance of a responsible person if the child is 16 and over.[62] If a parent or guardian fails to attend and breaches the parental attendance order, the youth offender panel may refer the matter back to court (see paras 19.82–19.84 on breach of a parental attendance order).

57 PCC(S)A 2000 s23(2).
58 PCC(S)A 2000 s23(3).
59 PCC(S)A 2000 s23(5), (6).
60 PCC(S)A 2000 s24(2); Referral Order Guidance 2018, Youth Justice Board, October 2018.
61 PCC(S)A 2000 s20(2).
62 PCC(S)A 2000 s20(1).

Change of address

19.49 The court which made the RO also has the power to amend the RO to specify a new YOT where it appears to the court, by reason of either a change or a prospective change in the child's place or intended place of residence, the child will no longer be residing in an area covered by the current YOT.[63]

Convictions for further offences

Sentencing options

19.50 If a child is convicted of another offence during the period of a RO, the youth court or adult magistrates' court (or Crown Court judge exercising their powers by sitting as a district judge[64]) has the following sentencing options for the further offence:[65]

- make an absolute discharge or conditional discharge order (this does not revoke the existing RO);[66]
- extend the existing RO compliance period up to a maximum of 12 months;[67]
- impose a further RO, YRO or other order (with or without revoking the existing RO);
- revoke the original RO (and if it is in the interests of justice to do so, re-sentence for the original offence).[68]

19.51 These powers apply whether or not the further offence(s) were committed before or after the RO was made. The Youth Court Bench Book and Referral Order Guidance (paras 9.27–9.39) provide guidance on the court's powers to deal with further offences.

Extending an existing referral order

19.52 If a child is convicted of another offence during the period of a RO, the court may deal with the further offence by extending the existing compliance period up to a maximum of 12 months, provided the

63 PCC(S)A 2000 s21(5).
64 Courts Act 2003 s66.
65 PCC(S)A 2000 s28(b); Sch 1 Part II.
66 PCC(S)A 2000 s28(b); Sch 1 Part II para 14(1)(b).
67 PCC(S)A 2000 s28(b); Sch 1 Part II para 10.
68 PCC(S)A 2000 s28(b); Sch 1 Part II para 14(2), (3).

defendant is under 18 years old and the existing order is for less than 12 months.[69] If the court extends the RO, in relation to any connected offence, the court may extend the RO or impose/make an absolute discharge order.[70] Where the court is exercising its power to extend a RO for a further offence, there is no statutory requirement for the child to have pleaded guilty to the further offence. The court has the power to extend a second or subsequent RO in the same way as for the original RO.[71]

19.53 If an RO has been extended but the contract has yet to be signed, this should be expedited and a panel held with minimal delay after the court hearing.

Imposing a further referral order or other order

19.54 The court may impose a new RO (second or subsequent RO) if a child is convicted of further offence(s) during the period of a RO and the discretionary RO conditions are met.[72] This will not have the effect of automatically revoking the existing RO(s) and the court may direct that the new youth offender contract run consecutively to the existing order and should not take effect until the earlier order has been revoked or completed, as this enables the existing RO contract and any related restorative justice programme to be completed.[73] Alternatively, the orders will run concurrently.

Revoking (and re-sentencing)

19.55 The court may revoke an existing RO (or any one or more ROs) if it appears to the court to be 'in the interests of justice' to do so.[74] This power exists whether the further offence(s) were committed before or after the RO was made.

19.56 Where a RO is revoked, the court has a discretion whether to re-sentence for the original offence if it is 'in the interests of justice'

69 PCC(S)A 2000 s28(b); Sch 1 Part II para 10(2); Referral Order Guidance 2018 paras 9.27–9.28.

70 PCC(S)A 2000 s28(b); Sch 1 Part II para 13(4).

71 Referral Order Guidance, Ministry of Justice and Youth Justice Board, October 2018, para 9.31.

72 PCC(S)A 2000 Sch 1 Part II para 14(1)(a); Referral Order Guidance 2018, paras 9.29 and 9.35.

73 Referral Order Guidance 2018, Youth Justice Board, October 2018, para 9.35; and *Sentencing children and young people: definitive guideline*, para 7.10.

74 PCC(S)A 2000 Sch 1 Part II para 14(2).

to do so.[75] The court may deal with the child in any way in which the original sentencing court could have dealt with the offence, assuming PCC(S)A 2000 s16 (compulsory and discretionary referral conditions) had not applied[76] but the court may not make another RO.[77]

19.57 When re-sentencing the child for the original offence, the court *must* take into consideration the extent of the child's compliance with the terms of the youth offender contract.[78]

Referral back to court by youth offender panel

Overview

19.58 The youth offender panel may refer the child back to court,[79] for any of the following four reasons:

1) breach of a referral order (see paras 19.60–19.70);
2) early revocation (see paras 19.71–19.74);
3) an extension of the referral order (see paras 19.75–19.78);
4) an application by the child to have the case referred back to court (see paras 19.75–19.78).

19.59 The appropriate court is a youth court acting in the local justice area in which it appears the child resides or will reside.[80] If a child has turned 18, the appropriate court is an adult magistrates' court in that area.

Breach of a referral order

19.60 The youth offender panel can return the child to court for breach of a RO. A child will be given a formal written warning for unacceptable failures to attend a panel or failing to satisfactorily complete elements in the contract.[81] Where two formal warnings are given and there is a further unacceptable failure to comply, breach action is likely to be initiated, although the first step is to convene a panel who may decide

75 PCC(S)A 2000 Sch 1 Part II para 14(3).
76 PCC(S)A 2000 Sch 1 Part II para 14(3).
77 *Sentencing children and young people: definitive guideline*, para 7.11.
78 PCC(S)A 2000 Sch 1 Part II para 14(4).
79 The appropriate court is a youth court acting in the local justice area in which it appears the child resides or will reside – PCC(S)A 2000 s22(2A).
80 PCC(S)A 2000 s22(2A).
81 PCC(S)A 2000 Sch 1 Part I para 9.6.

additional support will enable the child to successfully complete the contract or that the elements are too demanding and should be varied.[82] A panel might also be convened for a single serious breach of a contract.[83] Where a child is unwilling to address their non-compliance, then it is open for the panel to refer the offender back to court to consider re-sentencing.

19.61 The youth offending panel's reasons for referring the case back to court must be set out in a written report for the court.[84] These could include:

- failure to attend a panel meeting;[85]
- there is no prospect of agreement being reached on a youth offender contract within a reasonable period after the making of the RO;[86]
- the child unreasonably refuses to sign the contract[87] or an amended contract;[88]
- it appears to the panel that the child has breached the terms of the contract;[89]
- it appears to the panel that the child's compliance does not justify the conclusion that he or she will have satisfactorily completed the contract.[90] (See para 19.70 on the court's powers where it is satisfied as to completion of the contract.)

19.62 The court has the power to issue a summons or a warrant for the arrest of the child to secure their attendance at court,[91] once the child is brought to court the child may be released or remanded and the court may adjourn proceedings.[92]

Court's powers when dealing with a breach of a referral order

19.63 The court's powers when dealing with a referral to court for breach of a RO are:

82 PCC(S)A 2000 Sch 1 Part I paras 9.6–9.8.
83 PCC(S)A 2000 Sch 1 Part I para 9.6.
84 PCC(S)A 2000 Sch 1 Part I para 2.
85 PCC(S)A 2000 s22(2)(b).
86 PCC(S)A 2000 s25(2).
87 PCC(S)A 2000 s25(3).
88 PCC(S)A 2000 s26(8).
89 PCC(S)A 2000 ss26(4)(b), 5(b).
90 PCC(S)A 2000 s27(2)(b), (4).
91 PCC(S)A 2000 Sch 1 paras 3 and 4.
92 PCC(S)A 2000 Sch 1 Part I paras 4 and 9ZA.

- allow the RO to continue;
- extend the length of the RO up to a maximum of 12 months (see para 19.65);
- impose a fine up to a maximum of £2,500 (see para 19.65);
- revoke the RO (or each of the ROs) and re-sentence (see paras 19.66–19.69).[93]

19.64 The court must first decide whether it upholds the panel's decision and a child is found to have breached the conditions of his or her RO.[94] Where the child has turned 18, any breach of referral order proceedings will be heard in the adult magistrates' court[95] (see para 19.81 below).

Power to extend the referral order or fine

19.65 If it is proved to the satisfaction of the court that the child has failed, without reasonable excuse, to comply with the terms of the youth offender contract,[96] and the court does not revoke the order (see paras 19.66–19.69 on power to revoke and re-sentence), the court may order the child pay a fine (up to a maximum of £2,500),[97] or make an order extending the length of the RO (up to a maximum of 12 months).[98]

Power to revoke and re-sentence

19.66 If the court upholds the panel's decision to refer the child back to the court, it may revoke the RO.[99]

19.67 If the court revokes the RO, it has the power to re-sentence for the original offence and may deal with the defendant in any way in which the original sentencing court could have dealt but the court may not make a new referral order.[100] When re-sentencing the child for the original offence, the court *must* have regard to the circumstances of

93 PCC(S)A 2000 Sch 1 para 5. Revoking the referral order has the effect of revoking any related orders.
94 PCC(S)A 2000 Sch 1 para 5(1).
95 PCC(S)A 2000 Sch 1 para 4(1)(b)(ii).
96 PCC(S)A 2000 Sch 1 para 6A(1)(b).
97 PCC(S)A 2000 Sch 1 para 6A(2)(a).
98 PCC(S)A 2000 Sch 1 para 6A(2)(a).
99 PCC(S)A 2000 Sch 1 para 5(1), (2).
100 PCC(S)A 2000 Sch 1 para 5(5)(a).

the referral back to court by the panel and the extent of the child's compliance with the terms of the youth offender contract.[101]

19.68 A court may only revoke the RO and re-sentence if the child is present in court.[102] The court's the powers are not affected by the expiry of the compliance period of the youth offender contract.[103]

19.69 A decision to revoke a RO may be appealed to the Crown Court.[104]

Exception where court satisfied as to completion of contract

19.70 Where a court considers a referral from a youth offender panel in relation to the child's lack of compliance (and that the child will not have satisfactorily completed the contract).[105] If the court decides, contrary to the decision of the panel, that the child's compliance with the terms of the contract has, or will have, been such as to justify the conclusion that the child has satisfactorily completed the contract, the court has the power to discharge the RO (or each of the ROs).[106]

Early revocation

19.71 The youth offender panel may refer a child back to court if it appears to the youth offender panel to be in the interests of justice for the RO (or each of the ROs) to be revoked.[107] The circumstances in which the panel may make a referral for early revocation include the child making good progress under the contract.[108]

19.72 The panel refer may request the court to:

- revoke the RO (or each of the ROs); or
- revoke the RO (or each of the ROs) and to deal with the child for the offence(s) in respect of which the revoked order was made.[109]

19.73 A court re-sentencing a child following revocation of a RO has the powers set out in PCC(S)A 200 Sch 1 para 5(5) (see paras 19.66–19.69 on power to revoke and re-sentence).

101 PCC(S)A 2000 Sch 1 para 5(5)(b).
102 PCC(S)A 2000 Sch 1 para 5(6).
103 PCC(S)A 2000 Sch 1 para 5(6).
104 PCC(S)A 2000 Sch 1 para 6.
105 A referral under PCC(S)A 2000 s27(4).
106 PCC(S)A 2000 Sch 1 para 8.
107 PCC(S)A 2000 s27A(2).
108 PCC(S)A 2000 s27A(3).
109 PCC(S)A 2000 s27A(2).

19.74 If the court decides not to revoke the RO, the panel may not make a further referral for early revocation for three months.[110]

Referral back to court to extend order

19.75 The youth offender panel may refer a child back to court to extend the period of the RO if it appears to the panel to be in the interests of justice for the RO (or each of the ROs) to be extended.[111] The youth offender panel's reasons must be set out in a written report for the court.[112]

19.76 The court may, if it appears that it would be in the interests of justice to do so, having regard to circumstances which have arisen since the contract took effect, make an order extending the length of the compliance period but:

- by no more than three months; and
- the extension period must not cause the total length of the order to exceed 12 months.[113]

19.77 The court may only extend the period of the order if:

- the child is present in court;
- the youth offender contract has taken effect; and
- the compliance period has not ended.[114]

19.78 The court must also have regard to the extent of the child's compliance with the contract.[115] The court does not have the power to revoke and re-sentence.

Referral back to court requested by the child

19.79 There is no provision for the child to apply directly to the court for the order to be varied or revoked. However, at any time during the period of a youth offender contract, a child may request a progress meeting with the youth offender panel and, if the child wishes:

- the youth offender contract to be varied; or
- to be referred back to court with a view to the RO (or ROs) being revoked on account of a significant change in the child's

110 PCC(S)A 2000 s27A(4).
111 PCC(S)A 2000 s27B(1)(c).
112 PCC(S)A 2000 Sch 1 para 9ZC.
113 PCC(S)A 2000 Sch 1, paras 9ZD(1), (2).
114 PCC(S)A 2000 Sch 1, paras 9ZD(4).
115 PCC(S)A 2000 Sch 1, paras 9ZD(3).

circumstances (such as being taken to live abroad) which makes compliance with any youth offender contract impractical.[116]

19.80 The youth offender panel would then be able to refer a child back to court if it appears to the youth offender panel to be in the interests of justice for the RO (or each of the ROs) to be revoked[117] (see paras 19.71–19.74 on early revocation).

Referral back to court where a child has turned 18

19.81 Once a child has turned 18, any breach proceedings[118] or other hearings where the youth offender panel refers the matter to court, will be heard in the adult magistrates' court. If the court decides to revoke the order, then its powers when re-sentencing are limited to those available to the court at the time of the original sentence.[119]

Breach of parental attendance order

19.82 If a parent or guardian fails to comply with a parental attendance order to attend youth justice panel meetings (see para 19.48 on parental attendance), and their child is still under 18 at the time of such failure, the panel may refer the matter to a youth court acting in the local justice area in which it appears the child resides or will reside.[120]

19.83 The youth offending panel's reasons for referring the case back to court must be set out in a written report for the court.[121] The court has the power to issue a summons or a warrant for the arrest of the parent or guardian, to secure attendance at court.[122]

19.84 If the court is satisfied that the parent or guardian failed without reasonable excuse to comply with a parental attendance order and the court is satisfied that a parenting order would be desirable in the interests of preventing the child committing further offences, the

116 PCC(S)A 2000 s26C.
117 PCC(S)A 2000 s27A(2).
118 PCC(S)A 2000 Sch 1 para 4(1)(b)(ii).
119 *Sentencing children and young people: definitive guideline*, para 7.8.
120 PCC(S)A 2000 s22(2A).
121 PCC(S)A 2000 Sch 1 para 9B.
122 PCC(S)A 2000 Sch 1 para 9C.

court may make a parenting order for up to 12 months.[123] The making of this order can be appealed to the Crown Court.[124]

Criminal record

19.85 A RO is a criminal conviction and will form part of a person's criminal record. The conviction will be spent as soon as the order ceases to have effect – in other words, once the contract has been completed (see para 25.28 for a table of rehabilitation periods). The length of the order (the 'compliance period') begins on the date the contract is signed and takes effect.[125] However, where the court makes a compensation order, the conviction will only be spent when the compensation order is paid and the referral order is complied with.[126]

19.86 First convictions for certain offences can be filtered (deleted) from a criminal records after a period of time, depending on the seriousness of the offence (see paras 25.49–25.56 on filtering).[127]

123 PCC(S)A 2000 Sch 1 para 9D.
124 PCC(S)A 2000 Sch 1 para 9E.
125 PCC(S)A 2000 para 24(2).
126 Referral Order Guidance 2018, YJB, October 2018, para 3.43.
127 Rehabilitation of Offenders Act 1974.

CHAPTER 20

Youth rehabilitation orders

continued

Key points

- A youth rehabilitation order (YRO) is the umbrella community order available for children.
- YROs can be tailored to address the needs of an individual child, the risk or re-offending and the risk of harm.
- The level of intervention is based upon the seriousness of the offence, the risk of re-offending or of causing serious harm. Defence lawyers should ensure that all requirements are proportionate and necessary.
- A YRO is a sentencing option where the offence (or combination of offences) are serious enough to warrant such a sentence.
- A YRO with fostering or intensive supervision and surveillance should be considered as an alternative to custody when the custody threshold has been passed.
- Children who breach a YRO can be returned to court and wilful and persistent breaches can result in children receiving custodial sentences for non-custodial offences.

Introduction

20.1 The youth rehabilitation order (YRO) is a community order[1] that can be individually tailored to include a range of activity, supervision and programme requirements. The court will usually be guided by the recommendations in a pre-sentence report and the level of intervention is based upon the seriousness of the offence, the risk of re-offending or of causing serious harm.[2]

20.2 Courts should always guard against the risk that the 'menu of options' presents the temptation to impose disproportionate or unnecessary conditions:

> The court should take care to ensure that the requirements imposed are not too onerous so as to make breach of the order almost inevitable.[3]

1 Criminal Justice Act (CJA) 2003 s147.

2 See paras 20.18–20.19.

3 Sentencing Council, *Sentencing children and young people: definitive guideline*, 2107, para 6.26.

Availability

20.3 A YRO is available as a sentencing disposal for any child who is aged under 18 on the date the child pleaded guilty or a finding of guilt is made.[4] The offence does not need to be imprisonable, but a court may only make a YRO if it is of the opinion that the offence (or combination of offences) are **serious enough** to warrant such a sentence.[5]

20.4 A YRO with fostering or intensive supervision and surveillance are both 'community alternatives to custody'. An intensive YRO is a sentencing option when sentencing a child for an imprisonable offence, which crosses the custody threshold and a custodial sentence would have been merited[6] (see paras 20.86–20.106 on intensive YROs).

Restrictions on the use of a youth rehabilitation order

20.5 The court cannot make a YRO on a child who is currently subject to a reparation order or a YRO. The court may make a second YRO if a child is already on a YRO unless the court by revoking the existing order and makes a new order[7] (see paras 20.127–20.132 on convictions for further offences).

20.6 A court is *not* precluded from making more than one YRO provided they are imposed on the same day, so it is open to the court to revoke the existing order and impose two YROs (see para 20.15 on concurrent and consecutive YROs).

Court's duties

Making an order: conditions, requirements and length

20.7 A court may only make a YRO if it is of the opinion that 'the offence, or combination of the offence and one or more offences associated

4 Criminal Justice and Immigration Act (CJIA) 2008 s1(1).

5 CJA 2003 s148(1) – bold added. Also see Sentencing Council, *Sentencing children and young people: definitive guideline*, para 6.24.

6 *Sentencing children and young people: definitive guideline*, paras 6.32–6.33.

7 CJIA 2008 Sch 1 para 30(4).

with it, was **serious enough** to warrant such a sentence'.[8]. Even if a community sentence and any restrictions on the child's liberty are justified, the court is not obliged to make a YRO.[9]

20.8 Any requirement(s) must be the most suitable for the child and the subsequent restriction on liberty must be commensurate with the seriousness of the offence or combination of offences(s).[10] Courts are urged take care to ensure that the requirements, any subsequent restriction on liberty and the length of the order are proportionate and not too onerous so as to make breach of the order almost inevitable.[11]

20.9 Before making a YRO, the court must:

- consider the offender's family circumstances and the likely effect of such an order;[12]
- consider whether the proposed requirements are compatible if imposing two or more requirements, or two or more YROs;[13]
- ensure that any requirement, as far as practicable, avoids any conflict with the offender's religious beliefs; attendance at work, school or other educational establishment; and the requirements of any other YRO to which the offender may be subject;[14]
- ensure the offender is not already subject to another YROs or a reparation order, which precludes the making of a YRO unless the court revokes the earlier order.[15]

20.10 There are 15 available YRO requirements[16] (all ages refer to age at date of the plea of guilty or finding of guilt):

- activity requirement (maximum 90 days);
- supervision requirement;
- unpaid work (16 and 17 year olds only, 40–240 hours);
- programme requirement;

8 CJA 2003 s148(1) – bold added. Also see *Sentencing children and young people: definitive guideline*, para 6.24.

9 CJA 2003 s148(5).

10 CJA 2003 s148(2).

11 *Sentencing children and young people: definitive guideline*, para 6.26.

12 CJA 2003 Sch 1 para 28.

13 CJA 2003 Sch 1 para 29(1).

14 CJA 2003 Sch 1 para 29(3).

15 CJA 2003 Sch 1 para 30(4).

16 CJIA 2008 s1(1).

- attendance centre requirement (maximum 12 hours for children aged 10–13; between 12 and 24 hours for 14–15 year olds; and between 12 and 36 hours for 16-17-year-olds);
- prohibited activity requirement;
- curfew requirement (maximum 12 months and between two and 16 hours a day);
- exclusion requirement (maximum three months);
- residence requirement (16 and 17 year olds only);
- local authority residence requirement (maximum six months, but not for any period after young person attains age of 18);
- mental health treatment requirement;
- drug treatment requirement;
- drug testing requirement (14–17 year olds only);
- intoxicating substance requirement;
- education requirement.

For curfew and prohibited activity requirements, the court must consider imposing an:

- electronic monitoring requirement.

For an intensive YRO:

- fostering requirement (maximum 12 months, but not for any period after young person attains age of 18);
- intensive supervision and surveillance requirement.

20.11 The court must fix the period within which the requirements are to be completed.[17] YROs can last from six months to three years. There can be different lengths for different requirements (see paras 20.13–20.14 on the start date and end date of YRO).

20.12 The order must specify the local justice area in which the offender will reside,[18] and copies of the order should be provided to the child (or parent or guardian if aged under 14).[19]

Start and end date of youth rehabilitation order

20.13 A YRO usually commences on the day after the order is made.[20] A court may order for the YRO to take effect on a later date.[21] Where a child is currently on a detention and training order (DTO), the court

17 CJIA 2008.
18 CJIA 2008.
19 CJIA 2008.
20 CJIA 2008 Sch 1 para 30(1).
21 CJIA 2008 Sch 1 para 30(1A).

may order the YRO to take effect from the date the period of supervisions begins, or, on expiry of the order.

20.14 The court must specify the date on which each of the requirements is to be completed. If there is a combination of different requirements, they can have different end dates, but the court must specify the end date of the order. The total length of the order must be a maximum of three years.

Concurrent and consecutive orders

20.15 When a court is dealing with a child for two or more associated offences[22] it may impose separate YROs for each offence (but the court cannot combine intensive fostering, supervision and surveillance nor combine any intensive activity requirement with other requirements).[23] The court must indicate whether the requirements are to run concurrently or consecutively. The court must also take care not to exceed the statutory number of hours for a requirement.

Youth rehabilitation orders imposed in the Crown Court

20.16 The Crown Court can make YROs. When doing so, it can choose to authorise the youth court or adult magistrates' court to deal with any breach proceedings or applications to amend, vary or revoke the order.[24]

Age of the defendant

20.17 Unless otherwise specified, a YRO can be imposed on a child who has turned 18 years old (or will do so during the order) provided the defendant was under 18 at the time of conviction. Age restrictions on requirements are determined by age on date of conviction.

Youth rehabilitation order requirements

Introduction

20.18 The youth offending team (YOT) will make recommendations based upon the seriousness of the offence, the risk of re-offending or of

22 Associated means convicted in the same proceedings or is sentenced at the same time – PCC(S)A 2000 s161.

23 CJIA 2008 Sch 1 para 31(1).

24 CJIA 2008 Sch 1 para 36.

causing serious harm. The proposed requirements and level of intensity is based upon the AssetPlus assessment and the 'scaled approach', the underlying principle is that children who are more likely to reoffend and/or present a risk of serous hard should receive higher levels of intervention (see paras 17.98–17.101 on AssetPlus assessments and the scaled approach).

	Child or young person profile	**Requirements of order**
Standard	Low likelihood of re-offending **and** a low risk of serious harm	Primarily seek to repair harm caused through, for example: • reparation; • unpaid work; • supervision; and/or • attendance centre.
Enhanced	Medium likelihood of re-offending **or** a medium risk of serious harm	Seek to repair harm caused and to enable help or change through, for example: • supervision; • reparation; • requirement to address behaviour e.g. drug treatment, offending behaviour programme, education programme; and/or • a combination of the above.
Intensive	High likelihood of re-offending **or** a very high risk of serious harm	Seek to ensure the control of and enable help or change for the child or young person through, for example: • supervision; • reparation; • requirement to address behaviour; • requirement to monitor or restrict movement, e.g. prohibited activity, curfew, exclusion or electronic monitoring; and/or • a combination of the above.

Source: Sentencing Council, *Sentencing children and young people: definitive guideline*, p27.

20.19 Defence lawyers need to be alert to the risk that children who are assessed as having a high risk of re-offending or causing serious harm may receive a recommendation of a YRO with relatively onerous requirements.[25] The focus of the requirements should primarily be rehabilitative rather than punitive. Equally, children who are assessed as having a low risk of re-offending but have committed a more serious offence may have more punitive requirements.[26]

Activity requirement[27]

20.20 This is a requirement to participate in specified activities, including residential exercises, for up to a maximum of 90 days.[28] (There can also be an extended activity requirement of up to 180 days as part of an intensive supervision and surveillance order – see para 20.101.)

20.21 A court may only impose an activity requirement if:

- it has consulted with the YOT or local probation service;
- it is satisfied that it is feasible to secure compliance with the requirement; and
- there is provision for such activities in the local justice area where the defendant resides or is to reside.[29]

20.22 The order must specify the number of days the child is required to participate in an activity or each of the specified activities.[30] This may be an activity at a specified place(s); a specified activity; a residential exercise; a number of days the defendant is required to engage in activities as instructed by the responsible officer (this can include a residential exercise for up to seven days and must be specified in the order[31]). The total number of days specified in an activity requirement must not exceed 90 days.[32]

20.23 The activity requirement may include an activity whose purpose is that of reparation, this may involve contact between the defendant and persons affected by the offences in respect of which the order

25 *Sentencing children and young people: definitive guideline*, para 6.30.
26 *Sentencing children and young people: definitive guideline*, para 6.31.
27 CJIA 2008 s1(1)(a); Sch 1 paras 6–8.
28 CJIA 2008 Sch 1 para 6(1)(c).
29 CJIA 2008 Sch 1 para 8(3).
30 CJIA 2008 Sch 1 para 6(1).
31 CJIA 2008 Sch 1 para 7(3). The requirement to attend a residential exercise should only be given with the consent of a parent or guardian (para 7(4)).
32 CJIA 2008 Sch 1 para 6(1)(c).

was made.[33] If compliance with the requirement would involve the co-operation of a person (other than the child and the responsible officer), then the court cannot include this activity requirement unless the person consents to its inclusion.[34]

Supervision requirement[35]

20.24 The supervision requirement is a requirement to attend appointments with the responsible officer (or another person determined by the responsible officer).[36]

20.25 The supervision requirement lasts for the length of the YRO. The frequency of the appointments will be determined by the AssetPlus assessment completed by the YOT in accordance with the scaled approach. The Case Management Guidance recommends the minimum numbers of appointments:

Intervention level	Minimum contacts each month in first three months of order	Minimum contacts each month in remainder of order
Standard	2	1
Enhanced	4	2
Intensive	8	4

Source: Case Management Guidance Section 6: Use community interventions, Youth Justice Board, 15 October 2014, para 2.3.

Unpaid work requirement[37]

20.26 The unpaid work requirement is only available for defendants aged 16 or 17 on the date of conviction for the offence. The child is required to complete a minimum of 40 hours and up to a maximum of 240 hours unpaid work. A court must obtain and consider a pre-sentence report before forming any opinion as to the child's suitability for this requirement.[38]

20.27 A court may only impose an unpaid work requirement if:

33 CJIA 2008 Sch 1 para 8(2).
34 CJIA 2008 Sch 1 para 8(4).
35 CJIA 2008 s1(1)(b); Sch 1 para 9.
36 CJIA 2008 Sch 1 para 9(1).
37 CJIA 2008 s1(1)(c); Sch 1 para 10.
38 CJA 2003.

- the court is satisfied the defendant is a suitable person to perform unpaid work;
- there is provision to complete unpaid work in the local justice area where the defendant resides or is to reside.[39]

20.28 The child must perform unpaid work at such times specified by the responsible officer.[40] The hours of unpaid work must be completed within 12 months from the day the YRO starts[41] (although there is provision for this to be extended[42]). The YRO remains in force until the specified number of hours of unpaid work are complete (unless the YRO is revoked).[43]

20.29 The assessment of a child's suitability for unpaid work will take into account the fact that 16- and 17-year-olds are often required to complete unpaid work alongside adult offenders.

Programme requirement[44]

20.30 A programme requirement means the child must participate in a systematic set of activities ('a programme').[45] A court must obtain and consider a pre-sentence report before forming any opinion as to the child's suitability for this requirement.[46]

20.31 A court may only impose a programme requirement if:

- the programme has been recommended by the YOT or local probation service as being suitable for the child;
- the programme is available at the place or places specified.[47]

20.32 If compliance with the requirement would involve the co-operation of a person (other than the child and the responsible officer), then the court cannot include this activity requirement unless the person consents to its inclusion.[48]

20.33 The programme requirement must specify the place or places and the number of days the child is required to attend the

39 CJIA 2008 Sch 1 para 10(3).
40 CJIA 2008 Sch 1 para 10(5).
41 CJIA 2008 Sch 1 para 10(6).
42 CJIA 2008 Sch 2 para 17.
43 CJIA 2008 Sch 1 para 10(7).
44 CJIA 2008 s1(1)(d), Sch 1 para 11.
45 CJIA 2008 Sch 1 para 11(1).
46 CJA 2003.
47 CJIA 2008 Sch 1 para 11(3).
48 CJIA 2008 Sch 1 para 11(4).

programme.[49] This may include residing at the place specified in order to participate in the programme.[50] This might be group work or individually. The options available will usually depend on whether the YOT has established a programme provision to address the needs assessed in AssetPlus, for example, knife enabled crime, violence or victim awareness.

20.34 A programme requirement means the child will be required to comply with instructions given by, or under the authority of, the person in charge of the programme.[51]

Attendance centre requirement[52]

20.35 An attendance centre requirement means that the child must attend a specified attendance centre for a specified the number of hours.[53]

20.36 A court may only impose an attendance centre requirement if:

- an attendance centre is available for persons of the child's description, and provision can be made at the centre for the child; and
- the court is satisfied that the proposed attendance centre is reasonably accessible to the child, having regard to the means of access available to the child and any other circumstances.[54]

20.37 The order must specify the attendance centre and the number of hours the child is required to attend, this must be:

- 12–36 hours if the child is aged 16 or over on the date of conviction;
- 12–24 hours if the child is aged 14 or 15 on the date of conviction;
- up to 12 hours if the child is aged ten to 13 on the date of conviction.[55]

20.38 The child may only be required to attend the centre on one occasion on any day, up to a maximum of three hours on any occasion.[56] After the responsible officer notifies the child of the first time they are

49 CJIA 2008 Sch 1 para 11(1).
50 CJIA 2008 Sch 1 para 11(2).
51 CJIA 2008 Sch 1 para 11(5).
52 CJIA 2008 s1(1)(e), Sch 1 para 12.
53 CJIA 2008 Sch 1 para 12(1).
54 CJIA 2008 Sch 1 para 12(3).
55 CJIA 2008 Sch 1 para 12(2).
56 CJIA 2008 Sch 1 para 12(6).

required to attend the centre, the officer in charge of the centre will fix the subsequent hours.[57] An attendance centre requirement means the child is required to attend at the centre at the time notified and engage in occupation, or receive instruction, under the supervision of the officer in charge of the centre.[58]

Prohibited activity requirement[59]

20.39 A prohibited activity requirement means the child must refrain from participating in activities specified in the order on a specified day or days or during a specified period.[60] Examples of prohibited activities are not to enter licensed premises, or not to travel on the top floor of a bus or not to possess, use or carry a firearm within the meaning of the Firearms Act 1968.[61]

20.40 A court may only impose a prohibited activity requirement if it has consulted with the YOT or local probation service.[62]

Curfew requirement[63]

20.41 A curfew requirement means the child must remain at a place specified in the order for between two and 16 hours in any day.[64] The curfew requirement may only last for a maximum of 12 months.[65] The order may specify different places or different time periods for different days.[66]

20.42 Curfew times can be flexible to reflect age, maturity, risk level and a child's positive evening commitments.[67] Standalone curfews should only be used in exceptional cases, and longer curfews should only be used in highest risk cases and mostly only for 16- and 17-year-olds.

57 CJIA 2008 Sch1 para 12(5), (6).
58 CJIA 2008 Sch 1 para 12(7).
59 CJIA 2008 s1(1)(f), Sch 1 para 13.
60 CJIA 2008 Sch 1 para 13(1).
61 CJIA 2008 Sch 1 para 13(3).
62 CJIA 2008 Sch 1 para 13(2).
63 CJIA 2008 s1(1)(g), Sch 1 para 14.
64 CJIA 2008 Sch 1 para 14(2).
65 CJIA 2008 Sch 1 para 14(3).
66 Youth Justice Board, Case Management Guidance Section 6: Use community interventions, 15 October 2014, para 2.3.
67 Youth Justice Board, Case Management Guidance Section 5: Use reports, 15 October 2014, para 2.17.

20.43 Before imposing a curfew requirement, the court must:

- obtain and consider information about the place proposed to be specified in the order including information as to the attitude of persons likely to be affected by the enforced presence there of the offender.[68]

This would mean taking into consideration the impact on siblings, safeguarding and welfare considerations. The court should also consider domestic violence and mental health issues.

20.44 A curfew requirement must be electronically monitored, unless:

- in the particular circumstances of the case, the court considers it inappropriate to do so;[69]
- the court has the consent of any person (other than the offender) whose co-operation is required to ensure that the monitoring takes place;[70]
- the court is satisfied there are suitable arrangements available in the place the court proposes to specify in the order.[71]

20.45 Electronic monitoring may be considered inappropriate in certain types of accommodation, for example, in a hostel where electronic monitoring equipment is not suitable for use in a hostel (see paras 20.82–20.85).[72]

Exclusion requirement[73]

20.46 An exclusion requirement means that a child is prohibited from entering a place or area specified in the order for a specified period of time, up to a maximum of three months.[74] The order may specify the exclusion only operates during specific periods and may specify different places, for different periods or days.[75]

20.47 A clearly marked map should be given to the child so that they are made aware of the exact restrictions being imposed.[76]

68 CJIA 2008 Sch 1 para 14(4).
69 CJIA 2008 Sch 1 para 2.
70 CJIA 2008 Sch 1 para 26(3).
71 CJIA 2008 Sch 1 para 26(6).
72 Youth Justice Board, Case Management Guidance Section 6: Use community interventions, 15 October 2014, para 2.3.
73 CJIA 2008 s1(1)(h), Sch 1 para 15.
74 CJIA 2008 s1(1)(h), Sch 1 para 15(1), (2).
75 CJIA 2008 s1(1)(h), Sch 1 para 15(3).
76 Youth Justice Board, 'Case Management Guidance Section 6: Use of community interventions', 15 October 2014, para 2.3.

20.48 An exclusion requirement must be electronically monitored, unless in the particular circumstances of the case, the court considers it inappropriate to do so.[77] The court must:

- have the consent of any person (other than the child) whose co-operation is required to ensure that the monitoring takes place;[78]
- be satisfied there are suitable arrangements available in the place the court proposes to specify in the order.[79]

See paras 20.82–20.85 on electronic monitoring.

Residence requirement[80]

20.49 A residence requirement is only available for defendants aged 16 or 17 at the time of conviction.[81]

20.50 A residence requirement means the child must reside:

- with a specified individual who must consent to the order;[82] or
- at a specified place.[83]

20.51 The YRO may also specify that the child may reside at a place other than that specified in the order, with the prior approval of the responsible officer.[84] If this is not specified, then any change of address or any event in the child's life requiring the child to reside elsewhere would require an application to the court to vary the order.

20.52 Before imposing a curfew requirement, the court must consider the child's home surroundings.[85] A court may not specify a hostel or other institution as the place of residence except on the recommendation of a member of the YOT, a probation officer or a local authority social worker.[86]

77 CJIA 2008 Sch 1 para 2.
78 CJIA 2008 Sch 1 para 26(3)(b).
79 CJIA 2008 Sch 1 para 26(6).
80 CJIA 2008 s1(1)(i), Sch 1 para 16.
81 CJIA 2008 Sch 1 para 16(4).
82 CJIA 2008 Sch 1 para 16(1)(a).
83 CJIA 2008 Sch 1 para 16(1)(b).
84 CJIA 2008 Sch 1 para 16(5).
85 CJIA 2008 Sch 1 para 16(6).
86 CJIA 2008 Sch 1 para 16(7).

Local authority residence requirement[87]

20.53 This is a requirement that the child must reside in accommodation provided by or on behalf of the local authority.[88]

20.54 Given the potential interference with a child's Article 8 ECHR rights, it is not surprising that there is an additional safeguard before imposing this requirement. The pre-conditions for imposing a local authority residence requirement are:

- the child is legally represented during the sentencing hearing;[89] or
- funding for legal representation was withdrawn because of the child's conduct;[90] or
- the child has been informed of the right to apply for legal representation but refused or failed to apply for legal aid.[91]

20.55 A local authority residence requirement can only be imposed if the court is satisfied that:

- the behaviour which constituted the offence was due to a significant extent to the circumstances in which the child was living;[92] and
- the imposition of the requirement will assist in the child's rehabilitation.[93]

20.56 A court may only impose a local authority residence requirement if it has consulted:

- a parent or guardian of the child (unless it is impracticable to consult such a person);[94] and
- the local authority which is to receive the child.[95]

20.57 The order must specify the local authority in whose area the child is to reside.[96] The requirement may also specify the child is not to reside with a person specified in the order.[97] The requirement must be no

87 CJIA 2008 s1(1)(j), Sch 1 para 17.
88 CJIA 2008 Sch 1 para 17(1).
89 CJIA 2008 Sch 1 para 19(1)(a).
90 CJIA 2008 Sch 1 para 19(1)(b), (2)(a).
91 CJIA 2008 Sch 1 para 19(1)(b), (2)(b).
92 CJIA 2008 Sch 1 para 17(3)(a).
93 CJIA 2008 Sch 1 para 17(3)(b).
94 CJIA 2008 Sch 1 para 17(4)(a).
95 CJIA 2008 Sch 1 para 17(4)(b).
96 CJIA 2008 Sch 1 para 17(5).
97 CJIA 2008 Sch 1 para 17(2).

longer than six months and must not include any period after the child has reached the age of 18.[98]

Mental health treatment requirement[99]

20.58 A mental health treatment requirement means the child must submit to treatment during the period of the order by or under the direction of a registered medical practitioner or a registered psychologist[100] (or both, for different periods) with a view to the improvement of the child's mental condition.[101]

20.59 The court must be satisfied that:

- the child's mental condition requires and may be susceptible to treatment but does not warrant a hospital or guardianship order within the meaning of the Mental Health Act 1983;[102]
- arrangements have been made or can be made for the treatment intended;[103] and
- the child has expressed willingness to comply with the requirement.[104]

20.60 The specified treatment must be:

- as a resident patient in a care home, an independent hospital or a hospital (but not in hospital premises where high security psychiatric services within the meaning of that Act are provided);[105]
- as a non-resident patient at a specified institution or place;[106] and
- by or under the direction of a registered medical practitioner or registered psychologist (or both);[107]

but the order must not otherwise specify the nature of the treatment.[108]

98 CJIA 2008 Sch 1 para 17(6).
99 CJIA 2008 s1(1)(k); Sch 1 para 20.
100 A registered psychologist means a person registered as a practitioner psychologist in the register maintained under the Health Professions Order 2001: CJIA 2008 Sch 1 para 20(6).
101 CJIA 2008 Sch 1 para 20(1).
102 CJIA 2008 Sch 1 para 20(3)(a).
103 CJIA 2008 Sch 1 para 20(3)(b).
104 CJIA 2008 Sch 1 para 20(3)(c).
105 CJIA 2008 Sch 1 para 20(2)(a).
106 CJIA 2008 Sch 1 para 20(2)(b).
107 CJIA 2008 Sch 1 para 20(2)(c).
108 CJIA 2008 Sch 1 para 20(2).

20.61 While the child is under treatment as a resident patient, the responsible officer should supervise the child to such extent as may be necessary for the purpose of the revocation or amendment of the order.[109] There is also provision for circumstances in which the arrangements can be varied from those specified in the order, if the treatment can be better or more conveniently given elsewhere.[110]

20.62 There is no requirement that the court must have evidence from a registered medical practitioner approved under Mental Health Act 1983 s12.[111]

20.63 Concerns were raised when this provision was being enacted that requirements such as mental health (or intoxicating substance) treatment should not form part of a sentence because the treatment should already be available for the child to access voluntarily.

20.64 A child who has expressed a willingness to comply with the requirement must still consent to treatment while subject to a mental health treatment requirement.[112] There is a tension between a child voluntarily consenting to treatment and being subject to this requirement as part of a court order. Consequently, YOTs should not automatically consider a lack of consent to a particular form of treatment a potential breach.

Drug treatment requirement[113]

20.65 A drug treatment requirement means the child must submit to treatment, under the direction of the treatment provider,[114] with a view to the reduction or elimination of the child's dependency on, or propensity to misuse, drugs, during the period of the order.[115] 'Drug' means a controlled drug as defined by Misuse of Drugs Act 1971 s2.[116]

20.66 A court may only impose a drug treatment requirement if the court is satisfied that:

109 CJIA 2008 Sch 1 para 20(4).
110 CJIA 2008 Sch 1 para 21. The responsible officer must be notified in writing.
111 This requirement was removed by LASPO 2012 s82(2)(a).
112 For consent to medical treatment for children and young people – see https://www.nhs.uk/conditions/consent-to-treatment/children/
113 CJIA 2008 s1(1)(l); Sch 1 para 22.
114 The 'treatment provider' is a specified person having the necessary qualifications or experience – CJIA 2008 Sch 1 para 22(1).
115 CJIA 2008 Sch 1 para 22(1).
116 CJIA 2008 Sch 1 para 22(5).

- the child is dependent on, or has a propensity to misuse, drugs;[117] and
- the child's dependency or propensity is such as requires and may be susceptible to treatment.[118]

20.67 The court must also be satisfied:

- the arrangements for this requirement are in place in the child's local justice area;[119]
- arrangements have been or can be made for the treatment intended;[120]
- the requirement has been recommended to the court as suitable for the child by a member of the YOT, or local probation service;[121] and
- the child has expressed willingness to comply with the requirement.[122]

20.68 The specified treatment must be:

- as a resident in a specified institution or place; or
- as a non-resident at a specified institution or place, at such intervals as specified;

but the order must not otherwise specify the nature of the treatment.[123]

20.69 The court may also wish to consider a drug testing requirement (see paras 20.70–20.73 below).

Drug testing requirement[124]

20.70 This is not a standalone requirement and can only be imposed alongside a drug treatment requirement. It means the child must provide samples in accordance with instructions by the responsible officer or the treatment provider for the purpose of measuring whether there is any drug in the child's body.[125]

117 CJIA 2008 Sch 1 para 22(2)(a).
118 CJIA 2008 Sch 1 para 22(2)(b).
119 CJIA 2008 Sch 1 para 22(4)(a).
120 CJIA 2008 Sch 1 para 22(4)(b).
121 CJIA 2008 Sch 1 para 22(4)(c).
122 CJIA 2008 Sch 1 para 22(4)(d).
123 CJIA 2008 Sch 1 para 22(3).
124 CJIA 2008 s1(1)(m), Sch 1 para 23.
125 CJIA 2008 Sch 1 para 23(1).

20.71 A court may only impose a drug testing requirement if the court is satisfied that:

- the arrangements for this requirement are in place in the child's local justice area;[126]
- the order also imposes a drug treatment requirement;[127] and
- the child has expressed willingness to comply with the requirement.[128]

20.72 The drug testing requirement:

- must specify for each month the minimum number of occasions on which samples are to be provided;[129]
- may specify times at which and circumstances in which samples may be required to be provided, and descriptions of the samples to be provided.[130]

20.73 If the tests are not to be carried out by the responsible officer, the order must specify that the results are to be communicated to the responsible officer.[131]

Intoxicating substance treatment requirement[132]

20.74 An intoxicating substance treatment requirement means that the child must submit to treatment, as directed, with a view to the reduction or elimination of their dependency on, or propensity to misuse, intoxicating substances such as alcohol, during a period or periods specified in the order.[133]

20.75 'Intoxicating substance' means alcohol, or any other substance or product (other than a drug) which is, or the fumes of which are, capable of being inhaled or otherwise used for the purpose of causing intoxication.[134]

20.76 A court may only impose a intoxicating substance treatment requirement if the court is satisfied that:

126 CJIA 2008 Sch 1 para 23(3)(a).
127 CJIA 2008 Sch 1 para 23(3)(b).
128 CJIA 2008 Sch 1 para 23(3)(c).
129 CJIA 2008 Sch 1 para 23(4)(a).
130 CJIA 2008 Sch 1 para 23(4)(b).
131 CJIA 2008 Sch 1 para 23(5).
132 CJIA 2008 s1(1)(n), Sch 1 para 24.
133 CJIA 2008 Sch 1 para 24(1).
134 CJIA 2008 Sch 1 para 24(5).

- the child is dependent on, or has a propensity to misuse, intoxicating substances;[135] and
- the child's dependency or propensity may be susceptible to treatment.[136]

20.77 The court must also be satisfied that:

- arrangements have been or can be made for the treatment intended;[137]
- the requirement has been recommended to the court as suitable for the child by a member of the YOT, or local probation service;[138] and
- the child has expressed willingness to comply with the requirement.[139]

20.78 The specified treatment must be:

- as a resident in a specified institution or place; or
- as a non-resident at a specified institution or place, at such intervals as specified;

but the order must not otherwise specify the nature of the treatment.[140]

Education requirement[141]

20.79 An education requirement means that a child must comply with approved education arrangements during the period or periods specified in the order.[142] Approved education arrangements are those made by the child's parent or guardian and approved by the local authority (where the child resides or is to reside).[143]

20.80 A court may only impose an education requirement if the court:

- has consulted the local authority proposed to be specified in the order;[144]

135 CJIA 2008 Sch 1 para 24(2)(a).
136 CJIA 2008 Sch 1 para 24(2)(b).
137 CJIA 2008 Sch 1 para 24(4)(a).
138 CJIA 2008 Sch 1 para 24(4)(b).
139 CJIA 2008 Sch 1 para 22(4)(c).
140 CJIA 2008 Sch 1 para 24(3).
141 CJIA 2008 s1(1)(o), Sch 1 para 25.
142 CJIA 2008 Sch 1 para 25(1).
143 CJIA 2008 Sch 1 paras 25(2), (3).
144 CJIA 2008 Sch 1 paras 25(4)(a).

- is satisfied that it is the local authority's view that arrangements exist for the child to receive efficient full-time education suitable to the child's age, ability, aptitude and special education needs (if any);[145] and
- is satisfied that the education requirement is necessary for securing the good conduct of the child or for preventing the commission of further offences.[146]

20.81 The order must specify the period of this requirement, which must not include any period when the offender has ceased to be of compulsory school age.[147]

Electronic monitoring requirement[148]

20.82 This not a standalone requirement and can only be imposed alongside other requirements.

20.83 A YRO *may* include electronic monitoring as a means of securing a child's compliance with other requirements.[149]

20.84 Electronic monitoring *must* be imposed where a court imposes a curfew or exclusion requirement,[150] unless:

- in the particular circumstances of the case, the court considers it inappropriate to do so;[151]
- the court has the consent of any person (other than the child) whose co-operation is required to ensure that the monitoring takes place;[152]
- the court is satisfied there are suitable arrangements available in the area in which the relevant place is situated.[153]

20.85 An electronic monitoring requirement must specify the person responsible for the monitoring.[154]

145 CJIA 2008 Sch 1 paras 25(4)(b)(i).
146 CJIA 2008 Sch 1 paras 25(4)(b)(ii).
147 CJIA 2008 Sch 1 paras 25(5).
148 CJIA 2008 s1(2), Sch 1 para 26.
149 CJIA 2008 s1(2)(a).
150 CJIA 2008 s1(2)(b), Sch 1 para 2.
151 CJIA 2008 Sch 1 para 2(a).
152 CJIA 2008 Sch 1 para 26(3)(b).
153 CJIA 2008 Sch 1 para 26(6).
154 CJIA 2008 Sch 1 para 26(4).

Intensive youth rehabilitation orders

20.86 The two most intensive community-based sentencing options are YROs with fostering; and YROs with intensive supervision and surveillance (ISS).

20.87 Both intensive YROs are intended to be community alternatives to custody.[155]

Availability

Overview

20.88 A court may make a YRO with intensive supervision and surveillance or fostering if:

- the offence is an imprisonable offence;
- the offence, or combination of the offence and any associated offence(s), is so serious that a custodial sentence would have been appropriate:[156]

  > The offence must . . . cross the custody threshold and a custodial sentence must be merited before one of these requirements can be imposed.[157]

If the child is aged under 15 at the time of conviction, the child must be classed as a 'persistent offender' (see para 20.91 on persistent offenders).

Intensive orders for 10 and 11 year olds

20.89 If the child was aged under 12 at the time of conviction, the court must form the view that a custodial sentence would have been appropriate if the defendant had been aged 12.[158] This means that intensive YROs are only available if the child would be deemed a persistent offender (see para 20.90).

Intensive orders for 12 to 14 year-olds

20.90 If the child was aged 12 to 14 at the time of conviction, the child must be deemed to be a persistent offender for the offence or combination

155 *Sentencing children and young people: definitive guideline*, para 6.32.
156 CJIA 2008 s1(4)(b).
157 *Sentencing children and young people: definitive guideline*, para 6.33.
158 CJIA 2008 s1(4)(b).

of offences to cross the custody threshold[159] (see paras 21.76–21.78 on custodial sentences and persistent offenders).

Persistent offender

20.91 There is no statutory definition of 'persistent offender'. The question of whether a child has achieved a degree of persistence in his or her offending is a decision for the sentencing court. The Sentencing Council's *Sentencing children and young people: definitive guideline* provides guidance on the definition of 'persistent offenders'.[160] (See also paras 21.76–21.78 on custodial sentences and persistent offender.)

Crossing a significant age threshold

20.92 Where a defendant has crossed a significant age threshold, the starting point for determining the appropriate sentence is the child's age at the time the offence was committed.[161] This means that intensive YROs are only available if the child would be deemed a persistent offender (see para 20.90). For children who have crossed a significant age threshold and are appearing in the Crown Court where a custodial sentence is available, an intensive YRO may be a more severe sentence than the maximum the court could have imposed at the time the offence was committed, but in the author's view may be appropriate as a robust alternative to custody.[162]

Youth rehabilitation order with fostering[163]

20.93 An intensive fostering requirement means the child must reside with a local authority foster parent.[164] The court may only impose an intensive fostering requirement if the offence is imprisonable and the custody threshold is passed (see para 20.88). A court wishing to impose a YRO with fostering must obtain and consider a pre-sentence report.[165]

159 CJIA 2008 s1(4)(c).
160 At paras 6.4–6.10.
161 *Sentencing children and young people: definitive guideline*, para 6.2. See also paras 17.31 and 17.52–17.55 on available sentences.
162 *Sentencing children and young people: definitive guideline*, para 6.3.
163 CJIA 2008 s1(3)(b); Sch 1 paras 4, 5, 18, 19.
164 A local authority foster parent has the same meaning as it has in Children Act 1989 s105(1).
165 CJA 2003 s156(3)(b).

20.94 The pre-conditions for imposing an intensive fostering requirement are:

- is legally represented during the sentencing hearing;[166] or
- that funding for legal representation was withdrawn because of the child's conduct;[167] or
- the child has been informed of the right to apply for such representation but refused or failed to apply for legal aid.[168]

20.95 A court may only impose an intensive fostering requirement if the court is satisfied that:

- the behaviour which constituted the offence was due to a significant extent to the circumstances in which the offender was living;[169] and
- the imposition of a fostering requirement would assist in the offender's rehabilitation.[170]

20.96 A court may only impose an intensive fostering requirement if:

- it has consulted the child's parents or guardians (unless it is impracticable to do so);[171] and
- it has consulted the local authority which is to place the child with a local authority foster parent;[172] and
- arrangements for implementing the requirement are available in the area of the local authority which is to place the child.[173]

20.97 A fostering requirement must:

- be for a maximum of 12 months;
- not include any period after the child has reached the age of 18;[174]
- specify the local authority which is to place the child with a foster parent;[175] and

166 CJIA 2008 Sch 1 para 19(1)(a).
167 CJIA 2008 Sch 1 para 19(1)(b), (2)(a).
168 CJIA 2008 Sch 1 para 19(1)(b), (2)(b).
169 CJIA 2008 Sch 1 para 4(2)(a).
170 CJIA 2008 Sch 1 para 4(2)(b).
171 CJIA 2008 Sch 1 para 4(3)(a).
172 CJIA 2008 Sch 1 para 4(3)(b).
173 CJIA 2008 Sch 1 para 18(7).
174 CJIA 2008 Sch 1 para 18(2).
175 CJIA 2008 Sch 1 para 18(3).

a YRO with fostering must also include a supervision requirement[176] (but an intensive supervision and surveillance requirement cannot be combined with intensive fostering[177]).

20.98 If, during the period of the fostering requirement, no suitable local authority foster parent is available, the responsible officer may notify the child and place the child in alternative local authority accommodation, an application to amend or revoke the YRO must have been made or proposed.[178]

Youth rehabilitation order with intensive supervision and surveillance[179]

20.99 A YRO with ISS is intended to provide the court with an alternative to custody, and combines the most intensive youth rehabilitation requirements of up to 25 hours programmed contact time per week, with an electronically monitored curfew.

20.100 A court may only impose a YRO with ISS if the offence is imprisonable and the custody threshold is passed (see para 20.88). A court wishing to impose a YRO with ISS must obtain and consider a pre-sentence report.[180]

20.101 An ISS must include:

- an extended activity requirement (for a minimum of 91 days up to a maximum of 180 days);[181]
- a supervision requirement;[182]
- a curfew requirement;[183] and
- electronic monitoring (unless in the particular circumstances of the case, the court considers it inappropriate or the court does not have the consent of the person without whose co-operation it will not be practicable to secure that the monitoring takes place or arrangements for electronic monitoring are not available).[184]

20.102 An ISS may also include:

176 CJIA 2008 Sch 1 para 4(4).
177 CJIA 2008 Sch 1 para 5(1).
178 CJIA 2008 Sch 1 para 18(5).
179 CJIA 2008 s1(3)(a), (4), Sch 1 paras 3, 5.
180 CJA 2003 s156(3)(b).
181 CJIA 2008 Sch 1 paras 3(2).
182 CJIA 2008 Sch 1 paras 3(4)(a).
183 CJIA 2008 Sch 1 paras 3(4)(b).
184 CJIA 2008 Sch 1 paras 2, 26(3) and (6).

- any of the other YRO requirements (except fostering).[185]

20.103 The core elements of any ISS package should include:

- education, training (especially basic literacy and numeracy) and employment;
- interventions to tackle offending behaviour;
- reparation to victims or the community;
- assistance in developing inter-personal skills;
- family support;
- a curfew supported by electronic monitoring plus two surveillance checks a day; the existence of a tag may count as one of these contacts.[186]

20.104 The number of appointments (contacts) per week will be determined by the AssetPlus assessment completed by the YOT in accordance with the scaled approach. The National Standards for Youth Justice 2013 recommend the following programmed contact time:

ISS type	**Contacts per week**		
Extended ISS (180 days)	1–4 months	5–6 months	7–12 months
	25 hours	15 hours	5 hours
Band 1 ISS (91 days)	1–3 months	4–6 months	
	25 hours	5 hours	
Band 2 ISS (91 days)	1–2 months	month 3	4–6 months
	20 hours	10 hours	5 hours

Source: National Standards for Youth Justice 2013, Youth Justice Board for England and Wales, April 2013, para 8.22, Table 2: ISS model.

20.105 The extended ISS version of 180 days' specified activity is intended for use in exceptional circumstances only.[187]

20.106 The National Standards also provide that where a high intensity ISS is considered appropriate, delivery can be adjusted to suit the following circumstances:[188]

- *Junior version ISS (13 years or younger)*: 12.5 hours programmed contact time each week (of which seven and a half hours can be

185 CJIA 2008 Sch 1 para 5(1).

186 Youth Justice Board for England and Wales, National Standards for Youth Justice 2013, April 2013, para 8.24.

187 National Standards for Youth Justice 2013, para 8.23.

188 National Standards for Youth Justice 2013, para 8.23.

education) for three months, with support during evenings and weekends. This must be followed by a minimum of five hours a week for the next three months, with support during evenings and weekends.

- *Education, training and employment ISS*: Minimum of one programmed contact each week day (Monday to Sunday), totalling seven hours of contact per week for three months, with support during evenings and weekends. This must be followed by a minimum of three hours a week for the next three months, with support during evenings and weekends.

Management of youth rehabilitation orders

20.107 A YRO is managed by the responsible officer. The responsible officer is a member of the YOT or the probation service.[189] Where the YRO includes electronic monitoring, the YRO must include provision for making a person responsible for the monitoring.[190] Where the only requirement is an attendance centre requirement, the responsible officer is the officer in charge of the centre.[191]

20.108 While a YRO is in force, a child has a duty to keep in touch with the responsible officer, and must notify the responsible officer of any change of address.[192]

189 CJIA 2008 s4(1)(c) and (2).
190 CJIA 2008 Sch 1 para 26(4).
191 CJIA 2008 s4(1)(b).
192 CJIA 2008 Sch 1 para 5(5).

Amending, varying or discharging a youth rehabilitation order

Generally

20.109 A YRO can be amended by a youth court, adult magistrates' court or Crown Court[193] if the child or responsible officer applies to the appropriate court and certain conditions apply.[194]

20.110 A YRO can be revoked or discharged by a youth court, adult magistrates' court or Crown Court[195] (or revoked and the child re-sentenced) if it appears to the court that it is in the interests of justice having regard to all the circumstances.[196] These provisions apply where the offender is, for example, making good progress or responding satisfactorily.[197]

Youth rehabilitation orders made on appeal

20.111 Where a YRO was made on appeal from an adult magistrates' court, it is treated as having been made by a magistrates' court. Where a YRO is made on appeal from the Crown Court to the criminal division of the Court of Appeal, it is treated as having been made by the Crown Court.[198]

Breach and enforcement of youth rehabilitation orders

Breach of a youth rehabilitation order

20.112 A breach of a YRO occurs when the responsible officer is of the opinion that a child has failed *without reasonable excuse* to comply with a YRO.

193 See para 20.16. A youth rehabilitation order made by a Crown Court must be amended by the Crown Court unless the court made an order for the youth court or adult magistrates' court; CJIA 2008 Sch 2 para 14.

194 CJIA 2008 Sch 2 paras 13, 15–16.

195 See para 20.16. A youth rehabilitation order made by the Crown Court must be varied or revoked by a crown court unless the court made an order for the youth court or adult magistrates' court; CJIA 2008 Sch 2 para 12.

196 CJIA 2008 Sch 2 paras 11 and 12.

197 CJIA 2008 Sch 2 paras 11(3) and 12(3).

198 CJIA 2008 Sch 2 para 2.

- If a child fails to comply with his or her YRO, the child is given a warning ('the first warning').[199]
- If there is a further failure to comply during the 'warned period', which is 12 months starting on the day the (first) warning was given, another warning is given.[200]
- If the child fails a further time to comply with the order, the responsible officer must initiate breach proceedings (unless there are exceptional circumstances).[201]

Breach warning

20.113 When a breach occurs, the responsible officer must give the child a warning:

- describing the circumstances of the failure;
- stating that the failure is unacceptable; and
- stating that the child will be liable to be brought before a court if the order is breached on more than one occasion within the 'warned period' (or, where the first warning has been given, the child will be liable to be brought before a court if the child again fails to comply with the order within the warned period).[202]

20.114 The responsible officer must make a record of the warning as soon as practicable after the warning has been given.[203] Although there is no statutory requirement for this warning to be in writing, or for it to be given in the presence of a parent or guardian, YOT guidance provides 'a formal written warning must be issued within 24 hours' to a child who has not given an acceptable reason or explanation for failing to attend a statutory appointment.[204]

Enforcement

20.115 Enforcement is triggered where there have been three occasions during a 12-month warned period (starting on the day the first warning was given) that the child has failed without reasonable excuse to comply with the order, and where the third unacceptable failure to attend takes

199 CJIA 2008 Sch 2 para 3.
200 CJIA 2008 Sch 2 paras 3 and 4(1)(b).
201 CJIA 2008 Sch 2 paras 4(1)(c) and 4(2).
202 CJIA 2008 Sch 2 para 3(2).
203 CJIA 2008 Sch 2 para 3(3).
204 Youth Justice Board, Case Management Guidance Section 6: Use community interventions, 15 October 2014, para 2.25.

place after two formal warnings have been given (see para 20.118 on breach of a YRO). YOT guidance indicates breach action must be initiated within five working days, or two working days in the case of a child assessed as posing a high risk of serious harm to others.[205]

20.116 The responsible officer may also commence breach proceedings without giving two formal warnings.[206] This will only be appropriate in exceptional circumstances, or where there is a serious breach of the requirements of the order, such as an act of violence.[207]

20.117 If the responsible officer is of the opinion that there are exceptional circumstances which justify taking the child to court without two previous warnings having been given, the decision should be agreed by a manager and will be recorded on the child's file.[208]

Breach proceedings

20.118 The responsible officer may commence breach proceedings by laying an information, the court may issue a summons or (where the information is in writing and on oath) issue a warrant for the offender's arrest.[209] Failure to answer the summons can lead to the court issuing a warrant for the offender's arrest.[210]

20.119 Breach proceedings will usually start in the youth court[211] (or the adult magistrates' court if the child has turned 18[212]) in the relevant local justice area.[213] Where the original order was imposed by a Crown Court, breach proceedings will be heard before the Crown Court (unless the court directed that further proceedings take place before the youth court or adult magistrates' court[214]).[215]

205 Youth Justice Board, Case Management Guidance Section 6: Use community interventions, 15 October 2014, para 2.25.

206 CJIA 2008 Sch 2 para 4(3).

207 Youth Justice Board, Case Management Guidance Section 6: Use community interventions, 15 October 2014, para 2.25.

208 Youth Justice Board, Case Management Guidance Section 6: Use community interventions, 15 October 2014, para 2.25.

209 CJIA 2008 Sch 2 para 5(1).

210 CJIA 2008 Sch 2 paras 5(6)(b) and (7).

211 CJIA 2008 Sch 2 para 5(3)(a).

212 CJIA 2008 Sch 2 paras 5(3)(b).

213 The relevant local justice area is the local justice area in which the child resides, or is specified in the youth rehabilitation order – CJIA 2008 Sch 2 para 5(4).

214 CJIA 2008 Sch 1 para 36.

215 CJIA 2008 Sch 2 paras 5(2) and 7.

20.120 The first issue for the court to determine is whether it has been proved to the satisfaction of the court that the defendant 'failed without reasonable excuse to comply with the YRO'.[216] A child should not be deemed to have failed to comply with the requirement if he or she has refused to undergo surgery, electrical or other treatment if the court is of the opinion the refusal was reasonable having regard to all the circumstances.

20.121 The *Sentencing children and young people definitive guideline* provides guidance on how courts should deal with breaches (at paras 17.15–17.16). Once a breach has been admitted or proved, the court will have the following options:

- take no action and allow the YRO to continue;
- impose a fine (up to £2,500 or £500 if the child is aged under 14);[217]
- amend the terms of the order (by adding to or substituting for any existing requirement or requirements)[218] provided the total length of the order does not exceed three years;[219]
- revoke the YRO and re-sentence.[220]

Powers of the court on re-sentence following breach

20.122 A court re-sentencing the defendant for the original offence may deal with the defendant in any way in which the original sentencing court could have dealt with the child for that offence(s).[221] When re-sentencing the child, the court must take into account the extent to which the child has complied with the order.[222]

20.123 Where the court deals with the child by amending the terms of the original order, the following provisions apply:

- If the original YRO did not contain an unpaid work requirement, the minimum number of hours the court can impose is 20 (rather than 40).[223]

216 CJIA 2008 Sch 2 paras 6(1)(b).
217 CJIA 2008 Sch 2 para 6(2)(a) or 8(2)(a).
218 CJIA 2008 Sch 2 para 6(2)(b) or 8(2)(b).
219 CJIA 2008 Sch 2 para 6(6) or 8(6).
220 CJIA 2008 Sch 2 paras 6(2)(c) and 6(10) or 8(2)(c) and 8(10).
221 CJIA 2008 Sch 2 para 6(2)(c) or (8)(2)(c).
222 CJIA 2008 Sch 2 para 6(4).
223 CJIA 2008 Sch 2 para 6(7) or 8(7).

- The court may not impose an extended activity requirement or fostering requirement unless the original order already has such a requirement.[224]
- If the original order contained a fostering requirement and the court proposes a new substitute fostering requirement, the maximum length of the requirement is 18 months (rather than 12 months) starting from the date of the original requirement.[225]

20.124 If a defendant has turned 18 by the date of the first court hearing for breach, their case will be dealt with by the adult magistrates' court (or Crown Court).[226] If the court chooses to revoke the YRO and re-sentence, the court's sentencing powers are limited to those available at the time of the original offence (see para 20.134).

Willful and persistent non-compliance

20.125 Where a child willfully and persistently breaches a YRO, the court has greater powers if the court decides to revoke the order and re-sentence. Willful and persistent non-compliance has no statutory definition, the *Sentencing children and young people definitive guideline* provides this guidance:

> A child or young person will almost certainly be considered to have 'wilfully and persistently' breached a YRO where there have been three breaches that have demonstrated a lack of willingness to comply with the order that have resulted in an appearance before court.[227]

20.126 Where the court is revoking the original order and re-sentencing the offender for the original offence and the young offender has *willfully* and *persistently* failed to comply with a YRO,[228] the court may:

- impose a YRO with ISS (even if the original offence(s) were not imprisonable or did not cross the custody threshold);[229]
- if the original order being revoked is a YRO with ISS and the original offence was punishable with imprisonment, then the court may impose a custodial sentence;[230]
- if the order being revoked is a YRO with ISS and the original offence was not punishable with imprisonment (ie the child or young

224 CJIA 2008 Sch 2 paras 6(8) or 8(8).
225 CJIA 2008 Sch 2 paras 6(9) or 8(9).
226 CJIA 2008 Sch 2 para 5(3)(b).
227 *Sentencing children and young people: definitive guideline*, 2017, p34.
228 CJIA 2008 Sch 2 paras 6(12)–(15) and 8(12)–(15) apply.
229 CJIA 2008 Sch 2 paras 6(13) or 8(13).
230 CJIA 2008 Sch 2 paras 6(14) or 8(14).

person has previously breached a YRO and a ISS requirement was imposed for a non-compliance) the court has the power to impose a detention and training order not exceeding four months.[231]

This may result in a child receiving a custodial sentence for a non-imprisonable offence.

Convictions for further offences

Overview

20.127 Where a child is convicted of a further offence by a youth court or adult magistrates' court while a YRO is in force, the court cannot make a new YRO.[232]

20.128 Where the original YRO was made by a Crown Court, the youth court or adult magistrates' court dealing with the new offence must commit the child in custody or release on bail to appear before the Crown Court,[233] unless a direction was given to allow the youth court and adult magistrates' court to deal further proceedings relating to the YRO.[234] If such a direction was made, the youth court or adult magistrates' court may still commit the child in custody or release on bail to dealt with by the Crown Court.[235]

Powers of the court on re-sentence following further conviction

20.129 Following a further conviction, the youth court or adult magistrates' court, may, if it would be in the interests of justice to do so:

- revoke the YRO;[236]
- revoke the YRO and re-sentence for the original offence;[237]
- Alternatively, the court may allow the YRO to continue and impose a fine, conditional discharge, reparation order or parenting order for the new offence.

231 CJIA 2008 Sch 2 paras 6(15) or 8(15).
232 A new youth rehabilitation order cannot be made while another YRO is in force. CJIA 2008 Sch 1 para 30(4).
233 CJIA 2008 Sch 2 para 18(11).
234 CJIA 2008 Sch 1 para 36(1).
235 CJIA 2008 Sch 2 para 18(9).
236 CJIA 2008 Sch 2 para 18(3) or 19(3).
237 CJIA 2008 Sch 2 para 18(4) or 19(4).

20.130 A youth court, adult magistrates' court or Crown Court re-sentencing the child for the original offence may deal with the her or him in any way in which the original sentencing court could have dealt with the child for that offence(s).[238]

20.131 The court must take into account the extent to which the child has complied with the order.[239]

20.132 When revoking and re-sentencing, the court could impose two YROs – one for the original offence and another for the further offence (see para 20.15 – on consecutive and concurrent YROs).

Turning a significant age threshold

20.133 Where a child subject to a YRO turns 12, 15 or 18 between sentence and breaching the order or being convicted for a further offence, the court's powers when re-sentencing are limited to those that would have been available to the court on the date the child was convicted of the original offence. The sentencing court should also be further guided as a starting point for determining the appropriate sentence by the child's age on the date of the offence.[240]

20.134 Where a child has turned 18, the breach or further offence will be dealt with in the adult magistrates' court or Crown Court.[241] If the court revokes the YRO and re-sentences for the original offence, its sentencing powers will be limited to those available on the date of conviction for the original offence.[242]

Criminal record

20.135 A YRO will appear on a child's criminal record and will become spent six months after the last day the order is to have effect (see para 25.28 on rehabilitation periods).[243]

> The length of the rehabilitation period and any likely effects on the child or young person's future prospects should be taken into account

238 CJIA 2008 Sch 2 para 18(4) or 19(4).

239 CJIA 2008 Sch 2 para 18(5) or (19(5).

240 *Sentencing children and young people: definitive guideline*, 2017, paras 6.1–6.3. Also see paras 17.32–60.

241 CJIA 2008 Sch 2 para 5(3)(b) – in relation to breaches.

242 *Sentencing children and young people: definitive guideline*, 2017, para 7.19.

243 Rehabilitation of Offenders Act 1974.

when considering if the sentence is commensurate with the seriousness of the offence.[244]

20.136 First convictions for certain offences will be filtered (not disclosed on a criminal record check) after a period of time, (see paras 25.49–25.56 on filtering).[245]

244 *Sentencing children and young people: definitive guideline*, 2017, para 6.11.
245 Rehabilitation of Offenders Act 1974.

CHAPTER 21

Custodial sentences

continued

Key points

- Children should only ever receive custodial sentences as a measure of last resort.
- Children cannot receive suspended sentences.
- Where an offence crosses the custody threshold, the court should consider whether an intensive youth rehabilitation order (YRO) with intensive supervision and surveillance (ISS) or YRO with IF would be appropriate.
- The maximum custodial sentence in the youth court is a 24 month detention and training order (DTO).
- Children in the crown court can receive DTOs, long-term detention;[1] extended detention; detention for life; detention at Her Majesty's pleasure.

Imposing custodial sentences on children

Overview

21.1 Custodial sentences must only be imposed as a *measure of last resort*[2] when an offence is 'so serious that neither a fine alone nor a community sentence can be justified'.[3]

21.2 Before imposing a custodial sentence, the court must consider that no community order can be imposed, in particular a youth rehabilitation order (YRO) with intensive supervision and surveillance (ISS) or YRO with fostering.[4] The court must state its reasons why these alternatives are not appropriate before imposing a custodial sentence.[5]

1 Powers of Criminal Courts (Sentencing) Act (PCC(S)A) 2000 s91.

2 United Nations Convention on the Rights of the Child (UNCRC) Article 37; Sentencing Council, *Sentencing children and young people: definitive guideline*, 2017, paras 1.3 and 6.42.

3 Criminal Justice Act (CJA) 2003 s152(2).

4 *Sentencing children and young people: definitive guideline*, para 6.42.

5 *Sentencing children and young people: definitive guideline*, para 6.42.

Children receive sentences of detention not imprisonment

21.3 Children (and younger adults) cannot receive sentences of imprisonment – any person aged under 21 who receives a custodial sentence may only receive sentences of detention.[6] This does not prevent under 21 year-olds being remanded in custody, committed in custody for sentences or sent in custody for trial under Crime and Disorder Act (CDA) 1998 s51 or s51A.[7] Children who receive sentences of detention may be placed in a secure children's home (SCH), secure training centre (STC) or young offender institution (YOI):

- SCHs:
  - children aged 10–14 years
  - all children 10–11 years
  - particularly vulnerable 12–14 year olds (and sometimes older children up to 17)
- STCs:
  - children aged 12–17 years
  - 12–14 year old boys
  - 12–17 year old girls
  - vulnerable boys aged 15–17 years
- YOIs:
  - boys aged 15–21 years
  - under 18s held in separate units from 18–21 year olds[8]

21.4 Where a child is placed in the secure estate is determined by the Ministry of Justice Placement Service (see paras 11.112–11.117 on placements decisions). The decision about the most appropriate placement is based on the youth offending team's assessment of vulnerability using the Asset tool (see paras 17.98–17.101). Placement decisions can be challenged (see paras 11.11–11.119 on challenging a placement decision).

Measure of last report

21.5 The welfare principle requires the court to consider the impact of a custodial sentence. The Sentencing Council's *Sentencing children*

6 Powers of Criminal Courts (Sentencing) Act (PCC(S)A) 2000 s89(1).

7 PCC(S)A 2000 s89(2).

8 See paras 1.89–1.97 on the secure estate for children.

and young people: definitive guideline (2017)[9] sets out some of the welfare considerations that reinforce the importance that 'custody is a last resort':

- a custodial sentence could have a significant effect on the child's prospects and opportunities;
- children are likely to be more susceptible than an adult to the contaminating influences within a custodial setting;
- there is at higher reconviction rate for children who receive custodial sentences than non-custodial sentences;
- the effect on vulnerable children, particularly the risk of self-harm and suicide.

Deterrent sentences

21.6 The availability of deterrent sentencing for children has been a topic of some debate. The *Sentencing children and young people: definitive guideline* makes clear that until Criminal Justice Act (CJA) 2003 s142A is implemented, there is no statutory bar on courts using deterrent sentencing:

> . . . deterrence can be a factor in sentencing children and young people although it should be restricted to serious offences and can, and often will, be outweighed by consideration of the child or young person's welfare.[10]

21.7 Although deterrence sentencing is theoretically permissible, it is hard to conceive of a sentencing exercise when such a sentence could be compatible with the welfare principle (see paras 16.10–16.14 on welfare considerations).

Suspended sentences

21.8 Suspended sentences are not available for children. Custodial sentences may only be suspended for those aged 18 and above.[11]

Crossing a significant age threshold

21.9 The available sentencing disposals are determined by a child's age on the date of conviction (see paras 17.32–17.39 on crossing a

9 *Sentencing children and young people: definitive guideline*, 2017, para 6.49.

10 *Sentencing children and young people: definitive guideline*, para 1.10.

11 CJA 2003 s189.

significant age threshold between conviction and sentence). This may mean the maximum sentence available on the date of conviction is greater that that at the date of the offence. For defendants who turn 12, 15 or 18 between offence and conviction, the starting point is:

> [T[he sentence likely to have been imposed on the date at which the offence was committed.[12]
>
> [I]t will rarely be appropriate that a more severe sentence than the maximum that the court could have imposed at the time of the offences was committed should be imposed. However, a sentence at or close to that maximum may be appropriate.[13]

21.10 There is increasing recognition courts that courts should not consider turning 18 a 'cliff-edge' in relation to sentencing and young adults may receive more lenient sentences than older adults (see paras 17.46–17.47 on young adults).

Criminal record

21.11 Custodial sentences up to four years will become spent. Custodial sentences of six months or less are spent after 18 months, sentences over six months and up to 30 months are spent after two years, sentences over 30 months and up to four years are spent after three and a half years for children aged under 18 on the date of convictions (see para 25.24 on rehabilitation periods). Custodial sentences over four years and over are never spent.

Mandatory minimum sentences

21.12 Certain offences carry mandatory minimum sentences which are relevant for children as well as adults.

Bladed article/offensive weapon offences

Threatening offences

21.13 The following offences carry mandatory minimum sentences:

12 *Sentencing children and young people: definitive guideline*, para 6.2. Also see *R v Ghafoor* [2002) EWCA Crim 1857, and *R v DM* [2012] EWCA Crim 1649.

13 *Sentencing children and young people: definitive guideline*, para 6.3.

- threatening with an offensive weapon in a public place: Prevention of Crime Act (PCA) 1953 s1A;
- threatening with an article with blade/point in a public place: Criminal Justice Act (CJA) 1988 s139AA(1);
- threatening with an article with blade/point or offensive, weapon on school premises: CJA 1988 s139AA(1).

21.14 The minimum sentence for someone aged 16 or 17 on conviction is a four-month DTO. The minimum for those aged 18 and over on conviction a six months's custodial sentence.[14] For those aged under 16 on conviction, there is no minimum sentence.

21.15 For each of the offences, the court is not required to impose the minimum sentence if it is of the opinion that there are particular circumstances which relate to the offence or to the offender and it would make it unjust to do so in all the circumstances.[15]

Second knife offences

21.16 Criminal Justice and Courts Act 2015 s28 and Sch 5 amended PCA 1953 ss1 and 2 and CJA 1988 s139[16] create mandatory minimum custodial sentences for those aged 16 and over convicted of a second or subsequent offence of possessing a knife or offensive weapon under PCA 1953 s1 or of possessing an article with a blade or sharp point under CJA 1988 s139 (including possessing a bladed article on school premises under CJA 1988 s139A).

21.17 Certain pre-conditions are required:

- the offence must have been committed on or after 17 July 2015;[17] and
- the offender must have been 16 or over when the second offence was committed, and must have had at least one relevant previous conviction.[18]

Relevant previous convictions include simple possession and threatening offences under the PCA 1953 and the CJA 1988. As well as offences committed in Scotland, Northern Ireland or an EU member

14 PCA 1953 s1A(6) and CJA 1988 s139AA(8).
15 PCA 1953 s1A(5) and CJA 1988 s139AA(7).
16 Criminal Justice and Courts Act 2015 (Commencement No 2) Order 2015.
17 PCA 1953 s1(2A)(a) and CJA 1988 s139(6A)(b).
18 PCA 1953 s1(2A)(b) and CJA 1988 s139(6A)(c).

state which would have constituted the commission of a relevant offence in this jurisdiction and certain Armed Forces offences.[19]

21.18 The age of the offender, and the date of the previous offence are irrelevant, although may be an important consideration passing sentencing (see para 21.23 below).

21.19 The mandatory minimum sentence for someone aged 16 or 17 on conviction is a four-month DTO.[20] The mandatory minimum sentence for someone aged 18 and over on conviction is imprisonment for six months.[21] There is no minimum sentence for those aged below 16 on the date of offence.

21.20 The court must pass the mandatory minimum sentence unless it is of the opinion that 'there are particular circumstances which relate to the offence, to the previous offence or to the offender, and would make it unjust to do so in all the circumstances'.[22]

Sentencing guidelines

21.21 The Sentencing Council published *Bladed articles and offensive weapons: definitive guideline* in June 2018, which includes a separate guideline dedicated to children.

21.22 When sentencing offences which are subject to the mandatory minimum sentences, credit for guilty plea should still be given.[23] In addition, days spent on remand or subject to a qualifying electronic curfew should be reduced from the sentence.

21.23 When deciding whether to impose the a mandatory minimum sentence for a 'second strike' offence, consideration should be given to the seriousness of the first offence and the period of time that has elapsed between offending as this may impact on whether it is unjust to impose the mandatory sentence.[24]

21.24 The guideline refers to the statutory duty to have regard to the welfare of children and states that 'in certain cases the concerns about the welfare of the child may be so significant that the court considers it unjust to impose the statutory minimum sentence'.[25]

19 PCA 1953 (1ZA) and CJA 1988 s139AZA.

20 PCA 1953 s1(2C)(b) and CJA 1988 s139(6C)(b).

21 PCA 1953 s1(2C)(a) and CJA 1988 s139(6C)(a).

22 PCA 1953 s1(2B) and CJA 1988 s139(6B).

23 Sentencing Council, *Bladed articles and offensive weapons: definitive guideline*, 2018, p17; *Sentencing children and young people: definitive guideline*, 2017, para 5.21; see para 21.63.

24 *Bladed articles and offensive weapons: definitive guideline*, p19.

25 *Bladed articles and offensive weapons: definitive guideline*, p19.

21.25 The offence specific guideline must be read alongside the *Sentencing children and young people: definitive guideline* which provides comprehensive guidance on the sentencing principles and welfare considerations that the court should have in mind when sentencing children.[26]

21.26 Further, the case-law that applies to firearms (see para 21.36 below) that demands a holistic approach to considering whether to disapply the mandatory minimum sentence may also be relevant to these offences.

Firearms

21.27 Mandatory minimum sentences apply to most offences contrary to Firearms Act 1968 s5: s5(1)(a), (ab), (aba), (ac), (ad), (ae), (af), (c) and (1A)(a).[27]

21.28 The mandatory sentence only applies to those aged 16 or above on the date of the offence. For those aged under 16 on the date of offence there is no minimum sentence.

21.29 The mandatory sentence applies where:

- the offence listed above was committed on or after 22 January 2004 *and* the offender was aged 16, 17 or over 21 years of age when the offence was committed; or
- the offence was committed on or after 28 May 2007 when the offender was aged 16 or over *and* is aged 18, 19 or 20 at the date of conviction.[28]

21.30 Due to an inadvertent mistake when passing the initial legislation, the minimum sentence does not apply to those who committed the offence before 28 May 2007 and were aged 18, 19 and 20 on the date of conviction.[29] Prior to the Firearms (Sentencing) (Transitory Provisions) Order 2007,[30] the definition of 'appropriate custodial sentence' did not include sentences of detention. That order came into force on 28 May 2007.

21.31 For those aged 16 or 17, the minimum sentence is three years' detention. Therefore any child aged 16 or 17 on the date of the alleged offence must be sent to the Crown Court for trial.[31] The minimum

26 *Bladed articles and offensive weapons: definitive guideline*, p15.
27 Firearms Act 1968 s51A.
28 Firearms Act 1968 s51A(4)(a).
29 *R v Campbell* [2006] EWCA Crim 726.
30 SI No 1324.
31 Magistrates' Court Act 1980 s24(1B).

sentence is five years' imprisonment or detention in a young offender institute for those aged 18 or above.

21.32 The same minimum sentences apply to the following offences committed on or after 6 April 2007, where the firearm mentioned is a prohibited weapon under Firearms Act 1968 s5(1)(a)–(af), (c) and (1A)(a):

- Firearms Act 1968 s16 (possession of firearm with intent to injure);
- Firearms Act 1968 s16A (possession of firearm with intent to cause fear of violence);
- Firearms Act 1968 s17 (use of firearm to resist arrest);
- Firearms Act 1968 s18 (carrying firearm with criminal intent);
- Firearms Act 1968 s19 (carrying a firearm in a public place);
- Firearms Act 1968 s20(1) (trespassing in a building with a firearm); and
- Violent Crime Reduction Act 2006 s28 (using another person to mind a dangerous weapon).

21.33 Those aged 16 or 17 at the time of the offence and under 18 on the date of conviction have a minimum sentence of three years' detention under PCC(S)A 2000 s91.[32] Those aged 18 or over on the date of conviction are subject to a five-year minimum sentence.[33]

21.34 It shall be an aggravating feature where a person aged 18 or over uses a person under 18 to mind the weapon, and such a finding must be stated in open court as an aggravating feature.[34]

Exceptional circumstances

21.35 There can be no reduction to below the minimum sentence in order to give credit for a guilty plea. However, the court may depart from the minimum sentence in 'exceptional circumstances'.[35]

21.36 In *R v Rehman*[36] the Court of Appeal confirmed that in order to interpret the legislation in a manner compatible with European Court of Human Rights (ECHR) Article 3, the court should take a holistic approach and exceptional circumstances may relate to the offence and/or the offender. It is not necessary to show that one particular factor is exceptional – the court should consider all the

32 Violent Crime Reduction Act 2006 s29(3)(b), (6).
33 Violent Crime Reduction Act 2006 s29(5).
34 Violent Crime Reduction Act 2006 s29(11) and (12).
35 Violent Crime Reduction Act 2006 s29(6).
36 [2006] 1 Cr App R (S) 77.

circumstances involved and whether together they amount to exceptional circumstances.

21.37 The age of the individual must be a relevant factor when considering whether exceptional circumstances justify a lesser sentence. The Sentencing Council's remarks on other minimum sentences (at para 21.25 above) may also be of assistance.

Court's duties

Pre-requisites before imposing a custodial sentence

Legal representation

21.38 The court can only impose a custodial sentence if a defendant is legally represented[37] (unless the defendant has refused or failed to apply for legal representation having been informed of the right to apply, or legal representation has been withdrawn due to the defendant's conduct).[38]

Pre-sentence report

21.39 The court must obtain and consider a pre-sentence report before imposing a custodial sentence (see paras 17.103–17.104 on using an existing report).[39] A custodial sentence may only be imposed when the offence is 'so serious that neither a fine alone nor a community sentence is justified,[40] the court must then consider whether to impose a YRO with intensive supervision and surveillance or fostering[41] (also see paras 20.86–20.106 on intensive YROs).

Determining whether the threshold for a discretionary custodial sentence has been passed

21.40 A court must decide whether the offence(s) that the court is dealing with have crossed the custodial threshold and no other sanction is

37 PCC(S)A 2000 s83(2). Please note defendants aged 21 and over who are not legally represented can receive custodial sentences if they had previously received a sentence of imprisonment (PCC(S)A 2000 s83(1)). This does not apply to defendants aged under 21.

38 PCC(S)A 2000 s83(3), (4).

39 CJA 2003 s156(3)(a).

40 CJA 2003 s152(2).

41 *Sentencing children and young people: definitive guideline*, para 6.42.

justified.[42] To determine the seriousness of the offence, the court must consider:

- All information that is available about the circumstances of the offence, and any associated offence(s), including any aggravating and mitigating factors;[43]
- The culpability of the child defendant, their chronological, developmental and emotional age[44] as well as the extent of pre-planning, role, level of peer pressure or other coercion, awareness of the consequences of their actions;[45]
- The likelihood of further offences being committed (this will form part of the pre-sentence report);[46]
- The Sentencing Guidelines for children and young people and any offence specific guidance for children and young people).[47]

Duty to give reasons

21.41 A court must give reasons for making a decision that the threshold for a discretionary custodial sentence has been passed.[48] The court must state its reasons for being satisfied that no other sanction would be appropriate, in particular, why an intensive YRO with ISS or fostering could not be justified.[49]

Determining the length of a custodial sentence

Calculating the length of a custodial sentence

Once the court has determined the custodial threshold has been crossed, it must then determine the length of the sentence. The court must take the following steps:

1. Decide whether the custodial threshold is passed:
   - Refer to *Sentencing children and young people: definitive guideline.*

42 CJA 2003 s152(2); and *Sentencing children and young people: definitive guideline,* paras 4.7 and 6.42.

43 CJA 2003 s156(1).

44 *Sentencing children and young people: definitive guideline,* paras 4.8–10.

45 *Sentencing children and young people: definitive guideline,* para 4.5.

46 CJA 2003 s174(8).

47 Coroners and Justice Act 2009 s125(1) places a mandatory duty every court to follow any relevant sentencing guidelines when sentencing defendants.

48 CJA 2003 ss174(4)(b), 152(2).

49 *Sentencing children and young people: definitive guideline,* para 6.42.

- Refer to any offence-specific guidance for children and young people to assess whether custody is the most appropriate disposal.[50]
- Determine whether a fine or community disposal is appropriate.

2. If the court decides the custody threshold has been passed, consider whether an intensive YRO (with ISS or fostering) could be justified (see paras 20.86–20.106).
3. Refer to *Sentencing children and young people: definitive guideline* to determine length and any offence-specific guidance for children and young people.
   - If there is no child-specific offence guideline, the court may use the adult guideline with an appropriate reduction, half to two thirds of the adult sentence for 15 – 17 year olds and a greater reduction for those aged under 15,[51] taking into account the child's chronological, emotional and developmental age and maturity.
   - Individual factors may require the court to depart from any adult guideline (see para 21.42).
   - Courts are discouraged from imposing short custodial sentences (see para 21.46).
   - Custodial sentences will be particularly rare for children aged 14 and under (see para 21.47).
4. Determine any level of reduction for guilty plea (see paras 21.48–21.65).
5. State the amount of the reduction.
6. Apply the reduction.
7. Calculate any time spent on a qualifying curfew or in youth detention accommodation (21.66–21.67).
8. State the amount of the reduction.
9. Apply the reduction.
10. Follow any further steps in the offence-specific guideline to determine the final sentence.
11. Consider whether the custodial term is the shortest possible length (see para 21.45). Any case that warrants a detention and training order (DTO) of less than four months must result in a non-custodial sentence (see para 21.46).

50 Coroners and Justice Act 2009 s125(1) places a mandatory duty every court to follow any relevant sentencing guidelines when sentencing defendants. Also see *Sentencing children and young people: definitive guideline*, 'Custodial sentences' p28.

51 *Sentencing children and young people: definitive guideline*, para 6.46.

Using adult guidelines for determining custodial sentences for children

21.42 As a starting point, whenever sentencing a child, the court will refer to the *Sentencing children and young people: definitive guideline* and any offence-specific guidance for children.[52] If there is no child-specific offence guideline, the sentencer may consult the adult guideline as a 'preliminary consideration'[53] in deciding where custody is appropriate and if so, the appropriate length of sentence. Courts are given a wide discretion and encouraged to give greatest consideration to individual factors and may depart from the adult sentencing guidance.[54]

> When considering the relevant adult guideline, the court *may* feel it appropriate to apply a sentence broadly within the region of *half to two thirds* of the adult sentence for those aged 15–17 and *allow a greater reduction* for those aged under 15. This is only a rough guide and must not be applied mechanistically [emphasis added].

21.43 In most cases when considering the appropriate reduction, the child's 'emotional and developmental age and maturity . . . is of at least equal importance as their chronological age'.[55]

21.44 The court must give individualised consideration to the sentencing of a child:

> The individual factors relating to the offence and the child or young person are of greatest importance and may present good reason to impose a sentence out of this range.[56]

Shortest possible length

21.45 When a court passes a custodial sentence, it must be for the shortest possible term commensurate with the seriousness of the offence and any associated offence(s) taking into account the circumstances, the child's age and maturity.[57] In some cases, this will result in a non-custodial sentence because children cannot receive a DTO shorter than four months (see para 21.46).

52 Coroners and Justice Act 2009 s125(1) places a mandatory duty every court to follow any relevant sentencing guidelines when sentencing defendants. *Sentencing children and young people: definitive guideline*, p28.

53 *Sentencing children and young people: definitive guideline*, p28 and para 6.45.

54 *Sentencing children and young people: definitive guideline*, para 6.46.

55 *Sentencing children and young people: definitive guideline*, para 6.46.

56 *Sentencing children and young people: definitive guideline*, para 6.47.

57 CJA 2003 s153(2); and *Sentencing children and young people: definitive guideline*, para 6.43.

Short sentences are discouraged

21.46 Courts are discouraged from imposing short custodial sentences on children as they disrupt education, training as well as family relationships and support.[58] Where the determination of sentence length leads the court to conclude that only a short custodial sentence could be justified, this may lead the court to conclude that an intensive community sentence would be the most appropriate sentence. Any offence that warrants a DTO of less than four months 'must result in a non-custodial sentence'.[59]

Custodial sentences for children aged ten to 14 years old

21.47 Custodial sentences will be 'particularly rare for children aged 10–14'.[60] 13 and 14 year olds can only receive a DTO if they are a persistent offender (see paras 21.76–21.78 on persistent offender). If a custodial sentence *is* imposed, it should be for a shorter length of time than the equivalent sentence that a 15–17 year old would receive for the same offence.[61]

Determine the level of reduction for a guilty plea[62]

Overview

21.48 The maximum reduction for a guilty plea is *one-third*. This would be for a guilty plea at the first stage of proceedings, this is defined as the first hearing at the youth court or adult magistrates' court at which a plea is sought[63] although a plea at a later stage may still attract full credit (see paras 21.54–27.62).

21.49 The maximum level of reduction for a guilty plea indicated after the first stage of proceedings is *one-quarter* (subject to the exceptions).[64]

21.50 The maximum level of reduction should be decreased on a sliding scale to a maximum of *one-tenth* on the first day of trial and decreasing further, even to zero, if entered during a trial (subject to the exceptions).[65]

58 *Sentencing children and young people: definitive guideline*, para 6.47.
59 *Sentencing children and young people: definitive guideline*, para 6.43.
60 *Sentencing children and young people: definitive guideline*, para 6.48.
61 *Sentencing children and young people: definitive guideline*, para 6.48.
62 CJA 2003 s144.
63 *Sentencing children and young people: definitive guideline*, para 5.5.
64 *Sentencing children and young people: definitive guideline*, para 5.6.
65 *Sentencing children and young people: definitive guideline*, para 5.7.

Determining the level of reduction

21.51 The court should consider the principles set out in guilty plea guidance within the *Sentencing children and young people: definitive guideline.*[66]

21.52 It is worth noting that early indication of guilt – such as admissions in police interview, co-operation with the investigation and demonstrations of remorse – should *not* attract greater reduction for guilty plea but are potential mitigating factors.[67]

21.53 The strength of the evidence against a child should not be taken into account when determining the level of reduction.[68]

Full credit for a delayed guilty plea

Further information, assistance or advice necessary

21.54 Full credit should be given to children for pleading guilty after the first stage of proceedings:

- where there were particular circumstances which reduced the child's ability to understand what was alleged or otherwise 'made it unreasonable to expect the child or young person to indicate a guilty plea *sooner than was done*';[69]
- where it is necessary 'to receive advice and/or have sight of evidence' in order to understand whether a child is guilty of the offences charged (as distinguished from delays in order to assess the strength of the prosecution evidence and the prospects of a finding of guilt or acquittal).[70]

21.55 This would include cases where delay arises because an expert's opinion is required to advise on fitness to plead and/or effective participation, or to determine whether the child had a defence such as diminished responsibility[71] (see chapter 4 on effective participation and fitness to plead).

21.56 Where the court is determining the appropriate reduction, the court should take note that it may be more reasonable for a child to rely on legal advice not to enter a plea at an earlier stage, for example while waiting for more evidence or reports than an adult. Adults are

66 *Sentencing children and young people: definitive guideline*, paras 5.1–5.4.
67 *Sentencing children and young people: definitive guideline*, para 5.4.
68 *Sentencing children and young people: definitive guideline*, para 5.4.
69 *Sentencing children and young people: definitive guideline*, para 5.16.
70 *Sentencing children and young people: definitive guideline*, para 5.17.
71 *R v Markham and Edwards* [2017] EWCA Crim 739.

more likely to be able to make an informed decision based on the assessment of the evidence.[72]

21.57 There may be rare circumstances where a discount for a guilty plea is still applicable after the trial, where, for example the child has pleaded guilty to the factual basis of the offence and is running a defence on medical evidence, which both narrows the issues, and also shows that the child is admitting culpability.[73]

Newton hearings and special reasons

21.58 Where the child's version of events is rejected in a Newton hearing or special reasons hearing, the reduction should normally be halved. Where witnesses are called, further reduction may be appropriate.[74]

Finding of guilt for lesser or different offence

21.59 Where a child is found guilty of a lesser or different offence and has made an unequivocal indication of a guilty plea, the appropriate level of reduction for a guilty plea should be given depending on when the indication was made and whether any exceptions apply.[75]

Applying the guilty plea reduction to detention and training orders

21.60 As DTOs are for fixed, prescribed periods, the application of the guilty plea reduction to DTOs may result in a sentence that falls between two prescribed periods. If this situation arises, 'the court must impose the lesser of those two periods', even though '[t]his may result in a reduction than greater than a third in order that the full reduction is given and a lawful sentence imposed'.[76]

21.61 The reduction in sentence for guilty plea may reduce a DTO to less than four months and therefore reduce the sentence to a community sentence.[77]

Sentencing up 24 months following a guilty plea

21.62 The court may impose a detention and training order of up to 24 months even when a child has pleaded guilty, 'if the offence is one

72 *R v Markham and Edwards* [2017] EWCA Crim 739 per Sir Brian Leveson, at para 72.

73 *R v Markham and Edwards* [2017] EWCA Crim 739 at paras 70–73.

74 *Sentencing children and young people: definitive guideline*, para 5.18.

75 *Sentencing children and young people: definitive guideline*, para 5.19.

76 *Sentencing children and young people: definitive guideline*, para 5.9.

77 *Sentencing children and young people: definitive guideline*, para 5.10.

which, but for the plea, would have attracted a sentence of detention in excess of 24 months'[78] under PCC(S)A s91 (see paras 21.120–21.131 on section 91 long-term detention).

Applying the guilty plea guidance to mandatory minimum sentences

21.63 Whether the reduction for guilty plea guidance is applicable varies according to different offences:

1) *Firearms*: The reduction for guilty plea only applies to the minimum sentence under Firearms Act 1968 s51A provided it does not reduce the length of sentence below the required minimum term.[79]
2) *Knife offences*:[80] The reduction for guilty plea guidance applies. Where the starting point for a child who is aged 16 or 17 who has been found guilty under Prevention of Crime Act (PCA) 1953 s1 or s1A; or CJA 1988 s136, s139AA or s139A would be at least a four-month detention and training order, the court may take into account the guilty plea guidance and principles and 'impose any sentence that it considers appropriate'.[81] This means the court can impose a non-custodial sentence where a child aged 16 or 17 pleads guilty.[82]

Applying the guilty plea guidance to mandatory life sentences for murder

21.64 The general principles of the reduction for guilty plea are applicable in relation to mandatory life sentences for murder, including the exceptions. The guidelines are set out in the *Sentencing children and young people: definitive guideline* at paras 5.22–5.25.

21.65 When the court imposes a mandatory life sentence for murder, the maximum reduction is one-sixth of the minimum term and the maximum reduction must not exceed five years.[83]

Calculating reduction for time on qualifying curfew (tag) or remanded in youth detention accommodation

21.66 A child who has spent time on a curfew of nine hours or more with electronic monitoring qualifies for a reduction of any subsequent

78 *Sentencing children and young people: definitive guideline*, para 5.14 and see para 17.
79 *Sentencing children and young people: definitive guideline*, para 5.20.
80 PCA 1953 s1 or s1A; or CJA 1988 s136, s139AA or s139A.
81 *Sentencing children and young people: definitive guideline*, para 5.21.
82 Sentencing Council, *Bladed articles and offensive weapons: definitive guideline*, 2018, pp17–18.
83 *Sentencing children and young people: definitive guideline*, para 5.25.

custodial sentence. Only curfews with an electronic monitoring requirement (tag) meet the requirements. *Each day a child is subject to a qualifying curfew entitles them to half a day to be deducted* from any subsequent custodial sentence. The court must determine the number of days to be deducted (rounding up where necessary) and reduce the total sentence length.[84] (See also para 11.78–11.81 on electronic monitoring, time spent on curfew.)

21.67 If the court is imposing a detention and training order, the calculation for *each day a child is subject to a qualifying curfew entitles them to one day to be deducted* – following the principle in *R v Eagles* (see paras 21.96–21.97).[85]

Custodial sentences in the youth court

Overview

21.68 In the youth court, the only available custodial sentence is a DTO of up to 24 months. The adult magistrates' court has no power to sentence a child to a custodial sentence – if an adult magistrates' court dealing with a child considers that custody is an appropriate option, the court must remit back to the youth court for sentence.[86]

21.69 Ten and 11 year olds cannot receive a DTO. A DTO can be imposed on children aged 12–17 years old, but is only available for 12–14 year olds if they are deemed a persistent offender (see paras 21.76–21.79 on persistent offenders).

21.70 The youth court and adult magistrates' court have the power to commit grave crimes for sentence, even after a finding of guilt (see paras 17.11–17.13 on committal of grave crimes for sentence). The youth court and adult magistrates' court also have the power to commit children to the Crown Court for sentence if it appears to the court the criteria for the imposition of a sentence under CJA 2003 s226B would be met (see paras 17.14–17.15 on committal for sentence – dangerousness).

84 CJA 2003 s240A.

85 *R v Eagles* [2006] EWCA Crim 2368; *Sentencing children and young people: definitive guideline*, para 6.53; see para 21.

86 PCC(S)A 2000 s8(2).

Detention and training order

Overview

21.71 A DTO is a custodial sentence for children aged 12–17 years old. The first half of the sentence will be spent in custody and the second half will be spent in the community supervised by the youth offending team (YOT). The focus of these sentences should be to spend a lot of time involved in training and education to help children stop offending when their sentence is finished.

Availability

21.72 A detention and training order is the only custodial sentence available in the youth court. It is available for defendants aged 12–17 years old. Whilst the date of conviction determines the court's sentencing powers it will 'rarely be appropriate that a more severe sentence' than the maximum that the court could have imposed given the child's age at the time of the offence be imposed[87] (see paras 17.32–17.39 on crossing a significant age threshold). Therefore it would be rare for the youth court to impose a DTO on a child who committed an offence aged 10 or 11.

21.73 A DTO may also be imposed in the Crown Court, but the adult magistrates' court has no power to impose DTOs.[88]

21.74 DTOs are particularly rare for children aged 14 or under[89] and may only be imposed on children aged 12–14 years if they are deemed to be a persistent offender (see paras 21.76–21.79).[90] DTOs are not available for children aged ten and 11.[91]

Court's duties

21.75 A court may only impose a DTO if

- the child is legally represented;[92]
- the offence is imprisonable (see paras 21.85–21.86 on non-imprisonable offences for children);

87 *Sentencing children and young people: definitive guideline*, para 6.3.

88 See paras 17.16–17.18 on available sentences in the adult magistrates' court.

89 *Sentencing children and young people: definitive guideline*, para 6.10.

90 PCC(S)A 2000 s100(2).

91 PCC(S)A 2000 s100(2)(b)(ii) – requires an order by the to make detention and training orders available for 10 and 11 year olds.

92 PCC(S)A 2000 s83(2).

- 'a custodial sentence is unavoidable'[93] and the court has considered all alternatives to custody including an intensive YRO;
- a custodial sentence is a 'measure of last resort';[94]
- the court has taken into account that the appropriate sentence for most first-time offenders who plead guilty to an imprisonable offence will be a mandatory referral order (see paras 21.79–21.81 for children on the cusp of custody).

Persistent offender – 12–14 year olds

21.76 There is no statutory definition of 'persistent offender'. The question of whether a child has achieved a degree of persistence in his or her offending is a decision for the sentencing court.

21.77 The *Sentencing children and young people: definitive guideline* provides guidance to sentencers:

> A child or young person who has committed one previous offence cannot reasonably be classed as a persistent offender . . .[95]
>
> [A] child or young person who has committed two or more previous offences should not necessarily be assumed to be one. To determine if the behaviour is persistent the nature of the previous offences and the lapse of time between the offences would need to be considered.[96,97]
>
> If there have been three findings of guilt in the past 12 months for imprisonable offences of a comparable nature (or the child or young person has been made the subject of orders . . . in relation to an imprisonable offence [such as restorative justice disposals and conditional cautions]) then the court could certainly justify classing the child or young person as a persistent offender.[98]

21.78 A number of principles can be drawn from case-law and the guidance set out in the *Sentencing children and young people: definitive guideline:*[99]

- A court may take into account 'previous contacts with authority as a result of criminal behaviour' that involve admissions of guilt such as out of court disposals including restorative justice disposals and conditional cautions.[100]

93 *Sentencing children and young people: definitive guideline*, para 6.51.
94 UNCRC Article 37; *Sentencing children and young people: definitive guideline*, paras 1.3 and 6.42.
95 *Sentencing children and young people: definitive guideline*, para 6.6.
96 *R v M* [2008] EWCA Crim 3329.
97 *Sentencing children and young people: definitive guideline*, para 6.8.
98 *Sentencing children and young people: definitive guideline*, para 6.7.
99 Paras 6.4–6.10.
100 *R v DB* [2001] Cr App R 113; and *Sentencing children and young people: definitive guideline*.

- If a child has not had an opportunity to address his or her behaviour through meaningful intervention with the local YOT, then the court should consider whether an alternative sentence may have a reasonable prospect of preventing re-offending.[101]
- A court should take into consideration the nature of the previous offences and the lapse of time between the offences.[102]
- 'When a child or young person is being sentenced in a single appearance for a series of separate, comparable offences committed over a short space of time then the court could justifiably consider the child to be a persistent offender, despite the fact there had been no previous findings of guilt.[103] In these cases the court should consider whether the child or young person has had prior opportunity to address their offending behaviour before imposing one of the optional sentences available for persistent offenders only . . .'[104]
- The age of the child at the date of the offence is relevant if the child crosses a significant age threshold between the date of the offence and the date of conviction (see paras 2.9–2.10 on crossing a significant age threshold).
- 'Even where the child or young person is found to be a persistent offender, a court is not obliged to impose one of the optional sentences. The approach should still be individualistic and all other considerations still apply. *Custodial sentences must be a last resort for all children and young people* and there is an expectation that they will be particularly rare for children and young people aged 14 or under.'[105]

First time offenders on the cusp of custody

21.79 Youth courts dealing with children who have offended for the first time and have pleaded guilty to committing an offence 'which is on the cusp of custody' will have to decide whether to impose a mandatory referral order or a detention and training order (unless the court is considering a hospital order). In such cases the *Sentencing children and young people: definitive guideline* (and *Referral Order Guidance*[106]) advise youth offending teams 'to convene a Youth Offender Panel prior to sentence (sometimes referred to as a "pseudo-panel" or "pre-panel")' where the child

101 See, for example, *Sentencing children and young people: definitive guideline*, para 6.8.
102 *R v M* [2008] EWCA Crim 3329.
103 *R v S* [2000] 1 Cr App R (S) 18
104 *Sentencing children and young people: definitive guideline*, para 6.8.
105 *Sentencing children and young people: definitive guideline*, para 6.10.
106 *Referral Order Guidance*, October 2018, paras 3.22–3.27.

will be asked to agree an intensive referral order contract.[107] This is intended to give the court a meaningful alternative to custody and enables the sentencing court to consider a proposed contract when deciding between an intensive referral order or custody.

21.80 While an adult magistrates' court can impose a referral order, the court cannot impose a custodial sentence (see paras 17.16–17.18 on available sentences in the adult magistrates' court). In such cases the adult magistrates' court will remit the matter to the youth court.

21.81 Crown Courts are not bound by the mandatory referral order conditions[108] – the Crown Court has a wider number of sentencing options available for first time offenders who plead guilty, including intensive youth rehabilitation orders. and can sentence to any sentence that they can impose on a child.

Length

21.82 DTOs can only be imposed for specified lengths:

- 4 months;
- 6 months;
- 8 months;
- 10 months;
- 12 months;
- 18 months; or
- 24 months.[109]

Consecutive detention and training orders

21.83 A court may impose consecutive detention and training orders, to commence on the expiry of any other detention and training order, whether the order is imposed by the same court or by any other court.[110] The orders may be imposed on different occasions, each order must be for one of the specified lengths (4, 6, 8, 10, 12, 18 or 24 months) but there is no requirement that the aggregate length is one of the specified lengths[111] provided the consecutive terms does not exceed in total 24 months.[112]

107 *Sentencing children and young people: definitive guideline*, para 6.21.

108 The Crown Court does not have the power to pass a referral order, however a Crown Court judge has the power to reconvene as a district judge under Courts Act 2003 s66 – see paras 17.22–17.27 on remittal to the youth court.

109 PCC(S)A 2000 s101(1).

110 CDA 1998 s74(2)(b).

111 *R v N (George Michael) (a juvenile)* [2001] 1 Cr App R (S) 116.

112 CDA 1998 s73(5).

Crossing the custody threshold?

21.84 In determining whether the minimum four-month DTO threshold is reached, terms less than four months cannot be imposed consecutively so as to aggregate to four months.[113]

Non-imprisonable offences for children

21.85 A youth court dealing with a child for offences where the maximum adult sentence is three months' imprisonment have no power to impose a DTO because the minimum prescribed term is a four-month DTO.[114]

21.86 The following offences where this principle applies are therefore non-imprisonable for children:

- criminal damage (where the damage is below £5,000)[115] – maximum penalty: three months;
- failure to surrender[116] – maximum penalty: three months;
- breach of dispersal order[117] – maximum penalty: three months;
- motor vehicle interference[118] – maximum penalty: three months;
- being found on enclosed premises[119] – maximum penalty: three months;
- obstruct/resist a police constable in execution of duty[120] – maximum penalty: one month;
- drugs – class A – fail/refuse to provide a sample[121] – maximum penalty: one month;
- fail to stop for a constable in a section 60 designated area[122] – maximum penalty: one month.

113 *R v Ganley* [2001] 1 Cr App R (S) 17; *R v Kent Youth Court ex p Kingwell* [1999] 1 Cr App R (S) 263.

114 *P v Leeds Youth Court* [2006] EWHC 2527 (Admin). In *P*, the High Court quashed a four-month DTO imposed on *P*, a 17-year-old, for criminal damage where the maximum sentence an adult could have received was a three-month custodial sentence.

115 Criminal Damage Act 1971 s1(1).

116 Bail Act 1976 s6.

117 Anti-social Behaviour, Crime and Policing Act 2014 s39.

118 Criminal Attempts Act 1981 s9.

119 Vagrancy Act 1824 s4.

120 Police Act 1996 s89(2).

121 Police and Criminal Evidence Act 1984 s63B.

122 Criminal Justice and Public Order Act 1994 s60(8).

Maximum detention and training order sentencing powers

21.87 The youth court has the power to impose up to a 24-month DTO on children; by comparison, the adult magistrates' court has the power to impose up to six months' imprisonment on adults[123] (12 months' for two either-way offences sentenced consecutively[124]). To address the potential risk of injustice, that children could receive longer sentences than adults charged with the same offences, sentencers are limited to the maximum length of custodial sentence available for an adult (See paras 21.88–21.89).

One or more summary offences

21.88 When a court is dealing with a child defendant for one or more summary only offences 'the aggregate sentence is limited to a maximum of six months'.[125] This is because the maximum aggregate adult sentence is six months' imprisonment for summary only offences.[126] In such cases, 'the court *may* make a modest *additional* reduction to the *overall* sentence to reflect the benefits derived from the guilty plea'.[127]

Therefore in *B v Leeds Crown Court* a sentence of eight months DTO for two summary-only offences was quashed.[128]

Applying the guilty plea reduction (detention and training orders)

21.90 As DTOs are for fixed, prescribed periods, the application of the guilty plea reduction to DTOs may require the court to impose greater than a third reduction (see para 21.60). Credit for a guilty plea may reduce a DTO to less than four months and therefore reduce the sentence to a community sentence (see para 21.61) or the court may impose a detention and training order of up to the maximum of 24 months even when a child has pleaded guilty, 'if the

123 Magistrates' Court Act 1980 s133(1).

124 Magistrates' Court Act 1980 s133(2).

125 *B v Leeds Crown Court and another* [2016] EWHC 1230 (Admin); *P v Leeds Youth Court* [2006] EWHC 2527 (Admin).

126 Magistrates' Court Act 1980 s130(1).

127 *Sentencing children and young people: definitive guideline*, para 5.13.

128 [2016] EWHC 1230 (Admin).

offence is one which, but for the plea, would have attracted a sentence of detention in excess of 24 months' (see para 21.62).[129]

Credit for time on remand (detention and training orders)

21.91 The court determining the length of a DTO shall take into account any period for which the offender has been remanded in custody.[130] However, time spent remanded in youth detention accommodation will not be automatically deducted from a DTO as happens with other custodial sentences, because the provision that allows the custodial setting to deduct time served does not apply to DTOs.[131] Therefore, any time spent in youth detention accommodation must be taken into account by the sentencer when determining the sentence and calculating the length of the order.

21.92 This needs to be modified for DTOs to give effect to the principle in *R v Eagles*[132] which established that children are entitled to credit to time on remand, and that therefore the length of the DTO needs to be reduced by the court in order to reflect time already spent in a custodial setting.

21.93 The *Sentencing children and young people: definitive guideline* provides that:[133]

> A DTO can be made only for the periods prescribed – 4, 6, 8, 10, 12, 18 or 24 months. Any time spent on remand in custody or on bail subject to a qualifying curfew condition should be taken into account when calculating the length of the order. The accepted approach is to **double the time spent on remand** before deciding the appropriate period of detention, in order to ensure that the regime is in line with that applied to adult offenders. After doubling the time spent on remand the court should then adopt the nearest prescribed period available for a DTO. [Emphasis added.]

21.94 As DTOs may only be made for prescribed periods, the sentencer will be required to 'adopt the nearest prescribed period available'. Arguably, the court should take the same approach as with applying

129 *Sentencing children and young people: definitive guideline*, para 5.9.

130 PCC(S)A 2000 s101(8)(a).

131 CJA 2003 s240ZA deducts the number of days an offender was remanded in custody in connection with the offence or a related offence from the time they will served as part of the sentence of imprisonment or detention.

132 [2006] EWCA Crim 2368.

133 At para 6.53.

credit for guilty pleas, 'the court must impose the lesser of those two periods'.[134] The purpose of having prescribed periods for DTOs is to keep custodial periods for children as short as possible, and to do otherwise would be to treat them more harshly than adults.

21.95 The court should state the period that has been deducted from the order so the child being sentenced is fully aware that time spent on remand has been deducted.

Applying the reduction for qualifying curfew to detention and training orders

21.96 Children who spend time on bail with a qualifying curfew condition are entitled to have this time deducted from a custodial sentence.[135] A qualifying curfew condition for children is a curfew condition of 9 hours or more with an electronic monitoring condition (often called 'a tag').[136]

21.97 Criminal Justice Act 2003 s240A(3) sets out the approach a court should take to calculating the credit period for an adult offender. This needs to be modified for DTOs to give effect to the principle in *R v Eagles* (see paras 21.92–21.95 above). The court should calculate the credit period as follows:

> Step 1
> Add–
> (a) the first day on which the offender's bail was first subject to the relevant conditions (even if it was not a whole day),
> and
> (b) the number of other days on which the offender's bail was subject to those conditions (but exclude the last of those days if the offender spends the last part of it in custody).
>
> Step 2
> Deduct the number of days on which the offender, whilst on bail subject to the relevant conditions, was also–
> (a) subject to any requirement imposed for the purpose of securing the electronic monitoring of the offender's compliance with a curfew requirement, or
> (b) on temporary release under rules made under section 47 of the Prison Act 1952.

134 *Sentencing children and young people: definitive guideline*, para 5.9.

135 PCC(S)A 2000 s101(8)(b); and CJA 2003 s240A.

136 CJA 2003 s240A(12).

Step 3
From the remainder, deduct the number of days during that remainder on which the offender has broken either or both of the relevant conditions.[137]

Applying the reduction for a qualifying curfew while remanded to local authority accommodation

21.98 The statutory provision to credit time spent on bail subject to a qualifying curfew does not provide for children in an analogous position who are remanded to local authority accommodation with an electronically monitored curfew of at least nine hours a day (see paras 21.91–21.95 on qualifying curfew).[138] The Court of Appeal has approved crediting time spent on a qualifying curfew (or other restrictive conditions, if the sentencer considers it in the interests of justice). The only way such credit can be awarded is for it to be included in the calculation of sentence length and the sentence reduced accordingly by the sentencing judge.[139]

Release and supervision

Early release – home detention curfew (HDC)

21.99 Children serving a DTO of less than eight months are not eligible for early release. For children serving a DTO of eight months or more there is a presumption in favour of early release (unless their behaviour in custody is seriously violent or disruptive or they are charged with a sexual offence or certain serious offences of serious violence).[140]

21.100 Home Detention Curfew (HDC) under PCC(S)A 2000 s102(4) allows children to be released up to 4.5 months (135 days) before their conditional release date provided they have served a quarter of their sentence. Children released under s102(4) will be subject to an electronically monitored curfew from the date of early release until the half way point of the DTO.

137 CJA 2003 s240A(3).

138 *R v Secretary of State for the Home Department ex p A* [2000] UKHL 4, [2000] 2 AC 276.

139 *R v A* [2019] EWCA Crim 106.

140 PCC(S)A 2000 s102(4). Also see Youth Justice Board, Case Management Guidance Section 7: Custody and resettlement, 15 October 2014, para 6.6.

Supervision after release

21.101 A child on a DTO will be subject to supervision on his or her release at the half-way point until the end of the order (or longer if released on HDC).[141] The supervision requirements will be discussed with the child before the written notice of supervision,[142] setting out the requirements, is finalised and given to the child.

21.102 In deciding the supervision requirements, the non-statutory guidance, *Notices of supervision: guidance for youth offending teams* (updated 27 February 2018),[143] should be used. The guidance is intended to limit the use of punitive restrictions such as the imposition of electronic monitoring and ISS requirements on children released from custody on a notice of supervision.

21.103 During the period of supervision, the child will be under the supervision of a member of the YOT or a probation officer.[144]

21.104 If a child is aged 18 or over at the half-way point of a DTO of less than 24 months, the child will be subject to a period of extended supervision.[145]

Breach of a detention and training order

Overview

21.105 Where a child breaches any of the requirements in their notice of supervision, the child cannot be administratively recalled to custody – breach proceedings will need to be instituted and the matter dealt with by the youth court.

21.106 Breach proceedings can take place even after the period of supervision has ended (see paras 21.109–21.113 on breach proceedings) and must be dealt with in the youth court, even if the defendant has attained the age of 18.[146]

141 PCC(S)A 2000 s103(1).

142 The written notice is required by PCC(S)A 2000 s103(6).

143 www.gov.uk/government/publications/notices-of-supervision-guidance-for-youth-justice-professionals/notices-of-supervision-guidance-for-youth-offending-teams.

144 PCC(S)A 2000 s103(3).

145 PCC(S)A 2000 s106B.

146 *Sentencing children and young people: definitive guideline*, para 7.21.

Breach warning

21.107 When a breach occurs, the responsible officer must give the child a warning. Responsible officers are encouraged to implement a scaled response, for example a verbal warning (for issues such as lateness):

- first written warning;
- second written warning
- implementing formal breach proceedings.[147]

21.108 For very serious breaches, such as an act of violence against a member of staff, breach proceedings may be instituted immediately. However, throughout the licence period every effort should be made to help the child comply.[148]

Breach proceedings

21.109 The child may be summonsed or a warrant may be issued for their arrest to appear at a youth court in the local justice area where they reside (unless it is not known where the child resides).[149]

21.110 The first issue to determine is whether it has been proved to the satisfaction of the court that the defendant 'has failed to comply with the [supervision] requirements'.[150] Defence lawyers should be aware that the *Notices of supervision: guidance for youth offending teams* emphasises the need for requirements to be necessary and proportionate (see paras 21.101–21.104 on supervision after release).

21.111 Once a breach has been admitted or proved, the 'primary aim of the court should be to encourage compliance and seek to support the rehabilitation of the child or young person'.[151] The court will have the following options:

- impose a further period of custody of up to three months or the length of time from the date the breach was committed until the end of the order, *whichever is shorter*;[152]

147 Youth Justice Board, Case Management Guidance Section 7: Custody and resettlement, 15 October 2014, para 6.16.

148 Youth Justice Board, Case Management Guidance Section 7: Custody and resettlement, 15 October 2014, para 6.16.

149 PCC(S)A 2000 s104(1), (2).

150 PCC(S)A 2000 s104(3).

151 *Sentencing children and young people: definitive guideline*, para 6.12.

152 PCC(S)A 2000 s104(3)(a) and (3A); and *Sentencing children and young people: definitive guideline*, para 7.21.

- impose a further period of supervision up to three months or the length of time from the date the breach was committed until the end of the order, *whichever is shorter*;[153]
- impose a fine (up to level 3 on the standard scale): £1,000 (or £250 if the child is aged under 14[154]);[155]
- take no action.[156]

21.112 The 'maximum period' of further custody or supervision the court may impose is calculated from the date of the breach (failure to comply with supervision requirements).[157] If the breach or failure took place over two or more days, it is taken to have occurred on the first of those days.[158] A court may order a period of detention or supervision, or impose a fine even after the detention and training order has ended.[159]

21.113 Any order made following breach proceedings can be appealed to the Crown Court.[160]

Further convictions

21.114 Where a child is found guilty of a further imprisonable offence during the currency of a DTO supervision, the court sentencing the child for the new offence has the power to recall the child. The sentencing court will have the following options in relation to the original offence:

- impose a further period of detention (that does not exceed the period between the date of the new offence and the date when the original order would have expired);[161]
- take no action.

153 PCC(S)A 2000 s104(3)(aa); and *Sentencing children and young people: definitive guideline*, para 7.21.
154 See para 18.67 on fines and availability.
155 PCC(S)A 2000 s104(3)(b); and *Sentencing children and young people: definitive guideline*, para 7.21.
156 *Sentencing children and young people: definitive guideline*, para 7.21.
157 PCC(S)A 2000 s104(3A); and *Sentencing children and young people: definitive guideline*, para 7.21.
158 PCC(S)A 2000 s104(3B).
159 PCC(S)A 2000 s104(3C).
160 PCC(S)A 2000 s104(6).
161 PCC(S)A 2000 s105(1), (2); and *Sentencing children and young people: definitive guideline*, para 7.22.

21.115 Where the new offence is found to have been committed over a period of two or more days, the date for the purposes of calculating the further period of detention is the *last of those days*.[162]

21.116 Any further period of custody can be served consecutively or concurrently.[163] This period should not be taken into account when determining the appropriate length of the sentence for the new offence.[164]

Custodial sentences in the crown court

Overview

21.117 In the Crown Court, the following custodial sentences are available:

- Detention and training order (DTO);
- Long-term detention (PCC(S)A 200 s91);
- extended detention (CJA 2003 s226B);
- detention for life (CJA 2003 s226);
- detention at Her Majesty's Pleasure (PCC(S)A 2000 s90).

The court also has the duty to remit cases to the youth court (see para 21.122–21.126 and also has the power to defer sentence (see para 17.28).

21.118 Detention of public protection was abolished under Legal Aid, Sentencing and Punishment of Offenders Act (LASPO) 2012 s226(3).

21.119 In some cases, the Crown Court has the power to impose either a DTO or a PCC(S)A 2000 s91 sentence of long-term detention (see paras 21.128–21.129).

Section 91 long-term detention[165]

Availability

21.120 Long-term detention under PCC(S)A 2000 s91 ('section 91 long-term detention') is only available in the Crown Court.

162 PCC(S)A 2000 s105(4).

163 PCC(S)A 2000 s105(3)(a); and *Sentencing children and young people: definitive guideline*, para 7.23.

164 PCC(S)A 2000 s105(3)(b); and *Sentencing children and young people: definitive guideline*, para 7.23.

165 PCC(S)A 2000 s91.

21.121 A child aged 10 to 17 may be sentenced to section 91 long-term detention in the Crown Court if convicted of a grave crime[166] and neither a YRO or a DTO is suitable.[167]

Court's duties

21.122 A Crown Court dealing with a child who has been convicted of any offence (other than homicide) must remit the case to the youth court unless it would be undesirable to do so.[168]

21.123 The *Sentencing children and young people: definitive guideline* states that:

> In considering whether remittal is undesirable a court should balance the need for expertise in the sentencing of children and young people with the benefits of the sentence being imposed by the court which determined guilt.[169]

21.124 There are cases that are heard in the Crown Court where section 91 long-term detention may not be available or appropriate:

- If the child has pleaded guilty, the court should consider whether a referral order may be appropriate.
- If it is found that a CRO or a DTO is the more appropriate sentence.
- If a child who has been sent to the Crown Court for trial but pleads to a less serious offence that is not a grave crime the court has no power to impose section 91 long-term detention.[170]
- For defendants aged 10 or 11, and aged 12–14 who are not persistent offenders, 'the court should take into account the normal prohibition on imposing custodial sentences'.[171]

21.125 For a fuller discussion of the court's duty to remit cases to the youth court see paras 17.22–17.27.

21.126 Once the Crown Court has determined that remittal to the youth court is undesirable the court must decide that neither a YRO nor a DTO is suitable; then follow the steps set out at para 21.41 to determine the appropriate length of sentence.

166 PCC(S)A 2000 s91(1).
167 PCC(S)A 2000 s91(3).
168 PCC(S)A 2000 s8(2).
169 *Sentencing children and young people: definitive guideline*, para 2.15.
170 PCC(S)A 2000 s91(1).
171 *Sentencing children and young people: definitive guideline*, p9.

Children jointly charged with adults

21.127 Children who are sent to the Crown Court because they are jointly charged with an adult may not meet the criteria for imposing section 91 long-term detention (see for example para 2.124). In such cases, the youth court is likely to be the most appropriate sentencing court and the court must remit under PCC(S)A 2000 s8(2), especially following a guilty plea 'as referral orders are generally not available in the crown court but may be the most appropriate sentence'[172] (see paras 21.122 21.126 and 17.22–17.27).

Imposing a detention and training order or section 91 long-term detention

21.128 Sometimes, a court will have the power to impose section 91 long-term detention but following reductions proposes to impose a sentence of two years or less. In these circumstances, a detention and training order will usually be substituted, as it allows for greater supervision on release.

> It is possible that, following a guilty plea, a two-year detention and training order may be appropriate as opposed to a sentence of section 91 detention, to account for the reduction.[173]

21.129 For a fuller discussion of DTOs see paras 21.71–21.116.

Release and supervision – section 91 detention

21.130 Children serving custodial sentences under four years are eligible to be considered for early release on HDC. Those serving sentences of four years or more, who have previously breached a HDC or those previously recalled to custody on a long sentence will not be eligible for early release.[174]

21.131 If a child turns 18 during the first half of a custodial sentence of less than 24 months Under 18 year olds serving a custodial sentence of 12 months or less will automatically receive three months' supervision.

172 *Sentencing children and young people: definitive guideline*, para 2.16.

173 *Sentencing children and young people: definitive guideline*, para 6.56.

174 Youth Justice Board, Case Management Guidance Section 7: Custody and resettlement, 15 October 2014, para 6.16.

Extended sentence of detention (section 226B)

Overview

21.132 Extended detention or an extended sentence of detention is a sentence to protect the public from serious harm caused by the defendant committing further specified offences. The court can extend the licence period by up to five or eight years. The child will be released from custody between two-thirds and the end of his or her custodial term, and therefore will also spend longer in custody then if he received a determinate sentence.

Availability

21.133 Extended detention[175] is a sentencing option in the Crown Court if:

- the defendant is under 18 years old on the date of conviction;
- the defendant is convicted of a specified offence (see para 21.134);
- the defendant is found to be a dangerous offender (see para 21.135–21.137);
- the court is not required to pass a sentence of detention for life; and
- the appropriate custodial term would be four years or more.

21.134 'Specified offences'[176] are specified violent or sexual offences listed in CJA 2003 Sch 15.

Court's duties

Assessment of dangerousness

21.135 The legal test of dangerousness[177] requires the court to form the opinion that:

> There is a significant risk to members of the public of serious harm caused by the child committing further specified offences.[178]

175 CJA 2003 s226B.

176 CJA 2003 s224(2).

177 CJA 2003 s229.

178 CJA 2003 s226B(1)(b); and *Sentencing children and young people: definitive guideline*, para 2.4.

'Serious harm' means death or serious personal injury, whether physical or psychological.[179] A 'significant risk' is 'more than a mere possibility of occurrence'.[180]

21.136 The assessment of dangerousness should take into account:

- all available information regarding previous patterns of behaviour relating to the offence;
- any other information relating to the child;
- the fact that children have greater capacity for change than adults:

> Children and young people may change and develop within a shorter time than adults change and this factor, along with their level of maturity, may be highly relevant when assessing probable future conduct and whether it might cause a risk of serious harm.[181]

21.137 For a fuller discussion of dangerousness assessment for children see paras 21.159–21.161. A court considering making a finding of dangerousness will require a pre-sentence report[182] and the court should request the report writer to address dangerousness (see paras 17.89–17.93 on dangerousness assessment).[183]

Determining the appropriate custodial term

21.138 Extended detention is only available if the appropriate custodial term is four years or more.[184]

Determining the length of the extended licence

21.139 The extended licence period must be a period of such length as the court considers necessary to protect members of the public from serious harm occasioned by the commission of further specified offences.[185]

21.140 The 'appropriate custodial term' must be at least four years, and the 'extension period' must be at least one year and must not exceed five years for a specified violent offence and eight years for a specified

179 CJA 2003 s224(3).

180 *Sentencing children and young people: definitive guideline*, para 2.5.

181 *Sentencing children and young people: definitive guideline*, para 2.6; and *R v Lang* [2005] EWCA Crim 2864, para 17(vi).

182 *Sentencing children and young people: definitive guideline*, para 2.5.

183 Youth Justice Board, Case Management Guidance Section 5: Use reports, 15 October 2014, para 2.12.

184 *R v Finnerty (Daniel Mark)* [2016] EWCA Crim 1513.

185 CJA 2003 s226B(5).

sexual offence. The total term of the extended sentence of detention (custodial term and the extended licence period) must not exceed the maximum term of imprisonment for an adult offender convicted of that offence.[186]

21.141 When given an extended sentence, the child will usually be released at the two-thirds points of the custodial term.

21.142 However, where the custodial term of the extended sentence is ten years or more, or the sentence is imposed for an offence listed in Criminal Justice Act 2003 Sch 15B, the case must be referred at the two thirds point to the Parole Board, who will consider whether it is no longer necessary for the protection of the public for the defendant to be detained. However, the child cannot be detained beyond the end of the custodial term.

Detention for life (section 226)

Overview

21.143 Detention for life is a sentence that means the child must serve a minimum term before he or she can apply to the Parole Board for release on licence; there is no automatic release date and the child will only be released if he or she is no longer considered to be a risk to the public. The defendant will remain on licence for the rest of his or her life, subject to recall to prison if any of the their licence conditions are broken or they are considered to be a risk to the public.

Availability

21.144 The Crown Court must impose a sentence of detention for life[187] if:

- the defendant is aged under 18 on the date of conviction;
- the defendant is convicted of a specified serious offence; and
- the defendant is found to be a dangerous offender; and
- the offence is one in respect of which the child would apart from this section be liable to a sentence of detention for life under PCC(S)A 2000 s91; and

186 CJA 2003 s226B(7); and *Sentencing children and young people: definitive guideline*, para 6.58.

187 CJA 2003 s226.

- the court considers that the seriousness of the offence, or of the offence and one or more offences associated with it, is such as to justify the imposition of a sentence of detention for life.

'Serious offences'[188] are specified offences listed in Criminal Justice Act 2003 Sch 15 that are punishable by custody for life or detention for a period of ten years of more.

Court's duties

21.145 In deciding whether the criteria for detention for life are met, the sentencer must first assess whether a child is a 'dangerous offender' (see paras 21.135–21.137 above).

21.146 Even where the court is of the opinion that there is a significant risk to members of the public of serious harm caused by the child committing further specified offences:

> A sentence of detention for life should be used *as a last resort* when an extended sentence is not able to provide the level of protection that is necessary [emphasis added].[189]

21.147 The court should consider:

- the seriousness of the offence;
- the child's previous findings of guilt;
- the level of danger posed to the public and whether there is a reliable estimate of the length of time the child will remain a danger; and
- the alternative sentences available.[190]

Determining the minimum term (tariff) for detention for life

21.148 The court is required to set a minimum term to be served in custody before the defendant can apply to the Parole Board for release on licence.[191] The court should take into account in calculating the minimum term, an appropriate reduction that should be allowed for a plea of guilty (see paras 21.48–21.65) and care should be taken not to incorporate in the notional determinate sentence an element for risk that was already covered by the indeterminate sentence.[192]

188 CJA 2003 s224.

189 *Sentencing children and young people: definitive guideline,* para 6.59.

190 *Sentencing children and young people: definitive guideline,* para 6.59.

191 *Sentencing children and young people: definitive guideline,* para 6.59; PCC(S)A 2000 s82A(2).

192 *R v Lang* [2005] EWCA Crim 2864.

Detention at Her Majesty's Pleasure

Overview

21.149 The mandatory sentence for any child who pleads guilty or is found guilty of committing the offence of murder is detention at Her Majesty's pleasure.[193] As with detention for life, the child must serve a minimum term before he or she can apply to the Parole Board for release on licence; and will remain on licence for the rest of her or his life.

Court's duties

21.150 When sentencing a child who pleads guilty or is found guilty of committing the offence of murder the mandatory sentence is detention at Her Majesty's Pleasure.[194] The court must set a tariff or minimum period to be served before the child can apply to the Parole Board for release (see paras 21.165–21.172).

21.151 Where a child who is charged with murder is found unfit to plead and to have done the act, if the court makes a hospital order it must make a restriction order[195] (see para 22.38–22.45 on hospital orders with a restriction order).

21.152 The court also has a discretion to impose a sentence of 'detention at Her Majesty's Pleasure' under PCC(S)A 2000 s91 where the maximum sentence for an adult is one of life imprisonment. Given the court's powers under the dangerousness provisions to impose extended detention and detention for life (see paras 21.130–21.146) it would be exceptional for the court to exercise this discretion (see also paras 21.159–21.161 on imposing indeterminate sentences on children).

Determining the minimum term (tariff) for detention at Her Majesty's Pleasure

21.153 The starting point for the minimum term for children who commit murder is 12 years.[196]

193 PCC(S)A 2000 s90.

194 PCC(S)A 2000 s90.

195 Criminal Procedure (Insanity) Act 1964 s5(3).

196 CJA 2003 Sch 21; *Sentencing children and young people: definitive guideline*, para 6.60.

21.154 The court must take into account any aggravating or mitigating factors.[197]

21.155 Aggravating factors that may be relevant include:

a) a significant degree of planning or premeditation;
b) the victim was vulnerable because of age or disability;
c) mental or physical suffering inflicted on the victim before death;
d) the abuse of a position of trust;
e) the use of duress or threats against another person to facilitate the commission of the offence;
f) the victim was providing a public service or performing a public duty; and
g) concealment, destruction or dismemberment of the body.

21.156 Mitigating factors include:

a) an intention to cause serious bodily harm rather than kill;
b) lack of premeditation;
c) the offender suffers from a mental disorder or disability (not falling within Homicide Act 1957 s2(1) of the) which lowered their degree of culpability;
d) the offender was provoked in a way not amounting to a defence of provocation;
e) the offender acted to any extent in self-defence;
f) a belief by the offender that the murder was an act of mercy;
g) the age of the offender.

21.157 The court should also consider any previous convictions, whether the offence was committed on bail and if the offender pleaded guilty. See paras 21.64–21.65 on credit for guilty plea for mandatory life sentences for murder.

21.158 The court should take into account any period the child has spent on remand in connection with the offence or a related offence. The child will get no credit for time served on remand unless it is taken into account when setting the minimum term. The court should normally subtract the time for which the child was remanded from the tariff it would otherwise impose in order to reach the minimum term.

Imposing indeterminate sentences on children

21.159 Where children commit serious offences, the court has the discretion to pass a life sentence or extended sentence on a child that will last

197 CJA 2003 Sch 22 para 9.

for the rest of that child's life. In the author's view the courts should be encouraged to exercise this discretion rarely.

21.160 The UK is now the only country in Europe to allow for life sentences to be passed on those under the age of 18. The UK has been criticised by the UN Committee on Rights of the Child[198] and the Special Rapporteur on Torture for its passing of life sentences on children.[199]

21.161 Given what is now known about how adolescent brain's develop (see paras 3.31–3.36 on child and adolescent brain development), the changes to physiology and brain structure, and consequently the behaviour of someone under the age of 18. A child's behaviour is likely to be quite different to that same individual when they reach maturity. Life sentences and extended sentences require the court to assess dangerousness by considering the future risk presented by the child, which is an almost impossible task as they are undergoing a period of fundamental change. This is also emphasised by the *Sentencing children and young people: definitive guideline*, in particular para 1.7:

> Offending by a child or young person is often a phase which passes fairly rapidly and so the sentence should not result in the alienation of the child or young person from society if that can be avoided.

198 In its concluding observations on the fifth periodic report of the United Kingdom of Great Britain and Northern Ireland, the Committee recommended at paragraph 78(c) that the UK should abolish mandatory imposition of life imprisonment for children for offences committed while they are under the age of 18.

199 Report of Special Rapporteur Juan E. Méndez Report to the UN General Assembly 5 March 2015, A/HRC/28/68 at para 74. Aailable at: www.ohchr.org/EN/HRBodies/HRC/RegularSessions/Session28/Documents/A_HRC_28_68_E.doc.

CHAPTER 22

Hospital orders and other mental health disposals

continued

Key points

- The fact that a child is suffering from a mental illness relates to every aspect of their case, not just mitigation and sentence and should be fully explored at the outset of a case.
- Social services should provide support for children with mental health needs and this may be provided in the community rather than as part of a sentence.
- There are different disposals available on conviction and following a finding of unfitness to plead.
- There are different pathways for children suffering from a mental illness, mental health treatment in a residential hospital setting or a custodial sentence. The most appropriate pathway will require individualised consideration.

Introduction

22.1 It is important that if a child is suffering from a mental illness, that this is considered at the outset of a criminal investigation. If a child is suffering from a significant mental illness, there is a strong public interest in diverting the child away from the criminal justice system. Where possible, written representations should be made to the police and/or Crown Prosecution Service (CPS) to ensure that all relevant information in favour of the case being diverted is before the decision-maker (see para 7.130 on out of court disposals and children with mental illness).

22.2 In any case involving a child with a mental illness, it will usually be appropriate to instruct an expert to consider whether a child is fit to plead and able to effectively participate – alternatively, the expert can advise on modifications to the trial process (see para 12.53 on questions for an expert). If the child is fit to plead and then convicted, or the child is unfit to plead and found to have done the act or omission, the expert can provide advice on disposals. The expert report may also be able to provide guidance on what treatment might be available in the community or as a hospital in-patient. For this reason, it is particularly important to find a psychologist or psychiatrist who specialises in the particular needs of the child concerned – for example, if a child has Asperger syndrome, a psychologist or psychiatrist specialising in autism spectrum conditions may be able to recommend appropriate treatment, as well as insight into the condition to assist the sentencer.

22.3 This chapter will look at social services duties and mental health services; sentencing disposals where the defendant is fit to plead; and disposals in cases of insanity and unfitness to plead.

Terminology

22.4 Mental Health Act (MHA) 1983 s1(2) defines 'mental disorder' as 'any disorder or disability of the mind'.[1] Mental disorders may also be described as a mental illness or psychiatric disorder. Mental disorders include:

- depression;
- post-traumatic stress disorder (PTSD);
- autism spectrum disorder (ASD);
- attention deficit hyperactivity disorder (ADHD);
- psychosis;
- bipolar disorder;
- schizophrenia;
- conduct disorder.

(See paras 3.40–3.80 on relevance of background, common conditions and mental illness.)

22.5 A learning disability[2] falls within the MHA 1983 definition of 'mental disorder' if it is associated with 'abnormally aggressive or seriously irresponsible conduct'.[3]

Social services duties and mental health services

Generally

22.6 A child who is suffering from a mental illness may be able to access support from the Child and Adolescent Mental Health Service (CAMHS). Voluntary hospital admission may also be appropriate.

1 MHA 1983 s1(2).

2 See para 3.63 for the definition of 'learning disability'.

3 MHA 1983 s1(2A).

Local authorities

22.7 A child who is remanded to local authority accommodation or to youth detention accommodation is owed a duty by the local authority and is a 'looked after child'.[4] Alternatively, any child charged with a serious offence who is facing a custodial sentence would be deemed a 'child in need' and therefore a Children Act 1989 s17 assessment can be requested by anyone, including the child, their family, their lawyer, and the youth offending team.[5] A section 17 needs assessment enables the local authority to determine what help or support may be required. If, following the needs assessment, the child is found to be a 'child in need', then the local authority have a duty to prepare a care plan.[6]

22.8 The care plan will set out the support and intervention the local authority will provide,[7] for example it may include:

- *wrap-around support for the family, either through general personal support or a structured system such as multi-systemic therapy (MST);*
- *accommodation provided by the local authority with a foster carer, in a children's home or a secure children's home;*
- *therapeutic intervention, such as a course on sexual offending provided by specialist providers;*[8]
- *mental health assessments/interventions;*
- *substance misuse support;*
- *family counselling;*
- *education support.*

22.9 This should be discussed with the child and may depend on the availability of services or placements, as well as the child's ability and willingness to consent to treatment. A child who engages with support and treatment may be diverted away from the formal criminal justice system (see chapter 7 on out of court disposals) or, if charged and convicted, the child's engagement with support and treatment should be documented in the pre-sentence report or raised by the defence during mitigation. Evidence that the child is addressing his or her underlying problems may assist in avoiding a custodial

4 Legal Aid, Sentencing and Punishment of Offenders Act (LASPO) 2012 s104.

5 Children Act 1989 s17; and Framework for the assessment of children in need and their families (2010).

6 R *(K) v Manchester City Council* [2006] EWHC 3164 (Admin).

7 Also taking into consideration Care Act 2014 duties.

8 For example: GMAP; Lucy Faithfull; NCATS; National Society for the Prevention of Cruelty to Children (NSPCC).

or more onerous community-based sentence – for example, the child may receive a youth rehabilitation order without a mental health requirement because of the child's voluntary engagement with services.

Applications for bail or remand to local authority accommodation

22.10 A defence lawyer representing a child with a mental illness who is remanded to youth detention accommodation should consider making a further bail application. The Children Act 1989 requires local authorities to take all reasonable steps to avoid the need for children within their area to be placed in secure accommodation.[9] This duty is repeated for social workers supporting children who become looked after by virtue of their remand to youth detention accommodation.[10] A child who is living in the community and accessing support is ultimately less likely to receive a custodial sentence.

Interim hospital order

22.11 Alternatively, defence lawyers should consider whether to make an application for an interim hospital order (see paras 22.64–22.67 on hospital orders).

Sentencing disposals where defendant is fit to plead

Introduction

22.12 For children who have been convicted and are being sentenced, the following mental health disposals are available:

- youth rehabilitation order with a mental health treatment requirement;
- guardianship order (age 16 and over);
- hospital order.

The Crown Court also has the power to impose:

- hospital order with a restriction order.

9 Children Act 1989 Sch 2 s7.

10 LASPO 2012 s102.

22.13 Some children will be reluctant to be 'labelled' as having a mental illness and they will be concerned about the 'stigma' (see paras 22.61–22.71 on hospital v prison below). For this reason, it is important to ensure they receive specialist legal advice. Where a child is found unfit to plead, the court must appoint a lawyer to put a case for the defence[11] and this needn't be trial counsel.[12]

Youth rehabilitation order with mental health treatment requirement

22.14 A mental health treatment requirement might be considered if there are concerns about the defendant's mental health. A youth rehabilitation order with a mental health treatment requirement means that the child must submit to treatment during the period of the order.[13] The treatment is given under the direction of a registered medical practitioner or a registered psychologist,[14] or both for different periods, with a view to the improving the child's mental health condition.[15]

22.15 The child must have a treatable mental health condition. There is no requirement that the court must have evidence from a registered medical practitioner approved under MHA 1983 s12.[16]

22.16 For more details, see paras 20.58–20.64 on youth rehabilitation order mental health treatment requirements.

Guardianship order

Availability

22.17 The youth court or a Crown Court may make a guardianship order if the defendant is suffering from a mental disorder that warrants a guardianship order and a local authority (or any other approved person) are willing to receive the defendant into guardianship.[17]

11 Criminal Procedure (Insanity) Act 1968 s4A.

12 *R v Norman* (2008) EWCA Crim 1810 at para 34(iii).

13 Criminal Justice and Immigration Act (CJIA) 2008 Sch 1 para 20(1).

14 A registered psychologist is a person registered as a practitioner psychologist in the register maintained under the Health Professions Order 2001.

15 CJIA 2008 Sch 1 para 20(1).

16 This requirement was removed by LASPO 2012 s82(2)(a).

17 MHA 1983 s37(6).

22.18 A guardianship order is only available if the defendant is aged 16 or over.[18]

22.19 The defendant must have a mental disorder, but there is no requirement for the mental disorder to be treatable.

Court's duties

22.20 A court may only make a guardianship order if the defendant is convicted of an offence which is imprisonable in the case of an adult,[19] and:

- the court is satisfied, on the written or oral evidence of two registered medical practitioners, that the defendant is suffering from mental disorder;
- the defendant has attained the age of 16 years;
- the mental disorder is of a nature or degree which warrants his reception into guardianship;
- the court is of the opinion, having regard to all the circumstances including the nature of the offence and the character and antecedents of the defendant, and to the other available methods of dealing with him or her, that the most suitable method of disposing of the case is a guardianship order.[20]

22.21 The court may only make a guardianship order if it is satisfied that that a local social services authority, or any other person approved by the local authority, is willing to receive the defendant into guardianship.[21]

22.22 Where a court is minded to make a guardianship order, the court has the power to request a local authority to inform the court whether it or the approved person is willing to act as a guardian for the defendant and to provide the court with 'such information as it reasonably can' about how the local authority or the approved person could be expected to exercise their guardianship powers.[22]

22.23 If the court makes a guardianship order it may not impose a custodial sentence, a fine or youth rehabilitation order.[23]

18 MHA 1983 s37(2)(a)(ii).
19 MHA 1983 s37(1).
20 MHA 1983 s37(2).
21 MHA 1983 s37(6).
22 MHA 1983 s39A.
23 MHA 1983 s37(8).

Powers and duration of a guardianship order

22.24 A guardianship order provides the local authority or other person named as the guardian with three powers:

1) the right to decide where the person lives;
2) the power to require the person to attend specified places for medical treatment, work, education or training;
3) the power for a doctor, approved mental health professional (AMHP) or other specified person to visit the person where he or she lives.[24]

22.25 A guardianship order lasts for six months in the first instance. After this, it may be renewed for a further six months, and then for a year at a time.[25]

Variation or discharge of a guardianship order

22.26 The defendant has a right to make an application to the Mental Health Tribunal for the order to be discharged once in the first six months, once in the second six months and then once in every 12 month period after that.[26] Legal aid is available for all Mental Health Tribunal applications and is not subject to means testing.

Criminal record

22.27 A person who is receives a guardianship order will have a criminal record and the conviction will become a spent conviction (see paras 25.21–25.30 on spent convictions).

Hospital order (section 37 order)

Availability

22.28 The youth court[27] and Crown Court may make a hospital order under MHA 1983 s37 if the defendant is suffering from a treatable mental disorder and is convicted of an offence which is imprisonable in the case of an adult.[28] A hospital order means the defendant is admitted to a psychiatric hospital and is detained there for treatment for a

24 MHA 1983 ss40(2), 8.
25 MHA 1983 ss40(2), 20(2).
26 MHA 1983 ss66(1)(c); 2(c), (g).
27 *R (P) v Barking Youth Court* [2002] EWHC 734 (Admin).
28 MHA 1983 s37(1).

mental disorder. A hospital order is only appropriate for more severe mental health problems that are suitable for in-patient treatment.

22.29 A hospital order is available even if there is a mandatory minimum sentence[29] but not for offences, such as murder, where the sentence is fixed by law unless the court imposes a restriction order[30] (see para 22.49). A hospital order should be considered as an alternative to custody.

Court's duties

22.30 A court may only make a hospital order if the child is convicted of an offence that is imprisonable in the case of an adult,[31] and:

- the court is satisfied, on the written or oral evidence of two registered medical practitioners, that the defendant is suffering from mental disorder;
- the mental disorder is of a nature or degree which makes it appropriate for the defendant to be detained in a hospital for medical treatment;
- the court is of the opinion, having regard to all the circumstances including the nature of the offence and the character and antecedents of the defendant, and to the other available methods of dealing with him or her, that the most suitable method of disposing of the case is a hospital order.[32]

22.31 The court should hear evidence from the approved clinician who would have overall responsibility for the child (or the hospital managers).[33] When a court is considering whether to make a hospital order, the defendant should be legally represented.[34]

22.32 If the court makes a hospital order, it may not impose a custodial sentence, a fine, referral order, youth rehabilitation order or parental bind over.[35]

Powers and duration of a hospital order

22.33 A hospital order made under MHA 1983 s37 means the defendant will be detained in hospital for treatment for his or her mental

29 MHA 1983 s37(1A).
30 MHA 1983 s37(1) and Criminal Procedure (Insanity) Act (CP(I)A) 1964 s5(3).
31 MHA 1983 s37(1).
32 MHA 1983 s37(2).
33 MHA 1983 s37(4).
34 *R v Blackwood* (1974) 59 Cr App R 170, CA.
35 MHA 1983 s37(8).

disorder until the responsible clinician decides it is no longer necessary for the defendant to be detained or the patient is discharged by the mental health tribunal.

22.34 A hospital order lasts for six months in the first instance. After this, it may be renewed for a further six months, and then for a year at a time.

22.35 As with the interim hospital order, admission can take place within the period of 28 days beginning with the date of the order; and the court may give directions for the defendant's conveyance to, and detention in, a place of safety pending the admission. Should the admission to this placement no longer be available the secretary of state can order that the child be transferred to any other hospital that may be appropriate.[36]

Discharge of a hospital order

22.36 There is a right to apply to the Mental Health Tribunal to be discharged.[37] A patient can apply for discharge of the hospital order after six months and once in every 12-month period after that.[38] An application for discharge can also be made to hospital managers. Legal aid is available for all Mental Health Tribunal applications and is not subject to means testing.

Criminal record

22.37 A person who is receives a hospital order following a conviction will have a criminal record and the conviction will become a spent conviction (see paras 25.21–25.30 on spent convictions). A person who is receives a hospital order following a finding they were unfit to plead is not convicted, however a finding of fact is treated as a conviction for the purposes of the Rehabilitation of Offenders Act 1974, and therefore it may be disclosed on criminal record checks.[39]

36 MHA 1983 s37(5).
37 MHA 1983 s66(1)(b).
38 MHA 1983 s66(2)(b), (g).
39 Rehabilitation of Offenders Act 1974 s1.

Hospital order with a restriction order (section 41 order)

Availability

22.38 The Crown Court may make a hospital order with a restriction order if it is necessary for the protection of the public from serious harm.

22.39 The youth court or adult magistrates' court may commit a defendant aged 14 or over to the Crown Court with a view to a restriction order being made (see paras 22.41–22.42).[40]

Court's duties

22.40 A court may only make a hospital order with a restriction order if:

- the conditions for a hospital order are satisfied (see paras 22.30–22.32);[41]
- at least one of the medical practitioners has given evidence orally before the court;[42]
- the court is satisfied, having regard to the nature of the offence, the antecedents of the defendant and the risk of him or her committing further offences if set at large, that it is necessary for the protection of the public from serious harm so to do.[43]

Committal to the crown court

22.41 The youth court or adult magistrates' court may commit a child to the Crown Court with a view to a restriction order being made, if:

- the child was aged 14 or over on the date of conviction;
- the offence is imprisonable in the case of an adult;
- the conditions for a hospital order are satisfied (see paras 22.30–22.32);[44]
- it appears to the court, having regard to the nature of the offence, the antecedents of the child and the risk of him or her committing further offences if set at large, that if a hospital order is made a restriction order should also be made.[45]

40 MHA 1983 s43(1).
41 MHA 1983 s37(1).
42 MHA 1983 s41(2).
43 MHA 1983 s41(2).
44 MHA 1983 s37(1).
45 MHA 1983 s43(1).

22.42 If exercising this power, the child is committed in custody to the Crown Court or, the youth court or adult magistrates' court can direct that the child be detained in a hospital pending the hearing of the case by the Crown Court.[46]

Powers and duration of a restriction order

22.43 Once a restriction order is made, the patient remains detained in hospital until the secretary of state is satisfied that 'a restriction order is no longer required for the protection of the public from serious harm'.[47]

Discharge from a restriction order

22.44 A hospital order with a restriction order can be discharged by the secretary of state or Mental Health Tribunal. The secretary of state can discharge a patient conditionally or absolutely. If released conditionally, a patient can apply to the Mental Health Tribunal for an absolute discharge one year after their conditional discharge an may then apply every two years. An application for discharge can also be made to hospital managers. Legal aid is available for all Mental Health Tribunal applications and is not subject to means testing.[48]

Criminal record

22.45 A person who is receives a hospital order with a restrictions order following a conviction will have a criminal record and the conviction will become a spent conviction. A person who is receives a hospital order with a restriction order following a finding they were unfit to plead is not convicted, however, a finding of fact is treated as a conviction for the purposes of the Rehabilitation of Offenders Act 1974 and therefore it may be disclosed on criminal record checks.[49]

46 MHA 1983 s44.
47 MHA 1983 s42(1).
48 MHA 1983 s66(1)(b); MHA 1983 s66(2)(b), (g).
49 Rehabilitation of Offenders Act 1974 s1.

Disposals where the defendant is unfit to plead

Introduction

22.46 In the youth court and adult magistrates' court, where a child is found unfit to plead[50] the court has the following disposals available:

- guardianship order (age 16 and over); or
- hospital order.

22.47 In the Crown Court where a child is found not guilty by reason of insanity[51] or found unfit to plead and to have done an act or omission,[52] the court has the following disposals available:

- hospital order (with or without a restriction order);
- supervision order; or
- absolute discharge.

Hospital order (with or without a restriction order)

22.48 A hospital order is available for all offences where there has been a finding that the defendant is unfit to plead (see paras 22.46–22.47). A hospital order may only be made if the conditions set out in MHA s37 are met (see paras 22.30–22.32 on hospital orders).

22.49 Where a hospital order is passed the court must pass a restriction order under Mental Health Act 1983 s41 if the offence is one for which the sentence is fixed by law, such as murder or where the court finds the individual poses a risk of serious harm to the public (see paras 22.37–22.44 on hospital orders with a restriction order).[53]

Guardianship order

22.50 A guardianship order may only be made in the youth court if the defendant is aged 16 or over and the conditions set out in MHA 1983 s37 are met (see paras 22.17–22.27 on guardianship orders).

50 See paras 4.69–4.83 on unfitness to plead in the youth court and adult magistrates' court – MHA 1983 s37; and PCC(S)A 2000 s11.

51 CP(I)A 1964 s1.

52 CP(I)A 1964 ss4, 4A.

53 CP(I)A 1964 s5(3).

Supervision order

Overview

22.51 A supervision order requires the defendant to be supervised by a social worker or probation officer (a supervising officer) for a specified period no longer than two years.

Availability

22.52 The Crown Court may make a supervision order following a finding that the defendant is not guilty by reason of insanity or unfit to plead and that the defendant had done the act or omission charged.[54]

Court's duties

22.53 A court may only make a supervision order if the court is satisfied that:

- having regard to all the circumstances of the case, a supervision order is the most suitable means of dealing with the defendant;
- the supervising officer specified in the order is willing to undertake the supervision; and
- arrangements have been made for the proposed treatment.[55]

22.54 The court must also specify the length of the order (up to a maximum of two years).[56]

Treatment requirement of a supervision order

22.55 A supervision order may impose a requirement that the defendant undergoes treatment by or under the direction of a registered medical practitioner. The court may only impose a treatment requirement if:

- the court is satisfied, on the written or oral evidence of two or more registered medical practitioners (one of whom is approved for the purposes of MHA 1983 s12) that the mental condition requires and may be susceptible to treatment; but is not such to warrant a hospital order;[57] or
- the court is satisfied, on the written or oral evidence of two or more registered medical practitioners, that because of a medical

54 CP(I)A 1964 s5(2).

55 CP(I)A 1964 Sch 1A Part 2 para 2.

56 CP(I)A 1964 Sch 1A Part 1 para 1(1).

57 CP(I)A 1964 Sch 1A Part 2 para 4(2).

condition, other than his or her mental condition, the supervised person is likely to pose a risk to himself or herself or others; and the condition may be susceptible to treatment.[58]

22.56 The treatment need not be specified but it should be treatment as a non-resident patient under the direction of a specified registered medical practitioner.[59] It may be for the whole period of the order or that period as may be specified.[60]

Variation or discharge of a supervision order

22.57 The supervised person or supervising officer may apply to an adult magistrates' court or youth court to vary or discharge the supervision order.[61]

Reviews and breaches of a supervision order

22.58 Any application to review and vary the terms of the order can be made to a magistrates' court. An application to vary can be made either by the supervised person or by the supervising officer.[62]

Absolute discharge

22.59 An absolute discharge may be made where the court does not consider it necessary or appropriate to impose any punishment[63] (see paras 18.5–18.11 on absolute discharge).

Unfitness to plead and criminal records

22.60 Whilst a child who is found unfit to plead is said not to have a conviction for the offence, a finding of fact is nevertheless treated as a conviction for the purposes of the Rehabilitation of Offenders Act 1974 and therefore it will become spent (depending on the sentence) and be subject to the same disclosure rules as if the defendant had been convicted of the same offence. In relation to certain sex offences, if found to have done an act or omission, the notification requirements will be triggered (see paras 25.76–25.81 on notification requirements).

58 CP(I)A 1964 Sch 1A para 5(1).
59 CP(I)A 1964 Sch 1A paras 4(3), 5(3).
60 CP(I)A 1964 Sch 1A paras 4(1), 5(2).
61 CP(I)A 1964 Sch 1A paras 9–14.
62 CP(I)A 1964 Sch 1A para 11.
63 CP(I)A 1964 s5(2).

Hospital v prison[64]

Overview

22.61 There will be occasions when the defence advocate will need to advise a child about whether to consider a mental health disposal and becoming an in-patient in a psychiatric hospital rather than a custodial sentence.

22.62 First, it will be important to have sought expert advice and make full enquiries as to whether or not hospital is even a possible option. The threshold is high, the recommendation of two psychiatrists is required and a bed or placement will need to be found.

22.63 Second, even if a hospital pathway is possible, careful consideration will need to be given to whether or not it is the right option.

Interim hospital order

22.64 Consideration should be given to whether to remand the child to hospital before sentence. This will provide both the child and the professionals working with the child to see whether this is the most appropriate option.[65]

22.65 Under MHA 1983 s38, where the court is satisfied, on the written or oral evidence of two registered medical practitioners, that the child is suffering from a mental disorder and that there is reason to suppose that the mental disorder from which the child is suffering is such that it may be appropriate for a hospital order to be made, the court may, before making a hospital order or dealing with him or her in some other way, make an interim hospital order authorising his or her admission to a hospital as specified in the order.

22.66 In the case of a child who is subject to an interim hospital order, the court may make a hospital order without the offender being brought before the court if the child is represented by an authorised person who is given an opportunity of being heard and at least one of the registered medical practitioners is employed at the hospital which is specified in the order.[66]

22.67 Admission can take place within the period of 28 days beginning with the date of the order; and the court may give directions for his

64 This guidance has been drafted with the assistance of Dr Laura Janes, Legal Director, Howard League for Penal Reform.

65 MHA 1983 ss35–36, 38.

66 MHA 1983 ss35–36, 38.

or her conveyance to and detention in a place of safety pending the admission.[67]

Transfer to hospital

22.68 If a child is mentally unwell, the child may also be transferred to hospital or another specialist mental health facility – this can be done administratively if a child is on remand[68] or after receiving a custodial sentence.[69] If a child is liable to be transferred administratively anyway, it may be more appropriate to actively pursue a transfer to hospital during the criminal proceedings. There is a severe shortage of secure beds in hospitals particularly for adolescent patients, so this will avoid the child having to be transferred later and being at the mercy of both the hospital and prison systems.

Choosing between hospital and prison

22.69 Where a hospital disposal is not inevitable, very careful thought will need to be given to the pros and cons of the two pathways. In every case, it will depend on the child's wishes, feelings and personality. For example:

- Some children cannot bear the intensity of hospital treatment and the sense of intrusion into their thoughts. In some instances, the prospect of being forcibly medicated (even subject to the safeguards under the MHA 1983) is frightening. For others, the most worrying aspect of being in hospital is that it can result in being there for an unlimited amount of time, whereas a prison sentence is time-limited (unless the child has a life sentence). Those children find it is easier to 'keep their head down' and serve a determinate custodial sentence. However, they are likely to spend a lot of time alone in their cell.
- Some children find it difficult to spend long periods alone in their cell. They appreciate the greater opportunity for individualised care and attention in hospital. It means they are being cared for until they no longer require that care. They spend less time alone. There are greater opportunities to seek discharge from hospital than from prison. Less time is spent alone in a cell.

22.70 Everyone's experience of prison and hospital is different. A lot depends on where a child is placed, eg which mental health facility or part of the custodial estate. It is worth looking at reports by

67 MHA 1983 ss35–36, 38.

68 MHA 1983 s47(1) s49.

69 MHA 1983 s48(1) s49.

Ofsted (Office for Standards in Education, Children's Services and Skills) and Her Majesty's Inspectorate of Prisons for an up-to-date picture of treatment and conditions, as well as any initiatives that may be available. Placements in the secure estate are not decided by the court – the Youth Custody Service, a department of the Ministry of Justice, decides where to place a child in custody in accordance with its published policy[70] (see paras 11.112–11.119 on placement decisions).

22.71 Some of the key differences between prison and hospital are listed below.

Hospital	Custody
• Ongoing multi-disciplinary assessments available throughout stay. • Ongoing treatment from multi-disciplinary team usually including medical doctor, psychiatrist, psychologist, occupational therapist education and hospital based social worker. • The wards may be mixed-sex. • Full education available. • Advocacy (legal entitlement to an Independent Mental Health Advocate). • Flexible arrangements for contact and visiting compared to prison (you can make and receive calls at specified times). • There will be very unwell other young people around them. • Regular six-monthly multi-disciplinary 'care programme approach' (CPA) reviews – parents can usually come; youth offending team or probation also usually invited, may have a solicitor present (legal aid subject to means testing). Treatment targets are devised and set. Any issues or concerns can be raised.	• Assessments usually need to be brought in, can be delayed. • Treatment can often be delayed, depending on where detained, unlikely to have same level of multi-disciplinary level of care unless at a secure children's home. • Establishments not mixed-sex (except some secure children's homes). • Education available (but minimum requirement of 15 hours a week, not always met at young offender institutions). • Advocacy services available but no legal entitlement to them and may be more difficult to access. • Visiting restricted, parents must make appointments at young offender institutions (greater access at secure children's homes and secure training centres). • There may be unwell and disruptive children around them; may be exposed to violence.

70 HM Prison and Probation Service and Youth Custody Service, 'Youth Custody Service placement team: overview of operational procedures', September 2017.

Hospital	Custody
• Possibility of Mental Health Act 1983 s17 ground leave – can be at any point subject to progress (if on a restricted order requires Ministry of Justice approval).[75] • If serving a prison sentence but transferred to hospital and eligible for parole, the process is frozen until either discharged from section (parole hearing can take place from hospital). • Entitled to regular Mental Health Review Tribunals with free legal representation; depending on the order in place, there may be other options for discharge. • Legal duty on home health and local authorities to create and provide a discharge plan including after care (Mental Health Act 1983 s117); culture of care in mental health services means these plans are generally taken more seriously. • At 18: transfer to an adult hospital – rights and entitlements continue (as above).	• Sentence planning meetings take place at regular intervals, no entitlement to a solicitor present and no legal aid for this. • Opportunities for Release on Temporary Licence (ROTL) or other temporary release may be linked to length of sentence (including how much time has been served) and may be more difficult to achieve. • Duties for discharge planning do not automatically involve health; concerns reported by inspectorates of prisons and probation about the lack of accommodation and support in place before release. • At 18: transfer to an adult prison for girls or young adult section of a young offender institute (sometimes this is within an adult prison). Resources for young adults in prison are considerably less than for children in custody.

Source: Howard League for Penal Reform, 2018

71 MHA 1983 s17.

CHAPTER 23

Parenting orders and parental bind over orders

Key points

- A court must make a parenting order (PO) or a parental bind over order when sentencing a child under 16 (or give reasons for not doing so).
- A court may make a PO or a parental bind over order when sentencing a child aged 16 or 17.
- POs are also available when a court makes an anti-social behaviour injunction, criminal behaviour order or sexual harm prevention order on a child.
- If a court does not make a PO or a parental bind over order, when it has the duty to do so, it must give reasons.

Introduction

23.1 Any court sentencing a child aged under 16 has a *duty* to make a parenting order[1] (PO) or a parental bind over order.[2] Any court sentencing a child aged 16 and over has a *discretion* to or impose a PO or make a parental bind over order.[3]

23.2 The only exception is that a court cannot make a parental bind over order when imposing a referral order and there is a discretion on the court to impose a PO (see para 23.7).[4]

Parenting orders

Availability

23.3 A PO may be made when a child is convicted of an offence.[5] A PO may also be made if a criminal behaviour order or sexual harm prevention order is made on a child.[6]

1 CDA 1998 s9(1).
2 Powers of Criminal Courts (Sentencing) Act (PCC(S)A) 2000 s150(1).
3 CDA 1998 s8(2).
4 PCC(S)A 2000 s19(5)(b).
5 CDA 1998 s8(1)(c). The defendant must be aged under 18 at the time of conviction.
6 CDA 1998 s8(1)(b).

23.4 In any court proceedings, a PO may be made where:

- a child safety order is made,[7] or there is a failure to comply with a child safety order;[8]
- a parental compensation order in relation to a child's behaviour is made;[9] or
- a person is convicted of a failure to comply with a school attendance order or a failure to secure regular attendance at school of a registered pupil.[10]

Court's duties

23.5 In the criminal courts – the youth court, adult magistrates' court and Crown Court – if a child is aged under 16 when convicted of an offence, the court *must*:

- make a PO in respect of the parent or guardian if it is satisfied that the PO would be 'desirable in the interests of preventing ... the commission of any further offence by the child or young person';[11]
- state in open court that it is not satisfied and why not.[12]

23.6 The power to make a parenting order is discretionary when the court makes a referral order on a child aged under 16 (see para 23.10).[13]

23.7 If the child is aged 16 or 17 when convicted of an offence, the court has a discretion to make a parenting order if it is satisfied that the parenting order would be desirable in the interests of preventing the commission of any further offence by the child.[14]

23.8 A court granting an anti-social behaviour injunction, making a criminal behaviour order or sexual harm prevention order in respect of a child *must* in the case of 10–15 year olds (and *may* in relation to 16 and 17 year olds):

- make a parenting order if it considers it desirable to prevent any repetition of the kind of behaviour that led to the order being made;[15] or
- state in open court that it is not and why it is not.[16]

7 CDA 1998 s8(1)(a).
8 CDA 1998 s8(1)(a).
9 CDA 1998 s8(1)(aa).
10 CDA 1998 s8(1)(d).
11 CDA 1998 s8(1)(c), (2)(6)(b) and s9(1).
12 CDA 1998 s9(1)(b).
13 CDA 1998 s9(1A).
14 CDA 1998 s8(1)(c) and(6)(b).
15 CDA 1998 s8(1)(b), (6)(a) and s9(1B).
16 CDA 1998 s9(1B).

23.9 Before making a mandatory PO on a child under the age of 16, the court must obtain and consider information about the child's family circumstances and the likely effect of the PO on those circumstances.[17]

23.10 Where the court is considering making a referral order and a PO, the court must obtain and consider a report by an appropriate officer indicating:

- the proposed requirements for the PO;
- the reasons why those requirements would be desirable in the interests of preventing the child committing further offences; and
- if the child is aged under 16, the child's family circumstances and the likely effect of the PO on those circumstances.[18]

23.11 POs can last for a period up to 12 months and specify requirements, these must include attendance at counselling or guidance sessions for up to three months (and not more than once a week).[19]

23.12 The mandatory requirement for counselling or guidance does not apply if a PO has been made on a previous occasion, in these circumstances the court has a discretion include such a requirement.[20] The counselling or guidance requirement can be a residential programme if it is likely to be more effective than a non-residential course and that any interference with family life is proportionate.[21] Requirements specified in a PO should, as far as practicable, avoid any conflict with the parents' religious beliefs; and any interference with the times, if any, the parent or guardian normally works or attends an educational establishment.

23.13 When making the PO, the court must explain to the parent in ordinary language:

- the effect of the order and the requirements proposed to be included in it;
- the consequences of a failure to comply with any of those requirements; and
- that the court has power to review the order on the application either of the parent or of the responsible officer.

17 CDA 1998 s9(2)(b).
18 CDA 1998 s9(2A).
19 CDA 1998 s8(4).
20 CDA 1998 s8(5).
21 CDA 1998 s8(7A).

Reviewing a parenting order

23.14 While a PO is in force, the responsible officer or the parent may apply to the court to vary or discharge the order.[22] A PO can only be discharged with the consent of the court that made the order.[23]

Appealing a parenting order

23.15 A PO made by the youth court or adult magistrates' court can be appealed to the Crown Court. A PO made by the Crown Court can be appealed to the Court of Appeal. If an appeal is from a youth court acting in its civil jurisdiction, this can be appealed to the High Court by way of case stated.

Breach of a parenting order

23.16 If while a PO is in force the parent or guardian fails, without reasonable excuse, to comply with any requirement in the PO or directions given by the responsible officer, breach proceedings may be instituted. Breach of a PO is punishable by a fine not exceeding level 3: £3,000.[24]

Parental bind over orders

Availability

23.17 Courts have the power to bind over parents or guardians where a child is convicted of an offence and the court forms the view that using this power would be desirable in the interests of preventing the child committing further offences.[25]

23.18 There has been a decline in the use of parental bind overs since the introduction of parenting orders (see paras 23.3–23.16). In most circumstances a parenting order is likely to be more appropriate that a parental bind over.[26]

22 CDA 1998 s9(5).
23 CDA 1998 s9(6).
24 CDA 1998 s9(7).
25 PCC(S)A 2000 s150(1)(a).
26 *Sentencing children and young people: definitive guideline*, 2018, para 6.46.

Court's duties

23.19 The court *must* bind over parents or guardians of children aged under 16 provided the court is satisfied it would be desirable to prevent the child committing further offences.[27] The court *may* bind over parents or guardians of children aged 16 and over provided it would be desirable to prevent the child committing further offences.

23.20 Where the court does not make a parental bind over order and it has the power to do so, it *must* state in open court that it is not satisfied that such an order would be desirable to prevent the commission of further offences by the child and explain why.[28]

23.21 Parents or guardians can be bound over 'to take proper care of and exercise proper control over a child'[29] and enter into a 'recognisance' up to a maximum of £1,000.[30] A 'recognisance' is an undertaking given by a person before a court or magistrate to observe some condition. The court imposing the parental bind over order should specify the actions which the parent or guardian is to take.[31] Where the court imposes a community sentence on a child, the court may include a condition that the parent or guardian ensure that the child complies with the requirements of the sentence.[32]

23.22 The parental bind over order can be up to three years, and must end on the child's 18th birthday.[33] Parents or guardians must consent to the bind over order; if the parent or guardian unreasonably refuses to consent, the parent or guardian can be ordered to pay a fine up to a maximum of £1,000.[34]

Restrictions on use of a parental bind over order

23.23 The court cannot impose a parental bind over order if the court is making a referral order.[35]

27 PCC(S)A 2000 s150(1).
28 PCC(S)A 2000 s150(1)(b).
29 PCC(S)A 2000 s150(2)(a).
30 PCC(S)A 2000 s150(3).
31 Criminal Practice Directions 2015, para J.19.
32 PCC(S)A 2000 s150(2).
33 PCC(S)A 2000 s150(4).
34 PCC(S)A 2000 s150(2)(b).
35 PCC(S)A 2000 s19(5)(b).

Appealing a parental bind over order

23.24 A parental bind over order made by the youth court or adult magistrates' court can be appealed to the Crown Court.[36] A parental bind over order made by the Crown Court can be appealed to the Court of Appeal.[37]

36 PCC(S)A 2000 s150(8).
37 PCC(S)A 2000 s150(9).

CHAPTER 24

Ancillary orders

continued

Key points

- Courts will need to consider ancillary orders as part of the sentencing exercise.
- Children can receive criminal behaviour orders, anti social behaviour injunctions and anti-gang injunctions.
- Anti social behaviour injunctions and gang injunctions are civil proceedings and special rules apply in relation to legal aid.
- Children can receive deportation orders.
- Children can receive endorsements, penalty points and disqualification, even if they are under 16 or 17 years old and do not have a driving licence.
- Children can receive football banning orders.
- The notification requirements for certain sexual offences (also known as the sex offenders register) apply to children but for shorter periods than adults.

Introduction

24.1 This chapter will discuss ancillary orders available for children: criminal behaviour orders, anti-social behaviour injunctions and anti-gang injunctions; restraining orders; deportation orders; endorsements, penalty points and disqualification; football banning orders; and notification requirements for certain sexual offences.

Behaviour orders and injunctions

Anti-social behaviour orders

24.2 Anti-social behaviour orders[1] (ASBOs) made on conviction were replaced by criminal behaviour orders (CBOs) in 2014. Existing ASBOs remain in force, but cannot be extended; five years after commencement, on 20 October 2019, any post-conviction ASBO still in force will be automatically treated as a CBO.[2]

1 CDA 1998 s1C.

2 Anti-social Behaviour, Crime and Policing Act (ASBCPA) 2014 s33(4).

Criminal behaviour orders

Introduction

24.3 CBOs are intended to prevent a convicted person from engaging in behaviour that is likely to cause harassment, alarm or distress to any person.[3] A CBO may include prohibitions (conditions that prohibit the person from doing anything), as well as positive requirements (such as alcohol awareness, drug treatment or attendance at a recreational activity to encourage more positive use of the child's time) that allow the court to require the defendant to undertake positive activities to address underlying causes of the anti-social behaviour. The statutory framework and Crown Prosecution Service (CPS) guidance require the CPS to ascertain the views of the local youth offending team (YOT) before making a CBO application for a child (see paras 24.12–24.13 on precondition).

24.4 CBOs were introduced alongside other new powers to address anti-social behaviour: dispersal orders, community protection notices and public spaces protection orders. Breach of any of these orders is a criminal offence.

24.5 The applicant for CBOs is usually the Crown Prosecution Service (CPS) either on its own initiative or following a request from the police or local authority.

Guidance

24.6 Anti-social Behaviour, Crime and Policing Act (ASBCPA) 2014 Part 2 sets out the statutory provisions relating to CBOs. The other relevant guidance available is:

- Home Office statutory guidance 'Anti-social Behaviour, Crime and Policing Act 2014: Reform of anti-social behaviour powers statutory guidance for frontline professionals' (updated December 2017).[4]

3 ASBCPA 2014 s22(5).

4 Home Office, 'Anti-social Behaviour, Crime and Policing Act 2014: Anti-social behaviour powers; Statutory guidance for frontline professionals', 2017: www.gov.uk/government/publications/anti-social-behaviour-crime-and-policing-bill-anti-social-behaviour.

- 'YOT practitioner's guide: civil injunctions and the Criminal Behaviour Order' (published 10 July 2015).[5]
- CPS legal guidance on criminal behaviour orders, 'Criminal behaviour orders – youths'.[6]

24.7 It is recommended that local authorities – with the police and the local youth offending team (YOT) – should develop a tiered approach to anti-social behaviour, including diverting children from the justice system, restorative approaches and offering evidence-based voluntary support when needed (particularly family-based support), before an injunction or CBO is considered.[7]

Availability

24.8 A criminal court has the power to make a CBO when a person has been convicted of an offence.[8]

24.9 The Court of Appeal has provided guidance that CBOs should only be made in limited circumstances, and then only if tailored to the specific facts of the case:

> We are still in the early days of CBOs and the case law is not yet fully developed. Section 22 of the 2014 Act might on a literal construction be said to apply to a high proportion of cases in the criminal courts. Many offences are committed in public places and cause a degree of alarm and distress either to the victims or to members of the public who observe them . . .
>
> We do not believe that it was the intention of Parliament that criminal behaviour orders should become a mere matter of box-ticking routine . . . [S]uch orders are not lightly to be imposed; the court should proceed with a proper degree of caution and circumspection; the order must be tailored to the specific circumstances of the person on whom it is to be imposed; and assessments of proportionality are intensively fact sensitive.[9]

5 Youth Justice Board of England and Wales, 'YOT Practitioner's Guide: civil injunctions and the Criminal Behaviour Order', published 10 July 2015: www.gov.uk/government/publications/yot-practitioners-guide-injunctions-to-prevent-gang-related-violence.

6 CPS legal guidance on criminal behaviour orders: www.cps.gov.uk/legal-guidance/criminal-behaviour-orders.

7 See the Standing Committee for Youth Justice, Guide to the new anti-social behaviour powers, February 2015, p4.

8 ASBCPA 2014 s22(2). The CBO provisions came into force on 20 October 2014 and apply to all criminal proceedings commenced on or after that date (confirmed in *R v Simsek* [2015] EWCA Crim 1268).

9 *R v Kamran Khan* [2018] EWCA Crim 1472, paras 19–20.

24.10 The Court of Appeal noted the statutory guidance:

> . . . which states that the CBO 'is intended for tackling the most serious and persistent offenders where their behaviour has brought them before a criminal court'.[10]

24.11 The statutory guidance:

> . . . emphasises the importance of ensuring that the powers are used appropriately to provide a proportionate response to the specific behaviour that is causing harm or nuisance without impacting adversely on behaviour that is neither unlawful nor anti-social.[11]

Pre-condition

24.12 Before applying for a CBO for a child defendant (who will be under the age of 18 when the application is made), the prosecution must find out the views of the local YOT.[12] The CPS legal guidance on CBOs provides guidance on the process to find out the views of the local YOT.[13] It also provides the YOT with a template for recording their views.

24.13 Where the YOT 'raises objections which the reviewing lawyer considers do not address the issues in the case . . . prosecutors should be aware that YOT objections may be renewed in court'.[14] Where the prosecution have not received a response, the YOT's views will usually be invited during the proceedings.

Court's powers and duties

24.14 The court may only make a CBO against a defendant who has been convicted of an offence and the prosecution makes an application to the court (see paras 24.17–24.18 below).[15] The application must be made before the sentencing hearing is concluded 'as an application cannot be made retrospectively'.[16]

10 *R v Kamran Khan* [2018] EWCA Crim 1472, para 18. Referring to 'Anti-social Behaviour, Crime and Policing Act 2014: Anti-social behaviour powers; Statutory guidance for frontline professionals', 2017, p29.

11 'Anti-social Behaviour, Crime and Policing Act 2014: Anti-social behaviour powers; Statutory guidance for frontline professionals', 2017, p1.

12 ASBCPA 2014 s22(8).

13 CPS legal guidance on criminal behaviour orders, Annexe L.

14 CPS legal guidance on criminal behaviour orders – youths.

15 ASBCPA 2014 s22(7).

16 Magistrates' Court Sentencing Guidelines, Ancillary Orders, 5. Criminal behaviour orders: www.sentencingcouncil.org.uk/explanatory-material/item/ancillary-orders/5-criminal-behaviour-orders/.

24.15 The court may make a CBO if two conditions are met (emphasis added):

1) The first condition is that 'the court is satisfied, *beyond reasonable doubt*, that the offender has engaged in behaviour that caused or was likely to cause harassment, alarm or distress to any person'.[17]
2) The second condition is that 'the court considers that making the order *will help* in preventing the offender from engaging in such behaviour'.[18]

24.16 An order may only be made if it is in addition to dealing with the defendant for the offence by imposing a sentence or a conditional discharge.[19] A CBO cannot be combined with an absolute discharge.

Procedure for applying for a criminal behaviour order

24.17 The prosecution must serve a notice of intention to apply for a criminal behaviour order as set out in Criminal Procedure Rules (CrimPR) r31.3. The notice must:

- summarise the relevant facts;
- the evidence relied upon
- attach any statements not already served; and
- specify the terms of the proposed order.[20]

24.18 The Criminal Procedure Rules set out the form in which this notice should be served.[21] Compliance with the rules should not be considered a mere technicality,[22] although a failure by the prosecution to comply with the Criminal Procedure Rules may not cause a CBO to be invalid if no unfairness was caused.[23]

17 ASBCPA 2014 s22(3).
18 ASBCPA 2014 s22(4).
19 ASBCPA 2014 s22(5).
20 CrimPR r31.3(3).
21 CrimPR Part 31 Behaviour Order forms: www.justice.gov.uk/courts/procedure-rules/criminal/forms
22 *M v DPP* [2007] EWHC 1032 (Admin); and *R v Kamran Khan* [2018] EWCA Crim 1472, para 13.
23 *R v Nasser Asfi* [2016] EWCA Crim 1236.

Evidential test

24.19 CBO applications are civil proceedings and civil rules of evidence[24] apply.[25] The court may hear evidence from the prosecution or the defendant.[26] If hearsay evidence is relied upon, a hearsay notice must be served.[27] The evidence does not need to have been admissible in the original proceedings in which the defendant was convicted.[28] The court may take account of evidence of the convicted person's conduct going back up to one year before the commencement of the CBO provisions on 20 October 2014.[29] Special measures directions are available for vulnerable and intimidated witnesses.[30]

24.20 When the court considers the first condition – whether the defendant 'has engaged in behaviour that caused or was likely to cause harassment, alarm or distress to any person'[31] – the criminal standard of proof applies.[32]

24.21 The court must then consider the second condition – whether 'the order will help in preventing the offender from engaging in such behaviour'[33] – is met. The 'helpfulness' test was intended to simplify the anti-social behaviour regime, but in fact 'the legislative language is a shade less clear'.[34] The court will be guided, in particular, by the expertise of the local YOT in relation to how the proposed order 'will help' address a child's anti-social behaviour.

Adjournments

24.22 The court may adjourn the application even after the defendant has been sentenced (provided the notice of application was served in accordance with CrimPR r31.2).[35] However, it should be dealt with

24 Civil Evidence Act 1995.

25 *R (W) v Acton Youth Court* [2005] EWHC 954 (Admin).

26 ASBCPA 2014 s23(1).

27 CrimPR rr31.6–31.7.

28 ASBCPA 2014 s23(2).

29 ASBCPA 2014 s33(5).

30 ASBCPA 2014 s31.

31 ASBCPA 2014 s22(3).

32 This was established under the previous anti-social behaviour order legislation: *R (McCann and others) v Crown Court at Manchester; Clingham v Kensington and Chelsea RBC* [2002] UKHL 39, [2002] 3 WLR 1313.

33 ASBCPA 2014 s22(4).

34 *DPP v Bulmer* [2015] EWHC 2323 (Admin), para 21.

35 ASBCPA 2014 s23(3).

expeditiously – in *R v Kamran Khan*[36] a delay of several months was criticised by the Court of Appeal.

24.23 Where the application is adjourned, the court can make an interim order[37] (see paras 24.24–24.25 on interim orders). If the defendant fails to attend the adjourned hearing, the court may issue an arrest warrant or hear the application in the defendant's absence, provided the court is satisfied the defendant had adequate notice of the time and place of the adjourned proceedings (and the defendant was warned the court may hear proceedings in their absence).[38]

Interim criminal behaviour order (interim order)

24.24 Where the court adjourns the hearing of an application for a CBO (whether made with notice or without), the court may grant an 'interim order' until the final hearing of the application or until further order if 'the court thinks it just to do so'.[39]

24.25 In making an interim order, there is no requirement for the prosecution to have made an application or to have ascertained the views of the local YOT.[40] The court may include both prohibitions and positive requirements.[41]

Making a criminal behaviour order

The terms of the order

24.26 A CBO may include both prohibitions and positive requirements for the purpose of preventing the defendant from engaging in behaviour likely to cause harassment, alarm or distress.[42] Although the court is not obliged to include a positive requirement,[43] the court may wish to consider positive requirements that support the child in addressing the underlying causes of their anti-social behaviour.

24.27 Any requirements must, so far as practicable, avoid interfering with the times at which the defendant normally works or attends school or any other educational establishment; and must not conflict

36 [2018] EWCA Crim 1472, para 22.
37 ASBCPA 2014 s26.
38 ASBCPA 2014 s23(4), (5), (6).
39 ASBCPA 2014 s26(2).
40 ASBCPA 2014 s26(3).
41 ASBCPA 2014 s26(4).
42 ASBCPA 2014 s22(5).
43 *DPP v Bulmer* [2015] EWHC 2323 (Admin), para 23.

with the requirements of any other court order or injunction to which the defendant may be subject.[44]

24.28 In addition to any specified terms, the defendant must keep in touch with the individual or organisation responsible for supervising any requirement and to notify them of a change of address.[45] Failure to follow these requirements will amount to a breach of the CBO.[46]

24.29 Guidance on the appropriateness of prohibitions can be drawn from case-law arising from the ASBO regime: 'the guidance given in decisions of [the Divisional Court] and those of the Court of Appeal (Criminal Division) on ASBOs is of relevance when considering whether to make a Criminal Behaviour Order' provided it is modified to reflect the removal of the 'necessity test' and the additional procedural safeguards in ASBCPA 2014 s24.[47] The guidance given by the Court of Appeal in *R v Boness*[48] at paras 19–23 should be followed, in particular the four requirements derived from the previous Court of Appeal decision in *R v P (Shane Tony)*:

1) The terms of the order must be precise and capable of being understood by the defendant.
2) The findings of fact giving rise to the making of the order must be recorded.
3) The order must be explained to the defendant.
4) The exact terms of the order must be pronounced in open court and the written order must accurately reflect the order as pronounced.[49]

24.30 Prohibitions should not be too widely drafted so that they could cause a defendant to breach the order for behaviour that is neither unlawful nor anti-social.[50] In *R v Simsek*, the Court of Appeal made the following observations:[51]

> The scope of such a prohibition exposed the applicant to breach proceedings for being in possession of a wide range of items which are lawful and which bear no obvious relationship to the anti-social

44 ASBCPA 2014 s22(9).

45 ASBCPA 2014 s24(6).

46 ASBCPA 2014 ss24(6) and 30(1).

47 *R v Kamran Khan* [2018] EWCA Crim 1472, para 18 approving observations made in *DPP v Bulmer* [2015] EWHC 2323 (Admin), para 26.

48 [2005] EWCA Crim 2395.

49 *R v Kamran Khan* [2018] EWCA Crim 1472, para 14.

50 'Anti-social Behaviour, Crime and Policing Act 2014: Anti-social behaviour powers; Statutory guidance for frontline professionals', 2017, p1.

51 *R v Simsek* [2015] EWCA Crim 1268, para 18.

behaviour that formed the subject of the indictment. The final part of the prohibition, namely a prohibition on being in possession of any self-seal bags, is also patently too wide.

Proportionality

24.31 The court must consider the child's welfare, best interests and whether the proposed terms of the order are a necessary, proportionate or a reasonable interference with the child's human rights, primarily European Convention on Human Rights (ECHR) Article 8 (the right to private and family life).[52]

Positive requirements

24.32 When considering a positive requirement, the court must hear evidence about its suitability and enforceability from the person or organisation who will be responsible for supervising the order.[53] Before including two or more requirements, the court must consider their compatibility with each other.[54]

24.33 If making a positive requirement, the order must specify the person or organisation responsible for supervising the requirement.[55] This specified person or organisation has a duty to make the necessary arrangements for the requirement(s), to promote the offender's compliance and has a duty to inform the prosecution and the appropriate chief officer of police whether the defendant has complied or failed to comply with the relevant requirements.[56]

Length of order

24.34 For defendants who are children when the CBO is made, the CBO must be for a minimum of one year and not more than three years[57] (for adults the order must be for a fixed period of two years or more, or an indefinite period[58]). If the defendant is currently subject to another order, the new order may start on the day the previous order

52 *DPP v Bulmer* [2015] EWHC 2323 (Admin), para 47; *R v John James* [2016] EWCA Crim 676, para 18. Also see R *v Boness* [2005] EWCA Crim 2395.

53 ASBCPA 2014 s24(2).

54 ASBCPA 2014 s24(3).

55 ASBCPA 2014 s24(1).

56 ASBCPA 2014 s24(4).

57 ASBCPA 2014 s25(4).

58 ASBCPA 2014 s25(5).

ceases to have effect.[59] However, there is no other power to postpone the start of an order (for example, where the defendant receives a custodial sentence). The order may specify periods during which particular prohibitions or requirements have effect.[60]

Reporting restrictions (anonymity)

24.35 The reporting restrictions that automatically apply in the youth court under Children and Young Persons (CYPA) Act 1933 s49 do not apply to the making of a CBO[61] or to breach proceedings[62] (see para 24.52 below), although they still apply to the offence the child has been convicted of. The youth court (and adult courts) have a discretionary power to restrict reporting of the making of a CBO under CYPA 1933 s39.[63]

24.36 In *R (T) v St Alban's Crown Court*[64] the issue of reporting restrictions in relation to a child subject to an ASBO was considered. This case establishes the principle that the court 'should always consider granting an order to preserve the child's anonymity under CYPA 1933 s39'. The judge stated that:

> Whilst the court plainly does not have to refer to every factor which may weigh in favour of a section 39 direction being made, it is necessary, in my view, that it should briefly summarise the principal factors weighing in favour, even if the decision finally is that these factors are outweighed by the public interest in disclosure.[65]

24.37 The court must have regard to the welfare of the child[66] (see paras 24.38–24.39). For a wider discussion on automatic and discretionary reporting restrictions, see para 14.32 on civil cases and criminal behaviour orders.

Publicising criminal behaviour orders

24.38 If reporting restrictions are not imposed, it is open to the police and local authority to publicise the criminal behaviour order, by issuing a press release or informing the local community. The police or local

59 ASBCPA 2014 s25(4).
60 ASBCPA 2014 s25(6).
61 ASBCPA 2014 s23(8)(a).
62 ASBCPA 2014 s30(5).
63 ASBCPA 2014 s23(8)(b).
64 [2002] EWHC 1129 (Admin).
65 *R (T) v St Alban's Crown Court* [2002] EWHC 1129 (Admin).
66 CYPA 1933 s44(1).

authority must have regard to the impact publicity would have on the child's welfare:[67]

> When deciding whether to publicise a CBO, public authorities (including the courts) must consider that it is necessary and proportionate to interfere with the young person's right to privacy, and the likely impact on a young person's behaviour. This will need to be balanced against the need to provide re-assurance to victims and the wider community as well as providing them with information so that they can report any breaches. Each case should be decided carefully on its own facts.[68]

In most cases, the local YOT would be consulted before such a course is taken, in order to provide information about the likely impact of publicising the CBO.

Annual review of criminal behaviour orders on children

24.39 Any CBO made on a child must be reviewed by the police every 12 months from the day the order takes effect or is varied (provided the defendant will be under the age of 18 at the end of the review period and the order is still running and is not discharged).[69]

24.40 A review must consider:

- the extent to which the child has complied with the order;
- the adequacy of any support available to the child to help him or her comply with it;
- any matters relevant to the question whether an application should be made for the order to be varied or discharged.

24.41 Further guidance on how the review should be carried out is available in the statutory guidance.[70]

Varying or discharging a criminal behaviour order

24.42 An application to vary or discharge a CBO can be made by the person subject to it or the prosecution.[71] The power to vary a CBO includes a power to include an additional prohibition or requirement in the order or to extend the period for which a prohibition or requirement has effect.[72]

67 Children Act 2004 s11(2)(a).

68 'Anti-social Behaviour, Crime and Policing Act 2014: Anti-social behaviour powers; Statutory guidance for frontline professionals', 2017, p32.

69 ASBCPA 2014 s28.

70 'Anti-social Behaviour, Crime and Policing Act 2014: Anti-social behaviour powers Statutory guidance for frontline professionals', 2017.

71 ASBCPA 2014 s27(1).

72 ASBCPA 2014 s27(4).

Appealing a criminal behaviour order

24.43 An appeal against a CBO made by the youth court or adult magistrates' court is to the Crown Court.[73] A CBO made by the Crown Court may be appealed to the Court of Appeal (Criminal Division).[74]

Breach of a criminal behaviour order

24.44 It is a criminal offence to breach a CBO. A person who without reasonable excuse

(a) does anything he or she is prohibited from doing by a CBO; or
(b) fails to do anything he or she is required to do by a CBO,

commits an offence.[75]

24.45 The court's powers to deal with a defendant following a breach of a CBO are set out in ASBCPA 2014 s30. The Sentencing Council published a sentencing guideline for breach of a criminal behaviour order in October 2018,[76] but as there is no specific guidance in relation to children who breach CBOs, it should be read alongside the Sentencing Council's *Sentencing children and young people: definitive guideline.*[77]

Arrest and detention for breach of a criminal behaviour order

24.46 A child may be arrested for breach of a CBO.[78] If charged and refused bail, this can lead to children spending overnight in police custody (although there is a duty to transfer the child to local authority accommodation[79] this rarely happens in practice). Defence lawyers should be aware that in some cases the appropriate response to a breach is a youth caution and therefore court proceedings and unnecessary police detention can be avoided (see para 24.47).

73 Magistrates' Court Act 1980 s108(1), (3).
74 Criminal Appeal Act 1968 ss50, 9.
75 ASBCPA 2014 s30(1).
76 Magistrates' Court Sentencing Guideline – Breach of a criminal behaviour order; available at https://www.sentencingcouncil.org.uk/offences/magistrates-court/item/breach-of-a-criminal-behaviour-order/.
77 Sentencing Council, *Sentencing children and young people: definitive guideline*, 2017, p17 and para 6.46 on suggested reduction.
78 Breach of a CBO is a criminal offence – see para 24.44.
79 PACE 1984 s38(6) – see paras 6.195–6.204.

The decision to prosecute a breach of a criminal behaviour order

24.47 The CPS legal guidance on CBOs sets out the following considerations on whether or not to prosecute a child for a breach of an order:

> The public interest factors apply equally to youths as they do to adults, but in the case of youths, they must be balanced against the principles set out in the CPS legal guidance on Youth Offenders. Prosecutors must be able to show that the interests and welfare of the youth have been identified and balanced with the seriousness of the offence and any aggravating factors set out in the Code for Crown Prosecutors and relevant CPS legal guidance.
>
> Where a youth breaches a CBO, a youth caution may be appropriate. The CPS legal guidance on Youth Offenders states that youth cautions are intended to provide a proportionate and effective response to offending behaviour and can be used for any offence providing the statutory criteria are satisfied. Offence seriousness is determined by reference to the ACPO Gravity Matrix, which sets out the most prevalent offences, and provides them with a score of 1, 2, 3 or 4. The score may be raised or lowered by one level according to aggravating and mitigating factors which are set out in the Matrix.
>
> The Gravity Matrix score for breach of a CBO without any aggravating factors is 3 provided the breach was not a flagrant one. Where the breach was flagrant, then the expectation would be to charge, unless there were some very unusual circumstances. In the case of breaches of a CBO imposed following a conviction, the public interest will usually require a prosecution.[80]

Prosecuting a breach of a criminal behaviour order

24.48 Breach proceedings for children take place in the youth court, irrespective of which court made the original order. The defence of reasonable excuse is available and if raised must be disproved by the prosecution.

24.49 The penalties for breach on summary conviction are a maximum six months' imprisonment, or a fine, or both. Following conviction on indictment, a maximum of five years' imprisonment or a fine, or both. A conditional discharge is not available.[81]

24.50 For children (aged under 18 when the breach is brought to court) the maximum available sentence in the youth court is a 24-month detention and training order. However, following the principle that

80 CPS Legal Guidance – Criminal Behaviour Orders, Criminal Behaviour Orders – Youths: www.cps.gov.uk / https://www.cps.gov.uk/legal-guidance/criminal-behaviour-orders.

81 ASBCPA 2014 s30(2).

children should not receive longer sentences than adults,[82] it would rarely be appropriate to exceed a six-month detention and training order (see paras 21.87–21.89 on maximum detention and training order sentencing powers).

24.51 The Sentencing Council have produced a new sentencing guideline for breach of a criminal behaviour order,[83] but as there is no specific guidance in relation to children who breach CBOs, it should be read alongside the *Sentencing children and young people: definitive guideline*.[84]

Reporting restrictions

24.52 When dealing with a breach of a CBO, automatic reporting restrictions under CYPA 1933 s49 do not apply.[85] The court has a discretionary power to restrict reporting under Youth Justice and Criminal Evidence Act 1999 s45 where the defendant is under the age of 18. If it exercises this power, it must give its reasons for doing so.[86] See paras 24.35–24.38 on reporting restrictions and CBOs.

Anti-social behaviour injunctions (civil injunction)

Introduction

24.53 Anti-social behaviour injunctions (ASBIs) are civil injunctions.

Legal aid for respondents

24.54 Application, variation, discharge and appeal of ASBIs will all be covered by civil legal aid.[87] Eligibility for legal aid will require children appearing in the youth court to undertake a 'means test' to determine

82 *B v Leeds Crown Court and another* [2016] EWHC 1230 (Admin); *P v Leeds Youth Court* [2006] EWHC 2527 (Admin).

83 Magistrates' Court Sentencing Guideline – Breach of a criminal behaviour order.

84 *Sentencing children and young people: definitive guideline*, 2017, p17 and para 6.46 on suggested reduction.

85 ASBCPA 2014 s30(5).

86 ASBCPA 2014 s30(6).

87 Ministry of Justice, 'Anti-social Behaviour, Crime and Policing Act 2014: Changes to remuneration for legal aid service – Response to Consultation', January 2015, para 1.3. Note that on breach of ASBIs are covered by criminal legal aid see para 24.92.

whether they qualify for legal aid.[88] Respondents can check their financial eligibility for legal aid by using the online eligibility calculator.[89]

Guidance

24.55 ASBCPA 2014 Part 1 sets out the statutory provisions relating to ASBIs. The other relevant guidance available is:

- Home Office statutory guidance 'Anti-social Behaviour, Crime and Policing Act 2014: Reform of anti-social behaviour powers statutory guidance for frontline professionals' (revised December 2017).[90]
- 'YOT practitioner's guide: civil injunctions and the criminal behaviour order' (published 10 July 2015).[91]

24.56 It is recommended that local authorities – with the police and the local YOT – should develop a tiered approach to anti-social behaviour, including diverting children from the justice system, restorative approaches, and offering evidence-based voluntary support when needed (particularly family-based support), before an injunction is considered.[92]

Availability

24.57 The ASBI is a civil power and an injunction may be granted against a person aged 10 or over who has engaged or threatens to engage in anti-social behaviour.[93]

24.58 When considering applying for an ASBI against a child, the statutory guidance advocates informal approaches and therefore the availability of ASBIs against children should only be considered as a last resort:

88 Ministry of Justice, 'Anti-social Behaviour, Crime and Policing Act 2014: Changes to remuneration for legal aid service – Response to Consultation', January 2015, para 9.

89 www.gov.uk/check-legal-aid.

90 Home Office, 'Anti-social Behaviour, Crime and Policing Act 2014: Anti-social behaviour powers; Statutory guidance for frontline professionals', published 24 December 2017.

91 Youth Justice Board of England and Wales, 'YOT Practitioner's Guide: civil injunctions and the Criminal Behaviour Order', published 10 July 2015: www.gov.uk/government/publications/yot-practitioners-guide-injunctions-to-prevent-gang-related-violence.

92 See the Standing Committee for Youth Justice guide to the new anti-social behaviour powers, February 2015, p4.

93 ASBCPA 2014 s1(1).

> [I]t is a formal sanction and in appropriate cases professionals will want to consider whether an informal approach might be preferable before resorting to court action, especially in the case of under 18s. However, where informal approaches have not worked or professionals decide that a formal response is needed, they are free to apply to the court for a civil injunction.[94]

24.59 The ASBI is designed '[t]o stop or prevent individuals engaging in anti-social behaviour quickly, nipping problems in the bud before they escalate.'[95]

24.60 The following agencies can apply for a civil injunction:

- local authority;
- housing provider;
- chief officer of police for a police area;
- chief constable of the British Transport Police Force;
- Transport for London;
- Environment Agency;
- Natural Resources Body for Wales; and
- NHS Protect.[96]

Pre-condition

24.61 Before applying for an ASBI for a child (who will still be under the age of 18 when the application is made), the person applying for the injunction must find out the views of the local YOT and inform any other body or individual the applicant thinks appropriate of the application.[97]

24.62 Ascertaining the views of the local YOT should ensure informal approaches are explored before resorting to court action (see para 24.58):

> Although the consultation requirement does not mean that the youth offending team can veto the application, it is important that applicants fully consider and take into account representations from the youth offending team as part of developing good partnership working in cases involving young people.[98]

94 'Anti-social Behaviour, Crime and Policing Act 2014: Anti-social behaviour powers; Statutory guidance for frontline professionals', Home Office, 2017, p21.

95 'Anti-social Behaviour, Crime and Policing Act 2014: Anti-social behaviour powers; Statutory guidance for frontline professionals', Home Office, 2017, p20.

96 ASBCPA 2014 s5(1). Additionally, the Secretary of State or Welsh Ministers exercising security management functions have the power to apply for an injunction.

97 ASBCPA 2014 s14(1).

98 'Anti-social Behaviour, Crime and Policing Act 2014: Anti-social behaviour powers; Statutory guidance for frontline professionals', Home Office, 2017, p23.

24.63 This requirement does not apply to without-notice applications, however, if the without-notice application is adjourned, the applicant must consult the local youth offending exception and inform other relevant people.[99]

Court's duties

24.64 The court may make an anti-social behaviour injunction if two conditions are met (emphasis added):

1) The first condition is that 'the court is satisfied, *on the balance of probabilities*, that the respondent has engaged or threatens to engage in anti-social behaviour'.[100]
2) The second condition is that 'the court considers it *just and convenient* to grant the injunction for the purpose of preventing the respondent from engaging in anti-social behaviour'.[101]

24.65 Anti-social behaviour means 'conduct that has caused, or is likely to cause, harassment, alarm or distress to any person', however additional definitions may apply according to the agency applying for the ASBI.[102]

Procedure for applying for a civil injunction

24.66 An application for a civil injunction under this section must be made to a youth court if the respondent is a child otherwise the application is made in the High Court or the county court.[103] If there are linked respondents who are adults, the application must still be made in the youth court and adults will appear alongside children in the youth court.[104]

Without notice applications

24.67 An application for an injunction may be made without notice being given to the respondent. In these circumstances, the court has three options:

99 ASBCPA 2014 s14(2).
100 ASBCPA 2014 s1(2).
101 ASBCPA 2014 s1(3).
102 ASBCPA 2014 s2.
103 ASBCPA 2014 s1(8).
104 ASBCPA 2014 s18(2).

- adjourn the proceedings and grant an interim injunction; or
- adjourn the proceedings without granting an interim injunction; or
- dismiss the application.[105]

24.68 Given the importance of considering informal approaches before taking formal action, it would be rare for an ASBI to be sought without notice in relation to a child.

24.69 If the without-notice application is adjourned, the applicant must consult the local youth offending exception and inform other relevant people.[106]

Interim injunctions

24.70 Where the court adjourns the hearing of an application for an injunction (whether made with notice or without), the court may grant an 'interim injunction' until the final hearing of the application or until further order if 'the court thinks it just to do so'.[107]

24.71 An interim injunction made following a without notice hearing may not include requirements to participate in particular activities.[108] Subject to that, the court has the same powers whether or not the injunction is an interim injunction.[109]

Making an anti-social behaviour injunction

Length

24.72 An ASBI made against a child must be for a specified period and no longer than 12 months.[110]

Requirements and prohibitions included in the anti-social behaviour injunction

24.73 The injunction may include both prohibitions and positive requirements for the purpose of preventing the respondent from engaging in anti-social behaviour.[111]

105 ASBCPA 2014 s6.
106 ASBCPA 2014 s14(2).
107 ASBCPA 2014 s7(1), (2).
108 ASBCPA 2014 s7(1), (2).
109 ASBCPA 2014 s7(1), (2).
110 ASBCPA 2014 s1(6).
111 ASBCPA 2014 s1(4).

24.74 Any prohibitions and positive requirements must, so far as practicable, avoid interfering with the times, if any, at which the respondent normally works or attends school or any other educational establishment; and any conflict with the requirements of any other court order or injunction to which the respondent may be subject.[112]

24.75 In *R v Kamran Khan*,[113] the Court of Appeal emphasised the importance of the terms being precise and capable of being understood by the defendant (see paras 24.29–24.30 above on CBOs). Prohibitions should not be too widely drafted so that they could cause a defendant to breach the injunction for behaviour that is neither unlawful nor anti-social.[114]

24.76 When considering a positive requirement, the court must hear evidence about its suitability and enforceability from the person or organisation who will be responsible for supervising the order.[115] If it is proposed to include two or more requirements, the court must consider their compatibility with each other.[116]

24.77 An injunction that includes a requirement must specify the person (individual or organisation) who is to be responsible for supervising compliance with the requirement.[117] This specified person or organisation has a duty to make the necessary arrangements for the requirement(s), to promote the individual's compliance and has a duty to inform the prosecution and the appropriate chief officer of police whether the respondent has complied or failed to comply with the relevant requirements.[118]

24.78 In addition to any specific requirements, the respondent must keep in touch with the individual or organisation responsible for supervising any requirement and to notify them of a change of address.[119] These obligations have effect as requirements of the injunction.

Exclusion from home address

24.79 The court's power to exclude perpetrators of anti-social behaviour from their home, who use or threaten violent or there is a significant

112 ASBCPA 2014 s1(5).
113 [2018] EWCA Crim 1472.
114 'Anti-social Behaviour, Crime and Policing Act 2014: Anti-social behaviour powers; Statutory guidance for frontline professionals', 2017, p1.
115 ASBCPA 2014 s3(2).
116 ASBCPA 2014 s3(3).
117 ASBCPA 2014 s3(1).
118 ASBCPA 2014 s3(4).
119 ASBCPA 2014 s3(6).

risk of harm as a term of the ASBI does not apply to respondents who are children[120] – the court granting an injunction may not grant a prohibition excluding a child from his or her home.

Power of arrest

24.80 A court granting an injunction may attach a power of arrest to a breach of a prohibition or requirement of the injunction if the court thinks that:

- the anti-social behaviour in which the respondent has engaged or threatened to engage consists of or includes the use or threatened use of violence against other persons; or
- there is a significant risk of harm to other persons from the respondent.[121]

24.81 If the court attaches a power of arrest, the injunction may specify a period for which the power of arrest is to have effect and this can be shorter than period of any prohibition or requirement.[122]

Proportionality

24.82 The court must consider the child's welfare and best interests and whether the proposed terms of the order are a necessary, proportionate or a reasonable interference with the defendant's human rights, primarily Article 8 ECHR (the right to private and family life).[123]

Length of the injunction

24.83 A civil injunction made against a child respondent must be for a specified period and no longer than 12 months.[124]

Reporting restrictions (anonymity)

24.84 The reporting restrictions that automatically apply in the youth court under CYPA 1933 s49 do not apply to the making of a civil injunction[125] or to breach proceedings (see para 24.98 below). The youth

120 ASBCPA 2014 s13(1)(a).
121 ASBCPA 2014 s4(1).
122 ASBCPA 2014 s4(2).
123 *DPP v Bulmer* [2015] EWHC 2323 (Admin), para 47; *R v John James* [2016] EWCA Crim 676, para 18. Also see *R v Boness* [2005] EWCA Crim 2395.
124 ASBCPA 2014 s1(6).
125 ASBCPA 2014 s17.

court has a discretionary power to restrict reporting of the making of an order under Children and Young Persons Act 1933 s39.

24.85 The court should always consider whether to grant an order to preserve the child's anonymity under CYPA 1933 s39[126] (see paras 24.35–24.38 on reporting restrictions and CBOs).

Varying or discharging an anti-social behaviour injunction

24.86 The court may vary or discharge an injunction. The applicant (the person who applied for the injunction) or the respondent may apply to vary or discharge an anti-social behaviour injunction.[127] The power to vary an injunction includes a power:

- to include an additional prohibition or requirement in the injunction, or to extend the period for which a prohibition or requirement has effect;
- to attach a power of arrest, or to extend the period for which a power of arrest has effect.[128]

24.87 The application is to the court that granted the injunction. Except where the injunction was granted by a youth court and the respondent is now aged 18 or over, the application is to the county court.[129] If the respondent will be aged under 18 when that application is made, before making such an application, the applicant must:

- consult the local YOT about the application for variation or discharge;
- inform any other body or individual the applicant thinks appropriate of that application.[130]

24.88 If an application to vary or discharge the injunction under ASBCPA 2014 s8 is dismissed, the applicant party may not make a further application without the consent of the court or the agreement of the other party.[131]

126 *R (T) v St Alban's Crown Court* [2002] EWHC 1129 (Admin).
127 ASBCPA 2014 s8(1).
128 ASBCPA 2014 s8(3).
129 ASBCPA 2014 s8(2).
130 ASBCPA 2014 s14(3).
131 ASBCPA 2014 s8(4).

Appealing an anti-social behaviour injunction

24.89 An appeal against an ASBI made by the youth court is made to the Crown Court.[132] On appeal, the Crown Court may make:

- whatever orders are necessary to give effect to its determination of the appeal; and
- whatever incidental or consequential orders appear to it to be just.[133]

24.90 An order of the Crown Court made on an appeal under this section (other than one directing that an application be re-heard by the youth court) is to be treated for the purposes of applying to vary or discharge the injunction as an order of the youth court.[134]

Breach of an anti-social behaviour injunction

Overview

24.91 It is not a criminal offence to breach a civil injunction, however the sanctions available are robust. If a breach is proven, the court has the power to impose a supervision order or, as a very last resort, a civil detention order[135] of up to three months for 14 to 17 year olds[136] (adults can receive an unlimited fine or up to two years in prison).

Legal aid for respondents

24.92 Criminal legal aid is available for ASBI breach proceedings. Breaches of ASBIs made under the ASBCPA 2014 became criminal matters for legal aid purposes due to the risk of custody.[137] A solicitor authorised to undertake criminal work may apply for a criminal representation order to represent a child facing breach proceedings; civil

132 ASBCPA 2014 s15(1).

133 ASBCPA 2014 s15(2).

134 ASBCPA 2014 s15(3).

135 A detention order is detention in a secure training centre, young offender institution or secure accommodation – ASBCPA 2014 Sch 2 para 14.

136 ASBCPA 2014 s12, Sch 2 para 1.

137 Apply for legal aid for breach of Part 1 injunctions under the Anti-social Behaviour, Crime and Policing Act (ASBCPA) 2014 Guidance for providers ('Legal Aid applications for breach of Part 1 injunctions – Guidance'), Legal Aid Agency, version 2, May 2017, p3.

providers may apply for an individual case contract.[138] Legal aid for breach proceedings heard in civil venues is not means tested.[139]

Arrest and detention for breach of an anti-social behaviour injunction

24.93 Where there is a power of arrest attached to a provision of an injunction, a constable may arrest the respondent without warrant if he or she has reasonable cause to suspect that the respondent is in breach of the provision.[140] The respondent must be brought before a court within 24 hours of being arrested (disregarding Christmas Day, Good Friday and any Sunday).[141]

24.94 Where the injunction was granted by a youth court, the respondent must be brought before a justice of the peace (but if the respondent is aged 18 or over, before a county court).[142] If the respondent is under 18, the court must then remand him or her on bail to appear before the youth court that granted the injunction,[143] unless the child is suffering from a mental disorder and the court remands the person to a hospital or registered establishment.[144]

24.95 Alternatively, if there is no power of arrest, the person who applied for the injunction may apply for the issue of a warrant for the respondent's arrest if the person considers that the respondent is in breach of any of its provisions.[145] A judge or justice may issue a warrant if the judge has reasonable grounds for believing that the respondent is in breach of any provision of the injunction.[146] The power of arrest will require the respondent to be brought before the youth court that granted the injunction (or the county court, if the person is aged 18 or over).[147]

138 All applications for criminal legal aid should be submitted via the e-form portal. Firms without a criminal legal aid contract who wish to represent a client in a breach of part 1 injunction proceedings must apply for an ICC by emailing the NCT in Nottingham at: Nottinghm.NCT@legalaid.gsi.gov.uk.

139 Legal aid applications for breach of Part 1 injunctions – Guidance, Legal Aid Agency, version 2, May 2017 p3.

140 ASBCPA 2014 s9(1).

141 ASBCPA 2014 s9.

142 ASBCPA 2014 s9(3).

143 ASBCPA 2014 s9(6); Sch 1 para 2(1).

144 ASBCPA 2014 s9(6); Sch 1 para 6(1).

145 ASBCPA 2014 s10.

146 ASBCPA 2014 s10(3).

147 ASBCPA 2014 s10(6).

Prosecuting a breach of an anti-social behaviour injunction

24.96 Breach proceedings will be heard before the youth court where the original injunction was made (or in the county court the respondent is aged 18 or over). Breaches must be proved to the criminal standard.[148]

24.97 If a breach is proven, the court has the power to impose a supervision order or, if 'in view of the severity or extent of the breach, no other power available to the court is appropriate' a civil detention order of up to three months for 14–17 year olds'.[149]

Reporting restrictions (anonymity)

24.98 When dealing with a breach of an ASBI, automatic reporting restrictions under CYPA 1933 s39 do not apply.[150] The court retains a discretionary power to restrict reporting under CYPA 1933 s39 where the defendant is a child (see para 14.32).[151]

Anti-gang injunctions (civil injunction)

Introduction

24.99 The Policing and Crime Act (PCA) 2009 Part 4 sets out the statutory provisions relating to injunctions to prevent gang-related violence and drug-dealing activity. For the purposes of this book, these injunctions will be described as 'anti-gang injunctions'.

Legal aid for respondents

24.100 Legal representation for respondents in anti-gang injunction applications is covered by civil legal aid and criminal legal aid for breaches (see paras 24.54 and 24.92).

Guidance

24.101 The government has issued statutory guidance on *Injunctions to prevent gang-related violence and gang-related drug dealing: revised guidance.*[152] Local authorities are likely to have their own policy

148 ASBCPA 2014 Sch 2 para 1.

149 ASBCPA 2014 s12 Sch 2 para 1.

150 ASBCPA 2014 s17.

151 ASBCPA 2014.

152 'Statutory guidance injunctions to prevent gang-related violence and gang-related drug dealing: revised guidance', HM Government, May 2016.

documents addressing safeguarding of children who may be affected by gang activity. This may provide important guidance on how to approach the use of anti-gang injunctions, in particular, issues to consider for girls[153] and the approach to be taken given the recent prevalence of county lines gangs (see paras 13.14–13.16). Children exploited by county lines gangs should generally be viewed as victims rather than suspects or perpetrators of criminal drug-related activity.

24.102 There are specific issues when considering an anti-gang injunctions for 14 to 17 year olds.[154] Local authorities and the police (working with the local YOT) should consider what support and intervention can be put in place before an injunction is considered to safeguard the child and prevent them engaging in gang activity.[155]There is also a need to act proportionately and have due regard to the individual rights of potential child respondents, for example:

> It can be common for groups of children and young people to gather together in public places to socialise. Although some peer group gatherings can lead to increased anti-social behaviour and youth offending, these activities should not be confused with the serious violence of a street gang.[156]

It is important that injunctions are not used to infringe normal childhood behaviour.[157]

Availability

24.103 The anti-gang injunction is a civil order, and an injunction may be granted against a person aged 14 or over who has engaged in, has engaged in or has encouraged or assisted gang-related violence, or gang-related drug-dealing activity.[158]

24.104 An application may be made by the police (including the British Transport Police) or a local authority.[159]

153 'Statutory guidance injunctions to prevent gang-related violence and gang-related drug dealing: revised guidance', HM Government, May 2016 at paras 4.1–4.2.

154 'Statutory guidance injunctions to prevent gang-related violence and gang-related drug dealing: revised guidance', HM Government, May 2016 at para 3.2.

155 CBO guidance.

156 'Safeguarding children and young people who may be affected by gang activity', Greater Manchester Safeguarding Partnership: http://greatermanchesterscb.proceduresonline.com/chapters/p_sg_ch_yp_gang_act.html.

157 ECHR Article 8 and UNCRC rights.

158 PCA 2009 s34(2).

159 PCA 2009 s37(1).

Pre-condition

24.105 Before applying for an anti-gang injunction for a child (who will be under the age of 18 when the application is made), the person applying for the injunction must consult:

- any local authority that the applicant thinks it appropriate to consult;
- any chief police officer that the applicant thinks it appropriate to consult;
- the local YOT in whose area the respondent resides (and if it appears to the applicant that the respondent resides in the area of two or more YOTs, it must consult such of those teams as the applicant thinks appropriate); and
- any other body or individual that the applicant thinks it appropriate to consult.[160]

24.106 This requirement does not apply to without-notice applications.[161]

24.107 If however, the without-notice application is adjourned, the applicant must comply with the consultation requirement (see para 24.105).[162]

Court's duties

24.108 The court may grant an anti-gang injunction if two conditions are met (emphasis added):

- The first condition is that 'the court is satisfied, *on the balance of probabilities*, that the respondent has engaged in or has encouraged or assisted gang-related violence, or gang-related drug-dealing activity'.[163]
- The second condition is that 'the court thinks it is *necessary* to grant the injunction to prevent the respondent from engaging in, or encouraging or assisting, gang-related violence or gang-related drug-dealing activity; and/or to protect the respondent from gang-related violence or gang-related drug-dealing activity'.[164]

24.109 'Gang-related' means that it occurs in the course of, or is otherwise related to, the activities of a group that consists of at least three

160 PCA 2009 s38(2), (3).

161 PCA 2009 s37 and 39.

162 PCA 2009 s39(5).

163 PCA 2009 s34(2).

164 PCA 2009 s34(3).

people, and has one or more characteristics that enable its members to be identified by others as a group.[165]

Procedure for applying for an anti-gang injunction

Generally

24.110 An application for an anti-gang injunction under this section must be made to a youth court if the respondent is a child (an application is made in the High Court or the county court in any other case).

Without notice applications

24.111 An application for an anti-gang injunction may be made without notice being given to the respondent. In these circumstances, the court has two options:

- dismiss the application; or
- adjourn proceedings.[166]

24.112 If proceedings are adjourned, the court may make an interim injunction[167] (see paras 24.130–24.131) on interim injunctions without notice).

24.113 Given the importance of considering alternative approaches before taking court action, it would be rare for an anti-gang injunction to be sought without notice in relation to a child. If the without-notice application is adjourned, the applicant must comply with the consultation requirement before the date of the first full hearing[168] (see para 24.105 on consultation requirement).

Making an anti-gang injunction

Requirements and prohibitions included in the anti-gang injunction

24.114 The injunction may include both prohibitions and positive requirements for the purpose of preventing the respondent from engaging in, or encouraging or assisting, gang-related violence or gang-related drug-dealing activity; and/or to protect the respondent from gang-related violence or gang-related drug-dealing activity.[169] The prohibition or

165 PCA 2009 s34(5).
166 PCA 2009 s39(4).
167 PCA 2009 s41(2).
168 PCA 2009 s39(5).
169 PCA 2009 s34(4).

requirement may last up to two years, beginning on the date the injunction is granted.[170]

24.115 The prohibitions included in the injunction may, in particular, prohibit the respondent from:

- being in a particular place;
- being with particular persons in a particular place;
- being in charge of a particular species of animal in a particular place;
- wearing particular articles of clothing in a particular place;
- using the internet to facilitate or encourage violence or drug-dealing activity.[171]

24.116 The requirements included in the injunction may, in particular, have the effect of requiring the respondent to:

- notify the applicant of the respondent's address and of any change to that address;
- be at a particular place between particular times on particular days;
- present himself or herself to a particular person at a place where he or she is required to be between particular times on particular days;
- participate in particular activities between particular times on particular days.[172]

24.117 A requirement to be at a particular place between particular times may not be longer than requiring the respondent to be at a particular place for more than 8 hours in any day.[173]

24.118 Any prohibitions and positive requirements must, so far as practicable, avoid any conflict with the respondent's religious beliefs and avoid interfering with the times, if any, at which the respondent normally works or attends any educational establishment.[174]

24.119 The Court of Appeal[175] has emphasised the importance of the terms being precise and capable of being understood by the respondent (see paras 24.26–24.30 on terms of a CBO above).

24.120 In considering the terms of an anti-gang injunction, courts should weigh up the proportionality of prohibitions that have the effect of criminalising lawful behaviour and activities.

170 PCA 2009 s36(2).
171 PCA 2009 s35(2).
172 PCA 2009 s35(3).
173 PCA 2009 s35(4).
174 PCA 2009 s35(5).
175 See *R v Kamran Khan* [2018] EWCA Crim 1472 in relation to criminal behaviour orders.

Review hearings

24.121 The court may order the applicant and the respondent to attend one or more review hearings on a specified date or dates.[176] If any prohibition or requirement in the injunction is for longer than one year beginning with the injunction date, the court must order the applicant and the respondent to attend a review hearing and specify the date of the review hearing to take place within the last four weeks of the one-year period (whether or not the court orders them to attend any other review hearings).[177]

24.122 Where the respondent is a child on the date the injunction is granted, and any prohibition or requirement in the injunction is to continue for a period of at least four weeks beginning after the respondent's 18th birthday, the court must order the applicant and the respondent to attend a review hearing on a specified date within that period.[178]

24.123 The purpose of the review hearing is to consider whether the injunction should be varied or discharged.[179]

Power of arrest

24.124 A court granting an injunction may attach a power of arrest to a prohibition or requirement of the injunction, other than one which has the effect of requiring the respondent to participate in particular activities.[180]

24.125 If the court attaches a power of arrest, it may specify that the power is to have effect for a shorter period than the prohibition or requirement to which it relates.[181]

Proportionality

24.126 The court must consider the child's welfare, best interests and whether the proposed terms of the order are a necessary, proportionate or a reasonable interference with the defendant's human rights, primarily Article 8 ECHR (the right to private and family life).[182]

176 PCA 2009 s36(3).
177 PCA 2009 s36(4).
178 PCA 2009 s36(4A).
179 PCA 2009 s36(5).
180 PCA 2009 s36(6).
181 PCA 2009 s36(7).
182 *DPP v Bulmer* [2015] EWHC 2323 (Admin), para 47; *R v John James* [2016] EWCA Crim 676, para 18. Also see R *v Boness* [2005] EWCA Crim 2395.

Length of the anti-gang injunction

24.127 An AGI made against a child respondent aged 14–17 years, each prohibition or requirement must be for a specified period and no longer than two years from the day the injunction is made.[183]

Interim anti-gang injunctions

24.128 Where the court adjourns the hearing of an application for an anti-gang injunction and the application was made 'on notice' (the respondent was notified of the hearing in accordance with the rules of court), the court may grant an 'interim injunction' if 'the court thinks it *just* to do so' (emphasis added).[184]

24.129 An interim anti-gang injunction following an 'on notice' application may include any provision which the court has power to include in an injunction (including a power of arrest).[185]

24.130 Where the court adjourns the hearing of an application for an anti-gang injunction and the application was made without notice (see paras 24.111–24.113 on without notice applications for AGIs above), the court may grant an 'interim injunction' if 'the court thinks it *necessary* to do so' (emphasis added).[186]

24.131 An interim anti-gang injunction following a 'without notice' application may include any provision which the court has power to include in an injunction (including a power of arrest) except for a requirement to participate in particular activities.[187]

Reporting restrictions (anonymity)

24.132 The reporting restrictions that automatically apply in the youth court under CYPA 1933 s49 apply to the anti-gang injunction proceedings.

Varying or discharging an anti-gang injunction

24.133 The court may vary or discharge an anti-gang injunction following a review hearing,[188] or, on an application to vary or discharge the

183 PCA 2009 s36(2).
184 PCA 2009 s40(1), (2).
185 PCA 2009 s40(3).
186 PCA 2009 s41(1), (2).
187 PCA 2009 s41(3), (4).
188 See paras 24.121–24.123 on review hearings of anti-gang injunctions.

injunction by the applicant or the respondent.[189] An applicant applying to vary or discharge the order must notify the local authority, chief police officer, youth offending team(s) and any other body or individual that the applicant consulted[190] when applying for the anti-gang injunction (see paras 24.105–24.107 on consultation requirement).[191]

24.134 The court's power to vary an injunction includes power to:

- include an additional prohibition or requirement in the injunction;
- extend the period for which a prohibition or requirement in the injunction has effect (up to a maximum of two years from the day on which the injunction was granted);
- attach a power of arrest, or extend the period for which a power of arrest attached to the injunction has effect.[192]

24.135 There is no requirement to specify a date for a review hearing if the application to vary the injunction (to include a prohibition or requirement) is made at any time after the injunction has been in place for one year.[193] However, if the respondent was a child on the day the injunction was made, and any prohibition or requirement in the injunction is to have effect for a period of at least four weeks beginning with the respondent's 18th birthday, the court must order the applicant and the respondent to attend a review hearing on a specified date within that period.[194]

24.136 If the application is made by the applicant to granted on that person's application must before doing so:

a) consult the local YOT about the application for variation or discharge, if the respondent will be a child when that application is made;
b) inform any other body or individual the applicant thinks appropriate of that application.

24.137 If an application to vary or discharge an injunction is dismissed, no further application to vary or discharge it may be made by any person without the consent of the court.[195]

189 PCA 2009 s42(1), (2).
190 PCA 2009 s38(1), 39(5).
191 PCA 2009 s42(5).
192 PCA 2009 s42(3).
193 PCA 2009 s42(4).
194 PCA 2009 s42(4A).
195 PCA 2009 s42(6).

Appealing an anti-gang injunction

24.138 An appeal against an anti-gang injunction made by the youth court is to the Crown Court.[196] On appeal, the Crown Court may make:

- whatever orders are necessary to give effect to its determination of the appeal;
- whatever incidental or consequential orders appear to it to be just.[197]

24.139 An order of the Crown Court made on an appeal under this section (other than one directing that an application be re-heard by the youth court) is to be treated for the purposes of applying to vary or discharge the injunction as an order of the youth court.[198]

Breach of an anti-gang injunction

Breach

24.140 It is not a criminal offence to breach a civil injunction. If a breach is proven, the court has the power to impose a supervision order or a detention order on 14 to 17 year olds. If the respondent has turned 18, breach proceedings are dealt with in the county court.

Legal aid for respondents

24.141 Criminal legal aid is available for anti-gang injunction breach proceedings. A solicitor authorised to undertake criminal work may apply for a criminal representation order to represent a child facing breach proceedings; civil providers may apply for an individual case contract.[199] Legal aid for breach proceedings heard in civil venues is not means tested.[200]

Arrest and detention for breach of an anti-gang injunction

24.142 Where there is a power of arrest attached to an anti-gang injunction, a constable may arrest the respondent without a warrant if he or she has reasonable cause to suspect that the respondent is in breach of

196 PCA 2009 s46B(1).
197 PCA 2009 s46B(2).
198 PCA 2009 s46B(3).
199 See para 24.92.
200 These proceding are heard in the youth court sitting as a civil court.

the provision.[201] The respondent must be brought before a court within 24 hours of being arrested (disregarding Christmas Day, Good Friday and any Sunday).[202]

24.143 Alternatively, if there is no power of arrest, the person who applied for the injunction may apply for the issue of a warrant for the respondent's arrest if the person considers that the respondent is in breach of any of its provisions.[203]

Prosecuting a breach of an anti-gang injunction

24.144 Breach proceedings will be heard before the youth court where the original injunction was made (or in the county court if the respondent is now aged 18 or over).[204]

24.145 If the respondent is under 18 and brought before the youth court, and the matter is not disposed with,[205] the court has the power to remand him or her on bail, may remand the person on bail taking a recognisance, with or without sureties.[206] The court may also adjourn the matter for medical report to be prepared.[207]

24.146 An application for breach proceedings may be made by the injunction applicant.[208] Before making an application, the injunction applicant must consult the YOT previously consulted in relation to the injunction, and any other person previously so consulted.[209]

24.147 Breaches must be proved to the criminal standard.[210] If a breach is proven, before making an order, the court must consider a report from the YOT consulted by the applicant.[211] The court has the power to impose:

- a supervision order (with one or more supervision, activity or curfew requirement) for up to six months;[212] or

201 PCA 2009 s43(2).
202 PCA 2009 s43(4).
203 PCA 2009 s44(2).
204 PCA 2009 s43(7).
205 PCA 2009 s43(5), 44(4).
206 PCA 2009 Sch 5 para 2(2).
207 PCA 2009 s45.
208 PCA 2009 s46A, Sch 5A Part 1 para 1(1)(b).
209 PCA 2009 Sch 5A para 1(4).
210 PCA 2009 Sch 5A para 1(1)(b).
211 PCA 2009 Sch 5A paras 1(7) and 14(2).
212 PCA 2009 Sch 5A para 1(2)(a) and 2.

- if 'in view of the severity or extent of the breach, no other power available to the court is appropriate'[213] a detention order of up to three months for 14 to 17 year olds.[214]

24.148 A supervision order may include one or more of the following requirements:

- a supervision requirement;
- an activity requirement;
- a curfew requirement.[215]

The court's powers in relation to making a supervision order and powers if the respondent fails to comply with any requirement are set out at PCA 2009 Sch 5A Part 2 paras 2–13.

24.149 A detention order means being detained in a secure training centre, a secure college, a young offender institution or a secure children's home.[216] There is no provision for early release, so the child would serve the whole period, although the court has the power, on an application by the injunction applicant or the respondent, to revoke the order if it appears to be in the interests of justice to do so.[217]

Reporting restrictions (anonymity)

24.150 When dealing with a breach of an AGI, the automatic reporting restrictions under CYPA 1933 s49 apply.[218]

Serious crime prevention order

24.151 A serious crime prevention order (SCPO) may be made if a person is convicted of a serious offence or has been involved in serious crime and the court has reasonable grounds to believe that the order would protect the public by preventing, restricting or disrupting involvement by the person in serious crime in England and Wales.[219] SCPOs are *not* available for children.[220]

213 PCA 2009 Sch 5A para 1(7).
214 PCA 2009 Sch 5A paras 1(2)(b) and 14.
215 PCA 2009 Sch 5A Part 2 para 2(1).
216 PCA 2009 Sch 5A para 14.
217 PCA 2009 Sch 5A para 14.
218 They are not automatically disapplied.
219 Serious Crime Act 2007 ss1, 19.
220 Serious Crime Act 2007 s6.

Violent offender order

24.152 A violent offender order (VOO) is a civil order intended to protect the public from the risk of serious violent harm.[221] VOOs are *not* available for children.[222]

Restraining order

24.153 Restraining orders prohibit a defendant who as been convicted of an offence from doing anything for the purpose of protecting the victim of the offence, or any other person mentioned in the order, from further conduct which amounts to harassment or will cause a fear of violence.[223] In certain circumstances, restraining orders may be made following an acquittal.[224] Restraining orders may be made on children.

Deportation

Automatic deportation

24.154 A defendant who is not a British citizen who is convicted of an offence in the UK and receives a sentence of imprisonment of 12 months or more will be subject to the automatic deportation regime.[225] However, automatic deportation *does not* apply to children, 'where the secretary of state thinks that the foreign criminal was under the age of 18 on the date conviction.'[226]

24.155 Although described as automatic deportation it can still be challenged (see paras 24.159–24.163)

Recommendation for deportation

24.156 There are two further circumstances in which a person who has been before the criminal court may face deportation proceedings as a result. Firstly the court has a power to recommend deportation.[227] That power exists when a defendant, who is 17 or over and not a British citizen, is convicted of an imprisonable offence. The defendant

221 Criminal Justice and Immigration Act 2008 s98.
222 Criminal Justice and Immigration Act 2008 s99(1).
223 Protection from Harassment Act 1997 s5.
224 Protection from Harassment Act 1997 s5A.
225 UK Borders Act 2007 s32(4), (5).
226 UK Borders Act 2007 s33(3).
227 Immigration Act 1971 s6.

must be given a notice in writing seven days prior to the court hearing.[228] The test for whether to make a recommendation is whether the defendant's continued presence in the United Kingdom is to its detriment.[229] Where an offence has met the automatic deportation threshold it will not be necessary for judge to address it.

24.157 The more serious the crime and the longer the record, the more likely it is that there will be a recommendation for deportation.[230] It is unlikely that it will be appropriate to make a recommendation for deportation in respect of offences committed as a child, as offending by a child is often a phase which passes fairly rapidly,[231] children are generally considered less culpable than adults[232] and are more susceptible to change.[233]

24.158 The second circumstance is where the secretary of state considers the person's deportation is conducive to the public good.[234] The secretary of state can take into account a number of different factors in coming to this decision. These factors are set out in policies and extensive case law, which is beyond the scope of this book, but can include any criminal convictions, cautions or any contact with the police including allegations and acquittals. Offending behaviour committed as a child may be taken into consideration.

24.159 In the case of EU citizens, a recommendation for deportation:

> ... may not be taken against EU citizens (except if based on imperative grounds of public security) if they: [. . .]
>
> b) Are a minor, except if expulsion is necessary in the bests interest of the child."[235]

Challenging deportation or removal directions

24.160 A child facing deportation proceedings will have a right of appeal, if they make a human rights or protection claim.[236] Immigration advice

228 Immigration Act 1971 s6(2).

229 *R v Benabbas* [2005] EWCA Crim 2113; *R v Nazari* [1980] 1 WLR 1366.

230 *R v Nazari* [1980] 1 WLR 1366.

231 *Sentencing children and young people; definitive guideline*, para 1.7.

232 *Sentencing children and young people: definitive guideline*, para 1.5.

233 *Sentencing children and young people: definitive guideline*, para 2.5 and *R v Lang* [2005] EWCA Crim 2864.

234 Immigration Act 1971, s3(5).

235 Directive 2004/38/EC, Article 28; and Immigration (European Economic Area) Regulations 2006 SI No 1003 which extends the provisions to citizens of Norway, Iceland, Liechtenstein and Switzerland.

236 Nationality, Immigration and Asylum Act 2002 s82(1).

should be sought immediately if deportation is a possibility. Deportation is an exceptionally complex area of law which is outside the scope of this book, for further information see *Macdonald's Immigration Law and Practice.*

24.161 Where a child is looked after (or if the child is entitled to leaving care support) immigration advice should be funded by the responsible local authority. However, this is a complex area of law and the advice of a community care lawyer may be required where the local authority is unwilling to fund the private immigration legal fees.

24.162 Coram Children's Legal Centre runs a dedicated Migrant Children's Project advice line.

Driving offences, penalty points and endorsements

Penalty points, endorsement and disqualification

24.163 Obligatory endorsement (the mandatory requirement to impose penalty points for certain offences) applies equally to children as it does to adults. If the child is too young to drive or does not have a driving licence, the court is still able to impose the relevant penalty points. The exception is when the court finds 'special reasons'.

24.164 Some offences carry mandatory disqualification and others discretionary. When the court is considering discretionary disqualification, the sentencing principles should be considered and the adult starting point may appropriately be reduced. The child

> . . . should, if possible be given the opportunity to learn from their mistakes without undue penalisation or stigma, especially as a court sanction might have a significant effect on the future prospects and opportunities of the child or young person and hinder their re-integration into society.[237]

24.165 Reasons for keeping disqualification to a minimum may be:

- Where the child's employment prospects would be improved by the ability to drive, disqualification should be kept to a minimum.[238]
- Where a period of disqualification is imposed at the same time as a custodial sentence, a lengthy disqualification should be avoided as it may have an adverse effect on the child's chances of rehabilitation.[239]

237 *Sentencing children and young people: definitive guideline*, paras 1.5–1.6.
238 *R v Aspen* [1975] RTR 456.
239 *R v Russell* [1993] RTR 249.

- Lengthy periods of disqualification for those who seem incapable of leaving motor vehicles alone would be counterproductive.[240]

Newly qualified drivers

24.166 There is a two-year probationary period for all newly qualified drivers.[241] This means that the licence will automatically be revoked if the driver is convicted of an offence during the two years probationary period and receives six penalty points or more.[242] A newly qualified driver who has had their licence revoked will be required to re-take their driving test.[243]

24.167 In appropriate cases, a defence lawyer may seek to invite courts impose a short period of disqualification as an alternative to imposing penalty points to avoid automatic revocation of a newly qualified driver's licence and the requirement to take a new driving test.

Football banning orders[244]

24.168 Football banning orders may be made by a court when a defendant is convicted of a 'relevant offence', listed in Football Spectators Act 1989 Sch 1. These are usually offences committed while entering or trying to enter a football stadium or while travelling to or from a football match. Football banning orders can be made on children.

Orders relating to sexual offences

Sexual offences notification requirement (sex offenders register)

Overview

24.169 Children who commit certain sexual offences may be subject to notification requirements and are placed on the 'sex offenders register'.

240 *R v Thomas* [1983] 1 WLR 1490.
241 Road Traffic (New Drivers) Act 1995 s1.
242 Road Traffic (New Drivers) Act 1995 s2.
243 Road Traffic (New Drivers) Act 1995 s4.
244 Football Spectators Act 1989 s14A.

Automatic notification

24.170 Children who are cautioned for or convicted of, not been found to have committed the act but unfit to plead an offence listed in Sexual Offences Act (SOA) 2003 Sch 3 automatically become subject to notification requirements. This includes children found not guilty by reason of insanity or been found to have committed the act but unfit to plead.[245]

24.171 For a fuller discussion see paras 25.76–25.81.

Sentencing condition

24.172 In addition to the automatic requirements, certain sexual offences are subject to notification requirements if the defendant receives a custodial sentence of 12 months or longer. For example, the sentencing condition applies to offences relating to the possession of indecent images.

24.173 For a fuller discussion see paras 25.76–25.81.[246]

Barring

24.174 Children who commit certain sexual offences are automatically barred from working with children and vulnerable adults, this includes cautions and convictions (see paras 25.68–25.75).

Sexual harm prevention order

Availability

24.175 A court may make a sexual harm prevention order (SHPO) if the court deals with the defendant in relation to an offence listed in SOA 2003 Sch 3 or Sch 5, including where the defendant has been found not guilty by reason of insanity or found to be under a disability and to have done the act charged,[247] and the court is satisfied that it is necessary to make a SHPO for the purpose of:

- protecting the public or any particular members of the public from sexual harm from the defendant;[248] or

245 SOA 2003 s80(1)(c).
246 SOA 2003 s82(6).
247 SOA 2003 s103A(2)(a)(ii), (iii).
248 SOA 2003 s103A(2)(b)(i).

- protecting children or vulnerable adults generally, or any particular children or vulnerable adults, from sexual harm from the defendant outside the UK.[249]

24.176 A court may also make an order, following an application by the chief officer of police or the Director General of the National Crime Agency in respect of a person who:

- has received a youth caution or youth conditional caution;
- has a conviction (has pleaded guilty or has been found guilty);
- has been found not guilty by reason of insanity or found to be under a disability and to have done the act charged;[250]

if the court is satisfied that the defendant's behaviour since the appropriate date makes it necessary to make a SHPO, for the purpose of:

- protecting the public or any particular members of the public from sexual harm from the defendant; or
- protecting children or vulnerable adults generally, or any particular children or vulnerable adults, from sexual harm from the defendant outside the UK.[251]

24.177 Offences listed in SOA 2003 Schs 3 and 5 include:

- possession of indecent photograph of a child (Criminal Justice Act 1988 s160);
- sexual assault (SOA 2003 s3);
- exposure (SOA 2003 s66);
- voyeurism (SOA 2003 s67);
- threats to kill (Offences Against the Person Act 1861 s16);
- wounding/causing grievous bodily harm (Offences Against the Person Act 1861 s20);
- assault with intent to resist arrest (Offences Against the Person Act 1861 s38);
- assault occasioning actual bodily harm (Offences against the Person Act 1861 s47);
- burglary with intent to inflict grievous bodily harm or to do unlawful damage to a building/anything within it (Theft Act 1968 s9);
- arson (Criminal Damage Act 1971 s1);
- violent disorder (Public Order Act 1986 s2);
- affray (Public Order Act 1986 s3);

249 SOA 2003 s103A(2)(b)(ii).
250 SOA 2003 s103B(2).
251 SOA 2003 s103A(3)(b).

- harassment – conduct causing fear of violence (Protection from Harassment Act 1994 s4);
- racially or religiously aggravated wounding/causing grievous bodily harm (Crime and Disorder Act (CDA) 1998 s29);
- racially or religiously aggravated assault occasioning actual bodily harm (CDA 1998 s29);
- racially or religiously aggravated common assault (CDA 1998 s29);
- racially or religiously aggravated threatening behaviour (CDA 1998 s31(1)(a));
- racially or religiously aggravated disorderly behaviour with intent to cause harassment, alarm or distress (CDA 1998 s31(1)(b));
- exploitation of prostitution (SOA 2003 ss52 and 53).

24.178 Offences qualify even if the defendant had been cautioned, convicted of found to have done the act before the commencement of the SOA 2003, and includes offences committed in the UK or overseas.[252]

Court's duties

24.179 For a post-conviction SHPO, there is no requirement for an application to be made to the court. In appropriate cases, the prosecutor may wish to invite the court to consider making an order and the court may ask the pre-sentence report writer to consider the suitability of a SHPO on a non-prejudicial basis.

24.180 In order to make a SHPO, the court must be satisfied that the offender presents a risk of sexual harm to the public (or particular members of the public) and that an order is necessary to protect against this risk.[253]

24.181 The court is likely to take into consideration:

- the details of the offence;
- the offender's previous convictions; and
- the assessment of risk presented by the YOT worker in any pre-sentence report;
- the range of other options available to it in respect of protecting the public.

24.182 The court may want to consider:

1) Would an order minimise the risk of harm to the public or to any particular members of the public?

252 SOA 2003 s103B(3), (4).
253 SOA 2003 s103A(2)(b).

2) Is it proportionate?
3) Can it be policed effectively?[254]

24.183 The SHPO may only include negative prohibitions, and there is no power to impose positive obligations. Any prohibitions must be necessary for the purpose of protecting the public from sexual harm from the defendant and must be tailored to the individual defendant.[255] It may also prohibit foreign travel[256] and the defendant from engaging in particular activities on the internet. The SHPO may have effect for a fixed period (not less than five years) or until further order, but no order must be longer than necessary.[257] Given the need for a SHPO to be necessary and proportionate, that they must last a minimum of five years and the significant consequences of the notification requirements (see paras 25.76–25.81), it would appear to the authors of this book that they would rarely be imposed on children. The court should always seek guidance as to the necessity of a SHPO being made in relation to a child defendant from the relevant youth offending team.

Renewing or varying a sexual harm prevention order

24.184 A Sexual Harm Prevention Order may be renewed or varied on application to the court by the person who is the subject of the order or an interested chief officer of police.[258]

Breach of a sexual harm prevention order

24.185 The court's powers to deal with a defendant following a breach of a SHPO are set out SOA 2003 s103I. The Sentencing Council have produced a new sentencing guideline for breach of a sexual harm prevention order,[259] but as there is no specific guidance in relation to children who breach orders, the court's starting point should be the *Sentencing children and young people: definitive guideline.*[260]

254 Magistrates' Court Sentencing Guidelines, Ancillary Orders, 22 Sexual Harm Prevention Orders.

255 *R v Smith and others* [2011] EWCA Crim 1772; the Judicial College Crown Court Compendium (November 2017) at para *S7–13* provides examples of prohibitions approved in *Smith and others* and subsequent cases.

256 SOA 2003 s103D.

257 *R v McLellan* [2017] EWCA Crim 1464.

258 SOA 2003 s103E.

259 Magistrates' Court Sentencing Guideline – Breach of a sexual harm prevention order.

260 *Sentencing children and young people: definitive guideline.*

CHAPTER 25

Criminal records

continued

Key points

- All convictions and cautions are retained on the Police National Computer (PNC).
- Other information, such as arrests, acquittals and police intelligence and other non-conviction are all retained on the Police National Database (PND).
- Any information held on police records (police intelligence/non conviction data) is wiped when an individual turns 100. The police should review the data and only retain what is necessary for policing purposes. However, all convictions and cautions are retained until a person's 100th birthday.
- Convictions and cautions become 'spent' after a period of time, based on the sentence received.
- Spent convictions and cautions are not disclosed to others (employers, insurers, etc) unless they have permission to obtain a standard or enhanced Criminal Record Certificate (CRC) from the Disclosure and Barring Service (DBS)
- On a standard or enhanced CRC, all cautions and convictions are automatically disclosed, unless filtered.
- Any police intelligence (including allegations, arrests and acquittals) can be disclosed on an enhanced CRC if deemed relevant.
- Anyone can find out what information is recorded against him or her by the police by conducting a subject access request (SAR).

Introduction

25.1 This chapter deals with the effect of having a conviction, a caution or other disposal including any out of court disposals (see para 7.1 on out of court disposals) and any other information which is held on national police systems (referred to as 'police intelligence'). Having a criminal record may prevent people with childhood records pursuing certain careers, travelling to certain countries or accessing insurance and financial services.

25.2 It is important that solicitors and barristers and other professionals such as Youth Offending Teams (YOTs) are able to accurately explain the consequences of any contact with the criminal justice system. Knowing what the impact of a certain outcome will be may influence a child's decision in a case, for example whether to plead guilty or make admissions at the police station. Being able to explain the consequences of a certain outcome to an officer, the Crown Prosecution Service (CPS) or a judge may assist in mitigation or representations to make a different charging decision. This chapter will explain when and how a record is disclosed.

What is a criminal record?

25.3 A criminal record can refer to any information stored about an individual that relates to criminal activity. However, it is often used colloquially to refer to people who have unspent convictions or cautions (for an explanation as to 'spent' and 'unspent' see paras 25.21–25.30), as these will need to be disclosed to employers. Unless certain exceptions apply (see paras 25.31–25.63 for a fuller explanation of disclosure) if anyone, such as an employer, asks if you have a criminal record, you can say that you do not when all cautions or convictions you have are spent.[1] To know how long it takes for a conviction, caution, reprimand, final warning to be spent see para 25.21–25.30. There is also a disclosure calculator on Unlock's website (a charity dealing with criminal records for people with convictions) to assist in calculating at what point an individual's criminal record will become spent.[2]

25.4 Employers can carry out checks on their employees. When seeking employment, no one is required to disclose unspent convictions. There is no need to volunteer the information unless you are specifically asked, but many employers will ask. All employers are entitled to carry out a basic check on their employees, which will disclose unspent convictions, but nothing more than these. Employers are within their legal rights to take into consideration a person's unspent convictions when deciding whether to employ someone. However, a blanket policy against employing people with a criminal record is discriminatory, and will need to be justifiable.

1 Rehabilitation of Offenders Act (ROA) 1974 ss1 and 4.

2 www.disclosurecalculator.org.uk.

What information is retained?

Police National Computer

Overview

25.5 All convictions and cautions are retained on the Police National Computer (PNC). This includes conditional cautions, and previous out of court disposals such as youth reprimands and final warnings that are no longer used. Fixed penalty notices are also usually stored on the PNC (see paras 7.39–7.42 on fixed penalty notices).

25.6 In some cases, other information, such as acquittals or investigations, can be stored on the PNC, although such records are usually stored in local records (see police intelligence below para 25.57).

Weeding out

25.7 Previously there was a system of 'weeding out', whereby old offences could be deleted by the police. This practice ended in 2006, and all data is now retained. However, for anyone who received convictions or cautions prior to 2006 there is a chance that the data was deleted. This is more likely for very old and minor convictions or out of court disposals.

Stepping down

25.8 Between 2006 and 2009, the police operated a 'stepping down' procedure, where cautions, final warnings and reprimands could be removed from the PNC after ten years but retained on the Police National Database (PND), which could affect whether or not they would be disclosed in a DBS check (see para 25.57 on police intelligence below). The stepping down procedure was found to be unlawful in the case of *Chief Constable of Humberside v Information Commissioner*.[3]

25.9 Information that was previously 'stepped down' is nevertheless likely to appear in a criminal record check, as the disclosure officer will contact ACRO Criminal Records Office who have access to the stepped down information, so that it can be included on any check. The data held on the PNC is subject to the National Police Chiefs' Council guidance on 'Deletion of records from national police

3 [2010] 1 WLR 1136.

systems' that was issued on 19 May 2015.[4] This states that the PNC record is held until the individual is 100 years old.

Record deletion process

25.10 It is possible to apply for data to be deleted through the record deletion process. It is rare that records are deleted, and usually the process only applies to cautions, final warnings, reprimands or out of court disposals. It is highly unlikely that a conviction would be deleted, as it is possible to appeal a conviction to another court.

25.11 For the record deletion process, an application needs to be submitted to ACRO (the Association of Chief Police Officers Criminal Record Officer) by sending an application form, which can be downloaded from their website[5] and admissible applications will be passed to the chief officer of the force that owns the data (this will be the force who issued the caution or dealt with the matter). The chief officer of that force has the discretion, in exceptional circumstances, to delete the data. Paragraph 1.6.5 and Annex A of the National Police Chiefs' Council guidance lists the criteria for when to delete such data. The guidance states that it is for the Chief Constable to decide whether to delete a record, which will depend on the individual circumstances, Annex A gives examples of situations where it might be appropriate to consider deletion, these include situations where it was shown that no crime was committed, or where it was a malicious or false allegation, or where there is a 'wider public interest'. (See further, the Information Hub: self-help information on a wide range of issues that criminal convictions can affect.[6])

Police National Database

Overview

25.12 Police intelligence is recorded on local police systems but is retained on the PND. Police intelligence can be anything from an informal resolution of a criminal matter, such as triage (see paras 7.43–7.58 on informal diversion (no further action)); an acquittal for an offence; an

4 www.gov.uk/government/uploads/system/uploads/attachment_data/file/430095/Record_Deletion_Process.pdf.

5 www.acro.police.uk/Early_Deletion_of_Biometric_Information_Application.aspx

6 http://hub.unlock.org.uk/knowledgebase/retention-deletion-police-records/.

arrest that led to no further action being taken; or even an unsubstantiated allegation that the police never pursued.

Home Office Counting Rules

25.13 Whether or not a matter is recorded as a crime on the PND is governed by the Home Office Counting Rules.[7] Most matters that come to police attention and involve a criminal allegation are recorded as a crime. This is to ensure that there are valid statistics about crime, and that information is held about individuals that may become relevant in the future. The Home Secretary requires Chief Constables to produce regular data on the crime they record.[8] This means that, even where an allegation cannot be proven, details of that allegation and the alleged perpetrator (if known) will remain on the system.

Deletion of data

25.14 Locally held records – whether stored on electronic document management systems (such as the PND) or as paper records – are managed by the chief officer of the relevant force, in accordance with Accredited Professional Practice (APP) – Information Management issued by the College of Policing. This suggests that individual police forces should have review policies, where the data held is subject to scheduled reviews and information should only be retained if it is 'accurate, adequate, up to date and necessary for policing purposes'.[9] If not deleted, this data is also kept, until the record is wiped when the individual turns 100.

25.15 The Supreme Court confirmed in the case of *R (Catt and T) v ACPO and others*[10] that the retention of data on an individual police database interferes with the rights of that individual under Article 8 of the European Convention on Human Rights (privacy). However, the court found such interference to be a lawful one in the cases before it, as per Lady Hale:[11]

7 www.gov.uk/government/publications/counting-rules-for-recorded-crime.

8 Police Act 1996 s44(2) and (3).

9 www.app.college.police.uk/app-content/information-management/management-of-police-information/retention-review-and-disposal-of-police-information/.

10 [2015] 2 All ER 727.

11 At para 54.

> ... the policy of the Metropolitan Police in relation to these records was not unlawful, provided that it was flexible enough to allow for information to be deleted when retaining it would no longer serve any useful policing purpose.

However, *Catt* has now been successfully appealed to the ECHR.

Purpose of retention

25.16 Data is retained for a number of different purposes – eg it may be relevant to provide the government with crime statistics; or it may be relevant for intelligence purposes. The fact that the data is retained does not mean that it will be disclosed to a future employer – potential disclosure of the record is just one reason for retention.

25.17 Any data that is retained, however, can be disclosed to an employer in an enhanced criminal record certificate (CRC). The disclosure officer carrying out a check will make a decision at the time as to what is relevant (see further below para 25.57 on enhanced certificates/police intelligence). This means that there is no certainty for an individual who has data retained about him or her, as the individual will not know what may be disclosed to a future employer.

Obtaining a copy of your criminal record and information retained

Subject access requests

Overview

25.18 To obtain a copy of one's own criminal record, or what information is recorded about oneself, anyone can do a subject access request (SAR) under the Data Protection Act 1998. A reply should be expected within 40 calendar days. ACRO Criminal Records Office manage the PNC, and they will respond to requests as to what is held on the PNC. Such applications can be made online.[12]

25.19 Applications to discover what is held by local police forces (and therefore what is held on the PND) have to be made to the police force who hold and manage this data. A list of all of the police forces can be found on the ACRO website.[13]

12 www.acro.police.uk/Subject_Access_Online.aspx.

13 www.acro.police.uk/subject_access.aspx.

Enforced subject access requests

25.20 Unauthorised disclosure of an individual's record on the PNC is a criminal offence[14] as is coercing someone to apply for a SAR. This is known as an enforced subject access request.[15] This is to ensure that, for example, employers can only access the data they are entitled to from the DBS.

Spent convictions

Overview

25.21 The ROA 1974 introduced the concept of spent convictions. Once a conviction or caution is 'spent' it will not have to be declared to an employer, and an employer may not prejudice the subject in any way on the ground of it, unless certain exceptions apply[16] (see paras 25.31–25.63 on disclosure). Most convictions and all cautions become spent after a certain period of time. That period of time differs – see table on rehabilitation periods for time periods for convictions and cautions to become spent (at para 25.28).

25.22 How long it takes for a conviction to become spent depends entirely on the sentence received. Sentences received as a child are spent more quickly than adult sentences – typically they take half the time to become spent.

25.23 Some convictions are spent immediately, such as youth cautions, or absolute discharges.[17] Some are spent upon completion of the order or the sentence, such as a referral order, or a compensation order, which becomes spent once it is paid. Other sentences become spent after a certain period (rehabilitation period) which runs from the date the order is finished.

Rehabilitation periods

25.24 For custodial sentences – which includes detention and training orders – the rehabilitation period starts when the custodial sentence is finished, including any licence or training period. So, for example, a detention and training order of eight months has a rehabilitation

14 ROA 1974 s9(2).
15 Data Protection Act 1998 s56.
16 ROA 1974 s4(2) and (3), Sch 2 para 3(3) and (5).
17 ROA 1974 s5(4).

period of two years. Therefore, the conviction will be spent two years and eight months after sentence has been passed.

25.25 For non-custodial sentences, the rehabilitation period starts once the order is finished. Therefore a six-month youth rehabilitation order which has a six-month rehabilitation period will be spent one year after sentence has been passed.

25.26 Suspended sentences are treated the same as terms of imprisonment for the purposes of rehabilitation periods. The rehabilitation period will start once the order is finished.

Youth rehabilitation orders

25.27 When a community order or youth rehabilitation order is passed, the court should specify the end date of the whole order (which may have a number of elements to it). This is so it is clear when the conviction becomes spent. If the court fails to specify an end date, the conviction is spent two years from the date of conviction.[18]

Table of rehabilitation periods

25.28 The table below shows the rehabilitation period for each sentence.[19]

Table of rehabilitation periods for cautions, convictions and orders if person is aged under 18 at the date of conviction[20]

Sentence	Rehabilitation period (if under 18 when convicted)
Imprisonment over four years, life sentences, Imprisonment for Public Protection (IPP) or Detention for Public Protection (DPP) and extended sentences	N/A – these sentences are never spent
Imprisonment (over 30 months up to and including four years)	3.5 years
Imprisonment (including detention and training orders[21]) (more than six, up to and including 30 months)	Two years

18 ROA 1974 s5(3).

19 ROA 1974 s5(2).

20 ROA 1974 s5(2)(b).

21 ROA 1974 s5(8)(g).

Imprisonment (six months or less)	18 months
Youth rehabilitation order	Six months
Referral order[22]	None – the conviction is spent upon completion of the order
Compensation order	None – the conviction is spent upon payment of the order
Fine	Six months
Conditional discharge[23]	None – the conviction is spent at the end of the order
Absolute discharge	None. The conviction is spent immediately.
Reparation order	None – the conviction is spent at the end of the order[24]
Bind over[25]	None – spent at the end of the order
Hospital order[26]	None – spent at the end of the order
Youth conditional caution[27]	Three months
Youth caution[28]	None – spent immediately upon receipt

Table of rehabilitation periods for cautions, convictions and orders if person is aged over 18 when convicted[29]

Sentence	**Rehabilitation period (if over 18 when convicted)**
Imprisonment over four years, life sentences, IPP or DPP and extended sentences	N/A – these sentences are never spent

22 ROA 1974 s5(2)(a), (8).
23 ROA 1974 s5(2)(a), (8).
24 ROA 1974 s5(4)(b).
25 ROA 1974 s5(2)(a), (8).
26 ROA 1974 s5(2)(a), (8).
27 ROA 1974 Sch 1 para 1.
28 ROA 1974 Sch 1 para 1.
29 ROA 1974 s5(2)(b).

Sentence	Rehabilitation period (if over 18 when convicted)
Imprisonment (30 months to four years)	Seven years
Imprisonment (six to 30 months)	Four years
Imprisonment (six months or less)	Two years
Community order (over 18s only)	One year
Compensation order	None – the conviction is spent upon payment of the order
Fine	One year
Conditional discharge	None – the conviction is spent at the end of the order
Absolute discharge	None – the conviction is spent immediately
Caution[30]	Spent immediately on receipt of caution
Conditional caution[31]	Spent three months after caution issued

25.29 Therefore, a fine is spent six months or one year after it was imposed, regardless of whether it has been paid. A compensation order or spent on payment, and therefore if paid immediately will be spent immediately.

More than one previous conviction/dragging

25.30 Once a conviction or caution has become spent, it will remain spent. However, if someone is convicted of a further offence or offences, before their previous conviction(s) have become spent, none of those convictions will be spent until they all are, and therefore all offences are disclosable until the one with the longest rehabilitation period has become spent.[32]

30 ROA 1974 Sch 1 para 1.
31 ROA 1974 Sch 1 para 1.
32 ROA 1974 s6(2).

Disclosure of criminal record

Overview

Disclosure

25.31 There are two parts to disclosure.

25.32 First, the Police Act (PA) 1997 created a statutory scheme for the disclosure of criminal records, where required, in order to assess the suitability of a person for employment in particular types of position of trust or sensitivity, such as those involving contact with children, or suitability for the grant of particular types of licence or permit. When applying for a job an employer can apply for a basic, standard or enhanced criminal record certificate (CRC) depending on the position being applied for.

25.33 The DBS – previously the Criminal Records Bureau (CRB) – deal with most checks about a criminal record in England and Wales.[33] There are four types of certificate, and different matters may be disclosed in each certificate:

1) basic (see para 25.37);
2) standard (or CRC) (see para 25.40);
3) enhanced (or ECRC) (see para 25.41); and
4) enhanced with checks of barred lists (see paras 25.41 and 25.66).

25.34 Second, there is the exemption against self-disclosure. The ROA 1974 provides that, after a period of time, the criminal convictions of a person are in many cases 'spent'. This means, among other things, that that person is not obliged to disclose them in response to a question by, for example, a prospective employer. That prospective employer is also not entitled to make a decision prejudicial to the applicant by reference to them or to any failure on his or her part to disclose them. However, there are exceptions to this rule, set out in the Rehabilitation of Offenders Act 1974 (Exceptions) Order ('Exceptions Order') 1975.[34] Where the exceptions apply the applicant may be required to disclose information about spent convictions or cautions.

25.35 The protections are partially excluded for a range of positions, such as police staff and a range of positions working with children or

33 Which has powers under the 1975 order to disclose spent cautions and convictions, and under PA 1997 s113 to disclose other relevant information for enhanced checks.

34 SI No 102.

other vulnerable people.[35] For those positions all convictions and cautions except 'protected cautions' and 'protected convictions' must be disclosed. A 'protected caution' is defined in article 2A(1) of the Exceptions Order 1975. A 'protected conviction' is defined similarly in Article 2A(2) Exceptions Order 1975. Protected cautions and protected convictions mirror the 'filtering rules' and are explained more fully in paras 25.49–25.56 on filtering below.

Sensitive roles

25.36 There are some very sensitive roles that are entirely excluded from these protections, such as working as a constable or judicial appointments. These are covered by articles 3ZA and 4ZA of the Exceptions Order 1975 and there is a full list of the relevant roles listed in those Articles. For these roles, a candidate can be asked to disclose all past criminal information about himself or herself, and the filtering rules do not apply.

Basic certificate – criminal conviction certificate

25.37 Any employer can obtain a criminal conviction certificate (sometimes called a basic certificate) on a candidate, which will disclose all unspent convictions and conditional cautions[36]. Those convictions and conditional cautions are matters which the candidate will be obliged to disclose, if asked, for any role. See paras 25.21–25.30 above for ascertaining whether a matter has been spent.

Criminal record certificates

25.38 Under PA 1997 Part V, the DBS is required to issue a CRC or an enhanced CRC (ECRC) upon an application by the person to whom the information relates, if a 'registered person' certifies it is required for the purposes of an 'exempted question'[37].

25.39 'Registered persons' are, by PA 1997 s120, broadly those entered on a register maintained by the secretary of state containing the names of those who are likely to ask an exempted question. An 'exempted question' is a question about suitability for engagement in specified sensitive employment or activities.[38] The roles for which a standard CRC may be obtained are dealt with at paras 25.46–25.47 below.

35 Exceptions Order 1975 articles 3 and 4.

36 PA 1997 s112.

37 Subject to PA 1997 s113A(2A).

38 PA 1997 s113A(6).

25.40 The CRC must give 'the prescribed details of every relevant matter relating to the applicant which is recorded in central records' held by the police[39]: A 'relevant matter' is defined by PA 1997 s113A(6). Prior to 29 May 2013, this meant the disclosure of all convictions and nearly all cautions. However, since that date[40] a 'relevant matter' is defined more narrowly – now some cautions and convictions are 'filtered', and not disclosed (see para 25.49 on filtering below). Any conviction or caution that is not filtered will be disclosed.

25.41 PA 1997 s113B provides for the disclosure of additional information within an ECRC where it is required for the purpose of an exempted question which is asked for a prescribed purpose. Such purposes include considering the suitability of a person to engage in a regulated activity relating to children or vulnerable adults. In addition to the information that would be disclosed in a CRC, the ECRC should include any information held on local police records which the chief officer of the relevant police force reasonably believes to be relevant, and which in his opinion ought to be included in the certificate. This information is sometimes called 'soft intelligence' – see further para 25.57 on police intelligence/enhanced certificates below.

25.42 The criminal records disclosure regime was found to be incompatible with the Article 8 ECHR (right to respect for private and family life) in the case of *R (T) v Chief Constable of Greater Manchester Police.*[41] The Supreme Court found that it interfered with an individual's Article 8 rights and was not sufficiently nuanced to be in accordance with the law. It also held that the application of the self-disclosure scheme under the Exceptions Order 1975 was incompatible with Article 8. Following the judgment in *T*, a filtering regime was introduced (see para 25.49 below). However, recently the Supreme Court in *R (P, G and W) v Secretary of State for the Home Department*[42] found that the filtering regime is disproportionate in two ways. At the time of writing the government have not responded to the declaration of incompatibility made by the court. The Supreme Court has found that the disclosure of youth caution (or reprimand) on CRCs to be unlawful as well as other aspects of the scheme.

39 PA 1997 s113A(3).

40 Police Act 1997 (Criminal Record Certificates: Relevant Matters) (Amendment) (England and Wales) Order 2013 No 1200 art 3.

41 [2014] UKSC 35.

42 [2019] UKSC 3.

25.43 The Exceptions Order 1975 has also been found to be incompatible with Article 8 in the case of *R (R) v NPCC*[43] where it allowed a reprimand, in this case a reprimand for shoplifting when the applicant was 13 who was now 25, to be disclosed in applications to be a police constable. The High Court in *R (R) v NPCC*[44] also found that the employer, the police in that instance, was in breach of Article 8, in that they refused employment based purely on the fact that she received a reprimand for shoplifting aged 13. This was a disproportionate interference with Article 8, in part because the caution had no rational connection to employment for the police. The High Court found that there was little hope that an employer would act in a manner compatible with Article 8 and therefore it was essential that disclosure was only made when necessary, as per Mr Justice Green:[45]

> Indeed, the present case illustrates graphically how any assumption that employers will apply Article 8 type criteria in a fair, consistent and effective manner may be seriously misplaced.

Additionally, the court found that while there remained a uncertainty as to how retained data would be used, it 'leaves open the potential for misuse of the information'.[46]

Procedure for obtaining a DBS certificate

25.44 The procedure is as follows.

- The employer will send off the relevant form with the applicant's details to the DBS. The applicant needs to consent to this process, which can sometimes be completed online.
- The DBS will check the various databases and where there is an application for an ECRC also request further information from the Chief Constable of police forces which hold information on the applicant. Where there is a discretion about whether to disclose information, that decision is made by the Chief Constable.
- Where there is discretion over whether or not to disclose a matter and the Chief Constable of the relevant police force is considering whether to make such a disclosure, the police will often (though not always) write to the applicant for their representations on the proposed disclosure.

43 [2017] EWHC 2586 (Admin).
44 [2017] EWHC 2586 (Admin).
45 At para 14.
46 Para 74.

- The DBS will send the completed check back to the applicant (not the employer) with all relevant disclosure, allowing the applicant to check any inaccurate information, or to choose to withdraw from the application process, once the applicant knows what is disclosed.
- The employer will then expect the applicant to forward the certificate back to them.

25.45 DBS certificates can be obtained for both paid and voluntary positions, although that will usually affect the fee charged.

25.46 A full list of positions that are exempt from the protections and in respect of which a CRC be obtained can be found on the GOV.UK website.[47]

25.47 Common positions that are eligible for a standard CRC are:

- security;
- solicitor or barrister;
- accountant;
- vet;
- Financial Conduct Authority (FCA) approved person roles;
- football steward;
- traffic warden;
- locksmith (membership of Master Locksmiths).

25.48 Jobs that are eligible for an enhanced CRC include:

- working with children and/or vulnerable adults;
- teacher;
- social worker;
- NHS professional;
- carer;
- taxi driving licences.

Note: this list may include some college or university roles, especially if they involve placements working with children.

Filtering

25.49 For individuals who have a single conviction or cautions), their offences may be filtered from both enhanced and standard CRCs. When an offence is filtered, that means it will not be disclosed in a CRC or an ECRC. Convictions and cautions are filtered automatically – there is

47 www.gov.uk/government/publications/dbs-check-eligible-positions-guidance.

no need to apply for a matter to be filtered, it is an automatic process that means that filtered matters will simply not appear on the certificate.

25.50 Convictions are only filtered if the following apply:[48]

- the applicant has a single conviction;
- that conviction did not result in a custodial sentence;
- the conviction was not for an exempt offence.

'Exempt offences' includes any offences under Criminal Justice Act 2003 Sch 15. A full list of exempt offences can be found on the GOV. UK website.[49]

25.51 The 'multiple conviction rule' – which states that where an individual has more than one conviction) it is *not* filtered – even where an individual has two convictions that occurred out of the same incident both of those convictions will be disclosed.

25.52 All cautions, unless they are for an exempt offence as discussed above, are filtered. It does not matter how many cautions the applicant has received, nor if the applicant also has previous convictions – the applicant's cautions will still be filtered.

25.53 The age of the individual at the time of the offence is irrelevant in determining whether a conviction or caution *will* at some point be filtered. It is relevant for determining when a caution or conviction will be filtered.

25.54 Cautions are filtered two years after they are issued if received as a child, or six years after if received as an adult. This applies also to reprimands and warnings. Convictions are filtered 5.5 years after conviction, if under 18 on the date of conviction, and 11 years after conviction if over 18 on the date of conviction.

25.55 The filtering scheme was introduced after the Court of Appeal in the case of *R (T) v Chief Constable of Greater Manchester Police*[50] found the previous regime of retaining records to be unlawful.

25.56 The Supreme Court have found the filtering regime to be incompatible with an individual's rights under Article 8 (see para 25.42). The Justice Select Committee has criticised the filtering regime and the retention and disclosure of criminal records received as children in their report *Disclosure of youth criminal records* (October

48 PA 1997 s113A(6) as amended.

49 www.gov.uk/government/publications/dbs-list-of-offences-that-will-never-be-filtered-from-a-criminal-record-check.

50 [2014] UKSC 35.

2017),[51] and made a number of recommended changes to the government. At the time of writing, however, there is no indication whether any changes will be implemented.

Police intelligence and non-conviction data: enhanced certificates

25.57 When an enhanced CRC is obtained the DBS send enquiries to the police force which holds the records on the applicant. The chief police officer is responsible for considering whether to disclose further information. This exercise will usually be carried out by a disclosure officer. Other information held on police records, such as the PND, will be reviewed. There are two purposes to this review. First, the officer carries out a context check, by looking at the circumstances behind the convictions or cautions automatically disclosed, and if appropriate can provide more details about them. Second, information can be provided under 'other relevant information' on the ECRC. This can be any other information held about the applicant on crime records. .[52] The police will create crime records in line with the Home Office Counting Rules (see para 25.13). Crime records can be created where there is an allegation of a criminal offence even if that offence is not investigated or pursued. They will also exist where there has been an out of court disposal, including informal actions, such as triage, or a fixed penalty notice. If the individual denies the offence or has been acquitted of an offence that will not necessarily lead to the deletion of the crime record. Any such information can be disclosed in an ECRC, including acquittals.[53]

25.58 PA 1997 s113B states that the material should be disclosed if relevant to the prescribed purpose for the application, and further that the officer should have regard to any statutory guidance.[54] The Statutory Disclosure Guidance[55] currently in force was issued in August 2015, and provides that information should be sufficiently serious, current and credible before being disclosed. It also provides that consideration needs to be given to the impact of disclosure both on the applicant and others. In *R (L) v Commissioner of Police for the*

51 Disclosure of Youth Criminal Records: https://publications.parliament.uk/pa/cm201719/cmselect/cmjust/416/416.pdf.

52 PA 1997 s113B.

53 *R(AR) v Chief Constable of GMP* [2018] UKSC 47.

54 PA 1997 s113B(4A).

55 www.gov.uk/government/uploads/system/uploads/attachment_data/file/452321/6_1155_HO_LW_Stat_Dis_Guide-v3.pdf.

Metropolis[56] the Supreme Court concluded that this soft intelligence could only be included in the ECRC if that was compatible with the subject's rights under Article 8 ECHR (right to privacy and family life), and that if there was any doubt about that question, the subject should be given an opportunity to make representations about it prior to disclosure.

25.59 Usually where the police decide to disclose additional information over and above the convictions and cautions that will be automatically disclosed, they write to the applicant with the proposed wording in order to allow a chance for the applicant to make representations. Failure to do so will not automatically render the process unlawful; whether it is necessary to consult the applicant will depend on the facts of the case.[57]

25.60 Once the decision has been made as to what to disclose, the certificate will be sent directly to the applicant with the relevant information disclosed on it. The applicant can then provide the certificate to the employer.

25.61 Where the applicant disagrees with the discretion exercised by the police in disclosing information, the applicant has the right to complain to the Independent Monitor,[58] who will adjudicate on the decision to disclose the information. Included on the form are details of how to complain to the Independent Monitor, and how to complain if the information provided is inaccurate. The decision of the Independent Monitor can only be challenged by judicial review, where the court will consider the proportionality of the disclosure.[59]

Disclosure of acquittals and allegations

25.62 The credibility of the evidence is relevant to disclosure, the weaker the evidence is that the applicant committed the offence, the less likely it is that the matter will be disclosed. However, this is only one factor to be considered and there is no bar on disclosing acquittals: *R (R) v Chief Constable of Greater Manchester*,[60] where the court accepted that Article 6 of ECHR (right to a fair trial) was engaged, but that the disclosure of the acquittal was justified in that instance. Similarly

56 [2010] 1 AC 410.

57 *R (L) v Commissioner of the Metropolis* [2009] UKSC 3; *R (R) v Chief Constable of Greater Manchester* [2016] EWCA Civ 490 (paras 62–66).

58 PA 1997 s117A.

59 *R (LK) v Independent Monitor*, QBD, 17 June 2016 (unreported).

60 [2016] EWCA Civ 490.

allegations that were not prosecuted can be disclosed: *R (B) v Chief Constable of Derbyshire*.[61]

25.63 All crime records have an outcome code. These outcome codes are discussed at paras 7.17–7.18. Where a matter has not been proceeded with the outcome code may indicate the reason why, which may be relevant to disclosure. In particular since 2016, police can now record matters that were not prosecuted as not being in the public interest as 'Outcome 21' which indicates that they should not ordinarily be disclosed, see paras 7.19–7.25. However, ultimately even in these cases the decision will be made by the disclosure officer at the time.

Other consequences of recording and travel

25.64 The DBS is only one way in which information retained about an individual may be disclosed. Additionally information may be sought in relation to court proceedings, and in criminal cases any such information held on and individual could be disclosed to the court, subject to the rules on bad character applications. Certain jobs in the security services, police and high level government agencies require a more detailed 'vetting' process in which all information will usually be disclosed as dealt with at para 25.36 above Insurance companies will often ask about convictions, but they are only entitled to ask about unspent convictions. College courses are subject to similar rules as employers, and therefore some courses, where for example there may be a placement that involves working with children, will require an enhanced CRC.

25.65 When travelling abroad, some countries will ask for information about criminal records. What information they require is determined by the entry requirements of each individual country, and therefore it is not governed by UK law. Whether or not a conviction is spent is therefore unlikely to be relevant. Different countries have different criteria, and it is important to check whether you need a visa to enter the country, and then what questions will be asked about criminal convictions in the visa application. America operates a visa waiver system, where if travelling for a short period of time eligible people do not need a visa. However this does not apply to people convicted or even arrested for certain offences, who will then need to apply for a visa.[62]

61 [2011] EWHC 2362 (Admin).

62 http://hub.unlock.org.uk/knowledgebase/police-certificate/.

Barring

Overview

25.66 Courts no longer have the power to disqualify people from working with children. This process has been replaced by the Children's Barred List and the Adults' Barred List. If a person's name appears on these lists they are prevented from undertaking certain activities and work involving children and/or vulnerable adults. They are known as the 'Barred Lists' (children and adults).

25.67 There are two barred lists:

1) people who are prohibited from regulated activities with children, eg unsupervised contact with children, or work in certain establishments, such as schools; a full list of regulated activities can be found on the GOV.UK website;[63]
2) people who are prohibited from regulated activities with adults, eg providing health, personal, social care to adults; a full list for regulated activities for adults can be found on the GOV.UK website.[64]

The Barred Lists are operated by the DBS, who have a wide discretion who to place on these lists.[65] It was initially the Independent Safeguarding Authority who took these decisions, but that has been merged into the DBS.

Automatic barring

25.68 There are certain offences that will mean an individual will automatically be placed on the barred list without any discretion – these are generally serious sexual offences. They are often referred to as 'autobar' offences. The list of offences are set out in the Schedule to the Safeguarding Vulnerable Groups Act 2006 (Prescribed Criteria and Miscellaneous Provisions) Regulations Act 2009[66] (as amended) and a complete list of these offences is issued by the DBS.[67]

63 www.gov.uk/government/uploads/system/uploads/attachment_data/file/550197/Regulated_activity_in_relation_to_children.pdf.

64 www.gov.uk/government/uploads/system/uploads/attachment_data/file/216900/Regulated-Activity-Adults-Dec–2012.pdf.

65 This is governed by the SVGA 2006. Section 2 gives the DBS the authority to maintain the lists.

66 SI No 37.

67 www.safeguardingdurhamadults.info/media/13639/DBS-referral-guide-relevant-offences-for-England-and-Wales/pdf/Relevant_offences_for_England_and_Wales.pdf.

25.69 The list includes almost all sexual offences, regardless of the facts of the case; as well as serious offences such as murder.

25.70 If an individual receives a conviction or a caution for any of those offences, regardless of the age of the offender, the sentence received or the circumstances, that person will be on the barred list. While there is a right of appeal,[68] it can only be exercised if it can be shown that the DBS made a mistake about the type of offence that the individual was convicted of (ie that it was not an autobar offence) rather than an appeal regarding the circumstances of the offence.

Discretionary barring

25.71 There is a second set of offences that trigger consideration as to whether or not an individual can be placed on a barred list. If an individual commits one of these offences, the DBS will write to the individual to ask the individual to make representations as to whether they should be included. The DBS will then decide whether or not to include that individual on the barred list.

25.72 Further, even if an individual has committed no offence that triggers barring, the DBS can still make a judgment that an individual should be placed on the barred list if it receives information that it believes shows that the individual poses a risk to children or vulnerable adults. In those circumstances, the DBS again have to write to the individual to allow the individual the opportunity to make representations. The procedure in deciding whether an individual is put on the children's barring list is governed by Safeguarding Vulnerable Groups Act (SVGA) 2006 Sch 3 Part 1; and whether to place an individual on the adults' barring list is governed by Sch 3 Part 2 of that Act.

25.73 In any scenario where the DBS exercises some discretion as to whether to put an individual on the barred list, there is a right of appeal against that initial decision (under SVGA 2006 s4) to the Upper Tribunal.

25.74 Once an individual is on the barred list, providing the decision to be placed on the list is not successfully appealed, there is a minimum period that the individual has to remain barred, and this depends on the age of the individual. This period is as follows:

- under 18 – one year;
- 18–25 – five years;
- 25 plus – ten years.

25.75 After the minimum period, it is open to an individual to argue that due to a change in circumstances his or her placement on the barred

68 Under SVGA 2006 s4 to the Upper Tribunal.

list should be reviewed. While the DBS can refuse to do such a review, there is a right of appeal against a refusal to review, as well as a right of appeal against a negative decision following a review.[69]

Sex offenders register

Notification requirements

25.76 Notification requirements are often referred to as being placed on the 'sex offender's register'.[70] Notification requirements mean a person must notify the police of various personal details within three days, inform the police of any change of address or other personal details and of any foreign travel plans of three days or more.[71]

25.77 Children are subject to the same notification requirements as adults, however the periods of notification are halved (other than indefinite notification, which also applies to children). The length of notification periods are set out in the table below, see at para 25.80.

Automatic notification

25.78 A person is automatically subject to notification requirements if convicted or cautioned for an offence under SOA 2003 Sch 3.[72] This includes defendants who have been found not guilty by reason of insanity[73] or been found to have committed the act but unfit to plead.[74]

Sentencing condition

25.79 Certain sexual offences are subject to notification requirements if the defendant receives a custodial sentence of 12 months or longer.

Detention and training orders triggering notification requirements

25.79 Detention and training orders are treated as terms of imprisonment for the purposes of notification requirements (see para 25.80).[75] However, a detention and training order is made up of half detention

69 SVGA 2006 s4.
70 Sexual Offences Act (SOA) 2003 ss80–93.
71 SOA 2003, s83(1).
72 SOA 2003 s80.
73 SOA 2003 s80(1)(b).
74 SOA 2003 s80(1)(c).
75 SOA 2003 s131(a).

and training and half supervision, and it is only the detention and training part that is the equivalent to a term of imprisonment. In the case of *Slocombe*,[76] a 17-year-old was given a 12-month detention and training order, which consisted of six months' detention, and six months' supervision – this was treated by the Court of Appeal as the equivalent of six months' imprisonment (not 12) and therefore the length of the notification requirements were 3.5 years.

25.80 This analysis may have a bearing on whether the notification requirements apply at all. In *R v M*,[77] the defendants were convicted under SOA 2003 s13, which is subject to notification requirements only if a defendant is sentenced to a term of imprisonment of 12 months of more.[78] The defendants received detention and training orders of 12 months and 18 months, but following the analysis in *Slocombe*, this was the equivalent of six months' and nine months' imprisonment for the purposes of the notification requirements, and therefore the defendants were not subject to the requirements.

Length of notification requirements

Sentence	Length of notification requirements
30 months' imprisonment or longer (including life sentences) Hospital orders with restrictions	Indefinite
Less than 30 months', more than six months' imprisonment	Ten years (adult) Five years (child)
Six months' imprisonment or less Hospital order	Seven years (adult) 3.5 years (child)
Caution	Two years (adult) One year (child)
Conditional discharge	Length of conditional discharge
All other sentences	Five years (adult) 2.5 years (child)

21.81 For indefinite terms of imprisonment, there is a right to review after 15 years.[79]

76 [2005] EWCA Crim 2297.

77 [2010] EWCA Crim 42.

78 SOA 2003 Sch 3 para 22.

79 See: http://hub.unlock.org.uk/knowledgebase/information-sex-offence-notification-requirements.

APPENDICES

APPENDIX A

Youth court protocol[1]

YOUTH COURT BENCH BOOK APPENDIX A: MAGISTRATES ASSOCIATION PROTOCOL

This protocol is provided by the Youth Courts' Committee of the Magistrates' Association

The principal aim of the youth justice system is to prevent offending by children and young people, and a court must have regard to this principal aim as well as taking into account the welfare of the offender.

A court sentencing a young person must be aware of the obligations under a range of international conventions. These emphasise the importance of avoiding unnecessary criminalisation of you people whilst ensuring that they are held responsible for their actions and, where possible, take part in repairing the damage that they have caused. The youth court aims to promote reintegration rather than impose retribution.

The general principle must be that youth trials and sentencing take place in a youth court, separate from an adult court.

Unless there are truly exceptional circumstances, young people should appear at court in person before a youth court with magistrates or district judges (magistrates' court) trained in youth matters. Wherever possible, adult courts dealing with a young person with regard to bail should grant unconditional or conditional bail and adjourn the case to be heard in a youth court at the earliest opportunity.

Section 53 of the Criminal Justice and Courts Act 2015 gives magistrates the ability to send young offenders to the Crown Court for sentence following conviction if they consider that their sentencing powers (a detention and training order of up to two years in duration) are insufficient. There are very few offences which cannot, by law, be tried in the youth court. The exceptions include murder, attempted murder and manslaughter, and those offences which carry mandatory minimum sentences. Where a child or young person is jointly charged with an adult (someone aged 18 or over), the youth must be tried summarily unless the court considers it to be in the interests of justice for both the youth and the adult to be committed to the Crown Court for trial.

1 Youth Court Bench Book, Judicial College, August 2017 found at: www.judiciary.uk/wp-content/uploads/2016/10/youth-court-bench-book-august-2017.pdf/.

The youth court will:

- Engage with young people and their parents, guardians or carers
- Make the court less formal than the adult court
- Create an atmosphere which encourages dialogue and ensures that parents, guardians or carers understand their individual responsibilities in preventing further offending behaviour
- Develop mechanisms for the feedback of information to magistrates to enable sentencing to be as effective as possible in reducing further offending. The local authority, under Section 9 Children and Young Persons Act 1969, has a duty to provide the court with information on a young person's home surroundings, school record, health (including mental health) and character which it considers will assist the court. The youth court may request local authorities either to investigate or further investigate and provide the requested information.

This protocol provides advice only. Any decision with regard to the procedures to be adopted in each case will rest with the justices (having taken advice from the legal adviser) or the district judge (magistrates' court) taking into account all the circumstances of the particular case including the age, maturity and development – both intellectual and emotional – of the young person before the court.

This protocol has been adopted by the .... Youth Court Panel and will be effective from .... until further review.

1. Statutory duties

It is important to draw attention to the following statutory responsibilities of the youth court in relation to communication with children and young persons and their parents, guardians or carers. These responsibilities are in addition to the general duty for magistrates to give reasons for their decisions.

Rule 6 of the Magistrates' Courts (Children and Young Persons) Rules 1992 requires the court to explain to the child or young person the nature of the proceedings and the substance of the charge in simple language, suitable to their age and understanding.

Where a child or young person has pleaded guilty or been found guilty of an offence, Rule 11 of the same Rules imposes a duty on the court, before finally disposing of the case or remitting it to another court, to inform the child or young person, his parent or guardian or any person assisting them, of the manner in which it proposes to deal with the case. The court must then allow any of those people an opportunity to make representations. When making an Order, the court must explain to the child or young person the general nature and effect of the Order.

2. Court building and layout

Ideally, courthouses should provide:

- Separate entrances to the court for adults and youths Separate
- waiting areas for youths
- Separate waiting areas for witnesses

Changes to the layout of the court room will be made after consultation with the bench, justices' clerk, the court manager and youth court users.

The arrangement of furniture in the court may be changed from time to time to encourage children and young people and their parents, guardians or carers to participate in proceedings. It is essential for magistrates to communicate directly with children and their parents, guardians or carers and this can be achieved most effectively in a less formal atmosphere.

The defendant will not normally be in the dock, unless security considerations dictate otherwise (see section on secure docks below). All parties present in court will stand when the magistrates are entering or leaving the courtroom.

3. Secure dock

For courtrooms with a secure dock, subject to the court's discretion to order otherwise, a young person will be produced in the secure dock only if:

1. They have attained the age of 15; and
2. They are produced to the court from custody; and
3. He or she is charged with an offence of:
    i. A violent nature (other than common assault but including witness interference and offences specified in Schedule 15 of the Criminal Justice Act 2003), or
    ii. A sexual nature, or
    iii. Possession of a real or imitation firearm or other weapon

A young person will also be produced in the secure dock where the court so orders it of its own volition or upon representations.

A secure dock should be used for youths only in appropriate circumstances, and its use should not become the rule, even for those produced in custody. Only those charged with the most serious offences, or whose behaviour has given rise to serious concern, should be required to appear in the secure dock. The court's expectation with regards to use of the secure dock should be communicated to those bringing the young person into court from custody, where relevant.

4. Engagement

Youth court chairs have the opportunity to:

- Engage with young offenders and their parents, guardians or carers in focusing upon offending behaviour
- Create a youth court which is more open and commands the confidence of victims and the public
- Place a strong emphasis on using sentencing to prevent future offending Magistrates should understand when and how engagement should take place.

The following issues should be considered:

- Awareness of difficulties with communication experienced by many of the young people who appear in the youth court, including learning difficulties, developmental issues, mental health issues and issues of self-esteem
- Involvement of wingers, legal advisers, the press and victims as appropriate
- Handling of advocates ensuring the young offender speaks for themselves where appropriate and is questioned appropriately, taking into consideration their understanding and maturity
- Conducting engagement within an appropriate timetable
- Remembering to demonstrate active listening, using age-appropriate language and being aware of body language
- Managing any revised court layouts and assessing how these may affect court proceedings
- Upholding the dignity of the court

Ensuring pre-conviction that all participants understand their roles in court:

- Emphasising the importance and seriousness of the occasion
- Avoiding significant engagement at this stage

Engaging with parents, guardians and carers to focus upon issues regarding:

- Behaviour at home, school and/or work issues, interests and activities and peer group involvement
- Involvement in the care and control of the young person to ensure that informed decisions can be made regarding the appropriateness of parental orders

Assisting young offenders to understand the seriousness of their actions in order to promote responsibility and demonstrating that the court is concerned with the offender as an individual by passing an appropriate sentence in accordance with the Sentencing Council's

Definitive Guideline, *Overarching Principles – Sentencing Youths*, and any relevant offence-specific youth guidelines.

Engaging post-conviction with the young offender and their parent, guardian or carer to:

- Understand the motivation behind the offence
- Encourage the young person to accept responsibility for their part in the offence and to understand the consequences for themselves, their family and the victim(s)
- Address behaviour which may contribute to future offending

5. Defendants

The Chair should explain to the child or young person – and to any parent, guardian or carer in attendance – the roles of the various people present in court. Where a child or young person is not making a first appearance on the matter in hand (i.e. at a previously adjourned hearing or at a pre-trial review), the Chair should sensitively and appropriately check the understanding of the young person, and may decide to explain again.

The defendant's full name, address, date of birth and age will be confirmed, as will the identity of the guardian or carer. The defendant will be addressed by their first name alone from this point forward.

The legal adviser will explain to the child or young person the nature of the charge in ordinary language. The court will not proceed further until it is satisfied that the child or young person understands the allegations made.

Defendants will be required to stand in court to be identified, when the charges are put to them and when the court is disposing of the case. During the rest of the proceedings, they should be allowed to remain seated. Other court users should be seated throughout, apart from when the magistrates are entering or leaving the court. The young person should be seated next to their parent or guardian.

At the start of a trial, the Chair will check that the child or young person and any parent, guardian or carer in attendance understands the procedure to be followed, including the order of evidence and speeches..

The Chair should make it clear to defendants who have pleaded guilty or been found guilty that they may be asked questions during the course of the proceedings. The purpose of questioning is to:

- Ensure the bench has all the relevant information before disposing of the case and
- Encourage the offender to recognise his or her wrongdoing and to accept responsibility for it

Before finally disposing of a case, the Chair may, where appropriate, outline in open court the manner in which the court intends to deal with the case and may invite representations on the intended disposal.

The court will explain the nature and effect of its Order to the child or young person, and to his or her parent, guardian or carer, and will check the child or young person's understanding of the court's decision.

Consideration should always be given to the length of court sittings and how often it will be necessary to take breaks. This is particularly relevant to trials, and to those with identified learning difficulties.

6. Parents and guardians

It is essential that parents, guardians or carers attend court with their children. Magistrates expect the YOT to have made every effort to ensure such attendance. Despite the pressures of dealing speedily with an offence, there may be occasions when an adjournment is the best course of action to ensure that the parent, guardian or carer is made aware in person that the court takes the concept of parental responsibility very seriously. Not only can they provide essential information about the child, but some sanctions cannot be applied in their absence (e.g. binding them over to take care and control of their children; making them responsible for financial penalties).

Courts do have the power to summons a parent/guardian to court, and Legal Advisers will be able to provide further information. They also have the option of imposing a Parenting Order on a parent/guardian who is not present in court so long as an explanation is provided (e.g. in writing) of the effect of the

Order, the requirements included in it, the consequences which may follow if they fails to comply with the requirements and the power of the court to review the order on application. It is usually desirable to ensure both parents, where applicable, attend court and are involved in any parenting intervention.

Voluntary engagement with parents/guardians is preferable to a Court Order and the court would not be expected to give a Parenting Order where the parents/guardians are fully compliant with the support offered by the YOT on a voluntary basis.

The expectation should be that parents, guardians or carers also attend court with a 17-year-old defendant. Magistrates will need to balance the requirement to deal speedily with a case with the seriousness of the offence and the fact that a 17-year-old is still a child.

Parents, guardians or carers may be seated throughout the proceedings, but they should stand when the chair is announcing orders which affect them personally.

Where any unrepresented child or young person enters a plea of guilty, the bench's legal adviser will ascertain from any parent, guardian or carer in attendance that they are satisfied – on the basis of what he or she understands from the police and from the defendant – that the offence is properly admitted. The same will apply to offences to be taken into consideration.

Parents, guardians or carers should be encouraged to address the court before sentence.

7. Witnesses

Witnesses should be asked to stand whilst taking the Oath or Affirmation and thereafter should be invited to be seated whilst they give their evidence.

Trial preparation forms and hearings will identify when witnesses wish to give evidence under special measures. It is the role of the Chair to ensure that the inclusion of these measures in a trial does not create any impression that the fairness of the proceedings is compromised.

Witnesses will normally be allowed to remain in court after they have finished giving their evidence. However, this will be at the court's discretion. Should they be told to leave, Chair will give an explanation.

8. Victims

All victims should have the opportunity to attend youth court hearings, both trials and sentencing, if they wish to do so, unless the particular circumstances of the case mean that it would not be in the best interests of justice. If a victim is excluded, the Chair should explain why.

The alleged victims of a crime will usually be entitled to attend youth court proceedings as people directly concerned with the proceedings. On attending, they should be directed by court staff to liaise with the Witness Service about the practicalities of having access to the youth court.

A Victim Personal Statement will normally be presented by the prosecution. This should be considered during the sentencing exercise and could be used as a starting point for engagement with the young person in considering the consequences of their actions.

9. Looked after children

The youth court should always recognise the particular experiences and difficulties of young people who are looked after, and the need to protect their welfare. Looked after children should be accompanied in court by a carer who is fully familiar with their circumstances.

10. Attendance of others

The youth court is a closed court and only people directly involved in the case should normally be present. Other people should only be allowed into court with the express permission of the bench, having heard appropriate representations

11. Advocates

It is acknowledged that specialist youth training for all advocates practising in the youth court would be advantageous. At the very least, all parties in the proceedings should attempt to use plain language for legal and technical terms where possible, and should be familiar with this Youth Court Protocol.

12. Media

Members of the press are entitled to be present in the youth court.

The court may lift reporting restrictions where offenders have pleaded guilty or been found guilty and it is in the public interest to do so, but this should be exceptionally rare. The court may make such an Order on application, or of its own volition.

13. Working with Youth Offending Teams

It is essential that there is a relationship of open communication and trust between the youth court magistrates and the local YOT. The HMCTS/YJB booklet 'Making it Count in Court' is available as a download or a hard copy and can be ordered free of charge from www.yjb.gov.uk. This booklet contains ideas for liaison with YOTs, such as holding regular meetings between youth court panel chairs and YOT managers.

14. Monitoring

This Protocol will be reviewed by the Youth Court Panel on an annual basis.

APPENDIX B

Police recorded crime outcome codes[1]

Outcome groups reference table

Outcome Type	Outcome Description	Outcome Group
1	Charged/Summonsed	Charged/Summonsed
2	Caution – youths	Out-of-court (formal)
3	Caution – adults	Out-of-court (formal)
4	Taken into consideration (TIC)	Taken into consideration
5	Offender died	Prosecution prevented or not in the public interest
6	Penalty Notices for Disorder (PND)	Out-of-court (formal)
7	Cannabis/Khat warning	Out-of-court (informal)
8	Community Resolution	Out-of-court (informal)
9	Not in public interest (CPS)	Prosecution prevented or not in the public interest
10	Not in public interest (Police)	Prosecution prevented or not in the public interest
11	Prosecution prevented – suspect under age	Prosecution prevented or not in the public interest
12	Prosecution prevented: suspect too ill	Prosecution prevented or not in the public interest
13	Prosecution prevented: victim/key witness dead/ too ill	Prosecution prevented or not in the public interest

1 Extracted from 'Police Recorded Crime and Outcomes: Open Data Tables User Guide', Home Office, October 2016, p12.

14	Evidential difficulties: suspect not identified; victim does not support further action	Evidential difficulties (victim does not support action)
15	Evidential difficulties: suspect identified; victim supports action	Evidential difficulties (suspect identified; victim supports action)
16	Evidential difficulties: suspect identified; victim does not support further action	Evidential difficulties (victim does not support action)
17	Prosecution time limit expired	Prosecution prevented or not in the public interest
18	Investigation complete no suspect identified	Investigation complete no suspect identified
20	Action undertaken by another body/agency	Action undertaken by another body/agency
21	Further investigation to support formal action not in the public interest	Further investigation to support formal action not in the public interest

APPENDIX C

Criminal Practice Directions: extracts[1]

1 Criminal Practice Directions published October 2015, reproduced as amended at October 2018, found at: www.justice.gov.uk/courts/procedure-rules/criminal/rulesmenu-2015. © Crown copyright.

CRIMINAL PRACTICE DIRECTIONS 2015 DIVISION I: GENERAL MATTERS

3D VULNERABLE PEOPLE IN THE COURTS

3D.1 In respect of eligibility for special measures, 'vulnerable' and 'intimidated' witnesses are defined in sections 16 and 17 of the Youth Justice and Criminal Evidence Act 1999 (as amended by the Coroners and Justice Act 2009); 'vulnerable' includes those under 18 years of age and people with a mental disorder or learning disability; a physical disorder or disability; or who are likely to suffer fear or distress in giving evidence because of their own circumstances or those relating to the case.

3D.2 However, many other people giving evidence in a criminal case, whether as a witness or defendant, may require assistance: the court is required to take 'every reasonable step' to encourage and facilitate the attendance of witnesses and to facilitate the participation of any person, including the defendant (CrimPR 3.9(3)(a) and (b)). This includes enabling a witness or defendant to give their best evidence, and enabling a defendant to comprehend the proceedings and engage fully with his or her defence. The pre-trial and trial process should, so far as necessary, be adapted to meet those ends. Regard should be had to the welfare of a young defendant as required by section 44 of the Children and Young Persons Act 1933, and generally to Parts 1 and 3 of the Criminal Procedure Rules (the overriding objective and the court's powers of case management).

3D.3 Under Part 3 of the Rules, the court must identify the needs of witnesses at an early stage (CrimPR 3.2(2)(b)) and may require the parties to identify arrangements to facilitate the giving of evidence and participation in the trial (CrimPR 3.11(c)(iv) and (v)). There are various statutory special measures that the court may utilise to assist a witness in giving evidence. CrimPR Part 18 gives the procedures to be followed. Courts should note the 'primary rule' which requires the court to give a direction for a special measure to assist a child witness or qualifying witness and that in such cases an application to the court is not required (CrimPR 18.9).

3D.4 Court of Appeal decisions on this subject include a judgment from the Lord Chief Justice, Lord Judge in *R v Cox* [2012] EWCA Crim 549, [2012] 2 Cr App R 6; *R v Wills* [2011] EWCA Crim 1938, [2012] 1 Cr App R 2; and *R v E* [2011] EWCA Crim 3028, [2012] Crim LR 563.

3D.5 In *R v Wills*, the Court endorsed the approach taken by the report of the Advocacy Training Council (ATC) 'Raising the Bar: the Handling of Vulnerable Witnesses, Victims and Defendants in Court' (2011). The report includes and recommends the use of 'toolkits' to assist advocates as they prepare to question vulnerable people at court: www.advocacytrainingcouncil.org/vulnerable-witnesses/raising-the-bar

3D.6 Further toolkits are available through the Advocate's Gateway which is managed by the ATC's Management Committee: www.theadvocatesgateway.org/

3D.7 These toolkits represent best practice. Advocates should consult and follow the relevant guidance whenever they prepare to question a young or otherwise vulnerable witness or defendant. Judges may find it helpful to refer advocates to this material and to use the toolkits in case management.

3D.8 'Achieving Best Evidence in Criminal Proceedings' (Ministry of Justice 2011) describes best practice in preparation for the investigative interview and trial: www.cps.gov.uk/publications/docs/best_evidence_in_criminal_proceedings.pdf

3E GROUND RULES HEARINGS TO PLAN THE QUESTIONING OF A VULNERABLE WITNESS OR DEFENDANT

3E.1 The judiciary is responsible for controlling questioning. Over-rigorous or repetitive cross-examination of a child or vulnerable witness should be stopped. Intervention by the judge, magistrates or intermediary (if any) is minimised if questioning, taking account of the individual's communication needs, is discussed in advance and ground rules are agreed and adhered to.

3E.2 Discussion of ground rules is required in all intermediary trials where they must be discussed between the judge or magistrates, advocates and intermediary before the witness gives evidence. The intermediary must be present but is not required to take the oath (the intermediary's declaration is made just before the witness gives evidence).

3E.3 Discussion of ground rules is good practice, even if no intermediary is used, in all young witness cases and in other cases where a witness or defendant has communication needs. Discussion before the day of trial is preferable to give advocates time to adapt their questions to the witness's needs. It may be helpful for a trial practice note of boundaries to be created at the end of the discussion. The judge may use such a document in ensuring that the agreed ground rules are complied with.

3E.4 All witnesses, including the defendant and defence witnesses, should be enabled to give the best evidence they can. In relation to young and/or vulnerable people, this may mean departing radically from traditional cross-examination. The form and extent of appropriate cross-examination will vary from case to case. For adult non vulnerable witnesses an advocate will usually put his case so that the witness will have the opportunity of commenting upon it and/or answering it. When the witness is young or otherwise vulnerable, the court may dispense with the normal practice and impose restrictions on the advocate 'putting his case' where there is a risk of a young or otherwise vulnerable witness failing to understand, becoming distressed or acquiescing to leading questions. Where limitations on questioning are necessary and appropriate, they must be clearly defined. The judge has a duty to ensure that they are complied with and should explain them to the jury and the reasons for them. If the advocate fails to comply with the limitations, the judge should give relevant directions to the jury when that occurs and prevent further questioning that does not comply with the ground rules settled upon in advance. Instead of commenting on inconsistencies during cross-examination, following discussion between the judge and the advocates, the advocate or judge may point out important inconsistencies after (instead of during) the witness's evidence. The judge should also remind the jury of these during summing up. The judge should be alert to alleged inconsistencies that are not in fact inconsistent, or are trivial.

3E.5 If there is more than one defendant, the judge should not permit each advocate to repeat the questioning of a vulnerable witness. In advance of the trial, the advocates should divide the topics between them, with the advocate for the first defendant leading the questioning, and the advocate(s) for the other defendant(s) asking only ancillary questions relevant to their client's case, without repeating the questioning that has already taken place on behalf of the other defendant(s).

3E.6 In particular in a trial of a sexual offence, 'body maps' should be provided for the witness' use. If the witness needs to indicate a part of the body, the advocate should ask the witness to point to the relevant part on the body map. In sex cases, judges should not permit advocates to ask the witness to point to a part of the witness' own body. Similarly, photographs of the witness' body should not be shown around the court while the witness is giving evidence.

3F INTERMEDIARIES

Role and functions of intermediaries in criminal courts

3F.1 Intermediaries facilitate communication with witnesses and defendants who have communication needs. Their primary function is to improve the quality of evidence and aid understanding between the court, the advocates and the witness or defendant. For example, they commonly advise on the formulation of questions so as to avoid misunderstanding. On occasion, they actively assist and intervene during questioning. The extent to which they do so (if at all) depends on factors such as the communication needs of the witness or defendant, and the skills of the advocates in adapting their language and questioning style to meet those needs.

3F.2 Intermediaries are independent of parties and owe their duty to the court. The court and parties should be vigilant to ensure they act impartially and their assistance to witnesses and defendants is transparent. It is however permissible for an advocate to have a private consultation with an intermediary when formulating questions (although control of questioning remains the overall responsibility of the court).

3F.3 Further information is in *Intermediaries: Step by Step* (Toolkit 16; The Advocate's Gateway, 2015) and chapter 5 of the *Equal Treatment Bench Book* (Judicial College, 2013).

Links to publications

- www.theadvocatesgateway.org/images/toolkits/16inte rmediariesstepbystep 060315.pdf
- https://www.judiciary.gov.uk/wp-content/uploads/2013/11/5-children-and vulnerable adults.pdf

Assessment

3F.4 The process of appointment should begin with assessment by an intermediary and a report. The report will make recommendations to address the communication needs of the witness or defendant during trial.

3F.5 In light of the scarcity of intermediaries, the appropriateness of assessment must be decided with care to ensure their availability for those witnesses and defendants who are most in need. The decision should be made on an individual basis, in the context of the circumstances of the particular case.

Intermediaries for prosecution and defence witnesses

3F.6 Intermediaries are one of the special measures available to witnesses under the Youth Justice and Criminal Evidence Act (YJCEA) 1999. Witnesses deemed vulnerable in accordance with the criteria in YJCEA 1999 s16 are eligible for the assistance of an intermediary when giving evidence pursuant to YJCEA 1999 s29. These provisions do not apply to defendants.

3F.7 An application for an intermediary to assist a witness when giving evidence must be made in accordance with Part 18 of the Criminal Procedure Rules. In addition, where an intermediary report is available (see 3F.4 above), it should be provided with the application.

3F.8 The Witness Intermediary Scheme (WIS) operated by the National Crime Agency identifies intermediaries for witnesses and may be used by the prosecution and defence. The WIS is contactable at wit@nca.x.gsi.gov.uk/ 0845 000 5463. An intermediary appointed through the WIS is defined as a 'Registered Intermediary' and matched to the particular witness based on expertise, location and availability. Registered Intermediaries are accredited by the WIS and bound by Codes of Practice and Ethics issued by the Ministry of Justice (which oversees the WIS).

3F.9 Having identified a Registered Intermediary, the WIS does not provide funding. The party appointing the Registered Intermediary is responsible for payment at rates specified by the Ministry of Justice.

3F.10 Further information is in *The Registered Intermediaries Procedural Guidance Manual* (Ministry of Justice, 2015) and *Intermediaries: Step by Step* (see 3F.3 above).

Link to publication

- www.theadvocatesgateway.org/images/procedures/registered-intermediary-procedural-guidance-manual.pdf

Intermediaries for defendants

3F.11 Statutory provisions providing for defendants to be assisted by an intermediary when giving evidence (where necessary to ensure a fair trial) are not in force (because Coroners and Justice Act 2009 s104, which would insert sections 33BA and 33BB into the YJCEA 1999, has yet to be commenced).

3F.12 The court may direct the appointment of an intermediary to assist a defendant in reliance on its inherent powers (*C v Sevenoaks Youth Court* [2009] EWHC 3088 (Admin)). There is however no presumption that a defendant will be so assisted and, even where an intermediary would improve the trial process, appointment is not mandatory (*R v Cox* [2012] EWCA Crim 549). The court should adapt the trial process to address a defendant's communication needs (*R v Cox* [2012] EWCA Crim 549). It will rarely exercise its inherent powers to direct appointment of an intermediary but where a defendant is vulnerable or for some other reason experiences communication or hearing difficulties, such that he or she needs more help to follow the proceedings than his or her legal representatives readily can give having regard to their other functions on the defendant's behalf, then the court should consider sympathetically any application for the defendant to be accompanied throughout the trial by a support worker or other appropriate companion who can provide that assistance. This is consistent with CrimPR 3.9(3)(b) (see paragraph 3D.2 above); consistent with the observations in *R v Cox* (see paragraph 3D.4 above), *R (OP) v Ministry of Justice* [2014] EWHC 1944 (Admin) and *R v Rashid* [2017] EWCA Crim 2; and consistent with the arrangements contemplated at paragraph 3G.8 below.

3F.13 The court may exercise its inherent powers to direct appointment of an intermediary to assist a defendant giving evidence or for the entire trial. Terms of appointment are for the court and there is no illogicality in restricting the appointment to the defendant's evidence (*R v R* [2015] EWCA Crim 1870), when the 'most pressing need' arises (*OP v Secretary of State for Justice* [2014] EWHC 1944 (Admin)). Directions to appoint an intermediary for a defendant's evidence will thus be rare, but for the entire trial extremely rare, keeping in mind paragraph 3F.12 above.

3F.14 An application for an intermediary to assist a defendant must be made in accordance with Part 18 of the Criminal Procedure Rules. In addition, where an intermediary report is available (see 3F.4 above), it should be provided with the application.

3F.15 The WIS is not presently available to identify intermediaries for defendants (although in *OP v Secretary of State for Justice* [2014] EWHC 1944 (Admin), the Ministry of Justice was ordered to consider carefully whether it were justifiable to refuse equal provision to witnesses and defendants with respect to their evidence). 'Non-registered intermediaries' (intermediaries appointed other than through the WIS) must therefore be appointed for defendants. Although training is available, there is no accreditation process for non-registered intermediaries and rates of payment are unregulated.

3F.16 Arrangements for funding of intermediaries for defendants depend on the stage of the appointment process. Where the defendant is publicly funded, an application should be made to the Legal Aid Agency for prior authority to fund a pre-trial assessment. If the application is refused, an application may be made to the court to use its inherent powers to direct a pre-trial assessment and funding thereof. Where the court uses its inherent powers to direct assistance by an intermediary at trial (during evidence or for the entire trial), court staff are responsible for arranging payment from Central Funds. Internal guidance for court staff is in *Guidance for HMCTS Staff: Registered and Non-Registered Intermediaries for Vulnerable Defendants and Non-Vulnerable Defence and Prosecution Witnesses* (Her Majesty's Courts and Tribunals Service, 2014).

3F.17 The court should be satisfied that a non-registered intermediary has expertise suitable to meet the defendant's communication needs.

3F.18 Further information is in *Intermediaries: Step by Step* (see 3F.3 above).

Ineffective directions for intermediaries to assist defendants

3F.19 Directions for intermediaries to help defendants may be ineffective due to general unavailability, lack of suitable expertise, or non-availability for the purpose directed (for example, where the direction is for assistance during evidence, but an intermediary will only accept appointment for the entire trial).

3F.20 Intermediaries may contribute to the administration of justice by facilitating communication with appropriate defendants during the trial process. A trial will not be rendered unfair because a direction to appoint an intermediary for the defendant is ineffective. 'It would, in fact, be a most unusual case for a defendant who is fit to plead to be so disadvantaged by his condition that a properly brought prosecution would have to be stayed' because an intermediary with suitable expertise is not available for the purpose directed by the court (*R v Cox* [2012] EWCA Crim 549).

3F.21 Faced with an ineffective direction, it remains the court's responsibility to adapt the trial process to address the defendant's communication needs, as was the case prior to the existence of intermediaries (*R v Cox* [2012] EWCA

Crim 549). In such a case, a ground rules hearing should be convened to ensure every reasonable step is taken to facilitate the defendant's participation in accordance with CrimPR 3.9. At the hearing, the court should make new, further and / or alternative directions. This includes setting ground rules to help the defendant follow proceedings and (where applicable) to give evidence.

3F.22 For example, to help the defendant follow proceedings the court may require evidence to be adduced by simple questions, with witnesses being asked to answer in short sentences. Regular breaks may assist the defendant's concentration and enable the defence advocate to summarise the evidence and take further instructions.

3F.23 Further guidance is available in publications such as *Ground Rules Hearings and the Fair Treatment of Vulnerable People in Court* (Toolkit 1; The Advocate's Gateway, 2015) and *General Principles from Research – Planning to Question a Vulnerable Person or Someone with Communication Needs* (Toolkit 2(a); The Advocate's Gateway, 2015). In the absence of an intermediary, these publications include information on planning how to manage the participation and questioning of the defendant, and the formulation of questions to avert misunderstanding (for example, by avoiding 'long and complicated questions . . . posed in a leading or tagged' manner' (*R v Wills* [2011] EWCA Crim 1938, [2012] 1 Cr App R 2)).

Links to publications

- www.theadvocatesgateway.org/images/toolkits/1groundruleshearingsand thefairtreatmentofvulnerablepeopleincourt 060315.pdf
- www.theadvocatesgateway.org/images/toolkits/2generalprinciplesfrom researchpolicyandguidance-planningtoquestionavulnerablepersonor someonewithcommun icationneeds141215.pdf

Intermediaries for witnesses and defendants under 18

3F.24 Communication needs (such as short attention span, suggestibility and reticence in relation to authority figures) are common to many witnesses and defendants under 18. Consideration should therefore be given to the communication needs of all children and young people appearing in the criminal courts and to adapting the trial process to address any such needs. Guidance is available in publications such as *Planning to Question a Child or Young Person* (Toolkit 6; The Advocate's Gateway, 2015) and *Effective Participation of Young Defendants* (Toolkit 8; The Advocate's Gateway, 2013).

Links to publications

- www.theadvocatesgateway.org/images/toolkits/6planningtoquestiona childoryoungperson141215.pdf
- www.theadvocatesgateway.org/images/toolkits/8YoungDefendants 211013.pdf

3F.25 For the reasons set out in 3F.5 above, the appropriateness of an intermediary assessment for witnesses and defendants under 18 must be decided with care. Whilst there is no presumption that they will be assessed by an intermediary (to evaluate their communication needs prior to trial) or assisted by an intermediary at court (for example, if / when giving evidence), the decision should be made on an individual basis in the context of the circumstances of the particular case.

3F.26 Assessment by an intermediary should be considered for witnesses and defendants under 18 who seem liable to misunderstand questions or to experience difficulty expressing answers, including those who seem unlikely to be able to recognise a problematic question (such as one that is misleading or not readily understood), and those who may be reluctant to tell a questioner in a position of authority if they do not understand.

Attendance at ground rules hearing

3F.27 Where the court directs questioning will be conducted through an intermediary, CrimPR 3.9 requires the court to set ground rules. The intermediary should be present at the ground rules hearing to make representations in accordance with CrimPR 3.9(7)(a).

Listing

3F.28 Where the court directs an intermediary will attend the trial, their dates of availability should be provided to the court. It is preferable that such trials are fixed rather than placed in warned lists.

Photographs of court facilities

3F.29 Resident Judges in the Crown Court or the Chief Clerk or other responsible person in the magistrates' courts should, in consultation with HMCTS managers responsible for court security matters, develop a policy to govern under what circumstances photographs or other visual recordings may be made of court facilities, such as a live link room, to assist vulnerable or child witnesses to familiarise themselves with the setting, so as to be enabled to give their best evidence. For example, a photograph may provide a helpful reminder to a witness whose court visit has taken place sometime earlier. Resident Judges should tend to permit photographs to be taken for this purpose by intermediaries or supporters, subject to whatever restrictions the Resident Judge or responsible person considers to be appropriate, having regard to the security requirements of the court.

3G VULNERABLE DEFENDANTS

Before the trial, sentencing or appeal

3G.1 If a vulnerable defendant, especially one who is young, is to be tried jointly with one who is not, the court should consider at the plea and case management hearing, or at a case management hearing in a magistrates' court, whether the vulnerable defendant should be tried on his own, but should only so order if satisfied that a fair trial cannot be achieved by use of appropriate special measures or other support for the defendant. If a vulnerable defendant is tried jointly with one who is not, the court should consider whether any of the modifications set out in this direction should apply in the circumstances of the joint trial and, so far as practicable, make orders to give effect to any such modifications.

3G.2 It may be appropriate to arrange that a vulnerable defendant should visit, out of court hours and before the trial, sentencing or appeal hearing, the courtroom in which that hearing is to take place so that he or she can familiarise him or herself with it.

3G.3 Where an intermediary is being used to help the defendant to communicate at court, the intermediary should accompany the defendant on his or her pre-trial visit. The visit will enable the defendant to familiarise him or herself with the layout of the court, and may include matters such as: where the defendant will sit, either in the dock or otherwise; court officials (what their roles are and where they sit); who else might be in the court, for example those in the public gallery and press box; the location of the witness box; basic court procedure; and the facilities available in the court.

3G.4 If the defendant's use of the live link is being considered, he or she should have an opportunity to have a practice session.

3G.5 If any case against a vulnerable defendant has attracted or may attract widespread public or media interest, the assistance of the police should be enlisted to try and ensure that the defendant is not, when attending the court, exposed to intimidation, vilification or abuse. Section 41 of the Criminal Justice Act 1925 prohibits the taking of photographs of defendants and witnesses (among others) in the court building or in its precincts, or when entering or leaving those precincts. A direction reminding media representatives of the prohibition may be appropriate. The court should also be ready at this stage, if it has not already done so, where relevant to make a reporting restriction under section 39 of the Children and Young Persons Act 1933 or, on an appeal to the Crown Court from a youth court, to remind media representatives of theapplication of section 49 of that Act.

3G.6 The provisions of the Practice Direction accompanying Part 6 should be followed.

The trial, sentencing or appeal hearing

3G.7 Subject to the need for appropriate security arrangements, the proceedings should, if practicable, be held in a courtroom in which all the participants are on the same or almost the same level.

3G.8 Subject again to the need for appropriate security arrangements, a vulnerable defendant, especially if he is young, should normally, if he wishes, be free to sit with members of his family or others in a like relationship, and with some other suitable supporting adult such as a social worker, and in a place which permits easy, informal communication with his legal representatives. The court should ensure that a suitable supporting adult is available throughout the course of the proceedings.

3G.9 It is essential that at the beginning of the proceedings, the court should ensure that what is to take place has been explained to a vulnerable defendant in terms he or she can understand and, at trial in the Crown Court, it should ensure in particular that the role of the jury has been explained. It should remind those representing the vulnerable defendant and the supporting adult of their responsibility to explain each step as it takes place and, at trial, explain the possible consequences of a guilty verdict and credit for a guilty plea. The court should also remind any intermediary of the responsibility to ensure that the vulnerable defendant has understood the explanations given to him/her. Throughout the trial the court should continue to ensure, by any appropriate means, that the defendant understands what is happening and what has been said by those on the bench, the advocates and witnesses.

3G.10 A trial should be conducted according to a timetable which takes full account of a vulnerable defendant's ability to concentrate. Frequent and regular breaks will often be appropriate. The court should ensure, so far as practicable, that the whole trial is conducted in clear language that the defendant can understand and that evidence in chief and cross-examination are conducted using questions that are short and clear. The conclusions of the 'ground rules' hearing should be followed, and advocates should use and follow the 'toolkits' as discussed above.

3G.11 A vulnerable defendant who wishes to give evidence by live link, in accordance with section 33A of the YJCEA 1999, may apply for a direction to that effect; the procedure in CrimPR 18.14 to 18.17 should be followed. Before making such a direction, the court must be satisfied that it is in the interests of justice to do so and that the use of a live link would enable the defendant to participate more effectively as a witness in the proceedings. The direction will need to deal with the practical arrangements to be made, including the identity of the person or persons who will accompany him or her.

3G.12 In the Crown Court, the judge should consider whether robes and wigs should be worn, and should take account of the wishes of both a vulnerable defendant and any vulnerable witness. It is generally desirable that those responsible for the security of a vulnerable defendant who is in custody, especially if he or she is young, should not be in uniform, and that there should be no recognisable police presence in the courtroom save for good reason.

3G.13 The court should be prepared to restrict attendance by members of the public in the courtroom to a small number, perhaps limited to those with an immediate and direct interest in the outcome. The court should rule on any challenged claim to attend. However, facilities for reporting the proceedings (subject to any restrictions under section 39 or 49 of the Children and Young Persons Act 1933) must be provided. The court may restrict the number of reporters attending in the courtroom to such number as is judged practicable and desirable. In ruling on any challenged claim to attend in the courtroom for the purpose of reporting, the court should be mindful of the public's general right to be informed about the administration of justice.

3G.14 Where it has been decided to limit access to the courtroom, whether by reporters or generally, arrangements should be made for the proceedings to be relayed, audibly and if possible visually, to another room in the same court complex to which the media and the public have access if it appears that there will be a need for such additional facilities. Those making use of such a facility should be reminded that it is to be treated as an extension of the courtroom and that they are required to conduct themselves accordingly.

3P COMMISSIONING MEDICAL REPORTS

General observations

3P.1 CrimPR 24.3 and 25.10 concern procedures to be followed in magistrates' courts and in the Crown Court respectively where there is doubt about a defendant's mental health and, in the Crown Court, the defendant's capacity to participate in a trial. CrimPR governs the procedure where, on the court's own initiative, a magistrates' court requires expert medical opinion about the potential suitability of a hospital order under section 37(3) of the Mental Health Act 1983 (hospital order without convicting the defendant), the Crown Court requires such opinion about the defendant's fitness to participate at trial, under section 4 of the Criminal Procedure (Insanity) Act 1964, or either a magistrates' court or the Crown Court requires such opinion to help the court determine a question of intent or insanity.

3P.2 Rule 3.28 governs the procedure to be followed where a report is commissioned at the instigation of the court. It is not a substitute for the prompt commissioning of a report or reports by a party or party's representatives where expert medical opinion is material to that party's case. In particular, those representing a defendant may wish to obtain a medical report or reports wholly independently of the court. Nothing in these directions, therefore, should be read as discouraging a party from commissioning a medical report before the case comes before the court, where that party believes such a report to be material to an issue in the case and where it is possible promptly to commission it. However, where a party has commissioned such a report then if that report has not been received by the time the court gives directions for preparation for trial, and if the court agrees that it seems likely that the report will be material to what is in issue, then when giving directions for trial the court should include a timetable for the reception of that report and should give directions for progress to be reviewed at intervals, adopting the timetable set out in these directions with such adaptations as are needed.

3P.3 In assessing the likely materiality of an expert medical report to help the court assess a defendant's health and capacity at the time of the alleged offence or the time of trial, or both, the court will be assisted by the parties' representations; by the views expressed in any assessment that may already have been prepared; and by the views of practitioners in local criminal justice mental health services, whose assistance is available to the court under local liaison arrangements.

3P.4 Where the court requires the assistance of such a report then it is essential that there should be (i) absolute clarity about who is expected to do what, by when, and at whose expense; and (ii) judicial directions for progress with that report to be monitored and reviewed at prescribed intervals, following a timetable set by the court which culminates in the consideration of the report at a hearing. This is especially important where the report in question is a psychiatric assessment of the defendant for the preparation of which specific expertise may be required which is not readily available and because in some circumstances a second such assessment, by another medical practitioner, may be required.

Timetable for the commissioning, preparation and consideration of a report or reports

3P.5 CrimPR 3.28 requires the court to set a timetable appropriate to the case for the preparation and reception of a report. That timetable must not be in substitution for the usual timetable for preparation for trial but must instead be incorporated within the trial preparation timetable. The fact that a medical report is to be obtained, whether that is commissioned at a party's instigation or on the court's own initiative, is never a reason to postpone a preparation for trial or a plea and trial preparation hearing, or to decline to give the directions needed for preparation for trial. It follows that a trial date must be set and other directions given in the usual way.

3P.6 In setting the timetable for obtaining a report or reports the court will take account of such representations and other information that it receives, including information about the anticipated availability and workload of medical practitioners with the appropriate expertise. However, the timetable ought not be a protracted one. It is essential to keep in mind the importance of maintaining progress: in recognition of the defendant's rights and with respect for the interests of victims and witnesses, as required by CrimPR Part 1 (the overriding objective). In a magistrates' court account must be taken, too, of section 11 of the Powers of Criminal Courts (Sentencing) Act 2000, which limits the duration of each remand pending the preparation of a report to 3 weeks, where the defendant is to be in custody, and to 4 weeks if the defendant is to be on bail.

3P.7 Subject, therefore, to contrary judicial direction the timetable set by the court should require:

(a) the convening of a further pre-trial case management hearing to consider the report and its implications for the conduct of the proceedings no more than 6–8 weeks after the court makes its request in a magistrates' court, and no more than 10–12 weeks after the request in the Crown Court (at the end of Stage 2 of the directions for pre-trial preparation in the Crown Court);
(b) the prompt identification of an appropriate medical practitioner or practitioners, if not already identified by the court, and the despatch of a commission or commissions accordingly, within 2 business days of the court's decision to request a report;
(c) acknowledgement of a commission by its recipient, and acceptance or rejection of that commission, within 5 business days of its receipt;
(d) enquiries by court staff to confirm that the commission has been received, and to ascertain the action being taken in response, in the event that no acknowledgement is received within 10 business days of its despatch;
(e) delivery of the report within 5 weeks of the despatch of the commission;
(f) enquiries into progress by court staff in the event that no report is received within 5 weeks of the despatch of the commission.

3P.8 The further pre-trial case management hearing that is convened for the court to consider the report should not be adjourned before it takes place save in exceptional circumstances and then only by explicit judicial direction the reasons for which must be recorded. If by the time of that hearing the report is available, as usually should be the case, then at that hearing the court can be expected to determine the issue in respect of which the report was commissioned and give further directions accordingly. If by that time, exceptionally, the report is not available then the court should take the opportunity provided by that hearing to enquire into the reasons, give such directions as are appropriate, and if necessary adjourn the hearing to a fixed date for further consideration then. Where it is known in advance of that hearing that the report will not be available in time, the hearing may be conducted by live link or telephone: subject, in the defendant's case, to the same considerations as are identified at paragraph 3N.6 of these Practice Directions. However, it rarely will be appropriate to dispense altogether with that hearing, or to make enquiries and give further directions without any hearing at all, in view of the arrangements for monitoring and review that the court already will have directed and which, by definition therefore, thus far will have failed to secure the report's timely delivery.

3P.9 Where a requirement of the timetable set by the court is not met, or where on enquiry by court staff it appears that the timetable is unlikely to be met, and in any instance in which a medical practitioner who accepts a commission asks for more time, then court staff should not themselves adjust the timetable or accede to such a request but instead should seek directions from an appropriate judicial authority. Subject to local judicial direction, that will be, in the Crown Court, the judge assigned to the case or the resident judge and, in a magistrates' court, a District Judge (Magistrates' Courts) or justice of the peace assigned to the case, or the Justices' Clerk, an assistant clerk or other senior legal adviser. Even if the timetable is adjusted in consequence:

(a) the further pre-trial case management hearing convened to consider the report rarely should be adjourned before it takes place: see paragraph 3O.13 above;

(b) directions should be given for court staff henceforth to make regular enquiries into progress, at prescribed intervals of not more than 2 weeks, and to report theoutcome to an appropriate judicial authority who will decide what further directions, if any, to give.

3P.10 Any adjournment of a hearing convened to consider the report should be to a specific date: the hearing should not be adjourned generally, or to a date to be set in due course. The adjournment of such a hearing should not be for more than a further 6–8 weeks save in the most exceptional circumstances; and no more than one adjournment of the hearing should be allowed without obtaining written or oral representations from the commissioned medical practitioner explaining the reasons for the delay.

Commissioning a report

3P.11 Guidance entitled 'Good practice guidance: commissioning, administering and producing psychiatric reports for sentencing' prepared for and published by the Ministry of Justice and HM Courts and Tribunals Service in September 2010 contains material that will assist court staff and those who are asked to prepare such reports: www.ohrn.nhs.uk/resource/policy/GoodPracticeGuidePsychReports.pdf The guidance includes standard forms of letters of instruction and other documents.

3P.12 CrimPR 3.28 requires the commissioner of a report to explain why the court seeks the report and to include relevant information about the circumstances. The HMCTS Guidance contains forms for judicial use in the instruction of court staff, and guidance to court staff on the preparation of letters of instruction, where a report is required for sentencing purposes. Those forms and that guidance can be adapted for use where the court requires a report on the defendant's fitness to participate, in the Crown Court, or in a magistrates' court requires a report for the purposes of section 37(3) of the Mental Health Act 1983.

3P.13 The commission should invite a practitioner who is unable to accept it promptly to nominate a suitably qualified substitute, if possible, and to transfer the commission to that person, reporting the transfer when acknowledging the court officer's letter. It is entirely appropriate for the commission to draw the recipient's attention to CrimPR 1.2 (the duty of the participants in a criminal case) and to CrimPR 19.2(1)(b) (the obligation of an expert witness to comply with directions made by a court and at once to inform the court of any significant failure, by the expert or another, to take any step required by such a direction).

3P.14 Where the relevant legislation requires a second psychiatric assessment by a second medical practitioner, and where no commission already has been addressed to a second such practitioner, the commission may invite the person to whom it is addressed to nominate a suitably qualified second person and to pass a copy of the commission to that person forthwith.

Funding arrangements

3P.15 Where a medical report has been, or is to be, commissioned by a party then that party is responsible for arranging payment of the fees incurred, even though the report is intended for the court's use. That must be made clear in that party's commission.

3P.16 Where a medical report is requested by the court and commissioned by a party or by court staff at the court's direction then the commission must include (i) confirmation that the fees will be paid by HMCTS, (ii) details of how, and to whom, to submit an invoice or claim for fees, and (iii) notice of the prescribed rates of fees and of any legislative or other criteria applicable to the calculation of the fees that may be paid.

Remand in custody

3P.17 Where the defendant who is to be examined will be remanded in custody then notice that directions have been given for a medical report or reports to be prepared must be included in the information given to the defendant's custodian, to ensure that the preparation of the report or reports can be facilitated. This is especially important where bail is withheld on the ground that it would be otherwise impracticable to complete the required report, and in particular where that is the only ground for withholding bail.

APPENDIX D

Sentencing Children and Young People[1]

1 © Crown Copyright. Readers should refer to the version on the Sentencing Council website: www.sentencingcouncil.org.uk.

Applicability of guideline

The Sentencing Council issues this definitive guideline in accordance with section 120 of the Coroners and Justice Act 2009.

It applies to all children or young people, who are sentenced on or after 1 June 2017, regardless of the date of the offence.

Section 125(1) of the Coroners and Justice Act 2009 provides that when sentencing offences committed after 6 April 2010:

"Every court –

(a) must, in sentencing an offender, follow any sentencing guidelines which are relevant to the offender's case, and
(b) must, in exercising any other function relating to the sentencing of offenders, follow any sentencing guidelines which are relevant to the exercise of the function,

unless the court is satisfied that it would be contrary to the interests of justice to do so."

Guidance for sentencing children and young people set out in the 2006 robbery guideline and the 2007 sexual offences guideline, both produced by the Sentencing Guidelines Council, are replaced by this guideline.

Guilty plea section only

Section 144 of the Criminal Justice Act 2003 provides:

(1) In determining what sentence to pass on an offender who has pleaded guilty to an offence[1] in proceedings before that court or another court, a court must take into account:
   (a) the stage in the proceedings for the offence at which the offender indicated his intention to plead guilty, and
   (b) the circumstances in which this indication was given.

This section of the guideline applies regardless of the date of the offence to all children or young people where the **first hearing** is on or after 1 June 2017. It applies equally in youth courts, magistrates' courts and the Crown Court.

1 'Offence' includes breach of an order where this constitutes a separate criminal offence but not breach of terms of a sentence or licence.

Overarching Principles – Sentencing Children and Young People

Effective from 1 June 2017

Section one: General approach

Sentencing principles

1.1 When sentencing children or young people (those aged under 18 at the date of the finding of guilt) a court must[2] have regard to:

- the principal aim of the youth justice system (to prevent offending by children and young people);[3] and
- the welfare of the child or young person.[4]

1.2 While the seriousness of the offence will be the starting point, the approach to sentencing should be individualistic and focused on the child or young person, as opposed to offence focused. For a child or young person the sentence should focus on rehabilitation where possible. A court should also consider the effect the sentence is likely to have on the child or young person (both positive and negative) as well as any underlying factors contributing to the offending behaviour.

1.3 Domestic and international laws dictate that a custodial sentence should always be a measure of last resort for children and young people and statute provides that a custodial sentence may only be imposed when the offence is so serious that no other sanction is appropriate (see section six for more information on custodial sentences).

1.4 It is important to avoid "criminalising" children and young people unnecessarily; the primary purpose of the youth justice system is to encourage children and young people to take responsibility for their own actions and promote re-integration into society rather than to punish. Restorative justice disposals may be of particular value for children and young people as they can encourage them to take responsibility for their actions and understand the impact their offence may have had on others.

1.5 It is important to bear in mind any factors that may diminish the culpability of a child or young person. Children and young people are not fully developed and they have not attained full maturity. As such, this can impact on their decision making and risk taking behaviour. It is important to consider the extent to which the child or young person has been acting impulsively and whether their conduct has been affected by inexperience, emotional volatility or negative influences. They may not fully appreciate the effect their actions can have on other people and may not be capable of fully understanding the distress and pain they cause to the victims of their crimes. Children and young people are also likely to be susceptible to peer pressure and other external influences and changes taking place during adolescence can lead to experimentation, resulting in criminal behaviour. When considering a child or young person's age their emotional and developmental age is of at least equal importance to their chronological age (if not greater).

1.6 For these reasons, children and young people are likely to benefit from being given an opportunity to address their behaviour and may be receptive to changing their conduct. They should, if possible, be given the opportunity to learn from their mistakes without undue penalisation or stigma, especially as a court sanction might have a significant effect on the

2 This section does not apply when imposing a mandatory life sentence, when imposing a statutory minimum custodial sentence, when imposing detention for life under the dangerous offender provisions or when making certain orders under the Mental Health Act 1983

3 s.37(1) Crime and Disorder Act 1998

4 s.44(1) Children and Young Persons Act 1933

prospects and opportunities of the child or young person and hinder their re-integration into society.

1.7 Offending by a child or young person is often a phase which passes fairly rapidly and so the sentence should not result in the alienation of the child or young person from society if that can be avoided.

1.8 The impact of punishment is likely to be felt more heavily by a child or young person in comparison to an adult as any sentence will seem longer due to their young age. In addition penal interventions may interfere with a child or young person's education and this should be considered by a court at sentencing.

1.9 Any restriction on liberty must be commensurate with the seriousness of the offence. In considering the seriousness of any offence, the court must consider the child or young person's culpability in committing the offence and any harm which the offence caused, was intended to cause or might foreseeably have caused.[5]

1.10 Section 142 of the Criminal Justice Act 2003 sets out the purposes of sentencing for offenders who are over 18 on the date of conviction. That Act was amended in 2008 to add section 142A which sets out the purposes of sentencing for children and young people, subject to a commencement order being made. The difference between the purposes of sentencing for those under and over 18 is that section 142A does not include as a purpose of sentencing 'the reduction of crime (including its reduction by deterrence)'. Section 142A has not been brought into effect. Unless and until that happens, deterrence can be a factor in sentencing children and young people although normally it should be restricted to serious offences and can, and often will, be outweighed by considerations of the child or young person's welfare.

For more information on assessing the seriousness of the offence see section four.

Welfare

1.11 The statutory obligation to have regard to the welfare of a child or young person includes the obligation to secure proper provision for education and training,[6] to remove the child or young person from undesirable surroundings where appropriate[7] and the need to choose the best option for the child or young person taking account of the circumstances of the offence.

1.12 **In having regard to the welfare of the child or young person, a court should ensure that it is alert to:**

- **any mental health problems or learning difficulties/disabilities;**
- **any experiences of brain injury or traumatic life experience (including exposure to drug and alcohol abuse) and the developmental impact this may have had;**
- **any speech and language difficulties and the effect this may have on the ability of the child or young person (or any accompanying adult) to communicate with the court, to understand the sanction imposed or to fulfil the obligations resulting from that sanction;**

---

5 s.143(1) Criminal Justice Act 2003
6 s.44 Children and Young Persons Act 1933
7 ibid.

- **the vulnerability of children and young people to self harm, particularly within a custodial environment; and**
- **the effect on children and young people of experiences of loss and neglect and/or abuse.**

1.13 Factors regularly present in the background of children and young people that come before the court include deprived homes, poor parental employment records, low educational attainment, early experience of offending by other family members, experience of abuse and/or neglect, negative influences from peer associates and the misuse of drugs and/or alcohol.

1.14 The court should always seek to ensure that it has access to information about how best to identify and respond to these factors and, where necessary, that a proper assessment has taken place in order to enable the most appropriate sentence to be imposed.

1.15 The court should consider the reasons why, on some occasions, a child or young person may conduct themselves inappropriately in court (e.g. due to nervousness, a lack of understanding of the system, a belief that they will be discriminated against, peer pressure to behave in a certain way because of others present, a lack of maturity etc) and take this into account.

1.16 Evidence shows that looked after children and young people are over-represented in the criminal justice system.[8] When dealing with a child or young person who is looked after the court should also bear in mind the additional complex vulnerabilities that are likely to be present in their background. For example, looked after children and young people may have no or little contact with their family and/or friends, they may have special educational needs and/or emotional and behavioural problems, they may be heavily exposed to peers who have committed crime and they are likely to have accessed the care system as a result of abuse, neglect or parental absence due to bereavement, imprisonment or desertion. The court should also bear in mind that the level of parental-type support that a looked after child or young person receives throughout the criminal justice process may vary, and may be limited. For example, while parents are required to attend court hearings, this is not the case for social workers responsible for looked after children and young people. In some instances a looked after child or young person (including those placed in foster homes and independent accommodation, as well as in care homes) may be before the court for a low level offence that the police would not have been involved in, if it had occurred in an ordinary family setting.

1.17 For looked after children and young people who have committed an offence that crosses the custody threshold sentencers will need to consider any impact a custodial sentence may have on their leaving care rights and whether this impact is proportionate to the seriousness of the offence. For other young people who are in the process of leaving care or have recently left care then sentencers should bear in mind any effect this often difficult transition may have had on the young person's behaviour.

1.18 There is also evidence to suggest that black and minority ethnic children and young people are over-represented in the youth justice system.[9] The factors contributing to this are complex. One factor is that a significant proportion of looked after children and young people are from a black

8 Department for Education (2014) Outcomes for Children Looked After by Local Authorities in England, as at 31 March 2014. Statistical First Release 49/2014. [accessed via: https://www.gov.uk/government/statistics/outcomes-for-children-looked-after-by-local-authorities]

9 https://www.gov.uk/government/uploads/system/uploads/attachment_data/file/568680/bame-disproportionality-in-the-cjs.pdf

and minority ethnic background.[10] A further factor may be the experience of such children and young people in terms of discrimination and negative experiences of authority. When having regard to the welfare of the child or young person to be sentenced, the particular factors which arise in the case of black and minority ethnic children and young people need to be taken into account.

1.19 The requirement to have regard to the welfare of a child or young person is subject to the obligation to impose only those restrictions on liberty that are commensurate with the seriousness of the offence; accordingly, a court should not impose greater restrictions because of other factors in the child or young person's life.

1.20 When considering a child or young person who may be particularly vulnerable, sentencers should consider which available disposal is best able to support the child or young person and which disposals could potentially exacerbate any underlying issues. This is particularly important when considering custodial sentences as there are concerns about the effect on vulnerable children and young people of being in closed conditions, with significant risks of self harm, including suicide.

1.21 The vulnerability factors that are often present in the background of children and young people should also be considered in light of the offending behaviour itself. Although they do not alone cause offending behaviour – there are many children and young people who have experienced these circumstances but do not commit crime – there is a correlation and any response to criminal activity amongst children and young people will need to recognise the presence of such factors in order to be effective.

These principles do not undermine the fact that the sentence should reflect the seriousness of the offence. Further guidance on assessing the seriousness of an offence can be found at section four.

Section two: Allocation

(See also the allocation charts at pages 11 – 13 when reading this section.)

2.1 **Subject to the exceptions noted below, cases involving children and young people should be tried in the youth court.** It is the court which is best designed to meet their specific needs. A trial in the Crown Court with the inevitably greater formality and greatly increased number of people involved (including a jury and the public) should be reserved for the most serious cases.[11] The welfare principles in this guideline apply to all cases, including those tried or sentenced in the Crown Court.

This section covers the exceptions to this requirement.[12]

2.2 A child or young person must always appear in the Crown Court for trial if:
- charged with homicide;
- charged with a firearms offence subject to a mandatory minimum sentence of three years (and is over 16 years of age at the time of the offence); or

10 https://www.gov.uk/government/statistics/children-looked-after-in-england-including-adoption-2015-to-2016 (National table, figure B1)
11 *R on the application of H, A and O v Southampton Youth Court [2004]* EWHC 2912 Admin
12 s.24 Magistrates' Courts Act 1980

- notice has been given to the court (under section 51B or 51C of the Crime and Disorder Act 1998) in a serious or complex fraud or child case.

Dangerousness

2.3 A case should be sent to the Crown Court for trial if the offence charged is a specified offence[13] **and** it seems to the court that if found guilty the child or young person would meet the criteria for a sentence under the dangerous offender provisions.

2.4 A sentence under the dangerous offender provisions can only be imposed if:
- the child or young person is found guilty of a specified violent or sexual offence; **and**
- the court is of the opinion that there is a significant risk to the public of serious harm caused by the child or young person committing further specified offences; **and**
- a custodial term of at least four years would be imposed for the offence.

2.5 A 'significant risk' is more than a mere possibility of occurrence. The assessment of dangerousness should take into account all the available information relating to the circumstances of the offence and **may** also take into account any information regarding previous patterns of behaviour relating to this offence and any other relevant information relating to the child or young person. In making this assessment it will be essential to obtain a pre-sentence report.

2.6 Children and young people may change and develop within a shorter time than adults and this factor, along with their level of maturity, may be highly relevant when assessing probable future conduct and whether it may cause a significant risk of serious harm.[14]

2.7 In anything but the most serious cases it may be impossible for the court to form a view as to whether the child or young person would meet the criteria of the dangerous offender provisions without greater knowledge of the circumstances of the offence and the child or young person. In those circumstances jurisdiction for the case should be retained in the youth court. If, following a guilty plea or a finding of guilt, the dangerousness criteria appear to be met then the child or young person should be committed **for sentence**.

Grave crimes

2.8 Where a child or young person is before the court for an offence to which section 91(1) of the Powers of Criminal Courts (Sentencing) Act 2000 applies and the court considers that it ought to be possible to sentence them to more than two years' detention if found guilty of the offence, then they should be sent to the Crown Court. The test to be applied by the court is whether there is a **real prospect** that a sentence in excess of two years' detention will be imposed.

2.9 An offence comes within section 91 where:
- it is punishable with 14 years imprisonment or more for an adult (but is not a sentence fixed by law);
- it is an offence of sexual assault, a child sex offence committed by a child or young person, sexual activity with a child family member or inciting a child family member to engage in sexual activity; or

13 As listed in the Criminal Justice Act 2003 Sch.15

14 *R v Lang* [2005] EWCA Crim 2864, [2006] 1 WLR 2509

- it is one of a number of specified offences in relation to firearms, ammunition and weapons which are subject to a minimum term but, in respect of which, a court has found exceptional circumstances justifying a lesser sentence.

2.10 Before deciding whether to send the case to the Crown Court or retain jurisdiction in the youth court, the court should hear submissions from the prosecution and defence. As there is now a power to commit grave crimes for sentence[15] the court should no longer take the prosecution case at its highest when deciding whether to retain jurisdiction.[16] In most cases it is likely to be impossible to decide whether there is a real prospect that a sentence in excess of two years' detention will be imposed without knowing more about the facts of the case and the circumstances of the child or young person. In those circumstances the youth court should retain jurisdiction and commit for sentence if it is of the view, having heard more about the facts and the circumstances of the child or young person, that its powers of sentence are insufficient.

Where the court decides that the case is suitable to be dealt with in the youth court it must warn the child or young person that all available sentencing options remain open and, if found guilty, the child or young person may be committed to the Crown Court for sentence.

Children and young people should only be sent for trial or committed for sentence to the Crown Court when charged with or found guilty of an offence of such gravity that a custodial sentence substantially exceeding two years is a realistic possibility. For children aged 10 or 11, and children/young people aged 12 – 14 who are not persistent offenders, the court should take into account the normal prohibition on imposing custodial sentences.

Charged alongside an adult

2.11 The proper venue for the trial of any child or young person is normally the youth court. Subject to statutory restrictions, that remains the case where a child or young person is jointly charged with an adult. If the adult is sent for trial to the Crown Court, the court should conclude that the child or young person must be tried separately in the youth court unless it is in the interests of justice for the child or young person and the adult to be tried jointly.

2.12 Examples of factors that should be considered when deciding whether to send the child or young person to the Crown Court (rather than having a trial in the youth court) include:

- whether separate trials will cause injustice to witnesses or to the case as a whole (consideration should be given to the provisions of sections 27 and 28 of the Youth Justice and Criminal Evidence Act 1999);
- the age of the child or young person; the younger the child or young person, the greater the desirability that the child or young person be tried in the youth court;
- the age gap between the child or young person and the adult; a substantial gap in age militates in favour of the child or young person being tried in the youth court;
- the lack of maturity of the child or young person;
- the relative culpability of the child or young person compared with the adult and whether the alleged role played by the child or young person was minor; and/or
- the lack of previous findings of guilt on the part of the child or young person.

---

15 s.3(b) Powers of Criminal Courts (Sentencing) Act 2000, (as amended)
16 *R (DPP) v South Tyneside Youth Court* [2015] EWHC 1455 (Admin)

2.13 The court should bear in mind that the youth court now has a general power to commit for sentence (as discussed at paragraph 2.9); in appropriate cases this will permit a sentence to be imposed by the same court on adults and children and young people who have been tried separately.

2.14 The court should follow the plea before venue procedure (see flowcharts on pages 11 – 13) prior to considering whether it is in the interests of justice for the child or young person and the adult to be tried jointly.

Remittal from the Crown Court for sentence

2.15 If a child or young person is found guilty before the Crown Court of an offence other than homicide the court must remit the case to the youth court, unless it would be undesirable to do so.[17] In considering whether remittal is undesirable a court should balance the need for expertise in the sentencing of children and young people with the benefits of the sentence being imposed by the court which determined guilt.

2.16 Particular attention should be given to children and young people who are appearing before the Crown Court only because they have been charged with an adult offender; referral orders are generally not available in the Crown Court but may be the most appropriate sentence.

17 s.8 Powers of Criminal Courts (Sentencing) Act 2000

Child or young person charged alone or with other children and young people

(This is intended to be a reference tool only; for full guidance on allocation, particularly for grave crimes, please see pages 7 – 10.)

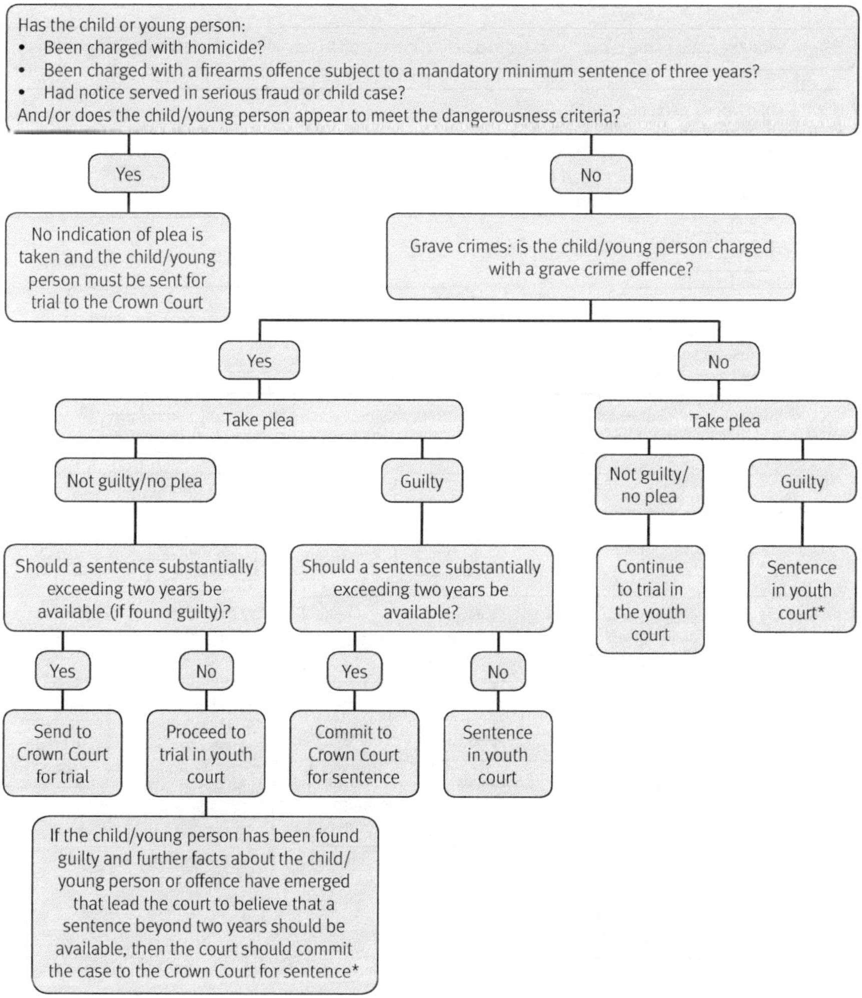

* If the dangerousness provisions appear to be satisfied the court must commit for sentence

Child or young person and adult charged as co-defendants where the adult is charged with an indictable only offence (or an offence where notice is given to the court under s.51B or s.51C Crime & Disorder Act 1998)

(This is intended to be a reference tool only; for full guidance on allocation, particularly for grave crimes, please see pages 7 – 10.)

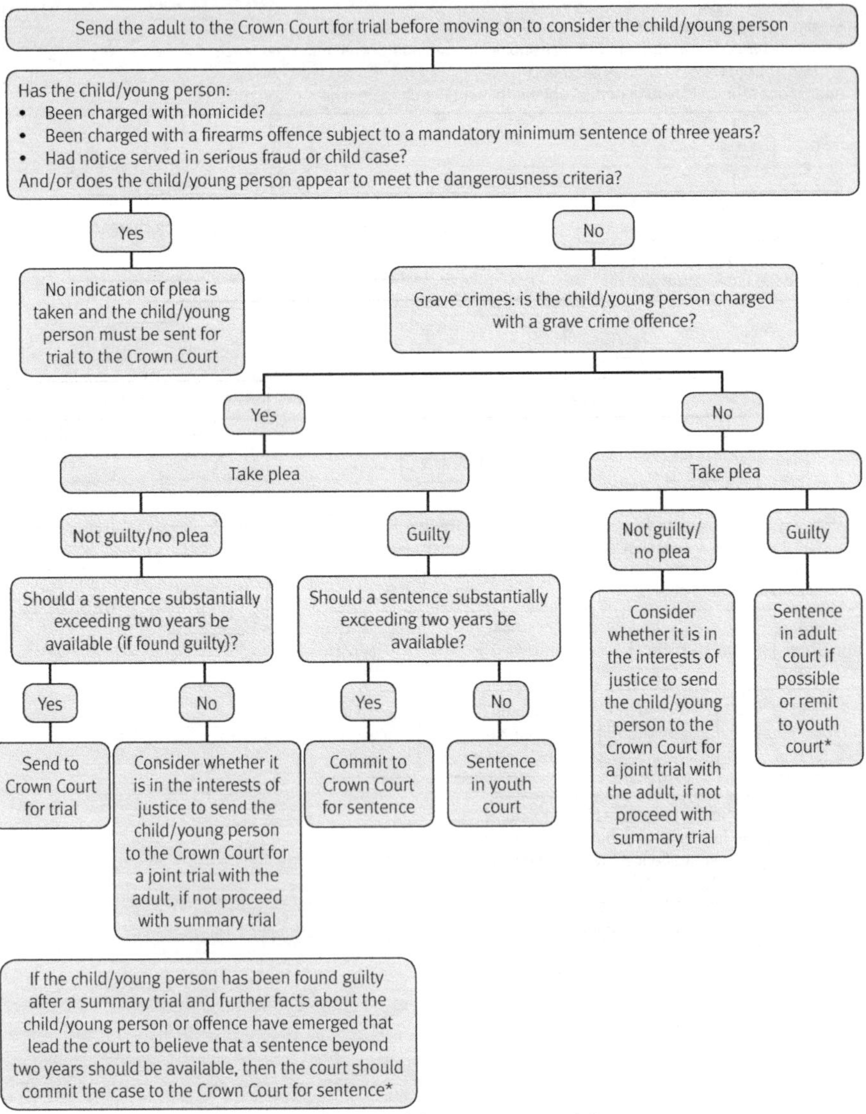

* If the dangerousness provisions appear to be satisfied the court must commit for sentence

Child or young person and adult charged as co-defendants where the adult is charged with either way offence

(This is intended to be a reference tool only; for full guidance on allocation, particularly for grave crimes, please see pages 7 – 10.)

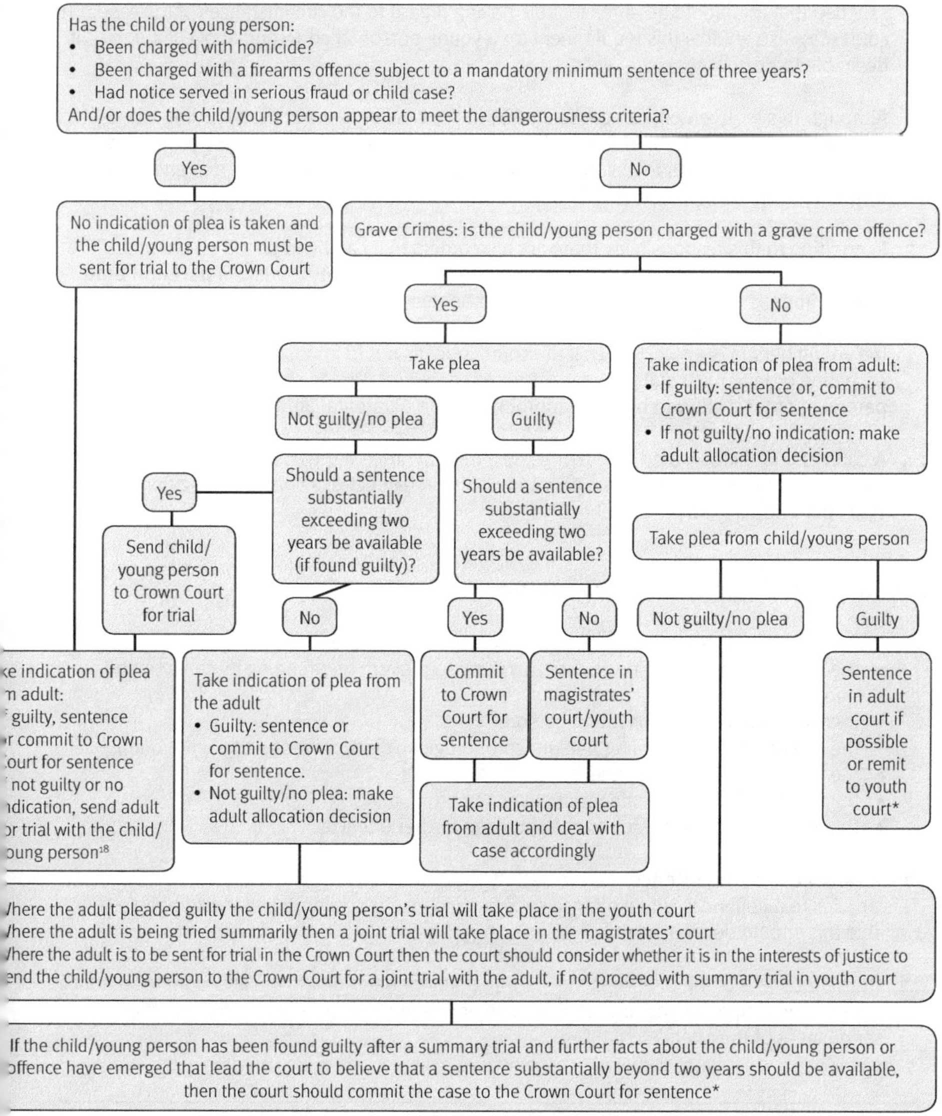

* If the dangerousness provisions appear to be satisfied the court must commit for sentence

18 s.51A(6) Crime & Disorder Act 1998

Section three: Parental responsibilities

3.1 For any child or young person aged under 16 appearing before court there is a statutory requirement that parents/guardians attend during all stages of proceedings, unless the court is satisfied that this would be unreasonable having regard to the circumstances of the case.[19] The court may also enforce this requirement for a young person aged 16 and above if it deems it desirable to do so.

3.2 Although this requirement can cause a delay in the case before the court it is important it is adhered to. If a court does find exception to proceed in the absence of a responsible adult then extra care must be taken to ensure the outcomes are clearly communicated to and understood by the child or young person.

3.3 In addition to this responsibility there are also orders that can be imposed on parents. If the child or young person is aged under 16 then the court has a duty to make a **parental bind over** or impose a **parenting order**, if it would be desirable in the interest of preventing the commission of further offences.[20] There is a discretionary power to make these orders where the young person is aged 16 or 17. If the court chooses not to impose a parental bind over or parenting order it must state its reasons for not doing so in open court. In most circumstances a parenting order is likely to be more appropriate than a parental bind over.

3.4 A court cannot make a bind over alongside a referral order. If the court makes a referral order the duty on the court to impose a parenting order in respect of a child or young person under 16 years old is replaced by a discretion.[21]

Section four: Determining the sentence

4.1 In determining the sentence, the key elements to consider are:
- the principal aim of the youth justice system (to prevent re-offending by children and young people);
- the welfare of the child or young person;
- the age of the child or young person (chronological, developmental and emotional);
- the seriousness of the offence;
- the likelihood of further offences being committed; and
- the extent of harm likely to result from those further offences.

The seriousness of the offence

(This applies to all offences; when offence specific guidance for children and young people is available this should be referred to.)

4.2 The seriousness of the offence is the starting point for determining the appropriate sentence; the sentence imposed and any restriction on liberty must be commensurate with the seriousness of the offence.

---

19 s.34A Children and Young Persons Act 1933
20 s.150 Powers of Criminal Courts (Sentencing) Act 2000 & s.8 Crime and Disorder Act 1998
21 s.9(1A) Crime and Disorder Act 1998

4.3 The approach to sentencing children and young people should always be individualistic and the court should always have in mind the principal aims of the youth justice system.

4.4 In order to determine the seriousness of the offence the court should assess the culpability of the child or young person and the harm that was caused, intended to be caused or could foreseeably have been caused.

4.5 In assessing **culpability** the court will wish to consider the extent to which the offence was planned, the role of the child or young person (if the offence was committed as part of a group), the level of force that was used in the commission of the offence and the awareness that the child or young person had of their actions and its possible consequences. There is an expectation that in general a child or young person will be dealt with less severely than an adult offender. In part, this is because children and young people are unlikely to have the same experience and capacity as an adult to understand the effect of their actions on other people or to appreciate the pain and distress caused and because a child or young person may be less able to resist temptation, especially where peer pressure is exerted. Children and young people are inherently more vulnerable than adults due to their age and the court will need to consider any mental health problems and/or learning disabilities they may have, as well as their emotional and developmental age. Any external factors that may have affected the child or young person's behaviour should be taken into account.

4.6 In assessing **harm** the court should consider the level of physical and psychological harm caused to the victim, the degree of any loss caused to the victim and the extent of any damage caused to property. (This assessment should also include a consideration of any harm that was intended to be caused or could foreseeably have been caused in the committal of the offence.)

4.7 The court should also consider any aggravating or mitigating factors that may increase or reduce the overall seriousness of the offence. **If any of these factors are included in the definition of the committed offence they should not be taken into account when considering the relative seriousness of the offence before the court**.

Aggravating factors
Statutory aggravating factors:
Previous findings of guilt, having regard to a) the **nature** of the offence to which the finding of guilt relates and its **relevance** to the current offence; and b) the **time** that has elapsed since the finding of guilt
Offence committed whilst on bail
Offence motivated by, or demonstrating hostility based on any of the following characteristics or presumed characteristics of the victim: religion, race, disability, sexual orientation or transgender identity
Other aggravating factors (non-exhaustive):
Steps taken to prevent the victim reporting or obtaining assistance
Steps taken to prevent the victim from assisting or supporting the prosecution
Victim is particularly vulnerable due to factors including but not limited to age, mental or physical disability
Restraint, detention or additional degradation of the victim

Prolonged nature of offence
Attempts to conceal/dispose of evidence
Established evidence of community/wider impact
Failure to comply with current court orders
Attempt to conceal identity
Involvement of others through peer pressure, bullying, coercion or manipulation
Commission of offence whilst under the influence of alcohol or drugs
History of antagonising or bullying the victim
Deliberate humiliation of victim, including but not limited to filming of the offence, deliberately committing the offence before a group of peers with the intention of causing additional distress or circulating details/photos/videos etc of the offence on social media or within peer groups

Factors reducing seriousness or reflecting personal mitigation (non-exhaustive)
No previous findings of guilt **or** no relevant/recent findings of guilt
Remorse, particularly where evidenced by voluntary reparation to the victim
Good character and/or exemplary conduct
Unstable upbringing including but not limited to: • time spent looked after • lack of familial presence or support • disrupted experiences in accommodation or education • exposure to drug/alcohol abuse, familial criminal behaviour or domestic abuse • victim of neglect or abuse, or exposure to neglect or abuse of others • experiences of trauma or loss
Participated in offence due to bullying, peer pressure, coercion or manipulation
Limited understanding of effect on victim
Serious medical condition requiring urgent, intensive or long-term treatment
Communication or learning disabilities or mental health concerns
In education, work or training
Particularly young or immature child or young person (where it affects their responsibility)
Determination and/or demonstration of steps taken to address addiction or offending behaviour

Age and maturity of the child or young person

4.8 There is a statutory presumption that no child under the age of 10 can be guilty of an offence.[22]

4.9 With a child or young person, the consideration of age requires a different approach to that which would be adopted in relation to the age of an adult. Even within the category of child or young person the response of a court to an offence is likely to be very different depending on whether the child or young person is at the lower end of the age bracket, in the middle or towards the top end.

22 s.50 Children and Young Persons Act 1933

4.10 Although chronological age dictates in some instances what sentence can be imposed (see section six for more information) the developmental and emotional age of the child or young person should always be considered and it is of at least equal importance as their chronological age. It is important to consider whether the child or young person has the necessary maturity to appreciate fully the consequences of their conduct, the extent to which the child or young person has been acting on an impulsive basis and whether their conduct has been affected by inexperience, emotional volatility or negative influences.

Section five: Guilty plea

This section of the guideline applies regardless of the date of the offence to all children or young people where the **first hearing** is on or after 1 June 2017. It applies equally in youth courts, magistrates' courts and the Crown Court.

Key principles

5.1 The purpose of this section of the guideline is to encourage those who are going to plead guilty to do so as early in the court process as possible. Nothing in this section should be used to put pressure on a child or young person to plead guilty.

5.2 Although a guilty person is entitled not to admit the offence and to put the prosecution to proof of its case, an acceptance of guilt:

a) normally reduces the impact of the crime upon victims;
b) saves victims and witnesses from having to testify; and
c) is in the public interest in that it saves public time and money on investigations and trials.

5.3 A guilty plea produces greater benefits the earlier the plea is made. In order to maximise the above benefits and to provide an incentive to those who are guilty to indicate a guilty plea as early as possible, this section of the guideline makes a clear distinction between a reduction in the sentence available at the first stage of the proceedings and a reduction in the sentence available at a later stage of the proceedings.

5.4 The purpose of reducing the sentence for a guilty plea is to yield the benefits described above and the guilty plea should be considered by the court to be independent of the child or young person's mitigation.

- Factors such as admissions at interview, co-operation with the investigation and demonstrations of remorse should **not** be taken into account in determining the level of reduction. Rather, they should be considered separately and prior to any guilty plea reduction, as potential mitigating factors.
- The benefits apply regardless of the strength of the evidence against a child or young person. The strength of the evidence should **not** be taken into account when determining the level of reduction.
- This section applies only to the punitive elements of the sentence and has no impact on ancillary orders including orders of disqualification from driving.

The approach

Stage 1:	Determine the appropriate sentence for the offence(s) in accordance with any offence specific sentencing guideline or using this *Overarching Principles* guideline.
Stage 2:	Determine the level of reduction for a guilty plea in accordance with this guideline.
Stage 3:	State the amount of that reduction.
Stage 4:	Apply the reduction to the appropriate sentence.
Stage 5:	Follow any further steps in the offence specific guideline to determine the final sentence.

Nothing in this guideline affects the duty of the parties to progress cases (including the service of material) and identify any issues in dispute in compliance with the Criminal Procedure Rules and Criminal Practice Directions.

Determining the level of reduction

The maximum level of reduction for a guilty plea is one-third.

5.5 **Plea indicated at the first stage of the proceedings**
Where a guilty plea is indicated at the first stage of proceedings a reduction of **one-third** should be made (subject to the exceptions below). The first stage will normally be the first hearing in the magistrates' or youth court at which a plea is sought and recorded by the court.[23]

5.6 **Plea indicated after the first stage of proceedings – maximum one quarter – sliding scale of reduction thereafter**
After the first stage of the proceedings the maximum level of reduction is **one-quarter** (subject to the exceptions below).

5.7 The reduction should be decreased from **one-quarter** to a maximum of **one-tenth** on the first day of trial having regard to the time when the guilty plea is first indicated relative to the progress of the case and the trial date (subject to the exceptions below). The reduction should normally be decreased further, even to zero, if the guilty plea is entered during the course of the trial.

5.8 For the purposes of this guideline a trial will be deemed to have started when pre-recorded cross-examination has begun.

Applying the reduction

Detention and training orders

5.9 A detention and training order (DTO) can only be imposed for the periods prescribed – 4, 6, 8, 10, 12, 18 or 24 months. If the reduction in sentence for a guilty plea results in a sentence that falls between two prescribed periods the court must impose the lesser of those two periods. This may result in a reduction greater than a third, in order that the full reduction is given and a lawful sentence imposed.

23 In cases where (in accordance with the Criminal Procedure Rules) a child/young person is given the opportunity to enter a guilty plea without attending a court hearing, doing so within the required time limits will constitute a plea at the first stage of proceedings.

Imposing one type of sentence rather than another

5.10 The reduction in sentence for a guilty plea can be taken into account by imposing one type of sentence rather than another, for example:

- by reducing a custodial sentence to a community sentence; or
- by reducing a community sentence to a different means of disposal.

Alternatively the court could reduce the length or severity of any punitive requirements attached to a community sentence.

5.11 The court must always have regard to the principal aim of the youth justice system, which is to prevent offending by children and young people. It is, therefore, important that the court ensures that any sentence imposed is an effective disposal.

5.12 Where a court has imposed one sentence rather than another to reflect the guilty plea there should normally be no further reduction on account of the guilty plea. Where, however, the less severe type of sentence is justified by other factors, the appropriate reduction for the plea should be applied in the normal way.

More than one summary offence

5.13 When dealing with more than one summary offence, the aggregate sentence is limited to a maximum of six months. Allowing for a reduction for each guilty plea, consecutive sentences might result in the imposition of the maximum six month sentence. Where this is the case, the court **may** make a modest *additional* reduction to the *overall* sentence to reflect the benefits derived from the guilty plea.

Sentencing up to 24 months DTO for offences committed by children and young people

5.14 A DTO of up to 24 months may be imposed on a child or young person if the offence is one which, but for the plea, would have attracted a sentence of detention in excess of 24 months under section 91 of the Powers of Criminal Courts (Sentencing) Act 2000.

Exceptions

Referral order

5.15 As a referral order is a sentence that is only available upon pleading guilty there should be no further reduction of the sentence to reflect the guilty plea.

Further information, assistance or advice necessary before indicating plea

5.16 Where the sentencing court is satisfied that there were particular circumstances which significantly reduced the child or young person's ability to understand what was alleged, or otherwise made it unreasonable to expect the child or young person to indicate a guilty plea **sooner than was done**, a reduction of one-third should still be made.

5.17 In considering whether this exception applies, sentencers should distinguish between cases in which it is necessary to receive advice and/or have sight of evidence in order to understand whether the child or young person is, in fact and law, guilty of the offence(s) charged, and cases in which a child or young person merely delays guilty plea(s) in order to assess the strength of the prosecution evidence and the prospects of a finding of guilt or acquittal.

Newton hearings and special reasons hearings

5.18 In circumstances where a child or young person's version of events is rejected at a Newton hearing[24] or special reasons hearing,[25] the reduction which would have been available at the stage of proceedings the plea was indicated should normally be halved. Where witnesses are called during such a hearing, it may be appropriate further to decrease the reduction.

Child or young person found guilty of a lesser or different offence

5.19 If a child or young person is found guilty of a lesser or different offence from that originally charged, and has earlier made an unequivocal indication of a guilty plea to this lesser or different offence to the prosecution and the court, the court should give the level of reduction that is appropriate to the stage in the proceedings at which this indication of plea (to the lesser or different offence) was made taking into account any other of these exceptions that apply. In the Crown Court where the offered plea is a permissible alternative on the indictment as charged, the child or young person will not be treated as having made an unequivocal indication unless the defendant has entered that plea.

Minimum sentence under section 51A of the Firearms Act 1968

5.20 There can be no reduction for a guilty plea if the effect of doing so would be to reduce the length of sentence below the required minimum term.

Appropriate custodial sentences for young persons aged at least 16 but under 18 when found guilty under the Prevention of Crime Act 1953 and Criminal Justice Act 1988

5.21 In circumstances where an appropriate custodial sentence of a DTO of at least four months falls to be imposed on a young person who is aged at least 16 but under 18, who has been found guilty under sections 1 or 1A of the Prevention of Crime Act 1953; or section 139, 139AA or 139A of the Criminal Justice Act 1988 (certain possession of knives or offensive weapon offences) the court may impose any sentence that it considers appropriate, having taken into consideration the general principles set out above.

Mandatory life sentences for murder

5.22 Murder is the most serious criminal offence and the sentence prescribed is different from all other sentences. By law, the sentence for murder is detention for life and the child or young person will remain subject to the sentence for the rest of their life.

5.23 Given the special characteristic of the offence of murder and the unique statutory provision in Schedule 21 of the Criminal Justice Act 2003 of starting points for the minimum term to be

24 A Newton hearing is held when a child/young person pleads guilty but disputes the case as put forward by the prosecution and the dispute would make a difference to the sentence. The judge will normally hear evidence from witnesses to decide which version of the disputed facts to base the sentence on.

25 A special reasons hearing occurs when a child/young person is found guilty of an offence carrying a mandatory licence endorsement or disqualification from driving and seeks to persuade the court that there are extenuating circumstances relating to the offence that the court should take into account by reducing or avoiding endorsement or disqualification. This may involve calling witnesses to give evidence.

served by a child or young person, careful consideration has to be given to the extent of any reduction for a guilty plea and to the need to ensure that the minimum term properly reflects the seriousness of the offence.

5.24 Whilst the general principles continue to apply (both that a guilty plea should be encouraged and that the extent of any reduction should reduce if the indication of plea is later than the first stage of the proceedings) the process of determining the level of reduction will be different.

Determining the level of reduction

5.25 In other circumstances:

- the court will weigh carefully the overall length of the minimum term taking into account other reductions for which the child or young person may be eligible so as to avoid a combination leading to an inappropriately short sentence;
- where it is appropriate to reduce the minimum term having regard to a plea of guilty, the reduction will not exceed one-sixth and will never exceed five years; and
- the maximum reduction of one-sixth or five years (whichever is less) should only be given when a guilty plea has been indicated at the first stage of the proceedings. Lesser reductions should be given for guilty pleas after that point, with a maximum of one-twentieth being given for a guilty plea on the day of trial.

The exceptions outlined at 5.16 – 5.18 apply to murder cases.

Section six: Available sentences

Crossing a significant age threshold between commission of offence and sentence

6.1 There will be occasions when an increase in the age of a child or young person will result in the maximum sentence on the date of *the finding of guilt* being greater than that available on the date on which the offence was *committed* (primarily turning 12, 15 or 18 years old).

6.2 In such situations the court should take as its starting point the sentence likely to have been imposed on the date at which the offence was committed. This includes young people who attain the age of 18 between the *commission* and the *the finding of guilt* of the offence[26] but when this occurs the purpose of sentencing adult offenders[27] has to be taken into account, which is:

- the punishment of offenders;
- the reduction of crime (including its reduction by deterrence);
- the reform and rehabilitation of offenders;
- the protection of the public; and
- the making of reparation by offenders to persons affected by their offences.

6.3 When any significant age threshold is passed it will rarely be appropriate that a more severe sentence than the maximum that the court could have imposed at the time the offence was committed should be imposed. However, a sentence at or close to that maximum may be appropriate.

26 *R v Ghafoor* [2002] EWCA Crim 1857, [2003] 1 Cr App R (S) 428
27 s.142 Criminal Justice Act 2003

Persistent offenders

6.4 Some sentences can only be imposed on children and young people if they are deemed a persistent offender. A child or young person **must** be classed as such for one of the following to be imposed:

- a youth rehabilitation order (YRO) with intensive supervision and surveillance when aged under 15;
- a YRO with fostering when aged under 15; and
- a detention and training order (DTO) when aged 12 – 14.

6.5 The term persistent offender is not defined in statute but has been considered by the Court of Appeal. In general it is expected that the child or young person would have had previous contact with authority as a result of criminal behaviour. This includes previous findings of guilt as well as admissions of guilt such as restorative justice disposals and conditional cautions.

6.6 A child or young person who has committed one previous offence cannot reasonably be classed as a persistent offender, and a child or young person who has committed two or more previous offences should not necessarily be assumed to be one. To determine if the behaviour is persistent the nature of the previous offences and the lapse of time between the offences would need to be considered.[28]

6.7 If there have been three findings of guilt in the past 12 months for imprisonable offences of a comparable nature (or the child or young person has been made the subject of orders as detailed above in relation to an imprisonable offence) then the court could certainly justify classing the child or young person as a persistent offender.

6.8 When a child or young person is being sentenced in a single appearance for a series of separate, comparable offences committed over a short space of time then the court could justifiably consider the child or young person to be a persistent offender, despite the fact that there may be no previous findings of guilt.[29] In these cases the court should consider whether the child or young person has had prior opportunity to address their offending behaviour before imposing one of the optional sentences available for persistent offenders only; if the court determines that the child or young person has not had an opportunity to address their behaviour and believes that an alternative sentence has a reasonable prospect of preventing re-offending then this alternative sentence should be imposed.

6.9 The court may also wish to consider any evidence of a reduction in the level of offending when taking into account previous offending behaviour. Children and young people may be unlikely to desist from committing crime in a clear cut manner but there may be changes in patterns of criminal behaviour (e.g. committing fewer and/or less serious offences or there being longer lengths of time between offences) that indicate that the child or young person is attempting to desist from crime.

6.10 Even where a child or young person is found to be a persistent offender, a court is not obliged to impose one of the optional sentences. The approach should still be individualistic and all other considerations still apply. **Custodial sentences must be a last resort for all children and**

28 *R v M* [2008] EWCA Crim 3329

29 *R v S* [2000] 1 Cr App R (S)18

young people and there is an expectation that they will be particularly rare for children and young people aged 14 or under.

Sentences available by age:

Sentence	Age of child or young person 10 – 11	12 – 14	15 – 17	Rehabilitation period
Absolute or conditional discharge or reparation order	✓	✓	✓	Absolute discharge and reparation: spent on day of sentence Conditional discharge: spent on last day of the period of discharge
Financial order	✓	✓	✓	Spent 6 months after the finding of guilt
Referral order	✓	✓	✓	Spent on day of completion
Youth rehabilitation order (YRO)	✓	✓	✓	Spent 6 months after the last day the order is to have effect
YRO with intensive supervision and surveillance or fostering	×	✓ For persistent offenders **only**	✓	Spent 6 months after the last day the order is to have effect
Detention and training order	×	✓ For persistent offenders **only**	✓	6 months or under: spent 18 months after the sentence is completed (including supervision period) More than 6 months: spent 24 months after the sentence is completed (including supervision period)
s.91 PCC(S) Act detention (grave crime)	✓	✓	✓	More than 6 months – 30 months: spent 24 months after sentence completed (including licence period) More than 30 months – 48 months: spent 42 months after sentence completed (including licence period) More than 48 months: never spent
Extended sentence of detention*	✓	✓	✓	Never spent

* If found guilty of a specified violent or sexual offence and the court is of the opinion that there is a significant risk to the public of serious harm caused by the child or young person committing further specified offences.

6.11 Some sentences have longer rehabilitation periods than others, for example referral orders are spent on the last day on which the order is to have effect.[30] Sentences can also have varying impacts on the future of children and young people; for example absolute or conditional discharges are not deemed to be treated as convictions other than for the purposes of criminal proceedings[31] and therefore may have a lesser impact on the child or young person's future prospects than other sentences. The length of the rehabilitation periods and any likely effects on the child or young person's future prospects should be taken into account when considering if the sentence is commensurate to the seriousness of the offence.

Breaches and the commission of further offences during the period of an order

6.12 If a child or young person is found guilty of breaching an order, or commits a further offence during the period of an order, the court will have various options available depending upon the nature of the order **(see Appendix one at page 32)**. The primary aim of the court should be to encourage compliance and seek to support the rehabilitation of the child or young person.

30 s.139 Legal Aid, Sentencing and Punishment of Offenders Act 2012
31 s.14 (1) Powers of Criminal Courts (Sentencing) Act 2000

Absolute or conditional discharge and reparation orders

6.13 An absolute discharge is appropriate in the least serious cases when, despite a finding of guilt, the court considers that no punishment should be imposed.

6.14 A conditional discharge is appropriate when, despite a finding of guilt, the offence is not serious enough to warrant an immediate punishment. The fixed period of conditional discharge must not exceed three years. Unless exceptional circumstances are found, a conditional discharge cannot be imposed if the child or young person has received one of the following in the previous 24 months: two or more cautions; or a conditional caution followed by a caution.[32]

6.15 A reparation order can require a child or young person to make reparation to the victim of the offence, where a victim wishes it, or to the community as a whole. Before making an order the court must consider a written report from a relevant authority, e.g. a youth offending team (YOT), and the order must be commensurate with the seriousness of the offence.

6.16 If the court has the power to make a reparation order but chooses not to do so, it must give its reasons.

Financial order

6.17 The court may impose a fine for any offence (unless the criteria for a mandatory referral order are met). In accordance with statutory requirements, where financial orders are being considered, priority must be given to compensation orders and, when an order for costs is to be made alongside a fine, the amount of the cost must not exceed the amount of the fine. If the child or young person is under 16 then the court has a duty to order parents or guardians to pay the fine; if the young person is 16 or over this duty is discretionary. In practice, many children and young people will have limited financial resources and the court will need to determine whether imposing a fine will be the most effective disposal.

6.18 A court should bear in mind that children and young people may have money that is specifically required for travel costs to school, college or apprenticeships and lunch expenses.

Referral orders

6.19 A referral order is the mandatory sentence in a youth court or magistrates' court for most children and young people who have committed an offence for the first time and have pleaded guilty to an imprisonable offence. Exceptions are for offences where a sentence is fixed by law or if the court deems a custodial sentence, an absolute or conditional discharge or a hospital order to be more appropriate.

6.20 A discretionary referral order can also be imposed for any offence where there has been a plea of guilty regardless of previous offending history. It should be remembered that they are not community orders and in general terms may be regarded as orders which fall between community disposals and fines. However, bearing in mind that the principal aim of the youth justice system is to prevent children and young people offending, second or subsequent referral orders should be considered in those cases where:

32 s.66ZB Crime & Disorder Act 1998

(a) the offence is not serious enough for a YRO but the child or young person does appear to require some intervention OR
(b) the offence is serious enough for a YRO but it is felt that a referral order would be the best way to prevent further offending (as an example, this may be because the child or young person has responded well in the past to such an order and the offence now before the court is dissimilar to that for which a referral order was previously imposed).

Referral orders are the main sentence for delivering restorative justice and all panel members are trained Restorative Conference Facilitators; as such they can be an effective sentence in encouraging children and young people to take responsibility for their actions and understand the effect their offence may have had on their victim.

6.21 In cases where children or young people have offended for the first time and have pleaded guilty to committing an offence which is on the cusp of the custody threshold, YOTs should be encouraged to convene a Youth Offender Panel prior to sentence (sometimes referred to as a "pseudo-panel" or "pre-panel") where the child or young person is asked to attend before a panel and agree an intensive contract. If that contract is placed before the sentencing youth court, the court can then decide whether it is sufficient to move below custody on this occasion. The proposed contract is not something the court can alter in any way; the court will still have to make a decision between referral order and custody but can do so on the basis that if it makes a referral order it can have confidence in what that will entail in the particular case.

6.22 The court determines the length of the order but a Referral Order Panel determines the requirements of the order.

Offence seriousness	Suggested length of referral order
Low	• 3 – 5 months
Medium	• 5 – 7 months
High	• 7 – 9 months
Very high	• 10 – 12 months

The YOT may propose certain requirements and the length of these requirements may not correspond to the above table; if the court feels these requirements will best achieve the aims of the youth justice system then they may still be imposed.

Youth rehabilitation orders (YRO)

6.23 A YRO is a community sentence within which a court may include one or more requirements designed to provide for punishment, protection of the public, reducing re-offending and reparation.

6.24 When imposing a YRO, the court must fix a period within which the requirements of the order are to be completed; this must not be more than three years from the date on which the order comes into effect.

6.25 The offence must be 'serious enough' in order to impose a YRO, but it does not need to be an imprisonable offence. Even if an offence is deemed 'serious enough' the court is not obliged to make a YRO.

6.26 The requirements included within the order (and the subsequent restriction on liberty) and the length of the order must be proportionate to the seriousness of the offence and suitable for the child or young person. The court should take care to ensure that the requirements imposed are not too onerous so as to make breach of the order almost inevitable.

6.27 The available requirements within a YRO are:

- activity requirement (maximum 90 days);
- supervision requirement;
- unpaid work requirement (between 40 and 240 hours);*
- programme requirement;
- attendance centre requirement (maximum 12 hours for children aged 10–13, between 12 and 24 hours for young people aged 14 or 15 and between 12 and 36 hours for young people aged 16 or over (all ages refer to age at date of the finding of guilt);
- prohibited activity requirement;
- curfew requirement (maximum 12 months and between 2 and 16 hours a day);
- exclusion requirement (maximum 3 months);
- electronic monitoring requirement;
- residence requirement;*
- local authority residence requirement (maximum 6 months but not for any period after young person attains age of 18);
- fostering requirement (maximum 12 months but not for any period after young person attains age of 18);**
- mental health treatment requirement;
- drug treatment requirement (with or without drug testing);
- intoxicating substance requirement;
- education requirement; and
- intensive supervision and surveillance requirement.**

* These requirements are only available for young people aged 16 or 17 years old on the date of the finding of guilt.

** These requirements can only be imposed if the offence is an imprisonable one AND the custody threshold has been passed. For children and young people aged under 15 they must be deemed a persistent offender.

Many of the above requirements have additional restrictions. Always consult your legal adviser before imposing a YRO.

6.28 When determining the nature and extent of the requirements the court should primarily consider the likelihood of the child or young person re-offending and the risk of the child or young person causing serious harm. A higher risk of re-offending does not in itself justify a greater restriction on liberty than is warranted by the seriousness of the offence; any requirements should still be commensurate with the seriousness of the offence and regard must still be had for the welfare of the child or young person.

6.29 The YOT will assess this as part of their report and recommend an intervention level to the court for consideration. It is possible for the court to ask the YOT to consider a particular requirement.

	Child or young person profile	Requirements of order[33]
Standard	Low likelihood of re-offending **and** a low risk of serious harm	Primarily seek to repair harm caused through, for example: • reparation; • unpaid work; • supervision; and/or • attendance centre.
Enhanced	Medium likelihood of re-offending **or** a medium risk of serious harm	Seek to repair harm caused and to enable help or change through, for example: • supervision; • reparation; • requirement to address behaviour e.g. drug treatment, offending behaviour programme, education programme; and/or • a combination of the above.
Intensive	High likelihood of re-offending **or** a very high risk of serious harm	Seek to ensure the control of and enable help or change for the child or young person through, for example: • supervision; • reparation; • requirement to address behaviour; • requirement to monitor or restrict movement, e.g. prohibited activity, curfew, exclusion or electronic monitoring; and/or • a combination of the above.

6.30 If a child or young person is assessed as presenting a high risk of re-offending or of causing serious harm but the offence that was committed is of relatively low seriousness then the appropriate requirements are likely to be primarily rehabilitative or for the protection of the public.

6.31 Likewise if a child or young person is assessed as presenting a low risk of re-offending or of causing serious harm but the offence was of relatively high seriousness then the appropriate requirements are likely to be primarily punitive.

Orders with intensive supervision and surveillance or with fostering

6.32 An intensive supervision and surveillance requirement and a fostering requirement are both community alternatives to custody.

6.33 The offence must be punishable by imprisonment, cross the custody threshold and a custodial sentence must be merited before one of these requirements can be imposed.

6.34 An order of this nature may only be imposed on a child or young person aged below 15 (at the time of the finding of guilt) if they are a persistent offender.

With intensive supervision and surveillance:

6.35 An order of this nature must include an extended activity requirement of between 90 and 180 days, a supervision requirement and a curfew requirement. Where appropriate, a YRO with intensive supervision and surveillance may also include additional requirements (other than a fostering requirement), although the order as a whole must comply with the obligation that the requirements must be those most suitable for the child or young person and that any restrictions on liberty are commensurate with the seriousness of the offence.

33 The examples provided here are not exclusive; the YOT will make recommendations based upon their assessment of the young offender which may vary from some of the examples given.

6.36 When imposing such an order, the court must ensure that the requirements are not so onerous as to make the likelihood of breach almost inevitable.

With fostering:

6.37 Where a fostering requirement is included within a YRO, it will require the child or young person to reside with a local authority foster parent for a specified period that must not exceed 12 months.

6.38 In order to impose this requirement the court must be satisfied that the behaviour which constituted the offence was due to a significant extent to the circumstances in which the child or young person was living, and that the imposition of fostering requirement would assist in the child or young person's rehabilitation. It is likely that other rights will be engaged (such as those under Article 8 of the European Convention on Human Rights)[34] and any interference with such rights must be proportionate.

6.39 The court must consult the child or young person's parent or guardian (unless impracticable) and the local authority before including this requirement. It can only be included if the child or young person was legally represented in court when consideration was being given to imposing such a requirement unless the child or young person, having had the opportunity to do so, did not apply for representation or that right was withdrawn because of the child or young person's conduct. **This requirement may be included only where the court has been notified that arrangements are available in the area of the relevant authority.**

6.40 A YRO with a fostering requirement must include a supervision requirement and can include other requirements when appropriate (except an intensive supervision and surveillance requirement). The order as a whole must comply with the obligation that the requirements must be those most suitable for the child or young person and that any restrictions on liberty are commensurate with the seriousness of the offence.

6.41 It is unlikely that the statutory criteria[35] will be met in many cases; where they are met and the court is considering making an order, care should be taken to ensure that there is a well developed plan for the care and support of the child or young person throughout the period of the order and following conclusion of the order. The court will need to be provided with sufficient information, including proposals for education and training during the order and plans for the child or young person on completion of the order.

Custodial sentences

A custodial sentence should always be used as a last resort. If offence specific guidelines for children and young people are available then the court should consult them in the first instance to asses whether custody is the most appropriate disposal.

The available custodial sentences for children and young people are:

34 Right to respect for family and private life

35 See paragraphs 5.28-30

Youth Court	Crown Court
• Detention and training order for the following periods: • 4 months; • 6 months; • 8 months; • 10 months; • 12 months; • 18 months; or • 24 months.	• Detention and training order (the same periods are available as in the youth court) • Long-term detention (under section 91 of the Powers of Criminal Courts (Sentencing) Act 2000) • Extended sentence of detention or detention for life (if dangerousness criteria are met) • Detention at Her Majesty's pleasure (for offences of murder)

6.42 Under both domestic and international law, a custodial sentence must only be imposed as a '**measure of last resort;**' statute provides that such a sentence may be imposed only where an offence is "so serious that neither a fine alone nor a community sentence can be justified."[36] If a custodial sentence is imposed, a court must state its reasons for being satisfied that the offence is so serious that no other sanction would be appropriate and, in particular, why a YRO with intensive supervision and surveillance or fostering could not be justified.

6.43 The term of a custodial sentence must be the shortest commensurate with the seriousness of the offence; any case that warrants a DTO of less than four months must result in a non-custodial sentence. The court should take account of the circumstances, age and maturity of the child or young person.

6.44 In determining whether an offence has crossed the custody threshold the court will need to assess the seriousness of the offence, in particular the level of harm that was caused, or was likely to have been caused, by the offence. The risk of serious harm in the future must also be assessed. The pre-sentence report will assess this criterion and must be considered before a custodial sentence is imposed. A custodial sentence is most likely to be unavoidable where it is necessary to protect the public from serious harm.

6.45 Only if the court is satisfied that the offence crosses the custody threshold, and that no other sentence is appropriate, the court may, as a preliminary consideration, consult the equivalent adult guideline in order to decide upon the appropriate length of the sentence.

6.46 When considering the relevant adult guideline, the court **may** feel it appropriate to apply a sentence broadly within the region of half to two thirds of the adult sentence for those aged 15 – 17 and allow a greater reduction for those aged under 15. This is only a rough guide and must not be applied mechanistically. In most cases when considering the appropriate reduction from the adult sentence **the emotional and developmental age and maturity of the child or young person is of at least equal importance as their chronological age**.

6.47 The individual factors relating to the offence and the child or young person are of the greatest importance and may present good reason to impose a sentence outside of this range. The court should bear in mind the negative effects a short custodial sentence can have; short sentences disrupt education and/or training and family relationships and support which are crucial stabilising factors to prevent re-offending.

36 s.152(2) Criminal Justice Act 2003

6.48 There is an expectation that custodial sentences will be particularly rare for a child or young person aged 14 or under. If custody is imposed, it should be for a shorter length of time than that which a young person aged 15 – 17 would receive if found guilty of the same offence. For a child or young person aged 14 or under the sentence should normally be imposed in a youth court (except in cases of homicide or when the dangerous offender criteria are met).

6.49 The welfare of the child or young person must be considered when imposing any sentence but is especially important when a custodial sentence is being considered. A custodial sentence could have a significant effect on the prospects and opportunities of the child or young person and a child or young person is likely to be more susceptible than an adult to the contaminating influences that can be expected within a custodial setting. There is a high reconviction rate for children and young people that have had custodial sentences and there have been many studies profiling the effect on vulnerable children and young people, particularly the risk of self harm and suicide and so it is of utmost importance that custody is a last resort.

Detention and training order (DTO)

6.50 A court can only impose a DTO if the child or young person is legally represented unless they have refused to apply for legal aid or it has been withdrawn as a result of their conduct.

6.51 If it is determined that the offence is of such seriousness that a custodial sentence is unavoidable then the length of this sentence must be considered on an individual basis. The court must take into account the chronological age of the child or young person, as well as their maturity, emotional and developmental age and other relevant factors, such as their mental health or any learning disabilities.

6.52 A DTO cannot be imposed on any child under the age of 12 at the time of the finding of guilt and is only applicable to children aged 12 – 14 if they are deemed to be a persistent offender. (See section on persistent offenders on page 22.)

6.53 A DTO can be made only for the periods prescribed – 4, 6, 8, 10, 12, 18 or 24 months. Any time spent on remand in custody or on bail subject to a qualifying curfew condition should be taken into account when calculating the length of the order. The accepted approach is to double the time spent on remand before deciding the appropriate period of detention, in order to ensure that the regime is in line with that applied to adult offenders.[37] After doubling the time spent on remand the court should then adopt the nearest prescribed period available for a DTO.

Long-term detention

6.54 A child or young person may be sentenced by the Crown Court to long-term detention under section 91 of the Powers of Criminal Courts (Sentencing) Act 2000 if found guilty of a grave crime and neither a community order nor a DTO is suitable.

6.55 These cases may be sent for trial to the Crown Court or committed for sentence only[38] (see section two for further information).

37 *R v Eagles* [2006] EWCA Crim 2368
38 s.3(b) Powers of Criminal Courts (Sentencing) Act 2000, (as amended)

6.56 It is possible that, following a guilty plea, a two year detention order may be appropriate as opposed to a sentence of section 91 detention, to account for the reduction.

Dangerous offenders

6.57 If a child or young person is found to be a dangerous offender they can be sentenced to **extended detention** or **detention for life**.

6.58 A sentence of extended detention may be imposed only where the appropriate custodial term would be 4 years or more. The extension period must not exceed 5 years in the case of a specified violent offence and 8 years in the case of a specified sexual offence. The term of the extended sentence of detention must not exceed the maximum term of imprisonment for an adult offender convicted of that offence.

6.59 A sentence of detention for life should be used as a last resort when an extended sentence is not able to provide the level of public protection that is necessary. In order to determine this, the court should consider the following factors in the order given:

- the seriousness of the offence;
- the child or young person's previous findings of guilt;
- the level of danger posed to the public and whether there is a reliable estimate of the length of time the child or young person will remain a danger; and
- the alternative sentences available.

The court is required to set a minimum term which must be served in custody before parole can be considered.

Detention at Her Majesty's pleasure

6.60 This is the mandatory sentence for any child or young person found guilty of committing a murder. The starting point for the minimum term is 12 years.

Appendix one: Breach of orders

Breach of a conditional discharge

7.1 If a child or young person commits an offence during the period of conditional discharge then the court has the power to re-sentence the original offence. The child or young person should be dealt with on the basis of their current age and not the age at the time of the finding of guilt and the court can deal with the original offence(s) in any way which it could have if the child or young person had just been found guilty.

7.2 There is no requirement to re-sentence; if a court deems it appropriate to do so they can sentence the child or young person for the new offence and leave the conditional discharge in place. If the order was made by the Crown Court then the youth court can commit the child or young person in custody or release them on bail until they can be brought or appear before the Crown Court. The court shall also send to the Crown Court a memorandum of conviction.

7.3 If the offender is convicted of committing a new offence after attaining the age of 18 but during the period of a conditional discharge made by a youth court then they may be re-sentenced for the original offence by the convicting adult magistrates' court. If the adult magistrates' court decides to take no action then the youth court that imposed the conditional discharge may summon the offender for the breach to be dealt with.

Breach of a reparation order

7.4 If it is proved to the appropriate court that the child or young person has failed to comply with any requirement of a reparation order that is currently in force then the court can:

- order the child or young person to pay a fine not exceeding £1,000; or
- revoke the order and re-sentence the child or young person in any way which they could have been dealt with for that offence.

If re-sentencing the child or young person the court must take into account the extent to which the child or young person has complied with the requirements of this order.

7.5 If the order was made by the Crown Court then the youth court can commit the child or young person in custody or release them on bail until they can be brought or appear before the Crown Court.

7.6 The child or young person or a Youth Offending Team (YOT) officer can also apply for the order to be revoked or amended but any new provisions must be ones that the court would have been able to include when the original reparation order was given. There is no power to re-sentence in this situation as the child or young person has not been found to be in breach of requirements.

Even when an offender has attained the age of 18 breach of a reparation order must be dealt with in the youth court.

Breach of a referral order (referral back to court)

7.7 If a child or young person is found to have breached the conditions of their referral order the court can revoke the referral order and re-sentence the child or young person using the range of sentencing options (other than a referral order) that would have been available to the court that originally sentenced them. If the court chooses not to revoke the referral order then it is possible to:

- allow the referral order to continue with the existing contract;
- extend the length of the referral order up to a maximum of 12 months (in total); or
- impose a fine up to a maximum of £2,500.

7.8 If an offender has attained the age of 18 by the first court hearing then breach proceedings must be dealt with by the adult magistrates' court. If the court chooses to revoke the order then its powers are limited to those available to the court at the time of the original sentence.

Commission of further offences whilst on a referral order

7.9 The court has the power to extend a referral order in respect of additional or further offences. This applies to not only a first referral order but also to any subsequent referral orders. Any period of extension must not exceed the total 12 month limit for a referral order.

7.10 If the court chooses not to extend the existing referral order or impose a discharge they have the power to impose a new referral order (where the discretionary referral order conditions are satisfied) in respect of the new offences only. This order can remain or run alongside the new order or the court may direct that the contract under the new order is not to take effect until the earlier order is revoked or discharged. Alternatively, the court may impose an absolute or conditional discharge.

7.11 If the court sentences in any other way they have a discretionary power to revoke the referral order. Where an order is revoked, if it appears to be in the interests of justice, the court may deal with the original offence(s) in any way that the original court could have done, but may not make a new referral order. Where the referral contract has taken effect, the court shall have regard to the extent of the child or young person's compliance with the terms of the contract.

Breach of a youth rehabilitation order (YRO)

7.12 Where a child or young person is in breach of a YRO the following options are available to the court:

- take no action and allow the order to continue in its original form;
- impose a fine (up to £2,500)(and allow the order to continue in its original form);
- amend the terms of the order; or
- revoke the order and re-sentence the child or young person.

7.13 If the terms of the order are amended the new requirements must be capable of being complied with before the expiry of the overall period. The court may impose any requirement that it could have imposed when making the order and this may be in addition to, or in substitution for, any requirements contained in the order. If the YRO did not contain an unpaid work requirement and the court includes such a requirement using this power, the minimum period of unpaid work is 20 hours; this will give greater flexibility when responding to less serious breaches or where there are significant other requirements to be complied with.

7.14 A court may not amend the terms of a YRO that did not include an extended activity requirement or a fostering requirement by inserting them at this stage; should these requirements be considered appropriate following breach, the child or young person must be re-sentenced and the original YRO revoked.

7.15 A court must ensure that it has sufficient information to enable it to understand why the order has been breached and should be satisfied that the YOT and other local authority services have taken all steps necessary to ensure that the child or young person has been given appropriate opportunity and the support necessary for compliance. This is particularly important if the court is considering imposing a custodial sentence as a result of the breach.

7.16 Where the failure arises primarily from non-compliance with reporting or other similar obligations and a sanction is necessary, the most appropriate response is likely to be the inclusion of (or increase in) a primarily punitive requirement such as the curfew requirement, unpaid work, the exclusion requirement and the prohibited activity requirement or the imposition of a fine. However, continuing failure to comply with the order is likely to lead to revocation of the order and re-sentencing for the original offence.

7.17 Where the child or young person has 'wilfully and persistently' failed to comply with the order, and the court proposes to sentence again for the offence(s) in respect of which the order was made, additional powers are available.

A child or young person will almost certainly be considered to have 'wilfully and persistently' breached a YRO where there have been three breaches that have demonstrated a lack of willingness to comply with the order that have resulted in an appearance before court.

7.18 The additional powers available to the court when re-sentencing a child or young person who has 'wilfully and persistently' breached their order are:

- the making of a YRO with intensive supervision and surveillance even though the offence is non-imprisonable;
- a custodial sentence if the YRO that is breached is one with an intensive supervision and surveillance requirement, which was imposed for an offence that was imprisonable; and
- the imposition of a DTO for four months for breach of a YRO with intensive supervision and surveillance which was imposed following wilful and persistent breach of an order made for a non-imprisonable offence.

The primary objective when sentencing for breach of a YRO is to ensure that the child or young person completes the requirements imposed by the court.

7.19 If an offender has attained the age of 18 by the first court hearing then breach proceedings must be dealt with by the adult magistrates' court. If the court chooses to revoke the order then its powers are limited to those available to the court at the time of the original sentence.

Commission of further offences during a YRO

7.20 If a child or young person commits an offence whilst subject to a YRO the court can impose any sentence for the new matter, but can only impose a new YRO if they revoke the existing order. Where the court revokes the original order they may re-sentence that matter at the same time as sentencing the new offence.

Breach of a detention and training order (DTO)

7.21 If a child or young person is found to have breached a supervision requirement after release from custody then the court may:

- impose a further period of custody of up to three months or the length of time from the date the breach was committed until the end of the order, **whichever is shorter**;
- impose a further period of supervision of up to three months or the length of time from the date the breach was committed until the end of the order, **whichever is shorter**;
- impose a fine of up to £1,000; or
- take no action.

Even if the offender has attained the age of 18 proceedings for breach of the supervision requirements must be dealt with in the youth court.

Commission of further offences during a DTO

7.22 If a child or young person is found guilty of a further imprisonable offence committed during the currency of the order then the court can impose a further period of detention. This period of detention cannot exceed the period between the date of the new offence and the date of when the original order would have expired.

7.23 This period can be served consecutively or concurrently with any sentence imposed for the new offence and this period should not be taken into account when determining the appropriate length of the sentence for the new offence.

Sexual Offences Guideline

Sentencing a child or young person for sexual offences involves a number of different considerations from adults. The primary difference is the age and level of maturity. Children and young people are less emotionally developed than adults; offending can arise through inappropriate sexual experimentation; gang or peer group pressure to engage in sexual activity; or a lack of understanding regarding consent, exploitation, coercion and appropriate sexual behaviour.

Below is a non-exhaustive list of factors that illustrate the type of background factors that may have played a part in leading a child or young person to commit an offence of this kind.

- Victim of neglect or abuse (sexual, physical or emotional) or has witnessed the neglect or abuse of another.
- Exposure to pornography or materials which are age inappropriate.
- Involvement in gangs.
- Associated with child sexual exploitation.
- Unstable living or educational arrangements.
- Communication or learning disabilities or mental health concerns.
- Part of a peer group, school or neighbourhood where harmful sexual norms and attitudes go unchallenged.
- A trigger event such as the death of a close relative or a family breakdown.

This guideline should be read alongside the *Overarching Principles – Sentencing Children and Young People* definitive guideline which provides comprehensive guidance on the sentencing principles and welfare considerations that the court should have in mind when sentencing children and young people.

The first step in determining the sentence is to assess the seriousness of the offence. This assessment is made by considering the nature of the offence and any aggravating and mitigating factors relating to the offence itself. **The fact that a sentence threshold is crossed does not necessarily mean that that sentence should be imposed.**

STEP ONE
Offence Seriousness – Nature of the offence

The boxes below give **examples** of the type of culpability and harm factors that may indicate that a particular threshold of sentence has been crossed.

A non-custodial sentence* may be the most suitable disposal where one or more of the following factors apply:
Any form of non-penetrative sexual activity
Any form of sexual activity (including penetration) without coercion, exploitation or pressure except where there is a significant disparity in age or maturity
Minimal psychological or physical harm caused to the victim

A custodial sentence or youth rehabilitation order with intensive supervision and surveillance* or fostering* may be justified where one or more of the following factors apply:
Any penetrative activity involving coercion, exploitation or pressure
Use or threats of violence against the victim or someone known to the victim
Prolonged detention/sustained incident
Severe psychological or physical harm caused to the victim

* Where the child or young person appears in the magistrates' court, and the conditions for a compulsory referral order apply, a referral order must be imposed unless the court is considering imposing a discharge, hospital order or custody.

See page 38.

STEP TWO
Offence Seriousness – Aggravating and mitigating factors

To complete the assessment of seriousness the court should consider the aggravating and mitigating factors relevant to the offence.

Aggravating factors
Statutory aggravating factors:
Previous findings of guilt, having regard to a) the **nature** of the offence to which the finding of guilt relates and its **relevance** to the current offence; and b) the **time** that has elapsed since the finding of guilt
Offence committed whilst on bail
Offence motivated by, or demonstrating hostility based on any of the following characteristics or presumed characteristics of the victim: religion, race, disability, sexual orientation or transgender identity
Other aggravating factors (non-exhaustive):
Significant degree of planning
Child or young person acts together with others to commit the offence
Use of alcohol/drugs on victim to facilitate the offence
Abuse of trust
Deliberate humiliation of victim, including but not limited to filming of the offence, deliberately committing the offence before a group of peers with the intention of causing additional distress or circulating details/photos/videos etc of the offence on social media or within peer groups
Grooming
Significant disparity of age between the child or young person and the victim (measured chronologically or with reference to level of maturity) (where not taken into account at step one)
Victim is particularly vulnerable due to factors including but not limited to age, mental or physical disability
Any steps taken to prevent reporting the incident/seeking assistance
Pregnancy or STI as a consequence of offence
Blackmail
Use of weapon

Mitigating factors (non-exhaustive)
No previous findings of guilt **or** no relevant/recent findings of guilt
Good character and/or exemplary conduct
Participated in offence due to bullying, peer pressure, coercion or manipulation
Genuine belief that activity was lawful

STEP THREE
Personal mitigation

Having assessed the offence seriousness, the court should then consider the mitigation personal to the child or young person to determine whether a custodial sentence or a community sentence is necessary. The effect of personal mitigation may reduce what would otherwise be a custodial sentence to a non-custodial one, or a community sentence to a different means of disposal.

Personal mitigating factors (non-exhaustive)
Particularly young or immature child or young person (where it affects their responsibility)
Communication or learning disabilities or mental health concerns
Unstable upbringing including but not limited to:- • time spent looked after • lack of familial presence or support • disrupted experiences in accommodation or education • exposure to drug/alcohol abuse, familial criminal behaviour or domestic abuse • exposure by others to pornography or sexually explicit materials • victim of neglect or abuse, or exposure to neglect or abuse of others • experiences of trauma or loss
Determination and/or demonstration of steps taken to address offending behaviour
Strong prospect of rehabilitation
Child or young person in education, training or employment

STEP FOUR
Reduction for guilty plea

The court should take account of any potential reduction for a guilty plea in accordance with section 144 of the Criminal Justice Act 2003 and part one, section five of the *Overarching Principles – Sentencing Children and Young People* definitive guideline.

The reduction in sentence for a guilty plea can be taken into account by imposing one type of sentence rather than another; for example:

- by reducing a custodial sentence to a community sentence; or
- by reducing a community sentence to a different means of disposal.

Alternatively the court could reduce the length or severity of any punitive requirements attached to a community sentence.

See the *Overarching Principles – Sentencing Children and Young People* definitive guideline for details of other available sentences including Referral Orders and Reparation Orders.

STEP FIVE
Review the sentence

The court must now review the sentence to ensure it is the most appropriate one for the child or young person. This will include an assessment of the likelihood of reoffending and the risk of causing serious harm. A report from the Youth Offending Team may assist.

See the *Overarching Principles – Sentencing Children and Young People* definitive guideline for comprehensive guidance on the sentencing principles and welfare considerations that the court should have in mind when sentencing children and young people, and for the full range of the sentences available to the court.

Referral Orders
In cases where children or young people have offended for the first time and have pleaded guilty to committing an offence which is on the cusp of the custody threshold, YOTs should be encouraged to convene a Youth Offender Panel prior to sentence (sometimes referred to as a "pseudo-panel" or "pre-panel") where the child or young person is asked to attend before a panel and agree an intensive contract. If that contract is placed before the sentencing youth court, the court can then decide whether it is sufficient to move below custody on this occasion. The proposed contract is not something the court can alter in any way; the court will still have to make a decision between referral order and custody but can do so on the basis that if it makes a referral order it can have confidence in what that will entail in the particular case.

The court determines the length of the order but a Referral Order Panel determines the requirements of the order.

Offence seriousness	Suggested length of referral order
Low	• 3 – 5 months
Medium	• 5 – 7 months
High	• 7 – 9 months
Very high	• 10 – 12 months

The YOT may propose certain requirements and the length of these requirements may not correspond to the above table; if the court feels these requirements will best achieve the aims of the youth justice system then they may still be imposed.

Youth Rehabilitation Order (YRO)
The following table sets out the different levels of intensity that are available under a Youth Rehabilitation Order. The level of intensity and the content of the order will depend upon the court's assessment of seriousness.

		Requirements of order
Standard	Low likelihood of re-offending **and** a low risk of serious harm	Primarily seek to repair harm caused through, for example: • reparation; • unpaid work; • supervision; and/or • attendance centre.

		Requirements of order
Enhanced	Medium likelihood of re-offending **or** a medium risk of serious harm	Seek to repair harm caused and to enable help or change through, for example: • supervision; • reparation; • requirement to address behaviour e.g. drug treatment, offending behaviour programme, education programme; and/or • a combination of the above.
Intensive	High likelihood of re-offending **or** a very high risk of serious harm	Seek to ensure the control of and enable help or change for the child or young person through, for example: • supervision; • reparation; • requirement to address behaviour; • requirement to monitor or restrict movement, e.g. prohibited activity, curfew, exclusion or electronic monitoring; and/or • a combination of the above.

YRO with Intensive Supervision and Surveillance (ISS) or YRO with Fostering

A YRO with an ISS or fostering requirement can only be imposed where the court is of the opinion that the offence has crossed the custody threshold and custody is merited.

The YRO with ISS includes an extended activity requirement, a supervision requirement and curfew. The YRO with fostering requires the child or young person to reside with a local authority foster parent for a specified period of up to 12 months.

Custodial Sentences

If a custodial sentence is imposed, the court must state its reasons for being satisfied that the offence is so serious that no other sanction would be appropriate and, in particular, why a YRO with ISS or fostering could not be justified.

Where a custodial sentence is **unavoidable** the length of custody imposed must be the shortest commensurate with the seriousness of the offence. The court may want to consider the equivalent adult guideline in order to determine the appropriate length of the sentence.

If considering the adult guideline, the court may feel it appropriate to apply a sentence broadly within the region of half to two thirds of the appropriate adult sentence for those aged 15 – 17 and allow a greater reduction for those aged under 15. This is only a rough guide and must not be applied mechanistically. The individual factors relating to the offence and the child or young person are of the greatest importance and may present good reason to impose a sentence outside of this range.

Robbery Guideline

This guideline should be read alongside the *Overarching Principles – Sentencing Children and Young People* definitive guideline which provides comprehensive guidance on the sentencing principles and welfare considerations that the court should have in mind when sentencing children and young people.

The first step in determining the sentence is to assess the seriousness of the offence. This assessment is made by considering the nature of the offence and any aggravating and mitigating factors relating to the offence itself. **The fact that a sentence threshold is crossed does not necessarily mean that that sentence should be imposed.**

STEP ONE
Offence Seriousness – Nature of the offence

The boxes below give **examples** of the type of culpability and harm factors that may indicate that a particular threshold of sentence has been crossed.

A non-custodial sentence* may be the most suitable disposal where one or more of the following factors apply:
Threat or use of minimal force
Little or no physical or psychological harm caused to the victim
Involved through coercion, intimidation or exploitation

A custodial sentence or youth rehabilitation order with intensive supervision and surveillance* or fostering* may be justified where one or more of the following factors apply:
Use of very significant force
Threat or use of a bladed article, firearm or imitation firearm (where produced)
Significant physical or psychological harm caused to the victim

* Where the child or young person appears in the magistrates' court, and the conditions for a compulsory referral order apply, a referral order must be imposed unless the court is considering imposing a discharge, hospital order or custody.

STEP TWO
Offence Seriousness – Aggravating and mitigating factors

To complete the assessment of seriousness the court should consider the aggravating and mitigating factors relevant to the offence.

Aggravating factors
Statutory aggravating factors:
Previous findings of guilt, having regard to a) the **nature** of the offence to which the finding of guilt relates and its **relevance** to the current offence; and b) the **time** that has elapsed since the finding of guilt
Offence committed whilst on bail
Offence motivated by, or demonstrating hostility based on any of the following characteristics or presumed characteristics of the victim: religion, race, disability, sexual orientation or transgender identity
Other aggravating factors (non-exhaustive):
Significant degree of planning
Deliberate humiliation of victim, including but not limited to filming of the offence, deliberately committing the offence before a group of peers with the intention of causing additional distress or circulating details/photos/videos etc of the offence on social media or within peer groups
Threat or use of a weapon other than a bladed article, firearm or imitation firearm (whether produced or not)
Threat to use a bladed article, firearm or imitation firearm (not produced)
Victim is particularly vulnerable due to factors including but not limited to age, mental or physical disability
A leading role where offending is part of a group
Attempt to conceal identity (for example, wearing a balaclava or hood)
Any steps taken to prevent reporting the incident/seeking assistance
High value goods or sums targeted or obtained (includes economic, personal or sentimental)
Restraint, detention or additional degradation of the victim

Mitigating factors (non-exhaustive)
No previous findings of guilt **or** no relevant/recent findings of guilt
Good character and/or exemplary conduct
Participated in offence due to bullying, peer pressure, coercion or manipulation
Remorse, particularly where evidenced by voluntary reparation to the victim
Little or no planning

STEP THREE
Personal mitigation

Having assessed the offence seriousness, the court should then consider the mitigation personal to the child or young person to determine whether a custodial sentence or a community sentence is necessary. The effect of personal mitigation may reduce what would otherwise be a custodial sentence to a non-custodial one, or a community sentence to a different means of disposal.

Personal mitigating factors (non-exhaustive)
Particularly young or immature child or young person (where it affects their responsibility)
Communication or learning disabilities or mental health concerns
Unstable upbringing including but not limited to: • time spent looked after • lack of familial presence or support • disrupted experiences in accommodation or education • exposure to drug/alcohol abuse, familial criminal behaviour or domestic abuse • victim of neglect or abuse, or exposure to neglect or abuse of others • experiences of trauma or loss
Determination and/or demonstration of steps taken to address offending behaviour
Child or young person in education, training or employment

STEP FOUR
Reduction for guilty plea

The court should take account of any potential reduction for a guilty plea in accordance with section 144 of the Criminal Justice Act 2003 and part one, section five of the *Overarching Principles – Sentencing Children and Young People* definitive guideline.

The reduction in sentence for a guilty plea can be taken into account by imposing one type of sentence rather than another; for example:
- by reducing a custodial sentence to a community sentence; or
- by reducing a community sentence to a different means of disposal.

Alternatively the court could reduce the length or severity of any punitive requirements attached to a community sentence.

See the *Overarching Principles – Sentencing Children and Young People* definitive guideline for details of other available sentences including Referral Orders and Reparation Orders.

STEP FIVE
Review the sentence

The court must now review the sentence to ensure it is the most appropriate one for the child or young person. This will include an assessment of the likelihood of reoffending and the risk of causing serious harm. A report from the Youth Offending Team may assist.

See the *Overarching Principles – Sentencing Children and Young People* definitive guideline for comprehensive guidance on the sentencing principles and welfare considerations that the court should have in mind when sentencing children and young people, and for the full range of the sentences available to the court.

Referral Orders

In cases where children or young people have offended for the first time and have pleaded guilty to committing an offence which is on the cusp of the custody threshold, YOTs should be encouraged to convene a Youth Offender Panel prior to sentence (sometimes referred to as a "pseudo-panel" or "pre-panel") where the child or young person is asked to attend before a panel and agree an intensive contract. If that contract is placed before the sentencing youth court, the court can then decide whether it is sufficient to move below custody on this occasion. The proposed contract is not something the court can alter in any way; the court will still have to make a decision between referral order and custody but can do so on the basis that if it makes a referral order it can have confidence in what that will entail in the particular case.

The court determines the length of the order but a Referral Order Panel determines the requirements of the order.

Offence seriousness	Suggested length of referral order
Low	• 3 – 5 months
Medium	• 5 – 7 months
High	• 7 – 9 months
Very high	• 10 – 12 months

The YOT may propose certain requirements and the length of these requirements may not correspond to the above table; if the court feels these requirements will best achieve the aims of the youth justice system then they may still be imposed.

Youth Rehabilitation Order (YRO)

The following table sets out the different levels of intensity that are available under a YRO. The level of intensity and the content of the order will depend upon the court's assessment of seriousness.

		Requirements of order
Standard	Low likelihood of re-offending **and** a low risk of serious harm	Primarily seek to repair harm caused through, for example: • reparation; • unpaid work; • supervision; and/or • attendance centre.

		Requirements of order
Enhanced	Medium likelihood of re-offending **or** a medium risk of serious harm	Seek to repair harm caused and to enable help or change through, for example: • supervision; • reparation; • requirement to address behaviour e.g. drug treatment, offending behaviour programme, education programme; and/or • a combination of the above.
Intensive	High likelihood of re-offending **or** a very high risk of serious harm	Seek to ensure the control of and enable help or change for the child or young person through, for example: • supervision; • reparation; • requirement to address behaviour; • requirement to monitor or restrict movement, e.g. prohibited activity, curfew, exclusion or electronic monitoring; and/or • a combination of the above.

YRO with Intensive Supervision and Surveillance (ISS) or YRO with fostering

A YRO with an ISS or fostering requirement can only be imposed where the court is of the opinion that the offence has crossed the custody threshold, and custody is merited.

The YRO with ISS includes an extended activity requirement, a supervision requirement and curfew. The YRO with fostering requires the child or young person to reside with a local authority foster parent for a specified period of up to 12 months.

Custodial Sentences

If a custodial sentence is imposed, the court must state its reasons for being satisfied that the offence is so serious that no other sanction would be appropriate and, in particular, why a YRO with ISS or fostering could not be justified.

Where a custodial sentence is **unavoidable** the length of custody imposed must be the shortest commensurate with the seriousness of the offence. The court may want to consider the equivalent adult guideline in order to determine the appropriate length of the sentence.

If considering the adult guideline, the court may feel it appropriate to apply a sentence broadly within the region of half to two thirds of the appropriate adult sentence for those aged 15 – 17 and allow a greater reduction for those aged under 15. This is only a rough guide and must not be applied mechanistically. The individual factors relating to the offence and the child or young person are of the greatest importance and may present good reason to impose a sentence outside of this range.

Index